Read Chapters 7-12

OFFICE DEVELOPMENT

Effectively Managing the Development Process

Robertson H. Short, Jr.

Development Publishing Company • Santa Barbara, California

Office Development
Effectively Managing the Development Process

By Robertson H. Short, Jr.

Published by:
Development Publishing Company
P. O. Box 4822
Santa Barbara, CA 93140-4822
(888) 308-6584
www.developmentpublishing.com

    All rights reserved. No part of this book may be reproduced or transmitted in any form or by any means, electronic or mechanical, including photocopying, recording or by any information storage and retrieval, without written permission from the author, except for the inclusion of brief quotations in a review.

© 2001 Robertson H. Short, Jr.

Publisher's Cataloging-in-Publication
(Provided by Quality Books)

Short, Robertson H. Jr.
    Office development : effectively managing the development process / Robertson H. Short, Jr. — 1st. ed.
    p. cm.
    LCCN: 00-191859
    ISBN: 0-9703879-0-3

    1. Office buildings—Design and construction.
I. Title.

TH4311.S56 2000   725'.23
                                        QBI00-826

Library of Congress Card Number: 00-191859

Manufactured in China

Contents

	Foreword	5
	About the Author	7
	Acknowledgments	8
	Disclaimer	9
1.	Introduction	11
2.	Observations, Thoughts and Philosophy	23
3.	Feasibility Analyses	29
4.	The Market Study	33
5.	The Site Study	55
6.	Political Environment	65
7.	Site Selection, Acquisition and Permitting	71
8.	Definitions and Project Economics	107
9.	Risk and Risk Management	111
10.	The Development Team	119
11.	The Pro Forma	125
12.	Development Financing	143
13.	General Design Comments	153
14.	Design Process	161
15.	Site Planning and Conceptual Design	181
16.	Floor Layout Design	197
17.	Marketing	207
18.	Site Design	215
19.	Structural Design	225
20.	Building Envelope Design	239
21.	Building Lobby and Elevator Design	269
22.	Acoustics	285
23.	Core Area Design	293
24.	Central Facilities Design	305
25.	Mechanical and Building Management Systems	321
26.	Electrical and Communication Systems	351
27.	Life Safety and Security Systems	365
28.	Leasing Team	375
29.	Leasing Strategies	381
30.	Tenant Space Development	387
31.	Lease Proposals	409

32.	Lease Negotiation	417
33.	Construction Contractor	433
34.	Project Schedule	443
35.	The Construction Process	461
36.	Asset and Property Management	479
37.	Conclusions	481
	Appendix A: References	485
	Appendix B: Notes on Feng Shui	487
	Appendix C: How Green Is My Building?	493
	Appendix D: Land Development	499
	Glossary	507
	Index	519
	Photography and Graphics Credits	527

Foreword

The creation of a new commercial property is one of the most exciting and personally satisfying activities in which one can participate in the business world. It begins with an idea or objective and results in a physical structure that will be a significant factor in the built environment for many years. This process is exciting to all involved, from the experienced real estate development executive to the novice in the field involved in acquiring a new facility to satisfy his or her organization's requirements. Unfortunately, it is this excitement and resultant over enthusiasm that is the Achilles' heel of the development business. Many projects have become economic or functional disasters because decisions were based upon the emotional appeal of the project rather than utilizing the discipline and controls essential to achieving a financially sound project that meets the original business objectives.

This book is the most comprehensive and authoritative text available for understanding and solving the many complex issues in the dynamic field of commercial development. It fills a void in the available texts in that it directly addresses the issues facing the Development Officer and clearly outlines the thought processes and decision-making that will lead to successful and profitable results. It is must reading for anyone undertaking a development project, and invaluable to those many individuals and firms who provide services to the development industry.

The genesis of this book occurred in the late 1990s when, after more than a decade of working off the excesses of the early 1980s, the commercial real estate market finally reached the point where new office building development became feasible. Recognizing that several of our otherwise highly qualified personnel would need to commence development responsibilities with minimal or no actual experience, I asked Bob Short to develop a seminar program to bridge this gap. When he was unsuccessful in finding a satisfactory text for this purpose, he began to create one utilizing the knowledge gained from his many years of developing outstanding commercial properties and his notebooks of information and references. His seminars were well received and filled an important need within our organization.

As Bob taught the seminars for our firm and others, and while he consulted on development projects for us in California, his text was expanded and revised until it became the quality work that it is today. Throughout the text, he added interesting references to issues from his prior projects to amplify points he was making.

Control of the process—from its start with thorough market, site, environmental and political evaluations through the financial analysis, design, construction, marketing and leasing of the project— is clearly explained. In addition to emphasis on effective control of the process, this text provides a wealth of technical data that can serve as a valuable resource for years to come.

A key element, not fully covered in other texts, is how to effectively control the architectural design so that project quality and costs meet the requirements of the market developed through the early market studies. It is an important iterative process that effectively utilizes the many and varied talents of the members of the development team.

While initial financial success is important to the viability of any firm, the developer must recognize that each project has an impact, for better or worse, on the community in which it is located. Bob shows how a well conceived, planned and executed development based on appropriate initial evaluations should become a long-term asset to both the developer and the community.

The text recognizes the current and future impact of technology and the Internet on the way the development business is performed and controlled. It points the way to the ever-increasing concerns, requirements for and benefits of energy conservation, enhancing the interior environment, promoting sustainability and recycling, and helping to minimize impacts to the overall environment.

One unique aspect of this book is that it incorporates a detailed Case Study of one our projects in Del Mar, California, the development of which paralleled the writing of the book. It was probably the smallest project that Bob was ever involved with, but one full of interesting and unusual issues. Each chapter of the text is followed by the relevant issues and solutions encountered throughout the Del Mar development process.

The reader of this book will come away with a depth of understanding of the development process and the myriad issues involved, and its direction for the future.

Michael V. Prentiss
Chairman,
Prentiss Properties Trust

About the Author

Bob Short has forty years experience in real estate, during which time he has been responsible for the development of fifteen million square feet of office and related space.

After several years in industrial construction and serving as partner in charge of engineering for a major Philadelphia architectural firm, Bob was responsible for the development of two major bank headquarters—First National Bank of Chicago and Crocker National Bank in San Francisco. He was responsible for extensive land purchases and sales, and directed the expansion and upgrading of the Crocker Bank branch system.

With Cadillac Fairview and its successor company, Prentiss Properties Limited, he was responsible for such projects as First City Center, Momentum Place and Pacific Place in Dallas, 780 Third Avenue in New York and the IBM building in Clear Lake, Texas, among others. He was also responsible for a large DoubleTree hotel and a major retail development that were associated with office building projects, and major office parks in Vernon Hills, Illinois, and Fontana, California.

Since forming R. H. Short & Associates in 1991 he has directed, or consulted on, the Federal Office Building in downtown Atlanta, and projects in San Jose, Sacramento, San Diego and Oakland, California. In addition, he has evaluated major land acquisitions and taught a series of seminars on office building development.

Bob has a BSME from Purdue University, an MBA from the University of Delaware, and is a registered professional engineer and a licensed real estate broker in several states. He has served as the Chairman of BOMI Institute, a Director of NACORE, and held a series of major positions in Building Owners and Managers International and the Pennsylvania and Illinois Society of Professional Engineers.

Acknowledgments

I am thankful to Mike Prentiss who provided me with my most challenging professional assignments, and lured me out of retirement to develop new projects again after the decade of absorbing the '80s overbuilding, and who challenged me to plan and present a seminar series on office building development.

I am grateful to Prentiss Properties Trust for their support and for providing the incentive and feedback for this book as I developed the series of seminars on office building development, and to the participants who helped me improve them.

I particularly appreciate the assistance of David Meyer and Joe Buskuhl of HKS Architects, David Habib of WDG-Habib Architecture, Martin Schlessinger of Blum Consulting Engineers, Mike Ernst of Prentiss Properties and Barbara S. Harris for their invaluable assistance in providing materials, advice and peer reviewing certain chapters to ensure that I did not make too many serious errors or omissions. Barbara Harris not only reviewed many chapters, but also copyedited the entire work. Special mention should be made of John Couvillion of Prentiss Properties who did such a fine job as the Development Officer on the Del Mar Gateway project used as the Case Study.

But most of all, I wish to thank the many co-workers, architects, consultants, contractors, material suppliers, brokers, attorneys and major tenants with whom I have shared so many successful projects—and who have taught me so much.

Disclaimer

This book is designed to provide information on the abilities and efforts of the Development Officer in controlling the process of conceiving, evaluating, designing, constructing and leasing a successful office development project. It is sold with the understanding that the publisher and author are not engaged in rendering legal, accounting, architectural, engineering or other professional services. If legal or other expert assistance is required, the services of a competent professional should be sought.

It is not the purpose of this text to reprint all the information that is otherwise available from authors and/or publishers, but instead to complement, amplify and supplement other texts. You are urged to read all available material, learn as much as possible about office building development, and tailor the information to your individual needs. For more information, refer to Appendix A and references included within the text material.

Every effort has been made to make this text as complete and as accurate as possible. However, *there may be mistakes*, both typographical and in content. Therefore, this text should be used only as a general guide and not as the ultimate source on this subject. Furthermore, this text endeavors to provide information that is current only up to the printing date.

The purpose of this text is help educate the relatively new development officer and provide supplemental information and/or different approaches to experienced development personnel. The author and publisher shall have neither liability nor responsibility to any person or entity with respect to any loss or damage caused, or alleged to have been caused, directly or indirectly, by the information contained in this book.

INTRODUCTION

One definition of real estate development is "...an idea or objective that through a complex process results in an occupied, income-producing structure." A successful development must have a clear set of objectives—a defined product to suit a defined market, intended for either long-term ownership or sales income, and projected to achieve a specified return in a given time frame. The objective must be pursued throughout the process with a clearly defined and understood strategy.

A process is a disciplined procedure that considers and evaluates all reasonably relevant data and, if performed properly, leads to a satisfactory conclusion. It has a finite beginning, an end and a feedback of the results.

This text was developed to provide a thorough working knowledge of the process of the development of office buildings in order to guide you, the Development Officer (often referred to as Development Manager), successfully through this complex interdisciplinary process. It was written at this time because the decade-long absence of office development resulting from the huge oversupply of the '80s had ended, but during that period young Development Officers and other real estate professionals lost the opportunity for many years of practical experience.

This text covers the broad scope of the information and decision-making required of the Development Officer, as well as provides a clear understanding of the principles underlying each issue or phase.

To accomplish a successful development it is of necessity a "hands-on" process that, due to the interrelationship of extensive issues and the many professionals specializing in their various disciplines, requires a constant and firm central control by the Development Officer. This control is essential to a successful project, as no other participant in the process has complete knowledge of the objectives and constraints, and how their work interrelates within that framework, except the Development Officer.

The ultimate role of the Development Officer is to set, and control achievement of, the overall objectives as briefly defined below:

- Set clear objectives for the project and each participant

- Determine the market feasibility and, if feasible, define the limitations

- Determine the political feasibility and regulatory issues, and define the strategies to overcome them

- Ascertain and manage the degree of risk

- Execute the plan by coordinating the design and construction of a product that will satisfy the identified market at a price that will produce an acceptable yield

- Develop and implement a strategy to market and lease the building effectively

- Accomplish the result in a timely manner, and within all economic constraints

This text is differentiated from others because it focuses directly on the individual Development Officer, rather than on a development company or the process as a whole, and the step-by-step role in understanding, defining and executing a project from beginning to end.

This work is addressed primarily to the relatively inexperienced Development Officer, although there is sufficient depth to be of value to more experienced developers. A few potential Development Officers are hired directly from the business schools into on-the-job training programs, but most enter this position after a proven record in the fields of brokerage, finance, architecture, engineering, construction, asset management or law. Regardless of the success in the original specialty, it is essential to develop an in-depth understanding of the other disciplines in order to effectively and successfully direct a development project. This book will provide that practical knowledge of the areas of development to which each reader has not been exposed, and the process of tying all of the issues and disciplines together effectively.

Additionally, this text is of considerable value to the many architects, engineers, consultants, contractors, attorneys, real estate brokers, asset and property managers, and officers of financial institutions whose work is directly related to commercial development. It provides a better understanding of the entire development process, the thought processes of their developer client, and how their specific expertise most effectively fits within the overall effort.

The specific objectives this work is intended to accomplish are:

- A working knowledge of each phase of the development process

- A thorough understanding of the basic principles underlying each phase

- Sufficient technical background in order to most effectively utilize the knowledge of the many professionals involved

- A technical reference to be consulted as various issues are addressed

- An improved confidence in, and the quality level of, the many important decisions and trade-offs the Development Officer must necessarily make

- An insight into some of the future directions of our industry

This text is divided into definable chapters in the general order in which their issues first arise in the course of a development project—from market, site, political and environmental studies, through extensive design issues, and to marketing, construction and leasing—but most importantly, it shows how they all tie together to achieve a successful project.

For study purposes each chapter is self-sustaining, but in actual practice the material covered in the separate chapters continually overlaps and interrelates with the material from most other chapters throughout this process. Each chapter covers material the Development Officer should understand as a basis for intelligent decision-making, and highlights those issues of greatest concern.

The text concentrates on background knowledge, the process and the necessary discipline rather than providing specific answers—there are none. In fact, nothing in development is an absolute—there are infinite variations of solutions in response to various conditions, and differing points of view are healthy, even necessary, for a successful project.

Throughout the various chapters we refer to documentation—from land evaluation and purchase agreements through entitlement processing, various contracts and leases—but most of it is not discussed in great detail. In fact, the total documentation for an office building project is monumental. It is important to set up an overall file format and index as early as possible, so that none of this important documentation will be misplaced. An excellent filing system outline is found in Chapter 6 of the *Real Estate Development Workbook and Manual* by Howard A. Zuckerman and George D. Blevins. (See Appendix A, References.)

While extensive effort by your attorneys is essential to the proper consummation of the documentation effort, you must control the timing, participate in the documentation, and approve every business issue. You must not only understand and approve each issue, but clearly disseminate the information that affects the work of each professional in a timely manner.

It is also important to lock in all agreements entered into as quickly as possible, as circumstances and organizations change. It is not unusual for agreed-upon issues to be returned to the table for renegotiations. Broken agreements and possible litigation can be disastrous for a project, as timing is usually essential to success.

This text dwells on details, and rightly so, because any given project will have thousands of details, which must be addressed and solved with reasonably satisfactory results and within an appropriate time. A major responsibility of the Development Officer is to constantly review all issues to ascertain that you are anticipating, understanding, evaluating and resolving all details, endeavoring to ensure that no details, or the interrelationship between details, are missed completely or resolved in a less than satisfactory manner. Many a project has been placed in jeopardy because of a lack of attention to details.

The importance of details notwithstanding, the successful Development Officer must continually step back and address the overall objectives of the project, as described earlier in this chapter. Just as a lack of attention to details can seriously harm a project, it is even worse to become so bogged down in details that you lose sight of the ultimate objective.

The text is periodically amplified through actual issues experienced by, or known to, the author. These experiences are differentiated from the basic text material by being set in beige background text boxes with a green border.

The text material is supplemented by a Case Study of an eight-story speculative office building in Del Mar, California. The site was acquired for the purpose of building an office building and a hotel. The primary developer was Prentiss Properties, who developed the office building, shared parking structure and the site work, while selling the hotel pad to a hotel developer. There was separate design, construction and ownership, but the site evaluation, political process and all site planning were performed cooperatively. The issues encountered and the decisions made are chronicled in detail in direct relation to each text chapter, and are shown at the end of the respective chapters. They are differentiated from the text by the green stripe along the leading edge of each page. The Case Study adds additional interest to the basic text material and provides examples of specific decisions along with the reasons therefore.

The primary focus of this text is the development of individual office property projects. While the land development of office or integrated parks is beyond the intended purpose, a description of the land development process is included as Appendix D because this information is important knowledge for the Development Officer to have.

Several subjects that are essential to a complete work on office building development—real estate principles, real estate law, taxes, asset and property management, and development accounting—have been intentionally omitted. Construction, while covered to the extent of defining the Development Officer's role, is not covered in depth. There are many good texts and correspondence courses available in real estate principles and real estate law for those whose academic background does not include such training. Asset and property management, as well as construction, are major fields that fill many textbooks in themselves, and cannot be appropriately covered herein. Taxes and accounting are subjects best left to the requirements of each firm.

It is important to stay current with all present and future trends in materials and designs, as well as political and social issues, such as energy reduction and sustainable design. Due to cost and the frequent lack of willingness for the marketplace to pay for cutting edge advances, it is often difficult for the commercial developer to be too far out in front on newer trends—but current knowledge of these trends is essential and every effort should be made to stretch as far toward these goals as economically feasible, as they are not only socially important but good business. When working with institutional or build-to-suit tenants, they will normally have the long-term approach that will permit the use of the most effective selection of materials and/or processes, as determined on a life cycle analysis.

Although the information in this book represents 40 years of experience through several current active projects, the reader must recognize that it only represents a base upon which to address and discover the best solutions to the various issues of the future, utilizing new technology as it becomes available. The rapidly increasing flow of information and management capabilities obtained through the Internet, and the multiple forms of improved communications, provide the opportunity to develop new managerial skills and procedures that will enable continual improvement of the entire process.

A major issue for real estate professionals has typically been the expending of significant time and effort to seek out the necessary information required for project evaluation. In the future, the information will be so freely available that the issue will become the need to verify it, reduce it to applicable information, convert that information into knowledge, and convert that knowledge into effective implementation.

The continuing improvement in communications technology has accelerated the simultaneous review of the various drawings and documents with participants in distant cities, and project management is now being controlled through web sites. Video techniques will make it increasingly feasible to see each participant during a meeting as well as the applicable subject material, and a video camera can effectively be used to carefully inspect a job site condition from afar.

Please note that neither this text, nor any seminars based on this text, are intended to provide answers to specific development issues— they are intended to provide a basic understanding and to assist you in learning the essential thought processes that will guide you in making good development decisions.

Finally, it is intended that the information included herein will help you to think broadly through a wide range of issues, to think of the entire project encompassing many disciplines, and to utilize your development team to its maximum potential.

CASE STUDY

This Case Study was a development of Prentiss Properties (PPL) and was recorded as the development project unfolded in order to provide real examples of the many issues that arise. The issues, processes and decisions—both good and bad—are described in considerable detail in order to amplify and supplement the text. Sections of this Case Study are at the end of the applicable text chapters, though not all chapters are addressed. This rigid order will at times differ from the natural flow of design and project decision-making, and it might not seem to flow smoothly, but each issue will be covered in the appropriate section. This Case Study will make the discussion issues come alive, so that the participant can relate to, or question, the decisions and their timeliness in relation to the theory of the text.

The subject project is located in the 114-acre San Diego Corporate Center in Del Mar, California, about 15 miles north of downtown San Diego. It is immediately beyond the intersection of the new east/west I-56, currently under construction, with the major I-5 interstate that connects San Diego with Los Angeles. The site is immediately south of Prentiss' two-building Executive Center Del Mar project that was in its final stages of construction as this opportunity arose, and is bounded by El Camino Real on the east, the I-5 freeway on the west, and by Valley Center Drive (also called by its former name of Carmel View Road on some documents) on the south side.

The immediate surrounding area has 1.5 million square feet of office buildings, a DoubleTree hotel, seven restaurants, auto services and extensive housing. It is approximately five miles north of La Jolla, the University of California at San Diego and University Town Center, a major concentration of office space and hotels. It is also 12 miles from San Diego State University and 16 miles from Lindbergh Field and downtown San Diego.

The site was announced as available through competitive bidding by Pardee Homes, the developer of San Diego Corporate Center, and developer of thousands of acres of residential and commercial development. Bids were originally solicited by January 30, 1998, but the site was not awarded to Prentiss until May 1, 1998.

The site, known as Lot #1, contains approximately 8.65 gross acres (5.93 net acres after subtracting a non-buildable drainage and freeway easement) and was then zoned as VC, Visitor Center, for a 500-room hotel. Because analysis has clearly and consistently shown since its original zoning in 1984 that a 500-room hotel was not feasible on the site, Pardee decided to entertain bids for development of a 150,000 gross square foot office building and a 200-room hotel. Closing on the land would be contingent upon achieving these entitlements. It was initially presumed that such a change would require going through a completely new planning and entitlement process. Adjacent office sites have a zoning FAR of 0.5, which is less than one half of that in the approved designation.

Due to Pardee's total involvement in this office park and the entire southern Del Mar area, they required approval rights for the selected hotel operator, the ultimate hotel owner and operator, and the design and material selections for the project. They also required the exterior material to be brick or an approved equal to complement the remainder of the park and, additionally, the right to participate in zoning and regulatory discussions. Their position was understandable since this site was the commanding entrance to the office park, and they are continually obtaining governmental approvals for the development of new tracts of land that they currently own. Pardee, a subsidiary of Weyerhauser, still owns thousands of non-entitled acreage of land for future residential development.

The Request for Proposals included the items below, several of which are shown in the figures on the following pages.

- Aerial photo showing the area from downtown San Diego to Del Mar, Figure 1-1
- Description of the Opportunity
- Site Specific Information
- Aerial Site Plan of San Diego Corporate Center, showing the Site (Lot # 1), Figure 1-2
- Parcel Map, Figure 1-3
- Location Map, Figure 1-4

This site, which is portrayed more clearly as the parcels numbered 1 and 2 in Figure 1-5, was of particular interest to Prentiss because:

- The site is immediately adjacent to the two-building, 110,000 sf Executive Center Del Mar complex that was to be completed in May 1998
- At the time of final bidding stages the current project was 70% leased at rates ranging up to 10% above pro forma
- There is virtually no speculative space available in the immediate area
- There are uniquely favorable traffic conditions that will be discussed in detail in the Market Study

Because Prentiss does not develop hotels, and since Pardee wanted only a single party on the land purchase contract, it was necessary to find a hotel developer. There was a developer in San Diego who had been working closely with some of the Pardee people on the site, so an effort was made to enter into an acceptable agreement with him. It soon became readily apparent that an agreement could not be reached, even with the early assumption of a land cost of only $19/ gross sf. When advised the project could not work at his proposed numbers, he stated that he could not contribute any additional funds to the purchase.

A relatively new firm, Waterford Development, consisting of experienced hotel developers who had a tentative understanding with Hilton was evaluated and accepted to jointly submit a proposal for the site. It was important to establish procedures quickly to insure:

- An agreement with a quality hotel chain and operator satisfactory to Prentiss and Pardee
- An acceptable agreement between the parties that would govern design of the buildings and site, fair and reasonable cost sharing, and the on-going operational relationship
- Assurance that Waterford could meet its financial obligations in a timely manner

As the proposal period advanced, the developer who was first considered put in a bid on his own at $25/gsf, ($1/gsf above our final price) and continually passed negative information to Pardee relative to our hotel developer, their ultimate hotel purchaser, and what both Marriott and Hilton were saying to him—all of which turned out to be false. It was just one more issue to resolve in the process of obtaining the site.

The selection of this project for a Case Study was fortuitous, as it encountered more issues than the author had ever encountered before for a project of this size, or almost any size. This project tended to prove "Short's Theory" that the complexity of a project doubles with the addition of each party exercising significant control over the process. For example, a speculative office building in a jurisdiction with straightforward entitlement and approval processes would have a complexity factor of "1," the developer being the sole decision maker. In a town with a difficult entitlement and permit process, such as San Diego, the complexity factor would be "2." In this project with design approvals by Pardee, a hotel developer with whom many decisions must be shared, Marriott who drove many design and timing issues, and Brandes (the lead tenant, as discussed later) who drove so many timing decisions, it reach a complexity factor of "32." While there is empirical evidence of the theory's accuracy, it has not yet been mathematically proven beyond a shadow of a doubt.

Introduction

Figure 1-1

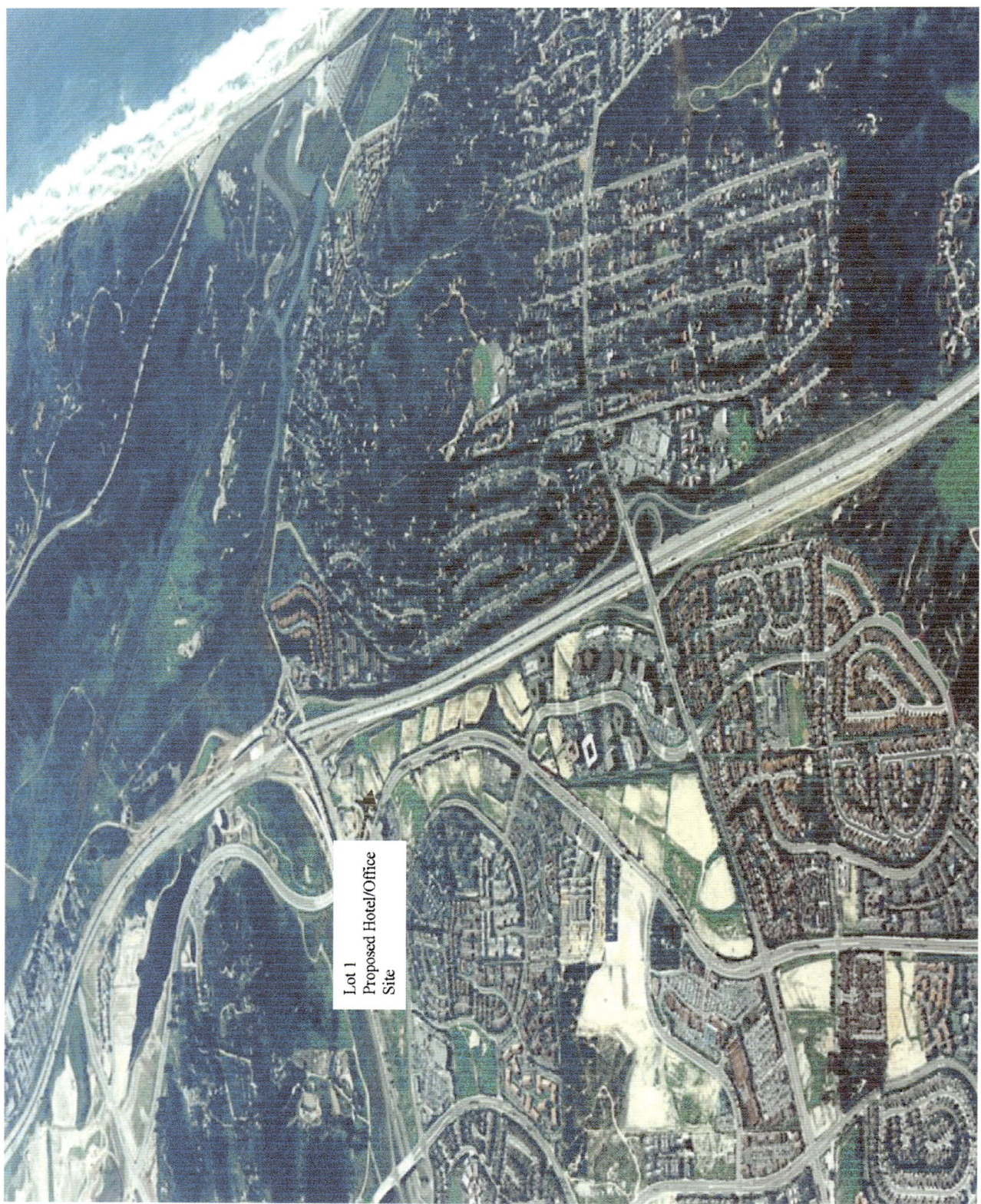

Figure 1-2

Parcel Map

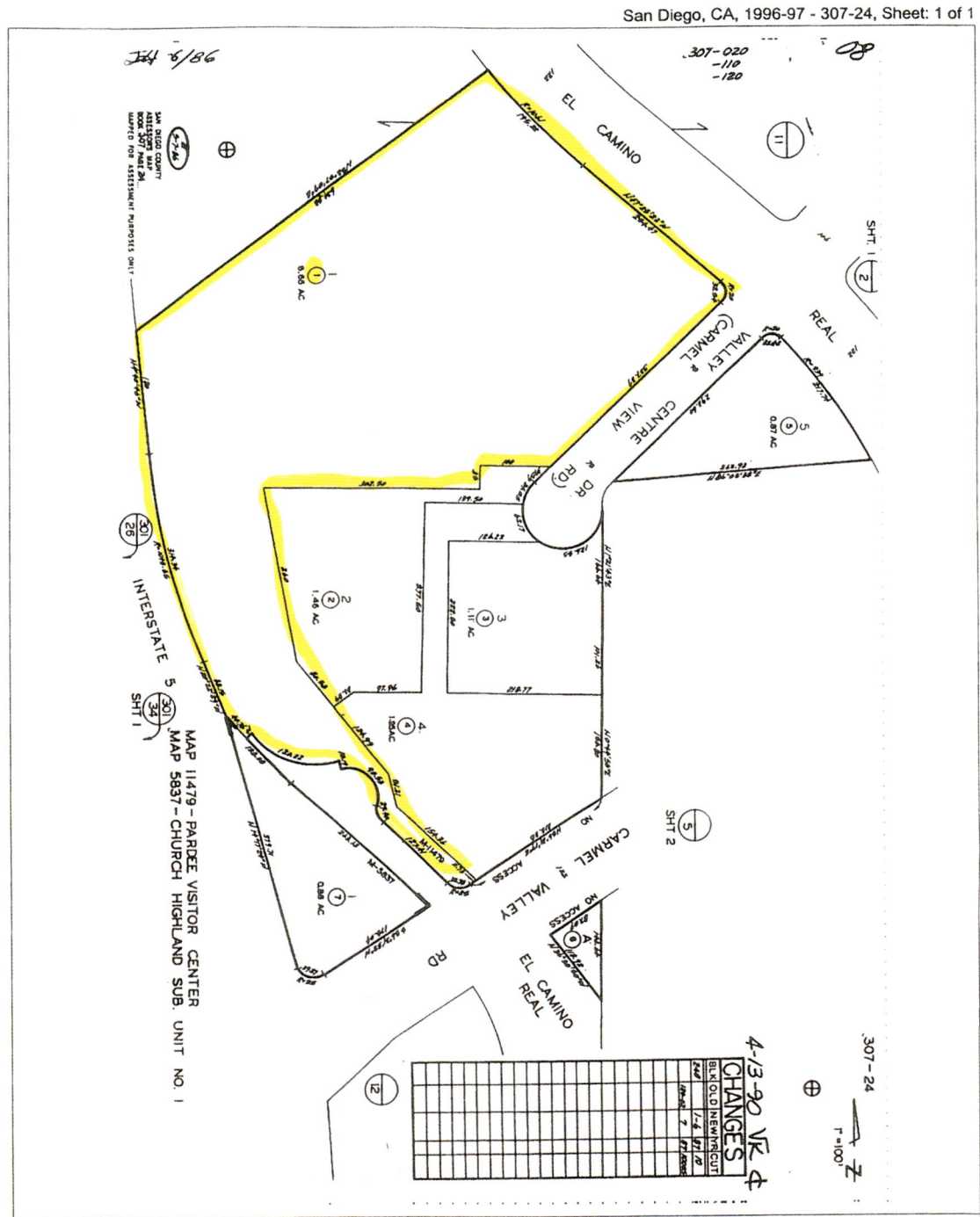

Figure 1-3

Figure 1-4

Introduction

1. Del Mar Gateway -
   Office - 8-Story, 161,500 RSF
   Prentiss Properties
2. Del Mar Gateway - Hotel
   Waterford Development
3. Brobeck, Phleger & Harrison -
   66,000 SF Office BTS
   Kilroy Realty
4. Safeskin Corporate HQ -
   240,000 SF - Proposed 3 & 4 Story
   Buildings - In Escrow
5. Kilroy Realty - SD HQ
   3-Story 55,000 SF
   Ground Breaking 30 Days
6. Executive Center Del Mar -
   4-Story 113,102 SF
   Prentiss Properties 95% Leased
7. Carmel Valley Corp. Ctr. -
   110,000 SF 100% Leased
   Kilroy Realty
8. Carmel Valley Centre I & II -
   110,000 SF - 94% Leased
   Spieker Properties
9. Doubletree Hotel
10. Accel BTS - Under Construction
    2-Story 40,000 SF Office Building
    Kilroy Realty
11. Advanced Information Resources
    70,000 BTS - 100% Leased
    3-Story Bldg. Complete Owner/User
12. Carmel Center - Kilroy Realty
    4-Phase Project - 135,000 SF
    5-Story Buildings
13. In Negotiations - Proposed
    Advanced Information Resources
    Expansion

Figure 1-5

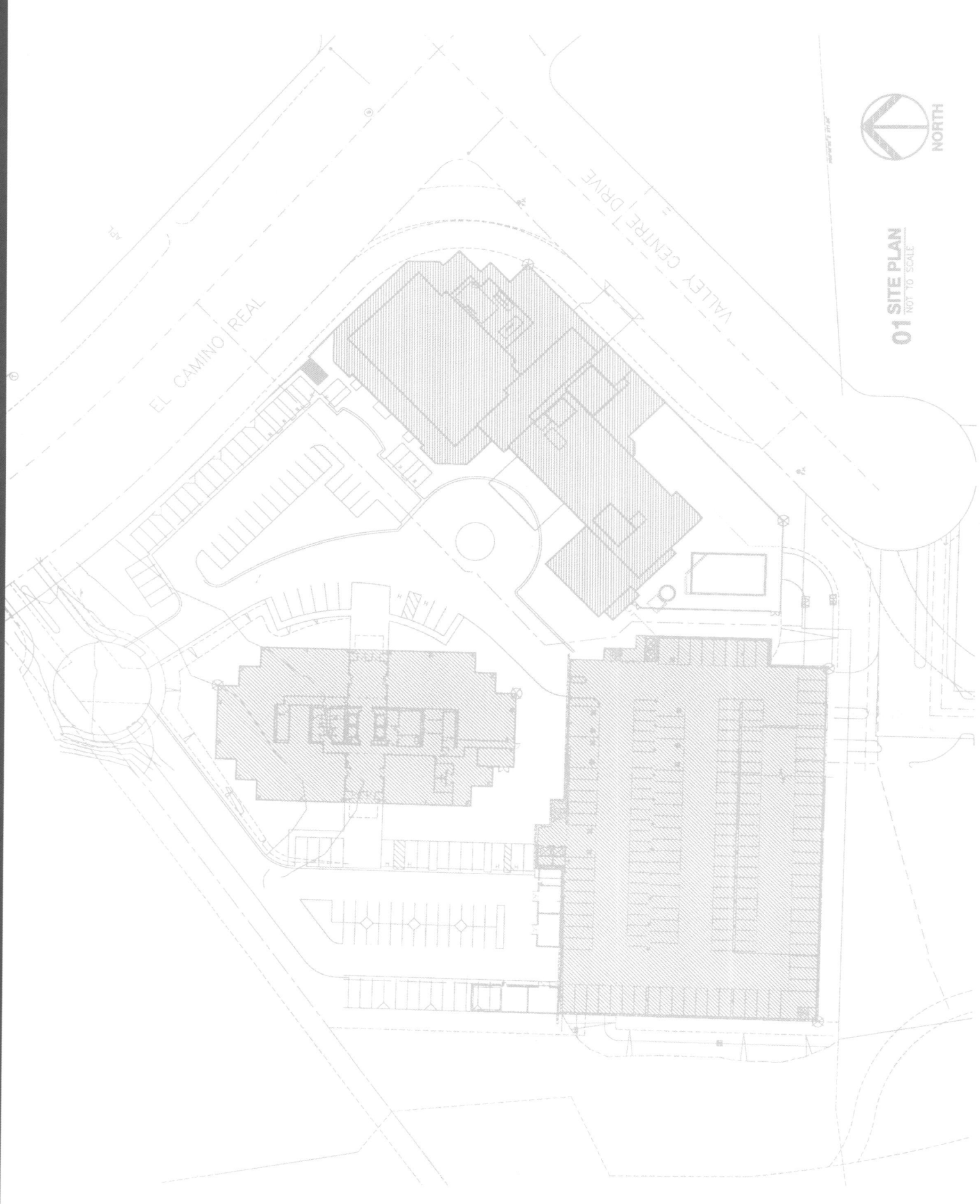

OBSERVATIONS, THOUGHTS and PHILOSOPHY

The successful project depends to a very large extent on the quality of performance of the Development Officer. The Development Officer defines and communicates the objectives, defines and communicates the strategy to accomplish those objectives and directs the execution of the strategy while endeavoring to achieve the highest quality performance from each team member. This requires substantial technical knowledge and, even more importantly, excellent people skills.

Development, like everything else in life, is approached with a combination of your overall philosophies, values and the impact of your past experiences. While different people have dramatically different value structures and experiences, the author's own thoughts on issues and beliefs indicated below have served him well throughout his development career.

What is Development?

- It is a project—it has an objective, a beginning, a process, an end, and the feedback of results
- It is a small operating business, wherein the successful project must meet all stated criteria, as well as bottom line results
- It is the creation of a profitable, habitable structure where none existed
- It's a financing vehicle to provide higher financial returns, or greater diversity, than alternate investments
- It is the disciplined common sense application of knowledge and principles—not rocket science

Keys to Successful Development

- Have a clearly defined objective—to achieve a product that satisfies the defined market, within the pro forma cost constraints
- Have a well-thought-out strategy
- Be accomplished with a single-minded focus

Project Control

- Projects are highly integrated—through many phases
- Development Officer must understand and be in control of each part of the project
- Thin organizations work best—one intermediate layer is the maximum—preferably none
- When delegating—clearly describe the delegated objectives, and obtain feedback of results
- It is essential to understand and monitor every dollar in the pro forma
- Success requires constant "hands on" control

Problems and Roadblocks

- Every project has them
- Problems must be considered solutions waiting to be found
- Don't believe that you cannot accomplish your objectives
- Never give up on an essential issue

- Creative brainstorming finds unusual solutions
- Stay focused on the objectives
- Address all issues with a positive attitude

The author came across the following quotation several years ago, cannot remember the source, and doesn't know the background of the author, but believes it is an invaluable philosophy toward life and work.

- Cross check information
- Listen more than talk—you never learn anything while talking
- Lead, push and encourage every team member to achieve excellence

Dealing with Professionals

- Treat them like professionals

ATTITUDE

"The longer I live, the more I realize the impact of attitude on life. Attitude, to me, is more important than facts. It is more important than the past, than education, than money, than circumstances, than failures, than successes, than what other people think or say or do.

It is more important than appearance, giftedness, or skill. It will make or break a company... a church... a home. The remarkable thing is we have a choice every day regarding the attitude we will embrace for that day. We cannot change our past... we cannot change the fact that people will act in a certain way. We cannot change the inevitable. The only thing we can do is play on the one string we have, and that is our attitude.... I am convinced that life is 10% what happens to me and 90% how I react to it. And so it is with you.... We are in charge of our attitudes."

— **Charles Swindell**

Style

- Check your ego at the door
- Understand your limitations
- Avoid trying to show off your knowledge
- You will never know as much as any of the consultants or other participants
- Encourage each team member to be creative—state and restate your objectives and concerns—not your own ideas or solutions
- Try to understand the limitations of each team member
- Demand team cooperation
- Don't be afraid to ask questions over and over until you understand all implications

- Recognize their superior knowledge of their fields
- Try to have just enough knowledge of their field to ask reasonable questions
- Their recommendations may be perceived by them to be the best technical solution, but they might not yield the result you are striving for in a given project
- Restate the project's objectives
- Keep asking questions until you get what you believe to be the best solution for the project
  ➤ Why?
  ➤ Why not?
  ➤ What is the benefit?
  ➤ What is the disadvantage or downside?
  ➤ What are the alternatives?

Observations, Thoughts and Philosophy

- Remember you are the *only one* who understands the entire project
    - Company objectives
    - Political implications and requirements
    - Economic constraints
    - Lending agreements
    - The market
    - Leasing commitments and requirements, and
    - The design and development of the project.
- The Development Officer's role is somewhat like a coach or conductor, he/she may not be able to perform each part or position, but must successfully lead the team
- But you must be demanding—push your professionals to excellence

Mistakes

- No unique, one-of-a-kind project has ever been built without many mistakes.
- The objective is to recognize, admit, control, correct and learn from each one.
- Failure to admit to, and address, mistakes can lead to greater problems later on.
- An automobile company spends four years or more in design and testing of a new model, then makes several hundred thousand units a year, and still has "lemons." Why would anyone think you could direct the design and construction of a one-of-a-kind building without mistakes?

> I found it was important to act toward each individual professional in a way that maximizes the results of his performance on the project and enhances his professional satisfaction. This usually means dealing with different ones in dramatically different ways. Quite a few years ago we engaged an architect, now deceased, who was one of the finest designers I have had the pleasure of working with, but he had a monumental ego with respect to his designs. If I had a concern about one of his design elements during a major project meeting, I would not discuss it in front of the others, but hold my comments until after the meeting was over. Later on, at his board, I would mention that what I hoped to accomplish was somewhat different from his proposal. I would say that I thought I knew what might solve the problem, and would work on it that night and come up with some ideas. We arranged to meet over a cup of coffee in the morning, where I would show him what I believed would be the best solution. He had such a poor regard for my design capabilities, and thought I might become enamored of my own ideas, that he would work long into the night, and before the morning meeting he had a range of excellent solutions that fully satisfied the project objectives.

Decision-Making

- Notwithstanding your efforts in encouraging the various professionals to produce their best recommendations—timely, well-thought-out and reasonable decisions must be made by the Development Officer. A feeling that the Development Officer is unable or unwilling to make decisions can demoralize a team.
- Decisions should, to the greatest extent possible, reinforce your belief in the team.

- Every mistake you make, if you learn from it, increases your value for future projects.

Understand the Risks

- Always try to recognize and face up to all risks—they won't go away

Be Realistic

- While you are striving for the optimal result, don't fall into the trap of believing that what you desire to have happen will happen—look for the hard reality—it is too easy to see everything through rose-colored glasses.

Integrity

- Long-term success, as well as your own sense of self-worth, is greatly enhanced by an unimpeachable set of ethical values, with your word being considered equivalent to a bond.
- The commercial real estate industry is really rather small, and you meet the same people over and over again. Any short-term advantage gained through a gray area of ethical behavior is lost many times over during your career.

will be wrong to some degree, must never be lost or combined with others, because your thought process can become untraceable.
- All paperwork must be processed properly and in a timely basis—no delays.
- Adhere to a reasonably detailed schedule at all times.
- Regardless of other commitments, focus on the project issues for some specific time each day to review all current requirements, open issues and time constraints.

Constructive interrelationships, integrity and always being true to your word will normally pay large dividends throughout your career. People will want to do business with you again and again. To the contrary, if they don't believe they can trust you, they will tend to avoid doing business with you. While this seems obvious in your own market area, the national commercial real estate business is smaller than one might think. I have done large lease deals in New York and Texas with California brokers, and in California with brokers from New York, Chicago and Texas. I have had as many as four large tenants in various parts of the country represented by the same interior designer, and have worked with the same contractor in several cities. You are very quickly known by your actions.

Discipline

- Error avoidance results from the continuous discipline of constantly reviewing each issue in an orderly, carefully-thought-out, step-by-step basis—and addressing each issue at the appropriate time.
- Each value of cost or income used in the originally approved pro forma, even though most

Preparation

The most important factor in real estate has been said to be "location, location, and location." In the development process, I believe it is "preparation, preparation, and preparation." **Always** be the best prepared person in every meeting, regardless of the subject matter.

Many years ago I served on the board of a not-for-profit organization in Chicago. One day I received a call from the director saying there was a budget bust of about $25,000 (a huge amount in those days) and requested me to try to convince a regular contributor to assist with the problem. I made an appointment for two days hence, but late in the afternoon before the meeting I realized I had no idea why this problem had occurred. I talked to our treasurer, took home the relative records and studied them until after 2AM. I understood the problem inside out and could answer any question our patron was likely to raise.

That morning after pleasantries, I said, "Clement, we have a short-term budget problem, and . . ." "How much do you need?" he asked. "We need $25,000, and it's because . . ." "OK, how is everything else going?" He never asked one question. Was it my body language? Did he sense I had all of the answers? Would he have contributed so readily if I was not prepared? I'll never know, but I believed it was because I was prepared.

Ever since that time I have believed that preparation was the key to success. I've rarely failed to achieve my desired results when fully prepared—rarely had very many questions. I believe completely in full preparation.

A final word: *The Development Officer is the one who has to make everything happen.*

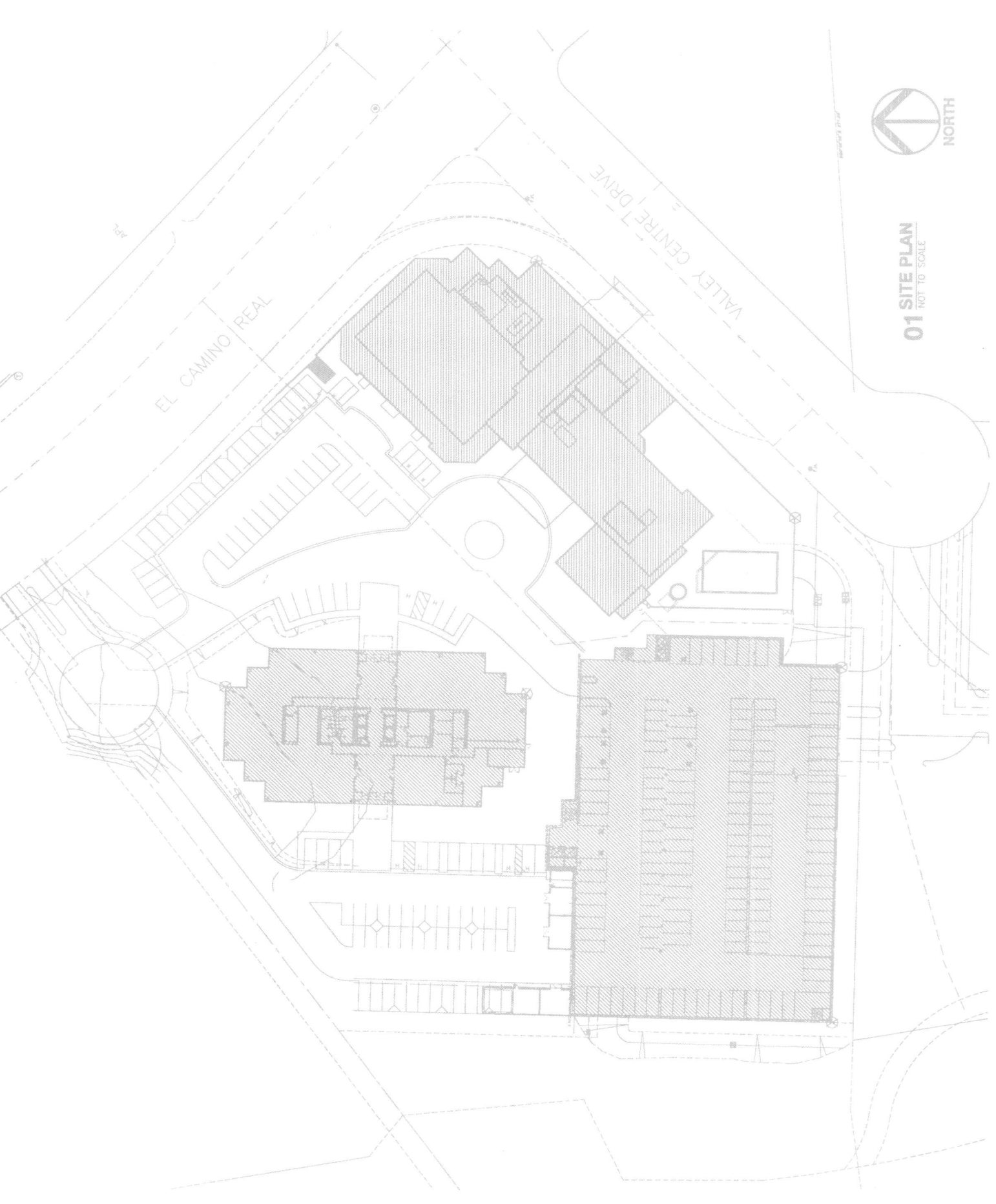

FEASIBILITY ANALYSES 3

Feasibility analyses are the most important evaluations made by the Development Officer, and the decisions based on them are the most important decisions to be made in a project. A Feasibility Analysis has three phases, which will be discussed in much greater depth in the three subsequent chapters.

- The Market Study—determines the economic potential of a proposed project
- The Site Study—defines the physical limitations on the project by zoning code and other issues, and explores the cost impact of the particular site
- The Political Environment—analyzes the political potential for a timely project, and the mitigation of community issues

This chapter provides an overview of the feasibility analyses, discusses sequencing them in stages of increasing depth, and shows how the information from these studies forms a basis for the design and marketing efforts.

Feasibility studies are used to determine the economic potential of a market area, a development site, and/or initiation of a development project in any given period of time. Market research identifies the opportunity and the income potential. The site, environmental and political evaluations primarily identify the potential cost and time constraints. A Feasibility Analysis should be performed in a very disciplined and open-minded manner—seeking the most factual and meaningful data possible—omitting any bias to "prove" the project to be feasible. Data collected should be validated by more than one source, if possible, and feasibility should always be measured against predetermined objectives and criteria.

If the economic potential is questionable, it is better to pass—there will always be another market, another site and another project. As negative information surfaces it takes significant courage to pull the plug after considerable funds have expended, **but if the desired objective is in jeopardy, it must be done.**

James Graaskamp provides an excellent definition of feasibility in *A Rational Approach to Feasibility Analysis* in 1973. Graaskamp stated, "A real estate project is feasible when the analyst determines that there is a reasonable likelihood of satisfying explicit objectives when a selected course of action is tested for fit to a context of specific constraints and limited resources." In other words, this definition states that feasibility provides only a reasonable likelihood of success, not a guarantee; it requires satisfying specific objectives that were established prior to the study, that it be feasible given a specific strategy and plan of action, and that it be performed within predetermined limited resources.

Feasibility studies are normally performed by the Development Officer, assisted by internal specialists—particularly the asset manager, leasing representatives and local property management—and the necessary external consultants discussed in later chapters. Formal feasibility studies by recognized real estate consultants are frequently required by lenders, but are rarely employed when internally determining project feasibility.

The depth of the necessary studies can be significantly reduced when the site to be purchased is already entitled for the type and scope of project anticipated. Not only are many of the environmental, regulatory and political issues already resolved, the total anticipated project development time is lessened, reducing market exposure. Alternatively, when there are substantial political and environmental issues, if the decision is to proceed anyway, the study should be in great depth, and the project should look for a return at least 100 basis points greater than a straightforward project to compensate for the greater time and risk.

These studies are normally performed in a series of stages, accomplishing the degree of depth deemed necessary to make the appropriate decisions at each stage. There must be satisfaction of a clear objective and recognition of a coherent strategy for the project to proceed at each decision point. Frequently the most sound and, sometimes, courageous decision is that a proposed project does not fit within the company's current operating or investment objectives. The sequential stages are:

- The first stage is more of a macro economic analysis to determine the degree of interest in a metropolitan area and, if so, the most attractive submarket, which is evaluated further prior to selection. The primary factors considered in this stage are a growing economy exemplified by increasing population and employment, reasonable and preferably declining vacancy, rising rental rates that would probably support new construction, and the appearance of a reasonably receptive political environment.

- The second stage, after selection of a submarket, requires a more extensive Market Study, identification of potential sites and their evaluation from both a site and a political standpoint. If it is determined that all defined issues can be reasonably resolved, site acquisition can proceed, excluding only the analysis of those site, environmental and political factors that can be treated as contingency issues in a land purchase contract.

- The third stage includes all of the factors from the market, site and political evaluations, as well as the information from the actual site planning and conceptual design. A strategy must be developed at this point to overcome the regulatory, political, environmental and site issues within acceptable cost and time parameters. All of this information, together with the conceptual design and estimated construction costs, is reflected in the pro forma for the project, which at this stage should include sensitivity analyses indicating the results of low, moderate and high forecasts of market conditions.

- The last stage is a final review of feasibility to determine if any market or other issues have changed from those identified in the third stage. This review should be made prior to closing on the land and committing the project to construction. It is better to have no project than the wrong project at the wrong time.

In addition to the important decisions regarding whether to enter a market, acquire land and initiate a project, a good Feasibility Analysis will provide the basis for strategies to overcome all identified issues, will provide the size, design quality and other information to serve as the Project Design Criteria, and will form the basis for developing an appropriate marketing program for the project.

The important information that will generally be included in a Feasibility Analysis, and the individual studies from which it comes, are outlined below. Certain of this information will be used in the acquisition and in setting marketing and leasing policies. The remainder will become the Project Design Criteria that will become the information provided to the design team as the basis for the design of the project, as discussed in detail in Chapter 14.

From the Market Study:

- Economic growth data for the metropolitan area
- Historical and projected data for office space, absorption, vacancy, rental rates and Tenant Improvements and inducements, for both the metropolitan area and the submarket
- Absorption rate and projected lease-up period
- Projected attainable rental rates
- Projected attainable stabilized occupancy
- Allowable construction cost based on the analysis of the achievable rental rates at an acceptable lease-up rate
- Size and type of most likely tenants
- Appropriate floor sizes and bay depths
- Appropriate building size

- The desired quality of the building to meet competition
- Ecological sensitivity of the community and prospective tenants
- Trends in use of rentable square feet per person
- Design building population densities
- Design requirements for structural floor loading, ceiling heights and electrical capacity
- Definition of rentable area
- Definition of shell and core construction vs. Tenant Improvements (TI)
- Projected tenant construction allowance and other concessions
- Acceptable methods of charging for electricity
- Desired parking ratios
- Adjacent tenant amenities, and those required on-site
- Labor pool to support target tenants
- Other relevant data

From the Site Study:
- Positive/negative marketing factors of the site—transportation, established office market and amenities
- Time, costs and strategies to mitigate the defined regulatory and environmental issues
- Zoning classification
- Permitted uses
- Maximum building height, bulk and density
- Unusual exiting or life safety requirements
- Site coverage
- Setbacks
- Building separations
- Traffic flow restrictions and requirements
- Minimum/maximum parking requirements
- Minimum landscape coverage
- Service dock requirements
- Special use limitations
- Special study costs
- Development, entitlement and permit fees
- Exactions and impact fees
- Off-site mitigation requirements and costs
- Utility and water management costs
- Abnormal soil, grading or other site costs
- Easements and other encumbrances
- Deed restrictions
- Discretionary review process and design review boards
- Real estate taxes
- Owner's associations
- Other relevant factors and costs

From the Political / Environment Evaluation:
- Definition of positive/negative political issues
- Strategy to overcome each negative issue
- Time, cost, strategies for, and probability of overcoming each negative issue

As stated at the beginning, each phase of the Feasibility Analysis will be studied separately in the following chapters to enhance the clarity of the discussion. All references to feasibility analyses in the Case Study will be incorporated in those chapters.

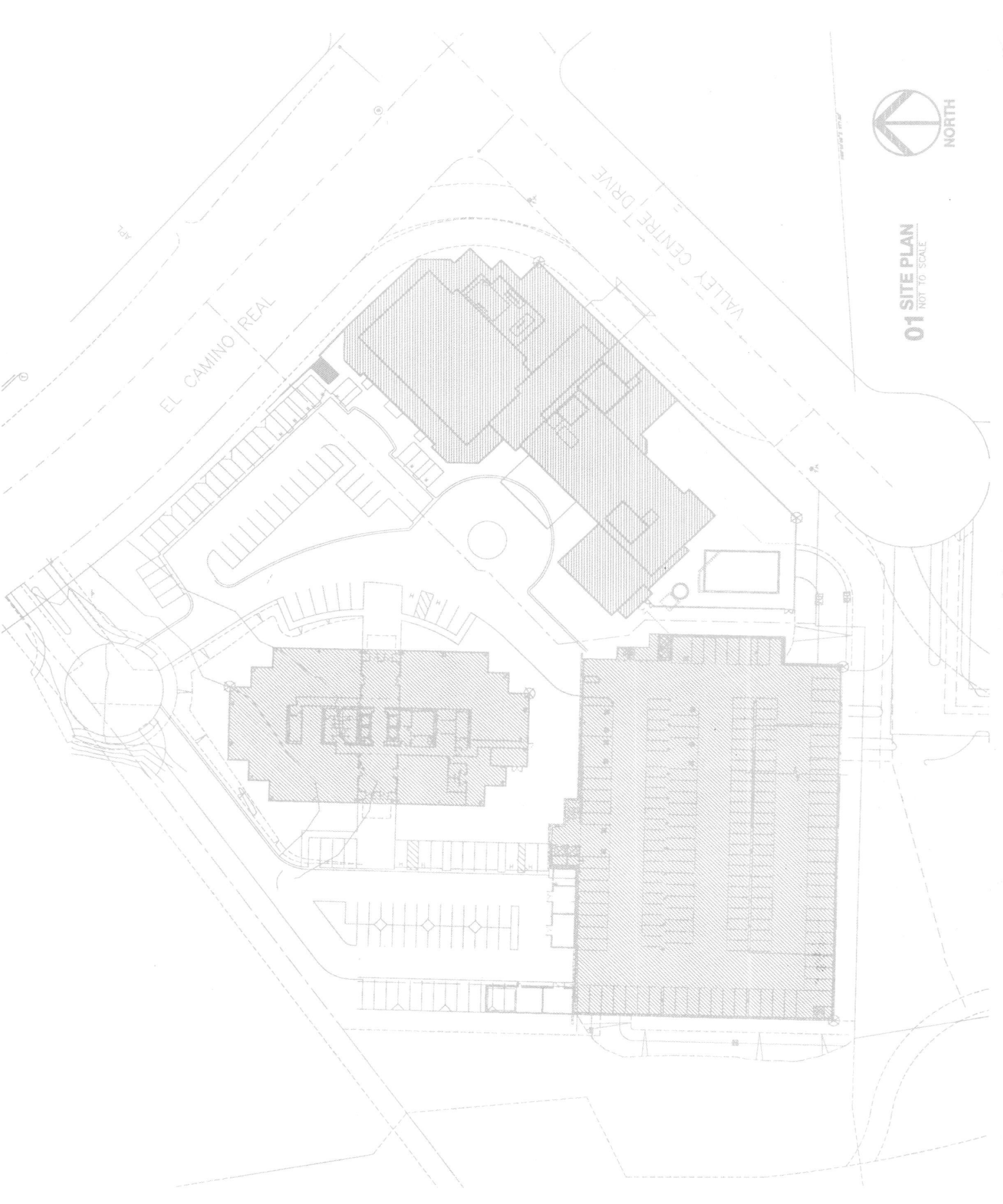

THE MARKET STUDY　　4

One of the two most important factors essential to an ultimately successful development project is a thorough and accurate market analysis—the other is successful leasing. The Market Study predicts the potential economic viability of a project, and successful leasing confirms it. It is the Development Officer's primary responsibility to ensure that this study is performed accurately and in a timely manner.

The study starts with the selection of a city and/or a proposed submarket, normally based on indications of a growing economy, reasonable vacancy and rising rental rates. In some cases, however, a site already will be under control, and the Market Study will be for the purpose of determining whether, when and/or how to proceed.

Many sources of market data are indicated, and the discussion in this chapter covers general economic trends, definition of market area, local definitions and practice, office market trends, demand analysis, office space supply, economic potential, the market cycle, product specific market data, amenities and services, marketing and site selection considerations. A brief discussion on the differences between speculative and build-to-suit projects is also included.

The decision to proceed with a project (or land acquisition) cannot be intelligently made without a full understanding of the market place in which the site is located. It is not only essential to understand the market as it exists, but to reasonably project the market through at least the entire development period, and preferably beyond. A smaller development on an entitled site may have a development period of 21 to 30 months, while it is not unusual for the development period of a larger project on a non-entitled site to be from four to six years or more—from site acquisition, through regulatory approvals, lead tenant negotiations, design, construction, and lease-up to a stabilized occupancy. The longer the development period, the more difficult the projections, and the greater the risk exposure of the project.

The extent of the Market Study may be reduced for a relatively small project on a previously entitled site when you are on the early part of the absorption phase of the market cycle. The shortened time horizon and market up-trend tends to limit the market risk.

In the event a decision is made to proceed, the most significant facts from the Market Study will be summarized and incorporated into the Feasibility Analysis along with similar facts from the site analysis and political environment, most of which then serves as Project Design Criteria. (See Chapter 14.) These criteria are one basis for the architect and design team to use in developing the conceptual designs, and will also be used as a basis for the preparation of an appropriate marketing plan.

Published and privately available economic, demographic and market data is available from sources such as Landauer Real Estate Forecast (www.landauer.com), Reis Reports, Inc. (www.reis.com), Data Resources, Inc., WEFA Group (formerly Wharton Econometrics (www.wefa.com), CB Commercial Torto-Wheaton (www.tortowheaton.com), ULI Market Profiles (www.uli.org), Cognetics Inc. (www.cogonline.com), Office Market Data Book by ONCOR International (www.oncorintl.com), Regional Financial Associates, Inc., and BOMA Experience Exchange Report (www.boma.org). Virtually all of these sources, as noted, and many others provide extensive data over the Internet, some only by subscription.

Governmentally generated data is available from various state and local offices of Economic Development or Management and Budget, U. S. Bureau of Labor Statistics, Bureau of Economics—U. S. Department of Commerce, and the U. S. Census Bureau. This data is available over the Internet.

Valuable local sources of market information are your asset and property managers, title companies, financial institutions, brokerage community, appraisers, redevelopment agencies, business development groups, chambers of commerce, local chapters of BOMA and IREM, economics departments of local universities, local library and local newspaper files. Some of this data may be available over the Internet, varying by source and location.

The extensive growth of information via the Internet may well reduce the information required from traditional sources, such as brokers. The successful developer will learn to sift through and evaluate the proliferation of information and turn it into effective knowledge. While brokers in general will be less important as a basic source of information, the better ones will retain their value through effective interpretation and projection of the data.

A good graphic method of evaluating the historic direction of growth, and frequently the reasons therefore, is through studying aerial photos displayed in approximately five-year intervals. Another such source are the newer electronic Geographic Information System (GIS) maps that in many areas provide extensive information, including landmarks, driving times, taxes, crime rates and other layers of information to help define and evaluate market areas.

Factors to consider in a market evaluation are discussed below. There are surely others, and many of these will not be necessary in any particular project.

General Economic Data and Trends

The first assessment is the viability of a city or metropolitan area and the most likely submarkets (to the extent that submarket data is available) as indicated by growth in population, employment and business locations.

National data on interest rates and Gross Domestic Product (GDP) growth, while not affecting the choice of a market, can raise a cautionary or positive flag as to development in general in the reasonably foreseeable future.

The following economic data does not have project specific use, but forms a background which, if it shows a healthy and growing economy in the area, will support and validate the likely long-term viability of a project, when that project is justified on the more site specific data. On the other hand, no growth, or slow growth, in the employable base will be a significant limit on the office market potential.

- Population growth
- Employment growth
- Office worker growth
- Available labor pool
- Demographic profiles
- Housing growth, availability and cost
- Retail sales
- Real estate values
- Corporate move-in/move-outs
- Business start-ups
- National and state GDP trends
- Interest rate trends

The available labor pool is an interesting factor. Significant available labor can be an important factor in encouraging in-migration of firms, but if too high it may indicate a lack of growth. It must be considered only in conjunction with other growth factors.

Define the Effective Market Area

When the economic data indicates a positive probability for a development in a given metropolitan area, the most attractive competitive submarket for your predetermined type of product must be selected. An office submarket is usually defined as a geographic area defined by vehicular driving times, transit availability and patterns, natural barriers, economic and demographic profiles, location of positive or negative elements, and competitive office districts.

Submarket data on growth available from the overall data collection above can usually be used to determine the most favorable submarket for your product. The most likely definitions of Dallas submarkets, for example, might be:

- Dallas CBD
- NW Dallas
- North Dallas
- Central Expressway
- Las Colinas
- Dallas/Fort Worth Airport
- Plano and beyond

If possible, try to identify whether information relative to your submarket has a historical correlation with national, state, or local economic data—as to whether it lags, leads, or coincides with those more rigorously tracked trends.

In every metropolitan area, for each product type, there is usually one dominant corridor of growth—although there may be one or more secondary corridors. The normal preference is to locate in the primary corridor, however, in some circumstances a secondary corridor may be attracting less competitive product and may be more compatible with your preferred target market.

Local Definitions and Practice

Before collecting specific market data it is important to learn and understand the definitions used in each local market, and verify that all data collected is consistent with these definitions.

- Total office inventory, or office stock, may or may not include corporate-owned buildings, build-to-suit buildings and governmental buildings, and usually does not include buildings smaller than some specified size. Within any market you may use any local definition, as long as it is consistent throughout the study.

- Space leased—the total area of leased space existing in the above-defined inventory.

- Space leasing rate—the total area of leases consummated in a given period. It is frequently erroneously used in place of absorption, which can greatly distort the market realities.

- Absorption—the total area of leases consummated in a given period, less space formerly used by each newly leased tenant, space not intended for immediate use, and still-leased space formerly used by tenants who are relocating from the market area.

- Demand—a prediction or extrapolated projection of the absorption of office space, usually over a several year period.

An example of the strength and durability of a development corridor can be found in Dallas. A study of high-end commercial development and upscale housing there since 1900 provides some interesting insights. At the turn of the century the most important residential direction was southerly. When Southern Methodist University was founded early in the century, on the north side of downtown, it created an almost immediate impact on that area by encouraging high-quality residential areas and supporting commercial development. From that time on, although modified somewhat by the development of DFW Airport, the primary development corridor has been almost straight north. From recent appearances it may soon reach Oklahoma. Many efforts have been made to alter the direction of the corridor, with minimal impact.

- Vacancy—space currently unleased, adjusted upward for uncommitted space in new or planned construction, space occupied by tenants committed to new construction or other spaces, space available for sublet and space that is leased but unused, and adjusted downward for buildings scheduled for demolition.

- Building class—a rough evaluation of building size and quality graded as A, B and C, and sometimes D, with plusses and minuses for further distinction. A+ is usually a high quality high-rise building, whereas A is a good quality newer building. B and lower are usually older, less well-located or inexpensively constructed buildings. Classifications can vary somewhat between various markets.

- Rentable area—the generally accepted standard nationally, frequently with a few local variations, is ANSI/BOMA Z65.1-1996, *Standard Method for Measuring Floor Area in Office Buildings,* available from Building Owners and Managers International. (See Appendix A.)

- Shell and core construction vs. Tenant Improvements—determined by current local market practice. (See details in Chapter 30.)

- Rental rates—it is necessary to understand whether the quoted rates are gross, gross less utilities or net rental rates as determined by local market practice. Gross rental rates normally include operating costs, utilities and real estate taxes. Net rental rates include no expenses, and is the income that covers the debt service and profit. Gross less utilities is self-explanatory.

Office Market Trends

The market data as discussed in subsequent paragraphs should be collected for the overall market, your selected submarket, and also for nearby submarkets that are partially competitive. It is rare that a submarket can maintain long-term viability when the overall market is stagnating or suffering with slow growth—they normally will not stay out of synchronization for too long. One should recognize the difficulty of collecting all of the desired data, as good information is often limited by poor records, and inconsistent and changing definitions. Nevertheless, it is essential to reconstruct this data in the most accurate manner possible.

The specific uses of market data are discussed in the following paragraphs on Demand Analysis, Office Space Supply and the Economic Potential. Collectively, these are the basis for a judgment as to whether the market will be acceptable over the projected development period so that it is appropriate to proceed with the purchase of property or to commence construction.

At this point you should note that virtually everyone in the business knows the direction and approximate intensity of the market at any point in time. The thorough analyst is the one who, by

---

My first exposure to an analysis sufficiently thorough to predict a strong market turn well in advance was in 1977 when I became responsible for the Crocker Bank properties. We had a major building in Los Angeles in which about one-half of the leases were going to expire in the next 18 to 24 months. Some of the major tenants had initiated negotiations to extend their leases. The market was generally depressed, and most of the individuals I consulted projected the market would remain more or less flat for several years. That assumption would result in re-leasing the space at approximately the current rental rates. Then John C. Cushman III provided me with his projection of the market. It was thorough and in great depth, considering factors such as employment growth rates that others ignored. I had never been exposed to such a quality analysis before. Based upon his recommendations we increased our rates by 40% and had no trouble re-leasing the building.

> Conversely, in Dallas in the mid-'80s no one either projected, or would believe, the impending real estate disaster. While Houston was savaged unexpectedly by the sudden drop in oil prices, developers in Dallas had time to evaluate the situation and react. The sad part is that by late 1983 or, at the very latest, early 1984 the information predicting the downturn was clearly visible—excessive inventories, new product coming to market much faster than net absorption, weakening quality of bank earnings, and slowing growth rates. Unfortunately, financing sources, most were from out of state, were awash in cash and still blinded by the mystique of Dallas. How many billions of value could have been saved by disciplined attention to the market?

correctly correlating and properly projecting the data, can reasonably predict the turns, and intensity of those turns, in the market. It is this ability to project the market turns that can create great wealth or, conversely, great losses.

Demand Analysis

Demand analysis is a prediction of the amount of office space that will be required during the anticipated term of a development project. It is, simplistically, the additional amount of office space required to house the anticipated additional number of office workers in the studied market(s) over that period, resulting from the net growth of workers in existing businesses and those from the inflow of new businesses. After studying all available data, there are two methods by which this prediction is computed—by projecting office worker growth and by studying and projecting space absorption—which are analyzed in parallel.

Demand analysis, like all other facets of the Feasibility Analysis, is studied with a rolling level of depth—sufficient at any point in time to make the various interim decisions. When investigating whether to enter a market, the study usually encompasses the overall market, and is initially completed only to a level necessary to determine whether there is a serious interest. Further study will determine the submarket(s) of interest and then, if acceptable sites are available, the study is concluded in depth with respect to the selected site(s).

The study of office worker growth will usually start with the recent history and an estimate of future employment levels by the local planning agencies. Where local agencies do not exist, or do not provide this service, projections can be obtained by analyzing estimated future data provided by the Bureau of Economic Analysis of the U.S. Department of Commerce and from historical data available from studying the applicable Standard Industrial Classification codes of the U.S. Bureau of Labor Statistics. Census Bureau data provides an indication of the overall population growth trends. The federal data is the underlying information used as a starting basis by the local planning agencies. The resultant projection of the growth of office workers must then be multiplied by an appropriate unit of rentable area per worker to obtain the projection of office space demand.

In many markets today the average amount of office space per employee is in the range of 175 to 250 rentable square feet per person, varying with type of operation. This unit space requirement may vary from city to city, between downtown and suburban markets and by industry group. An excellent source for current local information on square footage per person would be the local BOMA office, as well as other local real estate sources. There has been a recent trend toward "office warehousing" (where several employees share the same space, as their schedule requires), remote or home officing, and an increase in the trend toward open planning. While these trends have reduced unit office space requirements somewhat, and must be carefully watched, at this time it is not clear that it is going to have a further major effect on office space usage. An exception to the above averages is office space usage by large clerical or call center operations.

In addition to the study of workforce trends, a parallel analysis is made of the actual occupancy, vacancy and space absorption trends over the medium-term, preferably the past five or so years. Like the data above, it represents the result of existing business growth plus net business inflow, but also can be affected by obsolescence of older buildings and/or the shifting growth between submarkets.

Absorption data is frequently very uneven or erratic from year to year due to the varying availability of space, timing of major lease expirations and the individual move-in/out of significantly sized firms. In evaluating this data as a basis for projection, it is necessary to smooth it out to determine a reasonable annual average, growing on an annual basis generally in relation to its proportion of the increasing size of the base inventory. A "theoretical" absorption rate may then be projected through the anticipated development period. One caution: design-build space for a new tenant in town is absorption, but it may not have an impact on the speculative rental market.

The extrapolation of the theoretical future absorption **must never be accepted** in its raw form. The fact that it might well represent a long-term growth rate is irrelevant to the Market Study, as it does not indicate what is likely to occur in the immediate or near term future. Many a development analysis has incorporated such straight-lined data with disastrous results.

To effectively use this data, it is necessary to understand why absorption occurred, and stay alert for circumstances where the meaning of the data can be distorted by other events. For example, excessively low rental rates in other submarkets, excessive vacancy and low rental rates in higher or lower building classes and lack of available space in your submarket can give a falsely low absorption reading. Alternatively, low availability of space in adjoining submarkets and low rents in your submarket can indicate large increases in absorption that may not materialize as rental rates try to rise to the level that supports new construction.

The projection through the development period must be adjusted year by year based upon local information, some of it anecdotal, such as:

- Potential existing pent-up demand from firms unable to find space to fill their expansion needs
- Recent major expansions of space, which cannot be duplicated in the near future
- Knowledge or rumors of corporate relocations, downsizing or unusual projected growth
- General or locally specific economic data, which may increase or defer office worker expansion
- Potential competition from other submarkets or other building classes
- Change or stability in market lease rates and concessions
- The current position of the market in the market cycle

Another gauge to determine or measure the historical demand requirement is the annual amount of office space leased. This number is an important guide and may equate to absorption over a long enough period of time, but can be misleading. It will count space leased, but not yet occupied, in a new building while ignoring the vacancy created in the space that the firm is currently occupying.

A major factor affecting demand potential for the proposed project is the indicated demand in the specific industries and businesses that are most likely to relocate to your specific submarket. Such study may also identify potential lead tenants for a new project.

Data collected in the course of this study may frequently be contradictory. Determining absorption may provide differing projections, both year by year and in aggregate, when the appropriate adjustments are not made. When all of this data has been gathered, tested and evaluated, the ultimate assumption of demand for the specific submarket rests with the evaluation and "gut" belief of the Development Officer.

The demand analysis, like every other factor in the Market Study, must be updated throughout the predevelopment process, most particularly just prior to closing on the land and before commencing construction.

Office Space Supply

The study of office space supply correlates the information available on total office space inventory, potential new office space and vacancy rates. As with demand analysis, it may be looked at on an overall market basis and then more specifically evaluated for a selected submarket.

The method of inventory compilation may vary with the market. As indicated earlier, it is normally broken down into the class of building, i.e., from an A+ down to either a C or D rating. These ratings are a function of a building's quality, age, size, location and amenities. It is often further broken down between multi-tenant, owner/user and governmental office buildings, however, in some markets these latter two categories are either not specified separately or are omitted. Most markets also only list buildings above a specific size. The inventory lists each building by its location, indicating the size and unoccupied (or unleased) space.

In order to have a complete picture of supply, it is wise to analyze all potentially competitive building classes, such as A+, B+ and possibly even B. It is also necessary to analyze the supply in potentially competitive submarkets. These sources of indirect competition can become important in cases of major market imbalances. Buildings classified as B or B+ may not be directly competitive to your new project, but if there is too much vacancy in those categories a large enough rental rate discrepancy may be created that encourages tenants to accept the lower quality space. In a similar manner, rental rate disparity can cause market shifts between submarkets.

The known vacancy in your competitive classifications in the market or submarket must be adjusted for:
- Space available for sublet
- Rented space that is unoccupied
- Recent or planned corporate relocations or mergers
- Buildings that are planned for removal from inventory due to their obsolescence, or deterioration of their market area
- Competitive buildings under construction adjusted for the difference between any preleasing and the respective tenant's existing occupied space
- Projects in the predevelopment phase whose construction during your proposed development period can reasonably be expected

It should be specifically noted that for the last inventory adjustment indicated above, the accuracy of the projection varies greatly from state to state and jurisdiction to jurisdiction. In some areas of Texas, for example, it is very difficult to learn of planned projects unless information is obtained from a broker, design professional or government officials who may be aware of the plans due to the simplified and rapid approval process. On the other hand, in many jurisdictions in California the entitlement process is so lengthy and so public that there is a very clear record of the status of each project that may proceed ahead of, or following, yours and its position on the development timeline.

The historical vacancy rate, adjusted as deemed necessary, is studied to determine both its magnitude and its volatility. A stable vacancy rate, at a reasonably low level, indicates a stable market that has been remaining basically in balance. Recent changes in rental rates and/or concessions may indicate the likelihood as to whether the vacancy rate remains in its current range. A rising vacancy rate with falling rental rates is a major red flag, while the opposite is a very positive indicator, unless there is excessive new product coming online. If the vacancy rate is deemed to be too high or too low to be stable, the projection of office space supply must be adjusted accordingly.

It is important to note that the study of the former and current vacancy rate trend is a guide toward the stabilized vacancy rate assumption to be used in the project pro forma.

Economic Potential

The prior analyses have determined both a projection of the potential office space demand (absorption) for the selected submarket over the estimated development period, and based upon the best knowledge available, the estimated supply of the product over the same period. If these two figures are in a reasonable balance, and the vacancy level is currently in an acceptable range, there is a preliminary assumption that the project can be constructed within that period and be successfully leased if the project is in other respects competitive to the other product.

By comparing the size of the proposed project with the total supply anticipated during the development period, you obtain the mathematical percentage of the market represented by your project. The next step is to develop a matrix in which a comparison can be made of the proposed building with all existing and proposed competitive buildings on the basis of presumed quality, location, image, amenities, effective rental rates and any other relevant factors, in order to determine whether your project can be assumed to capture more, less or the same amount of space as your market share (the capture rate). Based upon the analysis of your capture rate of the available demand, a reasonable assumption can be made as to the most likely lease-up period for the building at competitive market rates, to reach the assumed stabilized vacancy.

A rule of thumb used by some developers, when more definitive market data is not available, is that the projected market demand in the submarket during the development period should be three to five times the rentable area of the proposed project in order to comfortably proceed with construction. This ratio presumes to provide a safety factor to allow for unanticipated competitive product and weaker than anticipated market demand, but is less satisfactory than a more rigorous evaluation.

A further study of the market data will indicate the current levels of rental rates, Tenant Improvements and other concessions, as well as the degree to which rates and concessions might change upward or downward within the proposed development period.

- Market rates in buildings most comparable to proposed project in location and quality
  - Face rates achieved
  - Rental escalation factors
  - Free rent
  - Tenant Improvement allowance value
  - Parking rates, if any
  - Other concessions or amenities
- Operating costs
- Trend in utility rates and operating costs
- Tax rates

Normally your proposed new office building will be classified as an A building and, therefore, primary emphasis will be placed on evaluating the buildings and market in that category. In a potentially difficult market careful attention must be paid to the A+ buildings as they might reduce their asking rent to lure away prospective tenants from your project thus requiring you to reduce your rents in order to maintain a spread and stay competitive. As discussed under Office Space Supply, the information from competitive submarkets should be carefully reviewed to determine if any competitive imbalances could affect the project economics.

From analysis of all of the above data, a set of initial leasing guidelines may be developed for the project.

Through a preliminary pro forma analysis (see Chapter 11) you can compute a presumed total project cost and initial returns using the economic income data assumptions derived above, and the estimated development and land costs. At this time you may have only a very preliminary understanding of certain of the zoning and site-induced costs pending further study. However, if the initial cash on cash and internal rate of return calculations appear satisfactory, an initial decision can be made to acquire the property, if not already controlled, and/or to proceed with a more rigorous evaluation of the site and political implications, and further refine the project assumptions and predicted economic returns.

Market Cycle

Contrary to opinions frequently expressed by persons trying to promote a development project, or during a long upward trend, the market cycle has never been legislated out of existence. The cycles will always occur—only the timing and severity are to be determined, and they are greatly affected by the national and state economies and interest rates.

The Market Study

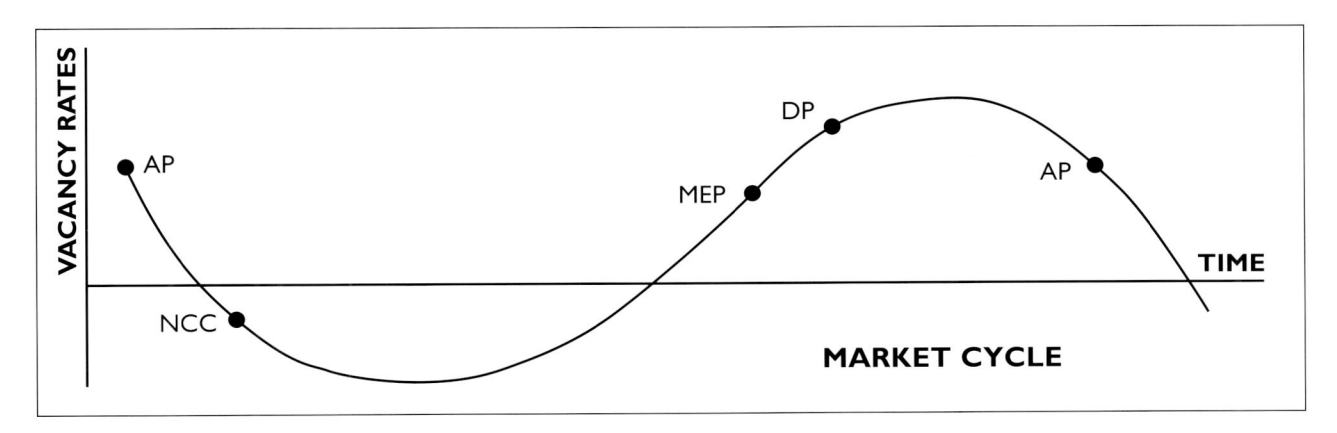

Figure 4-1

The phases of the market cycle are described below and are illustrated in the graph, in which the highest vacancy rate in the cycle is at the top of the graph and the lowest vacancy rate is at the bottom.

- Market Equilibrium Point (MSP)—supply and demand are in equilibrium, beyond which inventories continue to rise, and rental rates stabilize before starting to decline.

- Down Phase—overbuilt in relation to demand and vacancy rises past the point of market equilibrium. Rental rates decline and concessions rise. Very little construction occurs since lending is discontinued except for fully preleased buildings.

- Absorption Phase—economic adjustments and the lack of new product take effect. Excess inventory is absorbed and rental rates start to rise. New development activity soon commences. Most lenders do not reenter the market until this phase is well underway.

- New Construction Phase (NCP)—demand increases relative to supply, declining vacancy and rising rental rates create the conditions for new construction.

A more extensive discussion of the market cycle can be found in *Real Estate Development Workbook Manual,* by Howard A. Zuckerman and George D. Blevins (Prentice Hall, 1991). See Appendix A.

Misunderstanding the position in the market cycle at the time major decisions are made can be one of the most serious judgmental mistakes in evaluating a potential project. It has been my experience that effective rental rates (face rates less any over standard concessions) lag the cycle by three to six months.

In order to assess the position of the market cycle, it is recommended that data over five to ten years or more be collected, where available, for both the selected submarket and the metropolitan area covering office inventory, absorption, vacancy, rental rates, and leasing concessions (this latter data may have to be annotated). Graphing this data over time can assist in predicting the approximate current position in the market cycle, as well as projecting absorption, rental rates and concessions.

An example of data from a market analysis of the San Francisco CBD is shown on the following two pages. Note the inverse ratio of the vacancy rate and the weighted average of the gross rental rate over time as shown in Figure 4-1. The inventory shown in Figure 4-2 was distorted by the damage from the Loma Prieta earthquake. When the vacancy and gross rental rate trends are combined with the flat inventory, these graphs indicate a strong speculative office development market. Note that some basic information that we normally require is missing, but would not be critical to decision making in this instance:

- Absorption—can be deduced from the flat inventory and the declining vacancy.

- New product under construction—is always readily determined in San Francisco due to its very slow and public procedures, and specified annual limits on development

Office Development

San Francisco Central Business District 1981 thru YTD 1997
Class A Average Asking Rental Rates & Overall CBD Vacancy Rates

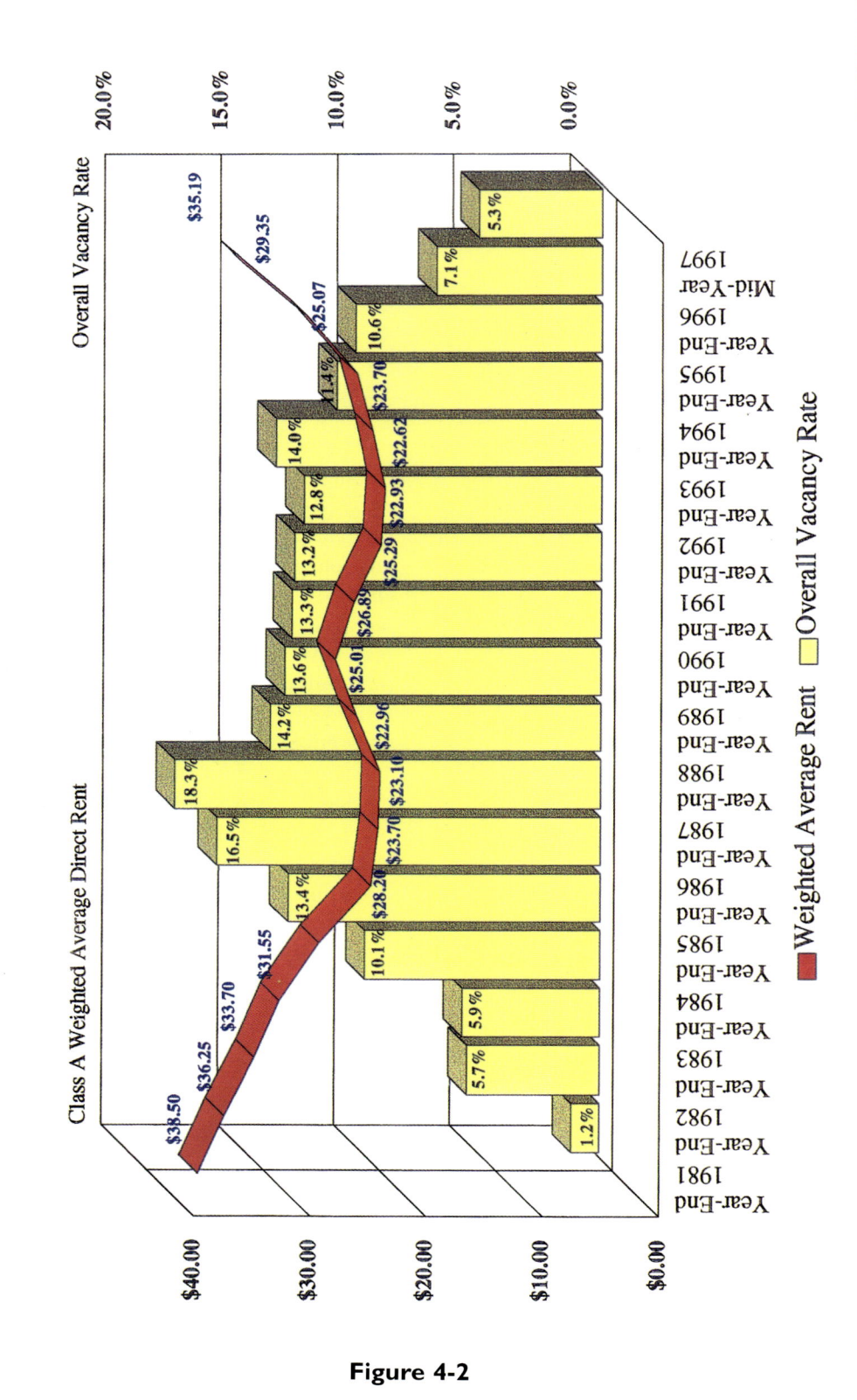

Year	Weighted Average Rent	Overall Vacancy Rate
Year-End 1981	$38.50	1.2%
Year-End 1982	$36.25	5.7%
Year-End 1983	$33.70	5.9%
Year-End 1984	$31.55	10.1%
Year-End 1985	$28.20	13.4%
Year-End 1986	$23.70	16.5%
Year-End 1987	$23.10	18.3%
Year-End 1988	$22.90	14.2%
Year-End 1989	$25.01	13.6%
Year-End 1990	$26.89	13.3%
Year-End 1991	$25.29	13.2%
Year-End 1992	$22.93	12.8%
Year-End 1993	$22.62	14.0%
Year-End 1994	$23.70	11.4%
Year-End 1995	$25.07	10.6%
Year-End 1996	$29.35	7.1%
Mid-Year 1997	$35.19	5.3%

Class A Average Asking Rental Rates are identified in blue-ink.

Figure 4-2

The Market Study 43

SAN FRANCISCO CBD OFFICE INVENTORY
1981 - 1997

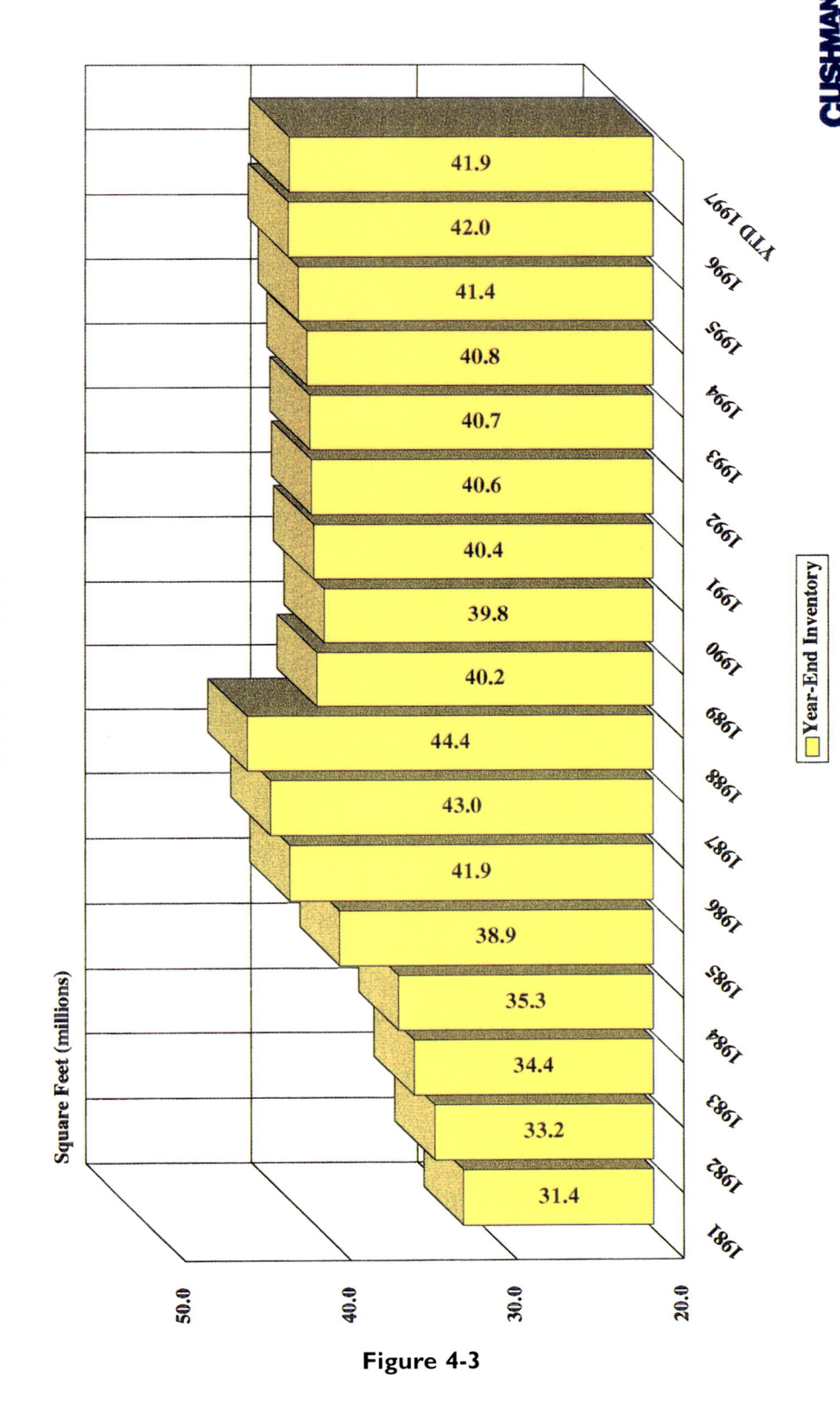

Square Feet (millions)

Year	Year-End Inventory
1981	31.4
1982	33.2
1983	34.4
1984	35.3
1985	38.9
1986	41.9
1987	43.0
1988	44.4
1989	40.2
1990	39.8
1991	40.4
1992	40.6
1993	40.7
1994	40.8
1995	41.4
1996	42.0
YTD 1997	41.9

Inventory fluctuates from 1992 - 1997, due to the commencement or completion of building renovations. In 1989, inventory damaged by the Loma Prieta Earthquake was extracted from our inventory statistics.

CUSHMAN & WAKEFIELD®
Improving your place in the world.℠

Figure 4-3

- Population growth—the important factor in the downtown of a metropolitan area of this size is the overall area growth.

It should be noted that positive trend lines alone are not sufficient to make a decision to go forward—it must be combined with knowledge of potential new competitive product, anecdotal market data and "gut" judgment.

On the other hand, negative trend lines would normally preclude going forward with a project unless there is a large preleased tenant, and maybe not even then. Even though a large committed prelease meets the pro forma numbers, leasing the remainder of the building at significantly less than pro forma rates might seriously dilute the overall net income.

- Quality of competitive buildings—compare important design features likely to attract or deter target tenants

- Ecological sensitivity of the community and prospective tenants

- Trend in rentable square feet (rsf) per person—there is some trend in back office operations toward greater population densities and higher electrical loads, affecting air conditioning and elevator capacity

- Potential of users requiring greater ceiling heights, higher structural floor loads and/or electrical capacity

> While a thorough market evaluation often seems like excessive effort, it is fully worth while in the long run. As with so many things, I learned this the hard way. Some years ago a broker convinced us, with insufficient verification, that there was a window of opportunity for a building of several hundred thousand feet in eighteen months. We jumped on the apparent opportunity, utilized a property we had acquired for a parking structure, and designed and constructed the building in the specified period. The problem was—there was no window, and the building struggled for several years. Upon reflection, it became obvious that we acted on inaccurate information. There had been sufficient information available at the time, had we properly investigated, to warn us not to proceed.

Project Specific Market Data

In addition to the primary market data, the following data collected in this Market Study provide essential information necessary to prepare the Project Design Criteria provided to the architect and the design team at the initiation of project design.

- Allowable construction cost based on the analysis of the achievable rental rates at an acceptable lease-up rate
- Size and type of likely tenants
- Floor size and bay depth to satisfy the prospective tenants
- Approximate building size
- Current and future developer competition
- Definitions of rentable area and shell and core construction
- Tenant Improvement allowances and other concessions
- Acceptable methods of charging for electricity
- Amenities required on-site
- Parking requirements—3 to 4 per 1000 rsf has been the general suburban norm, but some dense operations have required 5 to 8 per 1000 rsf. Many downtown locations have much lower requirements.

Amenities/Services

The survey of the immediate market area will describe the scope and type of retail and services available and, combined with the projected type of tenants, will indicate those that may be required as tenant amenities in order to achieve a successful leasing program. There is a trend, along with the trend to smaller projects, to provide less and less in the way of tenant amenities. The primary reason for this trend is that many tenant amenities have had a consistent earnings drag on office projects—many don't even cover operating costs, much less the initial construction cost and foregone rent—and doubt among developers as to how essential some of those amenities are to an effective leasing program. Typical retail and service amenities are:

- Luncheon clubs
- Mid-priced restaurants
- Fast food/take-out
- Banks, saving and loans or credit unions
- ATMs
- Health clubs
- Day care centers
- Newsstand/bookstore
- Flower stands
- Barber shop/hair salon
- Laundry/dry cleaner
- Shoe shine
- Fedex/UPS/Airborne pickup
- Convenience market
- Car wash and service area

It has frequently been perceived that the two most important amenities, in addition to food, are day care centers and fitness centers. Rather than an attempt to provide them, frequently arrangements can be made with nearby facilities. Dry cleaning pickup and car servicing can frequently be arranged with local providers at no cost to the building.

A recent book, *What Office Tenants Want*, a 1999 BOMA/ULI Tenant Survey Report, available from BOMA@boma.org, evaluates features, amenities, and services that attract and keep target market tenancies. Many of the results of this survey are surprising, as many of the amenities considered to be important by real estate professionals receive relatively low importance ratings—particularly in relation to certain building features and amenities. The table titled "Importance of and Satisfaction with Building Features, Amenities, and Services, by Category" is included as Figure 4-4. The book further breaks down this data by type of business and geographic location. (See Appendix A.)

Marketing and Site Selection Considerations

The following data that is collected and used as a guide to the specific site selection will also be used to help form a basis for positioning the marketability of the building, and a strategy for how the marketing program will be formulated and applied.

Relationship to Positive Factors:
- Visibility
- Public transportation
  - Trains or light rail
  - Bus
  - Airport
- Highway and road system
  - Highway interchanges
  - Traffic patterns
  - Degree of traffic congestion
  - Site ingress and egress
- Established office building market—equivalent or higher quality
- Major financial institutions
- Institutions of higher education
- Clubs, restaurants, hotels
- Public parking
- Retail
- Theater, cultural, entertainment
- Upscale residential—managerial decision makers
- General residential—employee pool
- Parks and other amenities
- Fire, police and other public services
- Availability of state of the art communications services
- Signage regulations

Importance of and Satisfaction with Building Features, Amenities, and Services, by Category

	Important (Percent)	Satisfied (Percent)
Locational Features		
Proximity to business services	87	98
Proximity to where employees live	81	95
Proximity to restaurants/retail/personal services	81	94
Proximity to clients	76	98
Proximity to public transportation	69	95
General Building Features		
Rental rates (including pass-throughs/escalations)	99	88
Operating expenses	98	87
Image and prestige of the building	95	92
On-site parking	94	80
Tenant improvement allowance	93	83
Cost of parking	91	75
Environmentally friendly building systems and materials	90	89
Disabled access	78	92
Covered parking	77	77
Tenant mix	73	92
Features of Building Exterior		
Appearance of building	98	93
Appearance of grounds/landscaping	98	92
Outside signage for your organization	71	80
Outside loading docks	53	82
Operable windows	40	61
Roof-loading capacity	23	90
Features of Interior Common Areas		
Appearance of entry lobby (style/finishes)	97	89
Buildingwide security systems after hours	97	85
Appearance of common areas other than lobby	97	84
Elevator service speed	88	72
Buildingwide security systems during work day	88	85
Features of Tenants' Office Suites		
Comfortable temperature	99	74
Indoor air quality	99	81
Acoustics/noise control	99	83
Power capacity	97	93
Tenant control of temperature	96	65
Security/controlled access	93	90
Proximity to restrooms	93	95
Flexible suite layout (e.g., easily reconfigured)	92	87
Cost of after-hours heating/cooling	89	79
Proximity to elevators	84	98
Building Amenities		
Food service	75	71
Banking/ATM	70	79
Convenience retail stores	64	81
Fitness center	53	58
Child-care facility	44	48
Concierge	41	77
Shared videoconference facility	38	60
Shared teleconference facility	34	64
Shared business services (e.g., data and word processing)	29	78
Building Management		
Quality of building maintenance work	99	89
Building management's ability to meet your needs	99	89
Building management's responsiveness	99	89
Effectiveness of communications with building management	99	86
On-site building management staff	93	90
On-site security guard	88	85

Figure 4-4

Source: BOMA/ULI—*What Office Tenants Want*

Relationship to Negative Elements:

- Industrial areas and manufacturing districts
- Overhead power lines
- Landfills
- Airport glide paths
- Sewage and water treatment plants
- Parking decks and rooftops
- Bus stations
- Slums
- Derelict hangouts
- Sexual preference areas
- Police station, jail, parole office
- Cemeteries

Retail Development

From the discussion under amenities, it is obvious the author is not in favor of rationalizing inclusion of retail components into a project, particularly without solid evidence of those amenities being necessary to a successful leasing program, or a market analysis that indicates the retail component would be economically viable in its own right.

Notwithstanding that caveat, many sites, by their size, location or absence of sufficient retail in the market area, offer a substantial demand for specific services. In such event, studies must establish that such services are not only viable in that location, but they will enhance the marketing acceptance of the project and the projected net income will increase the project's return.

Retail is a specialty that requires specific knowledge. The studies, when deemed appropriate, should be conducted by a brokerage firm specializing in retail or a retail consultant. Once the viability, scope and type of retail is established, a careful program must be undertaken and a designer retained who specializes in this field. It is not enough to attract retail tenants who will pay the asking rent, but the **right tenants** who will provide the best synergy to the overall retail complex.

Build-to-Suit Projects

When developing a project for a build-to-suit tenant the market analysis is performed in an entirely different manner, with many alternative objectives. A major portion, if not all, of the market analysis will be performed by the tenant, although you may participate and advise.

The most common criteria for site selection are access to an appropriate labor pool, good transportation, reasonably priced land of a size to accomplish any planned expansion, acceptable zoning, low real estate taxes, convenient access to their customers or suppliers if applicable, and sometimes, convenience to executive residential areas. For most companies the primary factor will be available labor pool, as the impact of unfavorable labor supply or quality can dwarf variances in occupancy cost.

The Development Officer should advise as to the future real estate value of any selected site, and if there is an ownership position by the developer, insist on a site that will retain its value.

In these projects, since the tenant is known, the design criteria are determined by a thorough evaluation of each functional operation by the user's management staff and interior planning firm, rather than market analysis. These studies will provide the information to establish building size, floor sizes, bay depths, ceiling heights, electrical capacity, parking ratios, building quality, on-site amenities and other relevant data.

Once again, the developer should advise as to whether any of these requirements or their arrangement will have a negative impact on the real estate value of the property in the future. There is usually a way in which to satisfy the user's requirements in such a way as to maintain long-term real estate value. If such cannot be accomplished, a developer with an interest in the project should insist on a very long-term lease or some adjustment in ownership obligations if the user vacates the property.

The type of Project Design Criteria restrictions obtained in the site studies and political evaluations are the same as in an investment feasibility study.

CASE STUDY

As discussed in the Introduction, the site is located in the high quality San Diego Corporate Center, immediately adjacent to Prentiss' Executive Center Del Mar, a 110,000 rsf office development in the lease-up phase when this opportunity was addressed. This new site has the best visibility in the area, and at six or eight stories will be the dominant office building. It must be a Class A building to properly relate to the site. As discussed in the Introduction, the freeway location is the best in the area, and the local access is excellent.

The graphs on the following pages, Figures 4-5 through 4-7, show the market status in Del Mar—indicating the Absorption, Effective Rents, and Vacancy from 1990 through 1997. The drop in absorption is a direct function of the lack of available product. Note the rising rents in 1997 coupled with the absence of vacancy.

The rapidly increasing market demand in the entire San Diego county area, as of the first quarter 1998 is shown by:

- Del Mar had 1,328,164 rsf of office space with a 1% vacancy
- North County (including Del Mar) had 7,305,511 rsf of office space with 6% vacancy
- San Diego County had 38,455,579 rsf of office space with 10% vacancy

The site is surrounded by quality housing, and the premier executive housing markets of Rancho Santa Fe, Fairbanks Ranch and Rancho Bernardo are within 10 miles. A shopping center is within two miles, A DoubleTree hotel is across the street, a Hampton Inn is currently under construction two blocks away, and several restaurants are within walking distance. The population growth in the immediate area since 1980, and projected to 2002 within radii of 3, 5, and 10 miles is shown on the graphs in Figures 4-8 and 4-9.

The site is located several miles north of the junction of the I-5 and I-805 freeways that defines the northern edge of the severe rush hour traffic, and the favorable traffic circulation will increase further with the imminent completion of the adjacent new I-56, which will connect the area to I-15 and the large residential areas to the east.

There was no data that indicated a negative change in the market within the assumed project period.

The rental rates for the adjacent project had risen from the pro forma rate of $1.95 to an average of $2.10, with some recent small tenants at $2.25, all with rental bumps, and exclusive of electricity. That project was 85% leased within the first month following the Certificate of Occupancy.

Since this new project was originally proposed to be a mid-rise structure with the best site in Del Mar, an initial pro forma rental rate of $2.10 (later increased to $2.25 as the market continued to improve) exclusive of electricity, was assumed increasing at 3% per year. It was later decided to include electricity in the base rent (see discussion later in this chapter and in Chapters 15 and 25) which added a further 15¢.

The Tenant Improvement (TI) allowance was running $33.50/ usf in the existing project which, increased at 3% per year, would require $35.50/usf for this project.

The brokers analyzed the market in the immediate area, which is primarily for small to mid-size professional and high tech tenants. In addition, traffic conditions might induce some larger tenants to relocate from University Town Center (UTC), five miles to the south. The brokers agreed with the rental and TI analysis and recommended the following criteria for the design of the building to satisfy the proposed tenancy in this market, which was agreed to.

The Market Study

NORTH COUNTY MARKET INFORMATION

DEL MAR HISTORIC OFFICE ABSORPTION

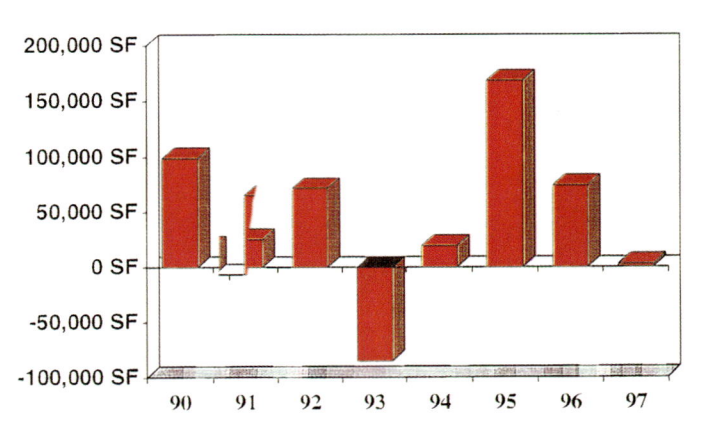

*Fujitsu Systems vacated 130,000 square feet in 1993, which offset 45,000 square feet of positive net absorption.

Prepared By Business Real Estate

Information contained herein has been obtained from the owner of the property or from other sources that we deem reliable. We have no reason to doubt its accuracy, but we do not guarantee it.

Figure 4-5

Office Development

NORTH COUNTY MARKET INFORMATION

HISTORIC OFFICE EFFECTIVE RENTS DEL MAR

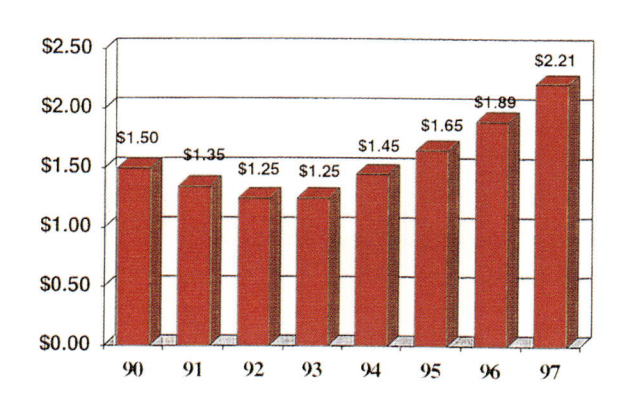

Year	Rent
90	$1.50
91	$1.35
92	$1.25
93	$1.25
94	$1.45
95	$1.65
96	$1.89
97	$2.21

Prepared By Business Real Estate

Information contained herein has been obtained from the owner of the property or from other sources that we deem reliable. We have no reason to doubt its accuracy, but we do not guarantee it.

NAI New America International

BRE Business Real Estate Brokerage Co.

Figure 4-6

The Market Study

NORTH COUNTY MARKET INFORMATION

DEL MAR HISTORIC OFFICE VACANCY

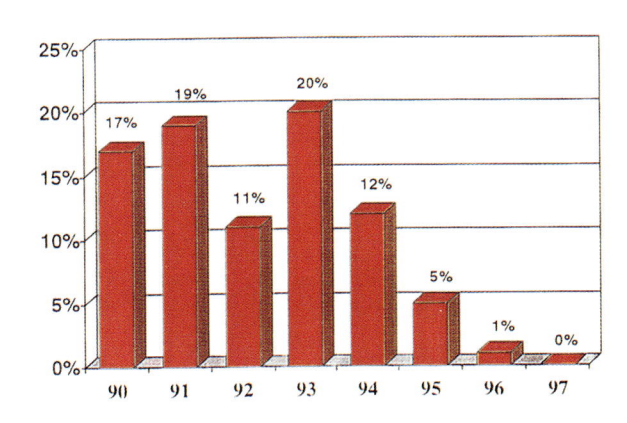

Year	Vacancy
90	17%
91	19%
92	11%
93	20%
94	12%
95	5%
96	1%
97	0%

Prepared By Business Real Estate

Information contained herein has been obtained from the owner of the property or from other sources that we deem reliable. We have no reason to doubt its accuracy, but we do not guarantee it.

NAI — New America International

BRE — Business Real Estate Brokerage Co.

Figure 4-7

POPULATION GROWTH - DEL MAR AREA

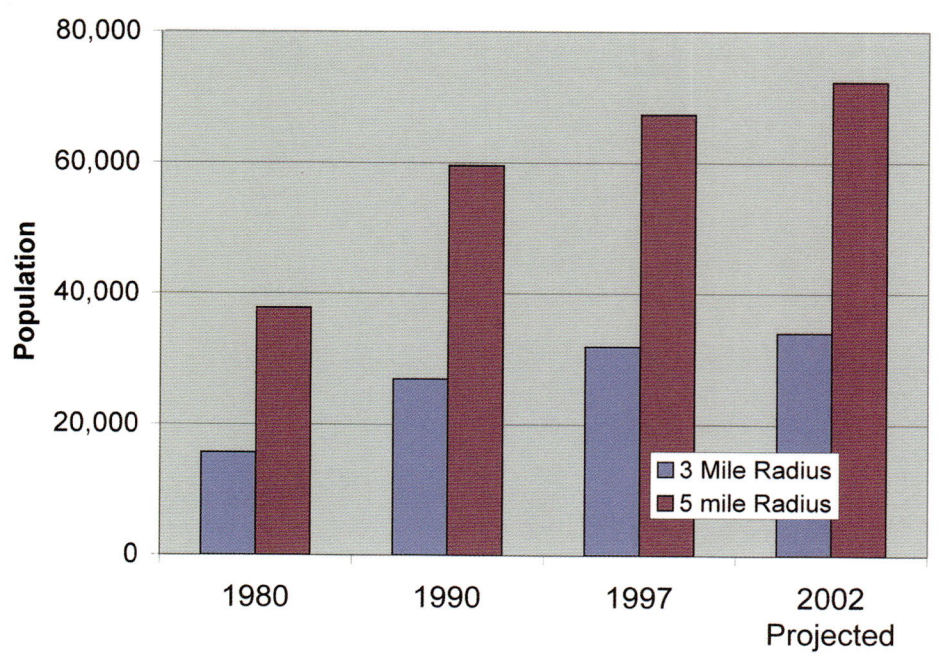

Figure 4-8

POPULATION GROWTH - DEL MAR AREA

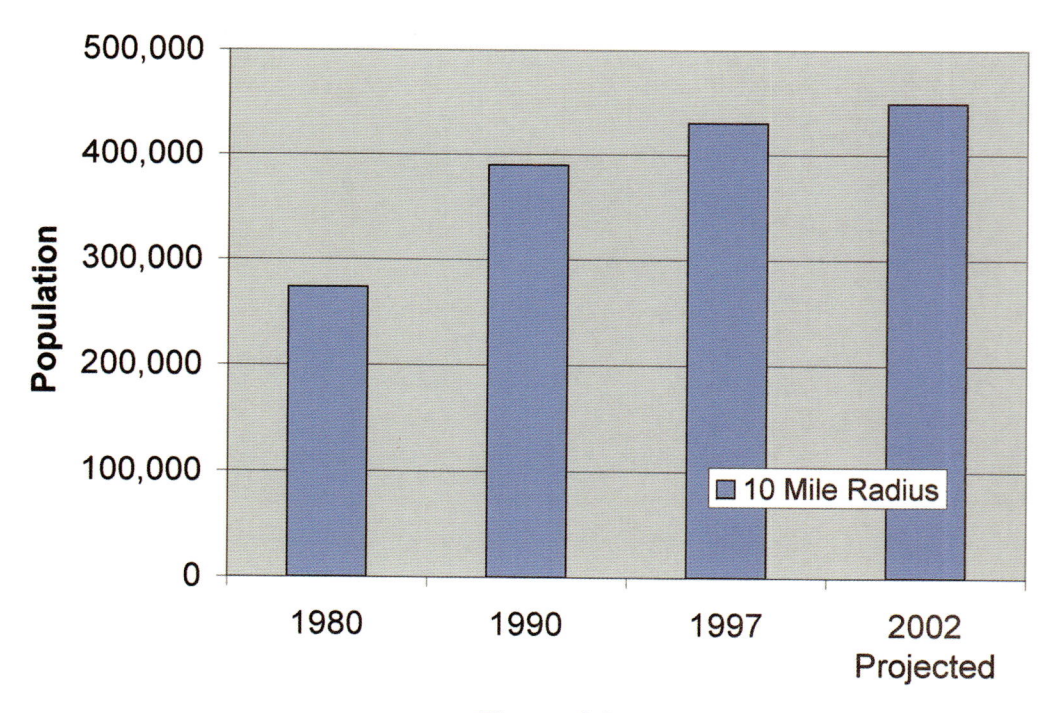

Figure 4-9

- Approximately 150,000 gross square feet
- Parking at four cars per 1000 gsf
- Maximum 20,000 rsf floor size
- Approximately 40-foot core to glass depth
- Minimum 9'0" ceiling height
- 50-pound floor live load plus 20 pounds for partitions
- Some tenants requesting six to seven w/usf of power available
- Multiple corner offices, if possible
- Granite façade—the Pardee agreement required brick, or approved upgrade

The market definition of rentable area was essentially in accordance with BOMA Standard. In conjunction with the brokers, the following break points between the shell and core construction and the Tenant Improvement work were agreed upon as shown below.

SHELL AND CORE VS. TENANT IMPROVEMENT DEFINITION

Function	Responsibility
Dry wall at columns and perimeter wall	TI
Drywall on tenant side of corridor/demising walls	TI
Ceiling grid support wires	TI
Ceiling grid and tile installation	TI
Lighting (except cores)	TI
Lighting and miscellaneous power grids	TI
Electric meters and wiring to floor electrical closets	Base Building (except for heat pump systems)
Heat pump refrigeration system	TI
Outside air riser and floor loop for heat pump system	Base Building
Condenser water loop for heat pump system	Base Building
Central HVAC system	Base Building
Main conditioned air riser and loop with central system	Base Building
Mixing boxes and floor air distribution (except core)	TI
Sprinkler risers and loops	Base Building
Sprinkler runouts and heads (except core)	Installed in base building, backcharged as preinstalled TIs. Head relocation is TI.
Smoke and heat sensors	TI
Finished tenant floor elevator lobbies	Base Building
Public corridors and finish	Base Building
Public area graphics	Base Building
Public toilet rooms	Base Building
Window blinds	TI. Frequently installed with base building as a preinstalled cost.
Tenant space development drawings (exclusive of sales layouts)	TI

The Executive Center Del Mar buildings had an air conditioning system based upon water source heat pumps, provided by the tenant as part of their TIs, with the building providing only the cooling towers and condenser water loop. The tenant paid for all of their electric energy costs on a separate meter. It was believed that with a larger building that might have to meet high rise codes, a central system would be more appropriate. This would increase the base building cost significantly, but an analysis indicated that the cost of tenant TIs would decrease by .80¢/usf for electrical and $3.20 /usf for HVAC. This would reduce the TI allowance to approximately $31.50/usf, which would offset about 85% of the added base building cost. A more detailed discussion of this issue is covered in Section 25.

Discussion with the brokers indicated that the project could be effectively marketed with the reduced TI allowance, since the actual TI costs would be lower than other buildings in the vicinity. It was also agreed that including the electricity cost in the base rental rate could be effectively marketed to the tenants.

There are no negative areas or elements in the vicinity of the site, and with all of the amenities nearby, there is no requirement for any on site beyond that provided by the hotel.

The project will have some additional advantages over a basic market demand analysis. The building at six to eight stories will have the best visibility in the market area, including views from two major freeways, and with the granite façade and other features will be the highest quality building north of UTC. In addition, the parking ratio which is above the average and adjacency to the new hotel are marketing advantages.

A hotel study was performed by Hospitality Valuation Services, a division of Hotel Consulting Services, Inc., and was very positive. It strongly recommended a hotel of 250 to 300 rooms and indicated a preference for a full, or partially-limited service hotel, but a suite hotel that would have virtually no services would also be successful. Although the initial assumption was for a suites hotel, Waterford's discussions with various hotel operators indicated a desire for significant dining and banquet facilities. Recommended operators appropriate to this site were Wyndham, Hilton and Marriott, with the economic numbers shown below for a Hilton Suites.

Year 10/1 TO 9/30	Occupancy Rate	Average Rate
2000/01	68%	$136.28
2001/02	76%	$147.75
2002/03	78%	$152.18
Stabilized	79%	$156.25

THE SITE STUDY

The site evaluation, or Site Study, is the second section of the Feasibility Analysis that defines the limitations on development and the costs involved in adapting to the site. It is used for the purpose of evaluating acquisition of a site, closing on a conditional commitment or option and/or determining whether or how to proceed with a site that is currently under control. The Market Study prepared in the prior chapter is used as a guide in the site evaluation process and determination of market limitations and opportunities. A proper Site Study clearly delineates the scope of what can be developed on the site and the various cost and time limitations placed upon the project.

This chapter will discuss planning and zoning, discretionary regulations, governmental charges and fees, redevelopment authorities, environmental site conditions, testing and verification of site conditions, legal and other site conditions, utility availability and the preliminary determination of site construction costs.

A thorough knowledge of the zoning, environmental and regulatory issues, as well as the physical limitations of the site, is essential before committing funds. This chapter discusses many of the issues that must be satisfactorily resolved before acquisition of a site or initiation of a project. Political issues, while in reality a site issue, are discussed in the following chapter due to their increasing importance and uniqueness.

Zoning attorneys, environmental consultants, geotechnical engineers, civil engineers, surveyors, arborists, historians and traffic engineers are frequently required to assist in these evaluations. Title companies and the planning and zoning department should be consulted early in the process. A preliminary title report listing all exceptions is an absolute requirement. Aerial photos are always valuable and electronic Geographic Information Systems (GIS) now have tax records, census data, crime statistics, water and sewer records, transportation information, driving times and much more valuable information in many metropolitan areas.

The site issues are normally all solvable, with the exception of certain high profile environmental issues, but frequently have a significant impact on cost and time. It is essential at this point to determine if any issues are not solvable at a reasonable cost and within an acceptable time. If so, it is time to explore an alternative opportunity.

In the event a decision is made to acquire a site, or to proceed with the project, the most significant data evaluated herein will be summarized and incorporated into the Feasibility Analysis. This study will also provide further data for the Project Design Criteria (see Chapter 14), and will provide essential cost data for the pro forma.

Site issues are divided into various categories, which will be discussed separately below. It should be noted that in addition to understanding and evaluating the feasibility and cost implications of each of these categories, it is necessary to as accurately as possible assess the time restrictions for inclusion in the overall project schedule. This will permit estimating the time at which the project will enter the market, so that information can be evaluated in the Market Study.

Planning and Zoning

Planning and zoning is a collection of written rules, requirements and standards that define the legal land uses and the specific limitations of development on a specific site. The Comprehensive General Plan is usually a 20-year or more plan that spells out the development goals and policies that guide and control desired land use and growth over that period. On the other hand, zoning laws are quite explicit as to what is permitted and under what circumstances. Significant zoning variations are normally not easily attained unless the governing jurisdiction is trying to promote a particular type of development, or unrelated prior changes have made the current regulations somewhat outdated. A compilation of applicable zoning requirements and other site issues, as listed below, becomes a major part of the feasibility study that then becomes part of the Project Design Criteria.

- Zoning classification
- Permitted uses
- Density—floor area ratio (FAR)
- Height and bulk limits
- Site coverage
- Setbacks—ground, upper levels
- Separation between buildings
- Minimum/maximum parking ratios, distance from parking to office
- Minimum required landscape coverage
- Exiting requirements and dead-end corridors
- Service dock requirements
- Special use limitations
- Off-site requirements
- Abnormal soil, grading or other site costs
- Unusual utility or water management requirements
- Deed restrictions, easements and encumbrances

Planned Unit Development (PUD)

When a site involves more than one project, and particularly when it entails more than one usage, an alternate to processing a project through the zoning regulations and other reviews is to process a request for a PUD. A PUD requires going through all of the zoning, EIR and discretionary reviews, but it does so for the entire contemplated project rather than for a single project at a time. When accepted by the local jurisdiction it sets the rules for all phases, supercedes the zoning requirements and avoids future EIRs and discretionary reviews unless the project is changed in some substantial way, or delayed beyond the contemplated development period.

Discretionary Regulations

While the zoning regulations above are specific, many jurisdictions currently have discretionary approval processes. While in theory these various boards function to accomplish certain specified public interests, in practice they are generally free to take any position that seems appropriate to them at the moment. These boards were established to protect elected officials from taking public pressure on design and other issues and, therefore, the officials are reluctant to override even onerous decisions. It is important to understand not only the number and scope of discretionary reviews, but the trend, or pattern, of their actions. Typical boards are:

- Urban design review boards
- Architectural review boards
- Other discretionary reviews

Governmental Costs and Fees

Required local fees have become a major factor in development cost in many jurisdictions. Many of these are fixed unit fees based on building FAR or land area, but some are related to the estimated cost to mitigate the actual or perceived issues that must be corrected. Among the types of fees are:

- Exactions—mitigation fees usually not specific to a particular public expense
- Impact fees—mitigation fees that are tied to mitigation of a specific governmental expense
- Development fees—usually payable to preserve a site's entitlements
- Building permit fees
- Off-site traffic mitigation—extra lanes, turning lanes, traffic lights, transit fees
- Miscellaneous fees—limited only by bureaucratic imagination

- Real estate taxes
  - In some locales real estate taxes may vary significantly by jurisdiction over a relatively small area, creating a relative lease rate advantage/disadvantage
  - Special tax districts for municipal improvements
  - Interest on development bonds used for infrastructure

Environmental Site Conditions (EIR/EIS)

Environmental protection and/or mitigation have become a major factor in assessing the cost and potential time delays for a project, and sometimes their prohibition. The Environmental Impact Report (EIR) or Environmental Impact Statement (EIS) is prepared at the developer's cost by a consultant approved or specified by the local governing body, but it becomes the local government's study. While it normally is for the purpose of exposing issues that must be mitigated, these reports are frequently used by opponents to delay approvals by critiquing the reports for possible errors of omission or commission. Some jurisdictions believe every minor irrelevant error must be corrected if pointed out by an opponent, even though there may be no substantive impact, requiring a revision and new public hearings thus delaying the project considerably.

All identified adverse environmental issues must either be waived or have approved mitigation measures borne by the developer—sometimes by taking corrective steps and sometimes by a mitigation payment. Another related issue is that the federal, state and local laws are so complex and frequently overlapping, that even after all governmental approvals have been received, opposition groups can tie up some projects in court for years.

Some environmental issues are extremely difficult and time consuming to resolve. As an example, the wetlands permitting process requires

> Be wary of sites with a known environmental issue of interest to local groups. It is not unusual for environmental groups to take multiple shots at stopping a project. A major hotel chain was trying to develop a large hotel along the coast in Santa Barbara County. One of the primary objections was that a portion of the project contained a Monarch butterfly resting place during their migration period, which the plan mitigated. Several environmental groups fought the project through the regulatory process and, when they failed that effort, filed suit to block the project. It was finally settled and the development permit authorized. It was reported that there had been significant donations to the opposition groups prior to the agreement.
>
> Unfortunately, by the time the development permit was received the economic conditions did not permit financing such a project. By the time the project became economically viable again the original development permit had expired, and the same groups opposed an extension. After another lengthy period, and another suit filed, the permit was finally reinstituted and the project proceeded.

approval from the Corps of Engineers, the EPA and the Fish and Wildlife Service. A recent survey showed that typically it requires at least one year to determine the mitigation of adverse impacts required. Other issues can involve six or seven approving agencies.

An environmental consultant is normally required. Even if a negative declaration, or amendment to an existing EIR, is achievable the consultant can guide you through the maze of regulations of overlapping agencies to identify and confirm issues. Primary environmental issues are:

> Constant vigilance is necessary where any environmental issues exist. ARCO set out to redevelop an obsolete petroleum pumping station into a golf course along the coast in Santa Barbara County. Apparently, after having received preliminary approvals to proceed, they spent a reported $11 million cleaning up the prior environmental degradation in order to receive their final permits to construct the golf course.
>
> Shortly prior to the anticipated approval someone found three endangered red-leg frogs in a small creek bed on the property and the project has been put on hold. Very few people believe those frogs were on the property at the time that the cleanup commenced.

- EIR/EIS if required—a negative declaration is frequently possible
- Sun studies
- Pedestrian wind studies
- Coastal commissions and controls
- Controlled waterways
- Flood plains
- Wetlands
- Open space
- Endangered species
- Critical and unique wildlife habitats
- Wildlife management
- Storm water management
- Designated natural landmarks
- Archeological resource surveys and protection
- Hazardous waste disposal—toxics, asbestos, PCBs,
- Underground tanks
- Water consumption
- Traffic
- Air pollution
- Noise

While most of these issues will not be factors in the typical development project, even where an EIR is not required, a traffic study is almost always a requirement of the local jurisdiction. They usually require the estimated number of daily trips, frequently the hourly trips, ratio of cars coming from different directions, left turn ingress/egress demand, locations of proposed curb cuts and estimated stacking at parking entrances.

Testing and Verification of Physical Site Conditions

Surveyors, soil testing laboratories, geotechnical engineers, hydrologists and civil engineers evaluate the site for problems that might affect the development and the costs for site work and foundation design. During the design phase, this information is used as a basis for design—particularly structural, civil and water control.

One investigation that has become virtually mandatory from a lender or ownership standpoint is the environmental survey. A Phase I survey is a historical record of uses at the site, chain of title, known environmental issues found in the vicinity, and any other information that can be found from existing records that may indicate the potential existence of hazardous materials that must be removed or otherwise mitigated.

Indications of automobile service facilities, dry cleaner establishments, underground tanks or any chemical source will normally require a Phase II study.

Typical studies required are:

- Environmental survey
- Surveys
  - Boundaries
  - Rights of way
  - Easements

- Topographical grades
- Utilities
- Flood plains and wetlands
- Existing structures

- Soil borings and analysis
  - Bearing capacity
  - Compaction
  - Base for road and walkways
  - Rock
  - Soil profile
  - Water table
  - Percolation tests

- Hydrology studies

- Seismic zone analysis

Legal, Special and Other Site Conditions

A thorough analysis of all available records and title information is essential to determine the existence of any issues that might preclude, or make difficult, the development of the site. Some of these are:

- Existing covenants conditions & restrictions
- Existing easements
- Other private covenants and/or deed restrictions
- Abandoned cemeteries
- Subdivision requirement
- Redevelopment areas
- Historical landmarks
- Special districts
  - Historical
  - Coastal
  - Design control
- Platting—Many jurisdictions will not permit more than one building to be constructed on one platted site. Replatting will be required prior to obtaining a building permit.
- Contiguous land uses

Utility Availability

The availability and capacity of utilities must be verified. Obtain "will serve" letters when there is any question as to their ability to serve your site. The distance of each utility service from the site, who will pay to run the service to the site, and the approximate cost should be determined in advance. Competitive suppliers should be investigated for each service, where applicable.

- Electrical power
- Gas
- Water—quantity, quality and consumption restrictions
- Sewage plant capacity
- Telephone companies
  - Fiber optic lines
  - Integrated Service Digital Network (ISDN) lines
  - Digital Subscriber Lines (DSL) or Asymmetrical Digital Subscriber Lines (ADSL)
  - Cable services
- Cable companies
  - Standard service
  - Direct Ethernet access to Internet providers
  - Telephone services

Demolition

Most sites are undeveloped or cleared land, but many are encumbered with existing structures. It is normal for an existing structure that can be economically removed for a newer structure to be old enough to contain asbestos, lead paint and/or PCBs, etc., as well as contaminants resulting from their use, such as petroleum products and chemicals. The toxic materials must be removed and disposed of using the proper hazardous material removal procedures before any demolition can occur. The vast majority of such buildings are low-rise structures that can frequently be demolished with a bulldozer, ball and crane, or similar equipment, and then hauled away. In other circumstances, usually with larger structures, more complex procedures are

> Demolition projects can be very large and varied. In the mid-1960s we demolished the 40-plus-story Morrison Hotel in the center of Chicago's loop to make way for the First National Bank building. In accordance with Chicago regulations, we scaffolded the entire building, and demolished it almost entirely by hand—one wall and one floor at a time. It took almost a year.
>
> In the mid-1980s we demolished the old Dallas Athletic Club in downtown Dallas. It was a heavy concrete structure with an Olympic sized swimming pool on the third floor. After extensive asbestos removal, and being thoroughly prepped, the building was demolished by implosion. In less than ten seconds there was a huge cloud of dust, and when it cleared, a large pile of construction debris, exactly where it was supposed to fall. The implosion was accomplished early on a Sunday morning when it did not interfere with any activities. Specialists from Baltimore were utilized; this was not a job for amateurs.

required, and some local jurisdictions have rather strict regulations.

Preliminary Site Work Cost

In addition to governmental fees, utility fees and costs and environmental mitigations, it is wise to have a rough estimate of the major costs resulting from an analysis of the physical evaluation of the site. Major potential cost issues are:

- Extensive grading—including exporting or importing fill
- Retaining walls
- Storm water management
- Rock excavation
- Abnormal foundation costs
- Site roadways
- Water or sewage treatment plants
- Demolition, including possible tenant relocation

Redevelopment Authorities

Redevelopment agencies were initially established to promote growth of a particular type in a particular place to solve a designated problem, most commonly in deteriorated sections of the downtown. Many have expanded their jurisdiction to many other areas, and some have become the zoning and planning czars for large areas of the city. Those who still pursue their original mandate frequently provide many positive incentives toward development they wish to promote, such as:

- Ombudsman—assist developer to maneuver through a maze of regulations and authorities
- Zoning variances
- Real estate tax abatement
- Site acquisition for lease to developer
- Favorable debt service rates
- Grants
- Parking
- Infrastructure

Other Governmental Services

- Police
- Fire
- Schools

All redevelopment agencies are not the same. They may vary with their charge or with the bureaucracy of their organization. I had the opportunity to watch three redevelopment agencies in action as they reviewed different projects. The redevelopment agency in San Jose, California, had a very clear plan and objective, and they worked very constructively and flexibly with developers to accomplish that objective in a way that made economic sense. Alternatively, in Los Angeles the agency had similar objectives but the agency was highly bureaucratic and highly rigid in the way they controlled the downtown area. They frequently required high fees and firm major decisions prior to the time such payment or decision may have been economically appropriate. The Pennsylvania Avenue Development Commission in Washington, D.C., was originally charged with promoting development along Pennsylvania Avenue in order to generally improve the rather rundown area between the White House and Capitol Hill. In exercising that role they demanded what I believed was excessively strict design control that may have satisfied their particular idea of appropriateness, but was not designed to achieve the original mandate that stemmed from President Kennedy's concerns resulting from his inaugural parade.

CASE STUDY

The area in which the project site is located is a largely built out 114-acre office, industrial and hospitality park, known as the San Diego Corporate Center. The center was developed under the North City West District Development plan. As previously mentioned, the site was formerly approved for a 500-room hotel with parking for 1000 cars under a Visitor Center Development Plan, all with an EIR and a Coastal Commission permit. All mitigation measures for that project, which were primarily turning lanes and traffic signalization, have been completed. It was decided to attempt to obtain approval for the project through a Substantial Conformance Review process, which had the advantage of saving approval time and minimizing the likelihood of new mitigation requirements resulting from a new EIR, or Coastal or Planning Commission review. It had the disadvantage, however, of requiring more work prior to submission and opened the project to certain local discretionary reviews.

The site was formerly a continuous slope that was modified by grading and fill some years ago into a site with three major plateaus at +80 feet, +71 feet and +60 feet as shown in Figure 5-1. The total extent of the grade is from +84 feet at the combined entrance with Executive Center Del Mar on El Camino Real to +55 feet at the only other feasible entrance on Valley Centre Drive. There will be extensive further grading to satisfy the requirements of the project.

There is a large non-buildable open space drainage and freeway easement that roughly parallels the freeway, which is along the bottom of Figure 5-1.

All necessary utilities are located in El Camino Real directly in front of the site, and some are duplicated in Valley Centre Drive. The utilities include gas, electricity at 12kv, telephone, cable, water, sanitary sewer and storm sewer. There is competitive telephone and high-speed Internet service offered by Pacific Bell and Time Warner. All of the utilities were accessed from El Camino Real except the site storm water drainage and the parking structure drainage, which went into Valley Center Drive.

There is a traffic light and turning lanes at the intersection of El Camino Real and Valley Center Drive. There is a break in the median across from the El Camino Real entrance, but no light or turning lanes.

Because this project was processed through a Substantial Conformance Review with the previously approved specific plan, there would be no specific height, density and site coverage limits—the limits being those approved in the prior project. The property line setback is 15 feet, and there is an adjacent 20-foot San Diego Gas & Electric (SDG&E) easement.

Because there was an EIR for the prior project, which has been fully mitigated, it was not believed that one, or any other significant special studies, would be required at this time. This assumption proved to be correct. Offsite work relative to traffic was included in the prior mitigation, and with the apparent equivalency, additional requirements were not anticipated.

The code required parking was 3.3 spaces per 1000sf for the office building and 1 per room for the hotel, plus 1 space per 80 sf for banquet and dining. The city of San Diego has no specific provision for "shared parking" reductions, but since the market driven requirement for parking is significantly greater than code, the proposed garage size was anticipated to be approved. San Diego does not recognize "one size fits all" parking layouts, but does permit up to 60% small car spaces. The standard stall size is 8'6" by 20 feet, and small car spaces are 7'6" x 15'0". The minimum parking width with two-way traffic is 61 feet. There is no specific requirement for a service dock.

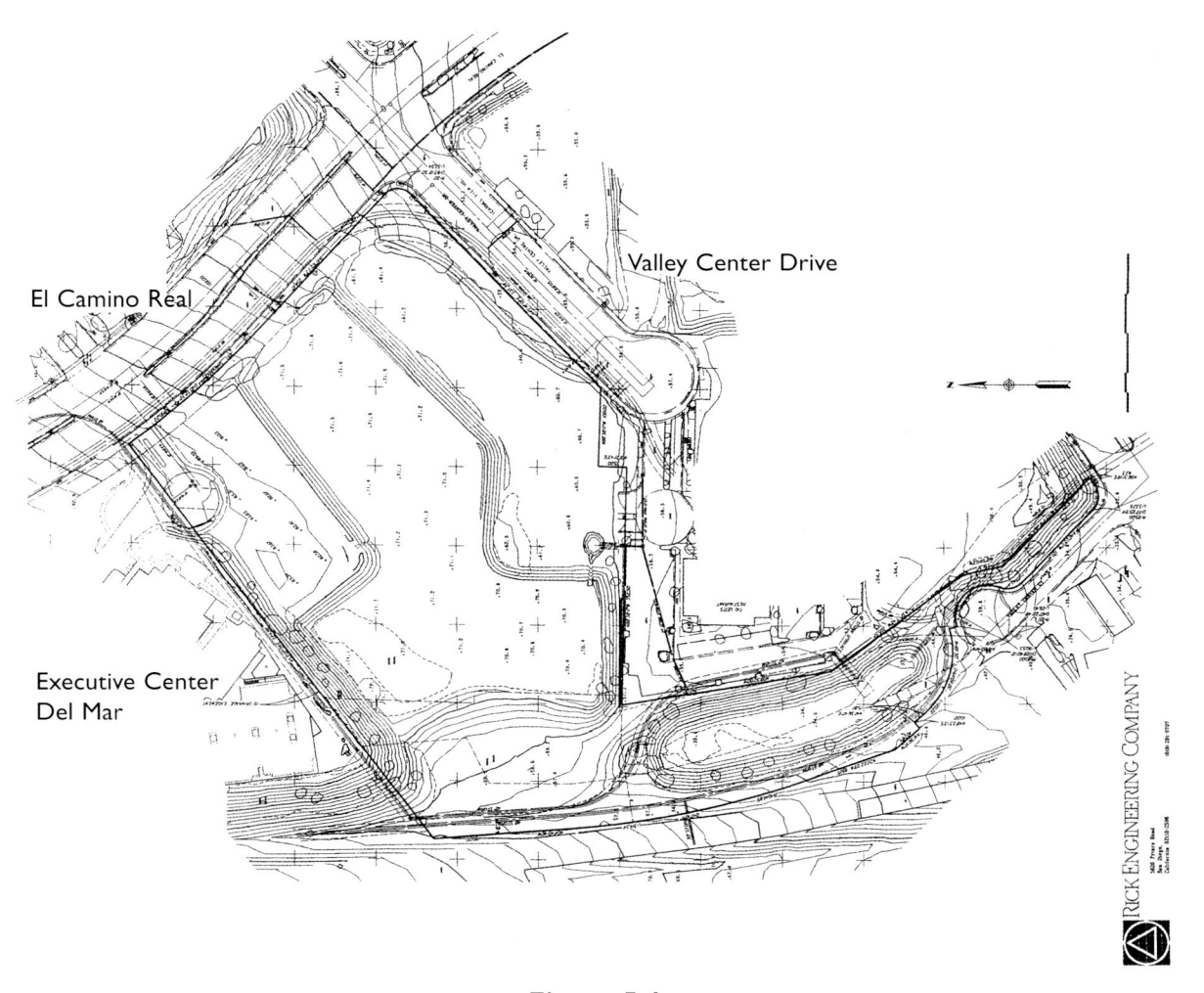

Figure 5-1

The cost of the impact fees and building permits are fixed and may be obtained directly from a printed schedule.

The structural engineer outlined in letter form the requirements to be submitted to several geotechnical engineering firms for soil test and analysis proposals. He recommended twelve test holes, four under each structure, 80 feet +/- deep, in order to establish certain seismic damping data, sensitivity to settlement, allowable spread footing and wall footing capacities, resistance to lateral loads, and other data. The assumed applied structural loads were:

	Max. Column Load
Office Tower	1000 kips
Parking Structure	600 kips
Hotel	1200 kips

The site is classified as being in a low to moderate zone of seismic activity. There were 12 test borings taken at the site ranging from 73.5 to 81 feet deep. The soils were a mixture of gravel/sand, silty gravels, silty sands, organic silts and organic silty clays. Water table was found at depths of 30 to 60 feet below the ground surface, which represented a depth of 57 to 60 feet below the upper pad and 30 to 37 feet below the lower pad. Among the recommendations in the soils report were:

- Backfill material to be placed in lifts not greater than 8", and be compacted to 90%.

- Exposed faces of fill slopes should be 2 horizontal to 1 vertical, or flatter.

- Shallow footing capacity of 4,000 psf for dead loads and long-term live loads, $\frac{1}{3}$ greater for short-term live loads. Coefficient of friction between bottom of footing and the prepared soil may be assumed to be 0.30.

- Mat foundations can use a nominal bearing pressure of 6,000 psf.

- Slabs on grade subject to vehicular traffic to be 6", 4" elsewhere, over compacted fill with 4" of free draining sand or crushed stone, and incorporating 6" x 6" welded wire mesh.

- Basement and retaining walls provided with drainage and imported non-expansive soils should be designed for the following lateral earth pressures.

EQUIVALENT FLUID WEIGHT (PCF)

Conditions	Level	3:1 Slope	2:1 Slope
Active	35	45	50
At-Rest	55	60	65
Passive	350	200	150

- Unrestrained (yielding) cantilever walls should be designed for an active equivalent fluid weight, restrained (non-yielding) walls should use at-rest, and passive values for slope conditions.

There were no known former uses of the site that might create contamination problems or archeological issues, but a Phase I environmental study was commissioned. The firm of Montgomery Watson was retained (contract amount of not to exceed $4,000) to perform the Phase I Environmental Site Assessment (Phase I ESA). This phase comprised:

- Historical Background Search—investigation of past land uses through review of aerial photographs, Sanborn insurance maps, chain-of-title search and other historical documentation.

- Regulatory Records Review—retaining a database retrieval firm such as Environmental Data Resources to access local, state and federal database records to document the status of any regulatory actions pertaining to environmental concerns at the site.

- Site Visit—performing site reconnaissance to describe and characterize the site, record on-site observations of current site physical characteristics, activities and operations, and provide a photographic summary of the property and complete a Phase I environmental assessment review form.

- Evaluation and Final Report Preparation—submitting a report of findings and, after review by PPL, submitting a final report.

The final report indicated no problems with environmental issues, and no mitigation issues were required.

POLITICAL ENVIRONMENT

In reality the evaluation of the political environment is a part of the site evaluation, and information gained here will be included in the Site Study portion of the feasibility study, but because of its nature, clarity is gained by discussing it separately.

A major role of the Development Officer is to judge at an early stage whether the political environment in a given community is appropriate for company objectives. Once a decision is made to proceed, the Development Officer must find the best approach to guide the project through the process. It should be noted that sometimes a project accomplished in a treacherous political environment can yield a high rate of return as alternate developments are faced with the same difficulties and may fall by the wayside.

The political attitudes toward development can vary widely from welcoming development with open arms and sometimes offering incentives, to a spoken or unspoken policy of deliberately strong resistance, with every conceivable variation in between.

Some communities have a natural resistance to development at virtually all times—they are frequently smaller idyllic towns, communities built up around people with a resistance to change and establishment values, coastal and mountain locations, communities whose character is unique and perceived to be harmed by change, and areas with heavy traffic, which is often from neighboring towns. These types of communities are also more likely to produce legal challenges to development from environmental or community groups, even when governmental approvals are obtained.

The attitude in other communities varies with general economic times and specifically the employment market conditions in the community. When jobs are of a particular concern, or the proposed development fills an accepted need, the community will tend to be receptive. In such communities at such times the process is frequently accelerated through appointment of project managers or ombudsmen to guide the project through the maze of regulatory bodies. When there is high employment, a high level of recent or current development, a rapid reduction of open and recreational space, and an increase in traffic, communities tend toward resistance. It should be noted that the public does not think in terms of advantages several years in the future, and the administrative bureaucracy does not always change their attitude and approach to project review along with the community's desires.

In addition to the dyed-in-the-wool environmental and historical preservation groups that seem to oppose every form of development, the most important issues that mobilize the average citizen seem to be increased traffic, loss of open space or views and the recent appearance of large or bulky buildings. Look for these signs and evidence of growing discontent when considering a project, as the typical opposition groups do not by themselves have the power they gain from an aroused citizenry.

The political environment defines the attitude of governmental and community groups to a potential project, and a thorough analysis should permit predicting the range of mitigation solutions, if any. In addition to reading about past issues, it is essential to talk to local politicians, business groups and even prominent slow-growth advocates.

Other good sources of information are attorneys, environmental consultants, chambers of commerce, business development groups, financial

When dealing with certain environmental, historical or purported consumer groups, it is important to try to understand their real objectives, rather than just their stated ones. We were planning a major building in downtown San Francisco in a vicinity that had significant historical implications. We went to the local historical preservation group during the very early phases of our design, endeavoring to understand and incorporate any issues they may have had. During the meeting we described the scope and objectives of our project and asked for their comments and suggestions. They requested inclusion of five specific objectives—preserving two buildings, restoring one and orienting our project to best showcase two others. All five suggestions were included in our design.

The efforts to obtain a building permit were endangered by a proposed anti-high-rise initiative, and we were endeavoring to obtain development approvals prior to the election. I went to the historical preservation group and requested that they support our project before the planning commission. They declined, saying that they never supported projects. I said that we could accept that, then asked them if they would go before the planning commission and merely state that they had requested us to include five features in our design and that we had incorporated all five. They declined again, and it became crystal clear that their concerns and objectives were not merely the promotion of certain historical values in the central business district, but merely to delay or prevent development. There was one benefit—they did not oppose the project before the commission.

The project picture shows the old bank hall that was preserved (several unattractive upper stories were removed to create a park on top of the bank hall), the much admired 111 Sutter building to the right, which was also preserved, and the new building in the background.

institutions, architects, political editorial writers, political leaders and newspaper files in the local library.

Where a site has not yet been acquired, strong political resistance will normally result in foregoing the effort and turning your evaluations to alternative properties. Where the site is already owned, or there is a compelling reason to build in that locale, mitigation of this resistance becomes essential.

Working personally with any receptive political figures, a broad public relations program, favorable articles and information planted in the media, and unearthing support wherever it can be found, are usually required to overcome the resistance.

Equally as important is to address the opposing groups early and often. While many developers avoid or try to go around opposition groups, the author believes it is much more productive to identify them, meet with them, describe your objectives, and try to understand their real issues (not just their stated ones), before they solidify their resistance after learning about your project through the papers or through leaks from the regulators. A small early concession may turn out to be more beneficial than major concessions offered after the resistance has hardened.

Issues and sources to study and evaluate relative to potential reasonable solutions or compromises are described below.

City/County Attitudes Toward Growth and Political Climate

- Liberal/conservative
- Pro/anti business and development

Frequent Negative Development Attitudes

Negative attitudes are intertwined with environmental and quality of life concerns, usually triggered by rapid growth problems locally or in nearby cities.

- LULU—locally unwanted land use
- NIMBY—not in my backyard
- BANANA—build absolutely nothing anywhere near anything
- NIMTOO—not in my term of office

Study the Political Environment

- Ask about past and present attitudes
- Fastest growing communities are most likely to create issues that arouse the public
- Prepare a strategy in advance

Demographics

- Prior, present and trends
- Projection 5, 10 and 20 years out

Identify Organizations That Might Oppose the Project

It is very important to know the opposition, and the primary concerns or objectives of each one. It is not unusual to be able to offer something attractive to attain either support or non-opposition.

- Sierra Club and other environmental groups
- Community Planning Council
- Historic preservation organizations
- Various neighborhood groups

Identify Organizations That Might Support the Project

There are organizations in every community who benefit from and have a vested interest in development and the additional business and jobs it brings. Identification of these groups and solicitation of their support is essential.

- Business council
- Chamber of commerce
- Taxpayers association
- Local businesses
- Labor unions
- Local press

Meet Key Persons—Personal Contact Is Essential

- Mayor/County manager
- City council/county supervisor who represents area of site
- All other council/supervisors if project may be controversial
- Director of planning and zoning
- Senior planner responsible for area
- Director of transportation/highways
- Director of building code enforcement

Identify Trade-offs

- Try to find trade-offs to satisfy as many groups as possible.

Development Assistance

- Mello-Roos bonds (California)
- Local and state revenue bonds

- Government funded parking, pedestrianways, etc.
- Redevelopment agency
- Conveyance of roadways, right of way, or land

Project control

- When there is political sensitivity to a project, team members should understand that **all discussions** with governmental, community organizations or the news media be initiated by, or cleared through, the Development Officer.

CASE STUDY

At the commencement of the project there were no known neighborhood or environmental groups that were likely to object to the project.

Early in the process the development team met with the Deputy Director, Development Services and a representative from the Special Projects, Economic Development Division to review the city's attitude toward the project and obtain their advice as to how to proceed. They were very positive, and suggested that some time could be saved by applying for a Substantial Conformance Review, since the total constructed area, maximum building height, number of average daily automobile trips and amount of parking spaces were equal to or less than the previously approved 500-room hotel. Their positive attitude was obviously driven by the anticipated tax revenue to be generated by the hotel portion of the project, as they accepted the fact that a 500-room hotel could not be financed.

There were no stated concerns by any regulatory authorities in the city of San Diego—only the necessity of obtaining approval to modify the project to a joint office-hotel project, presumably through the Substantial Conformance Review. The team was advised that approval on this basis would probably be granted if the project was approved by the local Carmel Valley Planning Board.

The project was submitted simultaneously to the city and the Carmel Valley Planning Board in October, 1998.

There was considerable surprise at the depth of resistance on the planning board, as it was believed that they were relatively benign. In retrospect, the team should have at least been prepared for resistance, as the buildings in the project were twice the height of most buildings in the office park, and as development increases in an area it is fairly normal for resistance to tend to increase. Their particular issues—which were basically height, density, view corridors and traffic—should probably have been anticipated, and been better prepared when they first arose. It might not have changed the timing or the outcome, however, it clearly would have been more prudent. This was a good lesson: Always prepare for the worst in the political arena.

At the first meeting with the planning board, after some discussion about height and density they scheduled a formal meeting for December 9. The board was led by a chairwoman who is not enamored by development of any size. Realizing that there might be more difficulty obtaining their approval than originally anticipated, a local consultant with strong community ties who apparently knew all of the active board members was retained, to assist in gaining their concurrence, or at least blunt their objections. It was clear that the resistance to the project, if any, would come from the planning board.

The only other potential political issues would come from the Coastal or Planning Commissions, who have the ability and inclination to apply discretionary mitigations in order to obtain their approvals, which are often quite unpredictable. Approval of these agencies would only be required if the Substantial Conformance Determination was not accomplished, or the project was otherwise opened to discretionary review.

A detailed discussion of the Substantial Conformance Review approval process is covered in Chapter 7.

EL CAMINO REAL

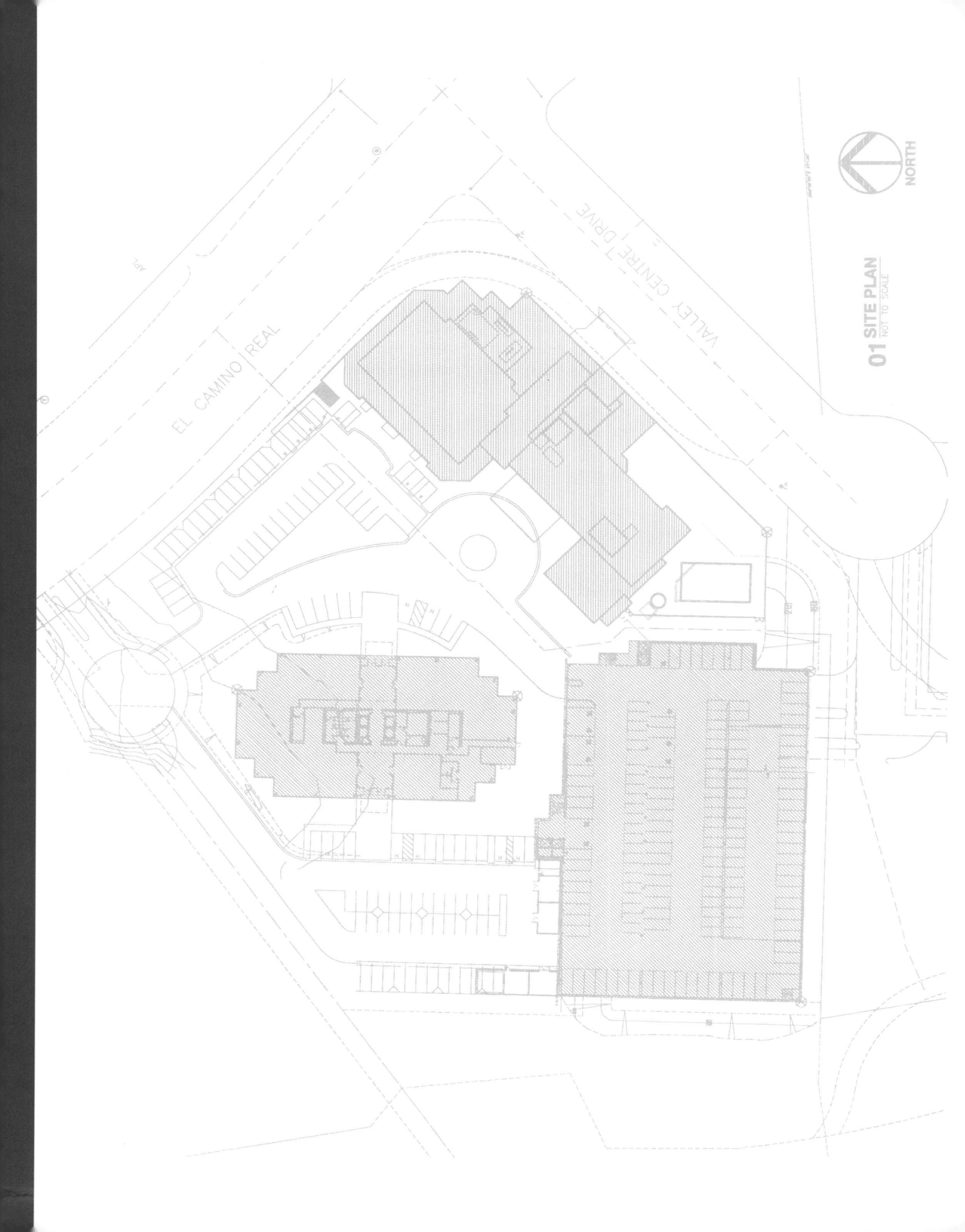

VALLEY CENTRE DRIVE

NORTH

01 SITE PLAN
NOT TO SCALE

SITE SELECTION, ACQUISITION and PERMITTING

Any consideration of a development site must be based on a clear set of objectives and a clear strategy. The type of product, general type of tenant, approximate project size and quality, method of financing, long-term hold vs. build-to-sell, and approximate timing should be determined in advance through an initial Market Study, subject to a more detailed analysis prior to actual site selection. The selection process should not commence without a reasonable understanding as to the market and the extent of the political and environmental issues.

This chapter will discuss the factors in site selection to accomplish predetermined criteria, the economic evaluation and price negotiation of a selected site, issues involved in the acquisition process and a brief comment on permitting and entitlements.

Consideration of a new development site is normally initiated in a particular city and/or its submarket when it is triggered either by the offer of an attractive site, a determination that the particular area has a positive combination of long-range growth and reasonably low vacancy of the preferred office product, or a desire to expand your operations into the particular area.

Sources of leads on possible sites are land brokers, aerial photography, local industrial development agencies, financial institutions, title companies, architects, attorneys, county planning and zoning departments, county plat books, county tax records, foreclosure reports and real estate tax services. A preliminary screening based on the chosen strategy will usually reduce the number of sites for serious detailed consideration down to a reasonable number.

A very important member of your team is the real estate attorney experienced in site selection and acquisition in the subject area, who can also recommend the most appropriate additional consultants. It takes a close cooperative working relationship to identify and solve the various legal and business issues, particularly without incurring excessive costs.

Site Selection

When looking for a site, or evaluating one, it is important to have the patience to search and evaluate until you identify a superior site, not just an adequate one. The superior site will undoubtedly cost a little more, but that can be more than made up through faster lease-up and/or higher rental rates.

The first issue is the general location and market for the preferred product—CBD, downtown, perimeter, suburban, or outlying—and the competitive submarket in which it is located.

A specific site should be evaluated for its relationship to various positive factors that would enhance the market for a proposed office building. There are many positive factors, which will vary in weighting depending on the type of market area and the type of product. Among those identified in the Market Study are:

- Visibility

- Public transportation
  - Trains or light rail
  - Bus
  - Airport

71

- Highway and road system
  - Highway interchanges
  - Traffic patterns
  - Degree of traffic congestion
  - Site ingress and egress
- Established office building market—equivalent or higher quality
- Major financial institutions
- Institutions of higher education
- Clubs, restaurants, hotels
- Public parking
- Retail
- Theater, cultural, entertainment
- Upscale residential—managerial decision makers
- General residential—employee pool
- Parks, other amenities
- Fire, police and other public services
- Availability of state-of-the-art communications
- Signage regulations

Factors that may be negative for a quality office development, and which must be carefully evaluated from a marketability standpoint are:

- Industrial and manufacturing districts
- Overhead power lines
- Landfills
- Airport glide paths
- Sewer and water plants
- Parking decks and rooftops
- Slums
- Derelict hangouts
- Bus stations
- Sexual preference areas
- Police station, jail, parole office
- Cemeteries

In many geographical areas location in the major growth corridor, convenience to the airport, freeway interchanges and relationship to established office markets of comparable or greater quality are the most important factors in determining the superior location available. The relationship of potential sites to these positive elements are best shown through aerial photography or the new GIS electronic maps available in many metropolitan areas. An increasingly important factor for many users is the availability of a substantial labor pool educated and suitable for their workforce. It is also very positive if the site has a slope of less than 5 degrees and the likelihood of natural drainage.

Once one or more sites are identified that appear to be located appropriately for a successful office development, the general market trends and the office market trends in that submarket, as discussed in Chapter 4, are studied in further depth to verify that a development on the site(s) would meet the profitability objectives.

When considering the acquisition of land, it is important to give full consideration to the market cycle, as discussed in detail in Chapter 4. Although no one can ever accurately judge the exact time of market turns, or their duration, the ideal time to purchase property for development is during the down cycle. This is because land prices tend to drop, and by the time the development process is completed the market should be in the absorption cycle.

For normal development, one should not buy more land than they can afford to retain through a down cycle. Those whose business is purchasing land for a long-term land investment are prone to attempt to find the bottom of the market and buy distressed properties whenever possible.

Based upon the completion of a satisfactory preliminary market analysis, preliminary investigations of the specifics of the site and the political environment, as covered in Chapters 5 and 6, should be initiated. If these preliminary investigations are positive, a site should be selected for evaluation and negotiation.

Some developers will retain real estate consultants to perform the necessary studies and prepare a Feasibility Analysis to evaluate the potential sites, while most have the capability to perform these analyses themselves, although independent reports may be required at a later date to satisfy potential lenders.

Site Evaluation

When acquiring land for development it is important that the land price be such that an office building(s) can be profitably developed, and that your costs will not put you at a disadvantage in relation to other competing developers and their projects.

There are two primary methods to arrive at an appropriate price to pay for a development site. In this chapter we are considering only the acquisition of land for one or several office building sites. Major land development will be covered in Appendix D.

The most common method of price determination is that of comparative sales, as prior sales data is normally readily available. It is necessary to compare each comparable with the site in question and make adjustments up or down so that the comparisons are on an equivalent basis. Some of the most common adjustments are:

- Date of the sale
- Size and shape of the parcels
- Whether purchased with or without full entitlements in place
- Flood plains or ground water
- Required water retention and detention
- Differences in zoning, particularly FAR variations
- Parking to be surface or structured
- Soil conditions
- Toxic waste assumptions
- Excessive cut and/or fills
- Utility availability
- Demolition and removal
- Highway or transportation access
- Convenience to positive market factors

The resultant price comparisons can be made on the basis of either the price per land square foot (usually adjusted to an effective land area by subtracting flood plain, excessive slope, etc.) or price per buildable square foot. While some developers commonly talk in terms of land square foot, the only cost basis that the author believes is meaningful is the buildable square foot, or the land square footage adjusted for the assumed zoning floor area ratio (FAR). This is the unit cost that ties directly into the economic pro forma for the project. The above notwithstanding, allowable FAR does not indicate whether the site can accommodate surface or structured parking, which can create a large variance in construction costs.

The second method is a residual pro forma analysis. In this method assumptions are made for all costs, market income, debt service and developer's desired return on investment, and the equation is solved for the maximum allowable land cost. Note that this type of analysis requires early assumptions of the cost of resolving many of the difficult site and political issues, as well as construction costs.

In addition to evaluating the appropriate price for the site, whenever possible the potential seller(s) should be investigated to determine everything possible about their needs and decision-making process, including their urgency or lack of it with regard to the sale. It is important to know whether the seller is likely to consider options, minimal non-refundable at-risk money on purchase contracts, or owner financing. This research can have an impact on how hard you negotiate and, in the case where more than one site is desirable, it might dictate which one you try to first acquire.

Site Acquisition

In spite of the extent of the preliminary investigations undertaken to this point, there are usually many largely unknown risks remaining before you are able to determine with certainty that the site can be developed profitably. The author is aware of several developments that took eight to ten years to obtain a site development permit, some that were greatly downsized and some that failed entirely. The impact of such an event is frightening—not only for the excessive costs involved, but the potential for a lower FAR than anticipated, and with no reasonable way to predict the market environment at the time the project is able to proceed.

Any purchase contract must make provisions for a thorough analysis of all of the factors described in the various sections of the Feasibility Analysis. It is important during the negotiation and evaluation period to maintain a strict discipline as to value, and not become caught up in the enthusiasm and competitive nature of making a deal.

Obviously, any site with entitlements that satisfy the objectives of the proposed development will greatly simplify the review process and the risk. Non-entitled sites, particularly where there are some political and environmental concerns, require more extensive feasibility studies, have inherently greater risk and require a return of at least an additional 100 basis points.

The most important factor in a land purchase contract is the amount of money at risk, and at what point it becomes at risk. The full purchase price should never be at risk, or subject to specific performance, until all studies are completed and evaluated, and a conscious decision is made to consummate the purchase. A Land Purchase Agreement should be recorded immediately.

The most effective way for the purchaser to protect against the myriad of uncertainties and risks is to enter into a purchase contract wherein the earnest money will be completely refunded after a stipulated period of time if the developer is unable to obtain a site development permit, which in his judgment will permit an economically feasible project, or the more saleable condition of a specified development size and type. As many sellers will object to what they consider in effect to be a free option, an alternative is to have a reasonable amount of nonrefundable earnest money that is forfeited after the evaluation period if the contract fails to close.

When negotiating with sellers over the conditions under which the funds become firm, it should be clearly pointed out that the land does not reach its potential value to anyone without reasonable entitlements. His alternate strategy would be to fund the cost of entitlements and then sell the land.

The method that is most frequently acceptable is to have the earnest money refundable after an agreed upon period of time if reasonably specific contingencies are not satisfactorily completed. Usually such contracts will have an option for a specified amount of hard earnest money to extend the evaluation period. Some examples of such contingencies are:

- FAR approval
- Zoning variances
- EIR approval
- Survey
- Soil tests
- Toxic waste tests
- Cost of utility availability
- Cost of access road connections
- Exaction (impact) fees
- Historic preservation issues
- Land spin-off
- Political and environmental issues
- Financing
- Site plan approval
- Many other due diligence issues

In addition to the above, and the discussion of the availability and terms of owner financing, many standard conditions must be part of any Land Purchase Agreement, such as:

- Marketable fee simple title
- Title search and title insurance commitment
- Prorations of taxes, operating costs, income and closing costs
- Encumbrances
- Design committee approval if covered by CC&Rs
- Material defects (if structures included)
- Condemnation proceedings
- Utility moratoriums
- Current leases and service contracts

- Brokerage responsibility
- Right of assignment
- Seller warranties on power to sell, violation of government regulations, etc.

After completion of all studies, and just prior to the expiration of the contingency period, one final review of the preliminary pro forma must be made to reverify the economic viability of the proposed project. Great discipline is required at this point to ascertain that the position in the market cycle still seems proper, and there are no major unknowns that could destroy the success of the project. Remember, it is always better to lose the earnest money and the cost of the studies than to enter into a losing project.

While frequently the desired parcel is for sale, or there is a willing seller, it is not uncommon for the most desirable site for your purpose to be held by a reticent seller. In such cases, creative efforts must be made to induce the seller to sell the land at a reasonable price. Some examples of this are joint ventures, tax free exchanges, property trades, ground leases with an option to purchase the land in a stipulated period of years at an agreed upon price, or a long-term ground lease, but the methods are limited only by the circumstances involved and your own creativity. Carefully listening to the proposed seller often yields clues to a successful solution. Ground leases, where unavoidable, must be carefully crafted as the term of the lease and its specific terms can impact the long-term economics of the project and create many issues with a prospective lender.

The most complicated site acquisition I ever experienced on a per square foot basis was the purchase of 3,500 square feet of land, occupied by Eddie Bauer, as part of the assembly for the Crocker Bank northern headquarters in San Francisco.

The site was critical to the Crocker project, and Eddie Bauer indicated a willingness to relocate if an equal or better location could be found. The Eddie Bauer site was on a long-term financing lease to an insurance company in Kentucky, so we had to negotiate with them as well.

The only alternative site that would satisfy Eddie Bauer was on Post Street, then occupied under lease by Abercrombie and Fitch, who were going through bankruptcy proceedings. The building was owned by a third party. It was necessary to negotiate with Abercrombie, and their primary lender, the First National Bank of Chicago, as well as the building owner.

When we thought we had negotiated an agreement, it was submitted to General Mills, Eddie Bauer's parent company. They rejected the agreement, saying that they needed an additional half million dollars to relocate. We were dismayed, as the cost was already a little too high. When we reassessed the transaction, we remembered that Eddie Bauer's requirements were for a 40-foot frontage and the new site was 50 feet wide. Our broker, Ed Plant, believed that a jewelry firm named Ciro's, who were losing their lease on the other side of Union Square, would pay as much as $60 triple net (this was 1977) per square foot for a nominal 10-foot-wide store.

We entered into an agreement with Ciro's which, when capped, had a value in excess of the half million that General Mills required. The purchase was consummated.

Multi-site Assemblies

Multi-site assembly creates an entirely new set of issues. It is not productive to acquire only one or a few of the sites that will not comprise a satisfactory development site, and information leaking out about an acquisition of one site can significantly increase the asking price for future negotiations.

One approach is to attempt to acquire each site contingent upon successfully acquiring the others. This approach might work for a small number of sites and may permit site evaluations to proceed more openly, but risks price increases that may preclude the acquisition entirely.

Another approach, or variations of it depending on the number of sites involved, is to contract for each site while attempting to keep the entire process secret. To have this approach work properly, it is necessary to make special provisions on all aspects of the transactions, such as:

- Retain a dependable real estate attorney experienced in assemblies
- Form several dummy corporations with no apparent relationship to you or each other
- Employ an individual broker, or a very small firm, as brokers are notorious for talking out of turn and leaving information unprotected on their desks
- Carefully select a title company because a pattern of land contracts can be noticed within a title company's plant, permitting information to be conveyed to outside parties

The above process must be carefully thought out and orchestrated, since in many states the real estate disclosure regulations place strict limitations on concealing information from a seller, which may suggest utilizing multiple brokers.

In multi-site assembly it is even more important to enter into purchase options or contracts with very low amounts of at-risk money, as development contingencies cannot be specified as clearly as in a single-site purchase. Even then, if the assembly takes too long, some of the option or contingency periods in the earlier contracts may expire prior to completion of the assembly.

A very difficult issue is how to keep the assembly from public notice and still accomplish an acceptable due diligence or feasibility review of the environmental, regulatory and political risks, particularly within the contractual time constraints. The best approach to this issue will vary with the type, location and political environment, but a generalized answer is to study the zoning and regulatory issues without site identification and to use a very limited and carefully-assembled support group—your attorney, a surveyor and a trustworthy environmental consultant—to study the other factors, thus minimizing exposure to potential issues while maintaining secrecy.

An example of a difficult multi-site assembly was undertaken in Dallas. It took us over two years to acquire a full downtown block that was desired as a headquarters site for Mercantile Bank (later Mbank). We later learned that Mercantile had previously tried to assemble that site, but had given up on the assumption that it could not be acquired.

The block was comprised of 19 separate parcels, two of which had 24 beneficiaries who had to agree to any sale, and several parcels were in family trusts. Because of the complexity and a concern for secrecy we retained a small two-person real estate firm, Bradley & Bradley, created five separate acquisition corporations and retained a small new title company, Plano Title. We were certain that if knowledge of our assembly was publicly known the cost would rise to a level that would preclude a cost-effective project. We encountered almost every kind of issue one can imagine during this assembly. A few of them are:

We gave the Bradleys the commission on a Friday and they decided to make one call before the weekend. Fortuitously, the party they chose to call on had received a purchase offer from McDonald's and the entire family was scheduled to meet that weekend to consider it. We were able to make a higher offer and acquire the property. We could never have completed a bank headquarters project block with a McDonald's on the corner.

One of the parcels with 24 beneficiaries had five of them overseas including one sailor on a ship in the South Pacific.

Another small parcel was owned by three cousins, one of whom was a bag lady with no telephone, who could only be reached through the bulletin board at her savings and loan, and the other two lived out of town. They refused to speak to each other and we finally decided to deal with each one singly, even though their ownership was an undivided interest. When we had purchase agreements from the other two parties, we advised the bag lady that if she didn't want to sell her interest to us we would go to court and file a partition suit to separate the interests. She then decided to sell. Incidentally, she passed away a few years later leaving an estate estimated at over $3 million.

One property was a bar inherited by a woman who had transferred the ownership to her new husband. When we entered into an agreement he took the money and apparently left the country. Another very interesting purchase was from the very forceful executor of a trust who thought he knew the market. When our broker arrived in his office, he said "Don't bother to sit down. Here is my price, take it or leave it." His price was 20% less than the price our broker had on a purchase contract in his pocket.

One of the sites contained an abandoned building that a small group of people wanted to retain as a historical edifice—it had been the first commercially air-conditioned building in Dallas. We didn't think many in the general public had any interest, and started demolition the day we closed on the contract to avoid having to go through a lengthy procedure.

The final, and the most difficult site was a corner property occupied by a small department store that was paying an exceedingly low rate with no rental escalation and a 40- or 45-year term remaining. Their rent was so low that we basically had to pay full land value to buy out their leasehold interest. The fee interest was in a spendthrift trust that precluded a sale, but the lease could be extended and renegotiated. Negotiation of this lease took over a year in order to obtain financable terms—and the lease payment was virtually based on the full value of the land. In other words, we paid for it twice. To add insult to injury the Historical Preservation Committee held hearings to determine if a demolition permit would be awarded. I listened for two hours to expressions such as "antiquity," "historic relic," "heritage," etc.—and the building was younger than I was at the time. We ultimately received the demolition permit, but the experience was rather deflating.

In spite of the excessive price for the last parcel, the average price of the assembly was below market for an equivalent site.

More information on this complex assembly is contained in the book, *Risk, Ruin & Riches—Inside the World of Big-Time Real Estate*, by Jim Powell.

Probably the most important traits required of the Development Officer in this type of assembly are thoroughness and the discipline to hold to the original site cost objectives.

Sometimes the potential to expand a single-site purchase into a multi-site assembly can result from seeing and acting upon an unusually attractive opportunity.

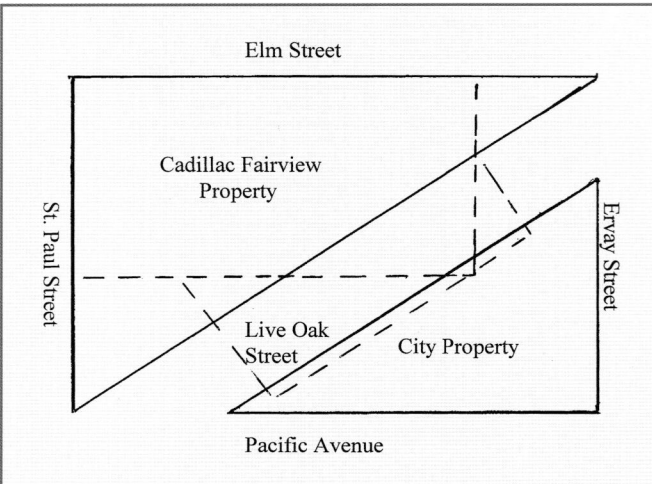

[Sketch: Block bounded by Elm Street (top), Pacific Avenue (bottom), St. Paul Street (left), and Ervay Street (right), showing Cadillac Fairview Property and City Property separated by Live Oak Street.]

We had a very interesting and unusual land assembly for what was to be the headquarters for the First City Bank in downtown Dallas. Our parent company had acquired two buildings in a block that was bifurcated by Live Oak Street and was unaware of the city's plans for that block.

As shown in the adjacent sketch, the city owned the smaller triangle, and had plans to close Live Oak Street, creating a transportation center. We did not believe that we could build an appropriate bank headquarters building on the portion of the site we were endeavoring to acquire, so we entered into discussions with the city to determine their objectives. Their plan was to ultimately build a subway through the downtown under Elm Street and out Live Oak Street to the northern suburbs. There would be a major subway station in the subject block under the section of Live Oak that would be abandoned. They wanted at least three covered bus shelters to facilitate access to and from the subway station, and they desired to have a park-like setting on most of the land they currently owned.

After extensive negotiation we entered into an agreement with the city to acquire their interests in the block and street and to provide the facilities they desired. We would build a complete subway tunnel to their specifications through the abandoned section of the street. We would design the future station, complete with ticket booth areas, platforms and circulation areas, as well as planned access to and from the street. As the station would not be built for several years, we filled the area above the tunnel with parking decks with knockout panels so that the station could be completed at a future date when the remainder of the subway was constructed. We would build three covered bus shelters and would create the park-like area where the city desired it.

The city agreed that the construction costs we undertook for the facilities they desired would be considered as partial payment for their interest in the land, against its appraised value. We agreed that we would keep our bank tower as far toward Elm and St. Paul Streets as possible to maximize the size of the landscaped area.

The building was located as shown with the dashed lines, the tower being the rectangular area and the angled lines representing the bank hall outline, with major columns on the centerline of and straddling the subway tunnel. Due to the slope of the site, access to the future subway station from Ervay St. was one level below the building lobby. The transit access from St. Paul Street was through a main building entrance, but immediately routed down to the lower level by escalator, in order to provide a separation between building and subway traffic, particularly after hours. The lower level was created as a retail area to support both the building and future transit passengers.

It was a very satisfactory deal for all parties, as we ended up with a full block in which to design the bank headquarters (see the adjacent picture with Thanksgiving Square in the foreground) and the city received all of the facilities they desired. An interesting footnote to the project is that the city never built the subway and there is an empty tunnel under that building to this date, with no projected use.

Permitting and Entitlements

Permitting is a thorough and orderly process required to satisfy all of the identified legal, zoning and political issues (plus a few occasional surprises) in order to qualify for the desired entitlements. It encompasses satisfying all zoning and other regulatory requirements, environmental studies and possible mitigations, review and comment by community groups and special bodies such as Coastal Commissions, Air Quality Control boards, Fish and Wildlife Commission, design and other discretionary review panels, and frequently many more.

Even when development is not envisioned to commence right away, it is prudent to proceed expeditiously to satisfy all of the political, environmental and regulatory issues so as to achieve entitlements for the proposed development before any change in political attitudes occurs.

Care should be taken, however, to carefully note the life of a development permit before a renewal application is required. Many a project has failed to obtain a permit renewal. Environmental and civic groups who objected to the initial permit may well object to the renewal, and may have more political clout at that later time. A further word of caution: there are many events that can override previously approved permits, such as a public referendum that affects the property, the addition of a newly declared endangered species, or other environmental occurrences.

Normally, a subdivision map or lot line adjustment is required in order to define separate individual parcels to permit different functions, financing or sale. The approval process for these often opens the project to further regulatory reviews with the potential for rejection or further mitigation.

The development permit and the tentative subdivision map are prerequisites for any further permits for the project.

CASE STUDY

SITE SELECTION

Site selection in this case was a non-issue, as the site was offered for sale as a site for a 150,000 gsf office building and a 200-room hotel through a bidding process in a location very desirable to Prentiss, as discussed in the Introduction.

ACQUISITION

The issues in the acquisition proposal, subject to a thorough Feasibility Analysis, were basically: (a) determining at what net price this was an attractive site, (b) entering into an acceptable agreement with an appropriate hotel developer, and (c) in addition to price, deciding what efforts were most likely to promote selection even if the proposal were not the highest bid.

One key to selection was to satisfy Pardee as to the quality office building that would be developed, as it is in the dominant location at the southern entrance to their office park, and they have additional sites to sell or develop in the future. In the adjacent project Prentiss had acquired plans prepared by Pardee, which were required to be used largely as is. The quality of those buildings was significantly improved without major changes to the façade, and was accomplished while not increasing the project costs. In addition, the project was completed on a shorter construction schedule than Pardee had anticipated. They were so impressed with the product that they leased a floor in one of the buildings and put their showroom on the first floor. In the process of working with Pardee, Prentiss was able to convey an impression of integrity, open discussion and a competence that they could accomplish the necessary rezoning in a reasonable period of time without creating any unnecessary negative reactions in the community. Additionally, Pardee's broker in the transaction was the leasing broker on the adjacent project and thought very highly of the development personnel, largely because of the quality of the product, the open relationship, quick decision making, fair attitude and prompt payment of commissions. It is believed the broker was a positive factor in Prentiss' behalf.

A second key to selection was to convince Pardee that Prentiss could provide the best hotel available, even though they would not develop it and would have no financial or operational involvement. A relatively new hotel development firm, Waterford Development, was selected largely based on the perceived quality of the personnel, their prior experience with other hotel developers, and the enthusiastic support of Hilton who was their initially proposed franchiser. A preliminary analysis of the market had indicated that a Hilton Suites or a Compact Hilton Commercial hotel would be the most successful operation in this particular market, due to the projected business traveler demand and the potential overexposure of Marriott. The next most likely selection for this particular market was assumed to be a Marriott Suites.

Jointly with Waterford, Hilton was originally proposed as the most appropriate selection. To satisfy Pardee with regard to the quality of the Prentiss team, a meeting was arranged with the hotel developer, Hilton management and the responsible Pardee management group at Hilton's headquarters in Los Angeles. At that meeting Hilton put on a good presentation as to their interest and proposed quality. In addition, Waterford's proposed equity partner and also a proposed purchaser/operator provided letters of extreme interest.

The third issue was the price that could be justified for the land in the competitively bid process. The minimum bid price was stated as $19/gross sf, and it was a certainty that due to the pressure of the current market, the site could not be acquired at that price. Pardee had reserved the right to consider factors other than price in their selection.

Due to the process involved, the desire to obtain the site and rising land values, a pure market analysis of value using adjusted sales data was not relevant; instead, the pro forma analysis approach to valuation was used.

To develop the pro forma the young start up architectural firm working on the existing adjacent project, Hanna Gabriel Wells, was selected to provide site evaluation, design schemes and an approximate schedule for the entitlement and design process, as well as very preliminary sizing and siting plans. The contractor building the current project was selected to prepare a preliminary cost estimate for the building, parking structure and site work based on the architect's information and a verbal description of desired quality.

At an early stage the possibility of two four-story office buildings was investigated, but it quickly became obvious that the site could not support three buildings. Later schemes where the hotel and office building were parallel to each other were evaluated, with the hotel oriented diagonally to the corner of El Camino Real and Valley Centre Drive. (Note that many of the drawings use the former name of Carmel View Road.) A preliminary scheme where the hotel was parallel to Valley Centre Drive, and adjacent to El Camino Real, with the office building at right angles to it was finally selected. The design on which the proposal was based, and submitted to Pardee, is shown in Figures 7-1 and 7-2.

The office building was assumed to be six stories, as that would avoid the penalties associated with high-rise codes that would occur if the highest floor line exceeded 75 feet above grade. The merits of the smaller floor size that would result if the building were eight stories would be studied at a later date.

During this evaluation a judgment was made that the parking structure size could be reduced by at least 10% from the separately calculated parking demands, due to a shared parking arrangement with the hotel. Later analysis showed the shared parking saving to be closer to 15%. Base building shell and core cost was assumed to be $57/gsf, and the parking structure was $7,625 per stall. The architectural and consultant fees were estimated at $5/building gsf.

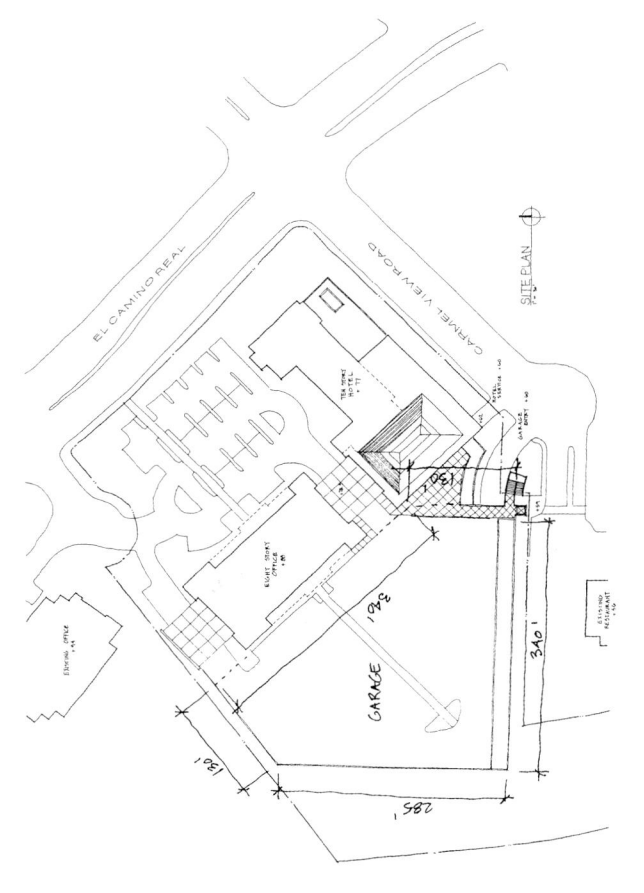

Figure 7-1

The amount Waterford would pay for the hotel pad, their contribution to the site evaluation efforts, site and parking design costs and the parking structure and site work construction costs were negotiated. An outline of the Land Sale Agreement with Waterford is appended at the end of this chapter.

As the design of the hotel developed, additional rooms and additional banquet space were added, which required additional parking spaces. The original deal with Waterford was for a fixed contribution to the parking structure, so it was necessary to negotiate a revision to the deal to provide for their paying a percentage determined by a formula, based on the gross parking requirement of each building.

Based on the above data, the current market experience and assumptions for the next two years, preliminary pro formas for the Prentiss portion of the project at various land cost assumptions were prepared, net of Waterford's land purchase price and

Figure 7-2

other contributions. A rental rate of $2.10/rsf per month (later increased to $2.25 due to continued rate increases occurring in the market), exclusive of electricity, was used for occupancy commencing approximately 24 months out, compared to a weighted average in the current project of $2.10, with the latest few leases at $2.25. TIs were increased from the current average of $33.50/usf to $35.50/usf. Operating expense assumptions were adjusted 7% from the current level to allow for the two-year escalation period.

There were several rounds of evaluations that included the office developer and hotel developer qualifications, the hotel franchiser, and the proposed land price. Prentiss was about ready to stop their bid at $23/gross square foot based on the pro forma analysis, but Waterford decided to increase their share to cover another dollar. It was finally agreed that $24/ gross sf for the land price was the maximum the venture would pay. At that land price, the Prentiss land cost was $34.90 per FAR foot, the estimated overall project cost was $205/rsf, and the projected free and clear return was 9.92%.

In spite of extreme pressures on Pardee management by several of the bidders, and it was learned that on an apples-to-apples basis the proposal was at least $600,000 or $1.60 per gross land square foot lower than the highest bidder, Prentiss was selected to negotiate a land purchase contract. The business judgment for this selection was undoubtedly based on the perceived certainty that the team would close and accomplish the project in a timely manner.

The Land Purchase Agreement called for Prentiss to acquire the entire site and resell the hotel pad to the hotel developer, pay an initial $150,000 of refundable earnest money, increase the earnest money to $300,000 and go firm with another $150,000 when all of the site-specific contingencies were satisfactorily resolved. An equal amount was placed in escrow by Waterford. The contract gave Pardee certain rights as to approval of the schematic design and participation in discussions with the political and regulatory bodies. A synopsis of the Land Purchase Agreement is shown at the end of this chapter.

In addition to all of the normal contingencies discussed in Chapter 5, the land purchase was also contingent upon receipt of a Substantial Conformance Determination, or other zoning approval that provided entitlements for at least the minimum project size specified, and the escrow would not close until approval of a tentative map dividing the property into the necessary separate parcels.

Necessary conditions to the Land Purchase Agreement were entering into an approved Land Sale Agreement and an approved Construction, Operation and Reciprocal Easement Agreement (COREA) with the hotel developer.

Resolution of the COREA was a more difficult issue than originally anticipated. Waterford repeatedly tried to renegotiate the scope of the parking required for the office building and the hotel and the cost sharing included originally in the Land Sale Agreement. One stated reason for these positions was their claim that the costs of the hotel were affected more than the office building by the changes required during the Substantial Conformance Review process, discussed later.

In addition, it was difficult to get Waterford to focus on the COREA for many months, apparently because they were having difficulty tying down their hotel operator and obtaining financing. Several extensions on submission of the COREA were requested and granted by Pardee. About three months before the anticipated closing, steady pressure was kept on Waterford to resolve all issues from the original draft submitted many months before.

Many issues were raised and negotiated, with an agreed upon COREA finally resolved the week of the land closing. Among the issues were:

- The total number of parking spaces required
- The amount of reserved parking spaces for the office building
- The amount of reserved parking spaces for the hotel
- Limits on parking permits issued to tenants
- Additional reserved valet parking area for special hotel events
- The percentage allocation of the operating costs for the parking structure and the site work

- Whether to support Waterford's efforts to change the CC&Rs to permit paid parking for the hotel guests
- Selection and payment of any parking operator, as well as operating procedures satisfactory to Prentiss, both prior to and after Prentiss commences charging for parking
- Method of allocating land real estate taxes, and the tax on the parking structure and site work improvements
- Proposition 13 protection for the hotel relative to the real estate taxes on the parking structure and the site work in event of a Prentiss sale
- Allocating depreciation to Waterford relative to their share of the cost of the parking and the site work (later waived by Waterford due to the planned sale to Marriott at Certificate of Occupancy)
- Makeup and decision-making of the Parking Advisory Committee
- Right to approve the maintenance budget
- The hotel's right to hold special functions on the top deck of the parking structure
- Sharing the costs of resubdividing the adjacent Lot 29

A synopsis of the COREA, as finally agreed upon is included at the end of this chapter.

Closing on the land necessitated juggling a maze of conflicting and difficult issues. It was necessary to close on the land as soon as possible so as to commence construction as soon as a grading permit was available in order to minimize the delay penalties in the 105,000 rsf lease to Brandes Investment Partners, as discussed more fully in Chapters 31 and 32. The various issues that had to be juggled were:

- It was necessary to execute the Brandes Lease prior to management and the lender approval to close on the land, but it could not be executed until approval of the lot line adjustment and grading permits were a certainty, so as to avoid excessive penalties. The negotiations with Brandes as to the landlord delay penalty issue were in progress until the last minute.
- The lease with Scripps Bank for the first two floors could not be executed prior to the Brandes Lease being executed, since top of the building signage could not be given away when it might be required for a major tenant if the Brandes Lease were not consummated
- It was necessary to complete the COREA to satisfy Pardee, the lender and Waterford's financial partner
- It was necessary to satisfy voluminous city issues in the third effort to subdivide the parcel for hotel and office ownership as discussed later in this chapter
- Extensive issues and delays were encountered in obtaining the grading plan approval, required prior to the approval of any other permits or the start of any work, as discussed under Chapter 14
- Obtaining Pardee's approval of the office building and the parking structure designs, which was much more difficult than anticipated
- Obtaining Pardee's approval to enter on the site prior to closing in order to prepare for the start of construction—general contractor's trailer, temporary power and communications, survey and staking for the grading
- Working out a compromise between the lender and Waterford's financial partner regarding guaranteeing payment for the shared structures, so the COREA could be executed
- Completing the construction contract that was delayed by the belated insistence by the law department on some form of consequential damages clause to help protect against damages in the Brandes Lease
- Satisfying all of the normal requirements of the lender and the normal closing issues
- Making contingency plans in the event Waterford and the lender could not close on time.

These issues were all resolved in a timely manner except that neither Waterford nor Prentiss' lender were in a position to close. The lot line adjustment was approved on September 2 and the land purchase closed on September 10. Grading was scheduled to start on September 13 pending receipt of the grading permit on the 10th, but was delayed a week as discussed under the Permitting section of this chapter. The funds for the closing were made out of pocket.

Technically the closing date would have been September 17, fifteen days after approval of the lot line adjustment, but since Waterford could not close their loan by then, and it was important to commence grading, the closing was a week early.

The delay of the Waterford closing was basically due to negotiations between Waterford, Orix (their proposed construction lender) and Marriott on an agreement to sell the hotel to Marriott at the Certificate of Occupancy. Orix was not satisfied that the construction costs were sufficiently firm, and the Orix Board did not want to close their loan until a takeout agreement was executed with Marriott.

Prentiss' lender, Société Générale, was going through an unusually long due diligence, as well as endeavoring to negotiate some cross-default provisions relative to other loans. They decided not close on the loan until the hotel sale closed and either a letter of credit or a satisfactory guarantee was in place to ensure the hotel's share of the parking structure and site work were paid in a timely manner.

Due to Waterford's failure to close, and they were technically in default, their delayed closing was made contingent on several issues in addition to their normal share of initial closing costs and the cost of the second closing. They were:

- Matching the lower façade of the hotel to the office building granite—they were intending to use a lower quality stone—and Prentiss' approval of the hotel elevation drawings.

- As the parking structure and site work were just ready for plan check submission at that time, closing was deemed conclusive evidence of their approval, subject only to advising them of any material changes resulting from final completion of the drawings, and any changes resulting from plan check review.

- Exhibit E of the Land Sales Agreement was revised to include certain additional soft costs, which Waterford was resisting, and removed all caps and approval rights of any cost increases. Prentiss recovered approximately $86,000 more of the soft costs and permit fees than contemplated in the original Exhibit E.

- Required payment of 50% of the $36,500 of the driveway costs for the shared entranceway to Executive Center Del Mar, which had been paid to Pardee on closing.

- Resolved the issue of relative payment guarantees between Société Générale and Orix, the Waterford financial partner.

- Closed the issue of how to share the depreciation benefits as the hotel would be sold to Marriott at Certificate of Occupancy, so the issue was mute.

- Agreed to divide all grading costs evenly as a site work cost rather than allocating it to the three structures plus the site work.

- Payment of interest at 10% on Waterford's share of the purchase price and any other funds owed by them at closing.

- Required the waiver of all contingencies and for Waterford to go firm on October 7, with a closing no later than October 29.

Approximately 10 days prior to the revised scheduled closing, Waterford advised they would again be unable to close on time. The two reasons were:

- Marriott would not execute the purchase agreement to acquire the hotel at the Certificate of Occupancy until completion of an acquisition and investment fund then being set up, so the fund could contract directly for the property.

- The financial partner, Orix, would not close and fund the venture agreement until Marriott executed the takeout purchase agreement and approved the GMP, which was not to be reviewed until the first week in November, and they were still insisting Prentiss provide a monetary guarantee to cover our completion obligations for the parking structure and site work.

It was disappointing that Marriott would not enter into the agreement and later assign it to the fund, but the decision was made at the CEO level not to increase the real estate on the balance sheet even for a short duration. There were other ways to solve this issue, but you can't reach that level of management for one isolated hotel deal. Marriott later showed their serious intent by offering to commit some of the money for the extensions.

Prentiss had taken the position with Orix repeatedly that the documents required constructing the parking structure and site work, but they had no intention of providing a guarantee. Prentiss was a publicly traded REIT and would be seriously harmed if they tried to renege on such a commitment, but to give them some comfort it was agreed to leave at least $8 million of equity in the project until the work was finished.

Waterford was told that a further extension would be considered if the agreed upon conditions were satisfactory. The next day a letter was received from their attorney saying the lot line separating our properties didn't conform to the building code, and they would not close until it was corrected (a two or more month process). This was a phony issue in which they were trying to get a free extension, since:

- The lot line as plotted by the civil engineer complied within an inch or two of the drawing provided by their architect
- They had reviewed and approved it after it was plotted
- The 3rd amendment to the Land Sale Agreement provided that they approved the site plan that contained the lot line as well as the legal description of the property

The only code issue they were concerned about was that one row of window glazing would require a higher fire rating unless the lot line was modified, which we had previously agreed to do.

Their position was rejected out of hand, and everyone was so angered at their ridiculous attempt to bluff that serious consideration was given to blowing them out of the deal when they defaulted at closing. Upon reflection, it was decided that the project was best served by not changing players, and a list of requirements for a possible extension was prepared. A major concern was that significantly delayed hotel construction might impact the ability to obtain a timely Certificate of Occupancy for the office building. They were not able to commit to close on October 29 and they were given two more days. When they still could not close because of Marriott's unwillingness to commit, a termination notice was issued.

The notice seemed to panic their primary financial partner, Interbank-Brenner, who visualized forfeiting their $450,000 deposit and other funds advanced to date. Interbank got all of the entities together on a conference call on November 5, at which it was agreed verbally to conditions to restore the agreement. In the meantime, it had been determined that Hilton no longer had any interest in the site, and it was clearly more important to obtain a firm hotel commitment than to explore theoretically more attractive alternatives. The conditions were:

- They would receive an extension to November 30, 1999 if:
  - They executed the revised agreement by November 8
  - Immediately released the $450,000 held in escrow
  - They paid another $450,000 outside of escrow, plus the interest due on the land purchase, by November 10

- They would be granted an option for a second extension until January 10, 2000, providing that by November 30 they:
  - Paid a further $450,000 outside of escrow, plus the interest due through November 30
  - Provided a letter from Marriott that they had agreed upon the terms of a purchase contract, and the only condition to executing the purchase contract was the closing of the investment fund
  - Provided a letter from Orix that they had agreed upon the terms of a sale agreement with Marriott, and the only condition remaining to funding the closing on the land was the execution of the contract by Marriott
  - Provided a letter from Pardee stating that their design was approved
  - There were a series of commitments required of them relative to the construction of the

hotel—location of barricades, limits on their use of the property after the office building requested a Temporary Certificate of Occupancy, the timing of construction of certain utilities, and holding Prentiss harmless from lease penalties and loss of rental income if they delayed our Certificate of Occupancy

There was second-guessing from the home office due to not declaring a default and taking the $450,000 deposit at the first opportunity. It was believed at the time that if the money was forfeited, Waterford's bankers might not have sufficient money remaining at risk to take the lead in forcing the hotel project to a satisfactory and timely conclusion. The overriding objectives were to get the hotel started and completed for the benefit of the project, and obtain the funds from the land sale and the hotel's share of common facilities. Certain decisions must be made by the individuals who are thoroughly familiar with and responsible for the negotiations, not by those observing from a distance.

Waterford complied with the requirements for the second extension in a timely manner, except for the approval by Pardee and the letters from Orix and Marriott. The Pardee personnel who were responsible for design were unavailable for a two-week period, so an extension was allowed for that requirement. At a meeting in early December the hotel designs were approved with a letter to follow. Unfortunately, at that meeting Pardee tried to reopen the issue of spandrel glass on the office building, which was rejected, as discussed in detail in Chapter 20.

The closing did not occur on January 10, as Waterford, their banker and Marriott still could not reach full agreement. On Tuesday the 11th the requirement of the commitments from Marriott and Orix were waived providing all monies currently due under the land purchase agreement were received along with the letter of credit for the hotel's share of the common facility development. At this time it was believed to be more important to receive the $6 million to cover these costs than to wait for an ownership agreement and a commitment on the start of hotel construction.

There was concern that since Interbank had essentially squeezed Waterford out of the deal by this time, that the return on the hotel might be a little too thin. If pressed too hard on obtaining these agreements, there was always the possibility they would reanalyze the risk versus returns and walk away from their earnest money and other advances.

Wall Street rejected Marriott's investment fund a few days after the money was received. Interbank and Marriott endeavored to enter into a venture to build the hotel. An alternate financial arrangement was required since, due to the collapse of the fund, they needed a construction loan with a five-year mini-perm. Orix would not make that type of loan and bowed out.

Apparently, Interbank and Marriott were having difficulty reaching a mutually satisfactory agreement, and were unable to find equity and financing that included an acceptable mini-perm. Interbank was unwilling to invest further funds so, when Marriott agreed to waive their right to purchase the hotel at completion, the project was sold to JMI, a local San Diego firm known to be interested in owning the hotel. Negotiations ensued to take over all prior obligations and retain Marriott as the operator.

The sale negotiations dragged on longer than anyone had anticipated. Due to their high regard for JMI, Pardee waived their right to buy back the hotel land, which was contractually permissible on March 10. In addition to their normal due diligence, the negotiations were periodically hung up on issues such as:

- Marriott had executed an apparently onerous management contract with Waterford, which JMI would not accept without significant modification

- JMI insisted that Interbank fund at closing all of the additional costs to be incurred due to the delay in the start of hotel construction, including barricade construction and contractual delays

- JMI's lender insisted that the minor boundary line adjustment be recorded prior to closing

- Prentiss had completed all of the necessary engineering, but would not process the boundary line adjustment until JMI put up an additional letter of credit to cover the applicable soft costs and the construction cost increases

The issues were resolved and JMI closed on the sale on June 9, 2000, with construction started on July 17.

PERMITTING

The permitting process was closely intertwined with the acquisition process, as the acquisition would not close without obtaining the approvals for the agreed minimum project size and an acceptable subdivision map. In addition, many of the design issues required for the city approvals also required Pardee's prior approval.

As a communication tool for the multiple parties, and guidance through the purchase, evaluation and entitlement process, an initial project schedule was immediately developed that was ready for review at the first formal project meeting, and included both permitting and front-end design issues. This schedule was updated and revised throughout the process.

The entitlement process, a joint effort between Prentiss and Waterford Development, the selected hotel developer, started with an analysis of the prior plan permit from 1984 for a Visitor Center. That approval was for a 500-room hotel with a 1000-car garage, and three restaurant pads with 350 additional parking spaces. That permit provided that since the proposed traffic was greater than originally anticipated, there were four traffic mitigation measures required, all of which had been constructed prior to purchase of the site. The restaurant pads and their parking had previously been separated from the hotel site. Two of the restaurants were in operation, with the third pad reserved for future use.

It was decided to endeavor obtaining approval for an eight-story 170,000 sf +/- office building and a 270-room hotel in order to maximize the benefit from the land cost. This was based on the position that the proposal was the best one for the site, and did not create any more issues than the originally approved project, due to:

- The hotel study showed that a 500-room hotel was not feasible, and for the city to obtain new revenues in the near future from its valuable hotel room tax, it was necessary to go with a 250 +/- hotel plus an office building.

- The originally permitted parking structure would have contained 320,000 sf for 1,000 cars, which when added to the 335,000 sf for the permitted hotel would be 655,000 sf of construction. The proposal for an office building of 170,000 sf, a hotel of 190,000 and a parking structure for 800 +/- cars at 315 sf per car would result in total constructed improvements of 612,000 sf.

- The average daily automobile trips for the proposed would be about 48 less than those for the 500-room hotel.

- The peak hour traffic was calculated as less than for the original plan permit.

As mentioned previously, city representatives recommended application through a Substantial Conformance Review, throughout which process they would support the project. This review process, if approved, would declare the project to be in substantial conformance with the previously approved project. They believed this was appropriate because the project included a hotel, which they really wanted, and the automobile traffic and gross developed space would not exceed the previous permit. Approval was deemed to be faster and would not open up the project to new discretionary requirements by the planning or coastal commissions.

A Substantial Conformance Review requires a much more complete initial submission, but once approved the project schedule could be reduced by several months and a negative declaration for the Environmental Impact Study would be virtually assured.

Prior to submission for the Substantial Conformance Review it was necessary to accomplish the following items:

- Complete the purchase agreement with Pardee

- Complete the Land Sale Agreement with Waterford Development

- Have at least a tentative hotel agreement with an acceptable chain and operator

- Develop mutually approved design schemes for the office building, hotel, parking structure and site

- Prepare sufficient cost evaluations to insure the proposed scheme met Prentiss' return objectives

- Obtain Pardee's approval of the hotel operator and the schematic designs

To pursue the design, schedule and costing effort necessary to obtain the approvals and establish that it was a viable project, HKS Architects was added to the design team and the general contractor was replaced, all as discussed in other chapters.

The request for a Substantial Conformance Review was presented to the deputy director of development services for the city of San Diego on October 9, 1998. At that time he assigned a project manager who had worked with the Waterford personnel on a prior project. While evidencing no concern from the city's point of view, the deputy director advised that Substantial Conformance Determination could not be accomplished without approval from the Carmel Valley Planning Board.

The materials prepared for submission to the city of San Diego for the Substantial Conformance Review, in addition to the application and ownership forms, included the drawings listed below, several of which are shown in the figures on the following pages.

- Engineering Map—800 : 1 scale
- Site Plan—Figure 7-3
- Grading Plan
- Topographic Map
- Landscape Concept Plan
- Elevation Plans—Figures 7-4 and 7-5
- Project Cross Section—Figure 7-6
- Floor Plans—typical floor on Figure 7-7
- Roof Plans
- Rendering—Figure 7-8

These materials were reviewed with the deputy director who found them satisfactory, but cautioned again that it would be necessary to have the approval of the Carmel Valley Planning Board before the city could make their ruling. A representative of Pardee sits on the planning board, and he recommended a preliminary presentation be made to the president of the association.

The proposal was informally submitted to the president and members of the Carmel Valley Planning Board with a request for their support of the project. There was some concern that too much of the parking structure would show from the freeway and that there might be too much traffic at the intersection of Valley Centre Drive (formerly Carmel View Road) with El Camino Real. To satisfy these issues, removal of the top level of the parking structure was agreed to, and a traffic study was provided that indicated the project would not create traffic congestion. The project was formally presented to the planning board in early November and their decision was scheduled for December 9, 1998.

The proposed project was also submitted to Pardee who retained certain approval rights from the Land Purchase Agreement. Pardee was generally satisfied but shared the same concern with regard to the exposed parking structure as expressed by the Carmel Valley representatives and would not approve a second level above grade.

At the first formal meeting of the board on December 9, there were a fair number of local citizens in attendance, including five or six who had connections to the contractor or brokers. There were many criticisms of the project, however, there was appreciation that the parking plans exceeded the minimum zoning requirements, since they were concerned that some existing projects have caused overflow parking on the streets. The comments included:

- There was too much density (they refused to accept the fact that the currently approved project had slightly greater density)

- The buildings were too tall (same comment as above)

- The hotel was too close to El Camino Real

- The project, primarily the hotel, blocked too much view of the bluffs to the south of the project

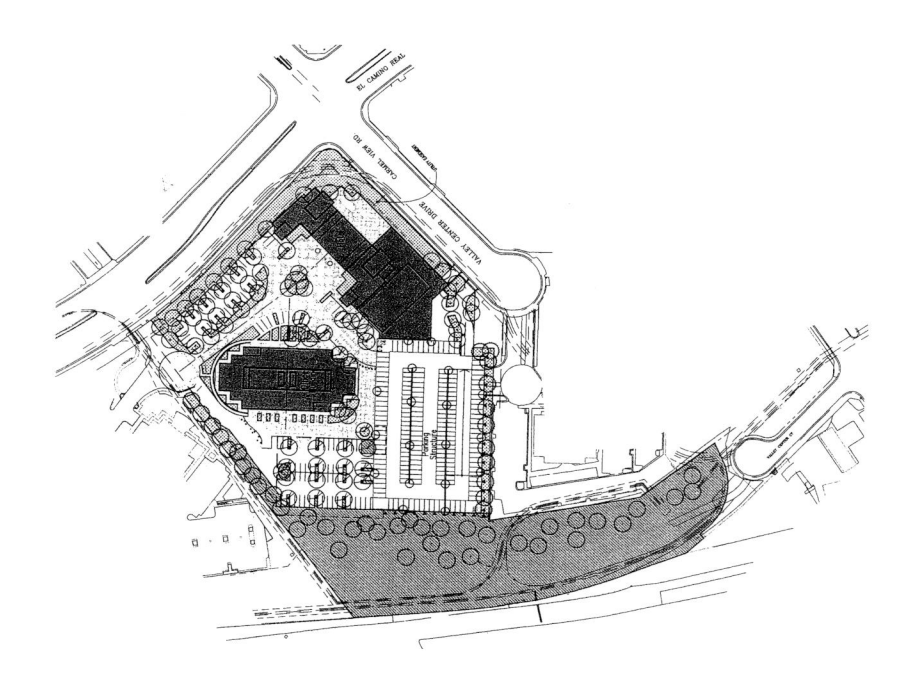

Figure 7-3

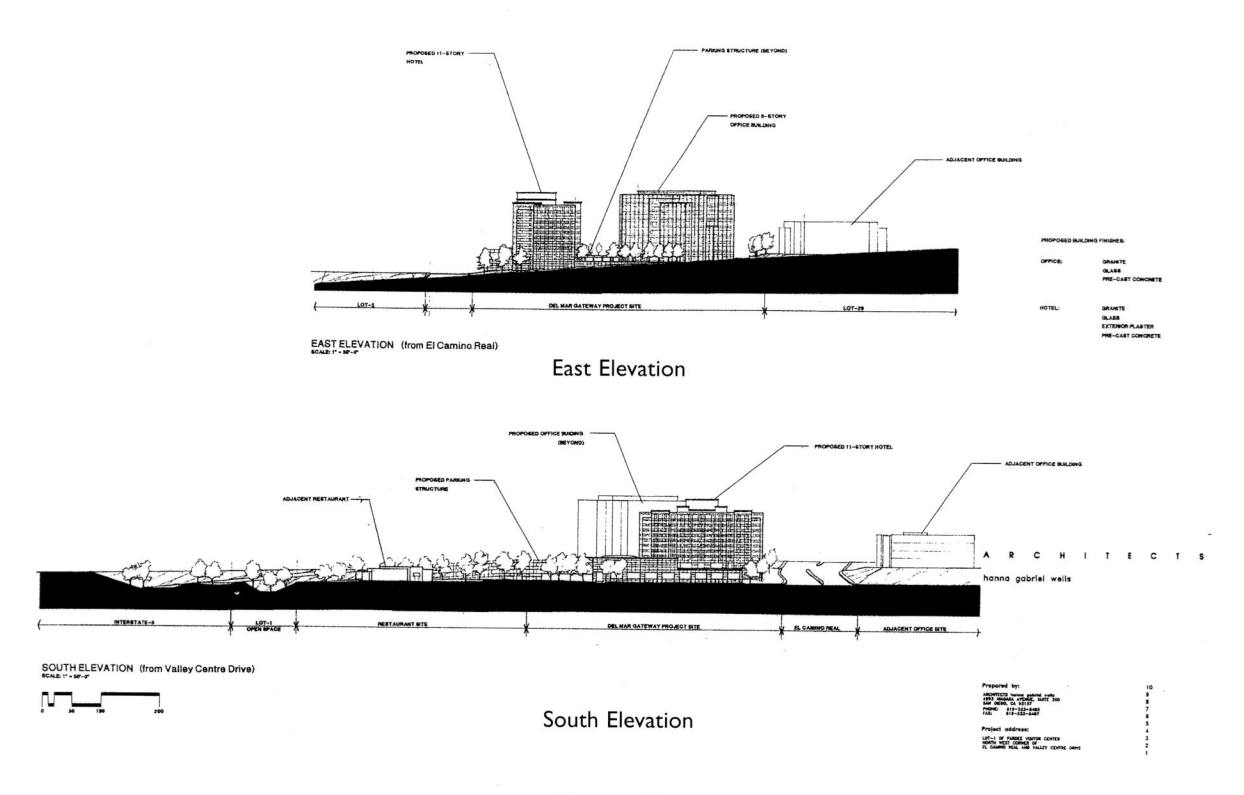

East Elevation

South Elevation

Figure 7-4

Site Selection, Acquisition and Permitting

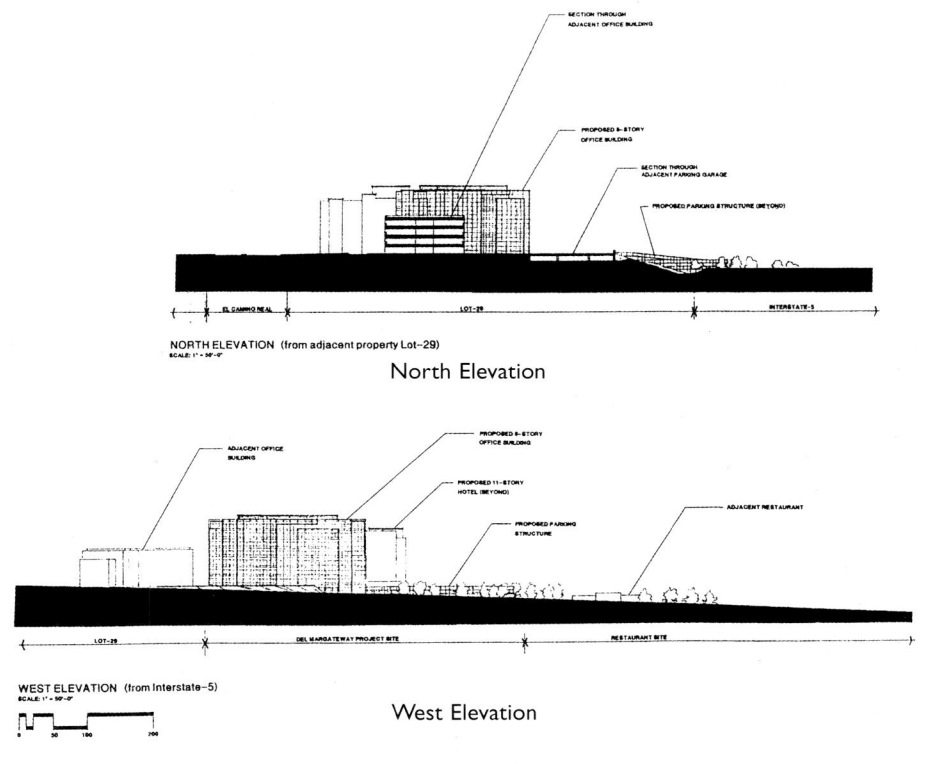

North Elevation

West Elevation

Figure 7-5

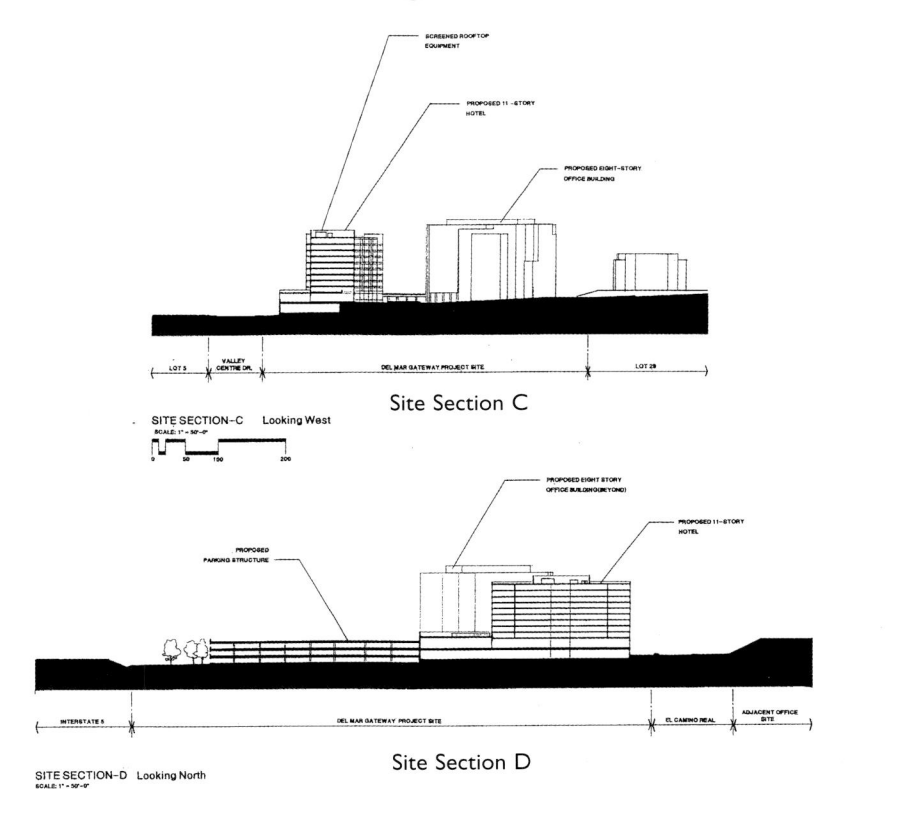

Site Section C

Site Section D

Figure 7-6

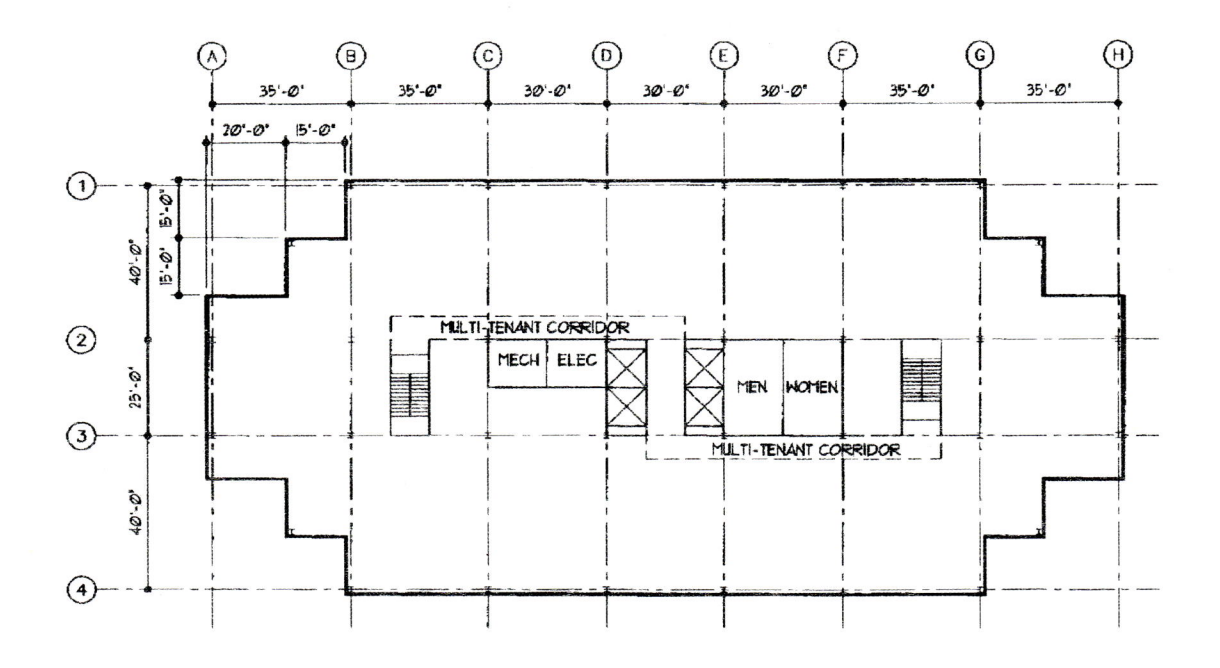

Third through Seventh Floor Plans

21,864 sf GROSS FLOOR AREA

SCALE: 1" = 30'-0"

Figure 7-7

Figure 7-8

when travelling south on El Camino Real (in reality the views are minimal while driving)

- The parking structure looked too large from the freeway
- They wanted to change the name to Carmel Valley Gateway

The chairperson of the planning board had even invited a representative of the Torrey Pines Planning Board to the meeting, even though Torrey Pines was across the freeway and to the south of the project, and had no jurisdiction. The closest homes in Torrey Pines are several miles away. This representative was opposed to the project in general, wanted the buildings limited in height to five stories, and wanted all of the roof structures and equipment screened to her satisfaction.

The board was split six to five in favor of sending a letter to the city requesting they not grant a Determination of Substantial Conformance. After some discussion they agreed not to send such a letter until after their next board meeting in January if there was agreement not to press the city for approval prior to that time. While the delay was not desirable, it was agreed to because it was felt that cooperation would strengthen the project's position with the city, and minimum work would be accomplished during the holiday period.

In the meantime one of the Waterford representatives met with an assistant city manager and received his full support, basically because of the new tax money the hotel would generate.

The city planning department representative met with the assistant to the councilman in whose district the project is located, and he was also supportive. He was aware of the Carmel Valley meeting, and felt as long as they were divided they could probably not block the project, but that was in conflict with previous information.

Since the city advised that approval of the planning board was needed in order to obtain the expedited Substantial Conformance Determination, several methods to satisfying their concerns were studied.

- Removing the top floor of the parking structure mitigated one concern.
- Redesigning the hotel, reducing the width of their tower by reducing the room sizes from oversized rooms to the standard size for Marriott, who by now was the likely operator. It added one floor, but improved the views.
- Relocating the hotel tower away from El Camino Real in one of two different ways as shown in Figures 7-9 and 7-10 in order to improve the perceived view corridors.

The location proposed in Figure 7-9 moved the hotel to the southwest corner of the property, and was rejected outright by Marriott because it had poor traffic access and exposure. The second approach kept the hotel adjacent to El Camino Real, but reversed the location of the tower and the banquet hall area. The structure was still as close to the road as before, but the first 117 feet from the road was the single story banquet facility. This scheme was acceptable to Marriott.

This proposed realignment of the hotel placed the hotel tower too close to the office building and reduced the size of the forecourt. The office building could not be moved to the west in order to gain additional space, as the configuration of the site and the requirement for a fire lane prevented this. The best solution at the time was to cant the office building at about 15 degrees by moving the north end to the west, as shown in Figure 7-11.

Presentation boards were prepared for the final meeting with the planning board to indicate the proposed solutions responding to their issues on view corridor and positioning the hotel too close to El Camino Real. In addition, a series of small meetings was arranged with various board members. To further communicate with the community the presentation boards were set up at a location where any resident who wished could drop by to view them prior to the final meeting. In addition, the consultant met with various board members and arrangements were made to have as many residents as possible favoring the project at the final meeting.

There were eight or nine residents who favored the project at the meeting, while there was apparently only one non-committee resident in attendance, other than a few former board members, who was not invited either by Prentiss or the board.

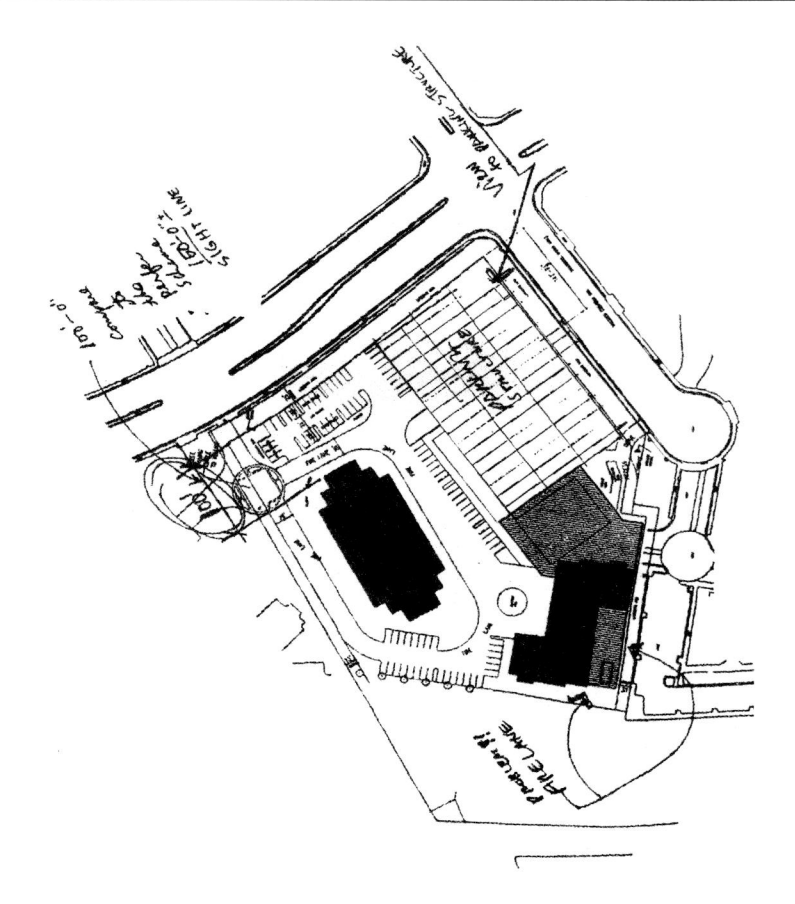

Figure 7-9

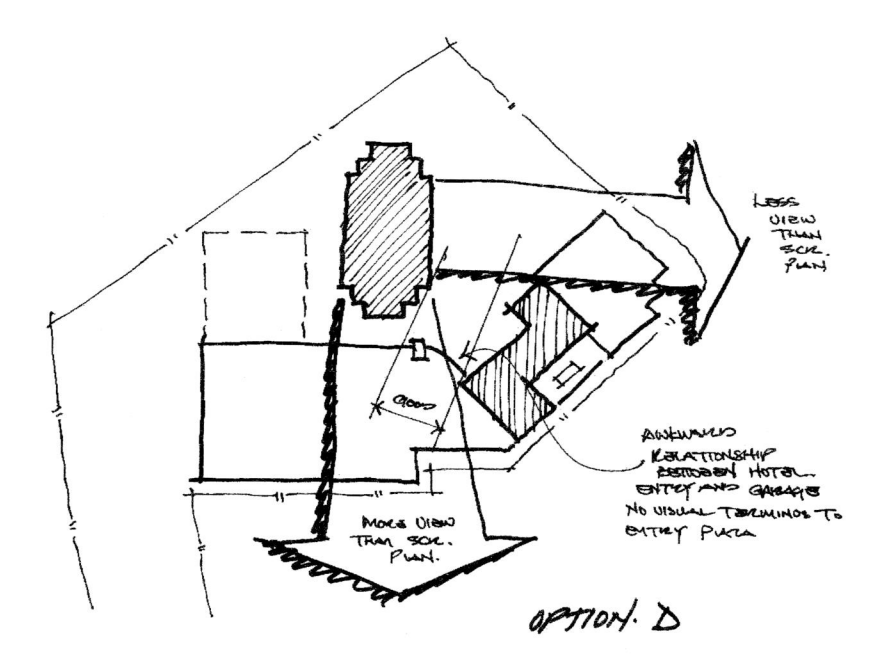

Figure 7-10

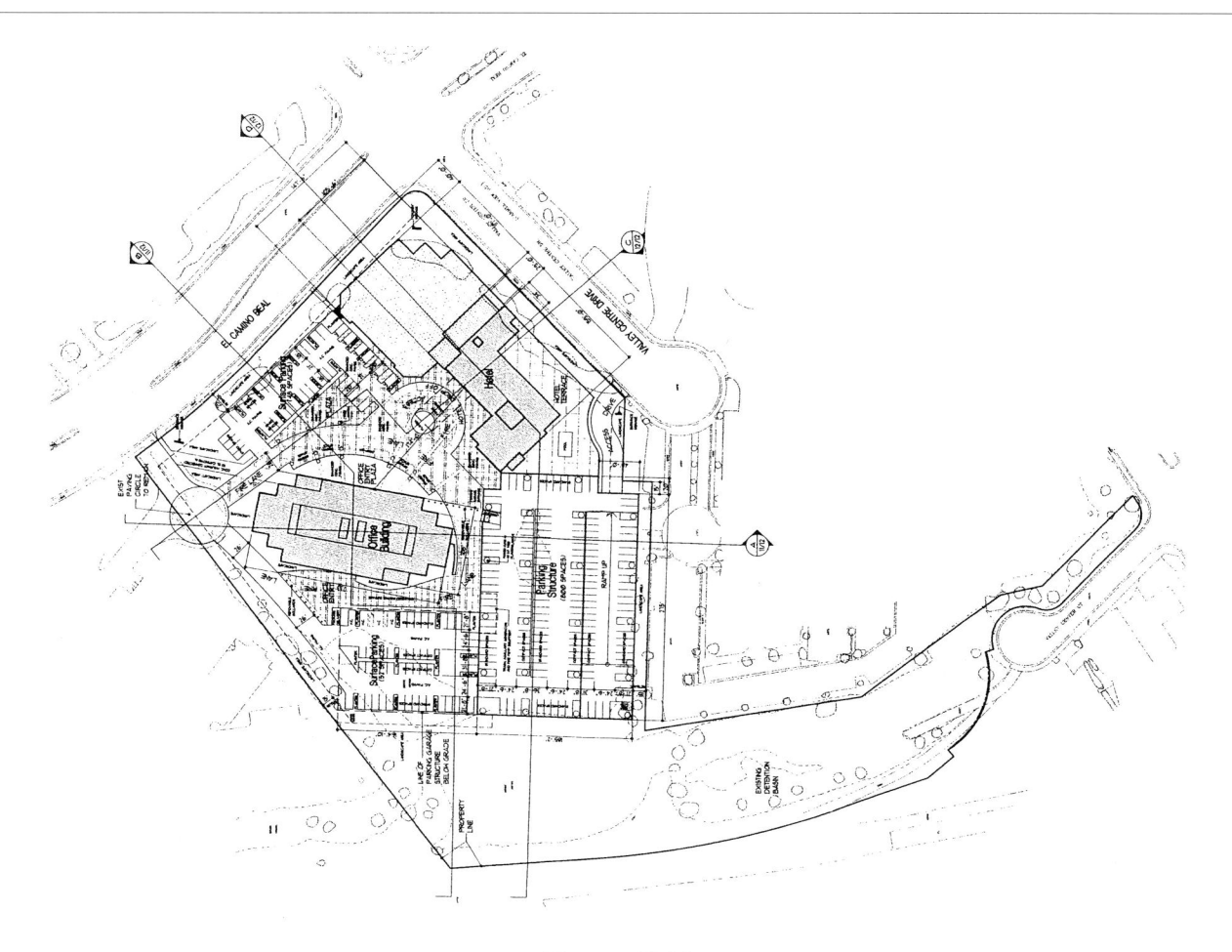

Figure 7-11

The chairperson suspected the audience was packed and directed that no one could speak who had any relation to the project or its participants. After considerable discussion, the board unanimously approved the revised designs and advised the city in a letter dated January 12 that they approved the project as revised. Their letter required the final changes agreed to in the meetings. As to the hotel:

- Distance from the El Camino Real curb to the east façade of the ballroom is to be 40 feet, 25 feet greater than the standard setback,

- Distance from the east edge of the ballroom to the east edge of the 7-story portion (stepped portion) of the hotel building is to be 117 feet

- Distance from the east face of the stepped portion to the 12-story portion of the hotel building is to be 29 feet

- Distance from the east face of the 12-story portion of the hotel to the western edge (width of tower) to be 129 feet

- Height of ballroom to be 18 feet, excluding parapet

- Height of the stepped portion of the hotel to be 54 feet above the ballroom, exclusive of parapet

- The height of the 12-story portion of the hotel from the building lobby floor will be 107 feet, exclusive of parapet

- The gross area of the hotel is to be 186,741 square feet

The association's approval letter listed requirements for the office building, also a result of changes agreed to during the meetings, which were:

- Distance from the curb at El Camino Real to the east face of the building is to be 138 feet
- Distance from the hotel entrance to the office building is to be 174 feet
- Height of building to be 109 feet, excluding the parapet
- The shape of the building was to be softened by stepping the building in plan, stepping the roof lines at the building ends and have balconies on the top floor to break up the horizontal planes
- Building orientation on site as previously depicted in Figure 7-12
- The building gross area to be 170,000 sf

The office building was angled at about 15° to the parking structure, as previously discussed, in order to accomplish the distances requested by the association. The details of these changes will not be discussed further in this chapter, as the understanding of these changes will flow better in Chapter 15, Site Planning and Conceptual Design.

The assigned city planning department project manager advised that any reasonable changes made to the plans approved by the planning board would be handled by her office and would not be returned to the planning board for comment.

After receipt of approval from the Carmel Valley Association, the planning staff had to coordinate their comments with the previously received comments from the various applicable departments and agencies. Several of the city agency reviewers objected to the issuance of a Substantial Conformance Determination, as they felt it was not consistent with city ordinances and procedures. To overcome this resistance, at the deputy director's suggestion a former city attorney was retained to research the entire history of the original approval process for the Visitor Center project and the impact of all applicable ordinances. The attorney wrote a letter on March 3 stating the scope of his research and his conclusions that the determination would be completely within all ordinances and practice, and could be approved. Approval was received on April 4, 1999, almost three months after receiving the planning board's approval. The justification as to Substantial Conformance with the Visitor Center project was:

- The proposed project provided the largest hotel that was currently commercially feasible
- 114 more parking spaces are provided than required by code, thus minimizing on-street parking
- There will be 48 less Average Daily Trips (ADTs) by automobiles than the permitted project
- There are 100 less parking spaces than the permitted project
- The maximum height and the lot coverage will be less than the permitted project
- Two smaller elements provide better view corridors than one larger structure
- There will be increased open space
- Conditional approval was received from the Carmel Valley Association

In addition to the city planning department's conceptual approval of Substantial Conformance, specific comments were received from the various affected departments, all of which were in line with the design intent.

The time required to obtain the general project approval through the Substantial Conformance Review process was much longer than predicted, but still required less time than if it had been treated as a new project, and there was considerably less risk. The Substantial Conformance Determination does not waive any applicable ordinances or regulations, and the approval letter listed specific fire, grading and landscape requirements.

As discussed in Chapter 15, the angular rotation of the office building required to obtain reasonable separation from the relocated hotel tower in order to satisfy the Carmel Valley Association was not a satisfactory solution. The building footprint was re-studied, and it was determined that by reducing the overall length by 17 feet and widening the building by about 5 feet the building could be aligned on the site as shown in Figure 7-12. The floor layouts were still satisfactory. This reduction in bulk, as well as increasing the distance from the El Camino Real curb, and the distance from the hotel entrance to the

Site Selection, Acquisition and Permitting

office building entrance from 174 feet to 184 feet further responded to the desires of the association.

It was then necessary to return to the planning department to request a revision to the Substantial Conformance Determination to incorporate this change, which was within the planner's authority. These changes were approved.

Further changes were required to the parking structure to resolve an insufficient separation from the hotel tower, as discussed further in Chapters 15 and 25.

Upon receipt of the Substantial Conformance Determination it was now necessary to separate the parcels for construction and ownership. The city initially advised this be accomplished through a commercial condominium separation rather than by a lot split through a tentative map, due to:

- The city of San Diego has been recently encouraging this procedure, presumably because it is less demanding on staff and commission time

- There was insufficient time left to follow the tentative map approval process and still commence construction so as to satisfy the occupancy requirements of our major tenant

- The deputy director clearly did not want for the project to go through the tentative map process,

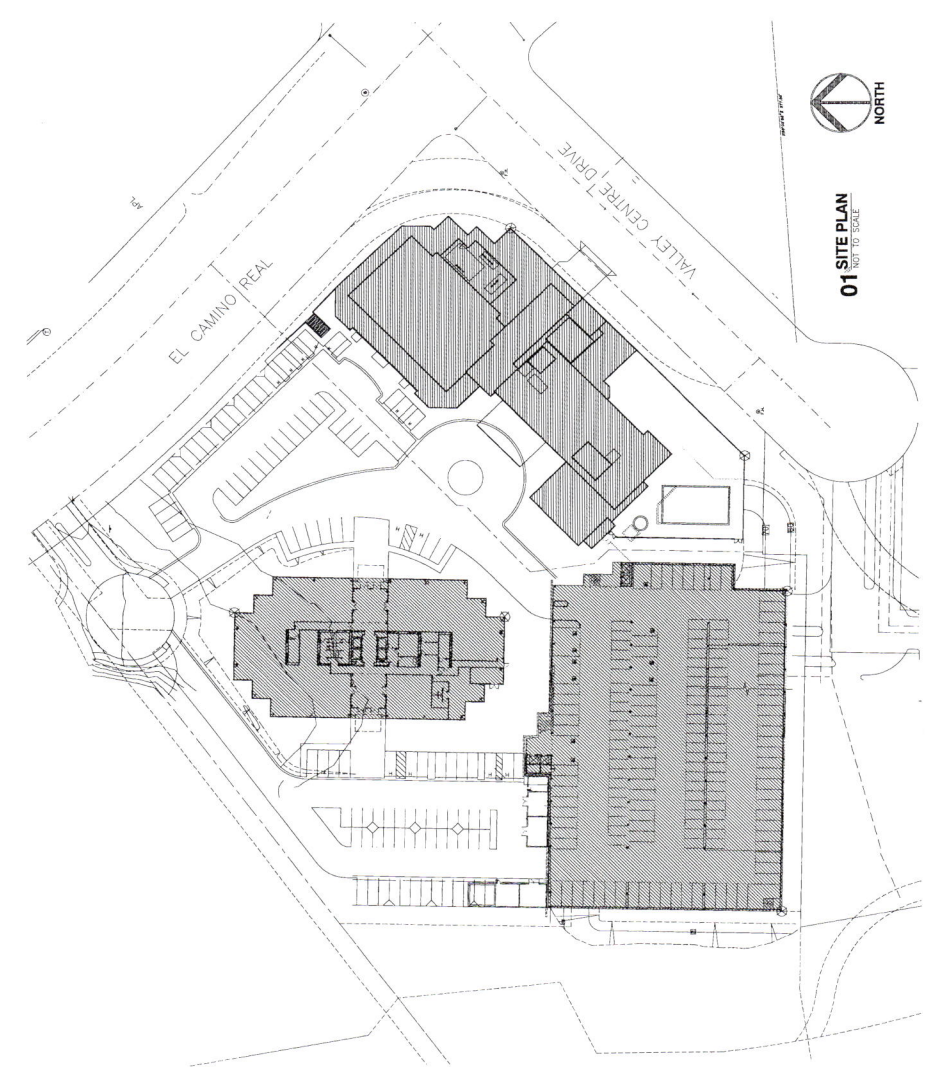

Figure 7-12

possibly due to the potential for second-guessing the Substantial Conformance Determination

- The tentative map process would require full review and approval of the Planning and Coastal Commissions, which might well open the project to new discretionary conditions and requirements

Unfortunately, the city had provided incorrect direction. When the submission reached the persons who actually process the commercial condominium lot splits, they advised that this could not be done when selling off a separate parcel. Further exploration with the right individuals finally produced a workable solution.

The adjacent property, Executive Center Del Mar, also called Lot 29 A and B, had been divided into two parcels to permit separate lenders or possible sale of one of the buildings in the future. Since that property abutted the new site, a lot line adjustment was proposed wherein the property line between the two existing buildings on Lot 29 would be removed and a property line inserted between the hotel parcel and the remainder of the new project. In this manner the contiguous land with single ownership (at that point in time) would still be divided into three parcels. This lot line adjustment could now be handled administratively. Nothing will prohibit requesting a new lot split on Executive Center Del Mar in the future when time and discretionary mitigations are not an issue. Waterford would participate in the costs of the future lot split as a substitute for the cost of a more extensive procedure at this time.

Approval of the lot line adjustment was essential to closing on the land and, since all other criteria for closing had already been met, escrow would close 15 days from city approval of the lot separation. Any delay in obtaining this approval would delay the construction start and impact the delay penalties under the Brandes Lease.

To obtain a lot line adjustment required submission and approval of a parcel map, which included:

- The site survey and description
- The proposed new parcel boundary
- All structures, driveways and walkways
- All easements and utilities, including a new easement around the office building to contain the new fire loop that will service the site
- Landscape and irrigation.

The initial estimate provided by the city for obtaining a lot line adjustment was 60 to 90 days when it was initiated in early June. This seemed too long and efforts were made to expedite the process. Obtaining this approval was more complicated than anticipated—even though the city was trying to expedite it for us. One of the problems was that the civil engineer was heavily overloaded with work and it was hard to get his full attention in order to provide all of the necessary information on the parcel map. Other issues were:

- Resolution of the easement for the fire water line loop. It was relocated several times before approval was obtained from the Fire Department, Water Utilities and Traffic and Safety. This caused a major delay even though the easement was entirely on only one of the proposed parcels.

- There is a 20-foot-wide 69 KV electrical power easement along both streets on which the site fronts, plus a nearly adjacent 5 KV utility easement. There were repeated conflicts with the street trees and the driveway, sidewalk and footings for the hotel.

- The engineering department procedures were ponderous and bureaucratic. Every time a change was made, even a minor note, the plans were re-circulated back to all reviewing parties.

Closing of escrow on the land was postponed from September 7 to 10 to be certain the lot line adjustment would be approved. Final approval of the plat was received on September 2, recorded on the 3rd and escrow closed on the 10th, waiving the 15-day period.

SYNOPSIS OF LAND PURCHASE AGREEMENT
Referred to as the Master Purchase Agreement

Date:	October 30, 1998
Seller:	Pardee Construction Company
Buyer:	Prentiss Properties Acquisition Partners, L. P.
Property:	Lot 1 of Pardee Visitor Center, San Diego County, including intangible property of Seller – rights, privileges, easements, contracts permits, licenses, etc. The gross area is 8.65 acres.
Purchase Price:	$9,043,046, or $24 per gross square foot ($35 useable).
Escrow Deposit:	$150,000 within 2 days of opening Escrow $150,000 within 2 days of the end of the due diligence period $150,000 within 2 days after receipt of a Substantial Conformity Determination Remainder at the close of Escrow.
Contingencies:	Within 45 days—approval of all title matters and tests desired by Buyer—soils tests, environmental, structural, percolation, water, oil, gas, mineral, radon, PCB or other tests.
	Receipt of Substantial Conformity Determination or other approval to construct agreed upon improvements.
	Approval of Subdivision Map dividing site into 3 parcels.
Requirements:	Within 90 days of opening of Escrow, Buyer will deliver to Seller an executed agreement to sell the Hotel Parcel to Waterford Development concurrently with the Escrow, and an agreement wherein Waterford will sell or lease the Hotel Parcel to a Hotel Owner, all subject to Seller's approval.
	Within 90 days of the opening of Escrow, Buyer will submit Conceptual Plans—site plan, grading plan, landscape plans, building elevations and material boards—to Seller, who in 15 days will in good faith approve or reject.
	Within 15 days after approval by Seller, Buyer will submit the approved plans to the City for Substantial Conformity Review. Seller may participate in any or all meetings with regulatory authorities. If a Substantial Conformity Determination, or alternate zoning approval is not obtained by 11/15/99, either party may terminate this agreement and all deposits are refundable.
	Within 30 days after receipt of the Substantial Conformity Determination, Buyer shall deliver to Seller copies of the Purchase and Development Agreements for its review and approval of Material Provisions.
	Within 30 days after receipt of Substantial Conformity Determination, Buyer will deliver to Seller the Construction, Operation, and Reciprocal Easement Agreement (COREA).
	Buyer will submit final plans for the Office Building, Hotel, Parking Structure and the Site work to Seller for final approval, which will not be unreasonably withheld.
Improvements:	The Office Building shall be between 6 and 8 stories, containing no more than 175,000 gross square feet.

The Hotel shall be between 7 and 12 stories, contain no more than 270 rooms and must be be operated by Hilton, Marriott or other operator approved by Seller.

The building exteriors shall have brick, granite or marble exterior with glass, or other first class building materials approved by Seller.

The Office Building shall have at least 4 parking spaces per 1,000 gross square foot and the Hotel shall have the number of spaces required by Code, all as adjusted for shared parking per accepted standards.

Close of Escrow: 120 days after Buyer's receipt of Substantial Conformation Determination, but in no event prior to 15 days following all approvals necessary for a Subdivision Map, but not later than 11/19/99.

Option to Repurchase Property: Seller has the option to repurchase the Site, or any Parcel thereof, on which construction has not commenced within 4 months after Close of Escrow.

Right of First Offer: Neither Hotel nor Office developer can sell the property prior to commencement of construction without providing Seller a Right of First Offer at the lower of the proposed sale price or the original land sale price.

Assignment: Either Buyer or Hotel developer may assign their rights to an entity at least 50% owned by the party or the parent of either party.

Completion: Buyer and Hotel Developer will cause construction to be diligently prosecuted to completion, which must occur within 36 months, subject to force majeure.

Common Driveway: Reimburse Seller $36,500 for their cost of the common driveway entrance with Executive Center Del Mar.

SYNOPSIS OF LAND SALE AGREEMENT

Date:	December 9, 1998
Seller:	Prentiss Properties Acquisition Partners, L. P.
Buyer:	Waterford Gateway, LLC
Property:	The Hotel Parcel, one of three parcels resulting from the division of Lot #1 of Pardee Visitor Center, San Diego County, including intangible property. All terms must be consistent with the Master Purchase Agreement.
Purchase Price:	$3,800,000
Escrow Deposits:	On opening of Escrow, $5,000 earnest money $295,000 on or before 12/9/98 $150,000 within 2 days after receipt of a Substantial Conformity Determination. Remainder one day prior to closing of the Master Purchase Agreement.
Contingencies:	Buyer has the same rights with respect to title, testing and inspection as Seller has under the Master Purchase Agreement.
Requirements:	Buyer and Seller will cooperate so that within 90 days of opening of Escrow, Buyer will deliver to Pardee an executed agreement to sell the Hotel Parcel to Waterford Development concurrently with the Escrow, and an agreement wherein Seller will sell or lease the Hotel Parcel to a Hotel Owner, all subject to seller's approval.
	Buyer and Seller will cooperate in obtaining any development approvals, subdivision and permits required.
	Buyer and Seller will cooperate so as to within 90 days of the opening of Escrow, submit mutually agreed upon Conceptual Plans—site plan, grading plan, landscape plans, building elevations and material boards—to Pardee, who in 15 days will in good faith approve or reject.
	Within 15 days after approval by Pardee, Buyer and Seller will submit the plans to the City for Substantial Conformity Review. If Substantial Conformity Determination, or alternate zoning approval is not obtained by 11/15/99, either party may terminate this agreement and all deposits are refundable.
	Within 30 days after receipt of the Substantial Conformity Review Determination, Buyer and Seller shall deliver to Pardee copies of the Purchase and Development Agreements for its review and approval of Material Provisions.
	Buyer and Seller will execute a Construction, Operation, and Reciprocal Easement Agreement (COREA) and Seller will deliver it to Pardee within 30 days after receipt of Substantial Conformity Determination.
	Seller will submit plans of the Hotel, Office Building, Parking Structure and Site work, mutually approved by Buyer and Seller, to Pardee for their approval.
Improvements:	Shall conform to limitations in the Master Purchase Agreement.
Close of Escrow:	As per the Master Purchase Agreement.

		Construction of Improvements:	The Buyer will construct the Hotel, the Seller will construct the Office Building, Parking Structure and Site work.

Construction of Improvements: The Buyer will construct the Hotel, the Seller will construct the Office Building, Parking Structure and Site work.

Seller will provide Buyer for its review and approval detailed plans and specifications for the parking structure, surface parking and other improvements on the Parking structure Parcel. Buyer will notify of its approval or disapproval thereof within 15 days, which will not be unreasonably withheld.

The cost of the Parking Structure will be divided 65% to Seller and 35% to Buyer.

The cost of the surface parking and Site Work will be divided 50% to the Seller and 50% to the Buyer.

Buyer and seller will cooperate in the construction as designated in the COREA.

Buyer will put an irrevocable Letter of Credit in Escrow to cover Buyer's obligations to fund the Parking Structure and the Site work.

If Seller defaults on construction of the Parking Structure and Site work, subject to cure rights, Buyer may construct those facilities and Seller will be liable for his share of the cost.

Cost Allocations: Certain costs will be allocated in accordance the table in Exhibit E, shown below.

	Estimated Cost To Prentiss	Waterford's Cost	% of Total
Due Diligence			
Legal	$ 20,000	$ 10,000	50%
Soil Engineer	$ 20,000	$ 10,000	50%
Environmental—Phase 1	$ 5,000	$ 2,500	50%
Land Subtotal	$ 45,000	$ 22,500	50%
Architects & Engineers			
Parking Architect Total*	$ 343,750	$ 120,313	35%
Civil/Geotech Engineer	$ 30,000	$ 15,000	50%
Parking Consultant	$ 20,000	$ 10,000	50%
Traffic Consultant	$ 15,000	$ 7,500	50%
Landscape Architect	$ 50,000	$ 25,000	50%
Site Architecture	$ 55,000	$ 27,500	50%
Architects & Engineers Subtotal	$ 20,000	$ 205,313	40%
Permit & Building Fees			
Entitlement Processing**	$ 30,000	$ 15,000	50%
Site Fees (FBA @ $51K/Acre)	$ 445,000	$ 222,500	50%
Parking Garage Fees	$ 90,000	$ 31,000	35%
Parking Garage Plan Check	$ 15,000	$ 5,250	35%
Permit & Building Fees Subtotal	$ 580,000	$ 274,250	47%
Construction			
Site Work	$ 1,000,000	$ 500,000	50%
Parking	$ 6,500,000	$ 2,275,000	35%
Construction Subtotal	$ 7,500,000	$ 2,775,000	37%
Total	$ 8,638,750	$ 3,277,063	38%

* Parking Architect costs are based on a 250,000 sf parking garage
** Includes $10,000 for Civil and $6,000 for landscape

Option to Repurchase Property:	As per the Master Purchase Agreement.
Right of First Offer:	As per the Master Purchase Agreement.
Assignment:	As per the Master Purchase Agreement.
Completion:	As per the Master Purchase Agreement.

SYNOPSIS OF COREA
CONSTRUCTION, OPERATION AND RECIPROCAL EASEMENT AGREEMENT

Date:	September 8, 1999
Parties:	Prentiss Properties Acquisition Partners, L. P. and Waterford Gateway, LLC
Effective Date:	To be recorded immediately after conveyance of the Hotel Parcel to Waterford.
Term:	99 years, except that easements included herein do not expire or terminate.
Site and Improvements:	Lot 1 of Pardee Visitor Center, San Diego County—divided into two parcels—the Hotel Parcel and the Parcel which contains the Office Building, the Parking Structure and all open area and surface parking not in the Hotel Parcel, collectively called the Parking Facilities.
	The Office Building and the Parking Facilities will be constructed and owned by Prentiss. The term Parking Facilities includes the Parking Structure and the Other Parking Facilities (surface parking and all site work). The Hotel will be constructed and owned by Waterford.
	Each party grants to the other non-exclusive reciprocal easements for pedestrian and vehicular ingress and egress, as shown on Exhibit E.
	Each party grants the other such easements as are necessary for the installation, operation and maintenance of public utility facilities necessary to service the improvements.
Designated Parking:	The Hotel will have approximately 50 dedicated parking spaces primarily for the use of check-in and check-out of Hotel patrons, located adjacent to the Hotel entrance, as shown on the parcel map as Exhibit C.
	Prentiss will reserve 160 parking spaces for the use the Office Building occupants, as shown on the parcel map as Exhibit D-1 through D-4. Ten are located in front of the Office Building, approximately 25 are located behind the Office Building, and the remainder on levels Plaza, B-1 and B-2 of the Parking Structure.
	Prentiss will issue a maximum of 690 parking permits to tenants, plus permits for necessary employees and service personnel.
	The Hotel may have a non-exclusive right to the use of parking spaces available to the general public, exclusive of the spaces in Exhibit D, in addition to those spaces shown on Exhibit C and any spaces allocated to Hotel employee parking.
	The Hotel may be allocated additional temporary valet parking spaces for special events, not more than 24 times per year, if such use will not unreasonably affect office tenants.
Construction:	Waterford agrees to construct the Hotel at its cost in accordance with all Agreements and the approved plans and specifications.
	Prentiss agrees to construct the Office Building and Parking Facilities (subject to reimbursement of Waterford's Allocated Share—35% for the Parking Structure and 50% for the Other Parking Facilities) at its cost in accordance with all Agreements and the approved plans and specifications.
	The parties agree to cooperate with each other to perform their work so as to not cause any unreasonable interference with the construction or business operation of the other party.

Prior to construction each party will submit to the other for approval a plan of the parcel showing utility connections, contractor's staging areas and other temporary facilities, workmen's parking area and any other access, along with a schedule indicating the approximate date(s) such areas will cease to be required.

Each party shall obtain all required permits and commence construction so as to complete construction no later than the dates set forth on the construction schedules attached as Exhibit H.

Maintenance: The respective parties will maintain the Hotel and Office Parcels and improvements in good condition.

Prentiss will maintain the Parking Facilities in first class condition, subject to reasonable wear and tear, and will earn a fee of 3% on all costs, with a minimum fee of $500 per month. Prentiss will prepare annual operating and capital budgets for joint approval.

The cost of all maintenance, repairs, utilities, insurance, real property taxes and capital improvements shall be split between the parties in accordance with the following Allocable Shares:

> Parking Structure: To be determined by a count of actual usage over a 12-month period commencing 6 months after the last Certificate of Occupancy.
>
> Other Parking Facilities: 50% each

Should Prentiss fail to maintain the Hotel's Dedicated Parking Spaces, the Hotel may, after notice and time to cure, the Hotel may assume responsibility for maintenance of these spaces.

Prentiss shall submit a maintenance and capital budget on or before October each year. The Hotel shall have the right to approve the budgets.

Should Prentiss fail to maintain the Parking Facilities, the Hotel may, after notice and time to cure, assume responsibility for the maintenance for this work. Prentiss shall then have those future rights.

Real Estate Taxes: The Hotel will pay all real estate taxes on the land under the Hotel Parcel. The real estate taxes on the land under the Office Building Parcel will be allocated 50% to the Office Building, 25% to the Parking Structure and 25% to all other Parking Facilities, the latter two treated as maintenance costs.

The Hotel will pay the real estate taxes on the improvements on the Hotel Parcel. The real estate taxes on the improvements on the Office Building Parcel will be allocated to the Office Building, Parking Structure and Other Parking Facilities on the basis of construction costs (initial tenant improvements will be allocated to the Office Building). The taxes applicable to the Parking Structure and Other Parking Facilities will be treated as maintenance costs. Prentiss will provide Proposition 13 protection on the real estate taxes on the parking structure and the site work for seven years.

Insurance: Each party will maintain no less than $10,000,000 of liability insurance on their respective properties, naming the other party as additional insured.

Each party will maintain all risk casualty insurance in an amount equal to at least 100% of the replacement cost, including earthquake coverage with no more than a 10% deductible. There are special conditions concerning earthquake coverage.

Required coverage may be made under umbrella policies.

Parking Operator: A Parking Operator, selected by both parties, renewable annually, will manage the Parking Structure, control ingress and egress, issue permits and collect revenues (only the Hotel will charge initially). The cost of the Parking Operator will be the obligation of the Hotel until such time as Prentiss elects to charge for parking – at which time the costs will be allocated according to revenue received.

Security Service: In the event that the parties mutually determine that security personnel are reasonably required they shall be provided in such numbers and hours as reasonably necessary.

Parking Services Advisory Committee: One representative each from Prentiss and the Hotel, to review and discuss Parking Facilities issues. Issues not agreed upon will be arbitrated.

Repair and Restoration: Certain reciprocal rights, see Agreement.

Condemnation: Certain reciprocal rights, see Agreement.

Signs: Hotel signage will be compatible with other exterior signs in the Project. The Hotel may have a monument sign at the main entrance, which in the sole discretion of Prentiss may be a separate monument or as part of a combination monument.

Lot Line Adjustment: To compensate Prentiss for utilizing its then existing subdivision of the adjacent Lot 29 (Executive Center Del Mar) to satisfy the requirements of this project, the parties will share equally the cost of restoring the subdivision line to Lot 29, up to a maximum cost of $50,000.

Arbitration: All joint operating decisions are subject to arbitration.

DEFINITIONS and PROJECT ECONOMICS

8

Projects are best understood through a complete knowledge of the various definitions and how the various numbers come together so as to achieve a complete understanding of the overall project economics. Different units of area are used by different persons, in different market areas, and for different reasons, and some people use "square feet" indiscriminately without any attempt at understanding the definitions. It is essential for the Development Officer to completely understand the units and to query persons who may appear to use them without a clear definition. Many of these definitions are included in this chapter.

Building area rentable definitions can vary significantly between various market areas, but the most generally accepted definition is the *Standard Method For Measuring Floor Area In Office Buildings*, ANSI/BOMA Z65.1-1996, developed by the Building Owners and Managers Association International. Their definitions are somewhat complex, so the author provides a simplified interpretation below.

Gross Measured Area: All above grade floor areas are calculated from the inside face of the outside glass lite to the inside face of the outside glass lite, and below grade areas are calculated from the inside faces of the structural walls, less parking areas and any portion of the loading dock that is located outside the building line. This is also referred to as gross square feet, or gsf.

Building Rentable Area (rsf): The gross measured area, less all major vertical penetrations, such as stairs, elevator shafts, flues, pipe shafts, vertical ducts, and their enclosing walls. Columns, openings for vertical cables, telephone distribution, and openings for plumbing lines *are not* major vertical penetrations.

Floor Rentable Area (rsf): The gross measured floor area, less the vertical penetrations, factored up to allocate all building common areas (main and auxiliary lobbies, atrium spaces at the level of the finished floor, health clubs, conference rooms, lounges or vending areas, lockers and shower facilities, mail rooms, fire control rooms, fully enclosed central mechanical and equipment rooms, and loading dock space within the building envelope).

Useable Area (usf): The measured area of tenant office or store space exclusive of all public corridors and central or shared facilities. Note that the usable area of a full floor tenant includes the area of the theoretical corridor, and usually the area of the elevator lobbies.

Rentable Area (rsf): The useable area factored up by a floor R/U (Rentable to Useable) ratio to incorporate the floor common areas (washrooms, janitorial closets, electrical and telephone rooms, mechanical rooms, elevator lobbies, and public corridors), and further factored up by a building R/U ratio to allocate proportionally all building common areas as discussed above under Floor Rentable Area.

The building rentable area should equal the sum of all the rentable areas, and also the sum of all of the floor rentable areas.

It is wise to require the architect to prepare a detailed set of floor plans that tie directly to the detailed area take-off calculations to ensure there are no misunderstandings.

Notwithstanding the calculation of rentable area, in most markets there are assumed acceptable "add on" factors (the amount by which the R/U ratio exceeds 100%), frequently in the range of 9% to 13% (up to 15% in very tall buildings), depending on the building size, height and special amenity features. Any ratio higher than the norm in that locale can incur rental rate penalties, while lower ratios are a plus to the leasing program.

Builders Gross Area (bgsf):

One definition that is sometimes ignored is the construction, or builders gross area that is used by construction contractors and is the area that must be used when calculating estimated building costs from a contractor's estimated cost per square foot. This differs from the gross measured area, above, in that it is always measured from the *outside* building dimensions, and can include covered walkways, overhangs, etc.

The following is a list of definitions that are used in the pro forma and for calculating the overall project economics.

Rental Income: All rentals projected to be received from the areas assumed to be leased and occupied.

Operating Costs: All costs of operation, including taxes, utilities, cleaning maintenance, insurance and management fees.

Rental Rate: The rental rate charged the tenant per rsf to cover debt service, all operating and utility costs and the developer return.

Net Rental Rate: The rental rate less the operating costs per sf.

Financing Rate: The melded rate of the permanent mortgage and other borrowings or internal cost of funds.

Monthly Expense: The sum of all costs incurred in any one month, including construction costs, TIs, financing costs, operating, and any other costs related to the project.

Break-Even Point: The point in time when the monthly rental income equals or exceeds the monthly expense (usually for a stipulated period of months to avoid a distortion through timing of TIs, commissions, construction contract closeout, etc.).

Total Project Cost: The total cost of the project as calculated in the pro forma, including all costs through the break-even point.

Unit Project Cost: Total Project Cost divided by the number of rentable square feet.

Stabilized Occupancy Rate: The percentage of the rentable area projected to be leased and rent paying at the completion of the project—the reciprocal is the **Vacancy Rate**.

Developer Markup: The number of basis points above the financing rate that the developer requires at the time of the initial lease-up, currently 200 basis points is recommended for an entitled site, and more for an non-entitled site.

The necessary net rental rate the project must achieve is:

$$\text{Net Rental Rate} = \text{Unit Project Cost} \times \frac{(\text{Financing Rate} + \text{Developer Markup})}{\text{Stabilized Occupancy Rate}}$$

Conversely, if you assume an achievable net rental rate and an achievable stabilized occupancy rate, you can compute the permissible unit project cost, and hence the permissible Total Project Cost. From this you can back out a target budget for construction cost, land cost or other variable.

Note that when the objective is to obtain a specific free and clear return, or desired return, rather than a return above the financing rate, a single number can be substituted to replace the financing rate plus the developer return. This desired return, as noted previously, would be significantly above the return on the purchase of a leased building to allow for the risk, and the premium would depend upon whether or not it was an entitled site.

One factor in the project economics that is not always treated in a consistent manner is vacancy cost. The generally accepted definition of vacancy cost is the cumulative negative income for the period between the substantial completion of construction and/or the occupancy permit, and the project's stabilized occupancy. In other words, the vacancy cost is total financing costs during the lease-up period, plus final construction and leasing costs, plus operating costs, less rental income.

Additional formulas frequently used for financial analysis and for lenders are shown below.

Debt Service Coverage Ratio = NOI / Debt Service

Loan to Value Ratio = Potential Loan Amount / Appraised Value

Break-Even Cash Flow Ratio = (Operating Expense + Debt Service) / Gross Income

Operating Expense Ratio = Operating Expense / Gross Income

Overall Cap Rate = NOI / Project Cost

Equity to Value Ratio = Invested Equity / Projected value

EL CAMINO REAL

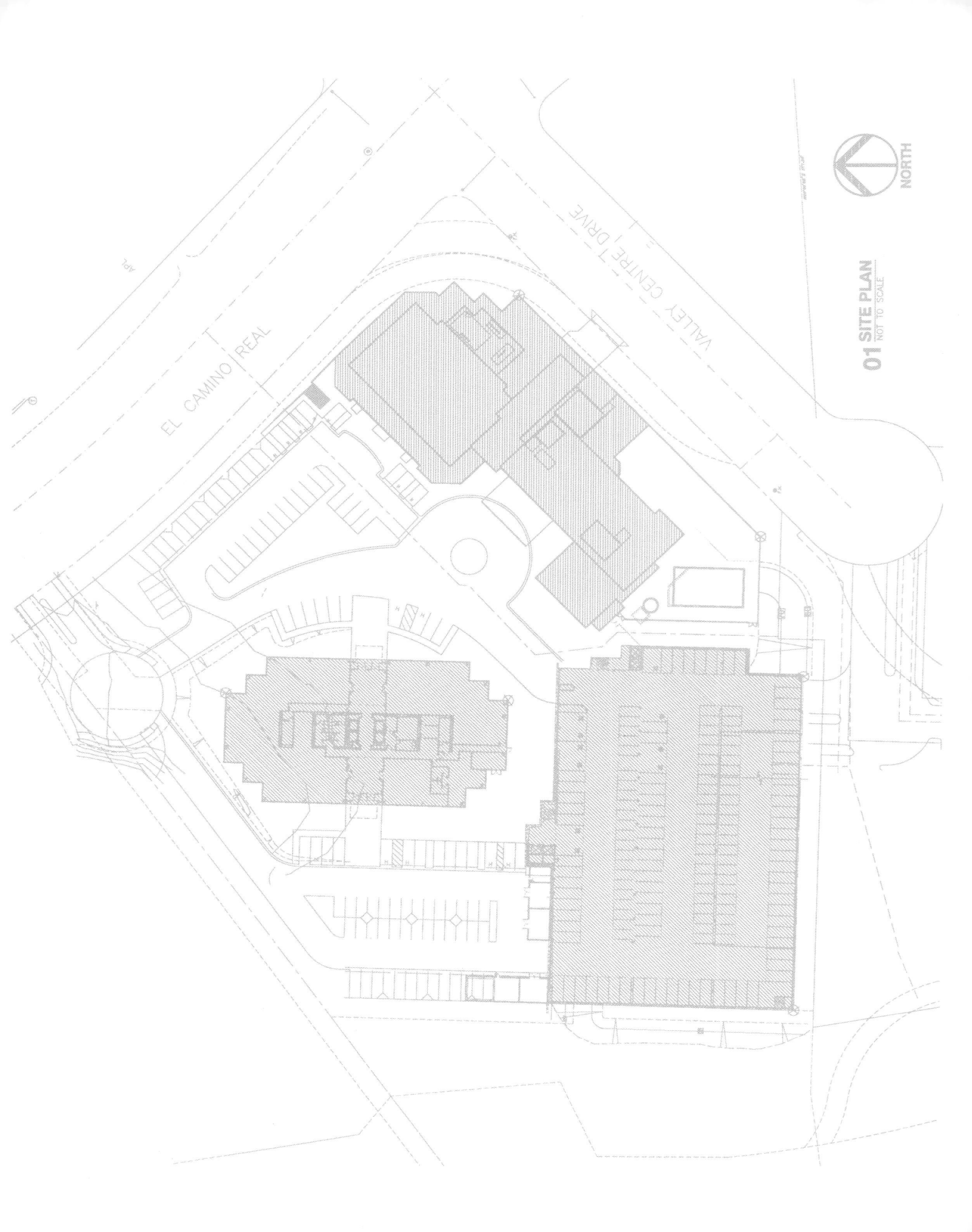

VALLEY CENTRE DRIVE

01 SITE PLAN
NOT TO SCALE

NORTH

RISK and RISK MANAGEMENT

There is substantial risk in every facet of the development of real estate—from excess unplanned costs, to time delays, to liability issues, to poor product design, to market deterioration—all while trying to recover monies expended over a considerable period of time without immediate return, and to achieve a desired return. This chapter will list and discuss a series of identified risks, their seriousness and some mitigation actions. At the end of this chapter the author will discuss the issues he considers to be the greatest risks.

The best protections against a reduced return are a thorough Feasibility Analysis that is prepared and presented as accurately and factually as possible, a high-quality development team, focused project control, and transferring as much risk as practicable to others.

The major cause of risk, other than an inadequate Feasibility Analysis, is the fact that the process occurs over a rather long period of time, with many people and firms participating, making all of the assumptions and projections subject to potential error. A smaller building designed and constructed on a site purchased with full entitlements may take 21 to 30 months to reach stabilized occupancy. A larger project planned for a non-entitled site in a location with some environmental or political uncertainty could take four to six years, or more, to reach that milestone.

The pro forma is the numerical analysis that represents the complete thought process of the Development Officer with regard to the project. The Feasibility Analysis is the source of the major income and many expense assumptions, while the other cost assumptions are prepared in conjunction with the consultants and contractors. A well-prepared pro forma will always have many assumption errors but, if thoroughly analyzed, the errors should tend to offset each other. A major failure usually results from omitting or not recognizing a significant cost.

To allow for the time lag return on the money, and the inherent development risk, it is a reasonable policy to require a return significantly above that required when purchasing an equivalent existing fully leased property. If the project site is purchased non-entitled, and there is some environmental or political risk, an additional risk factor of at least 100 basis points should be added to the desired return.

The proper approach to risk is to identify or recognize it, measure it where possible, and mitigate or minimize it, while constantly reviewing for additional potential risks. In fact, the Development Officer's primary responsibility is to manage risk, specifically to manage it through uncertainty.

The primary method of minimizing or mitigating as many risks as possible is by contractually transferring them to others through such actions as the Guaranteed Maximum Price (GMP) construction contract as discussed in Chapter 33: fixed price contracts for consultants, subcontractors and major vendors; insurance programs; bonding and indemnification; tenant leases; warranties and guarantees. The Development Officer should coordinate closely with the corporate risk manager as to all necessary procedures and a properly integrated insurance and risk management program.

Risks that are not transferable are minimized through a thorough Feasibility Analysis, a high quality development team and effective project management.

Following are some of the major risks and the methods to control or minimize them.

Site Acquisition

The primary protection prior to closing is to control the site through an option or a low "at risk" deposit on the land purchase contract, a thorough Feasibility Analysis and closing contingent upon a specified entitlement, if possible. The major risk point occurs at the time of closing the land contract. This is the time to reassess the Feasibility Analysis to ascertain that there is no significant change in the projections, as the accuracy of that study is the primary protection, and to reevaluate the preliminary pro forma.

Environmental, Political and Regulatory

The project economics are based upon an assumed start time to meet projected market conditions, and the cost of mitigating environmental, political and regulatory issues that were presumably known prior to site acquisition. The thoroughness and accuracy of the Feasibility Analysis is the primary protection against this cost risk, but the time required for mitigation and approval is more difficult to ascertain. A secondary protection is avoidance of the project when these risks are deemed to be very high. Any uncontrollable delay can have very detrimental consequences. As regulatory issues are more predictable, the most likely causes of delay are hazardous material and environmental issues, and political issues.

Design Risks

These risks are best controlled through assembling a quality design team, thoroughly analyzing all data and controlling the process of decision-making. The major risk issues that must be properly controlled during the design period are:

- Design costs—the actual cost of design is an issue that is best controlled by a clearly defined Project Design Criteria, fixed or per square foot professional contracts, a contract that clearly spells out each party's obligations, a requirement that no extra work is to be performed without prior approval and then only with an estimate of cost, and control of the process to avoid delays, changes or back-tracking.

- Excess project cost—a design for a product that exceeds the acceptable cost limitations is frequently correctable only by a project delay for redesign and the resultant quality imbalance that results from applying the cost reduction process to a fully detailed building. This risk is minimized by constant review of the design process by the Development Officer and the base line budget prepared and monitored by a qualified general contractor.

- Design errors—major risks can result from design errors. They can be partially mitigated by selecting firms with a proven design capability, a well-coordinated design process and established quality control procedures. The backup protection for the owner is the architect's errors and omissions insurance coverage, which should be project specific so that the coverage is not diluted by claims from other projects. The greatest exposure is usually in the structure, so the errors and omissions coverage for the structural engineer's policy should be arranged so as to provide additive coverage to that of the architect's.

- Poorly designed product—a product that does not meet market expectations can be a costly failure economically. The only protections to this risk are selection of highly qualified architects and consultants, a valid Project Design Criteria, and proper project control throughout the design process by the Development Officer.

Construction Commencement

Another major risk point occurs with the virtually irreversible decision to commence construction. It is again the time to reassess the Feasibility Analysis and pro forma to be reasonably certain the market projections still indicate the project will achieve an acceptable return at its projected cost.

Financing Issues

A primary method of avoiding a portion of the risk is through the use of non-recourse financing to the greatest extent possible, in order to transfer that portion of the risk to a lender.

National and international financial shocks can have a major impact on interest rates, primarily on the floating rate interim construction loan. The primary methods to mitigate this risk is through a hedging program if interest rates are anticipated to be volatile, and the negotiation of conditions for the earliest possible commencement of the permanent loan.

Construction Risks

While the base shell and core construction is the largest single element of cost, the author believes that with proper planning and control, and with a good project team, there should be relatively little risk of a major cost overrun after resolving the Guaranteed Maximum Price and the execution of fixed price or GMP contracts with subcontractors and major material vendors. The most significant risks in construction are:

- Subsurface construction—unanticipated excess rock, hazardous waste, antiquities, burial grounds, underground rivers, or other running water encountered during construction. The best protection is a thorough soil testing and analysis program, but because the testing is random there is always a chance of omissions.

- Change orders—primarily resulting from design changes during the construction period, poorly coordinated working drawings, uncontrollable delays due to labor disputes, or major construction errors or failures. The primary protections from the first two issues are a tightly controlled design and construction process and an architectural firm with proven quality control procedures. Frequently, major labor disruptions are not really controllable, but sometimes a contractor is able to negotiate an agreement to continue working and honor any contract that is ultimately negotiated.

- At the construction stage there should be provision of about 1% carried in the pro forma for design changes or other costs of the work requested by the owner or not reasonably included in the GMP, and this is in addition to the GMP contingency discussed below.

- Liability and property loss—liability is shifted to the contractors' and subcontractors' insurance coverage and indemnification as specified, backed up by the owner's excess liability and umbrella insurance coverage. The contractor's errors and omissions insurance provides additional protection against risk. Property loss to work in place or material on the job site during construction is protected by the owner/builder's risk insurance coverage as discussed in a subsequent paragraph. This policy should also cover materials in transit as it is frequently necessary to pay for and take title to materials prior to transit to insure their availability when required.

- Contractor and/or subcontractor default—this risk is normally transferred through requiring payment and performance bonds. It can also be mitigated by careful selection of each subcontractor, thorough and careful attention to the validity of each contractor's partial payment requests and waivers of liens, and obtaining the right of assignment of all contracts and material purchase agreements to the general contractor and/or the owner.

- The GMP will have an agreed upon contractor's contingency, usually from 1% to 2%, for the primary purpose of protecting the contractor against reasonably foreseeable job conditions, wage increases or estimating errors. This contingency will have reasonable conditions as to its use, and is sometimes carried separately outside the GMP.

Leasing

Even with a good market analysis and reasonable assumptions drawn from it, the market can change with dramatically negative results. Typical examples of negative impacts from a deteriorating market are listed below, and it is not uncommon that they all occur simultaneously, or in sequential order.

- Lower achievable rental rate

- Increased concessions

- Abnormally high lease commissions

- Slower lease-up
- Higher stabilized vacancy rate

Each market rate lease executed by a creditworthy tenant avoids a portion of the lease-up risk. Rental insurance covers lost rental income under many circumstances beyond control of the developer, and expense escalations in the leases protect against future operating increases. An overall project contingency is primarily to protect against the potential cost and income variances.

Liability Insurance

A well-thought-out and properly administered insurance program is essential to the successful risk management program for any development project. Each consultant, contractor, subcontractor, vendor or any entity participating in any activities on or related to the site is required to carry an appropriate amount of insurance as specified in the contract documents, in which the owner and developer, or any related entities are specified as additional insureds. The customary coverages are:

- Workers Compensation—including Statutory Coverage and Employer's Liability.
- General Liability, including:
  - Bodily Injury, per occurrence and aggregate
  - Property Damage, per occurrence and aggregate
  - Products and Completed Operations, for at least one year
  - Property damage, including Explosion, Collapse, and Underground
  - Contractual Liability (Hold Harmless coverage), Bodily Injury and General Liability
  - Any General Liability coverage should preferably apply to the specific project only
- Automobile Liability, aircraft and watercraft, if applicable, (owned, non-owned and hired). Bodily Injury per person and per accident and Property Damage per occurrence.

The policies must all have a waiver of subrogation and may not be cancelled without 30 day's notice to the additional insureds. Certificates of insurance are required for each policy, and it is an important part of risk management to periodically review each certificate to ensure that it is current.

An essential part of the risk management program is to ensure that the various contractors' and consultants' policies, and tenants', where applicable, are the first line of defense in any claim or suit. This protects the long-term cost of the owner's insurance program. The indemnification by all on-site entities, along with waivers of subrogation, further protects the owner and his program.

All policies are preferably based on a per occurrence basis, where practical, to insure that the coverage is not diluted through repetitive claims on other projects. At the end of the line in protection against insurable risks is the owner's excess liability and umbrella policies.

Builder's Risk Insurance

Builder's Risk Insurance is carried by the owner to insure against damage and/or destruction to the property in place, and collateral damages called soft costs. The hard cost portion, which currently may cost in the range of 6¢ per $100 of value, is best carried as an "all peril" or "all risk" policy, which means it covers any possible peril that could occur, except those explicitly exempted. The proceeds are provided to restore the project to the condition existing prior to the occurrence.

In computing the cost for the hard cost portion of the policy it is customary to exclude the land and foundations, as they do not normally constitute an exposure. There are specified deductibles for normal loss, flood and earthquake. The policy not only covers all necessary material and labor to restore the damage, but also debris removal and any equipment or anything else incidental to the construction process. It is important to cover material stored off-site or in transit to provide for the instances when it is desirable to acquire those materials in advance to control the construction schedule.

The soft cost coverage, currently about 10¢ per $100 of value, covers such items as consulting fees, interest and loss of rent from a delayed opening.

The policy covers the period through the final Certificate of Occupancy, or to a specified date certain. Partial occupancy should be permitted under the policy. The ongoing property and casualty insurance on the building must be carefully coordinated with the builder's risk policy to avoid any gap in coverage.

Completed Building

After completion there is considerable risk remaining that must be addressed.

- Improperly designed elements—the risk is transferred to the errors and omissions insurance.

- Malfunctioning equipment and improper workmanship—with proper contract documents the repair and/or replacement is normally covered for one year after substantial completion barring insolvency, which performance bonds are intended to cover. Longer term potential failures, such as roofing, glazing, etc. are usually covered by a manufacturer's warranty or a maintenance bond. Any latent defect responsibility in tenant leases should not exceed the period covered by contractors' obligations.

- Property insurance to cover the improvements against virtually all hazards.

- Loss of rental income—the loss of rent-paying tenancy due to damage, destruction or other specified circumstances are covered under rental insurance carried by the owner.

Primary Risk Concerns

Of all the risks encountered in the development process, the author believes that in a well-planned and controlled project, utilizing reputable and qualified consultants and contractors, the two predominant risks, which are the primary reason for carrying an overall development contingency in the range of 2% to 3% of Total Project Cost, are:

- Time—usually caused by misreading or encountering unforeseeable changes in environmental or political issues, or some major unanticipated construction delay due to labor strife or a job catastrophe

- Lease-up problems—the inability to accomplish the project's income objectives

While the above risks can be difficult, if not impossible, to predict in the beginning, recognition of their danger helps the Development Officer to observe clues as to their potential occurrence at the earliest possible time.

CASE STUDY

This project had all of the normal risk issues of any project, with some that were less and some greater than the norm.

The site acquisition risk was very low. The site was in an existing office park with a history of a lack of environmental issues, which were nevertheless covered by the 45-day investigation and testing period. Any political risk was mitigated by the fact that the Land Purchase Agreement provided for the refund of the deposit if the minimum agreed-upon project size and scope was not approved. The risk of the hotel developer not meeting his obligations appeared at the time to be limited to Prentiss' front end costs, as they did not have to close on the land without a firm hotel commitment.

The market risk is always very real, but in this case with the positive experience of leasing the two adjacent buildings, rental rates rising due to the shortage of acceptable space, and demand increasing, this risk appeared minimal.

The Substantial Conformance Determination, while taking longer than anticipated, was in an acceptable time frame and minimized timing risks, particularly related to the market, and its successful conclusion eliminated any further political risk.

The leasing risk was significantly reduced when a lease was entered into with a major tenant, Brandes Financial Partners, for over 100,000 rsf before completion of the schematic drawings or receipt of the Substantial Conformance Determination. The lease was expensive, as discussed in Chapters 31 and 32, and it reduced the cash on cash return by 28 basis points but the internal rate of return (IRR) increased by 11 basis points. This was a reasonable price to pay for the reduced lease-up risk. (The increase in the IRR was a quirk due to the re-leasing timing in the model.) The reduction of lease-up risk was partially offset by penalties in the lease for delayed occupancy and some construction cost risks that are discussed later. In order to partially mitigate severe delay penalties a compromise consequential damages provision was incorporated into the construction contract.

With over 62% of the building leased and still retaining the signage rights to the top of the tallest and best-exposed building in its market area, the lease-up risk looked very manageable. In fact, while still in the design phase an agreement was reached to lease 30,000 rsf on the first and second floors to a bank that wanted the signage rights. That lease was executed after obtaining regulatory approval the week the building permit was received.

The only remaining leasing risk was to be able to lease 20,000 rsf to small tenants with less than four-year terms, due to the expansion rights in the Brandes Lease, but the brokers were highly optimistic.

The Brandes Lease, however, did create a new potential risk, as Prentiss was now obligated to close on the land even if the hotel developer could not. Since it was the best hotel site in the San Diego area, this risk was believed to be acceptable.

Design cost risk was acceptable as all consultants were on fixed price per square foot contracts, even though the scope could change when trying to satisfy the requirements of two different types of buildings with two different developers on the same site.

The project had an interest rate risk as the loan was for a 75%-of-cost construction loan and three-year mini-perm with a rate floating with LIBOR.

While the major lease reduced the lease-up risk, it added some risk to the control of the construction costs. In order to come as close as possible to the tenant's lease commencement requirement of August 15, 2000, it was necessary to separately bid the majority of the construction work prior to approving a Guaranteed Maximum Price. The contracts let early were the curtain wall, structural steel, mechanical and electrical, fire protection, elevators, grading and concrete for the office building, and the retaining wall for the parking structure. In fact, all of those contracts were committed prior to even having an executed general construction contract or a building permit.

Due to delays caused by the changes to the hotel and Pardee approvals, the GMP for the parking structure and site work occurred even later, long after closing on the land and after construction started on the site work, major retaining wall and office building.

Subsurface construction risk was considered minimal since there has been so much work in the immediate area and the test boring results look consistently acceptable. The primary risk in this work would be excessive rock removal or unsatisfactory backfill material.

Change orders resulting from inadequate design drawings are always a potential issue, particularly when the major components are let separately and early, but it was a good architectural team and with diligence it was believed the problems could be held to a minimum.

The primary construction timing risk was completing construction in time to satisfy the occupancy requirements of the major tenant with minimum penalties, particularly if there were extensive bad weather conditions, as there was no *force majeure* with regard to the landlord delay penalties.

The lender was not prepared to close on the loan in time to commence construction, and in fact initially determined not to close prior to the closing of the land sale to the hotel. Since work commenced prior to placement of the Deed of Trust (a dummy Deed of Trust cannot be filed to protect the lender in California, as it can be in many other states) all liens against the project had priority over the construction loan, since every material and labor lien priority goes back to the first one on the job. It was necessary to agree to hold the title company harmless against such liens, so they could give a clean title insurance policy to the lender.

As discussed in Chapter 33, it was initially decided to accept some risk by not bonding many contractors, as the cost of delay in replacing a defaulting subcontractor was considered to outweigh the cost of replacing one. Before executing the construction contract, however, Swinerton & Walberg changed from individual bonding to an umbrella policy that gave them full freedom to solve a default in the most expeditious manner. Even though this would increase the GMP somewhat over the non-bonding approach, this was the best procedure, as it provided protection against both risks.

The closing on the hotel land and the start of its construction was delayed due to many open issues, primarily on Marriott's part. Several construction requirements were inserted into the extension agreement that protected obtaining a timely Certificate of Occupancy for the office building in spite of the delayed completion of the hotel. (See Chapter 7, under Acquisition.) The insurance program was the standard program Prentiss has established on a national basis, and is sufficiently conservative.

EL CAMINO REAL

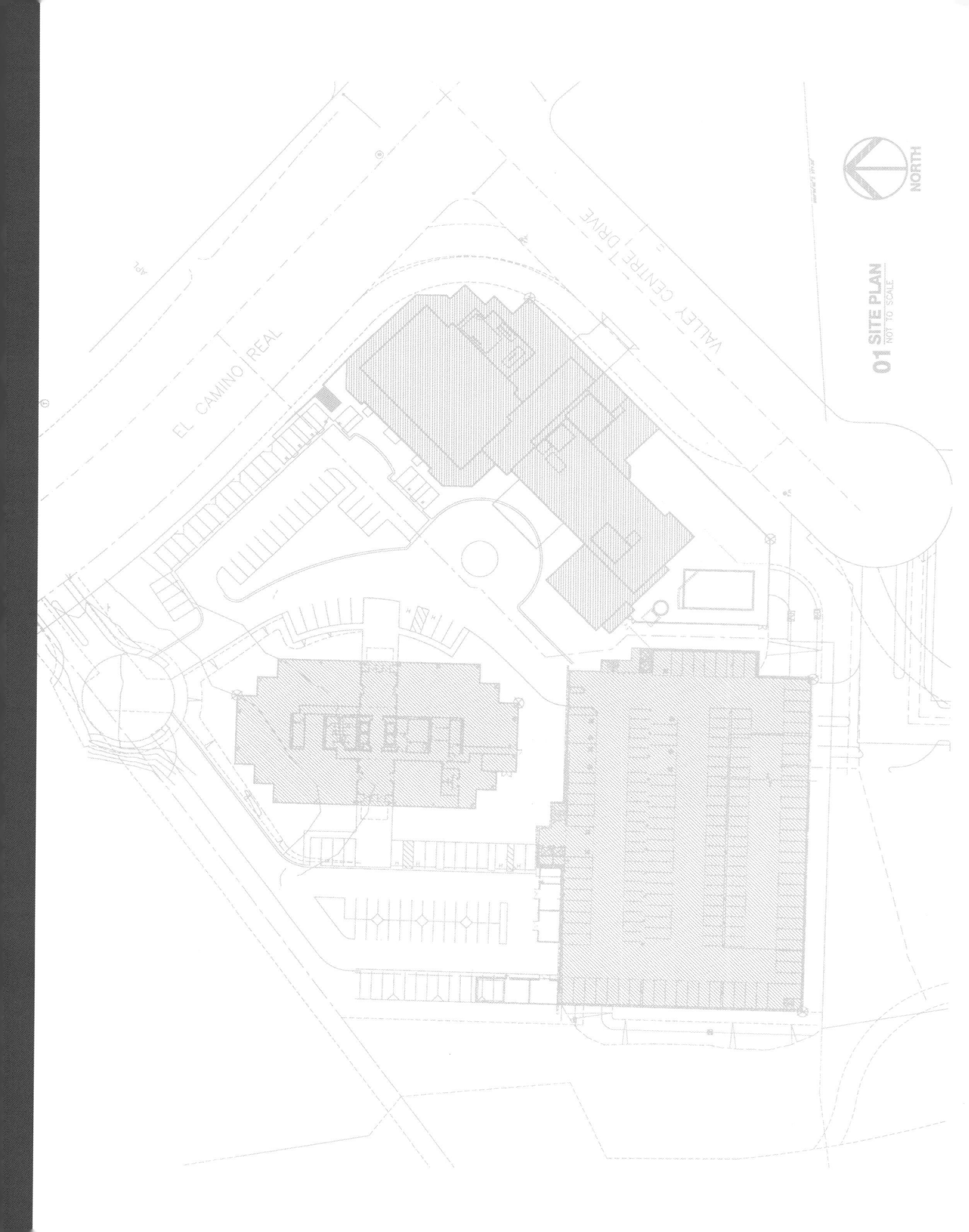

VALLEY CENTRE DRIVE

01 **SITE PLAN**
NOT TO SCALE

NORTH

THE DEVELOPMENT TEAM   10

This chapter lists the typical functions that must be performed on virtually every project. Depending on the size and complexity, on most projects multiple functions will be performed by a more limited number of professionals, rather than by retaining all of the individual specialists.

Selection of the various specialists, like the architectural selection discussed in Chapter 14, is based on their expertise in the type and size of project contemplated. Specialist consultants are particularly beneficial when there are complexities in the project that exceed the skills of the basic team. It is worth remembering that retaining the most highly qualified consultants adds very little, if any, cost premium and can add immeasurably to the quality of project decisions.

The Development Officer should always bear in mind, however, that regardless of the quality of the team and its enthusiasm for the project, there is always the potential for some conflict of interest. Each consultant or contractor has a contract with fixed, or otherwise limited, compensation and frequently encounters pressures from other assignments. On the other hand, you must be certain to see a sufficient number of proposed solutions to satisfy all of your concerns, and to obtain a product that satisfies all of the objectives. This conflict is rarely overt, but it does exist and may appear in justifications as to why further studies should not be initiated. There are times where excess complexity or an unusual number of studies occur, and you might discuss the issue with the consultant, and consider increasing the compensation, if reasonably warranted.

With the large number of members it is essential that each team member clearly understand the scope of his/her role and how it interrelates with the work of the other team members.

Marketing

- In-house marketing
- Marketing and public relations
- Brochure composition
- Model builders
- Photographers
- Printers

Site

- Planners (could be the architect)
- Environmental (EIR/EIS) consultant
- Surveyor—survey, topographical, utilities
- Hazardous waste consultant
- Civil engineer—roads, utilities, grading, waterways
- Geotechnical engineer
- Soils testing
- Traffic engineer

Legal and Management

- Corporate finance officer
- Corporate risk manager and/or insurance broker
- Zoning consultant
- General real estate legal
- Corporate staff or tax consultant
- Land use attorney

- Contract attorney—contracts and loan documentation
- Leasing attorney
- Appraiser
- Tax consultant
- Insurance agent or consultant
- Title company
- Surety

Leasing and Market Analysis

- Asset manager
- Leasing representative
- Interior space planner
- Office broker
- Retail broker

Design

- Architect (can be split between a design firm and a working drawing firm if there are sufficient reasons to do so)—the most common contractual arrangement is to include the structural, mechanical and electrical engineers in the architects contract, and frequently the landscape architect
- Structural engineer
- Mechanical engineer
- Electrical engineer
- Vertical transportation—elevator, escalator, window washing equipment (major projects only)
- Interior architect (analyze leasability of the design, prepare tenant layouts for leasing, and to prepare design drawings and working drawings for tenants where the market requires this service)
- Curtain wall consultant
- Testing labs—windows and façade
- Acoustical consultant
- Fire protection/code evaluation
- Window washing equipment—if not in vertical transportation
- Landscape architect
- Energy/building management systems (if mechanical engineer not qualified)
- Graphics
- Traffic and parking engineer
- Fountain design
- Roofing consultant
- Waterproofing consultant
- Lighting—special
- Communications consultant
- Retail consultant
- Retail space designer
- Restaurant designer
- Art consultant
- Audio/Visual consultant
- Property Management

Construction

- General contractor
- Major subcontractors—subject to approval of owner and sometimes negotiated
- Testing labs—soils, compaction, rock analysis, concrete, steel fabrication, steel erection, welding, wind tunnel (structural criteria and pedestrian wind issues on tall buildings), curtainwall (static pressure, air infiltration, static and dynamic water intrusion)
- Architect (shop drawings, field inspection, design clarifications, change orders, etc.)
- Tenant construction contractors
- Construction manager

Project Meetings

The scheduling and leading of project meetings is an important role of the Development Officer. The Development Officer should participate in all decisions and should attend and lead each meeting, since few meetings should be held that will not result in decisions. As many participants who can add to or benefit from each meeting should attend, while avoiding requiring attendance of those who will neither benefit nor contribute.

One of the most important features of a properly run design meeting is the fostering of open debate among the design professionals as to the interrelationships and trade-offs between conflicting solutions of various disciplines. Not only does this discourse usually lead to the best of many possible solutions, it provides important depth of understanding of the issues by the Development Officer.

The Development Officer should be fully responsible for the results and documentation of each meeting, and the setting of the agenda and time for the next meeting. When setting the agenda, it should be made clear to every participant what they are expected to accomplish prior to and/or present at the next meeting. Successful meetings are based upon:

- A specific meeting time
- Clear objectives
- A typed agenda
- Punctuality, required
- Following agenda—avoiding digression
- Minimizing interruptions
- Minimizing number of meetings
- An agenda for next meeting
- Objectives for each participant prior to the next meeting
- Minutes or memo of decisions

When you are concerned with some aspect of the performance or effectiveness of a team member, they should be counseled privately.

CASE STUDY

Portions of the development team were selected at the start of the land bidding process in order to make a preliminary evaluation of the site, obtain cost estimates in order to evaluate the price at which the site was economically feasible, and to analyze marketing and scheduling data. The team members are:

Hotel Developer	Waterford Development Company, a relatively new company started by experienced hotel development executives. They had an initial agreement of support from Hilton, but later changed to Marriott.
Architect for Office Building, Parking and Site	A joint venture between Hanna Gabriel Wells and HKS Architects, Inc. Randy Hanna was the architect of record for the first two buildings in San Diego. His work was excellent and he had a good rapport with the San Diego regulatory personnel, but his relatively new firm was believed to have insufficient depth for a mid-rise project such as this. HKS is a major firm with a long history on Prentiss projects and a well-staffed Los Angeles office. The initial concerns were valid, as ultimately the project proceeded with HKS as the sole architect.
Hotel Architect	Joe Wong of JWDA in San Diego.
Civil Engineer	Rick Engineering, civil engineer for the adjacent project and for all of San Diego Corporate Center.
Structural Engineer	Nabih Youssef & Associates.
MEP Engineers	Syska & Hennessy, Inc.
Landscape Architects	Wallace Roberts & Todd, who were very experienced with the city's approval process.
Parking Consultant	International Parking Design, Inc.
Elevator Consultant	Edgett Williams Consulting Group, Inc., with whom project personnel had successful past experiences.
Acoustical Consulting	Veneklasen Associates.
Traffic Consultant	Kimley-Horn, a well-regarded traffic consultant with major experience with the city of San Diego, whose traffic principal is also the traffic authority for a nearby town.
Environmental Consultant	Montgomery Watson.
Geotechnical Engineering	Kleinfelder.
Space Planner	Smith Consulting—performed well on Executive Center Del Mar, where they were a full-floor tenant.
Real Estate Broker	Business Real Estate Brokers—successfully represented Prentiss in the adjacent project and represented Pardee in the evaluation of bids for the site.

Attorney	Allen, Matkin, Leck, Gamble, & Mallory LLP have been doing most of the Prentiss work in Southern California for several years.
General Contractor	Swinerton & Walberg—selected jointly with Waterford.

01 SITE PLAN
NOT TO SCALE

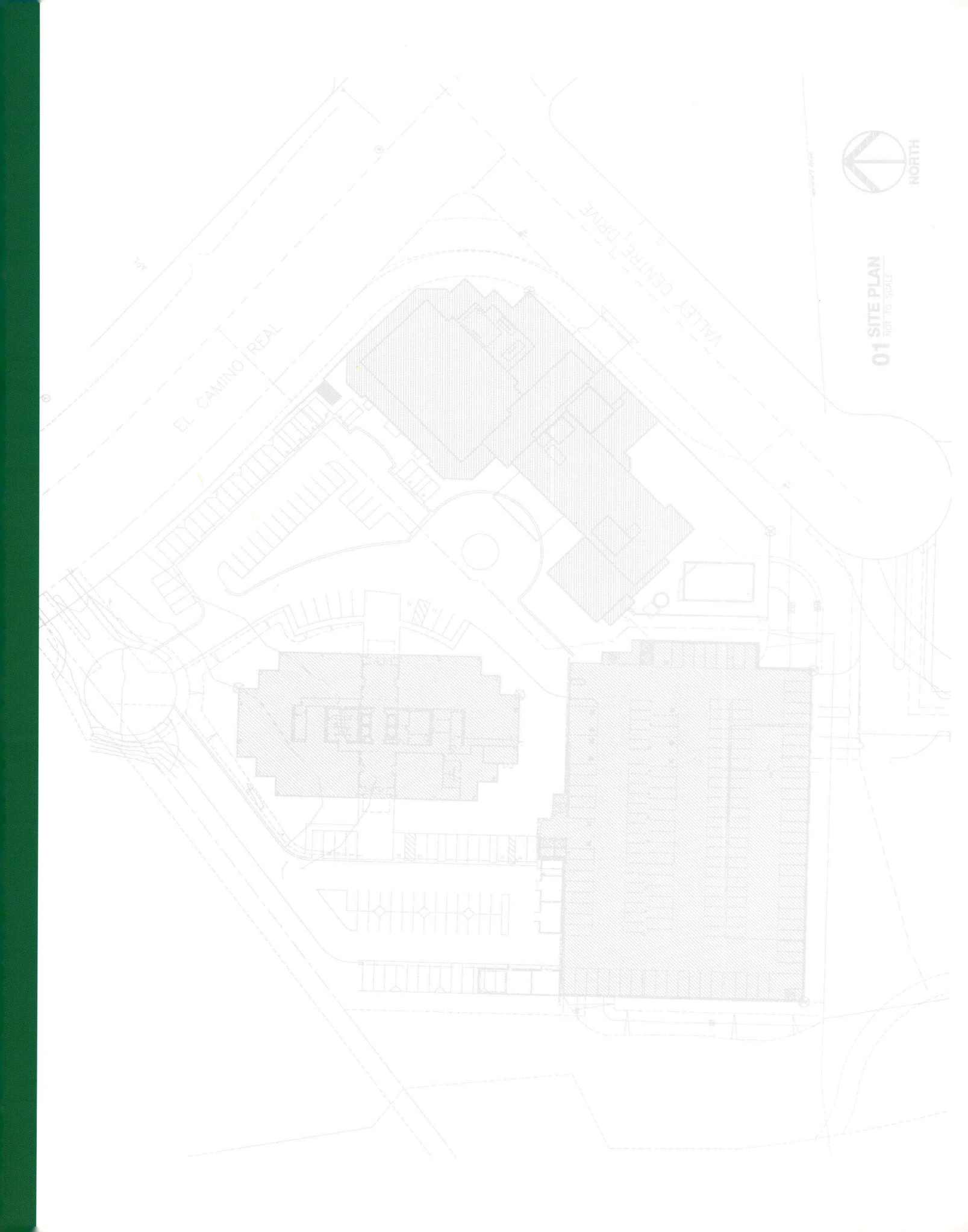

NORTH

THE PRO FORMA

The pro forma is the key tool through which the Development Officer evaluates the project potential, makes decisions and obtains any necessary management approvals. The Development Officer must prepare, revise as necessary and utilize it as a communication and management tool throughout the development period.

The pro forma is an analysis of the project's entire financial structure in order to compute the total project cost and the predicted returns. The author believes the one true measure of project success is the cash-on-cash return. Many people place great weight on the IRR, but that number uses assumptions much farther into the future, and it can vary widely with the assumptions and timing relative to the re-leasing period.

The pro forma allocates estimates of all known or anticipated project costs and income by the estimated time of their occurrence, so as to accurately compute the interest, vacancy cost, rental income, operating expenses and other costs that vary with time. The total project cost has been frequently defined as the maximum net cost as of the time that the pro forma has had three consecutive months of positive cash flow, called the break-even point. Use of the three consecutive month period tends to avoid possible distortion from delayed costs such as Tenant Improvements, leasing commissions or contract settlements that could indicate a false break-even point.

Contingencies are an essential element of the pro forma. The author recommends an initial hard cost contingency of 4% to 5%, reducing gradually as costs are fixed down to 1% to 2% at the time of the GMP, varying with the amount of money carried as allowances. In addition, there must be an overall project contingency of 2% to 3% to cover all other issues, particularly lease-up timing, rental rates and concessions. This overall contingency should not be reduced until the leasing reaches a point where the lease-up is fully predictable.

The Total Project Cost, as determined through the pro forma, is converted to a cost per rentable square foot, as the desired return multiplied by that cost must be equal to or less than the average net rental income after adjustment for projected vacancy. (See Chapter 8.) The various decisions made throughout the project must be constantly focused on that per rentable square foot cost.

A pro forma is a flexible tool that provides the essential basis for each of the major decisions over the term of the project development. The most common are:

- Initial project evaluation
- Sensitivity analyses
- Management project approval
- Lender or equity partner evaluations
- Final review prior to closing escrow on the land
- Final review prior to commencing construction
- Reevaluations due to major cost or market condition changes
- Measure of project performance

In other words, you can see that the pro forma review prior to each major step is an important form of risk control. If the project potential has turned negative, it is better to forego funds expended to date rather than lose greater sums by proceeding when the risk potential is too high.

A very preliminary pro forma based on initially available data is also of great assistance in the site selection and the conceptual design phases.

Once a pro forma is approved by senior management as a basis for proceeding with the project, that version of the pro forma should be set aside as an official document to remain unchanged as a basis for future comparison with pro forma revisions as the project progresses.

It is wise, many believe essential, for the Development Officer to perform the pro forma analysis personally rather than delegate it to an assistant or a pro forma specialist. It might take a little longer initially, but the total understanding of where every dollar of anticipated expenditure is allocated and the potential impact of any change are extremely important as the project progresses.

It is also very important to utilize the abilities of the persons on the development team with the greatest first-hand knowledge of the likely cost of each item. The architect, contractors, consulting engineers, property managers, brokers, finance managers, tax and insurance consultants, and many others must be consulted when preparing or revising a pro forma to obtain the most accurate data available.

The most important, and most difficult data to verify, are the market assumptions—prelease percentage, lease-up rate, net rental rate and concessions, as you are projecting the most volatile factors into the future. In some cases the prelease percentage is fixed, as it is a management requirement for initiating construction. Discipline is required to avoid slanting this market data in order to increase the projected return or to justify proceeding.

It is an essential criteria of any estimate or cost analysis that no element of cost be omitted. Many (if not all) numbers used in the pro forma will be wrong to some degree, but errors will normally tend to balance each other out. Costs that are missed entirely are the primary reason for major overruns.

As the project progresses changes will occur, and the Development Officer uses a working copy of the pro forma as a dynamic tool that is modified to reflect all new information and each significant project change, which is updated throughout the project, with a record as to the degree of variation from the official pro forma.

The basic shell and core cost (which to the surprise of most people is frequently less than 50% of total project cost) may either be spread equally over the construction period, one or two months behind the actual occurrence of the work to reflect the actual payment timing, or it can be spread on a bell curve developed by a contractor who has good timing data.

This chapter will discuss the five basic sections of a pro forma, listed below, and indicate the depth necessary to a successful pro forma study:

- Input Sheet
- Spreadsheet Calculations
- Executive Summary
- Project Cost Report
- Cash Flow Analysis

The input sheet is the most important part of the pro forma, because it includes every project assumption as to its amount and estimated timing. It is a graphic picture of the complete thought process of the Development Officer who prepared it. To minimize mistakes, the input sheet must serve as an extensive checklist, and be organized to reflect the approach by which Development Officers think their way through a project from beginning to end. The best-organized pro forma the author has seen was developed and is distributed by Financial Reporting, Inc. of Dallas, Texas.

The spreadsheet calculations from the input sheet data provide all cost information for the project and calculate any returns required by management or the Development Officer for the executive summary, or other project evaluation.

Another factor in the design of a proper pro forma is that the spreadsheet calculations be self-correcting and self-adjusting as information is added or modified. Every entry revision is a potential entry error, and the design must minimize these errors. The following are a few of the many examples that can illustrate this point.

- If the total building area is not changed and the non-rentable area changes, the rentable area will adjust.

- If the rentable has not been changed and the vacancy assumption or amount of space allocated to amenities is modified, the speculative rentable area will adjust and be reallocated.

- If the assumption as to the size of the preleased tenancy is modified, the speculative rentable area will adjust and be reallocated.

- If the lease-up period is changed, the speculative rentable area assumptions will be proportionately adjusted

- In the examples above, if the speculative rentable had been allocated into, say, 50% five-year leases and 50% ten-year leases, this allocation percentage, with its resultant cost impacts, will remain in place when the area is adjusted.

- If there is a timing change, such as adding a month to the construction schedule, the month in which each cost allocation falls will be adjusted accordingly.

A pro forma developed using a dynamic spread sheet program can be readily adapted to the automatic types of adjustments discussed above, while those developed using a data base program will have difficulty making the adjustments, and can require many repetitive manual entries for each revision.

After all costs are calculated and the total project cost is determined, the program should calculate the stabilized net rental income by multiplying the projected unit gross rental rate by the rentable area times the stabilized occupancy percentage, less the total of operating and utilities expense. Dividing the net rental income by the total project cost provides the cash-on-cash return.

The executive summary provides all of the financial information normally required by management or an investment committee to understand and approve or reject the economics of a project. This submission to management should also include the Market Study.

The project cost report shows a summary of the major costs in the project, although the Development Officer will normally use the cost totals directly from the spreadsheet calculations so that all costs will be shown.

The rental income and operating expense data, along with the projected market net rental rate and the expansion and renewal data are exported to the 10-year cash flow summary, which provides the projected economics of a project over time. The formats for these reports can vary widely and will not be shown here.

The cash flow summary normally runs 10 years from stabilized occupancy and includes all costs of owning and operating the facility, including all operating expenses and the cost of re-leasing commissions, TIs and vacancy periods at the termination of each initial lease. The sales values is based on using an assumed capitalization value multiplied by the projected income stream at the end of that period, less sales costs. An internal rate of return (IRR) is calculated from the initial expenditure on the project through the projected sale. An IRR is subject to significant variance based upon the timing of sale in relation to lease expirations, and the estimated re-leasing timing and costs.

An example of an executive summary is:

EXECUTIVE SUMMARY

Project Information

    Project Name
    Location
    Project Number, if applicable
    Revision No.
    Date

    Gross Square Feet
    Rentable Square Feet
    Useable Square Feet
    Retail Square Feet (included in above)
    Number of floors

EXECUTIVE SUMMARY (Continued)

Parking Spaces
    Structured
    Unstructured
    Total
Parking Ratio
Construction Loan Rate
Percent Preleased

Return Analysis
Stabilized Net Income
Total Project Cost (from Project Cost Summary)   Shown in $/RSF, $/GSF, and Total
Stabilized Cash-on-Cash Return   All returns should be presented on a best, worst and most likely case
    5-year average cash-on-cash return
    10-year average cash-on-cash return
    IRR

Time Line
Pre-Construction Period   Show these as Start, End, and Total Months
Construction Period
Lease-up Period

Leasing Assumptions
There should be separate columns for Pre-lease and Speculative tenants, and the estimates, particularly the lease-up period and the net rental rates, should be shown as best, most likely and worst cases.

Total Rentable Area
Stabilized Occupancy %
Prelease Area
Speculative Office Area
Retail Area

Gross Rental Rate—office
Initial Operating Expense—stabilized
Initial Utility Expense—stabilized   Some markets treat these as a separate tenant expense
Net Rental Rate—office
Annual Rent Increases, if applicable
Net Rental Rate—retail

Tenant Improvement Allowance
Other Concessions
Monthly Parking Rate
    Structured
    Non-structured
Amenities Provided   Health club, food service, day care center, etc.

A typical project cost report (or summary) is shown below. As a general rule each cost item would be shown as its dollar cost, % of total cost, $/GSF and $/RSF. This summary can be as detailed as required to be an effective evaluation tool. A complete listing of every cost line is obtained from the spreadsheet printout after calculating the input sheet data. It is this more detailed cost sheet that is normally used by the Development Officer for control.

PROJECT COST REPORT

Land	Normally includes all closing, legal, survey, site evaluation and demolition costs.
Design costs	
Permits and approvals	
Off-site work	
Exactions and impact fees	
Construction cost:	
Base building	
Parking	
Site work	
Tenant Improvements	
Testing and inspection	
Administrative costs	Assume this includes Construction Manager, FF&E and start-up costs. Other personnel and overhead charges may be specified.
Marketing	
Leasing costs	Includes lease commissions, leasing legal, leasing office (if any) and in-house commissions.
Financing costs	Includes loan placement fees, lender inspections, legal loan negotiation, appraisals, builders risk insurance, payment and performance bonds, and title insurance.
Interest expense	
Other development costs	Equipping costs, construction office, mockups, public corridor and elevator lobby construction, window blinds, graphics and signage, etc.
Operating and utility costs	
Rental income (negative expense)	
Vacancy expense	
Capital reserve	Some lenders want to see a capital reserve.
Development contingency	
Development fee	

The input sheet must include each and every factor that can affect the cost of a project. When the input is completed, the computer will make all of the calculations of costs and income prior to project completion. Many of the items in the sample input sheet shown below will not occur in every project. There will always be items that are not listed herein, however, so a good input sheet will have spare lines in each category to accommodate them. A well-designed input sheet will serve as a checklist to ensure that no costs are omitted altogether.

PRO FORMA INPUT SHEET

PROJECT DESCRIPTION
Developer
Developer address, phone & fax
Project name
Location
Project number
Revision number
Date

PROJECT ASSUMPTIONS
Land Area
    Purchased _____ sf, or _____ acres   Insert one and calculate the other.
    Ground lease _____ sf, or _____ acres   Insert one and calculate the other.

Building Areas
    Gross building area _____ gsf
    Factor _____ %   To convert architect's gross area to contractor's gross area.
    Rentable area _____ rsf, _____ % of gsf   Calculate one from the other.
    Useable area _____ usf, _____ % of rsf   Calculate one from the other.
    Retail area _____ rsf   Included in rentable area, above.
    Amenities area _____ rsf   Included in rentable area, above.
    Parking stalls _____ , or 1 per _____ rsf   Calculate one from the other.

Land Cost
    Purchase cost _____ / sf
    Ground lease _____ / mo. @ mo. no. _____

Construction Costs
    Building cost _____ / gsf, or _____   Calculate one from the other.
    Parking cost _____ / stall, or _____ / sf   Calculate one from the other.

Interest
    Predevelopment or land carry _____ %   Currently 30-day LIBOR + ___ % (see Finance Dept.).
    Interim interest _____ % @ mo. _____   As above. Provide for more than one rate change.
    Permanent debt service _____ %

Time line
    Entitlement Period _____ mos.
    Preconstruction _____ mos.
    Construction _____ mos.
    Lease-up _____ mos.   Best, most likely and worst cases for sensitivity analyses.

INPUT SHEET (Continued)

MARKET ASSUMPTIONS
Sensitivity Analyses

Certain income and cost estimates, particularly the net rental rates and the lease-up period should be input in a best, most likely and worst case for a market sensitivity analysis.

Prelease Tenant(s)

Lease area _____ rsf
Term _____ years
Net rental rate _____ / rsf, plus step incr.
   of _____ % or _____ / mo. @ mos.
   _____ , _____ , _____ , _____ , etc.
Commission rate _____ %
TI's _____ / usf
Expansions: _____ % of base lease area in
   mo. _____ @ _____ net rental rate / rsf,
   with a refurbishment rate of _____ / rsf
Renewals in mo. _____ @ market rate, or
   _____ / rsf, with refurbishment of _____ / rsf
Downtime _____ mos. prior to renewal term

Should have space for 2 or 3.

Speculative Tenants

Stabilized occupancy _____ %
5-year leases _____ % of spec rentable area
10-year leases _____ % of spec rentable area
Net rental rate _____ / rsf

If rental rates are quoted on a gross basis, the formulas will be revised to accommodate it. This must not be the highest achievable, as some space will be encumbered and some will be less desirable.

Step rentals _____ per mo. from mo. _____ ,
   or _____ / mo. annually,
   or _____ % annually
Commission rate—5-year terms _____ %
Commission rate—10-year terms _____ %
TIs _____ / usf—5-year tenants
TIs _____ / usf—10-year tenants
Expansions: _____ % of base lease area in
   mo. _____ @ _____ net rental rate / rsf,
   with a refurbishment rate of _____ / rsf
Renewals in mo. _____ @ market rate, or
   _____ / rsf, for _____ % of areas, with
   refurbishment of _____ / rsf
Downtime _____ mos. prior to renewal term

Retail Tenants

Lease area _____ rsf
Term _____ years
Net rental rate _____ / rsf, plus _____ %
   of sales over _____
Commission rate _____ %
TIs _____ / usf

Should have space for 3, expandable.

INPUT SHEET (Continued)

Amenity Tenants

    Lease area _____ rsf
    Income _____ @ initial occupancy, and
        _____ @ stabilized occupancy
    TI's _____ / usf
    Commission rate _____ %

Should have room for 3. Subsidized food service, health club, day care, etc.

Straight line between the two points.

Parking

    _____ / stall / mo.
    Transient income— _____ / visit
       @ _____ visits/mo.
       Annual increases _____ %
       Parking operating expenses @ $ _____
       per stall, increasing @ _____ % annually

Operating Expenses

    Stabilized operating exp. _____ / mo. /rsf

    Stabilized utility expense _____ / mo. / rsf
    Stabilized R. E. taxes _____ / mo. / rsf

Must not be underestimated, as a low estimate will ultimately reduce net income in gross leases.
If treated separately in lease.
If treated separately in lease.

Market Net Rental Rate: _____ / rsf @ end of construction period, increased by
  __ % / year, or by _____ / rsf / year

Will apply to first year of expansions or renewals unless overridden.

PROJECT COST INPUT
Land Costs

    Land purchase: area (sf) X _____ / sf,
       start in mo. _____
    Land expense to date: _____ @ mo. _____
    Ground lease—leased area (sf) X _____
       / mo., start @ mo. _____

Other Land Costs

    Easements: _____ / mo., start @ mo. _____
    Relocations: _____ in mo. _____
    Demolition: _____ in mo. _____
    Hazardous cleanup: _____ , start @
    mo. _____ , complete @ mo. _____
    Environmental studies _____ @ mo. _____
       to mo. ———
    Environmental mitigation: _____ ,
       start mo. _____ , complete mo. ____
    Surveys: _____ in mo. ____
    Legal acquisition: _____ in mo. ____
    Land interest: land carry interest X
       land cost to date

Cost to date for all land costs plus fees and exactions each mo. X interest rate through mo. (-1), i.e., start of construction.

INPUT SHEET (Continued)

Fees, Exactions and Zoning
    Traffic analysis
    Planning and zoning studies
    Exactions or impact fees _____ in mo. _____
    Off-site requirements _____ in mo. _____
    Legal zoning _____ in mo. _____
    Road & traffic controls _____ in mo. _____
    Development permit fees _____ in mo. _____
    Licenses _____ in mo. _____
    Private party exactions _____ in mo. _____

Construction Cost
    Building cost X gross area
        X factor, or _____ , spread over construction period
                Factor adjusts architect's gross to contractor's gross area. Costs may be spread straight line or on a curve. Can override assumptions.
    Parking unit cost X area / stall X no. of stalls, or _____ , spread over constr. period, or from mo. _____ to mo. _____
                May be spread straight line or curve. Can override assumptions.
    Site work
                If not in contractor's estimate or GMP.
        Utility constr. _____ , from mo. _____ to _____
        Utility relocate _____ , from mo. _____ to _____
        Grading _____ from mo. _____ to _____
        Water retention, detention and/or treatment from mo. _____ to mo. _____
        Hardscape and landscape _____ from _____ to _____ .
    Required public art _____ in mo._____
    Construction permit fees _____ in mo._____
                If not in construction estimate or GMP.
    Other construction
                If not in contractor's estimate or GMP.
    Curtain wall testing _____ in mo. _____
    Equipment _____ in mo. _____
    Window washing rig _____ in mo._____
    Construction office _____ in mo._____ to_____
    Security & energy mgt. _____ in mo. _____
    Graphics & signage _____ in mo. _____
    Window treatment _____ in mo. _____
    Public corridors and lobbies _____ in mo. _____
    Parking & dock equip. _____ in mo. _____
    Mockups _____ in mo. _____
    Construction mgr. _____ / mo. from mo. _____ to _____
    Devel. Officer _____ / mo., from mo. _____ to _____
    Other staff _____ / mo., from mo. _____ to _____
    Legal _____ in mo. _____

INPUT SHEET (Continued)

    Payment & perf. bonds _____ in mo. _____
    Testing _____ spread from mo. _____
        to _____
        Constr. contingency _____ % of total   Not be spread—used when required. May be carried
        construction cost   in GMP or separately.

Soft Costs
    Prelim. design for lender package
        _____ in mo. _____
    Architect and basic engineering
        Total design fees _____
        Allocate _____ % to entitlement
        _____ % to predevel, _____ %
        to design docs, & _____ % to construction
        services
    Predevel. spread from mo. _____ to _____
    % allocation X design fees

    Design documents spread from mo. _____
        to _____
    % allocation X design fees
    Alternative design calculation   Use when design will not be performed in one
        continuous period.

        Schematic Des. _____ % of Design Docs.,
        from mo. _____ to mo. _____
        Design Dev. _____ % of Design Docs.,
        From mo. _____ to mo. _____
        Working Drgs. _____ % of Design Docs.,
        from mo. _____ to mo. _____
    Constr. services – spread over constr. period
        % allocation X design fees
    Reimbursables _____ % X design fees   Spread over design & constr. periods, usually assume
    Other design consultants   10%.
        Soils testing _____ in mo. _____
        Soils engineering _____ spread from mo.
        _____ to _____
    Soils inspection _____ from mo. _____
        to mo. _____
    Civil engr. _____ spread from _____
        to _____
    Other consultants—all below will be
        totaled and spread from mo. _____
        to _____
    Elevator _____
    Parking _____
    Graphics _____
    Lighting _____
    Acoustical _____
    Fire, life safety & codes _____
    Curtainwall consultant _____
    Roofing consultant _____

INPUT SHEET (Continued)

    Interior leasing space planning _____
    Legal for contracts _____
    Other _____   Should be able to add others.
    Printing costs _____   If not included in the GMP.

MARKETING COSTS
    Marketing center constr., including
        furniture _____ in mo. _____
    Marketing center rent _____ / mo
        spread from mo. _____ to ___
    In-house commissions   Per company policy.
    Office operation _____ from mo. _____
        to _____
    Models _____ in mo. _____
    Renderings _____ in mo. _____
    Brochures and collateral _____ in mo. _____
    Advertising _____ in mo. _____ and _____
        in mo. _____
    Special events _____ in mo. _____
        and _____ in mo. _____
    Special site signage _____ in mo. _____
    Travel and entertainment _____ / mo.
        spread from mo. _____ to mo. _____

LEASING   All costs in this section occur a specified number of months prior to the occupancy date. All costs can be overridden if different from assumptions.

Pre-lease Tenant(s)   Should have space for 2 or 3.
    Rental income   Lease area X (net rental rate + operating cost + utilities + taxes) / 12, adjusted for rental steps.

    Occupancy _____ mos. after C of O
    TI's spread over _____ mos.   TI rate X lease area (in usf).
    Free rent for _____ mos.   Insert or leave blank, if none.
    Operating cost during free rent Y or N _____   If Y, will show as operating income.
    Lease signed in mo. _____
    Other concessions _____ in mo. _____
    Legal _____ / rsf X lease area, or _____ , in
        in mo. _____
    Leasing space planning _____ / usf X area
        (in usf)
    Commission   Commission rate X (Net rental, incl. all steps + operating + utilities) X leased area X term. Paid ½ at signing and ½ at rent commencement.

Speculative Tenants   Should have one group of tenants for each length term (i.e., 5 years or 10 years), occupying space equally in each month over the lease-up period. All expenses occur in negative months from occupancy.

    Total speculative area _____ rsf   Rentable area X stabilized occupancy %, less prelease area, less retail, less amenity area.

INPUT SHEET (Continued)

5-yr. leases _____ in rsf or %	Percent of 5-year leases X total speculative area.
10-yr. leases _____ in rsf or %	As above.
Lease-up period - _____ mos.	From C of O to Stabilized Occupancy.
Free rent for _____ mos.	Insert or leave blank, if none.
Operating cost during free rent Y or N	If Y, will show as operating income.
Net rental rate _____ / rsf,	Override if different from assumptions.
Rental steps _____ / mo. from mo. _____ , or _____ / mo. annually, or _____ % annually	Override if different from assumptions
Rental income	Monthly rent is (net rental + operating + utilities) X lease area / 12, starting after free rent, adjusted for steps.
Lease signing _____ mos. prior to occupancy	
Commission—5-year terms	Commission rate X (Net rental, incl. all steps + operating + utilities) X leased area X term. Paid ½ at signing and ½ at rent commencement.
Commission—10 year terms	As above.
TIs @ _____ / usf, spread over _____ mos., Prior to and including mo. of occupancy	TI rate (in usf) X lease area. Can override if different from assumptions.
Legal _____ / rsf X lease area, or _____	At time of lease signing.
Leasing space planning @ _____ / usf X lease area in usf	

Retail Tenants

	Should have space for 3.
Occupancy in mo. _____ after construction	
Leased signed _____ prior to occupancy	
Net rental rate _____ / rsf, plus _____ % over _____ in sales	Override if different from Assumptions
Rental income	Monthly rent is lease area X (net rental rate + operating adjusted for % used + utility) / 12.
Commission	Commission rate X (net rental rate + operating + utilities) X lease area X term. Paid ½ at signing and ½ at rent commencement.
TIs @ _____ / usf	TI rate X lease area (in usf). Can override if different from Assumptions.
_____ % of operating costs applicable	Retail self-performs many services.
Lease signed _____ mos. prior to occupancy	
Occupancy _____ mos. after constr. period	
Legal _____ / rsf X lease area, or _____ in mo. _____	

Amenity Tenants

	Should have space for 3
Occupancy _____ mos. after constr. period	
Lease signed _____ mos. prior to occupancy	
Income _____ @ initial occupancy, and _____ @ stabilized occupancy	Straight line between the two points. Can override if different from assumptions.
TI's @ _____ / usf	TI rate X lease area. Can override if different from assumptions.
Commissions	Commission rate X (net rental rate + operating + utilities) X lease area X term. Paid ½ at signing and ½ at rent commencement.

INPUT SHEET (Continued)

Legal _____ / rsf X lease area, or _____ in mo. _____

_____ % of operating costs applicable   Amenities self-perform many services.

Tenant Improvements (TIs)   Sum all TI costs for each month and for project total.

Lease Commissions   As above.

FINANCING COSTS   Equity treated the same as the applicable interim or permanent loan.

Interim loan fees _____ in mo. _____   Currently ½% to ¾%.

Interim loan interest _____ %   Interest rate times the cumulative funds expended each month from start of construction thru month. permanent loan commences. Currently 30 day LIBOR plus 150 to 200 basis points (See Finance Dept.).

Permanent loan fee _____ in mo. _____   Currently 1% to 2% refundable deposit if loan consummated.

Permanent loan debt service _____ % from _____ mo. after construction completion, or mo. of _____ % occupancy   Debt service rate X Total Project Cost to date each month. Starts either at construction completion, or other agreed upon occupancy rate, or fixed relationship to construction completion. Equity is computed at this rate for this purpose.

Legal fees—financing _____ in mo. _____ and _____ in mo. _____   Currently $30,000 for industrial and $50,000 for office.

Lender appraisal _____ in mo. _____   Currently $5,000 for industrial and $10,000 for office.

Title insurance _____ in mo. _____   Varies by state.

Lender inspection _____ in mo. _____ , plus _____ / mo. thru construction period $10,000 to $15,000 initially, and $600 to $800 per month.

Builders risk insurance _____ in mo. _____   Currently 6¢ / $100 of hard cost—do not include off-site and foundations in cost base. Soft costs @ 10¢ / $100.

Other insurance _____ in mo. _____   Usually an umbrella policy.

OTHER INDIRECT COSTS

Interim R.E. taxes _____ in mo. _____   Taxes based on % of funds expended on appraisal date, (usually 1/1/xx) X stabilized tax rate. Normally paid 2 times per yr.

Stabilized R.E. taxes   Stabilized tax rate X applicable portions of Total Project Cost to date. See Tax Dept. or consultant.

Operating costs _____ % in first mo. of occupancy   Spread from 40% @ initial occupancy to 100% at Stabilized Occupancy in direct proportion to occupancy each month. Adjust for partial allocation of cost for retail and amenity uses.

INPUT SHEET (Continued)

Utility costs @ _____ / mo.

Utility cost rate X lease area in occupancy. Only if separate in lease. Can override if different from assumptions.

Start-up costs _____ @ _____ mos. prior to end of construction period

Currently 25¢ / rsf.

Building FF&E _____ @ _____ mos. prior to end of construction period

Currently 25¢ / rsf.

Capital reserve _____

Required by some lenders. Do not spread—total only.

Development contingency _____ % of Total Project Cost

Do not spread—total only.

Development fee _____ % of Total Project Cost

Spread monthly based on total cost to date.

PROJECT INCOME
Office Rental Income
    Office net rental income

Summation of net rental income each month.

    Office operating expense income

Summation of each rsf-mo. of occupancy X (unit operating expense + unit R.E. tax + unit utility expense, as applicable).

    Office utility income, if applicable

Summation for each rsf-mo. of occupancy X unit utility expense, if separate.

Retail Income
    Retail net rental income

Summation of net rental income each month.

    Retail operating expense income, @ _____ % of base

Summation of each rsf-mo. of occupancy X (unit operating expense + unit R.E. tax + unit utility expense, as applicable).

    Retail utility income, if applicable, @ _____ % of base

Summation of each rsf-mo. of occupancy X unit utility expense, if separate.

Amenities Income
    Amenities net rental income

Summation of net rental income each month.

    Amenities operating expense income, @ _____ % of base

Summation of each rsf-mo. of occupancy X (unit operating expense + unit R.E. tax + unit utility expense, as applicable).

    Amenities utility income, if applicable, @ _____ % of base

Summation of each rsf-mo. of occupancy X unit utility expense, if separate.

Parking Income
    Parking revenue = rate per stall / mo. X rsf occupied, divided by rsf / stall
    Transient revenue = number of visits / mo. / 1000 X rsf occupied X _____ / visit

Other Income _____ / mo. start @ mo. _____

Antenna, communications, etc.

CASE STUDY

During the acquisition evaluations a series of pro formas were prepared to determine the land cost at which the project would be feasible. They were prepared using the typical industrial type pro forma, as no appropriate model was then available.

These preliminary pro formas changed with a series of new assumptions during the bidding process for the land, which considered various land values, contributions from a hotel developer and varying market assumptions. All analyses were based on a low rise 150,000 gsf building with four parking stalls per 1000 gsf, adjusted by a 10% reduction for shared parking with the hotel. The last several computations varied between a 9.92% and 10.02% free and clear return, and were accepted as sufficient to enter a purchase agreement for the land if accepted as the successful bidder. This was a relatively low risk decision, as there was no requirement to close on the land until all entitlements were received for the specified building and hotel size, and approval received on a Subdivision Map. Through further evaluation and refinements to the project assumptions, the pro forma was revised to yield projected returns of 10.55% cash-on-cash and 12.74% IRR.

As the project developed, the estimated cost was increased to convert the project to a high-rise with granite cladding and again to incorporate a central HVAC system, all as described in Chapters 14 and 15.

At a very early stage of the entitlement process, when the Brandes Lease opportunity arose and the economics were determined, it was necessary to obtain management authorization to enter into the lease, as it committed Prentiss Properties to acquire the land and construct the project. The pro forma submitted for this approval, shown below as the Approved Pro Forma, had a free and clear return of 10.27% and an IRR of 12.85%.

One questionable judgment was made when this pro forma was prepared. A construction cost number was used that was considerably less than then carried in the baseline budget prepared by the contractor. While it was believed costs could be reduced and there was a 5% construction contingency, the assumption turned out to be a stretch. A great deal of effort was made endeavoring to meet this number, but without total success. See further discussion in Chapter 14 under Baseline Budgeting.

The Approved Pro Forma was the officially approved Pro Forma for further comparison. Further design refinement, an increase in building size and a major decision to change to a central chiller refrigeration system (see Chapter 25) substantially changed many of the base numbers, and required a revision to the pro forma. The building increase and the chiller plant added $559,000 to the construction cost, and also increased the TI and brokerage costs. (An election was made not to make any correction to the optimistic cost assumptions noted in the paragraph above.) The above cost increases were more than balanced by the increased net rental income and the estimated reduction in utility costs. These changes resulted in an increase of the initial return to 10.47% and the IRR to 12.68%. The increase in the IRR is an aberration resulting from the 11-year Brandes Lease Term that extended the re-leasing and downtime costs beyond the standard 10-year analysis period. The cost side only of the pro forma is shown in the tabulation below.

The interest cost and the lease-up period rental income in the Approved Pro Forma are both excessive, as the construction of the pro forma required carrying the analysis to the end of a full year. The effective interest cost is the difference between the two.

For simplicity's sake, all of the Waterford land, permit and soft costs have been netted against the total costs for the respective category to show the resultant net cost to Prentiss. The construction costs are shown separately—both the total cost and the Waterford reimbursement—to match the discussion in Chapter 14.

The Final Pro Forma has a few items that are still estimates, as the final accounting numbers are not available. Any adjustments are not expected to be of any consequence.

The Final Pro Forma return would have been 10.60% based upon the originally assumed operating costs, but is 10.38% based on operating expenses that have been revised upward based on current cost information.

The closeness of the Total Project Cost between the Final and Approved Pro Formas masks significant variances—not an unusual occurrence. Note that the Total Project Cost per rentable square foot, the ultimate number on the cost side, remained almost constant from beginning to end. Some of the variances of note are:

- Net design costs were $150,000 over the estimate due primarily to increased civil and entitlement processing costs resulting from unanticipated entitlement and permitting issues, more extensive geotechnical effort due primarily to the soil nailed wall, and landscape and signage costs that were just higher than estimated.

- Due to a 5% construction contingency the final net construction cost was virtually even with the adjusted pro forma. The Brandes reimbursement was recovery of costs relative to their internal stair opening and emergency power that were included in base building construction cost. The SDG&E energy rebate was for exceeding their energy requirements.

- Administration fees exceeded the pro forma due to an incomplete initial estimate.

- Financing costs, exclusive of interest, exceeded the estimate by $60,000.

- Lease commissions exceeded the estimate by almost $170,000 due to higher rental rate achievement on the smaller tenants and a slightly increased rentable area. Leasing legal fees exceeded the estimate by $80,000, largely due to the difficult negotiation with Brandes.

- The largest variance was the positive one where the net of interest expense and rental income was significantly below the original projection. The fact that construction commenced almost simultaneously with the closing on the land and the early lease-up produced a break even prior to final construction cost expenditures becoming due reduced the interest costs significantly. It was noted previously that the Final Pro Forma covers a much shorter period of time after substantial completion.

A large number of variances that tend to balance out is more normal than unusual in a well-thought-out pro forma. In this case costs were clearly increased as a result of expediting the schedule to accommodate the Brandes Lease, but the resultant early lease-up income more than compensated.

It is of interest to note that the net construction cost is approximately one-half of the Total Project Cost. This is not unusual, and sometimes it is quite a bit less than half. This is surprising to some people who believe the base building construction is the major portion of development cost.

The Pro Forma

	APPROVED PRO FORMA	**ADJUSTED PRO FORMA**	**FINAL PRO FORMA**
Land Costs			
Land Purchase	$ 5,243,056	$ 5,243,056	$ 5,136,386
Closing, survey, etc.	40,500	40,500	128,151
	$ 5,283,556	$ 5,283,556	$ 5,264,537
Design Costs			
Architectural	$ 782,723	$ 782,723	$ 753,000
Other Consultants	79,000	79,000	230,558
Testing & Inspection	100,000	100,000	106,328
	$ 961,223	$ 961,223	$ 1,089,886
Permit Fees	$ 986,997	$ 986,997	$ 796,296
Construction—Shell			
Base Building	$ 11,062,952	$ 11,621,952	$ 12,153,814
Parking Structure	6,700,000	6,700,000	6,940,016
Site Work	1,000,000	1,000,000	1,496,880
Waterford reimbursement	(2,845,000)	(2,845,000)	(3,177,446)
Signage	40,000	40,000	55,000
SDG&E energy rebate	0	0	(40,000)
Other Improvements	87,808	87,808	Incl.
Brandes reimbursement	0	0	(97,000)
Contingency	786,148	786,148	0
	$ 16,831,908	$ 17,390,908	$ 17,331,264
Administrative Fees			
Salaries, incl. Acc't, T&E	$ 114,250	$ 114,250	$ 347,000
Developer's Fee	723,565	723,565	737,452
	$ 837,815	$ 837,815	$ 1,084,452
Insurance—Bldrs. Risk	$ 16,426	$ 16,426	$ 18,641
RE Tax—Construction	$ 100,000	$ 100,000	$ 69,000
Interest	$ 4,025,944	$ 4,025,944	$ 1,879,000
Financing Cost			
Loan Fee	$ 174,395	$ 174,395	$ 216,000
Appraisal, Legal, Insp.	89,000	89,000	112,500
	$ 263,395	$ 263,395	$ 328,500
Marketing Costs	$ 31,000	$ 31,000	0
Lease-up Costs			
Tenant Improvements	$ 5,094,305	$ 5,094,305	$ 5,123,094
Leasing Commissions	1,894,232	1,894,232	2,061,064
Space Planning / Legal	80,000	80,000	158,750
Signing Bonus—Brandes	1,025,000	1,025,000	1,025,000
	$ 8,093,537	$ 8,093,537	$ 8,367,908
Miscellaneous			
Less Year 2001 NOI	$ (2,317,819)	$ (2,317,819)	$ (1,006,402)
Capital Expenditures	25,070	25,070	40,000
	$ (2,292,749)	$ (2,292,749)	$ (966,402)
TOTAL PROJECT COST	$ 35,139,052	$ 35,698,052	$ 35,262,582
Rentable Square Feet	161,500	163,189	163,189
Cost per Rentable Square Foot	$ 217.58	$218.75	$216.08

01 SITE PLAN
NOT TO SCALE

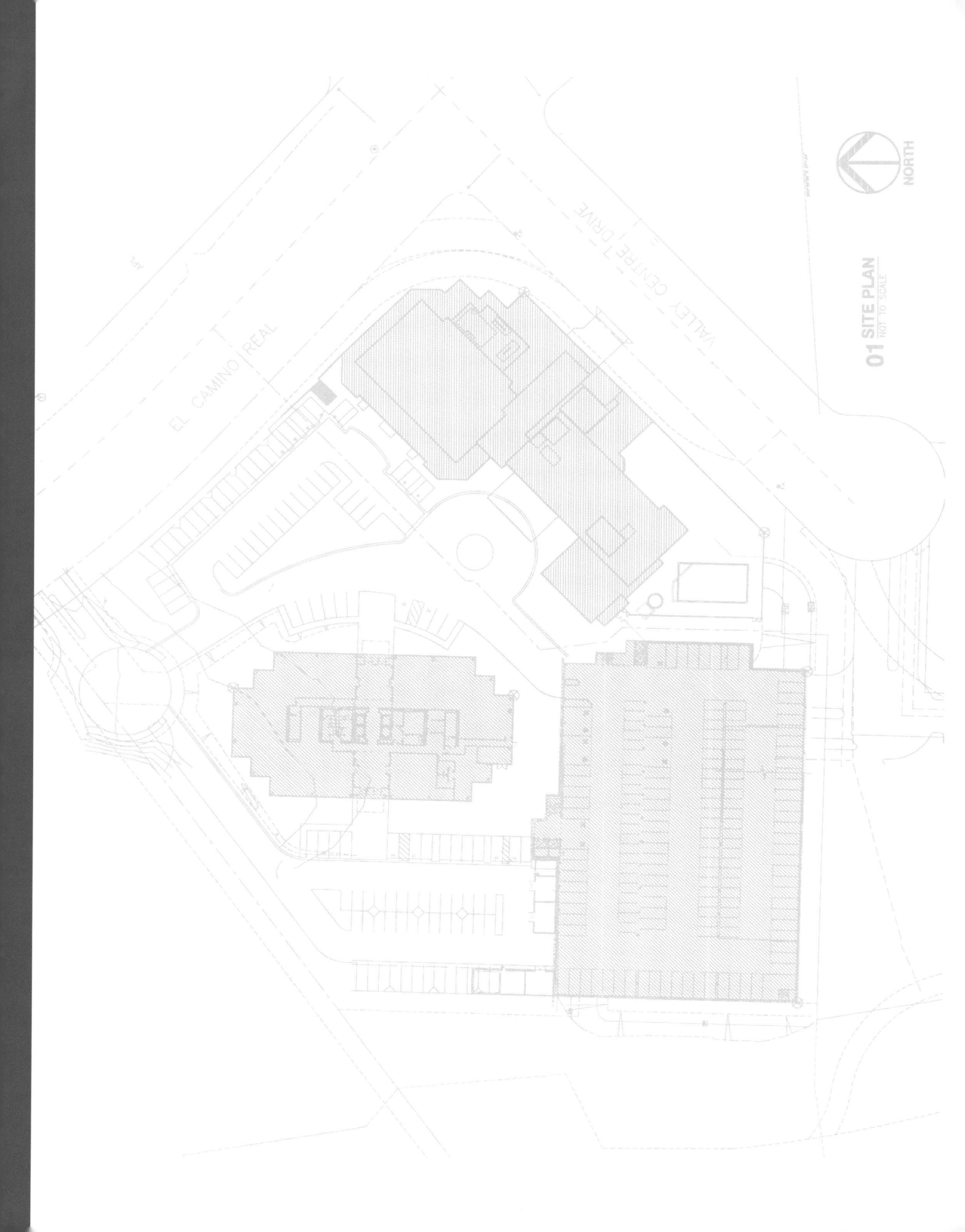

NORTH

DEVELOPMENT FINANCING   12

Financing is the lifeblood of the real estate development process. Few developers can proceed with the development of property of any size without external financing, and those who can do not want to tie up so much capital that they are precluded from other investments. The terms and conditions of the financing must provide the developer with sufficient flexibility to successfully build, market, manage and ultimately sell the project.

In this chapter, forms and sources of financing will be discussed, but the focus will be primarily on the administration of the construction loan and the permanent loan from the Development Officer's standpoint.

Availability and forms of financing vary widely with the type of real estate and with the current conditions in the financing markets. Not only do the forms of financing change with such conditions, but also interest rates, the length of the terms of loans, front-end pricing, various conditions and loan administration procedures. This chapter will try to provide an overview for the Development Officer in order to develop an understanding of the process and its requirements. There will be no attempt to cover the details of the extensive documentation involved, as that effort will be supported by a competent finance officer and real estate attorney.

There will also be no attempt to describe the many ways that financing can be structured, particularly the various forms of joint ventures, limited partnerships, REITs or securitization. This chapter will concentrate herein by describing the more common, or normal, methods of development finance.

A major issue in finance is the degree of risk and leverage. A recourse loan is one that reduces risk for the lender, as it is secured by a guaranty and/or other assets of the borrower, in addition to the real estate collateral. A non-recourse loan means that the developer is protected, as the lender only has recourse to the development property from which to recover the principal of his loan. As a practical matter, lenders virtually always limit the non-recourse obligation to a portion of the loan—the percentage determined by their lending policy, tenant credit, percentage of preleasing, evaluation of the project's value, the track record of the borrower, the amount of equity contributed by the borrower to the project and the financial market conditions.

Leverage greatly increases the potential return on the developer's invested capital, as long as the cash flow exceeds the debt service, and/or any current shortfall is exceeded by the appreciation of the property. When a project is too highly leveraged, and the cash flow does not cover the debt service, a reverse leverage can result in an early default and loss of the property.

Sources of financing may be located through mortgage brokers, mortgage bankers, banks, financial institutions, insurance companies, pension funds, mortgage Real Estate Investment Trusts (REITs), Real Estate Mortgage Investment Conduits (REMICs, mortgages on income producing property used as collateral for securities), other forms of securitization, private investors, yellow pages, newsletters and the Internet. Some of the financing newsletters are *Novick's Financial Newsletter*, *Crittendon Newsletter*, and *Fleet's Guide*. There are now several web sites offering to provide or arrange commercial financing.

No lender or investor should be approached without a complete "loan package," which provides a Feasibility Analysis, detailed description of the project, financial projections, and other evidence that the project has been thoroughly studied and that all risks have been evaluated and/or mitigated. A minimum financing package will include:

- Survey and legal description
- Preliminary plans, specifications, and a site plan showing the building and on-site parking
- Floor plans
- A pro forma showing an estimate of Total Project Costs including all indirect costs, profit and overhead, financing costs, land costs and contingencies
- A market and marketability analysis
- Zoning and environmental analysis
- Renderings, aerial photographs, and possibly a scale model, depending on project cost and size
- Market area maps showing location of the proposed project and competing buildings
- Financial statements of the developer
- Projections of income and expense

Land Financing

Non-recourse land financing is virtually impossible to obtain. The recovery of the loan principal and any accrued interest from raw land is a very risky proposition. Funds for the cost of the land, the due diligence and testing, and the front-end design are most commonly provided by cash or fully secured loans from financial institutions. Alternatives are seller financing, ground lease with an option to buy, joint ventures, limited partnerships or other forms of equity funding.

Equity

Equity is cash, or its most common substitute, a loan with a specified duration that is fully secured by other owned assets. Equity is an essential element in development financing, since it is difficult to obtain a loan on land as discussed before. Construction loans require some form of equity or recourse, and a permanent loan usually requires at least 20% to 25% equity, as there are few circumstances that a lender will lend more against the property.

External sources of equity are joint ventures and partnerships. A joint venture is usually an entity formed between a developer and a money source such as an insurance company, pension fund, real investment firm, or certain types of REITs. Partnerships are most often created wherein the developer as the general partner finds individual investors who wish to be limited partners. An alternate structure to a limited partnership is the Limited Liability Corporation. In each case the equity funds are provided in return for a share of ownership, or a share of the income stream, of the real property.

Equity sources are usually found through personal contacts, real estate investment brokers, financing newsletters, etc.

Construction Loans

Construction lending is inherently risky, and is usually provided by various financial institutions. Insurance companies and pension funds who provide construction loans usually tie them to a permanent mortgage loan, frequently with a participation in the project's net cash flow as discussed further in later paragraphs.

The primary risk in a construction, or interim, loan is that the cost of construction will exceed the amount agreed to in the loan, or that the project will otherwise not satisfy a takeout by the permanent lender. When the construction loan contains a mini-perm (a three- to-seven- year permanent loan) the risks of a permanent lender are added to those of the construction lender.

Construction loans usually require interest only monthly payments until 12 months after completion, with a floating interest rate and a firm termination date. They are almost never fully non-recourse, usually requiring all or a portion of the debt to be secured by other assets or guarantees. The developer will try to negotiate for as much of the loan as possible to be non-recourse so that a significant portion of the risk rests with the lender, freeing more loan capacity for other opportunities. A common arrangement is for the recourse portion of the loan to burn down to 50% at completion, with further reductions available based on achieving in-place rent sufficient to cover debt service. Most lenders will convert to non-recourse after the project achieves 1.25 to 1.4 debt service coverage.

Banks are the largest source of interim financing, as it is an extension of their primary function of short-term business financing, followed by the savings institutions. Bank deposits tend to be short-term and the rates they pay for the use of depositor's money varies with the market. Therefore, these loans must be at a variable rate with a spread (determined by risk) above their cost of funds, usually tied to an index. The most common index used for variable rate loans is the London Interbank Offered Rate (LIBOR), usually the current interest rate on three- to six-month Eurodeposits, or loans are based on a bank's prime lending rate, which is the rate the bank charges its most creditworthy customers.

A construction, or interim, lender treats the project as if they were the developer and therefore endeavors to mitigate as much of the time and cost risk as possible, as they may end up as the owner of the property. They attempt to protect their interest by carefully reviewing and approving the surveys, feasibility studies, site environmental assessments, appraisal, all site tests, pro forma, marketing analysis, contract documents and almost every other facet of the project.

If the loan has a mini-perm, or there is no takeout, when reviewing the pro forma and cash flow analysis, the construction lender acts like a permanent lender and usually looks for a minimum of a 7% vacancy assumption, management fees of 3%, capital reserves of at least 25¢ per square foot for office and 10¢ for industrial properties, and debt service coverage of 1.25 to 1.4 to one, based on a mortgage constant derived using seven- to ten-year treasuries plus 175 to 225 basis points with amortization over 25 to 30 years.

In many cases it is advisable to obtain a permanent loan commitment prior to approaching the construction lenders. Terms will be significantly better if a binding takeout is in place up front. After finding a willing construction lender, it will usually require at least 90 to 120 days to close the loan. The construction lender's requirements add significantly to the development cost by requiring:

- The developer to fund the cost of both the developer's and lender's legal costs—assume $50,000 for a routine office building

- Formal feasibility analyses

- Appraisals, probably $10,000 for a relatively small office building

- Lenders inspection—$10–15,000 initially for plan review, and probably $600 to 800 per month for inspection throughout the construction period for relatively small buildings

- Commitment fee of 1% to 3%

- Lenders title insurance policy—the premium varying by state

- Land released from any prior lien unless subordinated to the lender's satisfaction

The lenders requirements also impact the project with a long list of approval rights and procedures throughout the development period, which have a hidden cost impact. Among these approval rights are:

- All purchase and title documents, and clarifications of any issues included therein

- Promissory Note and Deed of Trust on the property

- Letters of credit and/or bonding of contractors

- All contract documents

- Notice to Proceed, GMP and all other contracts

- All plans not submitted prior to closing the loan

- Copies of all desired correspondence, inspection and test reports

- Security interest on all personal property, such as fixtures and equipment

- Insurance—including liability, automobile, workman's compensation, errors and omissions from all professionals, builder's risk, and loss of rental coverage, all with current certificates of coverage

- All loan draws, with specified holdbacks, frequently with a "down dated" endorsement by the title company required to protect against mechanics liens. Lenders often approve draws only on an approved schedule of the percent of construction completion irrespective of the funds expended

- All lien waivers
- Approval and assignment of leases
- Certificates of Occupancy
- Subordination of leases and estoppel certificates from each tenant
- Assignability of all professional contracts and construction documents to lender
- Letters from zoning department, and any other approval agencies, stating that the project meets all zoning regulations
- Estoppel certificates from a seller, governmental entity or anyone else who might have, or have had, some claim against the property
- Utility "will serve" letters
- Certificate of Completion
- As-built surveys

Among the precautions a construction lender takes to protect itself, unless the lender is providing a short-term permanent mortgage loans such as a mini-perm or a piggy-back loan, is to require the developer provide a commitment for a standby or takeout loan that insures the construction loan will be repaid.

To provide the construction lender with further comfort, they usually require a buy-sell agreement. This is a tri-party agreement wherein the construction lender, permanent lender and the developer agree that when all parties have met their predetermined obligations the permanent lender will buy the loan from the construction lender. The benefits of this arrangement are that the construction lender has an agreement that he will be taken out of the loan, the permanent lender has comfort that the developer will not shop for a less expensive permanent loan, and the developer has the peace of mind that both lenders are obligated to the deal.

Permanent Loan

The permanent loan, or mortgage, is a long-term loan placed on the property. The customary form is a promissory note that reflects the debt and a first Deed of Trust that automatically transfers the

---

To the Development Officer, satisfying the lender's requirements always seems difficult because, as lenders go through their due diligence trying to minimize their risk, they focus on issues the Development Officer does not think are important, or do not appear to be issues relative to the real world. Besides, the Development Officer is usually exceedingly busy resolving issues he does know are time critical and important. Notwithstanding the above, satisfying the lender and quickly closing the loan is a very important task.

My most painful experience with lenders was during the construction of First City Center in the early 1980s, when interest rates were out of sight. We entered into a construction loan with the Bank of Nova Scotia and had a permanent loan commitment from TIAA. The construction loan had options for interest at a function of the prime rate, LIBOR, or commercial paper. Negotiation of a buy-sell between TIAA and Scotia broke down, primarily over TIAA's non-recognition of the commercial paper component.

Concerned over the lack of a buy-sell, Scotia would send an extensive list of demands to me monthly with directions to obtain TIAA's concurrence of issues, which Scotia felt improved their risk situation. Naturally, when I tried to sell these issues to TIAA, I received nothing but lip service as the loan was not scheduled to close for two years. This act continued until the loan finally closed, and accomplished nothing except to wear down my nerves to the raw edge.

property to the lender in the event of specified defaults.

Permanent loans are most commonly made by life insurance companies, pension funds, saving and loans, mortgage REITs, mortgage limited partnerships, REMICs, and mortgage-backed securities. Loans are frequently accessed through mortgage bankers and mortgage brokers. Life insurance companies are appropriate for these long-term loans since their need for funds is easy to predict through long-term actuarial analysis. Others are investors interested in a consistent stream of funds.

The permanent loan is typically non-recourse and the only collateral is the ability of the land and its improvements to fully cover the debt service and the operating costs through varying market cycles over many years. In other words, the permanent lender evaluates the project on the assumption that he will be the owner. Additional risks assumed by the permanent lender that must be considered in setting his pricing are the maturity, risk premium, inflation premium and the default or credit-risk premium.

The market value of a commercial property is a function of the cash flow generated and the market capitalization rate at any point in time. The lender tries to mitigate his risk by thoroughly analyzing the appraisal, Market Study and the pro forma, lending no more than 75% to 80% of the anticipated value of the property, and in most cases requiring a specific amount of preleasing. In analyzing the pro forma the lender usually applies his own standards such as requiring the calculations to assume vacancy rates as high as 7%, using a management fee of 3%, allowances for capital reserves of at least 25¢ per square foot for office and 10¢ per square foot for industrial properties, and sufficient contingencies.

In evaluating whether to make the loan, or the amount of loan that satisfies their criteria, the lender will make their own calculations of the amount of cash flow the project will generate and compute the amount on the basis of their standards for loan to construction ratio and debt coverage ratio.

As mentioned earlier, since construction lenders want to receive their principal back within the desired period, it is easier to obtain a construction loan with a commitment from the permanent lender to take them out of their loan. A forward commitment such as this means agreeing to provide a permanent loan at a fixed interest rate one to two and one-half years ahead, with interest rates at that time unknown. To compensate for that risk, lenders have tended to charge a commitment fee of 1% to 3%. Recently, most have made the fee refundable if the agreement is consummated.

The types of loans can vary widely, limited only by the creativity of the lenders and the constantly varying market conditions. Formerly, the most common form was a fixed interest rate with a fixed debt service payment amortized over a 20, 25 or 30 year term, but currently it is difficult to find a lender willing to approve a term in excess of seven to ten years. These shorter term loans usually have a long-term amortization rate and a balloon payment at the end. Alternatives are variable interest rate loans tied to an index with a periodic and lifetime interest rate cap, and mini-perms that were discussed before. During certain economic periods lenders will require a participation in the cash flow in addition to the interest in order to justify the loan.

Another form, more common to corporate users, is a sale-leaseback or a sale-buyback. The advantages of this type of financing for a corporation with a strong balance sheet is a low interest rate and the availability of the capital for their business, while the buyer gets the income stream along with the depreciation benefit.

It is not uncommon for a specified percentage of the loan to be funded at the building completion and the funding increased as the leasing progresses. In such cases the loan might become fully funded when the cash flow covers the debt service and operating costs by 105%, or so, with leasing projections to reach the desired coverage range of 1.25 to 1.4.

To protect his interest in the project the lender will require the right to approve various documents and actions of the developer that were not reviewed and approved at the time of making the loan commitment. Among them are:

- Letters of credit and/or bonding of contractors that will survive the construction completion
- All contract documents
- All changes to the contract documents

- Notice to Proceed and all other contracts
- Assignability of all professional and construction contracts to lender
- Any desired construction inspection and test reports and/or correspondence
- Security interest on all personal property, such as fixtures and equipment
- Insurance—including liability, automobile, workman's compensation, errors and omissions from all professionals, builder's risk, and loss of rental coverage, all with current certificates of coverage
- Approval and assignment of each lease
- Certificates of Occupancy for each tenant
- Subordination of leases and estoppel certificates
- Certificates of Completion
- As-built drawings and surveys

Pre-closing requirements of the permanent loan include the following documents, which must be submitted and approved:

- Promissory note
- Deed to secure debt
- Legal description
- All contract documents
- Assignment of all of borrower's interest in the documents
- Commitment for title insurance
- Copy of all recorded title exceptions
- Any easements—utilities and others
- Insurance certification
- Appraisals
- Feasibility Analysis
- Certification of existence of the borrower
- Survey and surveyor's inspection report and certificate to lender's title insurer
- Copies of all final payments, or payments to date, with waivers of lien
- Parking letter, if applicable
- Zoning letter
- Copies of all executed leases
- Certification of environmental concerns compliance
- Tenant estoppel certificates
- Lease subordination, nondisturbance and attornment agreements
- Copies of service contracts
- Borrower's financial statements
- Uniform Commercial Code (UCC) financing statements
- Evidence of title

Some common clauses the borrower should focus on when reviewing the loan commitment and the loan document are described below. Some of these issues may be negotiated in a way that provides the borrower a little more flexibility, while fully protecting the lender.

Due-on-Sale Clause: Provides that if borrower transfers any portion of its interest in the property, lender in its sole discretion may accelerate the loan and make the unpaid balance and accrued interest due and payable.

Right-to-Transfer Clause: The right of the borrower to transfer his interest to another party subject to the approval of the lender, which approval will not be unreasonably withheld.

Acceleration Clause: The lender's right to accelerate the total unpaid balance in the event of default. The borrower can usually obtain a reasonable grace period.

Lock-in Clause: Provides that the loan cannot be prepaid for a specified period of time for any reason.

Prepayment Clause: A specified prepayment penalty for early loan payment—protects the lender who makes a loan in a high interest rate period from the borrower refinancing at a lower rate without some further payment to the lender.

Escrow Clause: Many lenders require that the borrower escrow funds monthly for real estate taxes and insurance. The interest on these funds should accrue to borrower.

Foreclosure and Right-of-Redemption Clause: Foreclosure is the last option for the lender to recover payment on a property that is in default. Borrower should be familiar with foreclosure regulations and any redemption laws.

Defeasance Clause: Gives the borrower the right to redeem the property after a default if the borrower pays off the total indebtedness to the lender.

Subordination Clause: Many lenders insist that either no secondary financing is allowed on the property, or they may require the right of approval of any secondary financing in order to ensure that the property is not burdened with too much monthly debt. This could prevent a sale with seller financing.

Release Clause: Stipulates that upon paying a certain amount of money the borrower can release a portion of the property the lender is holding as collateral.

Exculpatory Clause: Pertains to the personal liability of the borrower in case of default. The borrower should endeavor to negotiate all or a major portion of any personal liability out of the loan where possible.

Dragnet Clause: An open-ended clause in which the property stands as security for all obligations the borrower may have to lender—the note contemplated in the Deed of Trust and any other indebtedness to the lender.

Cross-Default Clause: A provision in which several pieces of property are pledged to the lender as collateral. If one of these loans is in default, it will trigger a default in the other properties.

Default Clauses: Outline what monetary and non-monetary events will trigger a default in the loan documents. The borrower will have a specified period of time to clear the default.

Non-Recourse Carve-out Clause: In the event of loss to a lender as a result of fraud, misrepresentation, waste, failure to insure, environmental issues and certain other conditions which vary with each lender, lender will reserve the right to have recourse beyond the collateral to the sponsorship.

Damage, Destruction and Condemnation: The lender usually insists on the receipt of all insurance proceeds under these circumstances, while they decide whether it is in their best interest to rebuild or restore the property. The developer clearly wants the proceeds used to immediately restore the property. Frequently, compromise language can be negotiated that will satisfy all parties.

CASE STUDY

When the project was initiated, the intent was to internally finance the initial portion of the work and then enter into a construction and/or a permanent loan in keeping with the current overall policies regarding project size and company-wide financing requirements.

During 1998, financial markets developed concerns regarding presumed overbuilding and overall earnings growth projections for REITs that caused a major drop in their stock prices, effectively preventing any new secondary offerings and causing lending institutions to tighten lending requirements. As a result, the company initially decided they would not go forward with this project without a financial partner or a pre-sale.

Giving full consideration to the continuing good leasing market in the area with rising rental rates, rising land prices, no obligation to close on the land unless entitlements were received, and even then, not until construction was ready to commence, it was concluded that the value of the interest would increase significantly with receipt of the final entitlements. It was agreed to proceed with the entitlements and the design while looking for an appropriate partner.

Several potential financial partners interested in participating in the project were found, but most wanted to purchase a one-half interest in the adjacent Executive Center Del Mar, along with either a one-half or full interest in the new building. Of the two who expressed the most interest, one was a firm also exploring the possibility of financing the hotel.

The Letter of Intent entered into with Brandes Financial for 100,000 rsf completely changed the approach to financing. The significant reduction of the lease-up risk led to foregoing the search for a financial partner in favor of a construction loan with a three-year mini-perm. An agreement was entered into with Société Générale who holds the mortgage on the adjacent Executive Center. The loan was for 75% of the pro forma project cost at 1.75% over LIBOR, after Prentiss puts their funds in first,.

An issue soon arose with Orix, the proposed construction lender for the hotel. The Purchase and Sale Agreement required Waterford (Orix) to put up a letter of credit at closing to cover the entire estimated obligation for their portion of the cost of constructing the parking structure and site work. Orix objected to putting up an L/C and insisted that Prentiss or Société Générale match any guarantee they made. Société Générale and Prentiss agreed to accept a guarantee rather than an L/C after reviewing the Orix financials, but would not provide a financial guarantee to cover funding their share. The rationale was that the agreements required them to build those facilities, and that was sufficient. The issue was tentatively resolved by guaranteeing that Prentiss Properties Acquisition Partners, the developing entity, would construct the parking structure and site work.

Another issue for the lender was that under California law, the first tradesman on the site determines the priority for liens—all future work at the site has lien right priority back to that time regardless of when that work occurs. If a Deed of Trust is not in place prior to the first tradesman on site, all liens have priority. In some states a dummy Deed of Trust may be filed prior to the start of work and later assigned to the lender, but not in California. There was no option, work had to commence prior to the time that Société Générale would be in a position to close the loan. The possibility of having one contract to cover the work up until the loan closing, and another one afterward was explored. This became impractical due to the timing and status of construction at the anticipated closing date. Prentiss indemnified the title company so that they could provide the lender with a clean title insurance policy.

There were extensive discussions with the lender over the issue of bonding the subcontractors. As discussed in Chapters 9 and 33, there was more concern over the risk of the time required to replace a defaulting contractor than the cost of such replacement. This issue finally went away when Swinerton & Walberg converted to an umbrella bond that provided full control over replacement of a defaulting subcontractor.

The depth of the review of the contract documents and market by Société Générale seemed excessive for a project that was 65% pre-leased in a very strong market where they were loaning only 75% of the cost.

Assembling and obtaining the necessary closing documents is always a major effort and most of it, must of necessity, be performed by the Development Officer. The Preliminary Closing Checklist consisted of 78 requests for information or execution. Many of these contained multiple requests for estoppel letters, evidence of various zoning and utility issues and information regarding each tenant and consultant, which increased the effective list to 110 documents.

The 4th Amendment of the Land Sale Agreement was prepared and sent to Waterford as part of the extension of time to close the contract. This extension agreement added significant requirements and obligations intended to ensure that no actions or delays by the hotel would impact receiving a Certificate of Occupancy for the office building. When Société Générale read the amendment, instead of being satisfied with the protections provided they became concerned and pressed for immediate assurances from the city that neither a construction delay nor failure to build the hotel would impact the Certificate of Occupancy. The Development Officer declined to pursue this request at that time because there were several permits outstanding, and it was not prudent to raise these issues while riding on the "Expedite" stamp that was based solely on the hotel tax benefit. When the last of the permits was received it was safe to approach the city and obtain a letter stating that delayed construction by the hotel would not affect the Certificate of Occupancy.

Another request was to obtain approval of the project from the Coastal Commission. The original Visitor Center plan with the 500-room hotel had been approved by the Coastal Commission. Since this project was approved as in Substantial Conformance with the original plan, the city advised that commission approval was not required. Approaching the commission for confirmation, particularly prior to completion, was considered risky as they had a reputation for opening up new discretionary issues. A letter was requested from the city stating that the Coastal Commission approved the project, or alternatively, that approval was not necessary. The city did not consider it a valid request. It was determined from the statutes that when a project within the commission's purview is approved through Substantial Conformance, the Coastal Commission is provided a copy of all relevant data and must respond within 30 days if they have any questions or objections. To avoid opening the question, the Development Officer verified the date the city had sent the information, and then checked the commission files and verified that a copy had been stamped "received." Based on this research, the city finally agreed to write a letter summarizing these events. Based on these last two city letters Société Générale finally closed on March 22, 2000.

Several of their requests became difficult issues to resolve, and were changed to post-closing items. Upon review of the ALTA survey the lender noted the setback between the hotel and the parking structure was 20 feet at one point, ten feet from each to the property line. They reviewed the city ordinances, determined that a rear yard setback must be 20 feet, and requested a letter from the city stating the relationship was acceptable. The city felt the request was unwarranted since a PUD establishes the requirements not the zoning ordinance and, due to the odd shaped lot, it was not clear where the rear yard setback would apply, even if applicable. They declined to write such a letter, saying their approval of the site development plan was full approval as shown. The Development Officer wrote a complete history of the site development plan and its approvals for the bank and its counsel, which was not accepted as sufficient protection. As of the publication of this book, this is still an open issue.

Another issue was the 20-foot-wide fire water line easement surrounding the office building. The "as-built" drawings showed a 4" encroachment into the easement by the soil nailed retaining wall for the parking structure. This encroachment resulted from an incorrect field layout. In addition, they became concerned that the fully approved tendrels for the wall (see Chapter 19) went into the easement well below the fire water line, and yet the easement permitted the city to remove anything within its boundaries to repair the line. Société Générale requested the easement be revised into a three-dimensional easement that remains above the tendrels, and moved 4" toward the office building. Trying to resolve this issue through an obviously overworked city engineering department was not a realistic possibility. Counsel will contact someone in the city attorney's office after receipt of the last of the Certificates of Occupancy to determine the best way to resolve this issue. At publication this remains an open item.

Closing a loan is never fun, and is sometimes downright frustrating. The Development Officer spent untold days trying to resolve the various issues on this loan.

GENERAL DESIGN COMMENTS 13

It is the objective and responsibility of the Development Officer to direct the creation of a building that is attractive, efficient, satisfies the defined Market Study, can be developed in the right time frame, and within the market-driven budget.

Architecture in General

The easiest type of project to develop is the cheapest building possible, and the next easiest (if you have a really fine architect and extensive funding) is a trophy building where image exceeds cost as the primary concern. The more difficult project is to spend just the right amount of money, in just the right places, to create the quality building that fits the defined market niche, so as to lease-up reasonably quickly at market rates. It is important (except in certain "touchy feely" areas) that the quality be spread equally throughout the project.

This chapter will provide an overview of the field of architectural design, objectives of a development project, the limitations imposed by codes and regulations, the use of standards and the control of the process.

Architecture is an interwoven relationship between a client's needs, the architectural response and the use of appropriate materials. Within a given location, site utilization is making the best use of the space and terrain available. In addition to the immediate site, the type of project and its design must fit appropriately within the character and built environment of the community. An office building development is normally significant in size and will exist for a long period of time—thus will have a long-term impact on the community, for better or for worse. A building that fits within the community has a much greater likelihood of being a profitable investment for many years. In other words, one could say that good commercial architecture produces a visually pleasing and functionally efficient structure, solves all of the project's defined restraints and satisfies the market objectives and community impacts within the approved budget.

The most interesting, and sometimes most expensive, feature is the geometry of the building, which is both its shape and degree of articulation. The shape tends to dictate the structure, while the degree of articulation affects the extent and details of the exterior skin. One of the most important issues in controlling project cost is the success in manipulating the geometry and structure simultaneously to accomplish an attractive and desired design with the simplest (and usually the lowest cost) structure. Since a totally plain, rectangular building is rarely appropriate for most markets, it takes a great deal of cooperation between the architect, structural engineer and Development Officer to achieve an optimum result. Materials will be discussed in detail in subsequent chapters.

The trend to very expensive, and sometimes ostentatious, buildings so evident in the late 1970s and the early '80s has lost favor. It is considered more prudent to have an attractive and efficient building, without excesses. Most tenants are looking for value rather than image, with emphasis shifting from appearance to substance and from expression of form to functional efficiency. In addition, most tenants recognize the link between a building that is pleasing and comfortable to work in and staff productivity.

Good modern architecture will always reflect and be driven by the client's functional needs, technological development, availability of new materials and techniques (including space age technology), environmental issues, demographics and serious social concerns. In other words, in each architec-

> An example of how perception of acceptable architecture can vary with individual entities, and with time, is the headquarters we developed for Mercantile Bank in Dallas in the mid-1980s. Named Momentum Place, after their advertising campaign, the building was a distinctive design by Philip Johnson and, in spite its appearance, it was a very economical shell and core. The bank, however, designed their bank hall with a six-floor atrium and the most extensive marble and cherry wood interior I have ever seen.
>
> The bank hall was so ostentatious that when the bank was in trouble late in the decade several banks that were considering a takeover advised that, if successful, they would not occupy the building as it did not fit their corporate identity. When Bank One did acquire Mercantile Bank they moved into the building but declined to use the executive facilities on the upper level of the atrium for the same reason.

tural era the built environment tends to reflect the knowledge and values of society at the time the buildings are created. Some of the ecologically sound social concerns becoming more obvious today are improved energy efficiency, natural light and air, plants to oxygenate the air, sustainability (i.e., recycled and recyclable products, wood from sustainable forests, etc.), healthier buildings and the desire for more personal comfort and control. It is the Development Officer's responsibility to insure that he and his consultants both recognize and implement those trends that are appropriate at any given point in time.

Any completed project will be evaluated on its:

- Identity—the design of the site, geometric shape, façade and entrance lobby

- Efficiency—cost, space utilization efficiency and operating costs

- Employee comfort—temperature, lighting, natural light, amenities and visual comfort, and other Interior Environmental Qualities (IEQ) outlined in Chapter 30 and discussed in various chapters

- Response to social and community objectives

Why is it important for the Development Officer to have an understanding of the many design disciplines, with their extensive details and variables, when great attention is given to selection of a competent design team? Some of the reasons are:

- The designers are undoubtedly competent—but not perfect

- The designers may not always fully understand all of your criteria

- You can formulate more effective questions

- It may be necessary to compromise with and modify the original design criteria to satisfy cost or other constraints

- It facilitates making the difficult decisions with a feeling of confidence

The purpose of this and the following chapters is not to prepare anyone to believe they can tell the design team how to design a building, but to impart certain information that will assist the Development Officer to understand the concepts, to understand the various recommendations received, and to be able to ask good questions of the many professionals involved in the project. There are no absolutes, no one correct answer to any issue, only reasonable judgments under specific circumstances. The design of a building is a constant series of trade-offs. As you evaluate each system and each material selection, you will be making the choice you believe best fits with the market and the pro forma.

Currently, many building sites are being purchased with completed plans that were prepared several years ago when market conditions precluded construction. The cost of reviewing and modifying these plans to comply with current codes, to benefit from current technology and to fit within each company's objectives are usually greater than contemplated. When evaluating such purchases, allow a significant sum for this work unless a thorough review of the drawings can be accomplished during due diligence. The standard AIA architectural contract calls for ownership of the contract documents by the architect. In such cases, without a release by the architect or indemnification from the owner, a significant unplanned cost could occur. In addition, in the due diligence period the remaining term on any entitlements and/or permits should be verified.

Codes and Regulations

Throughout the design process potential solutions are limited by local, state, and federal codes and/or regulations. The ADA is not a code, but a federal law and the impact must be carefully reviewed and understood. Most states have enacted their own handicap codes that generally mirror the ADA, but following those codes is not an automatic exemption from suit under the federal law. For the most part codes are rigid, but under certain circumstances variances are attainable.

Some of the most common national codes and standards used in different parts of the country are listed below. Individual jurisdictions incorporate various releases of current national and other codes, and have their own ordinances with additions and exceptions to these codes. California, in particular, has its own administrative code, and its Title 24 mandate for energy reduction. Some of the latest issues of the major codes of which the author is aware are noted herein, but care should be taken to always use the latest version, except when an earlier version is specified in the local code. Various national codes are prevalent in different areas of the country.

East of the Mississippi River and North of the Mason-Dixon Line

- Basic National Building Code (BOCA)—1996
- Basic National Mechanical Code—1996
- Basic National Plumbing Code—1996

Southeast

- Basic National Building Code (BOCA)—1996
- Standard Building Mechanical and Plumbing Code (SBC)—1994

West of the Mississippi River

- Uniform Building Code (UBC)—1994
- Uniform Mechanical Code—1994
- Uniform Plumbing Code—1994

National

- Federal Americans with Disabilities Act
- Federal OSHA
- National Electric Code—1999

Although office buildings are the safest structures that have ever been created from a life/safety standpoint, there is a constant trend toward adding additional safety features each time a code is revised. Recent code changes, particularly dealing with smoke control have added complexity to the final testing procedures. This complexity, when added to more detailed inspection and testing undertaken by the local jurisdictions, can add several weeks to the time required to obtain a Certificate of Occupancy.

Standards

There are thousands of standards covering almost every material, construction process and testing procedure used in construction. They are prepared by professional societies, testing laboratories and industry trade groups, and are incorporated into the project specifications where applicable. A few of these are listed below.

- American National Standards Institute (ANSI)
- National Electrical Manufactures Association (NEMA)
- National Electrical Contractors Association (NECA) Standard Manual
- American Society for Testing Materials (ASTM)
- Underwriters Laboratory (UL)
- Factory Mutual (FM), where applicable
- American Society of Heating and Air Conditioning Engineers (ASHRAE)
- National Fire Protection Association (NFPA)
- International Code Council (ICC)
- American Society of Civil Engineers (ASCE)
- Sheet Metal and Air Conditioning Contractors National Association (SMACNA)
- Institute of Electrical and Electronic Engineers (IEEE)
- Many other industry and professional group standards

ANSI is the official standards organization for the United States and is the sole U.S. representative member of the International Organization for Standardization (ISO), and is the recognized U.S. accrediting body for standards development and independent certification.

CAD and Technology

The extensive use today of highly efficient CAD systems has significantly changed and improved the design process. These systems are now being used by some firms from the conceptual design through the "as built" drawings at project completion. The new CAD systems speed the work in all design phases by improving coordination between the architect, consultants, contractor and subcontractors by simplifying design changes. Coordination drawings can now be sent by e-mail or through a web site from one office to another that has a complementary CAD system and a plotter.

The ease of transmitting the drawings, the ability to use 3-D images and modify materials and shapes all make it easier for the owner and architect to communicate on design proposals. **No development office should be without a compatible CAD system and, at the very least, a small 11" by 17" plotter.** An alternative to a plotter would be to have an arrangement with a printer wherein the desired plans could be e-mailed to them, with the prints delivered to you the same day.

Web site based project management on the Internet is now becoming the primary practical way to manage development projects from initial design through final closeout. Controlled by proper security, the entire team can communicate, in real time when appropriate, and effectively share drawings, documents and other data. In addition to the speed of transmission, accuracy is improved as each party is viewing the same information. Web cameras located strategically at the job site during construction provide a current photographic status to all team members. A few of the current web-based project management systems in use for development project management are Bid.com, Prolog, Cephren, BuildNet, Struxicon and Buzzsaw.

While presently used for general communication and to communicate with subcontractors during the bidding period, the industry is just beginning to learn how to utilize this new phenomenon. Simulation of new products and systems directly from manufacturers and testing them for applicability are in the early stages of experimentation and may soon become a major tool.

The author believes that in the near future major portions of the contract documents will be routinely contracted out to specialists, possibly the entire working drawings, even to firms in other parts of the world. (At present, shop drawing detailing for some contractors and material suppliers is being performed overseas.) Contract documents will also be transmitted from the web site directly to the design computers of major fabricators and manufacturers for use in the development of their shop and/or production drawings. These procedures will enhance the coordination and final checking of the contract documents.

In the not too distant future buildings will be almost completely designed by computers, and their operational features such as environmental systems and acoustical values will be completely modeled prior to construction, much like modern airplane design today.

Contract Documents

The Working Drawings (frequently called the Plans) and Specifications, when combined with the General Conditions and Supplementary Conditions, are collectively called the Contract Documents.

The working drawings depict the size, shape, organization and special details of the various elements of the building, and show their relationship and/or attachment to other building elements, permitting the Development Officer to visually understand the information presented.

The specifications, on the other hand, are filled with references to technical standards and to various manufacturer's model or reference numbers, usually with the notation ". . . or approved equal." It is very difficult for the Development Officer to understand the proposed end result by merely reading the specifications. The Development Officer must request the architects and engineers to explain and/or demonstrate clearly the quality of materials, installation and testing specified for each major item of material and equipment. Wherever exposed visual elements are specified, the Development Officer should insist on seeing samples or visual mockups, as discussed in various chapters of this text.

The General Conditions and Supplementary Conditions cover the design and construction responsibilities in general, as opposed to the item-specific descriptions in the specifications. They cover all business issues, and are considered an extension of the architectural and construction contracts.

There has been significant standardization within the industry in the preparation of the contract documents, and it is very important for the Development Officer to become familiar with them in order to rapidly find information you require.

- Drawings are organized in accordance with the ConDoc index sponsored by the AIA.

- Specification sections are organized in accordance with the master format sponsored by the Construction Specifications Institute (CSI).

- A relatively recent procedure, rapidly becoming an industry standard, utilizes a ConDoc notation system to tie the notes on drawing details directly to the appropriate specification section.

The Drawing Numbering System and the Masterspec Consolidated Table of Contents for the specifications, along with other more detailed documents, are available from the American Institute of Architects. (See Appendix A.)

Not only have the documents been standardized, but the increased use of factory-produced standardized parts will facilitate off-site construction with the benefits of minimizing on-site labor, reducing construction time and cost, and greatly improving quality control through factory inspection under controlled conditions.

Certification

While specifying a national standard for a given product provides a degree of confidence in the selection, there are still many issues relative to the ability of various alternative products to achieve the required results.

A recent trend intended to establish greater confidence in adherence to the specified standards is the certification of building products and components. This certification process was originally started at the federal government's instigation, primarily as an efficient way to ensure regulatory compliance in areas involving health and safety issues. A certification "mark" represents an approved program establishing compliance to a specified standard through testing, validating and auditing procedures.

Some manufacturers provide a certification "mark" based upon self-certification procedures, but most use trade industry or independent laboratories for third-party certification. Most of the standards groups listed provide certification. It is interesting to note that Underwriters Laboratory (UL), which has a long history of approving UL "listing marks" (indicating that a product meets specific safety requirements for fire, electric shock and casualty hazards), now offers a certification "mark" to certify compliance with a specific performance standard or condition.

Some additional testing laboratories providing third-party certification are Air-Conditioning & Refrigeration Institute (ARI), Air Movement & Control Association International (AMCA), American Architectural Manufacturers Association (AAMA), Builders Hardware Manufacturers Association (BHMA), Certified Ballast Manufacturers (CBM), International Association of Plumbing and Mechanical Officials (IAPMO), Intretek Testing Services (ITS) and NSF International (NSF).

Development Officer Issues

Several procedures the author believes important for the Development Officer to keep in mind in order to be most effective during this important and complex design period are:

- Prepare a detailed personal checklist prior to each meeting, listing all of the potential alternative methods, systems and materials likely to be discussed, since each meeting must have known specific objectives. This type of memory jogger permits intelligent questions that are essential to assist you in learning and understanding the reasons behind the various recommendations of the consultants, as well as to ensure that important issues are not overlooked.

- When discussing materials, finishes or any other visual issues, insist on seeing physical samples rather than viewing catalogues or listening to verbal descriptions, and insist on seeing completed installations in lieu of samples, wherever possible. (The author once bought a suit from a small sample and looked like a racetrack tout.)

- Ensure that the architects and engineers, as well as the Property Management specialists involved, explain and/or demonstrate the quality of materials, equipment and installation called for in the contract documents that is not clear from your own experience.

- Take full advantage of the experience and knowledge of the in-house construction managers when evaluating and selecting contractors and on decisions through the design period where their assistance will be invaluable in materials, design details and constructability.

- When dealing with operating issues, or considering varying finish materials and mechanical and electrical systems, be certain to involve asset managers, property managers and operating engineers, as they have a wealth of information as to how well certain equipment operates and its dependability, and how well various material finishes can be maintained and hold up in use.

- While it is important to utilize the knowledge of many individuals within the organization and outside of it, it is essential that all information that flows to and from the designers flows through the Development Officer. No matter how good or well-meaning the transmission of information may be, bypassing a single point of control can create problems or cause omissions.

EL CAMINO REAL

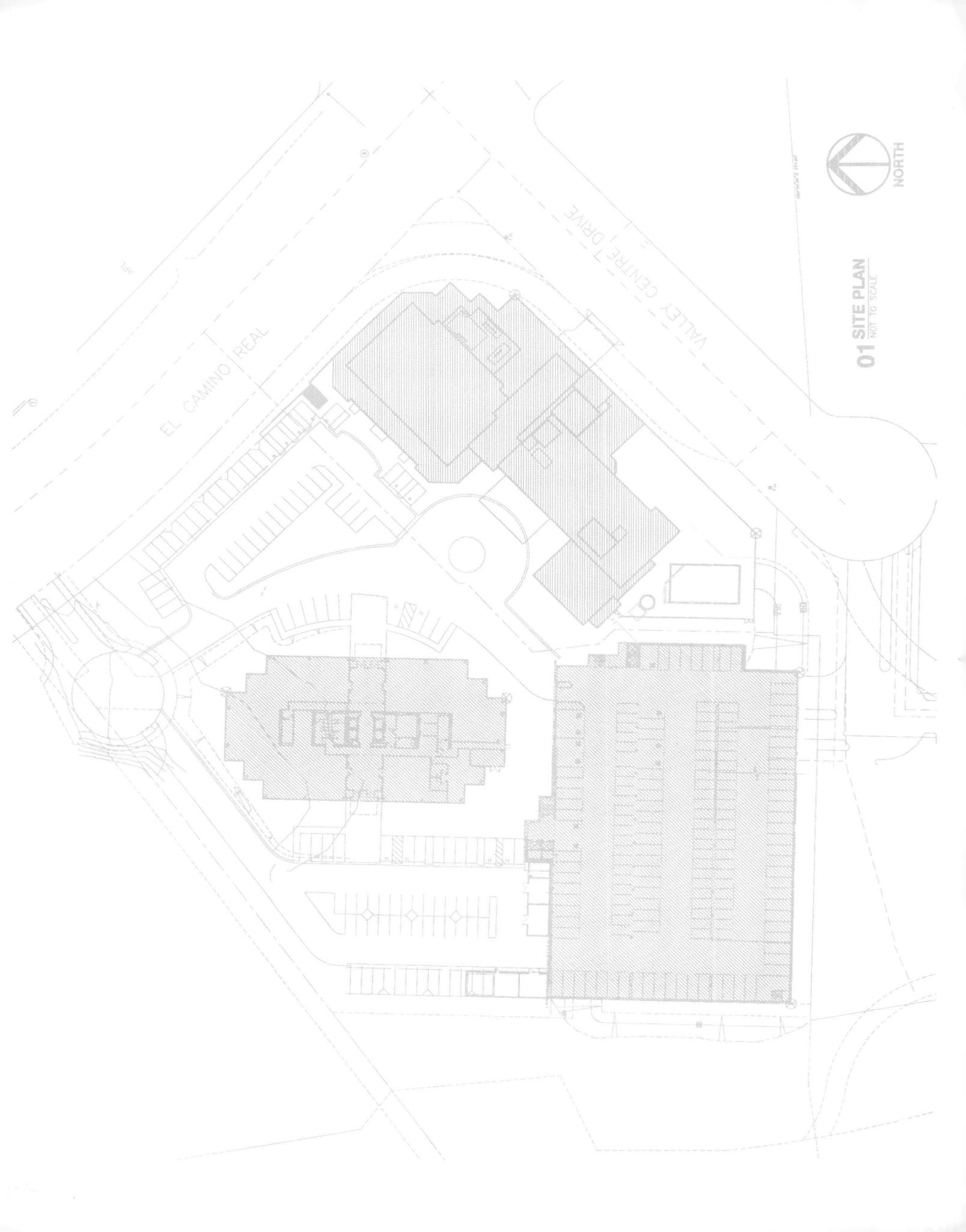

VALLEY CENTRE DRIVE

NORTH

01 SITE PLAN
NOT TO SCALE

DESIGN PROCESS

14

This chapter will cover the selection of the architect and the engineering consultants, the architect's contract, criteria necessary to define the project's requirements and limitations as determined from the feasibility analyses, the developer's objectives, a design overview, baseline budgeting, a description of the various phases of the work performed by the architect and the engineers, building permits and value engineering.

The Development Officer's first step is to select the key members of the design team and then communicate effectively to them the criteria and objectives that have been determined to this point.

Architect Selection

The selection of the architect can range from a currently exciting design architect to a technically competent one with more modest design capabilities that may be relatively local. Where practical, a local architect will usually be selected whose reputation and design flair fits with the company's and the project's objectives, and who has an acceptable working drawing capability, and successful experience working as part of the team with developers and negotiated general contractors. For most projects, working drawing skill is as important as design flair, as it impacts the ultimate building efficiency, long-term quality and cost control, as well as minimizing change order problems during the construction period.

The selection of the appropriate architect is a very important judgment in this process. Among the key issues to evaluate in this selection are:

- Design quality and style of the architect's work in relation to the objectives of the project.
- Experience with the type, size and design objectives of the project.
- Staff size and depth in relation to the size of the project, and their current workload.
- Verification that the proposed partner in charge, lead designer and project manager (or production manager) are experienced in projects of the type, size and scope of the intended project—particularly note their experience on their projects which you have considered in your evaluation. This is particularly important in this era where until recently few if any office buildings have been developed in the last decade.
- Location in, or experience in, the jurisdiction of the project can facilitate entitlement and permit processing procedures through knowledge of key regulators and reviewers.
- Location in relation to the Development Officer's office—convenience of interface.
- Experience with negotiated general construction contracts with GMPs and issuance of partial design packages to certain lead trades.
- Current technical level in CAD systems and use of Internet web sites for communication, compatibility with developer's CAD system and plotters.
- Procedures for quality control.
- Assess degree to which the firm tries to stay current with the latest trends in materials, techniques, use of sustainable and recycled products, and understanding of other political and social issues.

Recommendations of, and references on, architects and their skills and deficiencies can usually be obtained from qualified general contractors, subcontractors, respected brokers and building owners. From a short list of prospective architects, visit several recent projects to evaluate the design results against the stated objectives for each project.

In interview meetings try to verify the availability of current personnel for each of the projects presented to illustrate the firm's capabilities. If possible, have the persons proposed for your project handle the discussion of their responsibilities for each project presented. Too often, the senior principal does all of the presenting and then you never see him/her during the design process. Endeavor to evaluate the chemistry between key project members and yourself.

Whenever it is necessary to include your senior management, a lead tenant or a build-to-suit client in the architect selection, first reduce the list to no more than three candidates, all of whom you believe can properly achieve the project objectives. The interviews, including the question period, should be between one and two hours.

There are three basic methods employed in the selection of an architectural firm:

- Interview the firms, check all references, make a selection, and then negotiate a fee. When using this approach, it is wise to have a good handle as to what design fee is reasonable for the specified services for this type of project.

- During the interviews, discuss the proposed full service fees for the agreed upon services, the consultants they propose to include (such as elevator, roofing, curtain wall, parking, acoustical, and landscape) in addition to the standard structural, mechanical and electrical engineers, and the scope of work proposed for each consultant. Then select the architect with full consideration for their references and proposed fees, but with some final fee negotiation, as applicable.

- Proceed as above; select several firms you would be satisfied with, resolve the scope of services, and then competitively bid the fees.

The author prefers the second approach above, and definitely does not feel comfortable with the competitive bidding of the fees. There is the distinct possibility of buying the work too cheaply, and perhaps not ending up with the better architect.

One selection method not covered above is the design contest. The author personally believes this is the worst selection process because your decision is based upon an artwork from a designer who almost assuredly does not fully understand all of your criteria and objectives. In the contest time frame, it is difficult to address the many functional issues that will surface later, and accurate cost estimates are difficult to achieve.

The use of joint ventures of architectural firms is frequently prudent if done for the right reasons. Venturing because you couldn't decide which one to select, or because of internal disagreement, is the wrong approach to take. Bear in mind that there will always be some friction between venture firms, particularly if their skills overlap. There are times when it is appropriate because one firm has the design skills and/or reputation along with a small or weak production staff while the other firm can provide quality working drawings and construction administration. Another reason may be that the firm you prefer is located in a distant city and the regulatory or political climate in your site's locale seems to require a local architect. In that circumstance a venture with a well-connected local architect may be prudent.

If you do select two firms to joint venture, try to ensure that they have the personnel and company philosophies that will mesh well together. Let them understand the reasons that you selected each and then let them work out the leadership, the division of work and the fee split and submit their agreement to you. Query each separately to verify they are mutually satisfied—any problems that are evident should be corrected immediately or terminate the arrangement. If the two firms cannot work together harmoniously the project will be fraught with problems. There are occurrences where a selected architect suggests a specific venture partner to support areas where they believe they need greater expertise—these usually work well.

When using a negotiated general construction contractor, the contractor should also be retained at this point so that they may participate with the design team and provide essential cost, material and

> Frequently a joint venture architectural team is logical and successful in its performance. When we developed Momentum Place in Dallas, we and the bank jointly selected Philip Johnson as the design architect. Because the building was in Dallas and Philip in New York, and we did not believe Philip had a sufficiently large staff for the contract documents, we added HKS Architects to the venture. HKS had a proven record of producing quality contract documents in a timely manner.
>
> The marriage was successful, as each firm was fully cooperative and constructive, and the project went smoothly from the standpoints of schedule, cost control, quality of contract documents and construction.

schedule data and alternatives as the design progresses. (See Chapter 33.)

Engineering Consultant Selection

The primary engineering consultants—structural, mechanical and electrical—will be selected by the same criteria as used for the architect. Caution is recommended when using an architect's in-house engineers, as the Development Officer may lose control of important and timely transfer of information and opinions. With independent consulting engineers, selection should be made jointly with the architect—they must be able to work cooperatively together—but the engineer must understand that the owner wants undiluted opinions and analysis on all issues. Usually the major engineers are under contract to the architect for administrative purposes. Specialty engineers or consultants can be included in the architect's contract or contracted for separately, as desired.

It is almost as important to evaluate the perceived quality of the primary consulting engineers relative to your project as the architect. In addition to learning of their work in projects similar to yours, it is important to determine the creativity of the structural engineer in finding unusual solutions where required, as well as the quality of their working drawings. It is wise to clarify the quality of software programs the mechanical engineer uses to evaluate energy consumption alternatives for a proposed project, as there are many first cost/operating decisions to be made that affect the building envelope as well as the HVAC system. It is also important to determine their interest and experience in recycling and sustainability.

Many developers, such as the author, frequently prefer to bid design-build contracts for the mechanical, electrical and plumbing trades based upon design development documents prepared by the engineers. The mechanical and electrical engineers would normally prepare the design criteria, select major systems, locate and size the major equipment and distribution, and prepare design development drawings and a specification. A review of the contractor-prepared final engineering documents and a few site visits should be included. The design fees for these engineering services would be about 50% of a full service design. Where the general contractor or the owner has a quality MEP coordination capability, it is frequently advantageous to bid this work at the end of schematic design based upon a thorough design criteria and outline specification.

It is often prudent to use specialty design consultants who have important expertise at which the architect is less skilled. Frequently these services are included under the architect's contract—some of these are elevator, roofing, curtain wall, parking, acoustical and landscape design. All of these consultants provide total design services from schematic design to field supervision, where desired. Most often it is sufficient to use these consultants only during the schematic design and/or design development phases, with the architect being fully capable of providing all necessary remaining services through the working drawing and field supervision phases within the standard services covered in their agreement. When field supervision by these consultants is deemed necessary it can be performed on a per diem or hourly basis.

Architect's Contract

Design fees in the year 2001 for a low- to mid-rise office building, including structural, mechanical and electrical engineering would currently run from $2.50 to $4.00 per gsf, exclusive of specialty consultants, depending on the geographical location, quality, type and scope of the project. Of that, structural would be 35 to 40¢/gsf (but up to 55 or 60¢/gsf in seismic zones), and mechanical and electrical would be 40 to 50¢/gsf, with an additional 10 to 15¢/gsf for high-rise due to the more extensive life safety design. An open, free-standing parking structure would range from 85 to 90¢/gsf, and an enclosed or underground structure might run $1.25 to $1.50 per gsf. The structural fee for a parking structure would be about 30 to 35¢/gsf. The mechanical and electrical fee would be in the range of 5 to 7¢/gsf for a fully open structure, and probably 15¢/gsf for a mechanically ventilated garage. When the architect agrees to too low a fee, it may mean he has negotiated the engineer's fees down to the point where they are tempted to provide minimum analysis and creativity.

Each development company should have its own standard form of contract. For those who do not, the best source are the various contract forms of the Standard Agreement Between Owner and Architect, available from the American Institute of Architects (See Appendix A.) The author considers it important to modify these forms to include business issues deemed necessary to each development company. When using a standard contract form as a base, it is preferable to handle the business points directly, using counsel only for legal and liability issues. Excessive use of counsel increases cost without commensurate benefit.

Many issues must be considered in reaching a detailed understanding of the architect's obligations and responsibilities, and a clarification of business issues the author considers important to any developer. A checklist of the issues follows.

- Methods of payment
  - Cost per square foot—define square foot—usually the most appropriate
  - Fixed sum
  - Percent of construction cost—must define construction cost—not as good as the square foot approach
  - Hourly rate times multiple—multiples vary—use only for studies
- Services to be included under the architect's contract
  - Consultants—mechanical, electrical, structural, and landscape. Frequently, also vertical transportation, special lighting, and fire protection are included.
  - Zoning review and application
  - All necessary public hearings and presentations
  - Adaptations for major tenant—if not after significant completion of working drawings
  - Working design models and sketches
  - Permit applications
  - Lender changes
  - Fire insurance carrier requirements (when provided early in the process)
  - Separate bid packages, or fast track issues, if required
  - Telephone expense
  - Copying expense
  - Progress printing expense
  - Provide contractor with reproducibles of all drawings and specifications for reproduction of bid documents
  - Site observation—amount varies with project size
  - Shop drawings, samples, etc.
  - Job clarifications
  - Process change orders
  - Review monthly payments
  - Provide certifications required by lender
  - Final inspection and punch lists

- Certificate of Completion
- As-built drawings
- Post construction services—corrections, defects—a limit on hours is appropriate

• Professional errors and omissions and other insurance required
- Amount to be approved
- Errors and omissions provides more protection if it is per project coverage

• Services normally not included
- Geotechnical evaluation
- Soils testing
- Surveys
- Civil engineering— if major
- Testing laboratories
- Testing services
- Marketing models
- Renderings
- Approved travel outside metropolitan area
- Bid set printing
- Fees for permits, etc.
- Additions to scope—define computation of additional fee
- Resist any markups on direct costs

• Important business changes to AIA form
- Developer *must* own the contract documents
- Contract assignable to lenders
- Contract assignable to party to whom project is conveyed
- Architect cannot assign contract
- Architect can be terminated at any time—compensation limited to work performed
- Omit AIA provision that permits the architect the right to ask for any special services and, if owner does not provide them, contract directly for them

- Prefer individual project insurance coverage to aggregate coverage
- Liability and Workman's Comp insurance acceptable to your program
- Waivers of Subrogation
- Indemnification agreement

Design Process Initiation

The design process is initiated by the Development Officer providing the design team with the Project Design Criteria from the Feasibility Analysis discussed in Chapters 3, 4 and 5 plus additional preferences as to permissible budget, general quality of materials, preferred modules, retail and amenity requirements, schedule, insurance carrier requirements and known political and regulatory issues.

It should also be clearly stated whether the building is developed for long-term investment or sale, and whether emphasis should be placed primarily on construction cost, operating costs or on owning and operating cost evaluation. An important factor to consider relative to evaluating systems that affect operating costs is whether the leases will be gross, i.e., including utilities, or whether utilities will be billed separately.

At this point the Development Officer should clearly state any objectives regarding social and political issues such as healthier buildings, energy consumption, use of recycled materials, recycling during construction, other sustainability issues, general environmental concerns and desired compatibility with the local community. Review Appendix C, "How Green Is My Building," for more detailed discussion on most of these issues.

Always remember the more thoroughly the development team understands all of your objectives, the more effective they can be in accomplishing them.

The Project Design Criteria mentioned above is repeated here from Chapters 3, 4 and 5 for convenience.

PROJECT DESIGN CRITERIA

Allowable construction cost based upon attainable rental rates

Size and type of most likely tenants

Appropriate floor sizes and bay depths

Approximate building size

The desired quality of the building to meet competition

Ecological sensitivity of the community and prospective tenants

Trend in rentable square feet per person

Design building population densities

Design requirements for floor loads, ceiling heights and electrical loads

Definitions of rentable area

Definition of shell and core construction vs. Tenant Improvements

Projected tenant construction allowance and other concessions

Acceptable methods of charging for electricity

Tenant amenities required on-site

Desired parking ratios, with code maximum/ minimum

Zoning classification

Permitted uses

Maximum building area density in FAR (floor area ratio), height and bulk

Site coverage

Setbacks—ground and upper levels

Separations between buildings

Traffic flow restrictions and requirements

Minimum/maximum parking ratios, distance from parking to office

Minimum required landscape coverage

Exiting and dead-end corridor requirements

Service dock requirements

Special use limitations

Off-site mitigations and requirements

Special study costs

Development, entitlement and permit fees

Exactions and impact fees

Utility and water management information

Abnormal soil, grading or other site costs

Easements, and encumbrances

Deed restrictions

Discretionary review process and design review boards

Real estate taxes

Owners associations

Time, costs and strategies to mitigate the defined political, regulatory and environmental issues

Other relevant factors and costs

If all of the relevant information is not acquired during the Feasibility Analysis, the architect and civil engineer should assist in obtaining the remainder at the earliest possible time. Where there is a build-to-suit project, or a major prelease tenant, any special requirements of their tenancy must be included.

The allowable construction cost has been approximately determined from a preliminary pro forma. Whether the project is intended for a long-term investment or early sale can clarify the importance of long-term cost/benefit analyses.

Design Overview

Early in the process the design, utility and leasability of the building is determined as the basic design scheme is defined. The key elements of the aesthetics that most impact the leasing are listed below. Participation of the leasing, marketing and interior design personnel is important in making these evaluations at this stage.

- Outside landscape and lower level curb appeal
- Façade material and amount of exterior glass
- Lobby
- Floor size, bay depth module
- Efficiency of space layout
- Elevator quality and cab appearance
- Floor elevator lobbies
- Toilet room layout and quality

The early design period is the time in which the most effective cost control can be initiated as discussed later in this chapter. Value engineering is frequently thought of as a process occurring toward the end of the design when excessive costs are identified, however, in a properly planned project it occurs from beginning to end as discussed in a later paragraph in this chapter. Cost control is focused on (a) the most cost efficient structural system feasible, in keeping with desired design solutions, (b) efficient space utilization—i.e. the highest possible ratio of useable space to gross building area, (c) a thorough in-depth review of the mechanical, electrical and plumbing systems for compliance with owning/operating requirements, and (d) selecting all materials, particularly the building skin, and equipment in keeping with the desired quality and the budget. A quality contractor, with good conceptual estimating skills, is invaluable in providing good cost estimates and alternative solutions as design proceeds. Note that in (b) above, some people would use rentable instead of useable area to define efficiency, but wasted leasable areas such as oversized toilet rooms, janitor's closets, storage areas, and useless nooks in the core or in odd-shaped perimeter space are obvious to many knowledgeable users, who always check the ratio of the useable area to the rentable area.

As we discuss various design issues in the following chapters devoted to the different elements of design, we must recognize this text is specifically directed toward the development of speculative multi-tenant office buildings. The overriding issue throughout the design process is to make reasonable decisions for effectively serving a generic but specifically unknown tenancy, both initially and over time. For this reason, when faced with a range of materials, designs, systems or process selections, the choice will not necessarily be that which is better, but that which best satisfies the previously-defined market at a cost that permits the building to achieve an acceptable return from the unknown tenants.

Upgraded, or presumably more desirable, features must be saleable to tenants through an appropriate rental rate in order to recapture the cost.

As an example, in a market where the tenant pays electrical energy costs, a more expensive and efficient HVAC system might seem a logical choice, but if the target tenants will not give credit to the realization of operating savings, the extra expenditure will not provide an acceptable return.

While frequently extreme differences in quality exist between the various choices of materials, systems or processes, it is important to remember that each one of those choices is a proper selection for application to some building under some set of market and economic guidelines.

A build-to-suit building encompasses each one of the evaluative steps, issues and choices of a speculative building. The differences lie in the decision-making process. The tenant has known objectives and limitations against which each choice or decision may be tested. Therefore, more extensive return on investment analyses are performed as the tenant may well pay substantial initial premiums for long-term cost benefits or an improved working environment for its employees—potentially resulting in reduced turnover and/or absenteeism that might not be justified in a speculative building. One caveat when addressing a build-to-suit project is that while it is obviously necessary to accomplish all of the tenant's specific requirements, to the extent they can be accomplished by a building that could be successfully converted in the future to an efficient multi-tenant building, the long-term value of the real estate is enhanced.

The design of a building with a major prelease tenant creates issues somewhere between a speculative and a build-to-suit building. In this instance the primary issue is to accomplish as many of the objectives and desires of the major tenant as possible while keeping costs in line so the speculative space can be leased at market rates without diluting the overall return.

As we go through the design process, it is essential for the Development Officer to recognize that everything is interrelated—no decisions are made in a vacuum. In addition to cost implications, each choice or decision that is made will frequently require, prevent or modify another.

Design Phases

The phases into which the architectural contract is divided, and generally performed are outlined in the following paragraphs.

Schematic Design Phase

This phase is to define the scope and basic design of the project, defining all of the major architectural and structural features of the building, as well as basic assumptions regarding the environmental systems, sufficient for owner, lead tenant, and urban design approvals, and to prepare marketing information. The first portion of this phase is Site Planning and Conceptual Design, discussed in Chapter 15. It is important at this stage to have a careful analysis of the leasing efficiency of the proposed floor plan as discussed in detail in Chapter 16. There is only sufficient engineering accomplished during the schematic design to ensure that the proposed design can be accomplished. It generally involves about 10–15% of the overall design effort. This phase must be very carefully thought out to avoid backtracking and delays in later phases.

When a project is built-to-suit or has a pre-leased lead tenant who has contractual design approval rights, the developer should endeavor to limit those rights to issues which "... are not a natural derivation of the approved schematic design."

Toward the end of this phase it is important to address the Interior Environmental Quality issues, as discussed in detail in Chapter 30 and various other chapters, and prepare various energy consumption analyses to assist in the evaluation in the many first cost vs. operating cost decisions that must be made. The mechanical engineer should utilize an established comprehensive software program for these analyses. This data, when analyzed in conjunction with the ability to recover higher first costs in the marketplace and the developer's attitude toward social issues and energy consumption, will assist in making these decisions.

Design Development Phase

This phase, also called the preliminary design phase, involves sufficient engineering, architectural analysis and equipment definitions to indicate how the building is to be built, the quality of the components, and selection of the basic structural, mechanical, elevator and electrical systems. This phase usually involves 15–20% of the overall design effort.

There are many circumstances where regulatory requirements or good engineering judgments suggest sun shadow studies and wind tests for both structural and pedestrian level information at this stage of the design. Ground level wind currents

---

We had an interesting example of a build-to-suit project that was modified into a design creating long-term real estate value when we were asked to joint venture and develop a 400,000 square foot office building for IBM in Texas. IBM would lease the entire facility for ten years, with several five-year extension options.

This was a fast track project in which IBM had prepared layouts of the proposed building they wished to have developed. The location of the entrances, elevators and the initially-proposed floor layouts were such that this building would never be adaptable to anything but a single-user facility.

In spite of their protestations that this IBM division would use the facility for decades, we evaluated several different planning alternatives and came up with a scheme that fully satisfied the IBM operations, and yet was completely adaptable to a future multi-tenant building.

These changes to the design paid off handsomely for both ourselves and IBM, as the requirement for this facility was eliminated in less than seven years and, when it was necessary to put it on the market, it proved to be an economically sound investment.

should be replicated if there is reason to believe that unusual currents may be caused by the design. It would have been conducted earlier if required by an EIR or local planning review body. It is frequently advisable to have a wind tunnel test for tall buildings, usually considered as buildings in excess of 20 stories, to verify structural design conditions. These wind tunnel tests should include the building model and the surrounding buildings or terrain that might affect the direction and/or velocity of the wind.

Contract Documents Phase

This phase is when the working drawings and specifications are prepared, wherein the entire project is detailed in a way to describe to each trade how the building is to be built. It is in this phase that mockups of special details, and laboratory testing of components such as window wall sections are performed. This work involves about 35–45% of the overall design effort. The specifications supplement the working drawings and specify material selection, finishes, performance requirements, testing and any other information required to ensure that the products used and the installation methods follow the design intent.

It should be noted here that with a negotiated general contractor, a project is frequently fast tracked by starting construction when the working drawings are in the range of 40–65% completed. Site work, excavation, and subsurface construction can be started, and frequently long-lead-time material such as steel, elevators and curtain wall can be ordered. Most jurisdictions will issue a site or excavation permit to allow this fast tracking.

Bid and Negotiation Phase

The bid and negotiation phase can involve 5% of the design effort whether it is a conventionally bid project, or a series of bids by various trades throughout a GMP project. There are frequently many questions asked, alternatives submitted and evaluated, and clarifications issued.

Construction Administration Phase

Construction administration by the architect and engineers involves review and approval of shop drawings, technical brochures and catalogues, inspecting (contracts say "observation" for the architect's legal protection) the work for conformance with the contract documents, supplemental design details, processing change orders and work clarifications, recommending approval of payment requests, and inspection for the initial occupancy permits, final certification of completion and punch lists. This phase can involve from 20–30% of the overall design effort.

Merger of Phases by Developers

The phases of architectural work discussed above define the way a normal architectural contract is divided and describe the various phases through which work progresses. Historically, and a recommended procedure for one-time builders, a formal submission of the design work is made to the owner at the end of each design phase. At that time an estimate is made and, either changes will be requested by the owner based upon cost or design issues, or a formal notification is given by the owner to proceed to the next phase.

Experienced developers, who normally retain a general contractor as part of the development team, are frequently as concerned with time as they are with cost. In such cases it is normal to "roll" through the design phases in a way that best satisfies the desired progress of the project. It is not at all uncommon for a project to simultaneously have (a) the building lobby, elevator cabs and landscaping in either the schematic design or design development phase, (b) the majority of the shell and core work in the working drawing phase and (c) the grading and foundations under construction and the steel ordered from the mill. It is not uncommon, when time is essential, for the Notice To Proceed to be issued to the general contractor when the working drawings are 40% to 65% complete, sometimes even sooner.

These procedures are feasible because an experienced team knows when it is appropriate to make the various decisions, and a constant budget estimating and the value engineering process can satisfactorily control costs. Value engineering is discussed below and the Notice To Proceed is discussed in Chapter 35.

Building Permits

The contractor normally submits the contract documents to the regulatory authority for the plan check, but the process is a review of the architect's work product, and it is the architect who must answer questions and/or make any necessary changes to obtain approval.

It is quite common, where time is important, to break the documents into several different submittals—such as grading, foundations and basement construction, structural and the remainder of the documents. This permits construction to commence while the contract documents are being completed. In many jurisdictions a grading permit—which includes complete site grading, drainage, survey, easements, streets, utilities and minimal landscaping—is necessary before any building permit can be approved. It is not unusual that individual retaining wall permits, submitted with all details and calculations, must be approved prior to the start of grading.

To maintain a reasonable accuracy of the project schedule, it is essential early in the project to ascertain both the procedures followed by the approving jurisdiction and the current construction activity in the area. These combined factors will determine the most likely time period that must be allowed to obtain the necessary permits. The author has been involved with 50-story buildings that received completed plan-checks in less than four weeks and very small projects that have required three to four months.

Note that building permits, like development permits discussed in Chapter 7, can be rescinded under certain circumstances prior to vesting. Such circumstances can be a public referendum, new environmental information, or some other factor. Vesting usually is initiated by constructing some element that will become a permanent part of the improvement.

Cost Estimating, Value Engineering and Baseline Budgeting

Cost is a critical controlling factor in any development project. A procedure that is common with one-time builders and governmental agencies is, as discussed earlier, controlling costs by:

- Making a cost estimate at the end of each design phase, and then making design modifications as necessary to reduce costs that appear to be over the budget.

Be aware that building permits are still at some level of risk until they are vested. Vesting normally means the start of construction, as defined by the local jurisdiction

We were rushing to start a high-rise development in San Francisco for Crocker Bank, discussed previously, before an anti-high-rise initiative that was on the ballot was voted upon. We had received our foundation permits less than two weeks prior to election day, and we believed the initiative had a high likelihood of passing.

The site was almost completely covered with small older buildings and the normal procedure would have been to demolish the buildings and clear the site prior to commencing any construction. A review of the ordinances with our attorneys determined that demolition and site clearance would not vest our permits, however, the installation of permanent sheet piling installed to protect our subsurface construction would be considered as vesting. Many of my peers thought it strange that we would proceed in such an abnormal manner as to drive piling prior to demolition, and I took some ribbing until it was explained. We had reached the point where our attorneys were satisfied that we would have achieved vesting by election day, but the effort proved unnecessary, as the proposition failed. The precaution, however, was essential.

- Bidding the project on a lump-sum basis upon completion of the contract documents.

- If there are significant cost overruns at this point, usually discussions are entered into with the two or three low bidders, and value engineering is applied to identify sufficient changes to reach a contract amount that falls within the budget.

There are two weaknesses in this approach. First, the interim estimates are either made by the design team, who are notoriously poor estimators, or by contractors who are asked to make gratuitous estimates in return for being included on the bidders list. Neither of these approaches will normally have qualified "conceptual" estimators putting forth sufficient effort to provide an accurate cost projection.

(A "hard bid" estimator is one who makes a detailed takeoff of every item shown on the drawings or described in the specifications and estimates its price. A "conceptual" estimator is one who can visualize a building being constructed and estimate the various system elements that comprise the total cost from very preliminary information or drawings. Good conceptual estimators are few and far between.)

Secondly, when value engineering is utilized after the bids are received, it normally results in taking out the easiest savings in a way that does not require much rework of the drawings—such as removing finishes or specifying less expensive equipment. This tends to produce a product in which the quality is not consistent throughout, and some very desirable features may be lost. An example of this is where a significant cost reduction could result from a change of the building shape, but this might require major changes to and redrawing of the structural system and a major portion of the architectural details. A change such as that might have been the best solution if caught at the right time, but is rarely seriously considered this late in the project, so easier solutions are sought.

In what is considered the superior method for successful project development, we always recommend that the general contractor be selected simultaneously with the architect (selection process discussed in Chapter 33) to provide cost estimating, scheduling and knowledgeable information on various materials availability and relative costs to the design team.

The first issue for the general contractor to address is to review the owner's design criteria and evaluate the developer's desired quality and assumed cost of construction, in relation to the market driven breakpoint between the shell and core and the Tenant Improvements. After discussions between the Development Officer, architect and contractor regarding project scope and design, a target budget cost is set for the shell and core.

The general contractor, based on a full understanding of the objectives and further discussion with the architect, breaks the total square foot cost down by trade and/or function to create a baseline budget that is used by the development team to control the project cost from beginning to end.

In submitting the baseline budget, a good conceptual estimator will descriptively advise the limitations incorporated, such as skin materials, structural assumptions or type of HVAC system, necessary to meet the budget. Unique areas such as building lobbies and elevator cabs, for which there is little information at an early stage, are carried as allowances the team feels are reasonable, to be designed against when appropriate.

As the design proceeds, the conceptual estimator monitors the impact on cost of each system and all materials and equipment selected. As each system is developed, value engineering takes place, not only to ensure that the cost is in line with the baseline budget, but to guide the Development Officer as to whether the details and materials are consistent with the desired end product. If, after an initial value engineering is completed, the cost for a system appears to be over the baseline, a decision is made to further reduce the cost of that system, or conversely, to retain that quality of that system and reduce the cost of another. In this manner there is a continuous cost monitoring process that flows in parallel with the design process.

When this effort is properly performed, there should be no surprises at the time of the GMP and Notice to Proceed, and the project quality should be spread through the building in the manner desired.

Material Selection in General

There are extreme ranges of products for every material requirement in the building. It is important to remember that each one has an appropriate function in some building in some market. Each one has a cost and certain benefits, as well as its specific strengths and weaknesses. Some may impact operating costs, but others will not.

It is necessary for the Development Officer to evaluate the recommended materials that appear reasonable to the intended purpose and select those that are appropriate to the project's market and will provide an acceptable return.

CASE STUDY

Selection of the architectural firm came in two distinct steps. At the time Pardee decided to entertain bids on the proposed site the first two buildings in Del Mar, called Executive Center Del Mar, were in the final stages of construction on the adjoining site. That first site had been purchased along with the completed design drawings for the two office buildings. The original architect for the buildings was initially retained to evaluate modifications resulting from code changes since the contract documents were originally completed, as well as structural and interior changes necessary for the quality property Prentiss desired. There were unsatisfactory vibes from the beginning with the architect, and when his key designer left to form his own firm in the middle of the redesign, he was chosen to finish the work with his new firm. Requiring immediate architectural assistance to evaluate this new potential project for the purpose of determining our bid price for the land, the new firm, Hanna Gabriel Wells, was retained.

The office building was going to be at least 150,000 sf and would be either a mid-rise building of six stories, or a high-rise building of seven or eight floors. HGW had a design flair and they were experienced with processing developments through the system in the city of San Diego, but the firm was small and quite busy, so it was decided they did not have the depth to handle a project of this size alone. The Los Angeles office of HKS Architects, Inc. was selected as a good fit based on the many projects Prentiss had completed with their Dallas office. HKS is a very competent firm technically, but had no current work in San Diego, or experience with the city's approval process. Joint ventures are not normally recommended, but in this case it was believed each firm brought something the project required.

After some negotiation their proposal for $2.70 per gsf for the building and $1.23 per gsf for the garage, including all structural and MEP design, was accepted. The MEP, however, would be limited to design development and shop drawing review, as design/build electrical and mechanical contractors would be utilized. The allocation of the fee to the various project phases was:

Schematic Design	15%
Design Development	20%
Contract Documents	40%
Bidding / Negotiation	5%
Construction Administration	20%

HKS was very positive about the engineering consultants they recommended in their proposal and, after the interviews, everyone agreed. The structural engineer and parking consultant were particularly impressive, where the senior member of each firm takes the lead in the early schematic design analysis. Prentiss personnel had previous positive experience with Edgett Williams, the elevator consultant, and with Syska & Hennessy, the mechanical and electrical engineers, and were pleased to work with them again.

The architect proposed specialty consultants to provide full services for parking, acoustical, elevators, curtain wall and landscape architecture. It was determined to use the full services for the landscape architect, but limit the others to services primarily through the design development phase, as it was believed the architect could properly perform the working drawing portion of the work. A curtain wall consultant would have been utilized if a nonstandard curtainwall had been designed, but when a fully engineered and tested wall was selected, this expertise was not required.

The criteria for the office building were determined from the Market Study and Pardee's requirements from the purchase agreement. They were:

- Approximately 150,000 gross square feet

- Four parking stalls per 1000 gsf
- Approximately 40-foot core to glass depth
- Minimum 9'0" ceiling height
- 50 psf live load plus 20 psf for partitions
- Tenant power load of 6 to 7 w/sf were requested, but were to be reviewed further
- Multiple corner offices, if possible
- Maximum 20,000 rsf floor size, and
- Granite façade—the Pardee agreement said brick, or approved upgrade.

During the schematic design and entitlement phase several difficulties were encountered with the architectural team:

- HKS and Hanna Gabriel Wells did not seem to be meshing as well as had been hoped
- The responses of the Hanna firm were not as prompt as expected, as they were exceptionally busy and had not yet built up their staff
- The Hanna firm held on too long to certain design recommendations that had been rejected
- HKS showed their design capabilities by finding an excellent solution to the problem of the poorly angled building footprint that resulted from the approval process through the Carmel Valley Planning Board

Since HKS was the much stronger firm, a decision was made that the design would proceed more rapidly and effectively if HKS performed the architecture alone.

General contractors were interviewed shortly after selecting the architects, as discussed further in Chapter 33, and Swinerton & Walberg was selected.

Using compatible CAD systems, the architects set up a web site to facilitate transferring progress drawings to and from the consulting engineers, the contractor and the hotel architect.

Baseline Budgeting

The project costs went through an extensive series of adjustments. The early assumption while evaluating the potential land purchase was $60/rsf ($57/gsf) for a 150,000 gsf low-rise building. The assumption for the parking structure was $7,625 per stall, the major portion of which was to be above grade. The total number of projected spaces was reduced by 10% based upon shared parking with the hotel.

When the general scope of the project was reasonably well understood, Swinerton prepared three separate baseline budgets—office building, parking structure and site work—to use as a guide through the design process. The budgets were kept separate due to the cost sharing of the parking structure and site work costs with the hotel developer. As design decisions were tentatively made, Swinerton would advise the cost impact and, if acceptable, the design would proceed accordingly.

The baseline budgets and the pro forma grew in a series of major design changes:

- The office building was increased in size to 170,000
- It was changed to a high-rise structure with a granite façade at an estimated additional cost of $4/gsf as discussed in Chapter 15
- The increased size of the office building, and the additional rooms and banquet space in the hotel increased the parking requirement by 100 spaces
- The parking structure cost increased from $7,625 to $8,375 per space when an above ground level was rejected by Pardee and the city, and an estimated additional below grade level was required
- The site work had been underestimated, and the fire water line was not initially contemplated
- The HVAC design was changed from tenant installed heat pumps to self-contained DX units on each floor as a base building cost at an estimated increased base building cost of $4/gsf as discussed in Chapters 4 and 25
- A subsequent change from the DX units to a central chiller system, as a result of a favorable owning and operating analysis added $300,000
- A further increase in the building size added $260,000
- An additional $400 per space was added to the parking structure due to changes to satisfy the

hotel's requirement for an expanded deck, and Pardee's further changes

The contractor's baseline budget was somewhat higher than desired, but it was decided to accept is as a working tool and work cooperatively to reduce it. (As mentioned in Chapter 11, a lower number was used in the official pro forma.) This detailed cost estimate was used as a base for cost evaluations as the design progressed, endeavoring to reach completion with costs within the pro forma. Unfortunately, not only was the pro forma exceeded, but even the base line budget was exceeded, at least before the project construction contingency was included.

The GMP total construction costs (net of the Waterford reimbursement) were approximately $70,000 above the estimated pro forma after reducing the construction contingency to 1% to allow for construction issues.

By direct line comparison the GMP was about $770,000 over the baseline budget and $1 million over the adjusted pro forma, but after adjustment for the contingencies and the Waterford reimbursement, it was slightly less than the baseline.

There **is no excuse for not meeting your cost projections**, but there are always some issues that impact the process. While many cost reduction judgments were made, some of the issues that were not successfully mitigated after establishing the Approved Pro Forma were:

- The contractor erred on the concrete, miscellaneous metal and general conditions estimates, but unfortunately discovered them before the GMP was agreed upon.

- The Brandes Lease took away a great deal of the timing flexibility.

- It was decided to include $115,000 for bonding when the contractor entered into a blanket bond that provided full freedom to quickly find a replacement for a defaulting subcontractor, while at the same time protecting against any costs relative to such default. Initially it was intended not to bond most major contractors.

- The hotel requirements resulted in reducing the length of the parking structure, which placed more of it below ground and slightly reduced the efficiency.

- Pardee required enclosing an additional level of parking with berm, which effectively turned it into a below-grade floor.

- It was questionable to carry a pro forma construction cost number lower than the baseline budget, particularly with an expedited schedule.

- The end result shows the benefit of carrying a signficant contingency to provide for the unexpected.

The tabulation below shows the pro forma, after adjustment for the increased area and central refrigeration plant, the base line budget, Guaranteed Maximum Price and the final costs.

	Adjusted Pro forma	Base Line Budget	GMP	Final Costs
Site Work	$ 1,000,000	$ 1,182,000	$ 1,479,792	$ 1,496,880
Parking Structure	6,700,000	6,731,675	6,908,828	6,940,016
Base Building	11,621,952	11,731,714	12,016,028	12,153,814
Brandes Reimbursement	Incl. 0	Incl. 0	Incl. 0	(97,000)
GDG&E Credit	0	0	0	(40,000)
Signage	40,000	40,000	40,000	55,000
Other Improvements	87,808			
Subtotal	$19,449,760	$19,675,389	$20,444,648	$20,508,710

Less Credit from				
Waterford	(2,845,000)	(2,947,086)	(3,157,986)	(3,177,446)
Construction Contingency	786,148	786,148	172,867	0
Total	$17,390,908	$17,514,451	$17,459,529	$17,331,264
Variance from Base Line	($ 123,543)		($ 54,922)	($ 183,187)
Office Gross Area	172,567			
Office Building Unit Cost / gsf	$67.35	$67.98	$69.63	$70.43*
Office Rentable Area	165,189			
Office Building Unit Cost / rsf	$71.22	$71.89	$73.63	$72.88
Parking Structure Spaces	800			
Cost per Parking Space	$8,375	$8,415	$8,636	$8,675

* Adjusted for Brandes Reimbursement

Building Permits

The issue of various building permits became severe because the amount of work in San Diego was so great that the civil engineers, particularly the one on this project, were extremely busy and the city's reviewing agencies were so overloaded that permits were taking much longer than usual.

The grading permit is the key permit because it must be reviewed by seven agencies or departments plus the three utilities, and must be approved prior to any other permit being issued. There was a delay in starting the grading plan due to a series of changes to the parking structure required primarily to satisfy Marriott as to the sufficiency of the pool deck area, modifications to satisfy Pardee, and provision of a proper lot separation between the hotel and the parking structure. By the time preparation of the grading plan could go forward the civil engineer was already working weekends on other work. The plans for the grading permit were finally ready for submission on June 7.

The grading permit was processed in parallel with the lot line adjustment, discussed in Chapter 7, as together they determined the start of construction. The lot line adjustment was required as a condition of acquiring the property and to convey the hotel pad to the developer, and it was hoped to commence grading the day after closing on the land.

Even though the grading plan had an "Economic Expedite" stamp, due to the city's interest in accelerating receipt of the hotel tax proceeds, the estimate of time to approve this grading permit was 120 days which it was believed would create a problem satisfying the requirements of the Brandes lease and the Marriott desire, at that time, to open in time for the summer trade in 2000. A permit expediter was hired who was very familiar with the process and the city personnel, and the councilman for this area was contacted to request some assistance in expediting the permit. The councilman's office advised that they had a large number of complaints concerning processing time for permits and they would do what they could. They also suggested offering to retain an approved engineer to perform portions of the review work for the city, if the engineering department would approve. They did not. There was no obvious benefit from any efforts the councilman may have made in our behalf.

The same issues were encountered with delays in obtaining the grading permit that were experienced with the lot line adjustment (see Chapter 7), not surprisingly, because the civil engineer and many of the reviewers were the same people.

Major issues were the location of the easement for the fire water loop, which was changed twice to satisfy different departments, the possibility of relocating the storm sewer due to "soil nailing" issues discussed in Chapter 19, and issues with the SDG&E easement. The SDG&E easement issues included the encroachment of some hotel footings, trees required by the city that were in conflict with the easement, and details of the hotel's service driveway that crossed the easement. In fact, the grading permit was placed on hold after the initial review, until the fire loop, storm sewer and the issues with the SDG&E easement could be resolved. The SDG&E issues were resolved when the hotel redesigned the footings and the city dropped their request for the trees that conflicted with it. After study, it was determined that the storm sewer did not have to be relocated.

The same problems were encountered as before, wherein every change by one department, even the addition of a note, had to be circulated back to all of the other reviewers. It often took at least two days for a submittal to be transmitted to a department on an adjacent floor—and their policy forbade a developer's expediter from hand carrying the plans to save time.

Very late in the process the city advised that:

- Submission of an application to a state department in Sacramento for a Waste Water Verification Number was required, which was filed that same day using a personal check
- A recently revised city policy required filing a permit application for each retaining wall, which required the structural engineer to quickly complete all of the structural calculations
- The city would not start to estimate the amount required for the performance bond until the last approval was received

Frustrations reached their zenith in the last weeks when Traffic Safety, whose role is to evaluate and approve street barricades, their related signage and the street lights became an immovable obstacle. Almost three months after first reviewing the plans, the reviewer decided that the existing street lights should be replaced with a new city standard. Knowing that the schedule did not permit contesting what was believed to be an unreasonable request, the specified lights were immediately added to the plans. When the reviewer finally looked at the plans several days later, he told the engineers that he needed calculations prepared to indicate whether they would be satisfactory. The calculations were made and submitted the following day. After the engineer tried for three days to reach him—he did not return any telephone calls—a representative of development services was contacted for assistance. He immediately went to the reviewer who said that he had never seen the revised plans and calculations. An appointment was made for the reviewer to meet the engineer at the plan desk the following morning to review and approve the plans. After breaking two appointments, he finally reviewed the plans (it took ten minutes) and came up with a new series of issues relative to the barricades and temporary traffic signage, which would not be required for more than four months. development services was again requested to assist and they agreed to push through the permit without Traffic Safety approval if it was requested in writing. The request was made but, even though they had agreed to release it, it was held for another two weeks.

The permit was issued on October 11. It is interesting to note that the grading permit set incorporated 23 sheets, with the plan sheets at one inch equals twenty feet scale.

In the meantime, since all of the technical information had been approved by the individual departments, a judgment was made to commence grubbing and grading on September 20 without waiting for a grading permit.

The plans for the office building were submitted for building plan review on June 25. The hotel foundation plans were submitted for permit along with that submission so as to receive a special "Economic Expedite" stamp, as before.

The city was flooded with permit plan submissions since July 1 was the date on which all plans would have to conform to the 1998 CBC code (similar to 1997 UBC), instead of the 1994 UBC which had much less stringent seismic and smoke control requirements. Incidentally, a judgment had been made on this project that future value dictated the design be in accordance with 1998 CBC regardless of the timing of the submission.

The original estimate from the city was that it would probably require eight to ten weeks for the permit review. Any time in excess of eight weeks would delay the project unless delayed anyway by the grading permit.

San Diego has a procedure for "Express Plan-check," where for a premium fee of $95 per hour the reviewing departments would work some overtime in order to expedite the plan-check review. It was estimated the overtime fee could apply to anywhere from one to 200 hours. This was fine in normal times, but the staff was so overloaded almost every applicant paid the premium, which minimized the potential benefit. It was agreed to pay the premium even if only in self-defense and to reinforce the position as to the urgency of the requirement. As in the case of the grading permit, a permit expediter was hired to assist in accelerating the process. Even if she were unable to reduce the timing of the permit approval significantly, at least better information as to the status would be available.

The express plan-check turned out to be $9,000, which was immediately paid. It was estimated it could reduce the initial review time to six to eight weeks.

The comments when finally received were voluminous, but most of them were not too severe. The logjam in the civil engineering firm created by the grading permit and the lot line adjustment held up the necessary civil plan check activities that affected several trades in complying with their plan check corrections.

The most troubling comments were that the city took the position that the required exit paths on the roof and on the first floor did not meet their interpretation of the code. The roof had one stair exit and one hatch exit. The first floor had had one fire stair exiting directly to the outside and one exiting through the main lobby, all per UBC and CBC.

The roof issue was resolved by removing a significant portion of the penthouse and weatherproofing the equipment left uncovered. Since there were no enclosures on the roof except for the elevator equipment and chiller rooms, the exiting was deemed sufficient.

The first floor exiting was crucial, since if the second exit had to go directly to the outside it would have bisected the proposed bank hall, and would probably have prevented the consummation of the Scripps Lease. The issue was resolved by reversing the orientation of the toilet rooms so that there were no openings into the exit corridor. A short stub corridor was then added to service the toilet rooms. Additionally, it was necessary to use all wood doors to the first floor tenant spaces instead of glass so that the lobby could obtain a one-hour rating, permitting the second floor balcony to be acceptable as an exit path.

At the very last moment, a city reviewer requested a modification to the smoke control system. For some reason, which no one understood, the city would not permit smoke control issues to be set aside and treated for deferred approval, while processing the basic building permit. Trying to expedite this resolution, $300 was paid for the reviewer to make the final review over the weekend. He came back in on Monday with 29 comments, mainly notes he wanted added to the drawings, but he also insisted that the transfer switch for the emergency electrical generator be located in a separate room from the other electrical equipment, a request no one had ever heard of before. It was determined later that the reason for this becoming a last minute issue was that the city coordinator failed to distribute the plans to the person who reviews smoke control until the day before to the permit was to be obtained.

All of the answers to the original city comments had been returned to the city on September 28. Final approval was received on October 27, except for the fire suppression system, which was deferred.

The delayed resubmission and final plan check approval from the city endangered the schedule, since the foundation installation was required before building permit approval was possible. Filing separately for a foundation permit was explored, and it was learned that having two permit requests for a single project in the city in parallel would likely cause organizational chaos.

The contractor verified that the city would not physically approve the certified pad—relying on the inspecting geotechnical engineer. The contractor was then directed to complete the pad for certification and, after verifying that the reviewing structural engineer had no more comments on the footing design, was directed to excavate the footings and place the rebars. The contractor had discussed with the city's field inspector the possibility of providing a courtesy inspection prior to issuance of the permit, but they declined due to recent new procedures. Pouring the foundations was started the day after receiving the building permit.

The next critical permit was the one for the "soil nailed" retaining wall for the parking structure. By the time it was fully engineered there was less than a two-week window prior to the time its construction was required to start. While proceeding to push it through the review process, it was concluded that the first 4" layer of shotcrete could be considered as a temporary retaining wall and could safely start prior to receiving the retaining wall permit. The work started on October 26, and the permit was received on November 16th, when the work on first layer was about 60% complete.

One last-minute delay in the soil-nailing permit occurred when the city required the geotechnical engineer to make additional calculations to verify that the wall was designed in accordance with the seismic loads in the soils report without taking into consideration the resistance of the tendrels. They were satisfactory.

Due to the delays encountered in completing the plans for the parking structure and the site work resulting from the changes caused by the hotel and Pardee, as well as solving the structural issues resulting from uneven height retaining wall and seismic stresses, these plans were not submitted for plan check until September 22, 1999. The final approval was received on January 7 after extensive discussion of exiting, and whether concrete block walls of the stair tower should go to the open upper level.

Another issue arose during the city's review of the curtain wall shop drawings. They marked up the drawings to require 314 gusset plates be welded to the structural steel beams supporting the wall kickers. The structural engineer made an in-depth analysis that showed that the plates were unnecessary.

As a result of noting conditions inserted in Amendment #4 to the Land Sale Agreement with Waterford to protect against delays in the hotel development, the lender and certain individuals in the home office tried to pressure the Development Officer to immediately obtain an agreement from the city that if the hotel were delayed or not built, the Certificate of Occupancy would not be affected. He declined to do so, as that might cause the loss of the "Expedite" stamp, which was based solely on the desire for the hotel taxes. This issue was successfully addressed after all of the permits were in hand.

In retrospect, there were several errors in the handling of the permit process, specifically:

- Not exploring replacement of the civil engineer early in the process. He was selected because he had performed all of the work in the San Diego Corporate Center, and had all necessary information at the tip of his fingers, however, it should have been recognized from the early signs that he was not going to perform in a timely fashion.

- It should have been recognized sooner that termination of the local architect left no team member who had a working relationship with city staff.

- The development personnel should have been more personally involved with the city reviewing departments in order to more readily determine where the process could be expedited. Because there was no experience working with any of the city people, reliance was placed on the civil engineer and permit expediters.

These shortcomings and unanticipated difficulties notwithstanding, one way or another the construction commenced in time to ultimately achieve the desired schedule.

01 SITE PLAN
NOT TO SCALE

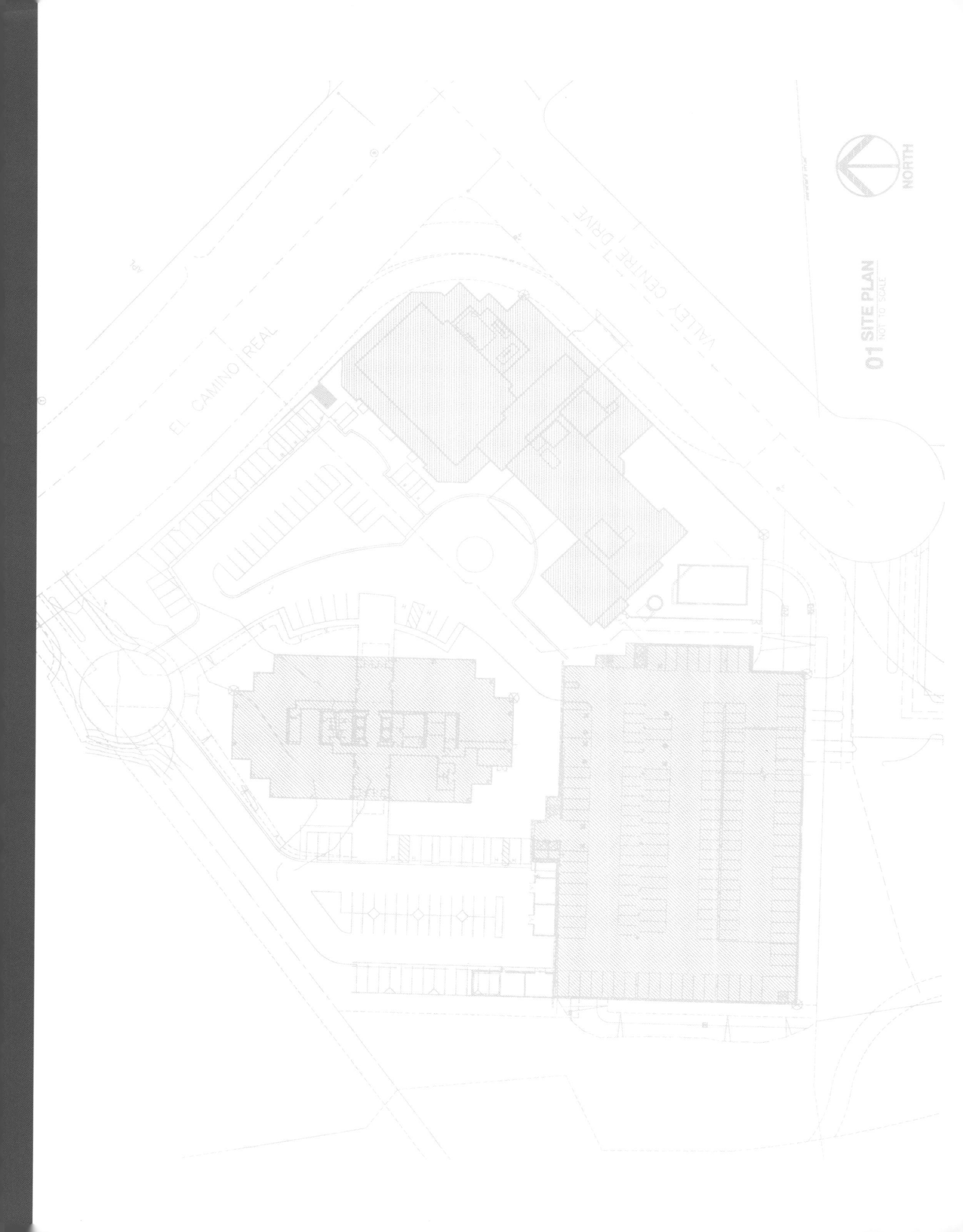

NORTH

EL CAMINO REAL

VALLEY CENTRE DRIVE

SITE PLANNING and CONCEPTUAL DESIGN

Site planning and conceptual design is exceedingly important as it sets the basic design of the project. If it is not thoroughly and properly evaluated, and appropriate decisions made at this point, inordinate backtracking is likely to occur throughout the design process.

Site planning and conceptual design (the first portion of the Schematic Design Phase) uses the Project Design Criteria from the Feasibility Analysis (discussed in Chapter 14) plus additional preferences of the developer as to materials, modules, retail and amenity requirements, known political and regulatory issues, the budget and schedule from the preliminary pro forma to define the general outlines of the project and its design. While site planning is also used in evaluating site purchase alternatives, this chapter will assume that the site has been acquired or committed to.

This chapter will describe the thought process through which the previously discussed criteria and other sources of information are transformed into a design solution.

For multi-building site planning, the approximate building sizes, building heights, floor areas and parking requirements are determined, and the process explores alternative arrangements to effectively provide:

- Use of the terrain to accomplish an aesthetically pleasing design relationship between the elements
- Appropriate highway and/or arterial exposure
- Initial visual impact from the entry point
- Good sight lines to and from each building
- Solar orientation to maximize the efficiency of the building environmental systems
- Acceptable traffic flow to and from the site
- Efficient automobile and pedestrian circulation
- Acceptable relationship of parking spaces or structure to building entrances
- Efficiency of the parking structure, if any
- Effective use of any major natural or proposed design features or views

The plan must take into consideration the platting of each building separately to avoid disruption to utilities, access, circulation, and the impact of any site limitations, in order to permit separate financing and/or ownership initially or in the future. The platted separation of shared parking facilities should be carefully evaluated. While planning for future phases is essential, be wary of efforts to prepurchase materials for future phases.

A single building site plan is much simpler in that it must consider all of the same factors, but is not constrained by the requirement of sharing the attributes and limitations of the site between multiple buildings.

The site planning and conceptual design are usually performed in parallel with the resolution of identified regulatory and environmental issues so the project may be fully entitled at the earliest possible time.

While site planning and building conceptual design may be discussed sequentially, and in fact site planning is initiated first, it is really an iterative process, with neither final until both are satisfied.

> Prepurchasing materials for future buildings to take advantage of volume pricing can sound attractive, but code and/or technological changes can create obsolescence.
>
> An insurance company in Dallas purchased sufficient lighting fixtures for an entire second office tower while they were constructing the first one. After storing the fixtures for many years, when the second tower was constructed the fixtures did not meet code, and the cost to properly modify them would have been greater than the cost of new fixtures.
>
> Another firm in Dallas, while constructing a major granite clad office tower, purchased all of the fabricated stone necessary for a duplicate building. Fifteen years later that stone is apparently still in storage in Dallas.

Traffic flow generated by the site may affect the location of acceptable curb cuts for ingress/egress points, ingress stacking lanes, permissibility of ingress/egress left turns and the necessity for new or increased signalization. These restraints, plus the importance of developing the most efficient parking structure possible (as discussed later in this chapter and in Chapter 25) where one is required, can have a major impact on the building design and location, and in some instances has been the most important factor driving the design solutions.

As the Project Design Criteria generally limits the building as to height, floor size, width (from the preferred bay depth plus the assumed core width) and, therefore, the building length, and the costs are constrained by the preliminary pro forma, the architect proposes several building envelope shapes that accomplish this criteria. There is a frequently stated view that a building should be designed from the "inside out," but since the major factors influencing the interior design are covered in the Project Design Criteria, the author believes it is generally better to tentatively accept an appropriate envelope prior to detailed study of the building interior.

In order to appropriately evaluate proposed building designs it is essential to understand the impact of height, shape and other factors on the cost efficiency of the building, in addition to those resulting from the use of materials of varying costs.

The first factor is height. It is obvious that the lower the height of the building, the greater the efficiency. A one-story building is not burdened with stairways, elevator shafts, or duct and pipe shafts. In addition, it has relatively low requirements to satisfy fire and life safety issues.

The reasons to increase the building height are the size and/or value of the land, or to reduce the floor size to one that satisfies the market. To increase the height, and along with it the unit cost, for any other reason will tend to make the building less economically viable.

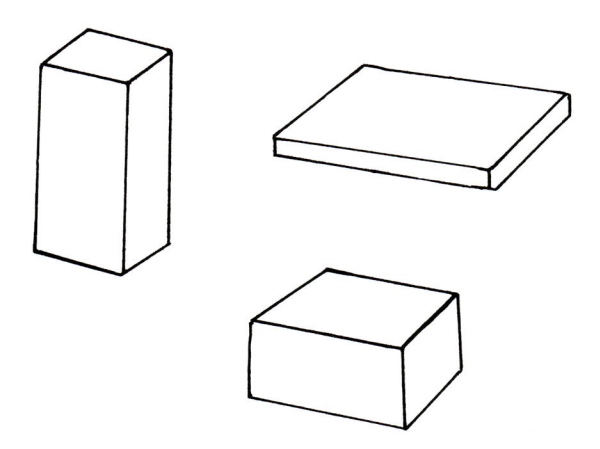

The height of the building has significant cost implications. As the height increases, the cost of vertical transportation and various shafts increase, while reducing the ratio of the rentable area to the gross area—thus increasing the cost per rentable square foot. The unit cost of the structure tends to also increase with height as it is supporting greater live and dead loads, in addition to resisting increased wind and seismic loads. Further, when any floor level exceeds 75 feet above grade in most jurisdictions, the building becomes subject to the high-rise code. High-rise requirements include expensive issues such as smoke control and emergency power for the various equipment. A tall building, while sometimes the result of actual or perceived ego, is normally justified only by the cost of land and maintaining the market-driven floor size. Note that most high-rise buildings are in very high land cost areas, and one- or two-story buildings are usually in very low cost land areas. A rough pro forma analysis will indicate where the trade-off occurs.

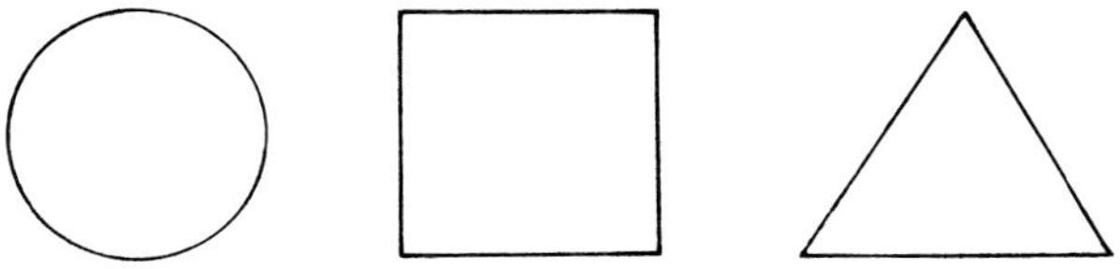

There are three basic geometric shapes—the circle, square and triangle, as shown in the diagram.

There are three basic ways to measure the efficiency of a building—the ratio of building skin (one of the most expensive components of the building) required for the given square foot area of the building, rentable and usable area ratios (previously discussed), and the layout efficiency of the tenant space. Since the circle has the smallest circumference for any given area, it will require the least amount of skin. Conversely, the triangle has the greatest perimeter per unit of area and will require the greatest amount of skin. The circle and the triangle are relatively inefficient shapes in which to layout office functions, therefore the square normally becomes the preferred choice due to the combination of unit cost and layout efficiency.

It should be noted that any curvature will affect the efficiency of tenant layouts to some degree, and the smaller the floor size the higher the ratio of skin to floor area.

The depth of a square with a central core is determined by using two times the desired bay width, as determined from the Market Study (and more thoroughly discussed in Chapter 16), plus the width of the building core. If a square of this dimension does not equal the desired floor size, the width must be either shortened or lengthened to achieve the appropriate size, thus creating a rectangle, the most common basic building shape.

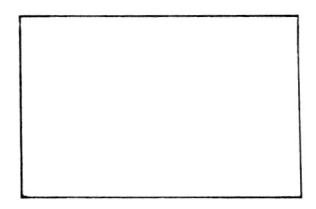

It is often considered desirable, for purposes of design or to create additional corner offices, to create one or more steps in the corners of the rectangular shape, as shown in the adjacent sketch. Note that the floor area is reduced, but the amount of building skin is unchanged. This increases the amount of curtain wall that must be provided per square foot, thus increasing the unit cost of the building. In addition, there may be some increase in the cost of the structural frame.

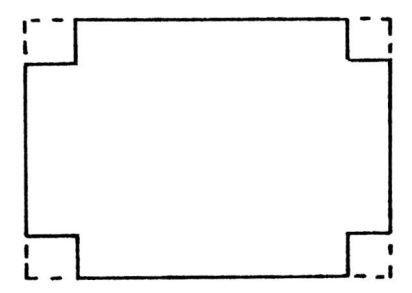

One current approach to insuring a relatively low-rise development while maintaining appropriate bay depths, yet providing sufficient space for very large tenants and for expansion, is to design the building with a central core between from two to four wings, as shown here. This form of design when created for a large tenant has the added benefit of maintaining future real estate value, or providing an exit strategy, by permitting future efficient multi-tenant usage.

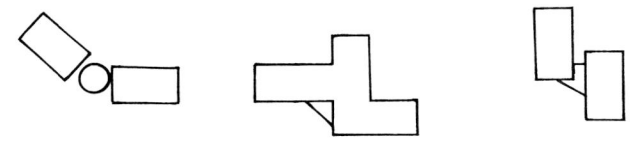

Because of limitations detailed more specifically in Chapters 19 and 20, the selected designs will tend to be either very simple in geometric form with façade articulation for aesthetic interest, or an interesting geometric form that will utilize minimal articulation. Frequently, the preliminary pro forma and the base line budget will indicate that certain materials are not affordable and the architect's attention is directed toward designs whose material costs can be accommodated.

Nothing in the above discussion of space and layout efficiencies is intended to indicate that unusual shapes or tall buildings may not be appropriate for any given project. The purpose is for you to recognize the factors that increase the project's cost so that you may apply a judgment as to whether those costs are justified by the benefits that are added.

Supplementing the earlier mention of solar orientation, consideration should be given to the design of shading elements to take maximum advantage of solar considerations in order to maximize the efficiency of the building's environmental systems. Consideration should also be given at this time as to whether the major mechanical and electrical rooms will be located remotely, on the roof, or within the building envelope.

When evaluating each design, ask extensive questions to determine how they will accomplish each objective indicated in the Project Design Criteria, and what trade-offs are required. This process should continue throughout all proposed design solutions and their revisions, until you are satisfied as to which scheme to develop further.

A common error by a Development Officer in this process is to too quickly approach a proposed design with suggested changes that might make it work satisfactorily. It is very normal for the architect (remember they are usually working on a fixed fee) to assume the Development Officer is indicating basic satisfaction with the scheme—and will tend to apply their efforts toward refining that design rather than considering and proposing alternative solutions that may be superior. It is much more effective to use questions and indications as to how the design may or may not meet the project objectives—and thus encourage the architect to use his creativity to find the best solution available.

Another area of caution to be alert to is when an architect seems to grasp a major design feature at an early stage and continue in that direction even when other factors surface that appear to conflict with that feature. It is not unusual for the architect to rationalize away other issues to avoid giving up the original idea. It is not that the initial design thought was not a valid or important one, it is just that changed information may indicate too many issues must be compromised to proceed with it. At some point the Development Officer must insist that another solution be found.

A relatively new concept to American architects and developers that should be given some consideration in this era of world commerce and finance is the oriental concept of *feng shui*. Based on my very limited knowledge of the subject, it is largely based on common sense. It is suggested that knowledge of this concept be gained, as major conflicts with its principles might negatively affect prospective oriental tenants or financiers. A brief overview of the subject is covered in Appendix B, which I suggest you read.

After tentatively selecting a conceptual design, it is now time to test the floor plan for leasability with a series of layouts by an interior planner familiar with the size and type of the most likely tenants. The space planner should test sample tenant layouts for small, medium and full-floor size tenants to determine whether the proposed floor plans can efficiently satisfy the range of tenant sizes contemplated by the Market Study. This would normally be performed by the interior design firm selected to assist in the leasing program, whose other responsibilities will include determining where less than full-floor prospects might best fit on the floor, and prepare preliminary space plans to submit along with the lease proposal. This is also the firm that will prepare space plans for tenants who have executed their leases, and do not wish to retain their own designer. A more thorough discussion of this subject is covered in Chapter 22.

Parking, and frequently landscape, requirements are included in the Project Design Criteria and can be major design issues. Obviously, parking on grade is the least expensive and will always be used where sufficient land permits. It should be laid out as efficiently as possible to permit maximum landscaping and clear circulation paths.

Where insufficient land exists for surface parking, or the land value is sufficiently high, structured parking should be provided with the least number of decks, and the greatest bay length, that are practical. The efficiency in square feet per parking space and the type of design resulting in a reasonable construction cost per square foot must be evaluated jointly to achieve the lowest possible cost

> Surface parking is much less expensive than structured parking, but it involves a trade-off with the amount of land available. A test calculation we made in San Diego in 1999 indicated the trade-off at one site. With estimated costs for structured parking at about $8,900 per stall, surface parking at $3,500 per stall and an assumption of 325 square feet per stall, the break-even point in project costs would occur when an additional three acres were allocated so as to permit surface parking. We built the structure.

per space. There are many types of designs for parking structures that are discussed in Chapter 25.

A parking structure should not be integrated with the building structure unless absolutely necessary. The column spacing for an efficient building is normally very inefficient for a parking structure, and the core provides a major impediment to traffic circulation. Excessive cost penalties can result. Several trade-off analyses should be considered in resolving this issue.

Inclusive of all relative utilities, a structured parking facility can cost several times the cost of surface parking. Giving consideration to the relatively high ratio of parking spaces to rentable area, structures can only be justified with high land costs or insufficient site area.

It is not unusual for the design of sufficient parking to have a major impact on the design of the entire project. Under certain circumstances the cost of additional parking to meet the market criteria may lead to a reduction of building size in order to find the least total project cost per rentable square foot. Some data on efficient parking module size is covered in Chapter 25.

Once the site and conceptual design seems to have reached a satisfactory solution, the remainder of the Schematic Design Phase may be completed and further design initiated as discussed in later chapters.

One factor that is frequently misunderstood by relatively inexperienced Development Officers is that in proposing and refining the conceptual plan, the architect is thinking in a macro or overview mode. Once the basic conceptual design is accepted, the architect then adjusts his thought process to look for issues on more of a micro level. This brings up issues not considered before, which may propose new solutions for issues you thought were resolved. This is a natural part of the process, and each change should be evaluated during the Schematic Design Phase on the basis of its merit and cost impact.

Build-to-Suit Projects

The importance of insuring that real estate value is maintained, or an exit strategy followed, was discussed previously in Chapters 4 and 14. It is during this phase that the designs must be thoroughly tested to verify that they satisfy both the user's requirements as well as those of the speculative real estate market.

CASE STUDY

This project is a classic case of integrating multiple issues in a single-site plan, and none can be considered final until all are resolved.

A series of design decisions had been made for the purpose of formulating a proposal to acquire the land, then it was necessary to basically start all over with the project design to be certain that each and every issue was thoroughly evaluated. Not much design work could be set until the type of hotel and the extent of its banquet, dining and other services were resolved. The type of hotel and facilities not only had a significant impact on the hotel footprint, but on the automobile traffic circulation and the required parking. The type of facilities also determines the time of day estimates necessary for the "shared parking analysis," which determines the total number of spaces that must be constructed, and the peak traffic load for planning approval purposes.

The early assumptions regarding the hotel were that it would be either a Marriott or Hilton suites hotel with minimum banquet and dining facilities. As a result of the economic study discussed in Chapter 4, the discussions with operators were broadened to include a full service hotel with banquet facilities, which would increase the parking requirements.

Patriot American, who owns the Wyndham chain, made a strong proposal for the project and was initially selected by Waterford over Hilton and Marriott, subject to approval by Prentiss and Pardee. Later, Patriot American backed out as the financial picture changed for hotel REITs, and was replaced with Marriott. Waterford, after a tentative agreement with Allegis, entered into a construction financing venture arrangement with Orix, USA to finance the project based on an intent to sell the hotel at or shortly after the Certificate of Occupancy.

The design was greatly affected by the desire to obtain the maximum impact from the prominence of the site and the building heights. They would be the tallest buildings north of UTC and the exposure to the freeway is unsurpassed. This is in addition to the necessity of providing a good visual impact from the entrance, efficient automobile and pedestrian circulation, a strong supporting relationship between the buildings, and a positive relationship with Executive Center Del Mar.

The early assumption that the hotel might best be located along Valley Centre Drive was reinforced with the inclusion of banquet and dining facilities. Servicing these facilities, as well as the normal hotel service, is best accommodated along the backside of the hotel at the lower level. The first floor and lobby of the hotel would be one floor (18' +/-) higher and facing, and approximately on the level of, the office building entrance, while the lower level would directly access the street.

Another early assumption that appeared to be valid was that access for visitor surface parking and hotel guests was best provided from the joint entrance on El Camino Real that is shared with the adjacent Executive Center Del Mar buildings. Not only did this entrance have direct access to the front lobby of the office building, but also to the hotel entrance and its planned valet parking service. Another factor is that it would be easier for the hotel transient clientele to recognize their destination with entrance signage provided at that point. Routing the total traffic flow through this entrance would have created a congested situation, so the bulk of the automobile access will be through Valley Centre Drive into a lower parking structure level, although southbound cars on El Camino Real would certainly enter the main entrance and flow behind the office building to the parking structure.

As in most projects, it was obvious that three potentially major cost factors (for which there are no visual or functional benefits) were the parking efficiency (i.e., the sf area per stall, which normally dictates the cost per stall), minimizing retaining walls, and the ability to minimize or avoid soil import/export. One step to increase the parking structure efficiency was to avoid placing the parking structure beneath the office building, as the office building columns always create parking inefficiencies. The shared use of the parking facility also tended to make this location unwise.

In the early site studies the two buildings were somewhat arbitrarily placed at right angles to each other, shown earlier as Figures 7-1 and 7-2, primarily because the designs in which they faced and were parallel to each other did not seem quite right. This approach left a somewhat triangular site for the garage. Analysis by the parking consultant showed that when using this available site the parking structure would require approximately 335 sf per stall, while a rectangular structure would reduce it to no more than 310 sf per stall, and probably less. Since the square foot construction cost of the parking structure would not necessarily be affected, and might actually be slightly reduced with rectilinear proportions, a significant amount could be saved. A further issue was to place the parking structure an appropriate distance from the office building so as to reduce the structural costs of providing lateral support for the building foundations, which was accomplished by locating it abutting the southern building line of the property.

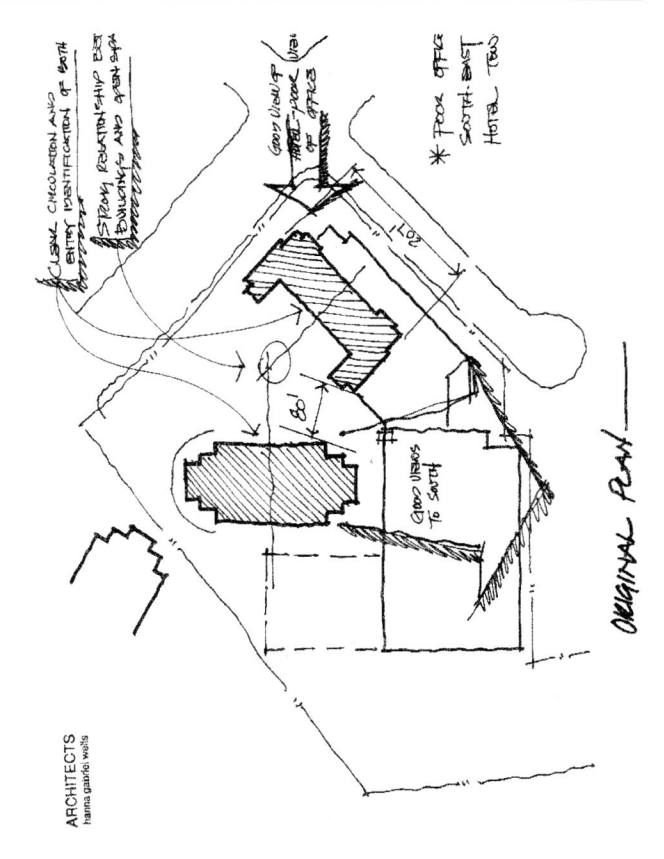

Figure 15-2

To achieve an efficient rectangular garage, it was necessary to rotate the office building approximately 22° +/- one way or the other from the original right angle orientation as shown in the following drawings labeled as Figures 15-1 and 15-2. The selection would not only affect how the office building would relate to the hotel and the overall site design and composition, but also to the Executive Center buildings.

The scheme in Figure 15-2 was selected because it related better to the hotel and the two adjacent office buildings and also created a better-organized site, principally because of one arrival point rather than two and a defined forecourt. This location scheme was further refined to obtain the necessary total of approximately 900 parking spaces, reduce interference between structures, and determine the best method to minimize the parking structure cost. Both schemes assumed some subsurface parking in an "L" shaped configuration, as shown lightly outlined in the figures. One cost reduction effort was to add an additional one-half

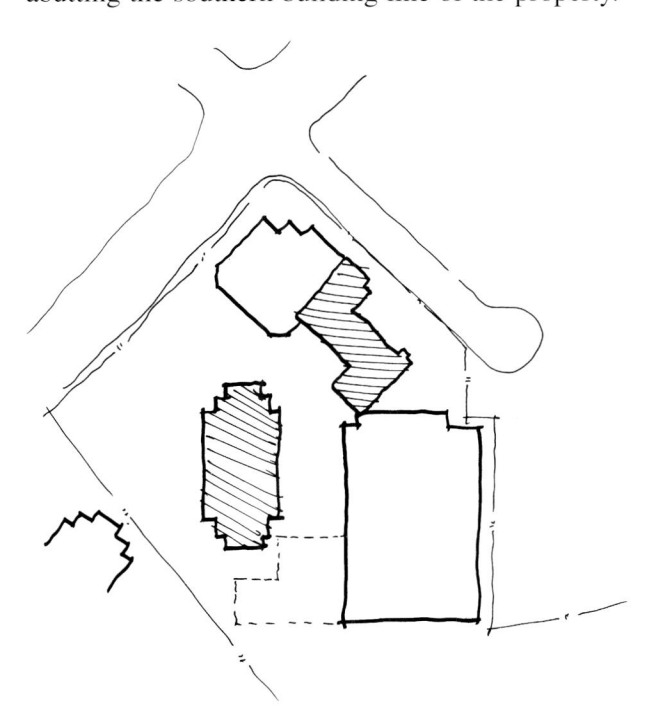

Figure 15-1

level to the top of the parking structure while eliminating the subsurface right angle configuration, as discussed further in Chapter 24. The 900 spaces were the estimated total requirement. Any surface spaces provided would be subtracted to determine the parking structure size. (It should be noted that the hotel required an additional 100 spaces over that originally anticipated due to the increase to 284 rooms and the larger banquet and dining facilities.)

The hotel design was originally proposed with a very strong top and all punched windows, see Figure 15-3, but was later revised to a top that would blend better with our office building, and the façade was softened somewhat.

of a floor would be almost 24,000 rsf, which the brokers thought was larger than desired for this market, but adding another floor would incur the high-rise premium. When an analysis of the project's projected traffic generation indicated that it compared sufficiently favorably to the project originally approved for the site to justify a building of up to 170,000 gsf, it was decided to proceed with an eight-story building of that size. This would provide 20,000 rsf floors, and the income from the additional building area would more than cover the high-rise construction premium plus the additional building area. (The unit land cost per gross building square foot was reduced by $4.11 due to the additional building area, versus the estimated high-

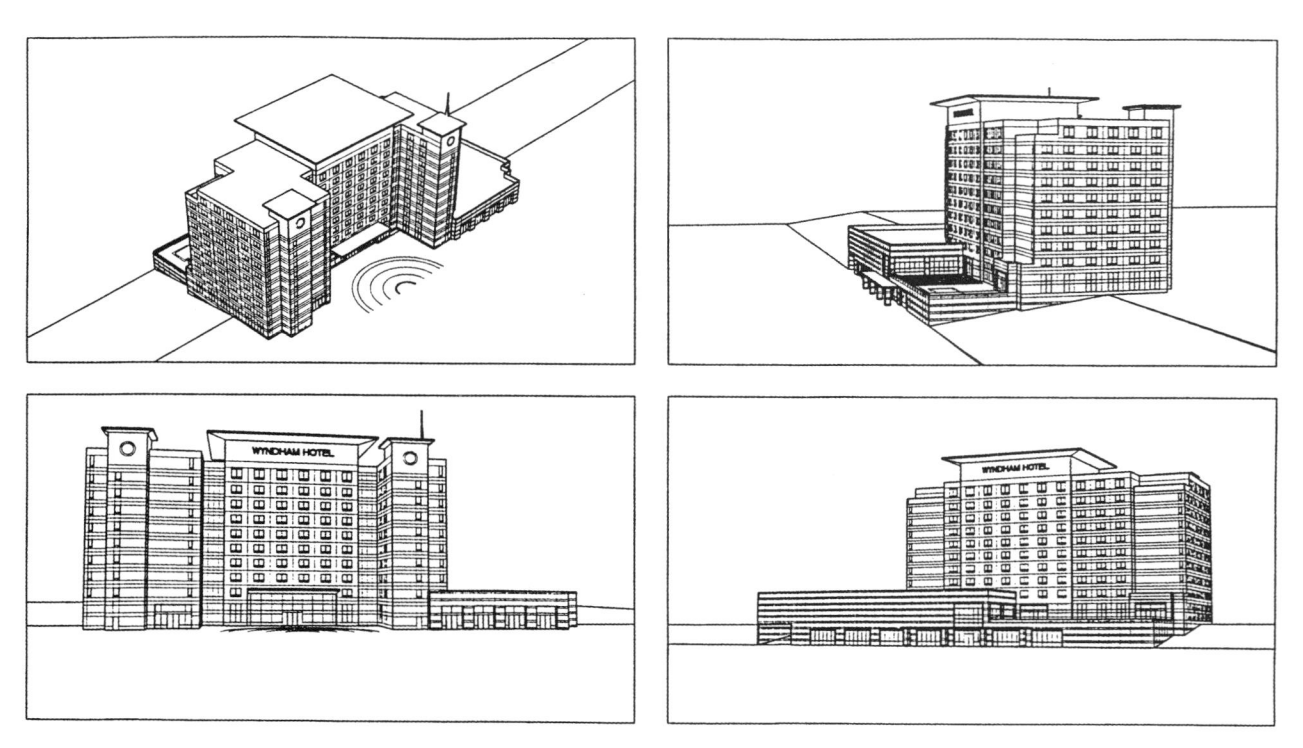

Figure 15-3

The initial criteria for the office building were taken from the Market Study and the Purchase and Sale Agreement, as discussed in Chapters 4 and 14.

Any building with the top-occupied floor line more than 75' above grade would require adherence to the high-rise building code, which would add significantly to the construction cost. With a building of 150,000 gsf limited to six floors, the rentable area

rise construction premium with granite façade of $4/gsf.) It would also require 80 additional spaces in the parking structure.

An eight-story brick building did not seem appropriate to the market analysis, so it was agreed to provide a granite and glass façade, possibly along with another material, that would come within our budget that at this point was $61/gsf. To accomplish

Site Planning and Conceptual Design

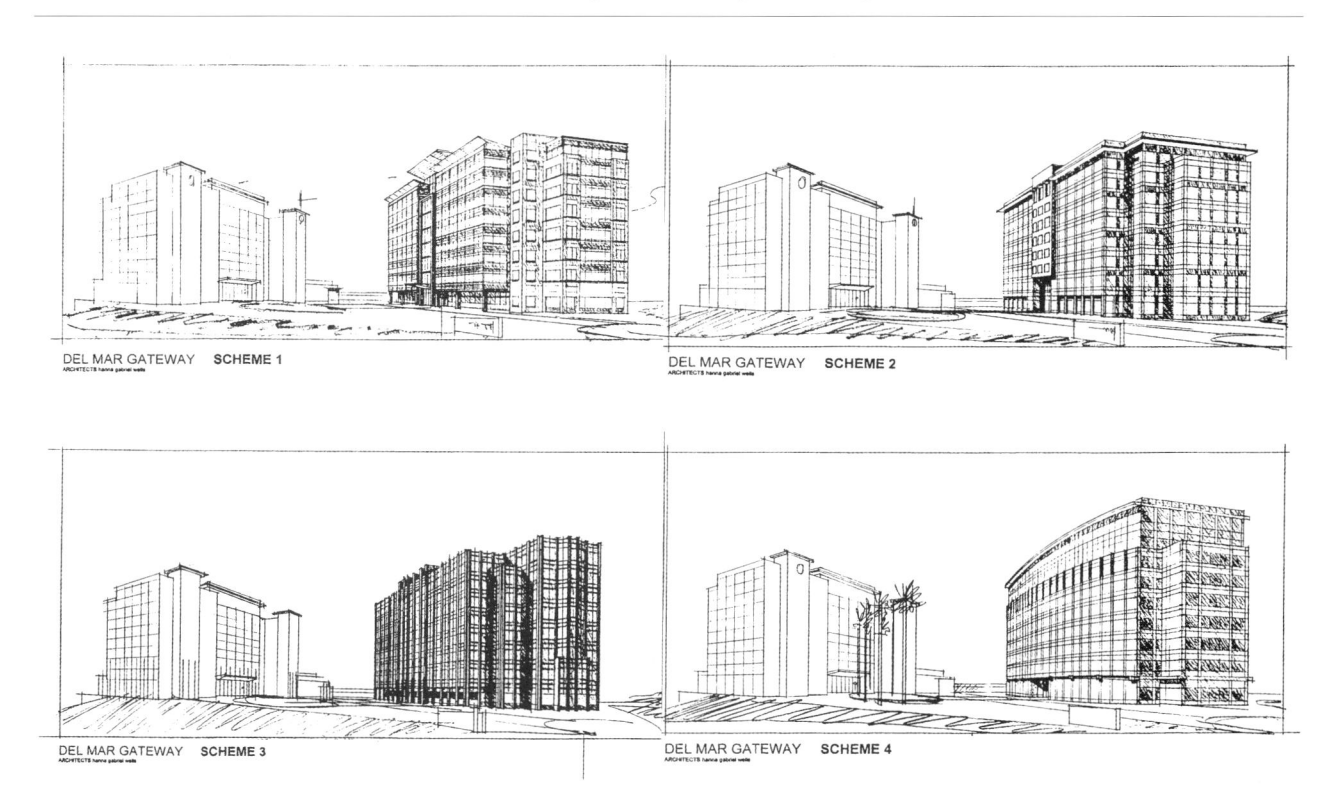

Figure 15-4

this, the structure would have to be relatively simple and the façade must have minimum articulation.

An early analysis by the structural engineer indicated that a steel structure with 30' x 40' exterior bays, with a 25' deep interior bay to provide the necessary transverse bracing for seismic loads, would be the most efficient to accomplish the preferred core to glass dimension. These proportions were believed to permit the structure to have either a moment frame or a brace frame solution as the design developed. Tenant layout evaluations determined that when providing extra corner offices, they should be 15' step backs to accommodate 15' x 15' offices.

The criteria were revised to add:

- An eight-story 170,000 gsf building
- Multiple corner offices of 15' x 15'
- Four elevators, including one swing car
- Presumed steel structure with 30' x 40' and 25' x 30' bays
- A granite and glass façade with minimum articulation

After several very preliminary schemes had been reviewed and the criteria clarified, the architects prepared eight schemes for review, which are shown on the following pages as Figures 15-4 and 15-5. Each scheme was accompanied by their respective floor plans, which were not considered necessary for presentation in this review, and a small Styrofoam model that assisted in evaluation of the designs. One example is shown in Figure 15-6.

Schemes 1, 2 and 7 were really variations of the same basic design, and some features from any of them could be used in a refined scheme. Scheme 3 was considered to have too much of an urban look and the articulation would surely be too expensive. Scheme 4, as well as Schemes 6 and 8 were not considered favorably because the lack of symmetry would probably add cost without any real benefit in this particular location, and the interior planning is more difficult for the tenants. Scheme 5 was the initial emotional favorite, but there was concern that there was significant additional curtain wall cost required, and that further additional cost would be required for catwalks to service the window washing and façade maintenance, due to the fenes-

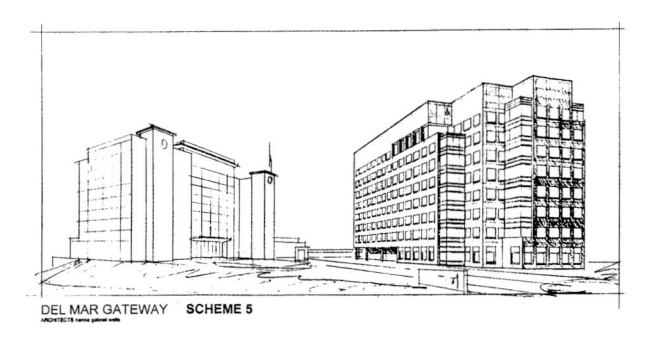

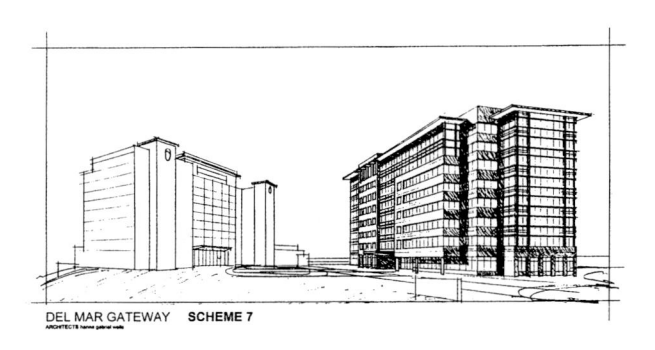

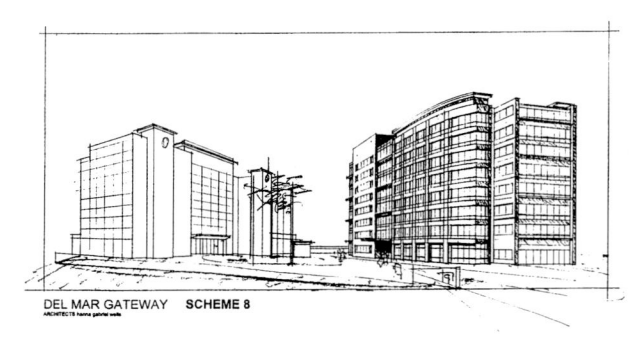

Figure 15-5

tration extending upward to hide the penthouse and rooftop equipment.

Scheme 1, without the heavy overhang, and Scheme 5 were selected for further design refinement and cost analysis to permit a design direction to be formulated.

Two variations of each of the above schemes were prepared and reviewed, as shown in Figure 15-7, along with the original Schemes 1 and 5. Some variation of Scheme 5A was initially preferred (lower left hand in the figure), as it seemed to have a little more character to differentiate it from other buildings, however, some simplicity from the original Scheme 5 would have to be retained for reasonable cost control. The treatment of the central bay above the entrance would be studied further to insure it is a positive visual element—but any further detailing would be subject to its cost impact.

Due to the new building orientation and the way it addresses the pedestrian traffic flow from the parking structure, it was decided to have only one main lobby for security purposes and, as a result, it was changed to a normal height for the first floor with a two-story atrium lobby at the front. The recessed covered walkway, or colonnade, from the parking structure end of the building to the main entrance was planned to run along the front side.

Further detail resolution was deferred until after the city entitlement approval process was concluded. The plans submitted to the city for the Substantial Conformance Review were sufficiently general, and void of as many details as possible, so

Figure 15-6

Figure 15-7

as to not restrict the ability to select preferred detailing later. Some features of Scheme 1A might yet be incorporated into the design, as the detailing appeared to be simpler.

The original assumption for the office building was to utilize a unitized curtain wall system for the skin if costs would permit. A steel or precast concrete truss system might be several dollars per sf less expensive, but could require extensive seismic engineering analysis and testing, particularly if a concrete truss were used due to its increased weight. The detailing and scope of glass vs. granite will be reviewed in great detail at a later date.

Syska & Hennessy proposed four HVAC schemes for discussion purposes, which are covered in more detail in Chapter 25. They were self contained direct expansion (DX) VAV air handling units on each floor, built-up DX units on either the roof or on grade, multiple rooftop chiller units, and a central centrifugal chiller plant. The first and last of the above schemes and were selected for an owning and operating analysis, including consideration of an economizer cycle. The results were that the estimated operating savings for the central centrifugal chiller plant, along with reduced TI costs, would more than pay for the additional $4/gsf of construction cost, so this enhancement was accepted. Both the baseline budget and the pro forma were adjusted to reflect these changes.

The baseline budget for the office building was priced at this point signficantly above the adjusted number then carried in the pro forma, and it was agreed an effort must be made to reduce it considerably as the design developed.

The refinement of the parking structure design omitted the subsurface right angle portion and replaced it with surface parking and a partial upper level—maintaining the requirement of approximately 800 spaces, as described in more detail in Chapter 24. There were two variations for the upper level—one where the top deck was lengthwise on the opposite side of the structure from the building, and the other was along the short side of the structure adjacent to the hotel. The latter scheme was selected, which yields 809 spaces at 303 sf per stall.

The top level would provide a second level above grade adjacent to the hotel, which is almost the same height as the ballroom. An effort was planned to have the façades read in a complementary manner.

Several methods were discussed concerning enhancing the parking structure appearance—including trellis elements, perimeter landscape elements on each deck level, and trees surrounding the perimeter of the structure.

The site design was impacted by the necessity to provide 90 to 100 surface parking spaces and a 26-foot-wide fire truck driveway loop around the office building. Combined with the necessary access drives, it became a relatively tight site. Landscape concepts were discussed, and any decision about a water feature was deferred until later when budget constraints were clearly known. The type of paving was deferred until later—but was likely to be textured or exposed aggregate concrete for the sake of economy. Recommended examples would be viewed. A preliminary budget of $270,000 was established for landscaping of both the site area and the parking structure. The landscape architect would prepare several schemes to fit within this budget.

After Wyndham dropped out it was determined that Marriott was very anxious to have their flag in this location and, fortunately, the footprint of the hotel did not have to be significantly changed. There was significant concern about the possibility that a substantial delay could occur to the project due to developing a design acceptable to Prentiss, Marriott and Pardee, and obtaining agreements that guaranteed financing. This scenario did not occur at that time, but there was a delay later on that affected closing on the hotel property as discussed in Chapter 7.

Pardee, who as the seller was concerned with how each project impacts their future land sales, generally approved the designs prior to submission to the city to initiate the Substantial Conformance Review process, but insisted that the added half floor of parking structure be removed and placed below ground.

The Pardee requirement to remove the top one-half floor from the parking structure, later also required by the Carmel Valley Planning Board, meant again redesigning the parking structure by either adding another basement level, or two levels beneath the surface parking area behind the office building that formed an "L" shaped structure. The "L" shape complicated the fire lane around the building, as the cost to build a parking deck that could handle fire truck weights would be prohibitive. The final solution was another lower level beneath the parking structure, as discussed in Chapter 24.

The site plan and a general outline of the office and hotel towers were prepared for submission to the city and the Carmel Valley Planning Board in the required form for the necessary approvals through the Substantial Conformance Review process.

As discussed in detail in Chapter 7, the hotel and site plan were significantly modified in order to satisfy the Carmel Valley Planning Board during the SCR process. The resulting site plan and rendering are shown here as Figures 15-8, (originally included as Figure 7-11) and 15-9, which is another view of the rendering originally shown as Figure 7-8.

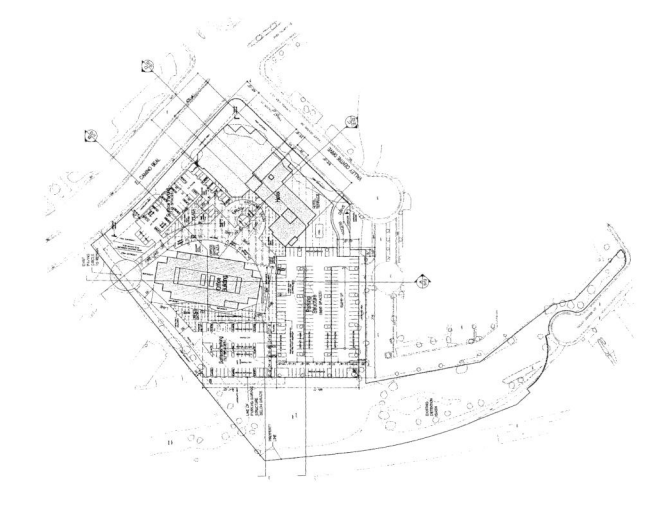

Figure 15-8

Figure 15-9

After receipt of the Substantial Conformance Determination, all of the guidelines imposed on the site and the buildings were carefully assessed and a fresh look at the overall design was initiated. The angular rotation of the office building and the cramped feeling of the forecourt resulting from the Substantial Conformance Review were unsatisfactory, so several other alternatives were studied, but it was felt they did not improve the project.

Finally, the preliminary floor plan was re-studied and it was determined that the overall length could be reduced by 17 feet, the width increased by 5 feet and it would still be an efficient floor plan. The core was widened by 2 feet and lengthened by 20 feet to accommodate the proposed brace framing system and to improve the efficiency of locating smaller tenants. The revised floor plan is shown in Figure 15-10. An analysis of the impact on smaller tenant layouts was satisfactory, and is discussed further in Chapter 16. The reduced length permitted orienting the office building to sit squarely with the parking structure, moving the building further away from El Camino Real, improving the forecourt and providing a cleaner and better organized solution, as shown in Figure 15-11. This variation from the approved orientation of the Substantial Conformance Determination was approved by the planning department, since all of the specified distances from El Camino Real and from the hotel were increased.

An unintended consequence of the revised orientation of the office building was that it was no longer at an angle that would induce most of the pedestrian flow from the parking structure to access the front of the building. Since there was no longer a compelling reason to have the planned colonnade, it was eliminated, reducing cost and adding rentable area. An issue with the lobby was also created. The lobby was designed to be two stories at the front with a single story at the rear of the building. It did not seem appropriate not to have the formal high-

Del Mar Gateway

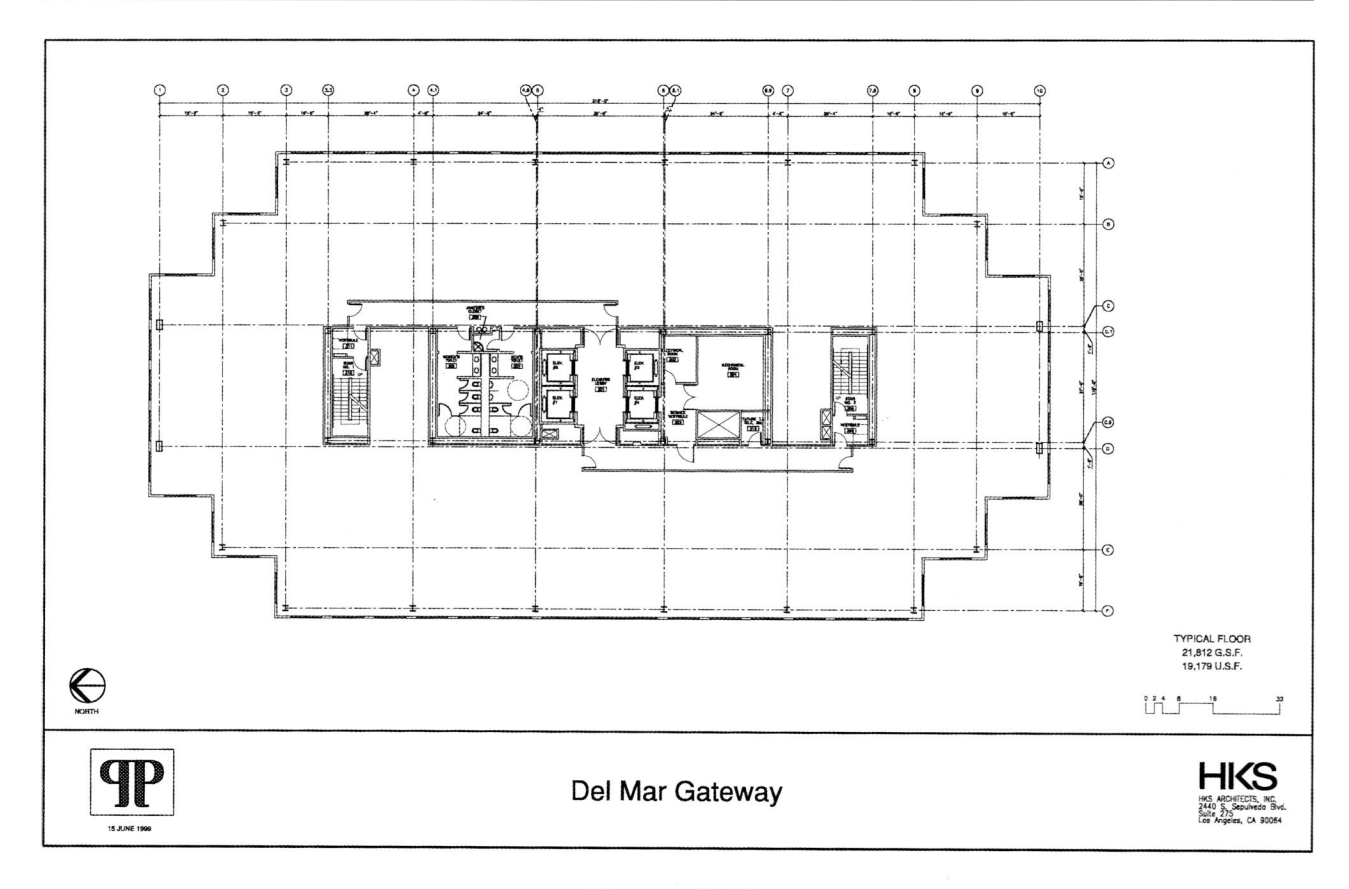

Figure 15-10

ceilinged lobby face the front of the building and the hotel, nor did it make economic sense to lose the rentable area required to have two-story lobbies on each side. The most appropriate solution would have eliminated the two-story lobby concept and raised the first floor height by 4 or 5 feet, with the same lobby height on each side, but this optimum solution was prevented by the height limitation placed on the building through the Substantial Conformance Determination.

With the site orientation set, efforts shifted to resolving the building design. The stepped ends of the building and the setbacks on two corners of the eighth floor were fixed and the budget was looking tight. The three variations of Schemes 5A and 1A best represented the objectives and the best features of each were combined. Efforts were concentrated on simplifying the façade, while retaining some flair, or character. This objective was primarily accomplished by differentiating the center bay on each side from the others through a series of recessed shadow lines, eliminating some granite, and recessing the glass line plane behind that of the granite. Different treatments for the corners were tried by interchanging some spandrel glass for granite. The final design of the façade is discussed more fully in Chapter 20.

The final size of the hotel banquet facilities was resolved, and a tentative verification of the total number of parking spaces was determined to be about 900. Approximately 90 spaces could be provided as surface parking, leaving about 810 to be provided in the structure. The variations considered in reaching the final parking structure design are left to Chapter 24.

The space between the building towers was studied both for visual impact and traffic circulation, and was believed acceptable. To accomplish the future lot split between the office building and the hotel a minimum of 20 feet is

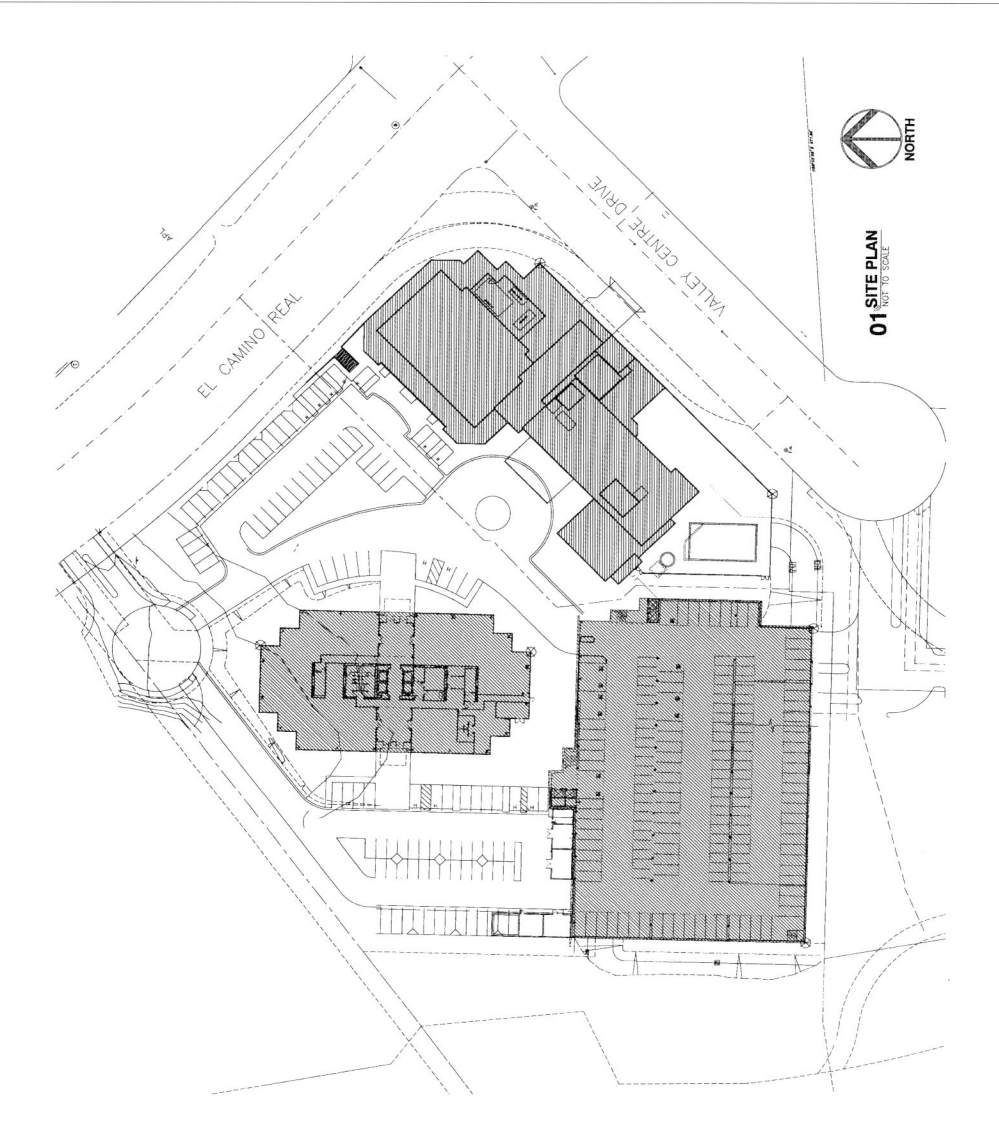

Figure 15-11

required between the hotel and the parking structure.

The necessary separation was further complicated by the fact that Marriott determined the pool and deck area to be much too small. The additional size requirement was first provided by relocating the parking structure entrance to the back side of the structure to permit extending the deck southward. Additional space was obtained by removing one 18'6" bay from the parking structure, replacing the lost spaces at the lowest level. Finally, an agreement was reached to extend their deck as far as necessary into the legal separation space—as this use would not affect the legality of the lot split.

After the required changes to the office building, hotel and parking structure, everyone was satisfied that it was a basic design and site plan that worked successfully for all concerned.

EL CAMINO REAL

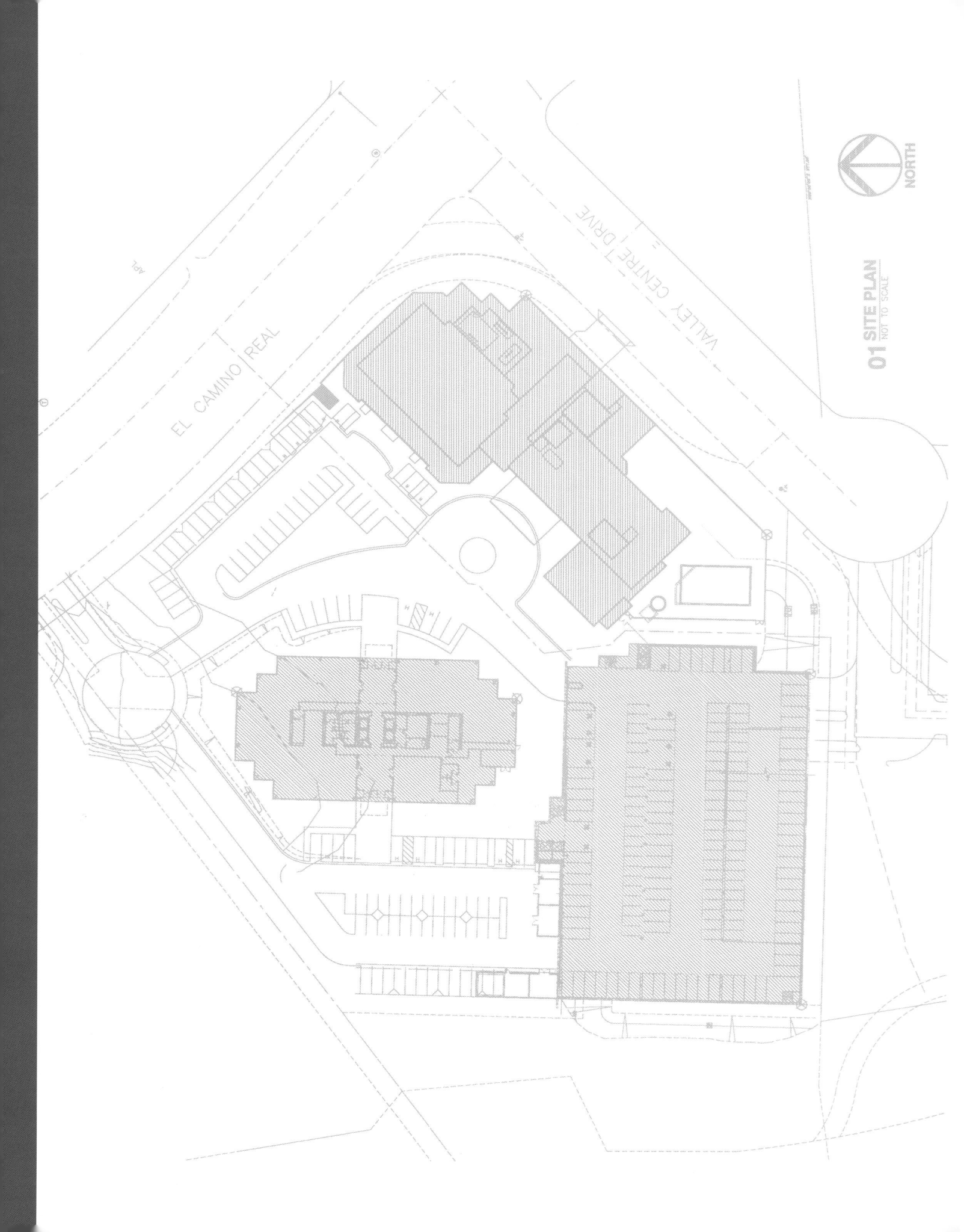

VALLEY CENTRE DRIVE

NORTH

01 SITE PLAN
NOT TO SCALE

FLOOR LAYOUT DESIGN 16

One of the more important marketing issues the Development Officer must address in building planning is to develop floor layouts that will be efficient for the various size and type of firms that are likely tenants for the building. It is important to resolve the basics of the floor plan as part of the Schematic Design Phase.

There are six main concepts in floor layout—floor size, bay depth, module, column location, corridor layout, and efficient use of the core that will be discussed in this chapter, along with test floor layouts and individual tenant space planning.

A major basis for this effort is derived from the Project Design Center as determined from the Market Study.

Floor Size

Simplistically, large tenants like very large floors, since they will require a lesser number of floors, with its resultant reduction in interfloor traffic and improved interaction efficiency (up to some reasonable maximum size). Smaller tenants prefer smaller floors, since they can have a more prominent position in relation to the elevator lobby, they do not feel lost on the floor, and they are closer to service facilities. Site size, setback and other zoning requirements will frequently set a maximum limit on the floor size. Notwithstanding any limitations, an optimum floor size for a downtown high-rise building with a high percentage of larger professional firms is in the 18,000 to 25,000 rsf

---

When developing the First National Bank of Chicago headquarters we encountered a difficult problem solving the conflicting criteria of very large, virtually column-free banking floors, with the top thirty floors requiring appropriate bay depths for speculative tenants. This was further impacted by the bank's desire to have a very distinctive design that would, in essence, be their international "logo." The lower bank floors were the full depth of the initial half-block site, and the building gradually curved upward to the start of the tenant floors. The solution was satisfactory in this instance, but it is not recommended for normal speculative office buildings.

range. Downtown buildings with a preponderance of smaller tenants would be in the 12,000 to 18,000 rsf range.

Suburban buildings catering to very large tenants can have floors of 40,000, or even 60,000 rsf. Construction of a third exit stairwell on large floors should be considered when the distance between the two basic stairs reaches 175–200 feet, even when not required by code. The extra stair can facilitate the layout of one-half floor or larger tenants while not affecting leasing of the remainder of the floor to smaller tenants. Frequently an extra pair of toilet rooms are deemed necessary on floors exceeding 40,000 rsf, and corridor lengths can become a problem after they exceed 80 to 90 feet in length. Many buildings put wet columns on large floors (hot and cold water, drain and vent piping) to facilitate a tenant locating water-using services, such as private toilet rooms, kitchens and dining rooms away from the core.

Bay Depth

Also called the core to glass dimension, bay depth varies in desirability depending on the tenant's size. There are varying opinions on optimum bay depths, but they do not range too widely. For medium to large tenants, the author believes 45' to 46' is close to optimum. This dimension was formerly based on a 15' band for perimeter offices, a 10' band for clerical and service, a 15' band for interior offices and conference rooms and a 5' to 6' circulation corridor. The increased use of computers has changed the historic 1:1 ratio of managers to clerical support, and the interior area

There are times when you follow your market information and gut feeling, and not the normal rules of thumb. In the early 1980s we had a site at 780 Third Avenue in New York that could be entitled for 500,000 square feet. The zoning rules at that time dictated that we could build out to the property line on the adjoining streets, but would have to step back several times in "wedding cake" fashion. By setting back far enough from the streets a straight shaft building could be constructed, but it was limited to 10,000 square feet of rentable area per floor. It would be a much more attractive building, but extremely inefficient. In spite of the calculated rentable area, only less than 8,000 square feet could be carpeted. The market data indicated it was a small tenant market, and an attractive building would be a very positive draw, so we proceeded on that basis with our fingers crossed. In spite of the assumptions, almost one quarter of the space was leased to Wang. The building was highly successful.

now tends to be used for cubicles for professional staff. The trend toward smaller cubicles has also created the need for team and/or conference rooms. The net result has been that the preferred overall dimension has not really changed. Bay depths larger than 46' are useable primarily for open planning.

For a mix of slightly smaller tenants, 41' to 42" works very well, and for much smaller tenants 30' to 36' seems to work well, as it keeps small spaces from being too narrow. Some buildings have offset the cores, such as 45' on one side and 35'–40' on the other to facilitate the layout of various office functions. A decision to offset the cores should be considered carefully to ensure the reasons are valid.

The author has always preferred the bay depths to be 31', 36', 41' and 46' because it permits a more satisfactory nominally 6' corridor, with the remainder of the space in even 5' modules for tenant layout. This extra will usually have to be integrated into the core depth in order to avoid impacting a proper planning module.

Module

The module is the repetitive square section of the floor that permits better organization of space. People have recommended everything from 4'0" to 6'0", on 1" increments, some with very convoluted reasoning. The 5'0" module has been the most commonly used over the last two decades, and is still the most common dimension for structural purposes, but the 6'0" and 4'0" modules are becoming more popular. Structural limitations, limits on overall dimensions and façade design sometimes dictate the choice. The module is intended to provide an organized layout where every partition that extends to the perimeter butts into either a column or a window mullion. The module was formerly used to arrange light fixtures on a repetitive pattern but, due to energy concerns, fixtures are now oriented more on a functional basis. The typical office sizes with differing modules, and their relatively similar areas, can be shown as:

TYPICAL OFFICE SIZES—VARIOUS MODULES

4 Foot	6 Foot	5 Foot	Office
12' x 12'	12' x 12'	10' x 15'	144–150 sf
12' x 16'	12' x 18'	15' x 15'	192–225 sf
16' x 20'	18' x 18'	15' x 20'	300–324 sf

During the 1980s, 12" x 12" fissured tile was considered the most desirable ceiling material for quality office space, and it works well with 12" wide or 24" wide light fixtures and the 4'0", 5'0" and 6'0" modules. Use of 24" x 24" ceiling tile has become much more acceptable and works particularly well with a 4'0" or a 6'0" module.

The ceiling support system should be run so that any partition on any module line can be properly braced, and lighting fixtures and air conditioning grilles and returns can be dropped into the module easily. Air diffusers at the perimeter and perimeter lighting, if any, must be properly coordinated with the module.

The increasingly extensive use of cubicles, the egalitarian tendency of some tenants toward placing managers offices inboard, and the use of corridors along the window line to create a lighter and more pleasant feel in the cubicle area have tended to reduce the importance of the planning module.

A further trend in office planning and layout is the use of smaller workstations for the individual worker, but providing group or shared space to promote interaction and shared creativity.

Column Location

Poorly planned column locations, usually the result of an unusual building shape or an attempt to reduce initial construction cost can impact the efficiency of the layout of tenant spaces by forcing wall locations or work stations to positions other than desired. This issue can be verified through testing with various tenant layouts.

Corridor and Exiting Layout

The core should be carefully laid out and tested for the ability to have a minimum amount of space dedicated to corridors, and also be able to fit in tenants of all sizes without exiting problems. Public corridors, as well as demising walls between tenants, are built from the floor to the slab above, or with a fire resistant lid, and must have at least a one-hour fire resistance rating.

The building codes drive the arrangements that limit the manner in which the floors may be laid out in an effort to satisfy the exiting requirements for all tenants. Public corridors must connect the exit stairways, which themselves must be separated by a minimum and maximum distance by code. The minimum separation in most jurisdictions is one-half the maximum diagonal of the building, with permissible dead-end corridors of 20 feet beyond the stairway entrance. Even where a dead-end corridor is permitted, it wastes space that might be conserved if more care were taken in the placement and layout of stairways and individual tenants. Some jurisdictions measure the distance between exits "as the crow flies" and some by "path of travel." It is often prudent to extend the distance between stairways further to facilitate accommodating smaller tenants, being careful to leave sufficient space beyond the stairways to permit efficient layouts outboard of the stairway.

A "Z" corridor, which goes through the elevator lobby and extends out in different directions to a stairwell from opposite sides of the lobby, is the most efficient solution for a multi-tenant floor. It is permitted under BOCA, and permitted under UBC if the elevator lobbies have smoke proof doors. Where "Z" corridors are not permitted, an additional corridor that parallels the elevator lobby is required. A "Z" corridor usually permits all core doors to have access to the corridor. The adjacent sketch shows a "Z" corridor with the four possible dead end corridors. In some jurisdictions where "Z" corridors are used, the smoke barrier doors at each end of the elevator lobby must have one leaf able to swing in each direction of travel, which can create a difficult design issue as discussed in Chapter 23 under Floor Elevator Lobbies.

In some cases, due to a large number of smaller tenants located on a floor with a less than optimum exit stairway location, an inefficient loop corridor will be required. Any increase in corridor length beyond the minimum corridor decreases the useable area, and thus increases the rentable/useable (R/U) ratio and the "add on" factor. If the add on factor exceeds the norm in the market, this excess may not be recoverable and require a downward adjustment in the effective rentable area.

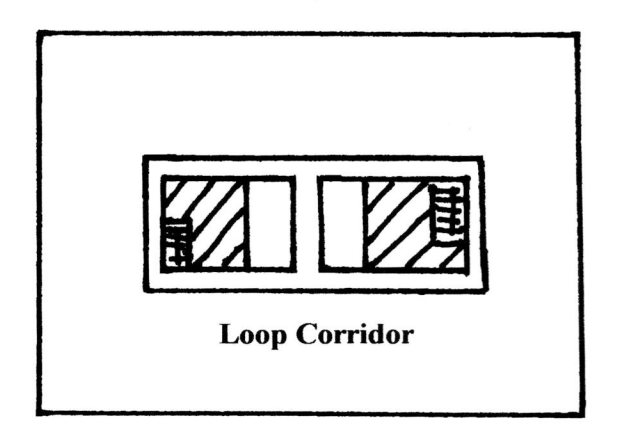

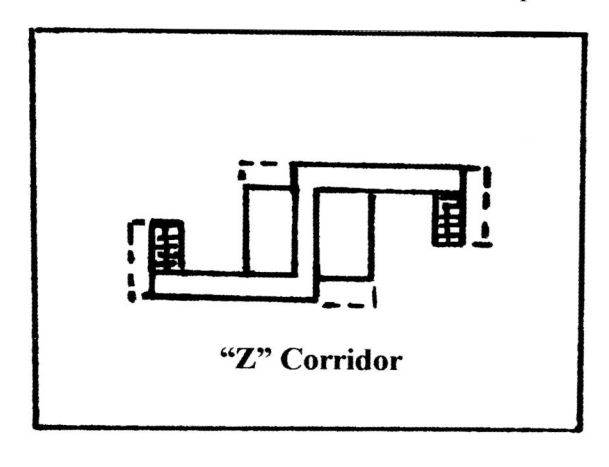

Loop Corridor

Another major code issue to address is that any tenant space exceeding 3,000 sf under UBC (5,000 sf under BOCA) must have a second exit to the corridor with access to a second exit stair. When a second exit is required, the two must be separated by ½ the diagonal of the tenant's space. Again, some jurisdictions measure this distance "as the crow flies" and some by the "path of travel." Even when a tenant occupies less than 3,000 sf the single exit must be located so that it permits the occupant to travel to either of two different exits.

Even when an exit corridor is approved for permitting of the base building, some tenant layouts may require additional rated exit corridors. Exiting requirements vary with projected population, but most jurisdictions require that personnel must not pass through more than one room beyond the one in which they are located before reaching a rated corridor. Exiting plans are now required in most jurisdictions as part of permit approval of tenant plans.

On the ground floor most jurisdictions require one exit from a stairway to go directly to the outside while the other one may exit through the building lobby. A few require that exits from both stairways go directly to the outside. This second regulation

"Z" Corridor

makes it difficult to provide quality first floor space to a major user, but the first approach may require that the building lobby have a one-hour rating.

One must always be alert to unusual local regulations. In Burbank, and some other jurisdictions in California, if the distance between a wall and a core is 12 feet or less, the space is deemed to be a corridor, and everything in that area must be of one-hour fireproof construction for the entire length of the space.

Efficient Use of Core

A core width is normally dictated either by the number of elevators in each bank, the length of the stairwell and vestibule, mechanical room sizing or the toilet room dimensions. The outside to outside width of the core is usually about nine feet times the number of elevators in a row, and varies with the type of structure. If a core is not laid out carefully, there may be relatively unusable areas in between fixed functions. In addition, when a lower rise of elevators drop off, there is further open space in the core. Consideration should be given to ensure that such spaces are of appropriate proportions for use as file rooms, computer centers, break rooms, libraries, etc., which are important space requirements that should be located as centrally as possible.

As mentioned earlier, the most effective core design is to split the stairwells out further to provide better egress conditions for locating smaller tenants, more useable interior space for major functions, limited only by the necessity of providing efficient space between the stairwell and the perimeter of the building.

The following sketch shows the first cut at a core with a freight elevator. If each floor had a mechanical room, it could be located behind the electrical and telephone closets, or they could be rearranged to have straight through mechanical room. The stairwells will almost assuredly be placed further away from the core elements to create effective space for smaller tenants.

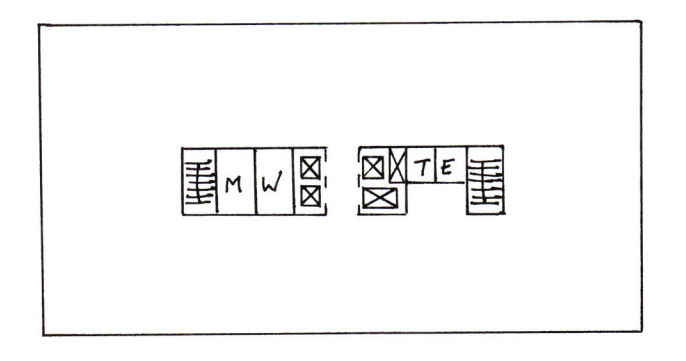

Some buildings place the entrance and elevator shafts at one end or on a corner of the building. The author believes this should only be done when absolutely necessary due to an unusual site configuration, or to satisfy a particular tenant requirement. Even so, it should be studied very carefully to ensure that in the future the building could be effectively leased to a mix of smaller tenants.

Test Floor Layouts

In spite of all the thought and analysis put forth in developing a floor layout, it should never be accepted without a series of test layouts by an interior space planner familiar with the various size and types of tenants most likely to be prospects for the building. The analysis includes not only the efficiency of the space for the tenant's use, but the ability to fit in smaller tenants while satisfying all regulatory requirements. Some developers send their initial floor layouts to three or four space planners for comment, rather than selecting one to work with from the beginning.

Test space layouts are a working tool, and need to be accurate, but not artistic. The layout in Figure 16-1 is almost hand traced over the proposed floor plan, but clearly makes its points. Note that a tenant located in the lower left hand space has access to only one exit direction and could not be expanded without failing to meet the requirement for the exit door separation.

Figure 16-2 on the following page is drawn in a more polished manner, but the information is no clearer. Note the length of the dead end corridors required to accomplish the positioning of reasonably sized tenants. This layout indicates a problem obtaining the required tenant exit door separation was improved by moving the stairwell one-half bay further outboard from the core.

It is important to point out that if certain spaces are difficult to lease due to their shape, orientation, or of an unnecessarily large size, rental rate concessions may be required that will reduce the average rental income for the building.

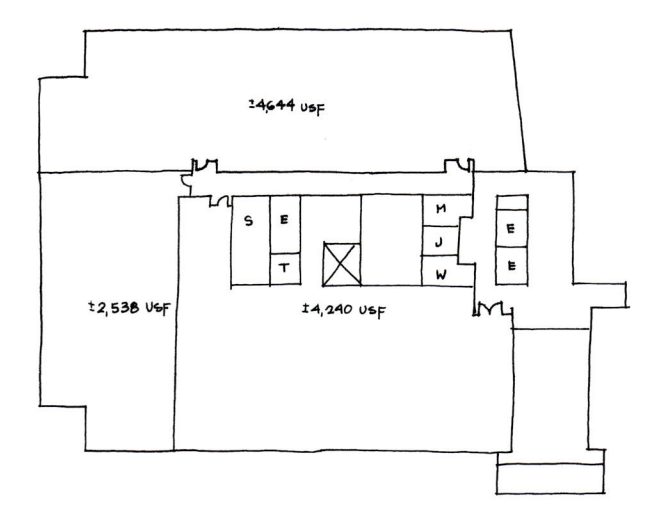

Figure 16-1

The test layouts are used to verify the appropriate distance between exit stairwells and from each stairwell to the end curtain wall, and the location of other core elements, in order to best facilitate the fitting of small and medium sized tenants on the floor.

Individual Tenant Space Planning

While not the primary responsibility of the Development Officer, it is important to understand some of the issues that may arise as tenants plan their space, even though the base building layout is designed to meet code and facilitate tenant locations. Within the tenant space, most jurisdictions require an exit plan, which indicates the number of occupants in different areas and their path of exit. A common requirement is that an occupant load of ten or more from a given area may only pass through one other room before reaching a rated exit corridor; populations in excess of 50 persons from an area must have two paths of exit. This type of requirement frequently forces a tenant to build or extend rated exit corridors within their space.

Normal practice when leasing to a full-floor tenant is for the base building to optionally construct the elevator lobby, but never the remainder of the corridors. The tenant is provided with the TI allowance for what would have been the standard corridor useable area, and they construct the exiting required in accordance with code.

THIS SHOWS THE BENEFITS OF THE 1-1/2 BAY SETBACK WITH RESPECT TO GETTING SUITE EXITS REQUIRED CODE DISTANCE APART.

Figure 16-2

CASE STUDY

A few test layouts were prepared on the first proposed floor plan, two of which are shown as Figures 16-3 and 16-4. The evaluation of the layouts indicated there might be some problems with tenants who exceed 3000 usf in the upper right hand and lower left hand corners of Figure 16-3.

The stairwells were moved out 10 feet each from the initial design, and the mechanical room was moved from one side of the core to the other to provide more flexibility in the core. These core changes, when combined with the previous widening of the core by two feet so the brace framing would not negatively impact the toilet rooms, created a very efficient floor plan while helping to make the brace frame structure both more efficient and more acceptable.

The final core to glass bay depth was 42'6". The original target was 40'0", but when the floor plan was reevaluated in order to square up the building within the site plan it was determined that 42'6" was fully satisfactory. When the floor plans were accepted the final area tabulation shown in Figure 16-5 was prepared.

The building module is 5'0". In the typical bays the module is measured from the centerline of the vertical granite to the mullion between the two lites of glass. In certain central and corner bays the nominal glass width is increased to 5'0" in order to maintain the module. See Chapter 20 for further discussion.

The revised floor plan was tested (two of the layouts are shown here as Figures 16-6 and 16-7) and were found to be very efficient for both full-floor tenants and small tenants. The column-free space between the core and the perimeter increases the efficiency of all layouts.

Note that the floor plans show the smoke proof doors at each end of the elevators swinging outward. This was the way the base building was approved, along with the "Z" corridors. When tenant layouts were reviewed with the city, it was determined that a "Z" corridor could not be used for exiting unless

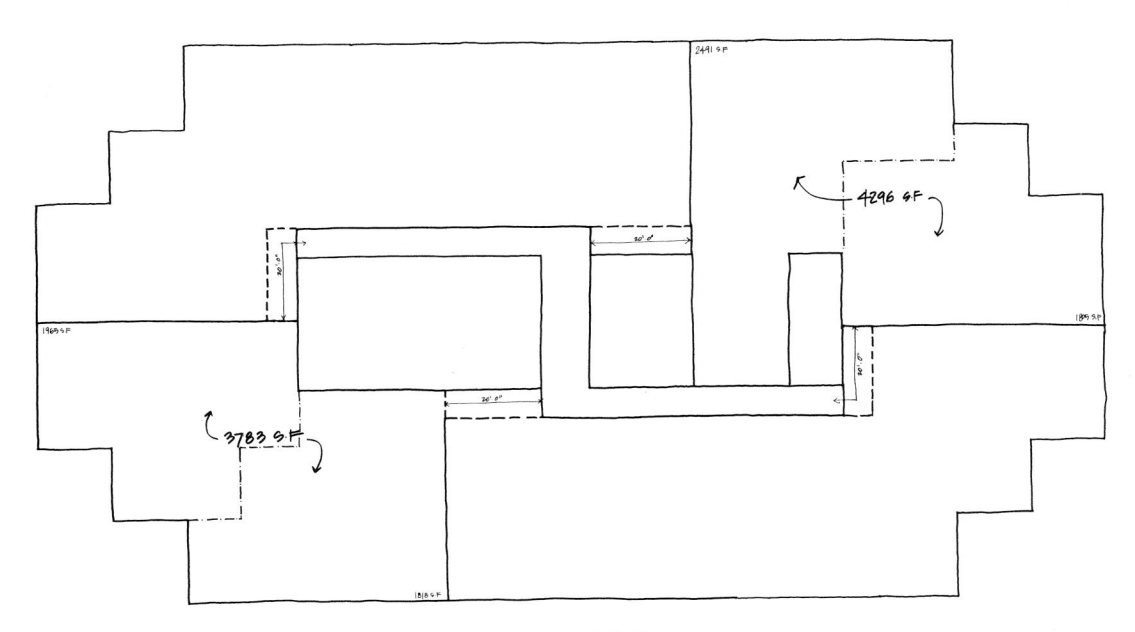

Figure 16-3

Del Mar Gateway
HKS Project No. 6244

7/1/99

NO CORRI-DORS FLRS 2-8; NO ELEV. LOBBIES FLRS 4-8 Floor	Gross Measured Area	Building Common Area	Adjusted Gross Measured Area	Vertical Penetration	Floor Rentable Area	Floor Common Area	Floor Usable Area	Pro Rated Building Common Area (0.029744)*fra	Adusted Rentable Area	Building R/U Ratio
1	21,320	4,985	16,335	945	15,390	1411	13,979	458	15,848	1.13
2	21,320	0	21,320	1856	19,464	1784	17,680	579	20,043	1.13
3	21,812	0	21,812	1051	20,761	1613	19,148	618	21,379	1.12
4	21,812	0	21,812	1051	20,761	1613	19,148	618	21,379	1.12
5	21,812	0	21,812	1051	20,761	1613	19,148	618	21,379	1.12
6	21,812	0	21,812	1051	20,761	1613	19,148	618	21,379	1.12
7	21,812	0	21,812	1051	20,761	1613	19,148	618	21,379	1.12
8	20,867	0	20,867	1051	19,816	1613	18,203	589	20,405	1.12
TOTAL	172,567	4,985	167,582	9,107	158,475	12,873	145,602	4,714	163,189	1.12

Rentable Efficiency 95%
Usable Efficiency 84%

Figure 16-4

one door at each end of the lobbies swung in the direction of traffic. This was changed so that one swung inward and was held open against the lobby wall, and the other swung 180° and was held open against the corridor wall. Balancing wood panels were used for visual balance as discussed further, including a sketch, in Chapter 23.

With a prelease tenant taking five floors, and another one taking the entire second floor, only one multi-tenant corridor plus the first floor exit corridors were included in the base building cost. The contractor was asked to price a typical corridor, complete with carpeting, lighting with a 2' x 2' direct/indirect fixture, full ceiling and several receptacles, which was $44,000.

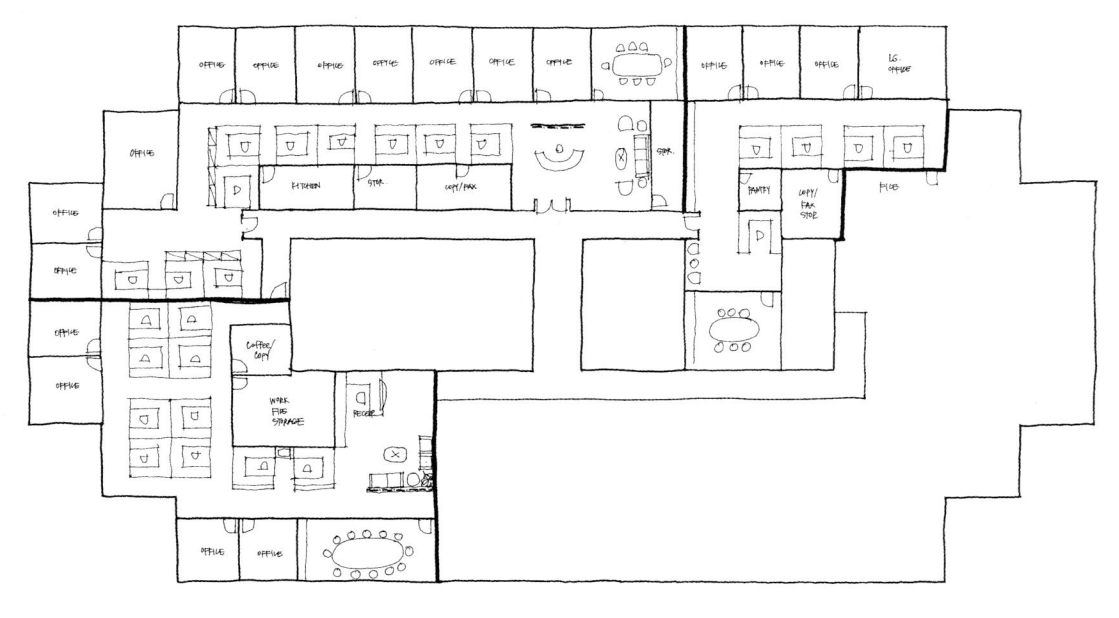

Figure 16-5

Floor Layout Design

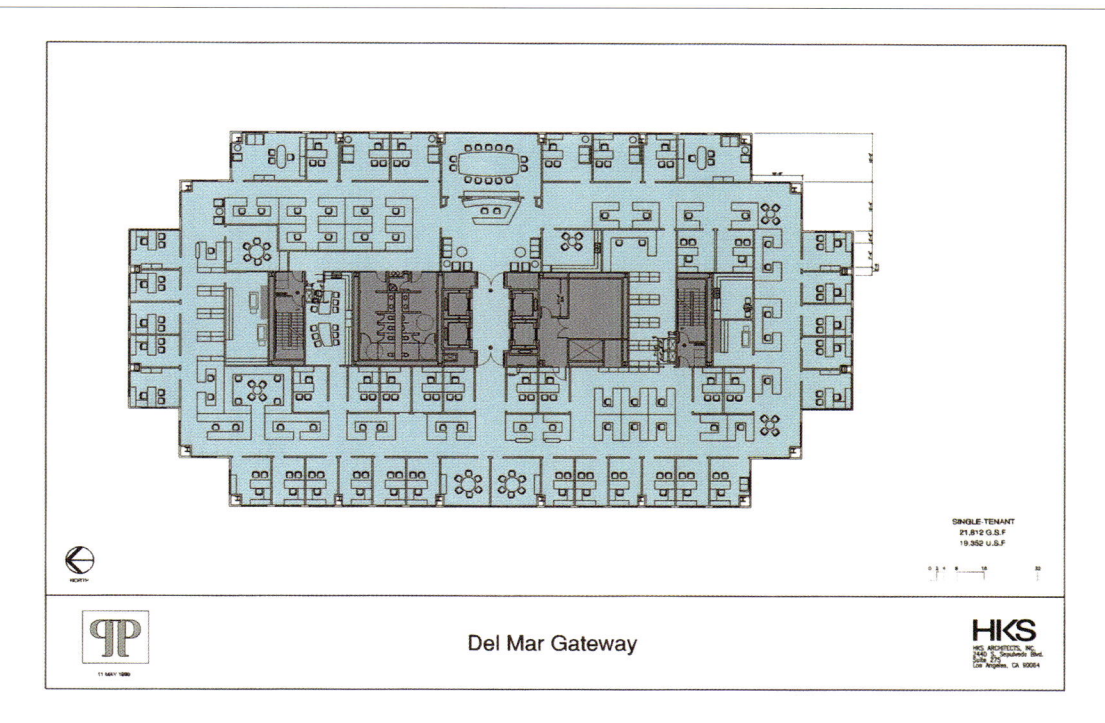

Figure 16-6

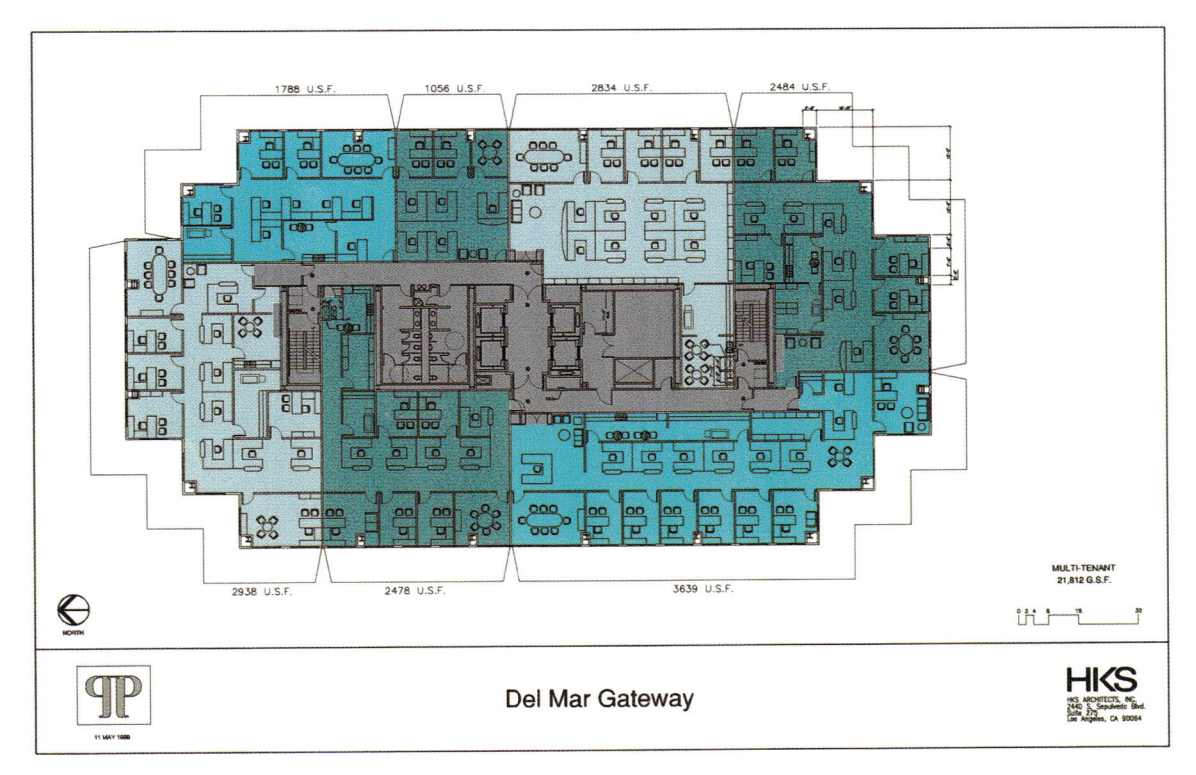

Figure 16-7

EL CAMINO REAL

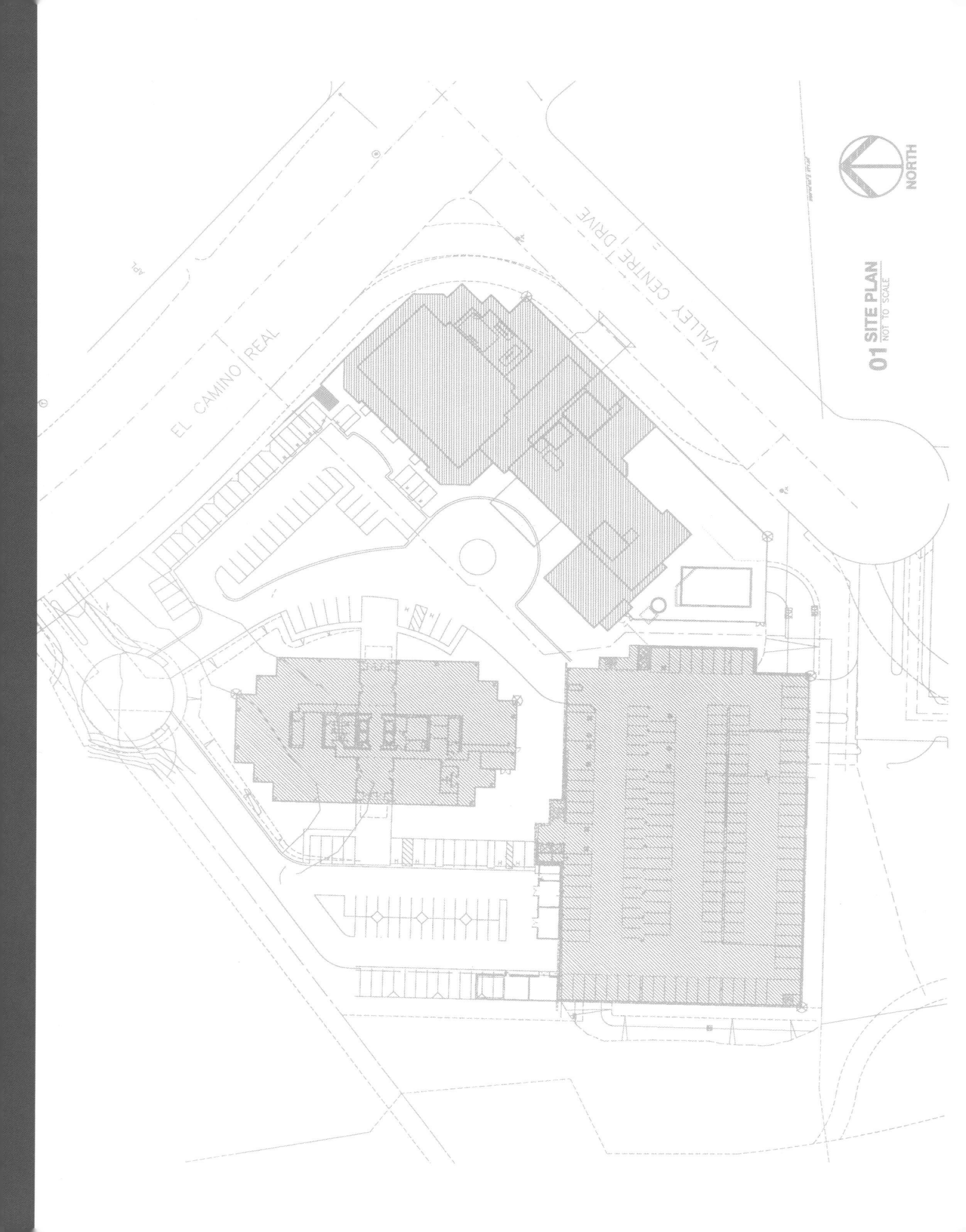

VALLEY CENTRE DRIVE

01 SITE PLAN
NOT TO SCALE

NORTH

MARKETING

17

Marketing is the concept of reaching a large number of potential customers and, sometimes, the public at large to create a sense of good will toward the firm or a project. Marketing is both corporate (i.e., general in nature) or product specific—in this work we will discuss only product specific marketing.

We will show in this chapter how the building design and the marketing and site specifics from the Market Study are the base for development of the marketing program. We will discuss the most common tools and methods utilized to reach the tenant base in order to have an economically successful project.

The type and scope of the marketing effort is determined by the company's stature in the marketplace, the project size and physical exposure, and the current status of the market. It is aimed both at the brokerage community and at potential users. A reasonable range for a marketing budget would be from 0.1% to 0.25% of project cost.

The arsenal of tools from which to choose, depending upon the budget and the project's needs, are discussed below. In addition to applying your own judgment as to which marketing elements to utilize, evaluate the competition in your market area, noting which elements are being utilized by other developers, and try to evaluate which techniques seem to be effective. In a marketplace in which you are unfamiliar, the opinions of the brokerage community, and possibly a public relations firm, will be extremely helpful.

The marketing program must have a clear objective and a coherent strategy. It must be based on an understanding of the market, the particulars and financial objectives of the project, and it must take advantage of the positive factors while minimizing or putting the proper spin on the negative factors.

The list of amenities to be provided in the project and the positive and negative relationship factors identified in the Market Study will have a major impact on the scope and direction of the marketing program. They are repeated here for reference.

Relationship to positive elements

- Visibility
- Public transportation
  - Trains or light rail
  - Bus
  - Airport
- Highway and road system
  - Highway interchanges
  - Traffic patterns
  - Degree of traffic congestion
  - Site ingress and egress
- Established office building market—equivalent or higher quality
- Major financial institutions
- Institutions of higher education
- Clubs, restaurants, hotels
- Public parking
- Retail
- Theater, cultural, entertainment
- Upscale residential—managerial decision-makers
- General residential—employee pool
- Parks, other amenities
- Fire, police and other public services

- Availability of state of the art communications services
- Signage regulations

Relationship to negative elements
- Industrial areas and manufacturing districts
- Overhead power lines
- Landfills
- Airport glide paths
- Sewage and water treatment plants
- Parking decks and rooftops
- Bus stations
- Slums
- Derelict hangouts
- Sexual preference areas
- Police station, jail, parole office
- Cemeteries

A marketing schedule or time line should be developed to coordinate with the project schedule, as the most effective use of publicity, ads, brochures, marketing center, etc. occurs when the timing is right. At the point when brokers and prospective tenants are most interested in a new project, the marketing materials must be available.

Public Relations

A public relations firm can be useful in establishing a positive attitude toward the project in the community, in the political arena and in the press. A PR firm can help you to capitalize on a unique marketing tool such as a name architect, a larger floor plate, a high tech building or an historical site, that can justify press releases. Don't confuse public relations with marketing—they are not the same but work in tandem.

Interesting press releases that obtain broad news coverage are far more effective than advertising.

Models

Models have formerly been the most effective way of conveying the design quality and details of a building to brokers and prospective tenants, but they are also one of the more expensive ways. Their greatest value is in marketing centers and in photographs for brochures where a picture of the model can be digitized into a picture of its future site. The greatest advantage of a model is for very large projects when it is imperative to attract a major pre-lease tenant. Models continue to be a significant advantage during the construction period, until the form of the building begins to take shape.

Models can be anywhere from a scale of ¼" to ¾" equals one foot, depending on the building size and type of detailing you are trying to show. A full building model is the most common type, and sometimes a second model is desired to show some special features. Most models show basically exterior features, although some feature lighted interiors. When the project is a multi-building project, a site model can be effective in showing both the initial and ultimate project. Professional model makers are located in most major cities. Where preleasing is not an important issue, and most of the leasing will take place after construction is well along, the expense of a model is questionable.

It is important to remember that model making has a long lead time. The exterior architecture must be essentially resolved before the work can begin. Delay in choosing exterior materials, color, etc. can hold back work on the model(s).

CAD Generated Computer Programs

It is now feasible to develop a CAD generated program that can be transcribed onto a CD-ROM or a tape, and this may well become the primary visual tool used to sell a project. This can show the entire project from an overview of the entire area, the site plan and the building from several prospectives. It can then "walk" the prospective tenant through the site, into the lobby, into the elevator and then into a finished floor that shows the tenant and base building finishes. The program can be artistically developed with plantings, art and scenes of surrounding areas. It can show any positive features of the project including amenities and the interior and exterior environmental systems and controls.

Renderings

Renderings are probably the most frequently used method of conveying the design of the project, prior to completion. Pictures of the rendering are essential for brochures or other printed material, if models are not available. Some architects prepare renderings for their projects, but it is normally more effective to use a professional rendering artist, usually an artistically inclined architect, who does nothing but building renderings. In addition to the full building, renderings of the building lobby, unusual views, and other special features are helpful to the leasing program.

Marketing Center

A good marketing center is a very effective, but costly, way to present a large, high quality building to the brokerage community and prospective tenants when preleasing is a major issue for the project. A marketing center can be located on site, where it can continue as a project leasing office throughout the lease-up period, or it can be located where it would best attract the targeted market. The center should be constructed of materials to be used in the project, particularly those materials which have the most aesthetic impact, such as a wall of the façade material, and an area representing the building lobby materials. The center would house the project model(s), material samples, all printed material, and usually office space for the leasing representative.

The purpose of a marketing center is to dramatize the project. It should be well thought out as to traffic flow, lighting, impact and drama.

A frequently used substitute for a real marketing center is a conference room, in either the owner's or the leasing broker's office suite, that is tailored to provide some feel for the finished product. It would

---

When Cadillac Fairview opened their office in Dallas we were completely unknown in that business community and local developers initiated a negative campaign about the invasion of Canadian developers. Our first project was the 50-story First City Bank building and, although we did have the bank as a lead tenant for 25% of the building, we needed to find an appropriate way to put our story before the market.

We elected to develop a full-scale marketing center, which consisted of two offices, a reception area, two models and various material samples. The marketing center itself was constructed largely of the materials to be used in the project.

One of the models represented the complete building and it was about seven feet tall at a scale of 1/8 inch equals one foot. The other model consisted of the lower levels only, indicating the bank hall, landscaped areas and the various entrances to the project—at a scale of ½ inch equals one foot. The models were lighted inside, occupants were represented, and there was an interesting presentation to go with them.

When developing an expensive marketing center, it is very difficult to know with any certainty whether the money spent will bring a reasonable return. It was only our newness to the market and size of the project that led us to present such an expensive facility. While it is hard to evaluate the benefit in the long term, we did make one 15-year lease of 125,000 square feet at full pro forma rental rates prior to starting construction based solely on the reaction of the partners in the law firm to our marketing center presentation. I believe we also gained significant credibility within the business and governmental communities.

In contrast, at the Del Mar Gateway project used as the Case Study, our basic marketing tool was a small brochure prepared by the brokers, and that was not complete until the building was over 90% leased.

contain the brochures, sample boards of the materials to be used in the project, and have all of the project literature. It should have the ceiling system, light fixtures, wood doors, hardware, carpeting and any special detailing that would be found in the completed building. Under some circumstances such a facility would be beneficial on-site, usually when several buildings will be built on-site in sequence.

Material Sample Boards

Sample boards should be both interesting and attractive, but also understandable. Separate boards prepared for each important subject convey the message more clearly than too many materials on one board. One board should contain only the exterior materials, arranged to feature the most prominent one. A separate board would be effective for the lobby materials, including the material for the elevators and elevator doors. One board should represent the materials in the toilet rooms. If the interior materials such as the ceiling, light fixtures, doors, hardware, carpet and perimeter window treatment are not displayed in the marketing center samples, they should be mounted on a separate sample board. The effectiveness of the boards can be significantly improved with an attractive backing and/or border or frame. If the boards are not artistically done they will lose most of their value.

Brochures

Brochures are the marketing staple of every new building project. Contrary to the models and marketing centers, which are intended to attract tenants to a project not yet started or sufficiently completed, the primary purpose of the brochures is to induce prospective tenants to visit the site, and to remember the features when evaluating between several alternative buildings. Some brochures are a simple tri-fold from an 8" by 11" printed sheet, which I don't believe normally expresses the quality that was intended to be conveyed. It is important that the brochure, while not overly expensive, must not look cheap. Better brochures consist of a primary folder with a place for additional materials, such as the renderings, aerial photography or a location plan, floor plans, pictures, tenant work letter, descriptions of the project and its special features, the benefits of the location, and information on the company. Brochures should at a minimum contain pictures of the rendering(s), aerial photography or location plans, and floor plans, and the base colors used in the brochure should be reminiscent of feature materials used in the project or those identified with the owner. Project size and available funds determine the scope of the brochures.

Brochures are deceptively difficult to produce. They can be costly and they are not effective unless they depict the unique features of the project. Since models and/or renderings are photographed for use in the brochures, they must be completed before the brochures can be created, and the models and renderings cannot be completed until most of the major design issues are resolved

The promises made in brochures as well as the layout of the pages may need to be approved by the owner, which can require a further lead time. A consensus on the project identification (name) and the logo to be used, if any, is important.

Photographs

Photographs used in the marketing literature should be made with care. When photographing an existing building, it would be wise to use an architectural photographer, who specializes in portraying a building in its most attractive light. In a new project their primary benefit would be to display the surroundings, at least until the building is sufficiently completed to where a photograph can be a sales tool.

Direct Mail

Direct mail has historically been a reasonably successfully method of keeping the project in front of brokers and potential tenants. It is often combined with brochures, project status updates, announcements of new leases and other facts of interest. Prospective tenants can be obtained from a list of all tenants in the market area whose leases expire within the next two or three years, plus those who for other reasons you believe might be interested in your building. Direct mail is being replaced by e-mail.

Internet Site

An Internet home page is becoming an essential marketing tool and can show anything that can be put in a brochure, and contain all or parts of the CAD generated computer program discussed previously. Descriptions of positive building features and leasing updates, as well as remote cameras that show actual physical construction progress can be included. Brokers can be induced to review the site periodically by sending them enticing e-mail messages that merely require them to click on a key word to access the site. Promoting usage by potential prospective tenants is more difficult, but could possibly be accomplished through e-mail or direct mail. One caveat, to obtain repeat hits it will be essential to keep the site fresh with new and interesting information.

Advertisements

Although ads do not ordinarily sell a specific prospective tenant, they do reinforce the reality of a project still under construction or still available for lease. We are a visual people and out-of-sight is still out-of-mind. Consider color ads in broker guides and local trade papers that concentrate on real estate news. Other print media, outdoor advertising, direct mail, radio and/or TV may be tried if appropriate information can be obtained on reader or listener profiles.

I believe ads are most effective when there is some newsworthy event such as a milestone in the construction progress, newly signed tenants, or some feature of the building that might generate some public interest.

Ads should be an extension of the marketing center ambiance, the brochure design, and the quality of the project. A good ad can be used again and again.

Tombstones

Some marketing experts believe that tombstones representing signed leases are the most effective form of advertising. They verify actual leasing activity and the quality of the tenants.

Events

Events such as ground breaking, marketing center open house, topping out, and grand opening of the building are common with highly visible projects. These events must be well planned so that brokers feel they must attend and prospective tenants want to attend. Although the leasing team may be responsible for the events, a PR firm can be very helpful, and may be essential. The costs are significant enough that you will want to monitor the plans to make certain that good results are obtained—those results being high attendance, positive response to the project and press coverage of the event.

Brokerage Contacts

The most effective way to reach the brokerage community is through personal contact by your in-house leasing representatives and/or your selected office broker. Depending on the market size, each office broker should be contacted, either personally or through a key contact, and preferably meeting with the appropriate brokers in each office at one of their regular staff meetings at their offices. Other ways of reaching brokers and keeping your project in front of them are:

- **Broker parties**—usually a cocktail party held in the marketing center, if any, to help them to focus on the appearance and features of the project.

- **Video tapes or CD-ROMs**—either mailed to them, or handed out at a party or other face-to-face meeting. Hopefully they will familiarize themselves with the features of the project at their desk.

- **Handouts**—pens, mouse pads or other trinkets that a broker might keep on his desk as a reminder of your project.

- **Internet home page**—properly designed and interesting, it must be developed into an effective method of keeping the brokerage community informed regarding your project. A current project in Nashville, Tennessee, has three cameras located around the site, and every day the status of construction can be viewed on a current basis.

- **E-mail**—although a relatively new form of communication it has proven to be a highly effective way to contact the brokers at very low cost, and may be the best way to direct their attention to your home page.

Relatively few tenants do not use brokers, so being constantly in front of the different brokers greatly enhances the times your building will be shown to a prospect.

Potential Tenants

Notwithstanding whether you have a broker, you or other members of your firm should personally contact anyone believed to be a potential tenant for the project.

In the 1980s, radio and television spots were tried by building owners in Houston and other cities attempting to reach prospective tenants, in addition to going through the brokerage community. Those were very difficult times, when it was worth trying anything, but I am not aware that such advertisements were highly successful. General public newspapers are sometimes used, but I believe they are more likely to be of benefit only for very unusual projects.

Site signage, particularly when a picture of the rendering is added when the building is designed, is one way of reaching the general public, particularly decision-makers whose homes may be convenient to the site. Another version is to use billboards, but I believe the main value of these is when you have a multi-building site, and you may be attempting to attract build-to-suit tenants.

CASE STUDY

The marketing of Del Mar Gateway is greatly enhanced not only by its general attractiveness and high market demand for office space in Del Mar, but by its relationship to so many positive elements, as noted below.

- At eight stories tall it will have the highest visibility in its market area.

- Highway access is excellent. It is located at the intersection of I-5, the major north-south route to Orange County and Los Angeles, and the almost finished I-56, which will lead directly to I-15 and major residential centers to the east. It is in an area of reasonably free-flowing traffic, above the congested area that stops several miles to the south at the intersection of I-5 and I-805. Ingress and egress are very good.

- While there is minimal commuter rail service, there is bus service and reasonable access to Lindbergh Field in San Diego.

- It is located in an established high-quality office market.

- It has convenient access to the University of California at San Diego and San Diego State University.

- It is adjacent to the upscale Marriott, a DoubleTree is diagonally across the street and a new Hampton Inn is a block away.

- Parking at 4 per 1,000 gsf will be among the highest in the area.

- There are several adjacent restaurants, and two retail areas with multiple restaurants are located within two miles without requiring freeway access.

- There is ready access to such upscale residential areas, popular with managerial personnel, such as Rancho Santa Fe, Fairbanks Ranch, Rancho Bernardo, La Jolla and Carlsbad.

- There is almost unlimited access to general residential areas.

- Fire and public safety services are first rate.

- State-of-the-art communications are available in El Camino Real, including competing telephone high-speed Internet access service.

- Reasonable signage, including top of the building, are permitted.

- There are no negative elements that impact the project.

The early prelease of 100,000 sf to Brandes Financial, while still retaining signage rights to the top of the building simplified the marketing effort. The primary challenge was thought to be leasing the spaces subject to expansion options. This turned out to be a non-issue.

The lease to Scripps Bank followed soon thereafter and provided the project with another amenity, as well increasing the preleased area to over 80%.

A rendering of the project and material sample boards were prepared. The broker started to prepare a nice quality brochure, but when the Scripps and Heritage Golf leases occurred so quickly, they settled for a single-page flyer. There was considered to be no need for models, a public relations effort or a marketing center.

A web site, www.delmargateway.com, was established early. It included:

- Rendering
- Location maps and directions to the site
- Nearby amenities
- Site Plan
- Overall description of project
- Office building description and specifications
- Floor plans

- Stacking plan showing the space committed to Brandes
- Office space brokers
- Contact information
- Development team
- Pictures looking from building site

It was intended to keep the site up to date with all current leases, noting the location of remaining space updated weekly, but it was deemed unnecessary.

18

SITE DESIGN

Site work incorporates all work necessary to adapt the site to accept the final building product, and provide all necessary services to it, as well as the parking areas and the landscaping. This chapter will discuss design features relative to the Building Elevation, Grading, Storm Water Management, Traffic and Roadways, Parking, Utilities, Structural Base and Landscaping.

Building Elevations

An important early decision is the elevation of the building pads and the entry level of the building and any parking structure, particularly on projects that will ultimately contain more than one building. These decisions can have a major impact on sight lines, cut and fill costs, acceptable slopes of roadways and site drainage.

Grading

Grading is the overall sculpting of the site to accommodate the various functions. It must provide a level pad for the building, facilitate the water management program, provide appropriate sight lines and promote an aesthetically pleasing landscape design. Every effort is made to accomplish the grading by balancing out the cut and fill so as to avoid the costly importing or exporting of soil. Berms are used to avoid retaining walls, control water flow, adjust elevations, control views, provide noise and wind barriers, blend with the natural features of the site and minimize safety hazards.

Environmentally, it is better to minimize grading to avoid the airborne particulate matter and to retain the natural topsoil wherever possible.

Storm Water Management

Storm water management is a major part of the site and grading work. Water must drain away from the building in all directions to protect the building from damage in heavy rainfall periods. Many projects have an operable storm water system available adjacent to the property. In such instances, the number and spacing of storm water inlets should be carefully planned and should be laid out simultaneously with the streets to facilitate coordination with the curbs and gutters. Grading then directs all of the runoff to these inlets.

In a new requirement that may spread, the Los Angeles Regional Water Control Board has issued regulations, subject to state approval, that would require treatment or temporary storage of rain water prior to its leaving the site even when a storm water system exists. The rules, which would require treatment of 27,000 gallons of rainwater per acre of parking or other hard surface, are an attempt to reduce the emptying of contaminants into the storm water system and thence into environmentally sensitive areas. An alternate solution would be a percolation system that would ensure the water entering the ground rather than entering the system.

Where a sewer system does not exist the water is carried away by overland flow or through open channels or swales. The ultimate destination of storm water is normally covered in governmental plans for each drainage basin, and the drainage plan for each project must comply. Any permanent and temporary ponding, plus provision for facilitating aquifer recharge, is usually dictated by this plan. The civil engineer will have knowledge of the particular requirements in a specific location.

Energy dissipation, or the effect of the speed of the water runoff, must be carefully controlled where water passes over highly erodable soil. One means of controlling peak water runoff is by use of detention ponds, as many jurisdictions require that peak runoff after development must not exceed that which existed before. Detention ponds temporarily store storm water and then release it, or bleed it off, at an acceptable flow rate.

Retention, as opposed to detention, is the impoundment of runoff, which is then gradually percolated into the soil or released to the atmosphere. Retention ponds can be a major aesthetic feature while serving a significant role in storm water management. Retention ponds treat the water by removing suspended materials and providing contact with aquatic vegetation for removal of nutrients. Some ponds provide both retention and detention through the use of weirs to regulate flow versus retention.

Traffic and Roadways

Traffic is the major issue for most suburban office building developments. Existing traffic counts and projections of the traffic increases that are estimated to be caused by the project are normally required, frequently back to the freeway or major highway on and off ramps. Curb cut locations for ingress and egress are often negotiated with the local authority as those that create the least disruption to the flow of traffic. These curb cut locations can impact the way the site is laid out. Extra lanes, turning lanes, stacking lanes and traffic controls are often required to mitigate any congestion caused by the increased traffic created by the project.

The interior roadway system should be located so that it can provide an aesthetically attractive entrance with good visibility and, traffic flows permitting, provide the most direct ingress to the building. Clear and understandable access should be provided to the building entrance for visitors, and to the general parking areas for the employees, in the shortest and most direct manner possible. There must be provision for two means of egress, and emergency egress and fire lanes must be acceptable to the fire department. Multiple lanes should be provided at the egress points, particularly if there is a traffic controller, to avoid an exiting bottleneck.

Where the building cannot justify an internal loading dock, an external loading area should be provided that permits efficient truck access without interference with the automobile or foot traffic. Whether internal or external space is available, property management should assist in determining the size and location of the loading dock and screened trash handling and recycling areas.

Roadways and parking areas provide an opportunity to use recycled materials—crushed reclaimed concrete as a base in lieu of newly quarried stone, and blacktop using recycled tires as a major component.

Parking

Where surface parking, or even a parking structure is required, it is frequently the dominant land use. In a suburban building the parking surface(s) area will normally exceed the gross building area by 30% to 60%. Parking should always be laid out with a clear circulation pattern, preferably more or less balancing surface parking around the building to minimize walking distances. Short-term visitor parking should be located convenient to the main building entrance, and handicap and vanpool parking, by regulation, must be convenient to an entrance. The surface parking and roadway system should be laid out as efficiently as possible—the paving is costly and is less visually pleasing than green space. Dead end parking aisles should be avoided wherever possible. Although double-loaded building lobbies do take up extra useable area, the added convenience to employee access from parking areas can be very important. Further information on car sizes, parking stalls and parking modules are described in detail under Central Facilities in Chapter 24. Many jurisdictions now require a specified ratio of bike racks to car spaces, frequently requiring enclosed racks.

Where a parking structure is required, its location and proportions must be carefully analyzed to ensure that it is as laid out as efficiently as possible, as they are very expensive. It is not unusual for the best solution for a parking structure to drive other facets of the site layout and building design.

The parking lighting will be the dominant light source on the site as minimum light levels throughout must be maintained. The most common light sources due to their efficiency are high-intensity discharge (HID) lamps. These include high-pressure sodium that has a warm yellow to orange to red tone, and metal halide, which has more of a bright white to blue color. The light band from the high-pressure sodium fixture is very narrow, making it hard to discriminate between shades of color of illuminated objects, while metal halide provides reasonable color differentiation. Both types are very energy efficient, but generally, high-pressure sodium has been preferred because of their long lasting lamps (12,000 to 15,000 hour life) and the fact that their efficiency does not drop off as rapidly with time. Another type of HID lamp is the mercury vapor, which is frequently used for landscaping and sign lighting. The mixing of light types should be avoided.

Many jurisdictions now require that the parking area be provided with a minimum number of appropriate trees so as to provide a specified percentage of shade, computed after fifteen years growth.

Utilities

The other utilities—potable water, electricity, gas, sewer, telephone and cable—are located at their most accessible point from which they are brought onto the site. The issue of how much of the utility extension is paid for by the utility is sometimes negotiable. There is now, at least theoretically, competition among electricity suppliers that must be investigated, however, they will probably all use the same local distribution system. Whenever electricity can be brought in from a loop, or from two different substations, the dependability of the service is greatly improved.

There is currently telephone competition existing in many markets, and before long there will be cable competition. Both provide high-speed Internet access. Provision must be made to bring all available services into the building to provide the competitive benefits to your tenants, and particularly to be able to provide the fastest and most reliable Internet access.

Structural Base

An acceptable structural base is required for the building pad, parking areas, roadways and walkways. The most common is a stone aggregate base, but some soils indicate the use of lime treatment or a chemical treatment such as geobase, a slurry mixture of soil, high calcium fly ash and lime spread over the area and roto-tilled to a depth of 8" to 10". As previously mentioned, recycled crushed concrete serves as an environmental substitute for stone aggregate.

Landscaping

Dollar for dollar, good landscaping can have the largest impact on the perception of quality and building appearance. People relate positively to plants, flowers, flags and water features. Elevation changes with walls, berms, sculpted grading and raised planters add interest. Decorative paving indicates a place of entrance and/or special interest. Lighting for landscape, steps and grade changes, walkways, building façade and parking areas can create an attractive atmosphere in the evening, as well as improving safety.

The largest costs of landscaping are the grading, hardscape, irrigation and drainage systems, and soil preparation. Many people make the mistake of using all small plantings that will not reach their intended design impact for several years. This approach can be "penny wise and pound foolish," since the most critical period for any building is its initial lease-up. During initial construction, upgraded plantings at the site entrance, building entrances and any visual focal point can be an important factor in attracting tenants.

It is important to give full consideration to the appropriateness of plant materials and the conservation of water. Indigenous native plants will normally be hardier and require less water and maintenance. Irrigation systems, where possible, should be drip systems. Where extensive irrigation is required, such as where there are large lawns, consideration should be given to the possibility of reclaimed water when available.

Fountains, waterfalls and reflecting pools are very attractive, but care must be taken in the design, particularly if they are over occupied spaces or parking space. Fountains and water features are the most expensive item in landscape on a per square foot basis, and can be a costly maintenance item. Attractive paving designs at pedestrian entrances and automobile drop off points, particularly when bordered by flowers, give a sense of welcome.

An attractive hardscape area is important for employee breaks and outdoor lunches, as well as for smokers. The area should have sufficient benches or walls of a height suitable for seating, and well-located trash receptacles. The arrangement of seating walls and plantings can create the perception of partially secluded area for personal comfort. It is also beneficial to provide several electrical outlets for the potential use of food or coffee carts.

In urban areas the hardscape or plaza areas serve not only the employees, but also the general public. If properly designed they can be a positive leasing amenity. To be successful, a plaza must be attractive to people and make them comfortable. Multiple levels, sufficient seating, attractive plantings, water features and the availability of food services all tend to draw people to a plaza. A plaza that does not attract people and add to their enjoyment will result in funds expended with minimal return.

Many people consider sufficient seating to be the most important item for a plaza—but people prefer to sit on walls, stairs and fountain edges rather than benches. It seems people like to discover their own location of a place to sit.

Public art, whether required by the zoning code or desired by the owner can be an important element of the overall landscape and building design. I have always believed that public art is good when it receives an emotional reaction from the viewing public, whether the reaction is positive or negative. If it creates no emotional reaction, it has not accomplished its purpose. When a code requires a stipulated amount to be spent on public art, say 1% of hard costs, they will usually allow elements of water features, attractive hardscape, or landscaping to count toward part of that financial obligation.

The best of all worlds is accomplished when the landscape and building complement each other to provide a unified feeling.

Value Engineering

Value engineering for site work should consider:

- Balance of cut and fill
- Minimize retaining walls
- Use natural drainage wherever possible
- Reduce the amount of paved surface
- Locate buildings for the shortest distance for utility lines
- Use the contours of the land
- Upgrading plantings only where they have an impact

I was fortunate to be the project manager for the development of the First National Bank of Chicago headquarters, now Bank One Center. The tower was constructed on the north half of the block, and a multi-level plaza was built on the south half where the prior bank building was located. At the time of construction, Illinois law prevented branch banking so all banking activities were required to occur in this building. In order to provide three public banking floors, none of which was more than one floor from the entrance level, a major portion of the plaza was depressed so that the lower level had outdoor access.

The plaza was designed and operated to maximize the interests and activities of the public. The plaza had several intermediate levels, a small personal banking facility, a major fountain, extensive seating on the seating walls and steps, and a Chagall mosaic (shown in the picture as an elongated box prior to its installation). In addition, several restaurants ringed the plaza on the lower level, outdoor dining was provided on the intermediate levels when weather permitted, and there were popcorn, hot dog and flower carts. Entertainment was provided most weekdays during the lunch hour and occasionally at 5 PM on evenings when the department stores were open, but obviously not during the winter period.

CASE STUDY

The initial basic site design is very important in that in San Diego a grading permit is required prior to approval of the building permit, and requires a sign-off by many agencies and departments. It must show all easements, slopes, retaining walls, drainage, utilities, driveways, building pads, parking, irrigation and minimal landscaping. This plan was delayed as the hotel changed some of its requirements resulting in changes to the parking structure, and Pardee made certain other changes, which significantly affected the site plan.

The site design was based on the final site plan shown in Figure 15-11 after adjustments were made to solve certain issues, such as the hotel pool deck, reduction of the parking structure floor plate, and provision for a subdivision map.

The site steps down in both southerly and westerly directions, with a freeway and drainage easement on the western edge.

The office building was set at a final elevation of 79'0", the hotel lobby at 76'6" and the hotel basement at 61'6". The plaza entrances to the parking structure are at 78'0" and the lower entrance to the B-2 level of the parking structure, directly off of Valley Centre Drive, is at elevation 56'8". The final elevations were set to minimize any significant slope changes between the structures and to minimize cut and fill so as to reduce export of material, and the necessity for an excessive amount of retaining walls. The net export of soil was 11,000 cubic yards.

The office park has a completed roadway system and any traffic controls required for the prior Visitor Center project had already been installed. Only the interior roadways were required for this project.

Installation of several retaining walls was unavoidable. There is one wall about 275 feet long along the bank between the project and Executive Center, varying in height from 18" to 9'6". Another wall extends for 240 feet between the east side of the hotel surface parking area and hotel along the El Camino Real easement, ranging in height from zero to 8 feet. There are two 25-foot-long walls defining the hotel truck dock entrance that vary in height from 2 to 7 feet. All of the walls are constructed in Geogrid block, as they are both attractive and less expensive than concrete block.

The parking was planned at 4 per 1,000 gsf for the office building and 1 space per room, plus 1 space per 80 sf for banquet and dining for the hotel. Shared parking calculations indicated a requirement of approximately 900 spaces, as discussed in more detail in Chapter 24. There is convenience surface parking provided adjacent to the hotel and behind the office building with an approximately 800-car parking structure.

All utilities—water, gas, electric, telephone, cable and sewers—serving the office building are located in El Camino Real, except for the storm sewer discussed separately. There are actually competitive telephone companies with service in the street. The hotel will take all of its services from Valley Centre Drive.

The fire department required a fire lane loop around the office building to provide complete fire truck access. This was accomplished by re-arranging the surface parking behind the office building—making one bay narrower and limited to one-way traffic, so the other will be wide enough to satisfy the fire truck passage. A special reader will be provided at the entrance gate to permit the truck's electronic signal to open it. Removable bollards will be placed to permit the trucks to circulate between the office building and parking structure, while preventing use of this path by automobiles.

To avoid the installation of at least two very-expensive double-check valve assemblies the city was granted a 20-foot wide easement for the 12" fire line, which would run from El Camino Real through our entrance driveway, around the office building and back to the main in El Camino Real. There are three hydrants located on this loop. There are also three existing fire hydrants around the perimeter of the site on El Camino Real and Valley Centre Drive.

The 4" water and 1" gas lines both feed into the north end of the building. They pass through the water meter with a backflow preventer and gas meters, respectively, which are located just north of the building below the circular divider that separates the traffic between Executive Center Del Mar and Del Mar Gateway. There is a drop in elevation of 5'6" from the roadway to the ground level at the location of the meters that, with landscaping, makes them relatively inconspicuous.

Two 6" sanitary waste lines come out of the east side of the office building and connect to an 8" PVC waste line that connects into the main sewer in El Camino Real.

The storm drainage system consists of 18" PVC collector mains, one in the forecourt between the two buildings and one behind the office building to drain the site, plus storm drainage from the office building roof. They were planned to come together between the hotel and the parking structure, and then run down between them to the storm main in Valley Centre Drive. The soil-nailed wall (discussed in Chapter 19) prevented the main serving the west surface parking area from traversing between the office building and the parking structure, so it was rerouted to run directly through the drainage easement to a storm drain by the freeway.

The electrical power is fed by two 4" conduits for the high voltage 12kv service to the 4000-amp transformer where it is stepped down to the 480/277-volt building service. The transformer is located adjacent to the north wall of the parking structure. Ten 4" conduits extend from the transformer room to the main electrical room located at the southwest corner of the building, which has outside access for the utility company.

The diesel-driven emergency fire pump and 26,000-gallon fire water storage tank serving the office building are located along the west side of the surface parking area that is west of the office building. They were originally planned to be adjacent to the north wall of the parking structure, but the weight of the water tank was too heavy a load for the soil-nailed retaining wall of the parking structure. Their planned location was interchanged with the trash and recycling areas.

The emergency generator serving the office building is located adjacent to the diesel-driven fire pump. Two 4" conduits feed from the generator to the emergency transfer switch, which is located in a small room separate from but adjacent to the main electrical room.

Six 4" conduits are provided from the street to the main communications room on the first floor for telephone and cable service.

The trash and recycle cubicles are located along the north wall of the parking structure adjacent to the generator room, and the loading area, consisting of two outside berths, is located near the northwest corner of the office building.

The roadways through the site and the surface parking areas are asphalt concrete paving over an aggregate base, with a rolled concrete curb.

The area at the front entrance of the office building is decorative concrete for the full 27-foot width of the lobby, and extending from the lobby doors to the far end of the parking spaces in front of the building, a distance of about 55 feet. The paving is a mixture of rectangles of two concretes, primarily "French Gray" top seeded with exposed aggregate of Arizona Coral, and accent areas of "Tawny Pink" with aggregate as above. A 7'8" strip down the center contains two dark-gray medium sandblasted benches and alternate areas of the French Gray concrete, and planter beds with green ground cover. There will be four multi-trunk purple orchid trees on each side of the entranceway, with planting beds set into the walkway area. Large beds of India Hawthorn (dark green leaves, pink flowers, about 2 to 2½ feet high), New Zealand Flax (2½ feet tall, variegated maroon/dark green leaves, small reddish/orange flowers) Sea Lavender (large green leaf ground cover, lavender flowers) and Sea Pink Thrift (6" high ground cover, small pink flowers), and seasonal plantings are on each side of the walkway.

The landscaped area between the front of the office building (upper right), the hotel (left) and the hotel surface parking area (bottom) is shown in Figure 18-1.

The back entrance of the office building is the same except that the abutting trees are Evergreen

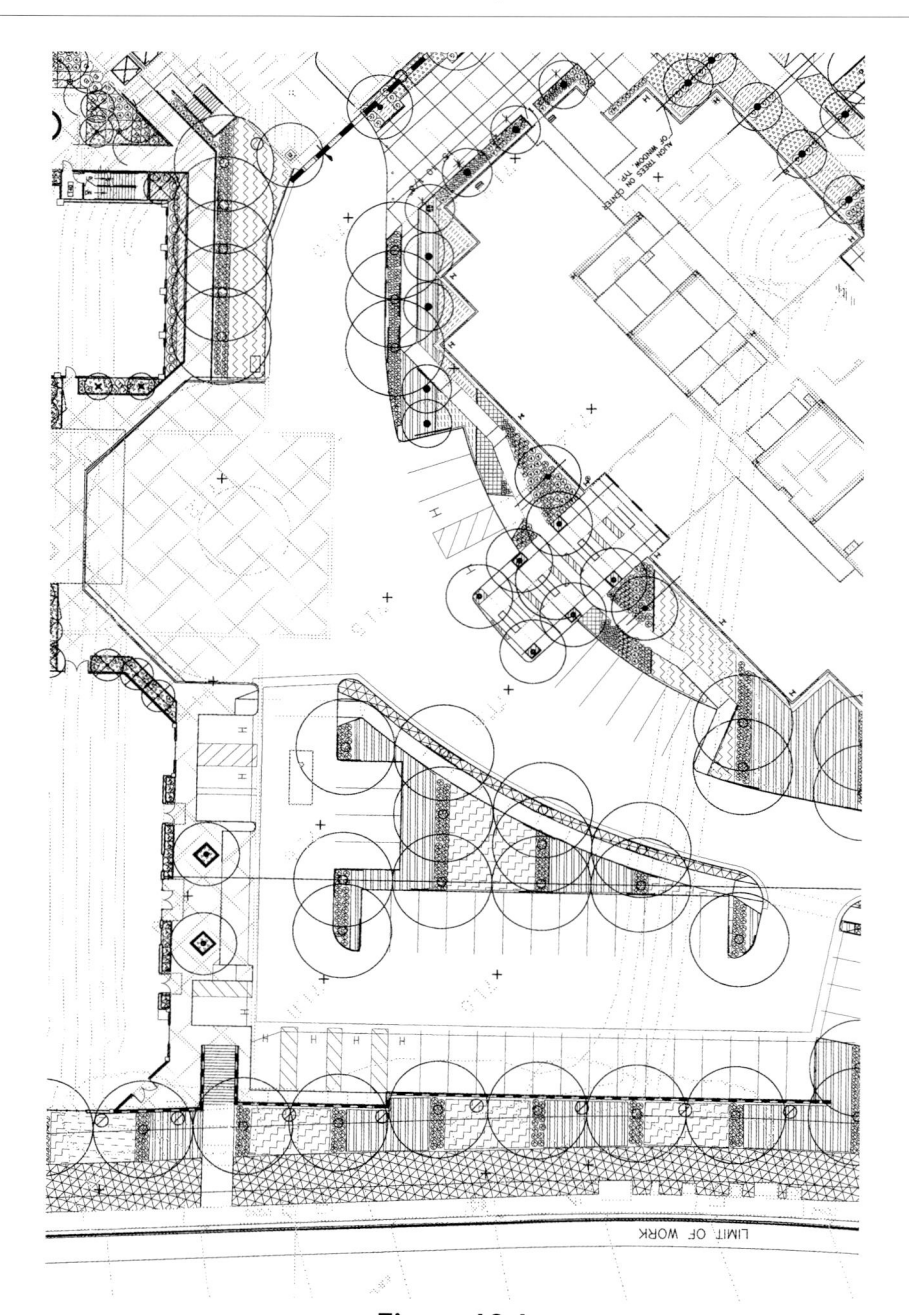

Figure 18-1

Pears (about 20 feet tall, dark green leaves, white flowers), due to the different sun conditions. These trees also extend along the entire west side of the building and around to the southeast corner of the building.

The paving along the front of the hotel is the same French Gray matching the entrances of the office building. There will be a fountain at the hotel front entrance that is not shown on the site work permit set, as it will be designed and installed by the hotel.

The area between the office building and the parking structure is paved with broom finish standard gray concrete with long accent strips of the Tawny Pink concrete with a sandblasted finish. This area serves as a pedestrian courtyard with trees and some benches, as well as the fire truck loop, which is restricted to other traffic by removable bollards.

This area also serves as a walkway between the parking structure stairs and elevators and the office building. The bike racks are located in this area near the elevators. San Diego Red Bougainvillea will grow up the screening on that face of the parking structure.

All other walkways are the broom finish standard gray concrete with accents of the sandblasted Tawny Pink.

The landscaping was selected primarily from indigenous drought-tolerant plants that require a minimum amount of watering. There is a complete irrigation system, however, on a timer to ensure that the plantings look attractive all year long. The selected plants flower mainly in the spring/ summer, some like the Star Jasmine and Sea Lavender bloom through the fall, and the India Hawthorn continue to bloom into the winter. Some plants will be interchanged to increase the amount of color in the winter.

There is a landscaped bank that separates this project from the Executive Center. It is lined with alternating groups of four Torrey Pines that are evergreens and four California Sycamores that are deciduous. These trees will grow to be 35 to 40 feet tall. The planting area beneath is covered with Pride of Madeira (3½ to 4 feet tall, grayish/green leaves, blueish/lavender flowers), Creeping Rosemary (18 inches high, greenish/gray, pink flowers) and Mexican Sage shrubs (ranging from 2 to 4 or 5 feet in height, with little blue and purple flowers).

New Zealand Christmas trees, evergreens that get to be 20 to 25 feet tall, are skirted up 8 feet and located in the center of the surface parking lot behind the office building and along the face of the parking structure. They are a gray/dark green with clusters of red flowers.

The area north of the office building and along the east side consists of repeating bands of Carmel Creeper (low spreading ground cover with dark green leaves and small violet/blue flowers), and Archtostaphylos (greenish/gray with pink flowers, about 18 inches high), separated by hedges of India Hawthorn. The northern area also contains Eldarica Pines, a gray/green evergreen that reaches about 30 feet in height.

The combined monument sign for the hotel and the office building is located adjacent to the entrance from El Camino Real. Surrounding the monument sign and extending to the interior drive is a planting area about 30 feet wide and 65 feet long, a heavy planting of shrubs that step down and away from the center line of the monument. The centerline row is Pride of Madeira, followed by parallel rows of India Hawthorn, New Zealand Flax, Sea Lavender and another row of New Zealand Flax. It provides a multi-color effect with a mixture of light green/heavy gray with maroon leaves and blue violet and yellow flowers in the spring and summer.

The area surrounding the hotel surface parking area is lined with Eldarica Pine, and they continue down and around the hotel. The planting areas have the same alternating parallel strips of Carmel Creeper and Archtostaphylos as the areas around the office building.

The immediate area of the hotel entrance has Star Jasmine (18-inch high ground cover, dark green leaves and white star-shaped flowers), Bird of Paradise (5 to 10 feet, dramatic leaves fanwise around the trunk, purplish/gray flower on a stem), Mexican Palm and Areca Palm, as well as two small fountains. Three 40-foot flagpoles are immediately adjacent to the entrance.

A row of Eldarica Pines is along the west side of the parking structure and around to the south side, with a continuous row of Hopseed Bush (reddish/green foliage, which grows to about 15 feet tall) to screen the parking structure from the freeway. There is a general ground cover of Creeping Rosemary and clusters of Mexican Sage and Pride of Madeira. New Zealand Christmas trees are included in planter pots on the upper deck of the parking structure to comply with code.

The area between the parking structure and the hotel pool deck is planted with alternating clumps of Pride of Madeira, New Zealand Flax, Bird of Paradise, Coreopsis (12 inches high, medium green leaves, yellow flowers) and India Hawthorn. San Diego Red Bougainvillea is planted to climb the walls.

The hotel strongly desired palm trees along the street sides of the hotel to provide more of a vacation setting and to highlight the resort portion of their business. Pardee rejected this request as inconsistent with the CC&Rs.

There is a 20-foot-wide SDG&E easement that extends from the property line to within five feet of the hotel and surface parking area. This created an issue in that the Substantial Conformance Determination and the city standard for this area required the planting of street trees along each street in the general area where the easement was located. The utility consultant attempted to negotiate with SDG&E to modify their position, but the utility was adamant that no trees were permitted in their easement. An additional issue arose wherein two column footings for the hotel were proposed to extend up to 72" into the easement, which was totally rejected, and they were redesigned.

The city landscape plan reviewers solved this dilemma by agreeing that street trees along the adjacent streets would not be required. This entire area on both streets was then planted with sod.

The landscape designer's original interpretation of the code's tree requirements for parking areas indicated that 40-square-foot tree beds would be required "in the parking areas," within 30 feet of each car, which would eliminate a significant number of spaces. The city landscape officials were additionally helpful in regard to the tree requirement in the surface parking areas. They agreed that by placing trees immediately adjacent to the parking area that it would count as trees "in the parking area" in order to meet the code. They further agreed that their requirement in the surface lot west of the office building could be satisfied by placing the trees in 6'3" by 6'3" tree wells turned 45°, so as not to eliminate any spaces. These changes resulted in a saving of nine parking spaces.

The lighting for the surface parking areas is provided by single and double, as required, low-pressure sodium fixtures on 20-foot poles to provide an average of 2+ foot-candles with a minimum of 0.2 foot-candles. Each fixture has two 90-watt lamps. There was a preference to use metal halide lamps, as it has a much better color rendition, but requirements of the city of San Diego for the use of metal halide are so stringent that enough fixtures could not be placed, without disrupting traffic, to provide satisfactory light. Apparently they believe high intensity metal halide lamps will interfere with the nearby observatories on top of the mountain. The problem with low-pressure sodium is the inability to differentiate between colors.

There are a series of bollards along all walking paths. They are 8" diameter cast aluminum, 42" high with two 32-watt compact fluorescent lamps (CFLs) shining through a louvered opening. They were planned to be metal halide lamps, but the city requires walkway lighting to extend all the way to the street as part of the emergency egress path and be on the emergency power system. Metal halide lamps are not acceptable for this purpose as, after a brief power interruption, they take about 10 minutes to warm up. A 35-watt PAR 20 lamp tree accent uplight is placed under each tree.

The bids on the site work originally came in at $1,700,00, which was much too high. After a value engineering effort, the cost was reduced to $1,480,000. The primary reductions were:

- Eliminating most of the originally proposed sandblasted finish on the exposed aggregate.

- Placing the 4" concrete pedestrian walkways over native soil rather than over the 4" Class II aggregate base.

- Placing the 6" concrete walkways in heavy traffic areas over native soil rather than over 6" Class II aggregate base.

- Placing 6" asphalt concrete pavement over native soil within the city water loop easement rather than 3" asphalt concrete over 4" Class II aggregate base. The remainder of the pavement stayed as specified at 3" of asphalt concrete over the 4" aggregate base.

- Reducing the amount of site lighting.

- Reducing the number and size of certain plants, however, there was a slight increase in the storm drainage cost due to the longer run to avoid the soil-nailed wall.

The structural changes to the paving outlined above were the result of the geotechnical engineer conducting additional testing in those areas.

STRUCTURAL DESIGN   19

The structure represents a major portion of the base building construction, usually running in the range of from 25% to 35% of the shell and core construction cost. Successful value engineering of this work, when coordinated with the impact of the architecture on the structure, can be a significant factor in effective cost control.

The foundation supports the building and the substructure resists the very considerable pressure of the soil surrounding it. The superstructure, or structural frame, supports the floor loads of the building and resists the horizontal forces of wind and, in some cases, seismic forces. Tall buildings are, in fact, designed for the desired degree of sway at the top under design wind force conditions.

This chapter will discuss various features of excavation and retention, foundations, substructures, reinforced concrete, the structural frame, structural efficiencies and fire resistance.

Excavation and Temporary Retention

When excavating for basements, foundation structure or other deep cuts, it is normally necessary to support and retain the adjoining soil to resist its sliding and overturning forces while the work is in process. This support, depending upon the system, can be either temporary and removed for salvage, or permanently incorporated into the structure. There are many methods used to provide earth retainage; the most economical selection is chosen based on the depth and width of the excavation, soil conditions, amount of rock or existing abandoned concrete substructures, water table level, the potential of flowing water and other conditions. Some of the more common methods of retainage are described below.

- Timber and plywood—plywood braced by lagging or timbers can be used for relatively shallow excavations.

- Sheet piling—heavy corrugated steel driven around the sub-surface site to prevent the earth from caving in until the structural walls can be built.

- Precast concrete soldier beams that are drilled into the ground.

- Soldier beams and lagging—"H" beams that are driven or drilled into the ground about 6–10 feet apart, with 2", 3" or 4" by 12" lumber wedged between them.

- Tie-back sheeting—long holes are drilled at a downward angle from the upper part of a soldier beam or other type of support, a long rod with an anchor on the end is inserted, and the hole is filled with concrete, often with an expanded mass at the end for greater resistance. Lagging is installed as above.

- Rock anchors—same as a tieback, but the holes are drilled into rock.

- Soil-nailing—similar in concept to tie-backs, but in this case the steel tendrels, spaced on a grid, are inserted in holes drilled downward at an angle, and filled with concrete. The holes are sometimes splayed for greater resistance. The tendrels hold a wire mesh that reinforces a shotcrete wall. Drainage boards are usually installed behind to prevent the build up of water pressure. The soil-nailing proceeds in predetermined layers as the excavation is accomplished.

- Slurry walls—usually a low slump concrete mix of chemically treated soil that is pumped into a trench or auger drilled holes to retain limited soil pressure and limit water intrusion.

- Cofferdam—vertical sheeting with internal bracing at various depths.

Under many soil conditions, structural retainage can be omitted by "laying back" the soil away from the hole at a slope at which the soil will sustain itself. This slope at which the soil is stable is determined by the geotechnical engineer and detailed in the soils report. After the permanent foundation or subsurface construction is completed, the soil is then backfilled against the work. While this is normally much less expensive, if the slope is low and there is significant depth to the excavation, the amount of area required to lay back the soil may be too great for the site or might cover so much area that it would delay other work until the backfill has been completed.

The importance of proper excavation retainage cannot be overemphasized, as there is a legal responsibility to protect neighboring property and streets, and hold them harmless from any damage resulting from your work.

Retaining Walls

Permanent free-standing walls that resist the sliding and overturning forces of the soil are called retaining walls. They are most commonly reinforced concrete or concrete block, and the diameter, amount and size of reinforcing bars, and the size of the footing are designed to resist the overturning moment of the soil. A retaining wall should always be drained on the soil side to prevent the build up of hydrostatic pressure. An alternate is to use precast concrete elements, which are often less expensive and can make a more attractive wall if exposed to view.

Another approach is to use permanent soil-nailing as a retaining wall. Steel tendrels must be coated with a plastic sheath, or other permanent corrosion protection, to prevent deterioration over time if an installation of this system is to be permanent. It is also important to provide complete drainage to prevent the build-up of hydrostatic pressure. It is recommended that the shotcrete be installed in two layers with waterproofing in between.

Foundations

The type of foundation and substructure is defined, or at least limited, by the soil conditions as determined by core drillings and analysis of the samples. Soil can vary from non-compacted old fill, silty clay with high water tables, to good compacted clay, to various types of rock. The tests provide a soil profile over the length of the drilled hole, locate the water table levels, and provide the data to compute the bearing capacity of the soil or rock at various levels. Whatever the type of soil, the geotechnical engineer must determine the allowable bearing or friction capacity of the material (i.e., the weight it will support). The structural engineer uses these recommendations to design the building foundations.

Foundations must resist both overturning and uplift forces as well as supporting the building, and seismic requirements can impose additional conditions, as some soils tend toward liquefaction during seismic disturbance. Special foundation issues must be addressed when encountering unusual soil conditions such as the expansive clay found in Texas, California and other southwestern states.

Various types of foundations are utilized based on the most economical solution, depending on the type of soil, rock, bearing capacity, the load of the building they must support and other factors. Some common methods are:

- Grade beams—a reinforced concrete beam, often called spread footings, they are wider than the wall they support.

- Column footings—a reinforced concrete base for the columns to rest upon.

- Caissons—a structural support whose bottom can be inspected prior to installation. They are usually reinforced concrete columns placed in holes that were drilled or dug in the ground.

- Pilings—a structural support whose bottom cannot be visually inspected prior to installation. This definition is becoming blurred, in the case of poured concrete, with the availability of remote visual inspection. Pilings are usually steel pipes, H-beams, precast concrete or wood driven into the ground or poured concrete. As in the case of caissons they support the structure through a combination of friction and direct bearing and resist uplift through friction.

When poured concrete pilings are used and the hole is not self-supporting throughout the process, it is usually performed by pouring the concrete into either permanent or retractable steel shells. When using retractable shells, care must be taken to measure the height after each pour to check for potential voids.

- Column caps—a base for a column located over a caisson or piling.

- Piers—a concrete column bedded into rock.

- Mat, or raft—a thick, heavily reinforced concrete slab over the entire building footprint, with the building resting or floating on this broad surface. Usually used on old fill or filled-in formerly water-covered areas, where pilings would be excessively long, or where an earthquake could create liquefaction in silty soil.

- Aggregate or geo-piers—a procedure used in certain swampy or high water table sites. Alternating layers of slurry and aggregate are placed in drilled holes and each layer is densified under high pressure with a cone-shaped head to not only compress the aggregate, but to expand it against the walls of the hole. It functions only in compression—steel cages must be added if the piers are subject to uplift forces. Footings, column caps or shear walls are installed on top of the pier.

There are times that it may be more economical to remove a strata of poor soil and replace it with engineered fill, in order to provide proper support for spread footings, rather than support the building on caissons or piling.

Substructure

The substructure walls are normally reinforced concrete, but can also be precast concrete or gunite. In most office building projects the site is relatively level, permitting the soil pressures against all sides of the subsurface area to be resisted not only by each wall face alone, but also by cross bracing provided by the beams and structural floors between them. If a substructure is built on a sharply sloping site, special retaining wall provisions must be included in the foundation design.

The footings or other support structure may require several analyses to determine the most efficient way to support the desired structure. It should also be noted that sometimes ground water can interfere with construction, and it may be necessary to install a ground dewatering system—consisting of pipes drilled down below the lowest excavation level, and pumps to expel the water. In many soil conditions, below-grade construction is much more costly than above-grade construction and, therefore, evaluations are required as to the best location of various services such as parking, loading docks, mechanical rooms and certain occupied areas.

Perimeter and slab waterproofing are of significant concern for below-grade areas and must be carefully designed. Where there is any doubt as to water penetration, sumps with automatic pumps should be installed at low points. Where the lowest slab is on grade, care should be taken to provide proper drainage out from under and away from the slab. It is not uncommon to utilize a waterproofing consultant for wet subsurface conditions. Under some water conditions additional structural resistance from sidewall and slab uplift must be provided to counteract hydrostatic pressure.

Careful planning and coordination is required to ensure that there is no unintended interference between utilities and subgrade services and footings and the caps for the caissons, pilings and piers.

Reinforced Concrete

Concrete will resist stresses by itself only in pure compression, and reinforcing steel (rebars) is required for it to have any resistance to tension, shear or torque loading. Rebars are also called deformed bars because the fabrication process deforms the steel creating the uneven surface necessary to bond effectively with the concrete. The size, spacing and cover of rebars is carefully designed to provide the strength required for each member to resist the anticipated forces.

The concrete is Portland cement and aggregate mixed with water. Admixtures and plasticizers are frequently added to insure proper performance under special circumstances or under certain weather conditions. The aggregate is used to produce an economical mix consistent with workability and consistency for placement. The structural engineer specifies the concrete mix, the percentage of each element of material in the concrete, to provide the stipulated strength under specific conditions. The ready-mix plant must advise of any variation they use due to temperature or other conditions.

The consistency is determined by a slump test, wherein a cone is filled with concrete taken from the ready-mix truck, turned upside down, and the slump is measured when the cone is removed. If there is insufficient slump the concrete will probably not properly fill all voids in the form and around the rebars. Too much slump usually means insufficient aggregate and/or too much water, increasing the probability of cracking. The concrete is also tested for the correct compression strength. Some of the samples are tested after seven days for a preliminary assessment of strength, and the remainder are given a final break test after 28 days to verify whether it met the design criteria.

Lightweight aggregates are now used extensively, and are practically a necessity for tall reinforced concrete buildings. These aggregates are obtained by expanding, calcinating, or sintering materials such as blast furnace slag, shale, slate and clay. The unit weight of lightweight aggregate concrete ranges from 90 to 115 pound per cubic foot, as compared to 140 to 150 pounds per cubic foot for normal concrete.

Concrete generates a heat of hydration due to the exothermic chemical reaction between the cement and the water. Curing is usually controlled by a water spray or light ponding. When the concrete section is 3 +/- or more feet thick, special precautions and additives are required due to the propensity for expansion cracks during hardening. At those thicknesses the heat cannot fully dissipate into the soil or the air.

A recent trend that is gaining favor involves the replacement of up to 50% of the Portland cement with Class F fly ash. Fly ash is a pozzolan, having cementitious properties when in the presence of the cement-water chemistry. It has many improved properties such as durability, less shrinkage, less creep, less heat of hydration and less chemical deterioration. One issue that must be allowed for in its use is that it has a slower rate of strength gain, which often means forms must be left in place for a longer period of time.

A major environmental benefit of using the fly ash is that it is a byproduct of coal burning power plants, much of which currently goes into the nation's landfills. In addition, the making and use of Portland cement creates great amounts of CO_2 that is purported to be a major factor in global warming. For every ton of Portland cement replaced by fly ash, about a ton of off-gassed CO_2 is saved.

Structural Frame

The structural frame consists of the columns (or in some cases structural walls) and beams, reinforced by the floor framing. The frame carries the weight of the building, plus a floor live loading discussed below, and must resist the dynamic loads. The vertical loads may be carried by steel, reinforced concrete, composite steel and reinforced concrete, pre-stressed concrete columns, or by reinforced concrete walls. Horizontal or dynamic, wind and seismic loads are carried by the moment frame (the connections between the columns and the beams), shear walls (usually the concrete core walls) and brace framing ("K" or "X" bracing in portions of the perimeter or core, and/or the beam and column frame in the core).

In seismic zones, and possibly in geographic zones with extreme storm winds, the use of moment frame construction will tend to increase the unit cost of the steel by several hundred dollars per ton. This increase is due to the additional detailing, welding and inspection required. Normally, one would attempt to use brace framing to the greatest extent possible, but there is reasonable concern by some owners whenever brace framing limits visibility from some windows on the perimeter, or where the interior braces limit internal flexibility.

Frequently, a building uses a combination of the above systems, such as a perimeter steel frame and floor structure and a reinforced concrete core (slip form in taller structures), that has a much better ability to resist the wind loads.

Wind loads are normally calculated from known conditions in the site location, however, for very tall buildings, over 20 stories, or those with unusual geometry, the wind tunnel tests recommended in Chapter 14 are very important to the structural design. The test model is modified to take many pressure readings on the model's façade in order to verify or modify the initial structural design assumptions. The model is placed in a model of the surrounding buildings and terrain, which is placed in a wind tunnel and tested at 15° increments of rotation to ascertain any impact that may result from the wind directions and/or velocity against the building.

schedule and fabrication that can delay the start of construction, unless an early mill order is released. It is not uncommon, however, that site preparation and substructure construction timing coincides with the structural steel lead-time to mitigate that issue. A steel structure is much more cost effective if standard rolled "H", "I" and channel sections can be used rather than the more labor intensive sections built up from rolled plate. However, sometimes built-up sections are the only way to satisfy some structural conditions.

A reinforced concrete frame with a flat slab is usually limited to no more than a 30-foot column spacing, however, other systems consisting of beams or joists can economically span in excess of 40 feet. Concrete framing formerly had some practical height limitations, though improvements in the design of concrete structures combined with the development of higher strength concrete mixes

> Some years ago the John Hancock building in Boston had so many glass failures that a hazardous condition was created in the surrounding streets, resulting in completion being delayed several years until the problem could be solved. No one knows how many millions were involved in the repairs, delays and the myriad of lawsuits.
>
> The failure was reported to be that the bite of the window frame on the glass lite was insufficient to retain the glazing under certain wind conditions. The window wall had been successfully tested, however, the failure occurred when the structural frame twisted under certain wind conditions, creating an untested condition on the glazing frames. It was reported that the tower had a wind tunnel test, but that it was not complete, as it did not replicate the surrounding structures.

The geometry of the building is a major factor in the structural system selected, but the most common solution for office buildings is structural steel perimeter frame with concrete shear walls and/or brace framing at the core. Reinforced concrete stairwell and elevator framing walls can be used as shear walls when located on a column line and tied into the beams and columns.

Steel buildings are much easier than concrete frames to modify later in order to meet some critical tenant need, like increased floor loading or new penetrations. While steel is usually faster to erect, it can have long lead times for shop drawings, mill

has permitted reinforced concrete structures in excess of 1500 feet in height. The mass of concrete has damping characteristics that enable it to absorb more external forces, reducing sway in tall buildings and improving occupancy comfort. In some cases the ability of the concrete mass to hold heat can improve the efficiency of the building's environmental systems.

In two-story, and in some cases three-story, buildings built for lower end usage, a tilt-up concrete wall can be utilized at significant cost reduction, but it has many design limitations.

> We have discussed the fact that the structure is a major factor in the building construction cost, and one for which there is no marketing credit, only the necessary stability of your building. Although alternative structural analyses are frequently straightforward, it pays to remain very open-minded to unusual suggestions when the building has a somewhat irregular configuration.
>
> During the Momentum Place design we went through a series of analyses on different structural systems. One of those that the contractor was very positive about was a concrete slip form exterior for the tower with a steel core and steel extensions at the lower levels for the bank hall. This proposal was counter to any intuitive reaction that we or the designers had with regard to an efficient structural scheme. We had the contractor go back over his analysis three or four times before we were convinced that it was the least expensive system for our project. The real key toward the solution being so effective was the punched window system on the corners of the tower, as shown in the picture.
>
> The building was built using that system and our structural costs came in exactly as projected, and helped to make the building shell and core very economical. The picture, from the *Engineering News Record,* shows the building under construction, and the magazine had an extensive article on the structural analysis.

Obviously a thorough analysis must be made to select the best combination of structural elements, and good structural engineers are getting more flexible and clever all the time. The structural engineer should evaluate both structural steel, reinforced concrete and various composite framing systems to select the one best suited for the project, considering cost, bay sizes, construction time, future flexibility, etc.

Floor Structure

One of the most effective floor structures in an office building consists of steel beams with a concrete deck poured over corrugated steel decking. As stated above, reinforced concrete is also used, but the smaller bay size and lack of flexibility in the future tend to reduce the frequency of its use in general purpose office buildings. There was a major effort some years ago to use (and still used to a minor degree, but rarely in a speculative building) a special steel decking below the concrete that served as a distribution means for telephone and electrical wiring, called an electrified floor system, but the author has never seen a reputable analysis that justified the higher initial cost with life cycle cost savings. Some small newer buildings are utilizing a steel frame with wood joists hung from the beams, but they are considered to be a lower quality in the marketplace and may even have cost penalties when consideration is given to the cost of protective drywall and the impact on the sprinkler system to obtain an acceptable fire rating. Factors in floor design are:

- **Floor load**—this is the weight the floor supports. The most common criteria for general office buildings is 50 psf for the live load (people and furniture) and 20 psf for partitions. Reinforced concrete floors are more likely to be 80 to 100 psf, at least partially to allow for the difficulty of reinforcing any required areas in the future. Sometimes it is wise to have 100 psf live load in the core (where the spans are shorter) for file rooms and libraries. Some special users with dense or heavy equipment may want 100, or even 150 psf throughout for flexibility.

- **Span**—the distance from the centerline of the perimeter column to the core structure. Choosing a span for layout efficiency is discussed in Chapters 4 and 21. Note that an analysis on one building showed that by increasing the span from 40 feet to 45 feet, the overall structural steel cost increased by 10% to 12.5%, but this is not necessarily typical.

- **Column location**—the best column locations are at the perimeter and in the core walls. Columns within the tenant space are an impediment to tenant layouts, and such locations should be minimized. Spacing is important, as the number of columns (except where spacing would create excessive spans) tends to increase the cost of the frame.

- **Floor construction**—the most common floor construction in mid- to high-rise buildings is composed of lightweight concrete (90–115 pounds per cubic foot) with wire mesh over corrugated metal forms, and strengthened by using studs welded to the steel beams to attain a composite construction between the steel and the concrete. In high-rise buildings the floor weight can be a significant factor. In low-rise buildings hard rock concrete may be more cost effective.

Structural Efficiency

Some rules of thumb to minimize structural costs are:

- The closer the frame is to a square or circle, the more effective
- Brace the frame through the core, where possible
- Keep columns in a straight line
- Avoid offset columns, where the column load is carried on a beam
- Minimize cantilevers
- Keep spans reasonable
- Keep live loads reasonable
- Use standard steel sections and minimize the use of built-up sections

The weight of steel is a major factor in project cost. As a bit of guidance—on several prior all-steel structures the author was familiar with, the weight of steel in a three- or four-story building ran from 8.5 to 10.0 psf, a 20-story building was 13.5 psf, and on a 49-story building was approximately 22 psf. In seismic areas the amount of steel is increased. At current uncomplicated fabricated steel unit prices of $1,500 to $1,700 per ton, the cost impact can be readily estimated. Moment frame unit costs will be considerably higher in seismic areas.

Fire Resistance

The three main national building codes—BOCA, SBC and UBC have extensive regulations concerning resistance to fire, flame spread, exiting, separations, smoke control, fire suppression, alarms, firemen's access and many other issues that affect life safety in structures. Careful study of the appropriate code, along with any exceptions in the local code, is required to establish the requirements for each building.

Structures are divided into five types, ranging from Type I (the highest) to Type V (the lowest), depending primarily on height, occupancy, use, floor size and setback from adjacent structures. As a general rule, high-rise office buildings (above 75' in height at the floor line of the highest occupied floor, in most cases) are in Type I and normally have a fire-resistance requirement of two hours, and low-rise office buildings are in Type II with a fire-resistant requirement of one hour. Under some circumstances, a building with a fully approved sprinkler system can reduce its fire-resistance rating by one hour. Steel structures may acquire their fire rating through encasement in gypsum board, concrete, or sprayed-on fireproofing. The floors, stairwells and exit paths must maintain a similar rating.

A façade must maintain a code-approved fire resistance if it is less than 20 feet from a property line. In such case, non-reinforced glass may not be used unless an approved water curtain is provided to either the inside or the outside of the glass lites.

It is important to note that proper fire resistance consists of not only the resistance of the primary elements, but negating any potential flame bypass, such as by providing fire stops where the façade joins the structure and at all floor penetrations. Stairwells and building shafts must have the same fire resistance as the main structural elements.

The codes provide that certain elements in a building be either noncombustible or maintain a specified maximum flame-spread rating. These are defined as:

- A noncombustible material is one that will not burn, ignite, support combustion, or release flammable vapors when subjected to fire or heat, usually specified as 1350° F for five minutes, or a material having a core or structural base meeting the above with a surfacing not over 1/8" thick, which has a flame-spread rating not higher than 50.

- Flame-spread ratings are obtained by measuring the extent and rapidity with which flames spread over their surfaces under test conditions specified in ASTM standards, and are a guide in the selection and use of finishing materials. Flame-spread ratings are specified by the codes for

---

When designing the 28-story Two First National Plaza building in Chicago, across the street from the bank headquarters, we were having difficulty obtaining a satisfactory floor plate without encroaching to within ten feet of the adjacent synagogue. To locate the façade this close would prevent the installation of normal vision glass due to the required fire rating. As we did not wish to use wire glass or glass block, the fire protection engineers proposed placing a dry type sprinkler head above each glass lite, to be actuated by a temperature sensor.

The building commissioner agreed to approve our request if it passed an approved laboratory fire test that established equivalency to the approved materials in the code. The first test at the Underwriters Laboratory failed. Motion picture film of the test indicated that the water tended to part into rivulets, leaving portions of the surface unprotected from the flames. The engineers revised their design to include a surfactant (a soap product) in the water stream to ensure full coverage. On the subsequent test the system passed and approval was obtained.

When the building was undergoing the necessary tests for the Certificate of Occupancy, we requested approval to test the external sprinklers without the use of the surfactant. The inspector flatly refused, demanding it be tested as designed, and would not even listen to our concerns. When the test was run on a Sunday morning the surfactant created a layer of foam about 15 feet high around the base of the building, spilling out into the street. The inspector smiled when he said, "Is this why you wanted to modify the test?"

different circumstances, for example public assembly rooms, corridors, exitways and the like. Building codes may require interior finishes with a flame spread rating of not more than 25.

Roof Structure

The roof deck of an office building is normally a concrete deck with the insulation and roof membrane on top of it as discussed in detail in Chapter 20. For many buildings with unusual shaped tops, the architectural feature is a screen-like façade, with the real roof a flat slab below.

CASE STUDY

The early assumption was to use a steel frame—they are generally more satisfactory for an office building. At the proposed size it was deemed to be no more costly than concrete, and functionally much more flexible.

Both moment frame and brace frame were analyzed. Brace frame creates elements, such as "K" and "X" bracing, to take the reactions, which will create some impediments that might affect tenant layouts or their unobstructed views, while a moment frame takes the reactions in a welded connection between the columns and the beams. A brace frame will require about the same tonnage as a moment frame, but will cost several hundred dollars less per ton, due to the reduced shop and field welding from that required by the moment frame. Brace framing normally saves both shop and field erection time.

At the start of the design, the San Diego building code still recognized the 1994 UBC Code, but they had adopted the 1998 California Building Code (CBC), essentially the same as the 1997 UBC, effective as of July 1, 1999. The new code contains more stringent seismic requirements and would increase the construction costs somewhat. The project could have beaten the deadline for use of 1994 UBC, however, a decision was made that long-term value would be enhanced by following the latest codes.

Preliminary bay size assumptions were to use 30' x 40' for the exterior bays because it accomplished the desired core to glass dimension and is a very efficient span in both directions. There may be cantilevers of a few feet to adjust the rentable area, or to provide some articulation. A central bay of 25' x 30' was proposed to facilitate the brace framing in resisting the transverse wind and seismic loads. This dimension would also accommodate the stairwells with their smoke-free vestibules required under the high-rise code. These bay sizes could work with a concrete frame if steel prices had continued to rise out of sight.

An analysis of the floor plan indicated that the structure would probably be a combination of brace framing and moment frame. It also indicated that the brace framing would interfere with some desired core door locations and would create some undesired interference in tenant layout. This, when combined with the estimated cost premium of several hundred dollars per ton for the extra welding and inspections required by the moment frame, dictated a further study.

Three changes, selected for other reasons, turned out to be fortuitous for the structural design.

- The building was shortened by about 17 feet to better orient the building on the site, as discussed in Chapters 7 and 15

- The building was widened by five feet to avoid any loss of floor space from the change above

- The core was lengthened by 20 feet to improve the ability to efficiently place small tenants on the floor, as discussed further in Chapter 16

As a result of the above, the core was widened by two feet, which prevented the brace framing from impinging on the toilet room layout and stairwell vestibule.

The above changes improved the ability to provide bracing in both the longitudinal and transverse directions, thereby virtually eliminating moment frame connections and providing a workable core. A typical brace section used in this design is a modified "K" brace turned sideways, as shown in Figure 19-1. The brace-framing plan is shown diagrammatically in three dimensions in Figure 19-2, with the red indicating the interior braces. The exterior framing is braced through the floor beams from the interior brace frames. The net result of the changes to the structural frame was estimated to be a savings of $80,000. The details of

Structural Design 235

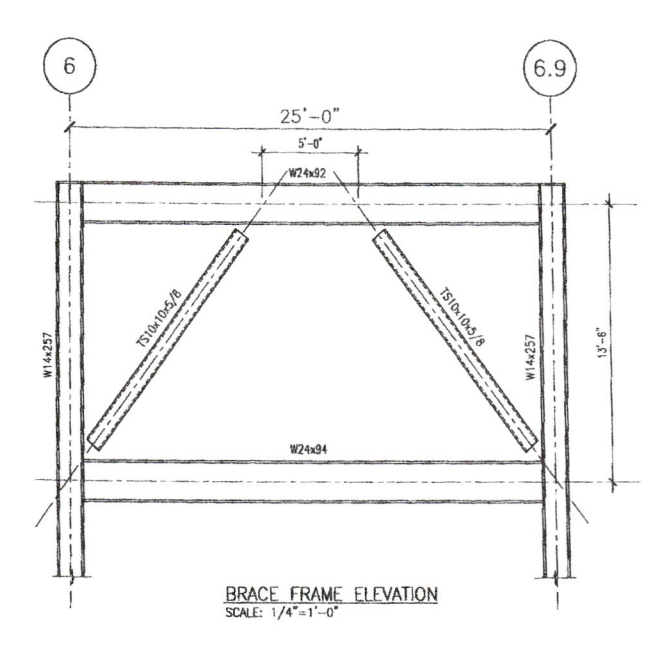

Figure 19-1

the brace framing were fine-tuned later to permit more flexible core door locations and facilitate the mechanical duct distribution.

This new structural layout has columns only at the core and on the perimeter—no interior columns. Further analysis permitted elimination of some of the columns at the step backs at each end of the building.

The floor structure is designed for 60 psf live load and 20 psf for partitions on the exterior bays, with 100 psf live load and 20 psf for partitions in the core bay and 10 feet beyond. The beams will be 2" deep on nominal ten-foot centers. The typical structural floor plan is shown as Figure 19-3, which also indicates the brace-frame members by the red lines. The floor-loading diagram is shown as Figure 19-4.

The typical slab edge overhangs the perimeter beams by 1'10". Because the slab edge must carry most of the weight of the curtain wall, it was detailed with a size ⅜" bent steel plate welded to the beam and bent up to form the face of the slab edge to provide support for the wall connections. This detail also called for 4-foot #4 rebars to be welded to the bent plate, which must be installed in the field. After all of the curtain wall connection load points were known, the structural engineer was requested to reevaluate this detail, due to the extensive amount of difficult field welding involved.

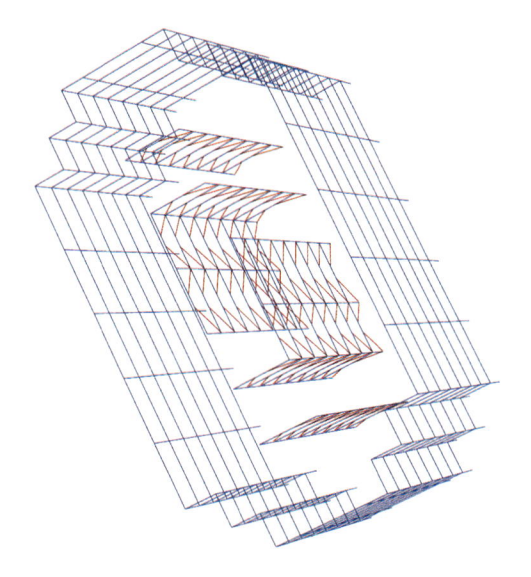

Figure 19-2

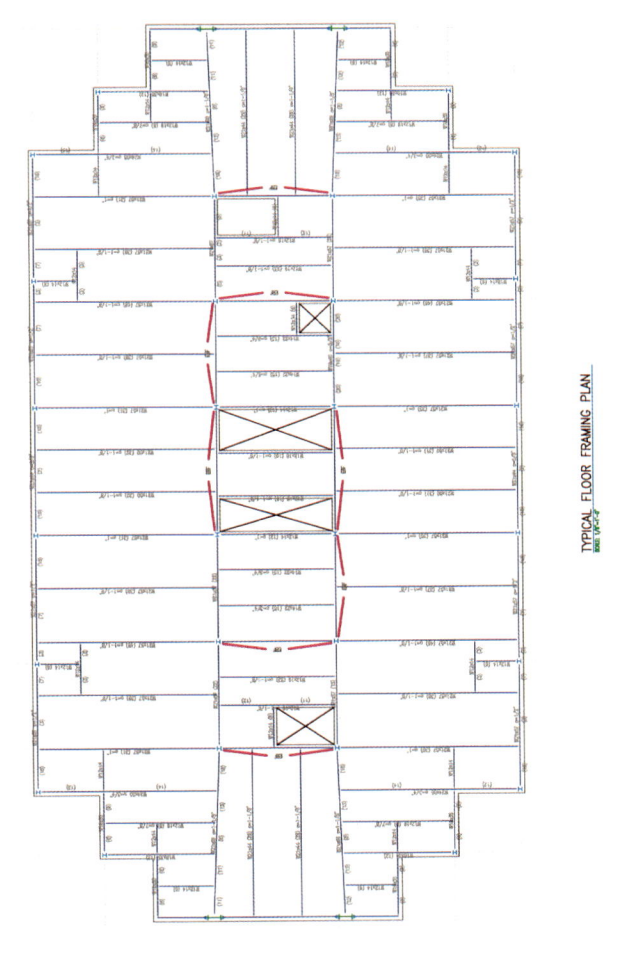

Figure 19-3

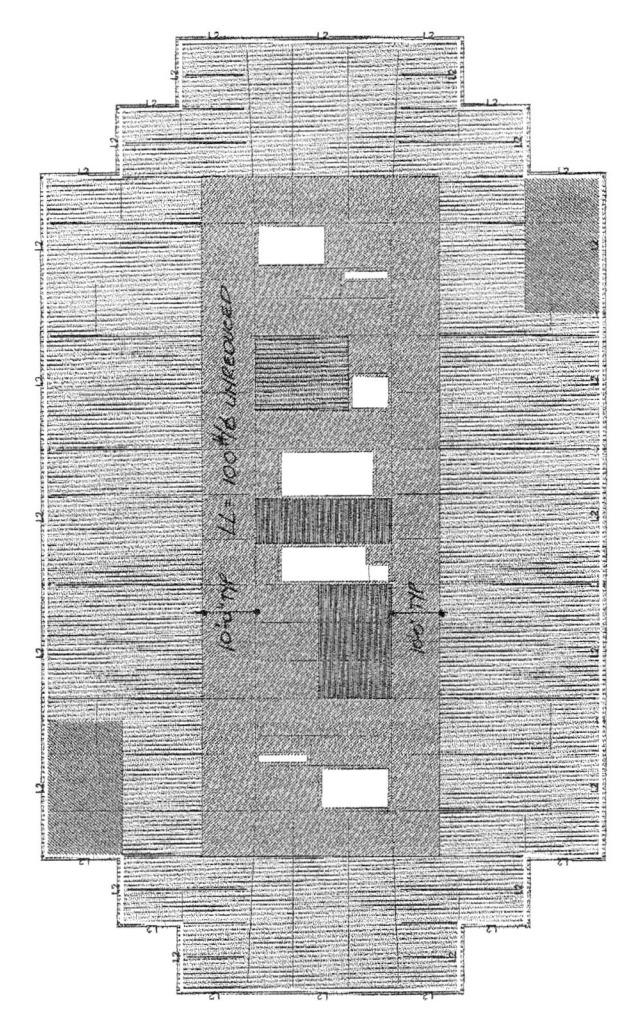

Figure 19-4

The revised analysis resulted in new details that used "hooked" rebars, on 18" centers. At each curtain wall mullion connection, every 7'6", two threaded rebars with double nuts attaching them to the bent plate were specified, eliminating all of the welding.

At the same time, the city marked up the curtain wall shop drawings to require that 314 welded steel gusset plates be added to the steel beams to reinforce where the curtain wall kickers were braced. This seemed excessive, so the structural engineer was requested to make a complete analysis of these beams at maximum wall loads. The result was that no gussets were required.

The building floor-to-floor height was 13'6", which, with the 21"-deep structural beams, permitted a 9'0" ceiling. The final weight of the steel structure was 14.1 pounds/sf, which was slightly more than the 13.45 pounds/sf anticipated.

The structural steel bids came in almost exactly on our baseline budget—the unit price of $1,217 per ton was somewhat lower than anticipated and offset the higher steel weight. The overall steel cost was $9.80/gsf.

In order to meet the construction schedule, the steel was bid and contracted for while the drawings were in the city for permit review and the mechanical drawings were being completed. Changes required by the completion of these items changed some beams and added some others, resulting in an increase of almost $80,000. While there was some premium due to the change order, most of this cost would have occurred even if included in the bid package.

The roof structure is a poured reinforced concrete deck.

The office building is supported on spread footings. The separation between the office building and the parking structure was carefully reviewed to avoid any unnecessary lateral pressure on the subsurface walls of the parking structure.

The parking structure consists of three 61'6"-wide longitudinal parking bays 260 feet long, constructed of post-tensioned concrete. The northernmost two are flat and the southern bay is the ramp. The two flat bays are post-tensioned as a unit and the ramp, naturally, is post-tensioned separately. The perimeter walls are designed with partial shear walls near the center of each side for seismic resistance.

Analysis of the parking structure indicated a somewhat more difficult structural issue than the office building. The long north wall had to withstand an earth pressure with a retaining wall height in excess of 40 feet, while the south wall was only 15 feet below grade, counting footings, due to the sloping site. A more common underground structure on a relatively level site results in a structure that reinforces each retaining wall through cross-bracing from one wall to another, while this project had a gross imbalance of forces to restrain. This was further complicated by the fact that the structure was designed for seismic stresses that required, as mentioned above, at least partial shear walls on all four sides.

The alternatives considered for the design of this structure were:

- Build a reinforced concrete retaining wall along the north wall, turning the corner at the east and west walls, which would require temporary shoring in order to construct it. The parking structure would then be a free-standing structure behind the retaining wall, and would only carry seismic and its own structural loads.

- A variation of the first alternative would be to construct a permanent "soil-nailed" retaining wall that would be accomplished in approximately six-foot steps from the top, and would not require temporary shoring. A separate design/build contractor would install this work under a retaining wall permit.

- The third alternative would be to design the north wall and portions of the east and west walls for both soil resistance and seismic resistance. This would either require temporary shoring (which was impractical) or laying back the soil on a 2/1 slope between the location of the wall and the other building foundations. This solution would require extensive temporary storage of large quantities of earth on the site, estimated at 6,000 to 7,000 cubic yards, probably delaying the start of the foundation work. In addition, the footing sizes would be excessive.

The first alternative was deemed too costly, and the other two were selected for a detailed estimate. There was not a significant cost difference between the second and third methods. The soil-nailing approach, however, would save important time due to avoiding the soil layback and storage that was important due to potential penalties under the Brandes lease.

The soil-nailing estimate included a water-resistant wall—a continuous "boot" (fluid-applied membrane), drainage board, bottom drains and a rubber float finish. In addition, the comparative estimate could well have underestimated the soil storage for alternative number three, with the possibility of removal and return of large quantities of earth. The cost of soil-nailing could be reduced by requiring a less highly-finished surface. The soil-nailing required that some special fittings be used to set the north-south post-tensioning of the decks in the approximately 6" gap between the retaining wall and the structural columns, but the cost impact was considered insignificant.

There were several issues to resolve before soil-nailing could be considered, in spite of its schedule advantages:

- The rods would interfere with installation of the main storm sewer that was located between the parking structure and the hotel. It would be necessary to relocate this line around the other side of the parking structure. (Later found to be unnecessary when it was determined that the soil-nailed wall did not have to extend along the east side of the structure.)

- A 20-foot-wide easement for the fire water line loop is located between the structure and the office building, which easement would be penetrated by the soil nailing rods. The fire department and bureau that handles the city's utility easements agreed to permit this penetration if the rods were sufficiently below the level of the fire water line, and if calculations indicated the line would not be subject to settlement or creep due to installation of these rods. Investigation by the geotechnical engineer established that they would not cause a problem.

- It was necessary to verify that appropriate rods for the soil-nailing wall could be installed so as not to interfere with the foundations of the hotel at its closest corner.

- Certain city maps indicated a geological fault in the vicinity of the parking structure, but the geotechnical engineer convinced both the city and Prentiss that there was no danger of liquefaction in this area.

These issues were all resolved satisfactorily, and the decision was made to proceed with a soil-nailed retaining wall. The soil-nailing contract was awarded on a design/build basis to Schnabel Foundation Company. They performed all engineering calculations and design for review and approval by the structural and geotechnical engineers as well as the city. When Schnabel was completing their calculations, they concluded there was a serious issue created by the 26,000-gallon fire water storage tank located adjacent to the wall. They recommended either a thicker wall, or at least partially support the tank on piers or pilings. A quick analysis indicated a premium of at least $45,000. The issue was resolved by interchanging the water tank with the trash and recycle cubicles, moving the heavy load farther from the retaining wall.

The construction procedure for this wall was:

- The grade elevation prior to construction was seven feet lower than the proposed top of the retaining wall. This issue was addressed by grading the earth up to the desired elevation first, then cutting it back for the retaining wall.

- Excavated to a depth of approximately five feet at a time for the full width of he wall to install the wall in five-foot vertical sections.

- Drilled 8" holes on five-foot horizontal centers at an average length of 35 feet (40 feet where the shear wall is located) in the top row, stepping down as the wall went deeper until they were 15 feet long in the bottom row. The holes were angled downward at about a 15° angle and splayed slightly in some areas.

- Inserted and grouted 1⅞" diameter steel tendrels, coated with a 7 to 12 mm epoxy coating, the length of the hole. Four-foot rebars were wired top and bottom to hold them in position during the grouting.

- Placed two-foot-wide vertical strips of perforated Miradrain 6000 every five feet horizontally for drainage and then installed heavy 6" x 6" welded wire mesh reinforcing.

- Installed approximately 4" of shotcrete (sprayed structural concrete).

- Installed a 12' x 12" x ½" steel plate with a hole in the center over the exposed end of each tendrel. A nut screwed on the tendrel to hold it firmly, but not stressed.

- Waterproofed the surface with a cold-applied Liquid Boot mastic.

- Repeated the above steps to the bottom of the wall.

- Provided a horizontal perforated pipe at the bottom to drain away all water from behind the retaining wall.

- Erected scaffolding, installed reinforcing bar cages and applied an additional 8" of shotcrete to complete the structural wall.

- The surface was finished to match a steel trowel finish sample provided at the job site. It was a little uneven, but since it was to be about 12" beyond the structure it was concluded to be satisfactory, and it saved quite a bit of money.

When Pardee insisted on berming the south side of the parking structure ten feet above proposed grade, this created another shear/seismic stress conflict. This was resolved by using masonry retaining walls between the columns. Two inches of structural clearance were provided at the sides and top of these walls to avoid the interrelationship between the retaining and seismic stresses.

BUILDING ENVELOPE DESIGN 20

The building envelope consists of the façade (fenestration), or building skin, and the roof—the exterior of the building that protects it from the elements while being the major factor in the aesthetics of the building's design. The building envelope must admit natural light, resist transmission of heat and cold, retain heat in cool weather, adjust daylight while controlling glare, and it must repel water and control air infiltration. It must perform all of these functions well, within an allowable cost limitation. In addition to these functional attributes, it creates the character of the building and, frequently, its perception of quality in the marketplace.

This chapter will discuss the various façade or fenestration systems, glazing, various opaque materials, detailing, sealants, testing and maintenance. The roof structure and its various components, drainage and alternative membranes, as well as top-of-building signage, are discussed at the end of this chapter.

FAÇADE or FENESTRATION

Approval of façade selection and design is one of the more interesting and difficult decisions the Development Officer must make in the design process. The cost trade-offs between materials, geometry and your best assumption as to the marketability of the product are difficult at best. The façade is what the public sees and identifies as your building. In addition to the façade's cost, its weight and shape affect the cost of the structure, and any unique shape can affect the space efficiency of the building. The decision is not only impacted by the market and your own preferences, but by the natural and built environment in which it is located.

The façade is the combination of vision glass and opaque facing material that, combined with the geometry, defines the architecture of the building. From a marketing standpoint, the largest amount of vision glass consistent with good energy practice or energy code requirements should be provided, which usually limits the vision glass to approximately 40% of the façade in the more extreme climates. In temperate climates 50% vision glass is reasonable. This calculation should address only the curtain wall area of occupied floors, ignoring the surface of roof screening or exposed lower levels. Due to energy restraint on the extent of vision glass, spandrel glass or other lighter colored panels are frequently used to accomplish a particular set of desired proportions, or to give the façade a lighter feeling. The façade is hung onto the steel or concrete frame, or is fastened to a masonry or reinforced concrete wall in which the windows are inset into punched openings.

In addition to the selected materials and the basic geometry of the building, the degree of articulation provides interest to the building's appearance. An example is the way the windows are set into the façade. The glazing is much thinner than the building wall. If the windows are set flush with the outside of the façade, then the extra wall thickness is made up with drywall or, sometimes, with a metal extension of the window frame. If the window is set back into the wall, most people will agree that the building gains in interest, but the setback, if greater than 3" to 4", is often framed with the exterior skin material or specially extruded elements. This not only adds a significantly greater amount of the expensive skin, but it can add expensive details. Protrusions, such as columns or mullions protruding from the surface, or reveals of any type have the same type of cost impact. The increased surface area of the skin resulting from these protrusions or recesses is called the articulation factor (AF). In early budget analyses an estimate frequently used for the articulation factor is 1.10.

When evaluating design proposals, keep in mind that the cost of the skin equals the total skin surface area times its unit cost. The total skin surface is the perimeter of the building multiplied by the height and the articulation factor. The ratio of the skin surface area to the gross building area represents the efficiency—a number below 0.40 is reasonably efficient. The total cost of the skin divided by the rentable area represents the true impact of its cost to the project.

The Development Officer must recognize that a speculative office building, in a normal market, can rarely, if ever, afford a visual appearance created by the combination of an unusual geometric shape, significant articulation and upgraded surface materials. In many cases only one, but frequently two, of these visual appearance approaches can fit within a competitive budget. This choice can impose a difficult design decision on the Development Officer very early in the design sequence.

Most buildings are clad with a curtain wall, defined as an exterior building wall that carries no floor or roof loads. There are two general categories of curtain walls—window wall and a column cover and spandrel system.

The window wall is usually manufactured and installed by a window wall contractor. It most often consists of a "stick" system utilizing vertical and horizontal framing members with infill panels and glazing, as shown in Figure 20-1. The vertical members (2), or mullions, are installed first, and attached to the anchors (1), followed by the horizontal rails (3 and 5) that are connected to the mullions. The spandrel panels (4) and vision glass (6) are installed between these structural members. The interior mullion trim (7) is installed last. The panels are usually installed as an outside glazing system. Shipping and storage of these members is relatively simple and the installation is straight-forward. The mullions and rails usually have weep holes or wicks to permit the release of some of the water that might leak into the system.

A higher quality version of a window wall system is the unitized curtain wall, wherein the infill

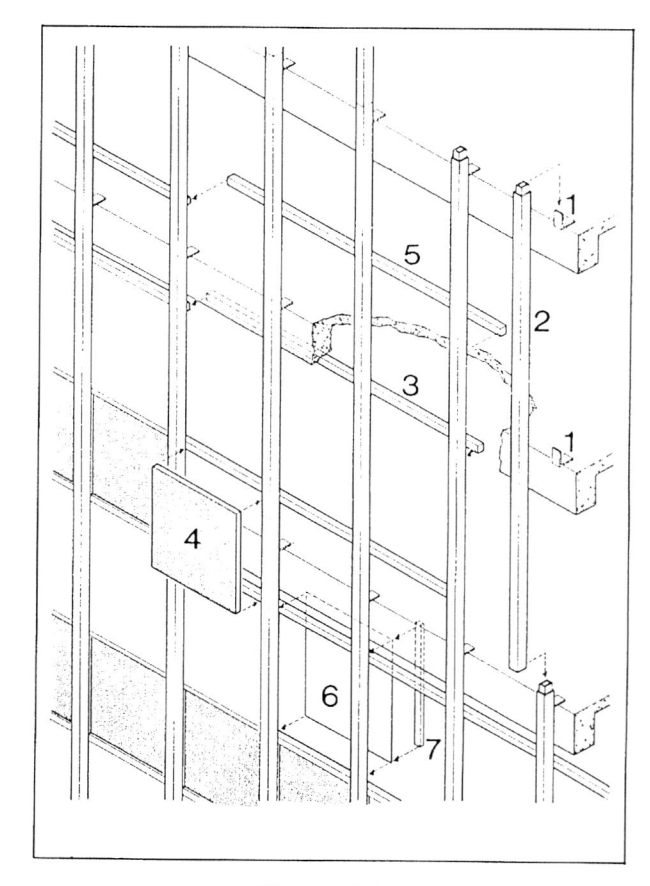

Figure 20-1

members are shipped as complete preglazed members. These units are more difficult to ship but reduce the number of construction lifts and provide for shop inspection rather than relying on field labor. An additional value is that, due to assembly control and unit stability, the pressure and infiltration tests of unitized sections will more accurately replicate the results of resistance to stresses on the installed wall.

The column cover and spandrel type of curtain wall, Figure 20-2, consists of column covers (1), spandrel panels (2), and glazing infill (3) with each normally hung independently from the structure by structural clips, or anchors. The spandrel panels, which are usually steel trusses or precast concrete finished or backing panels, are installed first, followed by the column covers and then the glazing frames and glazing. Sometimes entire wall sections are fabricated into a unitized wall section to simplify erection and minimize field connections.

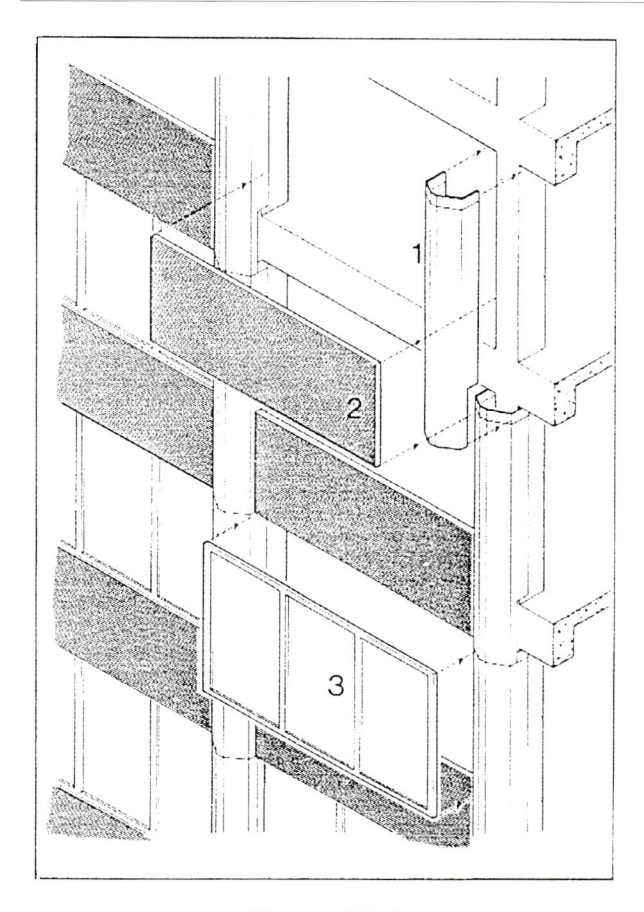

Figure 20-2

Vision Glass, or Glazing

Glazing is an exceedingly important visual element of the façade as the building appearance reflects the architectural blending of the glazing with the other elements to accomplish the desired architectural objective, and utilizes to best advantage the color, size, reflectivity and detailing of the vision glass element. The glazing can be in the form of a continuous row of glass and metal mullions between the perimeter columns, linear glazing with butt joints, or individual windows with frames or "punched" openings in walls. As stated previously, the area of vision glass should be selected to balance marketing and energy consumption concerns.

As social concerns about energy consumption increase, greater insulating, reflective and shading combinations will be used to permit maintaining the large amounts of vision glass that are so important to the interior space. The glazing and framing methods are selected based upon trade-offs between appearance, energy impact, interior environmental and marketing issues. The selection must consider:

- Structural integrity
- Visual appearance—color and/or reflectivity
- Capacity to insulate, or the rate of heat transfer, measured as the "U" factor—it is almost always less than 1.0—in BTUs per hour per square foot per °F temperature differential
- Visible light transmission (VLT)—the percentage of visible light that enters the space
- Ultraviolet transmittance—stated as a percentage of UV energy blocked from entrance to the space
- Shading coefficient—the ability to reduce solar heat gains, lower values indicate better performance
- Emissivity (E)—the ability to reflect heat, the lower values indicate better performance
- External and internal shading methods

Designing the façade for energy efficiency is a major issue, for which there is a range of solutions to evaluate. The geographical region in which the project is located partially determines the design direction to accomplish the most efficiently comfortable interior environment.

- The colder northern, or heat-dominated, region increases the importance of the "U" factor, with less emphasis on solar heat gain coefficients. "U" factors of 0.35 or less are desirable in these colder regions.
- In the southern, cooling-dominated, region cooling is the primary issue so emphasis is placed on low shading coefficients. A shading coefficient of 0.4 or lower and "U" factors of 0.75 or lower are reasonable.
- In the central, or mixed-climate regions, "U" factors of 0.4 or lower and solar heat gain coefficients of 0.55 or lower are desirable. Spectrally coated low-e coatings (discussed below) are one good method to offer temperature control, reduce glare and reduce cooling loads without sacrificing visible light into the space.

To accomplish the necessary energy requirements glass, in most climates, is insulated and either tinted and/or heat absorbing, with varying reflective values. A standard insulated glass panel has an R-value of R-2, but a recent trend to low emissivity, or low-e, coatings (a microscopically thin layer of metal or metallic oxide) can improve the rating to R-3. Another recent feature is to use an inert gas, such as Argon, between the glass lights, achieving efficiency gains of up to 10%. In certain warm or temperate climates single glazing may be satisfactory, since the benefit of insulated glass is primarily in the heating cycle.

There is frequently some confusion as to the resistance to thermal transmission being referred to both by the designation of R-value and by "U" factor. R-value is the direct inverse of the "U" factor or heat transfer rate. An R-value of R-2 equals a "U" factor of 0.50.

In extremely cold climates there are triple-glazed systems, three layers of glass with two insulating spaces between them that offer R-values up to R-8 or even R-10. In cold climates, it is essential to design the window frame with a thermal break (discussed below) to prevent the conduction of heat through the frame, saving energy and preventing condensation or frost on the inside of the frame. The higher the "U" value (and the lower the R-value), the higher the heat transfer rate and the lower the energy efficiency of the building. The range of impact on energy efficiency can be shown by the fact that "U" values can range from 1.04 for single-glazed units down to 0.18 for triple-glazed units with ½" air spaces between each lite.

The detailing of the frame can significantly affect the energy loss, in addition to preventing leakage and providing the proper bite on the glass lite. A double-glazed unit with a standard aluminum frame has an overall "U" factor of 0.87, while a frame with a thermal break might have an overall "U" value of only 0.63. A wood or vinyl unit might have a "U" factor of 0.56.

Thermally efficient aluminum windows are often designed in the form of a "sandwich" that places insulating material between the exterior and interior surfaces of frame and sash members. The insulating material interrupts the heat conduction pathway through the window, and is therefore

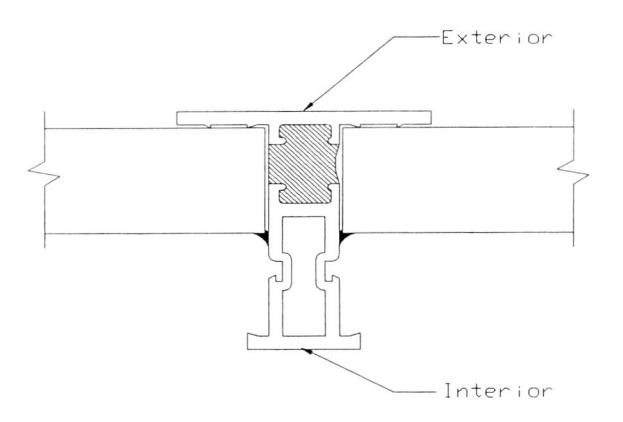

Figure 20-3

known as a "thermal break." Without this insulating medium the building's heat would be more rapidly dissipated through the metal elements to the outside. (See Figure 20-3.) A common thermal break system, known as poured and debridged (P&DB), involves the pouring of a liquid polyurethane formulation into a specially designed cavity built into the frame or sash extrusion. Once the material has properly cured, a section of aluminum forming the cavity is removed (debridged) to form the thermal barrier. While the polyurethane can usually withstand the tensile and compressive forces, it is frequently reinforced with a series of "dog bone" connectors encased within the polyurethane that ties the outer and inner frames structurally. Trim pieces are snapped into the side grooves, after the glass or filler panel is in place, to hold them firmly in position.

Another newer trend where both heat loss and solar gain are major factors is to provide insulated windows with operable shading between two lites of glass to reflect the maximum amount of solar energy and reduce energy requirements. This is particularly effective with a low-e window system. This approach is quite expensive.

Heat-absorbing glazing limits heat gain from solar radiation. Infrared radiation is absorbed by the outer lite, converted to heat, and is then conducted and radiated away from the building, reducing the cooling load and eliminating hot spots. The result, however, can be significantly limited amounts of visible light passing through, which can give the general appearance of a darker, colder feeling even though the lighting level and temperature are within a normal range.

Highly reflective glass can provide a good resistance to solar heat gain, but permits a very low level of visible light transmission, and is considered visually undesirable by many communities. In some jurisdictions it is not permitted under the codes. This glass should never be used in public spaces, such as restaurants, as after dark the reflection will be reversed into the room.

Consideration of natural light transmitted into the workspace can become a trade-off with many common energy reduction solutions. The primary drawback to tinted and heat-absorbing glass is the impact on transmission of light into the workspace. All tinted glazing, even that designed to block only infrared light, changes the appearance of the facility and blocks some visible light. The amount of tinting used depends on how much visible light is desired in the workspace—how dark an appearance is acceptable—versus how much solar energy needs to be blocked. For energy purposes, the warmer the climate in which the facility is located and the greater the ratio of cooling to heating costs, the higher the level of tinting should be specified, if this approach is used.

Low emissivity (low-e) coatings function as selective filters, allowing most visible light through while blocking at least half of the infrared solar heat gain. These coatings reduce heat gain in the summer and heat loss in the winter. The coatings also block 60-80% of the ultraviolet radiation, while reducing glare. The additional transmission of natural light improves visibility, can reduce the necessary lighting levels, and produces what is perceived to be a higher quality of light. As with all other applied coatings, low-e glass can be applied to the glass lite, but acceptable long-term performance requires it be installed within an insulated or laminated glass panel to protect the coating. The premium for low-e glazing is reduced where insulated or laminated glazing is required for other reasons. The low-e glazing tends to provide better quality natural light to the space.

It was reported that a study by the Center for Building Performance, School of Architecture, Carnegie Mellon University indicated that 13 different health complaints from office workers increased with the distance from the window and natural daylight. This may be a strong reason to consider low-emissivity glazing, since reducing the width of a building is not normally an acceptable option.

Unlike most materials that are structurally designed with a factor of safety that must be exceeded prior to failure, the structural design of glass is designated as a percent breakage for a given size lite of a certain thickness under the specified design pressure conditions. Large lites whose breakage resistance is marginal in relation to the desired thickness may be heat-strengthened, a partial stress-relieving process, or fully annealed. Wind pressures on the glazing can be calculated using local data, but on a taller building, or one with an unusual configuration, it should be verified in a wind tunnel test of a building model. The most extreme pressure condition on a glazed section is the vacuum pulled on the lee side of a corner when the wind is raking across that corner. The angle that causes the extreme condition and the severity is determined through testing, but is usually between 30 and 60 degrees.

The glazing should also be analyzed for conditions that cause high heat stresses, where the sun shines on a portion of the lite for a significant period of time, while remainder of the lite is in shadow. These conditions are more common in heat absorbing glass and can be accentuated by deep articulation of the façade or interior insulating blinds.

Vision glass is the weakest point of acoustical resistance in the building envelope. Insulated glass provides some acoustical resistance, varying with the thickness of the air or inert gas space (usually a 1" void is required for significant attenuation). Laminated glass will improve the acoustic resistance to a much greater extent than standard insulated lites. Buildings located near freeways, airport glide paths or other noise generators should be acoustically modeled prior to selection of the glazing, at least on the sides facing the noise source.

Interior shading, discussed in Chapter 30, is an essential part of solar control—venetian blinds and drapes being the most common. Two-tone blinds are available if some heat collection is desirable—one side reflects light and heat while the other absorbs heat and re-radiates it through the space. Where individual control is not required, motorized blinds on a photocell controller is quite effective. HVAC engineers tend to exclude the solar resistance or shading value of interior shading from their calculations, as their use is not predictable..

Infiltration also impacts the energy efficiency where operable windows are used, with infiltration directly related to the window type—how well it is constructed, and how well it is gasketed. Most well constructed windows have infiltration rates of less than 0.5 cfm per square foot of window opening. The impact of operable windows on the HVAC system is discussed in Chapter 25.

The design of the window frame should incorporate a clean, neat detail for the interface of the inner face of the frame with the interior perimeter drywall—a detail that is frequently overlooked.

In Europe, a new form of building envelope, called the "climate wall," is a curtain wall of sorts that allows air to circulate between glass panels. The moving air provides fresh air to the building, a layer of insulation and an exchange medium for heat transfer. In the winter, air warmed by the sun reduces the need for heating it. In the summer the night air is drawn into the building to provide both fresh air and cooling.

Opaque Façade Materials

A wide variety of opaque materials are used to complement the vision glass. Some of the materials commonly used for the opaque portion of the façade in the general order of their perceived quality are discussed below. In addition to their aesthetic appearance and cost, an evaluation of façade materials should include an analysis of their:

- Heat transmission, or "U" value—between 50% and 60% of the surface will be opaque facing material, and the "U" value can vary considerably with the material, the insulation provided and the detailing. Current practice would normally require that sufficient insulation be provided so the "U" values will be a minimum of 0.075 and 0.080.

- Heat capacitance (defined as Btu / ft^2 / °F)—the ability to retain heat in the surface material, usually a direct function of mass.

- Availability—some materials are difficult to readily obtain in sufficient quantities of a suitable range of color and pattern, and some require long distance or high cost shipping.

- Annual maintenance cost—as discussed later, maintenance is an important factor in life cycle costing.

Mixture of Materials

Mixing façade materials has become more common as some architects find that use of several opaque elements in the façade can provide a much more attractive design than a single material. The use of spandrel glass or a lighter color material can create a lighter and friendlier design, and can permit an architect to achieve more creative design solutions and varied proportions.

Use of multiple materials can also be a way to reduce overall costs by using a sufficient amount of the more expensive material to create the image of higher quality, and less expensive materials elsewhere.

Stone

Granite, marble and limestone are the most common stone selections for building façades. Some flat granite pieces can be as thin as 2 cm, but 3 cm is more common, and marble and limestone tend to be at least 3 cm thick. Finishes can be polished, honed (almost polished, but matte finish), flamed (rough texture achieved by passing a flame over the stone pieces) or saw cut. Manual stone cutting is now reserved for monuments. Stone is usually mounted on steel framing sections or rough precast concrete panels (a bond breaker is required between the stone and the panel due to differential expansion), which are then fastened to the structural frame. To avoid the high cost of purchasing and shipping solid granite pieces, the appearance of solid pieces of stone is created by pinning and epoxying two or more pieces of 3 cm stone together with a mitered joint. The joint can barely be seen on close inspection, and from any distance it looks like a thick block of stone.

Granite on the exterior is usually flamed or polished. Some prefer polished stone because it has a deeper and richer appearance and can be washed in the same manner as the windows. Flamed is preferred by others because it exposes the real color and texture of the stone. Frequently, a very attractive façade combination uses both polished and flame-finished pieces—it provides a striking contrast while maintaining a compatible aesthetic relationship. Flamed finishes should be avoided on light-colored granite as it tends to look more like concrete from a distance. Honed finishes should be

> The cost of exterior wall materials can vary extensively due to local market circumstances, and even international monetary imbalances, in addition to the normal cost differences for various systems.
>
> We mentioned previously a 400,000 square foot development that we joint ventured with IBM. The original plan was to use articulated precast concrete, but its cost was rather high due to current market demand. Since it was in 1985, and the dollar was exceptionally high in relation to the Italian lira, we were able to buy granite as our façade material at a cost that was slightly less than we had budgeted for the precast.
>
> At the time we were designing the IBM building we had a major building façade undergoing fabrication in Italy. Because of the fast track schedule on the IBM project, we estimated the square footage, compiled the list of assumed standard piece sizes, then called our fabricator in Italy and negotiated a price over the telephone. Two weeks later we sent a draftsman to Italy with our elevation drawings so that the price could be confirmed and fabrication started.
>
> We had a very nice looking building exterior, erected on time and within budget, and the IBM the operations that were housed in the facility were very pleased with a result.

Strange things can occur in pricing of large quantities of natural materials such as stone. Very early in the design process for Momentum Place in Dallas, Philip Johnson selected a particular stone, which we fully agreed with. It had the desired color range, but more importantly, had interesting striations that were appropriate for the large expanses of stone at the base, as shown below.

Unfortunately, an Italian fabricator, aware of this choice, entered into a venture with the quarry for the exclusive right to provide the stone. The budget prices then quoted were significantly higher than anticipated. When we became aware of this arrangement, we initiated a search for an alternate stone that would satisfy Philip's design objectives, and found one almost as satisfactory that came from the mountains of Brazil.

A visit to the quarry convinced us there was a consistent vein, which could be quarried at a rate that would meet our schedule. While there, we learned that a high-rise building in London was being clad with the stone. We went to London, viewed the project, and were satisfied that it was acceptable, even though we still had a preference for the original selection.

We then directed all of the potential bidders to mock-up the Brazilian stone as well as the original selection, if possible. When the prices were received, and the mock-ups evaluated, we were able to buy the preferred stone at the price we had initially budgeted, for a savings of almost $2 million. The trips were obviously worthwhile.

carefully analyzed if proposed for the façade because they have neither the intensity of color of the polished finish nor the rough natural texture of the flamed finish. Honed is an excellent choice for flooring as it is more cleanable than flamed and less prone to slipping than polished. Saw-cut (like it sounds, it is used just as it comes from the large diamond-tipped saws) is more likely to be used in landscape design.

Marble is normally used on the façade with a polished or saw-cut finish. Again, the polished has a darker and richer appearance. Honed marble is used on interior flooring.

Limestone is most often used with a saw-cut finish. Note that limestone and marble are much more porous than granite, which can make cleaning more difficult, and water penetration can create severe problems when the material is exposed to repetitive freezing conditions.

The structural integrity of a proposed stone should be verified by testing or established experience. The quarrying sizes should be checked early in design. Most European blocks, when trimmed are slightly over 4' x 5' x 5', which would make 2.5' x 5' or 2' x 5' piece sizes quite efficient, and any 3' long piece very inefficient. Minimizing the number of different piece sizes and shapes will reduce fabrication costs. Most thin-stone fabrication (2 to 3 cm) has historically been accomplished in Italy or Spain, but recently some domestic companies are fabricating thin sections.

Additional cautions are required when purchasing stone, or any other material, from an overseas source. The author recommends an independent local expediter be retained to monitor the stone quality on a regular basis. The quality control starts with the architect visiting the fabrication plant prior to any fabrication to choose samples that represent the extremes in color range, striations, and granular size that are acceptable. The pieces are then cut in half, one for the plant and one for the job site, marked as to the range it represents, and signed by the architect. The expediter then checks the pieces as they are fabricated against these samples. By the time unacceptable material would arrive at the job site, it would usually be too late to obtain replacements and meet the construction schedule.

The expediter also keeps a running total of each piece fabricated to compare to the agreed-upon schedule. Not only is the total count important, specific pieces are needed at specific times in accordance with the construction schedule. When setting the schedule, give full consideration to the estimated shipping time, and the fact that ocean shipping is not as dependable time-wise as domestic shipping.

Spandrel Glass

Tinted glass with an insulated backing is frequently used to match or complement the vision glass. It can be a very powerful design element by creating a lighter feel to the building and/or permitting different proportions, as opposed to all of a single opaque material. In addition, it will normally have a lower unit cost than many high-quality materials.

Spandrel glass can range from 0% to 20% of the façade, with vision glass 40% to 50% and other opaque material the remaining 40% to 60%.

When all spandrel glass is used as the opaque surface in conjunction with vision glazing, it creates an all glass building. If well designed, an all glass building can accomplish a sleek and modern look, but it is only as good as its detailing.

Precast Concrete

The ability to create quality details with precast concrete has improved significantly in recent years. Optimal piece sizes to maximize shop efficiency and minimize the number of lifts, and a limited number of different piece sizes and shapes to reduce fabrication forms and handling, are major factors in controlling cost. Interest can be added to the design by a wide range of colors and textures with exposed aggregate, concrete coloring and articulation. New methods are constantly being developed to improve the decorative value of concrete and to simulate other natural materials. Precast systems also benefit from the opportunity for good shop control and ease of erection, even though shipping is bulky and costly and the structure must carry the greater weight. Some precast panels have insulation sandwiched inside.

Frequently, there is insufficient competition for precast work due to relatively few fabricators in many areas and the high cost of transportation, which makes bidding risky. Often times, negotiating a contract during the design phase can be beneficial if the proposed costs meet your expectations.

Cast-in-Place Concrete

In much the same manner as precast concrete, the appearance of cast-in-place concrete is being improved to where it is much more acceptable as an exposed finish material. There have been several projects where the forms have been carefully designed so that the form joint marks create the desired design on the finished surface.

Glass Fiber Reinforced Concrete (GFRC)

GFRC is a Portland cement-based composite with alkali-resistant glass fibers randomly dispersed throughout. Its advantages are moldability to replicate complicated forms and ornamental details, and it's lightweight (as much as 80% lighter than precast concrete thereby reducing structural loads). GFRC can readily create cornices and other heavy looking designs, as well as sculpted shapes.

Glass fibers and cement slurry are simultaneously sprayed into a mold to form the sections. Due to differential expansion and contraction, window sections must be separately connected to the structure. The number of molds must be minimized to avoid major cost premiums.

Architectural Metal

A variety of metal panels, with many different finishes, are available. Aluminum may have a polished or natural finish protected by a sealer or anodized finishes that may vary from clear to quite dark. Aluminum or steel, painted or coated with a material such as Kynar, are frequently used. A relatively recent coating with significantly increased environmental resistance is Polyvinylidene Fluoride (PVDF). These PVDF fluoropolymers are reported to have excellent color and gloss retention and resistance to thermal, chemical and ultraviolet conditions.

Forming, shaping or extruding are used to achieve articulated or textured finishes. Stainless steel, bronze or Corten can only be afforded on trophy or specialty buildings. Titanium has been recently used on an institutional building to take advantage of its lightweight, interesting color and space-age image, but its economics are not known to the author at this time. Metal panels are usually installed mounted on a steel frame or as infill in a window wall assembly. Metal panels are also light in weight in relation to other materials, but can be somewhat more susceptible to damage.

Tile Panels

A newer trend is using tiles of stone, thin brick, porcelain and ceramic tile products either laid up or in prefabricated large panels. Porcelain may be the most durable and have the widest range of colors and patterns. Stone tiles of 12" x 12" or 18" x 18" can offer reduced costs of stone due to recovery of a higher percentage of useable material from the raw quarry stock and utilizing thinner material. The primary concern with using a natural material in small square pieces is the difficulty in keeping the overall appearance within an acceptable range, unless it has a relatively fine grain and a consistent color. Unless carefully installed, variations in the protrusion of the individual tiles can create a disappointing appearance. Another potential problem for thin-set stone is that leakage can cause staining and efflorescence.

One installation method is to fasten a 5/8" or ¾" fiberglass substrate over building paper to the studs with mechanical fasteners, and then lay up the tile with a Portland cement based latex mastic and fill the joints with grout. Tiles are also laid up over a cement plaster scratch coat. A more expensive alternative would be to fasten the tiles with mechanical fasteners.

Brick

There are bricks of many different colors, hardness and porosities. Due to varying porosity, the selected brick should be tested to determine the best sealer to use. Frequently it is wise to use a consultant for this purpose. Thin-face bricks are now in common usage, and brick can be installed in large prefabricated panels or laid up individually. Hardened bricks with very low porosity should be used for horizontal surfaces or decorative paving. The use of jumbo brick up to three times the size of standard brick is now being used to reduce the installation cost.

Exterior Insulation and Finish Systems (EIFS)

Best known by the trade name DRIVIT, EIFS gains economic advantage through combining weatherproofing, thermal insulation and an attractive all-in-one integrated composite wall cladding system. It is comprised of a finish and a base coat of stucco-like material applied over a foam insulation reinforced with fiberglass mesh for stability that is attached with an adhesive fastener to the building substrate, usually a stud wall sheathed with cement or gypsum-based boards. The synthetic stucco coatings can even resemble metals or stone, and provide wide choices of color and texture. The ability of the insulation board to be sculpted or shaped provides an opportunity for architectural interest.

There have been many problems associated with EIFS through water damage and structural failures due to water penetration through the material, primarily at terminations, penetrations and perimeters. In addition to water leaks, there has been a problem in some climates with water vapor penetration and condensation. There is great concern as to the perception of quality and the ability to obtain a long-term satisfactory performance and appearance.

There is recent evidence, however, that improved detailing and better quality installation resulting from the recent standards by the EIFS Industry Members Association has made this a better product. These standards, called water-managed EIFS, provide for constructing a cavity, or air space, between the insulation and the sheathing and a water barrier on the outside of the sheathing, all held together with mechanical fasteners instead of adhesives. In addition, better details are recommended for terminations where the EIFS meet other materials and penetrations.

Stucco

Basically, stucco is a residential type of construction usually used on low-end one- or two-story buildings. It consists of several coats of cement plaster sprayed over expanded metal lath that is attached to the studs or to a substrate. The cement can include colored dyes, or the finished surface can be painted.

Detailing

The appearance of the opaque wall is greatly affected by the range of color and imperfections, and the consistency of the quality of workmanship. For materials such as stone, and even some brick, a mock-up is recommended in the fabricator's plant, preferably using full size pieces, on which the architect will mark approval of those units within the acceptable range, and mark his rejection on those deemed to be outside the range. Any fabricated units outside the range are not accepted for installation. A similar range mock-up is often kept at the job site, but the most effective control is frequent inspection at the plant to avoid construction delays that may result from rejection of material at the job site. Sealing and grouting details are approved in a similar manner, and the mock-up is kept at the job site.

Similar mock-ups, usually kept at the point of fabrication, are advisable for precast concrete, poured-in-place concrete, and GFRC. In addition to color range, these mock-ups focus on the quality of workmanship and finishes.

In addition to the visual material choice, proper wall insulation, vapor barrier, flashing, caulking and details are critical to the performance of any wall system. There are curtain wall consultants who do nothing but advise on the functional details of façade design, and their utilization is frequently a wise investment.

A wall must be carefully designed to keep water out of the building, minimize air infiltration and protect the studs, clips and other members that connect it to the structure. The accomplishment of a satisfactory water resistant wall is a combination of the specific detailing and the appropriateness of the selected sealants.

There are basically two concepts for designing a curtain wall—fully sealed walls and rain screens. A fully sealed curtain wall tries to ensure that no water will enter its outer perimeter for any reason at any time. If any crack in the sealant occurs, there will be a leak at any time the outside pressure exceeds the pressure inside the building or when capillary action occurs. Once inside, the water really has no place to go. This type of wall tests the "memory" capabilities of the sealant as it is constantly working and moving due to temperature changes and the relative movement of the elements of the wall over a long period of time. As a matter of fact, it is virtually impossible for a sealant to maintain a perfect seal over time due to the movement and some degradation of the sealant itself.

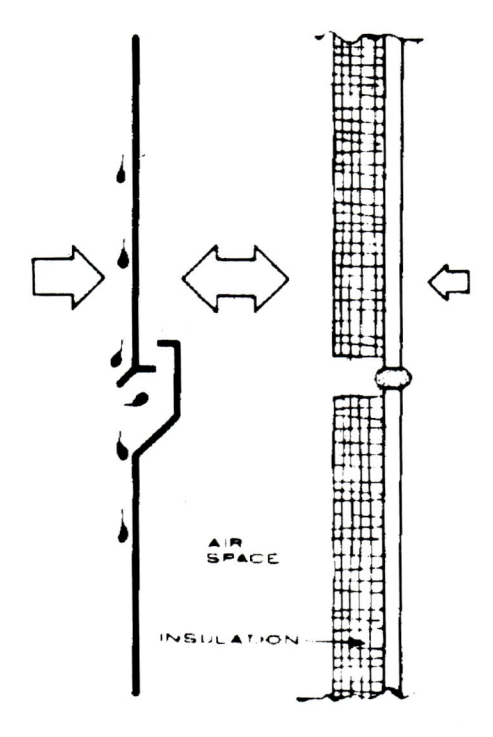

Figure 20-4

A rain screen (or pressure-equalized wall construction) consists of two walls—the outer wall facing the elements, an air cavity in between and a fully sealed inner wall. This system is illustrated in Figure 20-4 showing the pressure equalizing principal. The outer wall permits water entrance, but such water that may enter the cavity tends to flow down the inside face of the rain screen and is channeled outside through drain holes by flashing placed every two or three floors or at each fire stop. The cavity space will maintain a pressure equal to that outside the building. Even with small imperfections in the inner sealant, there should be no significant leakage into the building. There must be no penetrations through the inner wall with this type of construction, not even electrical outlets.

Sealants

Careful selection and installation of the sealant is an essential element in achieving a successful wall. The selected sealant must have been tested extensively under the temperature variations anticipated at the site. Proper installation requires clean, dry joints and the installation of a plastic rope into the joint that will not bond to the sealant. The sealant is then caulked carefully into the joint following the manufacturer's recommendations, particularly as to joint width, cleanliness, temperature at the time of installation and the thickness of the application. The sealant works properly when bonded only to two opposite surfaces, permitting it to stretch and compress in a linear manner, as shown in Figure 20-5.

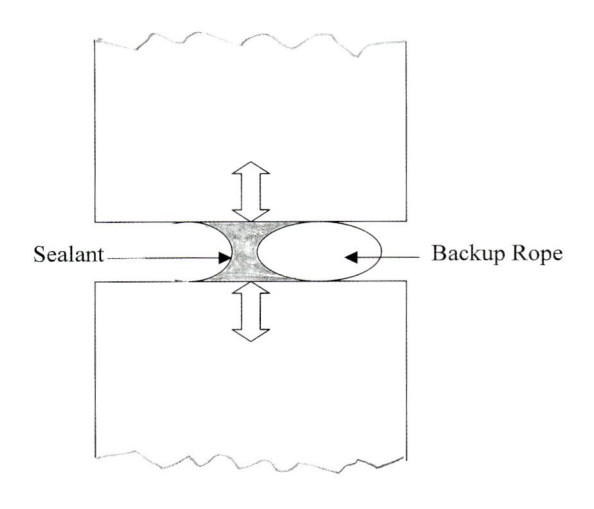

Figure 20-5

Testing

Unless a curtain wall is very standard, or is for a building of less than nine or ten stories, and is using familiar details, a wall-section test is recommended. The test usually comprises a wall section with a minimum height of one window element and two spandrels with a width of at least 20 feet if a full column-to-column width is not practical. A cross section of a typical chamber is shown in Figure 20-6. The pressure test is accomplished with a negative static pressure of one and

Building Envelope Design

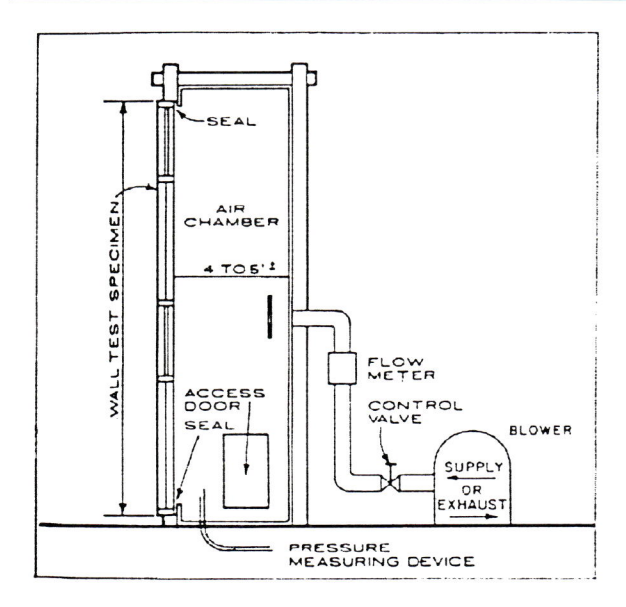

Figure 20-6

one-half times the design pressure to check the structural integrity of the glass, frame, spandrel panel, column cover and the connectors, as well as the complete assembly. This test is conducted by pulling a vacuum inside of the test chamber, of which the tested wall section is the front face, as shown.

A variation of the pressure test is to have two chambers with the test wall section between them. The chamber on the interior face is maintained at building temperature and the other chamber may simulate extreme outside design conditions. The vacuum is pulled in one chamber while the other remains at atmospheric pressure.

The unit is also tested statically for air and water penetration, and dynamically for water penetration. The static water penetration test utilizes a water spray of about 2.5 gallons per square foot over the entire face of the wall section while it is under the static test pressure described above. The dynamic test is usually conducted by simultaneously spraying water in the same manner on the wall section while the wall is being subjected to the pulsating pressure generated by engine driven propellers. This pulsation tries to simulate the worst kind of varying pressures the wall may encounter during varying storm and wind conditions by constantly flexing the panels, connectors and sealant.

The worst structural design condition on a wall is at a corner on the leeward side of the most prevalent high velocity wind direction. The vacuum caused by the passing wind creates the maximum design-pressure condition.

A word of caution relative to the schedule is necessary when a wall test is contemplated. The test must be consummated utilizing the elements proposed for installation in the wall. This means completely detailing the wall, manufacturing the mullions, rails, anchors, trusses and any other items, and purchasing the glazing and opaque element. The lead time for this process can be extensive and must be incorporated in the schedule from the start.

Maintenance

Contrary to some common views, every façade needs periodic maintenance—from cleaning to inspection to replacement of the sealant. Frequency of cleaning of the exterior surfaces will vary from location to location dependent upon climatic conditions and atmospheric cleanliness.

Vision glazing should be washed in accordance with local standards for Class A office buildings—but not less than twice per year. For all-glass buildings, the entire surface should be washed at the same time to avoid streaks or other unsatisfactory conditions. Joint sealant should be replaced and mullions coated every 10 to 15 years.

Metal panels should be cleaned every 3 to 4 years, the surface recoated and joints sealed every 10 to 15 years. Polished stone may be cleaned every 3 to 4 years, or may be cleaned with the windows at any scheduled cleaning.

Stone (other than polished), precast and brick should normally be cleaned every 10 to 20 years varying with the porosity, and joints should be checked for resealing at the same time. EIFS or stucco will probably require joints to be sealed and cracks repaired every 10 years and resurfacing every 15 years or so.

Appropriate provision must be made for window washing and exterior maintenance, while satisfying ever more stringent OSHA regulations and good practice. Solutions can run all the way from fully automated equipment, to davit sockets

> Curtain wall testing is rejected by many developers because of its significant cost and considerable time delay. Remember that you must design the system, contract for it, prepare shop drawings, construct and/or purchase the sections required for the test and satisfactorily complete the test prior to fabrication proceeding with a certainty that there would be no changes. Normally, neither the window wall contractor nor the developer wish to take the chance of fabricating the extrusions and other materials prior to the results of the test.
>
> Notwithstanding these concerns, window wall testing can be very important. On the First National Bank of Chicago building we found that certain support brackets were inadequate, and if constructed without the test, a serious problem could have occurred.
>
> There are many well-documented curtain wall failures such as the many corner windows in the Chase Manhattan building that failed under negative pressure when the wind was about 60 degrees to the face of the building, and the extensive leaks in the chapel at the Air Force Academy and the IDS center in Minneapolis.
>
> I'm not familiar with the testing or lack of it on the three buildings listed above, but they illustrate the unbelievable cost that can result from curtain wall failure. It tends to make the cost of testing appear to be very inexpensive insurance.

for portable rigs, to tiebacks, or to nothing at all if the exterior can be serviced from the ground. Vertical tracks to guide the scaffolding, or tieback buttons on the skin that engage a track on the rig, are required above certain heights to ensure that a wind cannot blow the scaffold away from the building and endanger the workers. Extensive safety features and electrical interlocks are required on taller structures.

The parapet height should be reviewed in light of the types of maintenance work anticipated, as the equipment must be raised above this level. Provision must be made for walkways to be installed to prevent damage to the membrane from any anticipated maintenance work. Usually, property management and/or competent maintenance companies should be consulted in order to accomplish an efficient and satisfactory system.

ROOF

The roof deck of an office building is normally a concrete structural deck with the insulation and roof membrane on top. For many buildings with unusual shaped tops, the architectural feature is a screen-like façade, with the real roof a relatively flat slab below.

A less than satisfactory roof creates many problems for the building and its tenants. A successful roof is dependent upon proper selection, design and installation. The key factors the Development Officer must consider in the design and selection of the roof are:

- Climatic conditions
- Shape, size and use of roof
- Proper membrane selection, as discussed below
- Firm attachment at the perimeters
- Membrane protection
- Drainage
- Flashing design
- Insulation
- Proper coordination of all elements of the roof assembly
- Quality of installation
- Quality and term of warranty available
- Cost

A roofing system basically consists of a supporting roof deck, appropriate fastening system,

> The preparation for window washing and curtain wall maintenance in most buildings is limited to providing davit sockets to support scaffolding that is provided by the exterior maintenance contractor.
>
> On many large or irregular shaped buildings, the equipment is very complex machinery requiring careful design and testing. On the First National Bank of Chicago the motorized scaffold had to be capable of initiating its drops from two different roof levels, the higher one accessed by hydraulic lift. On each end of the building the scaffolding had to telescope outward as the platform descended, and back in as it ascended, due to the curved configuration at the ends.
>
> On Momentum Place in Dallas (see picture), the motorized platform had to be capable of not only going down the four sides of the 60-story building, but traversing laterally from the center to the drop positions. On the front side it had to access five different planes of the façade, two at right angles, and on two drops had to step out fifteen as the building increased in size as pictured. On the back side it had to step out twenty feet on three different drops. This motorized platform was considered to be so unique that the Canadian Broadcasting Company made an hour-long documentary describing its development.
>
> At the World Trade Center in New York City the motorized platform was designed to wash the windows automatically. The only human participation is to transfer it from one drop to the next one and index it for the proper drop. The equipment has been replaced, but the system is reported to be working satisfactorily.

vapor retardant, insulation, roof membrane, and a protective surface. Various types of membranes and the other components of the roof assembly are discussed below.

The protection over the deck that shields the interior of the building is the roof membrane. There are many types and styles of membranes, whose choice is dependent on variables such as cost, weight, anticipated frequency of maintenance, type and length of desired warranty, roof size, deck type, extent and intensity of sunlight, temperature extremes and variation, desired reflectivity, desired "U" factor, snow and ice, and extreme wind conditions. The project conditions are analyzed in the light of the desired life span and the experience of the architect, contractor and owner.

U.S. Intec, a subsidiary of GAF Building Materials, has developed software called Roof Advisor to assist in the selection of the proper roofing material to satisfy various conditions. This program may be downloaded from the Internet at www.paybackestimating.com/usinyec. It asks a series of questions (some of which are weighted by your judgment) about criteria listed in the above paragraph and provides several roof system choices ranked in order of preference.

Roofing membrane systems, over an insulating material with a "U" factor as called for in the energy budget, can be classified as:

- Built-up roofing
  - 4-ply bitumen roofing—a standard for many years is being gradually replaced in many applications by modified bitumens, single-ply membranes and spray systems. It consists of a series of layers of bitumen (asphalt or coal tar pitch), alternated with glass fiber felt layers. Aggregate, usually gravel, protects the roof membrane from impact, abrasion and ultraviolet energy.
  - Modified bitumen roofing—combines newer formulations with traditional installation techniques used in built-up roofs. The asphalt is modified using various polymer ingredients that improve low-temperature flexibility, and is reinforced for additional strength and stability.
  - Hybrid systems—a combination of conventional built-up glass plies with a surface ply of an SBS-modified bitumen.
- Single ply—there are many variations as discussed below. Many authorities recommend that membranes less than 60 mils be avoided as the cost savings may not be beneficial in the long run. With flexible sheet membranes, great care is required to ensure overlapping seams resist dynamic wind uplift loads, thermal movement and foot traffic. The types are:
  - Thermoplastics—plastics that can be readily seamed by either welding with a hot air gun or with solvents (which include high levels of VOCs) to become a monolithic sheet. They include:
    - Polyvinyl chlorides (PVCs)—versatile and are resistant to extreme weather conditions. Have good seaming capabilities.
    - Chlorinated polyethylenes (CPEs)—usually reinforced with scrim. Good weather resistance, resistant to oil, chemicals, and ozone. Flexible and can be pigmented. Most often made in thinner sections, such as 40 to 48 mils.
    - Thermopolyolefins (TPOs)—a blend of polypropylene and extruded polystyrene, usually reinforced with polyester fabrics, are among the newer roofing products. Good flexibility, readily weldable, good impact and puncture resistance, and blends with colorant.
  - Thermosets—based on rubber polymers. They are bonded by liquid contact adhesives (also high in VOCs) or a seam tape adhesive in order to form a seal at the overlaps, as they can not be welded.
    - Chlorosulfonated polyethylene (CSPE) or "Hypalon"—a synthetic rubber compound that self-cures when exposed to ultraviolet radiation. It is resistant to weathering and ozone, and is available in many colors. It is adaptable to a variety of roof shapes.
    - Ethylene propylene diene monomer (EPDM)—a vulcanized-cured material, reinforced with polyester. Available in either black or white, it has low temperature flexibility and is resistant to ozone, ultraviolet, and abrasion. It is resilient.
- Spray and fluid applications
  - Spray polyurethane foam (SPF)—a two-component liquid that forms a closed-cell mass that provides a seamless membrane. It has an insulation value of R-6 per inch of thickness, conforms to any shape roof and attachments, and can be applied over a wide variety of substrates, including old roofing systems. CFC-free blowing agents are expected to be available in a few years.
  - Hydrotech protected roof membrane—a hot rubberized asphalt compound, applied evenly over the roof in fluid form to a depth of approximately $3/16"$. Satisfactory for both dead flat roofs, and those roofs holding standing water.

In addition to the type of roof membrane, roofs are also generally referred to by the method of attachment to the roofing substrate.

- Fully adhered systems—bonded with adhesives, giving the roof a light weight with great resistance to uplift. The finished surface of the adhered roof is smooth.

- Ballasted systems—are loosely attached and generally held in place with gravel, pavers or cement-covered insulation. Slope must be 2:12 or less. Roof heights and proximity to high wind zones should be evaluated.

- Mechanically fastened systems—using weather-protected individual membrane plates or batten bars to connect the membrane to the structure through the insulation. Not subject to slope limitations, they work well on most roof structures.

While roof materials may be discussed individually, a proper roofing installation is an integrated system that includes proper coordination of the membrane, attachments, flashings, insulation and the deck itself. Product incompatibility can greatly decrease the life expectancy.

When evaluating the roof design it is necessary to consider factors such as building height, wind exposure, climatic conditions and its extreme ranges, anticipated foot traffic, aesthetics, energy consumption, likelihood of frequent modifications, severity of the impact of water damage, and cost. It is frequently advisable to include a roofing consultant on the design team to ensure these important decisions are properly made.

Great weight should be given to the length and quality of the warranty when making a selection of roofing material and application contractor. The warranty should be for at least 20 years, cover both labor and material, not be limited only to "gale force" winds (only 32 mph), and must be through a financially strong and established surety. A careful review of the qualifications and conditions is necessary to ensure that normal and reasonable maintenance practices will not invalidate the warranty. A review by Property Management is prudent.

Good drainage and membrane protection are essential to maintaining the integrity of any roof. The drainage slope will vary with the membrane selected. In addition to the primary roof drains, overflow scuppers or overflow drains with separate drain lines are required, set about 2" higher than the primary roof drainage system to protect against blockage in the primary system, that would permit standing water that could overload the roof system.

In some high-rise buildings the roof and drainage system is designed to "store" a given amount of water on the roof in a heavy storm, for gradual release over time, in order to reduce the size of the roof drain lines. In such case the trade-off is the extra expense of the roof structure vs. the savings in sizing of the drain lines.

Some single-ply membranes are heavy enough to serve as their own protective coating, but other membranes will require metal, tile, tar and gravel, ballast or concrete to protect it. If other than concrete is used, protective maintenance pathways must be laid over the roof membrane to protect it from damage during normal maintenance and equipment operations.

Flashings must be properly designed and carefully installed, and must accommodate differential movement between the roof and the wall system. Comprehensive guide details are available from the National Roofing Contractors Association, but may have to be adjusted for conditions on a specific project.

While most concern is directed toward the forces on and leaks through the roof, a major design issue is wind-induced uplift, where the wind velocity creates a low air pressure above the roof, while the building exerts a positive pressure from inside. The worst conditions are created at the roof edges, which must be thoroughly anchored. ASCE-795 provides design requirements as well as updated national wind speed maps.

Sufficiently sized retaining curbs should be provided around the cooling towers and any other water-using equipment with sufficient internal drainage, and around all penetrations. Hose bibbs should be provided at about 50–60 foot intervals along the perimeter for maintenance and window washing, and electrical outlets should be similarly provided for various maintenance functions and possibly for signage.

Several roof jacks should be installed to permit future satellite or line-of-sight communications, as well as future additional electrical service, so as not to disturb the integrity of the roof at a later date.

Where setbacks occur facing tenant space, the roof should be covered with a decorative material such as tile, brick or special aggregates. The parapet should be kept to a minimum height in such spaces, using a handrail or transparent panels to provide for personnel safety, otherwise the tenant's view would be hindered.

Roof insulation is as important as the membrane itself. Most roofing insulation is formed into rigid boards for ease of handling and durability. In addition to controlling heat transfer, the insulation can help control or eliminate condensation, provide fire resistance at the roof plane, and acts as a clean level substrate for roofing membranes. No single insulation is best for all roofs—they must be evaluated on their compatibility with bitumens and adhesives, impact resistance, fire resistance, moisture resistance, thermal resistance, stable R-value (or its inverse, the "U" value) over time, attachment capabilities, dimensional stability, and component stability (compatibility with other roofing materials). Common roofing insulation materials, in the general order of their R-value (highest to lowest) are: polyisocyanurate, extruded polystyrene, mineral fiber, glass fiber, expanded polystyrene, cellular glass, perlite and wood fiberboard.

Polystyrene applied directly to the deck without a thermal barrier is currently being promoted as a roofing insulation. In addition to an R-value stable over a long period of time, it is purported to withstand exposure to foot traffic, freeze and thaw cycles and moisture absorption.

It is becoming much more important in some climates to install double-insulated roofs, using materials such as polyiso, in order to greatly increase the "U" value and reduce the heating and cooling load on the building systems. The lesser number of stories in the building, the more impact the roof insulation has on the efficiency of the building's environmental systems. The "U" value is the overall coefficient of heat transmission and represents the flow of Btu/hour/square foot/°F difference in temperature across a building section.

A newer trend is toward "white roofs," or "reflective roofs," that reflect or divert solar heat in locations where air conditioning is a significant factor. Insulation can be decreased if the roof surface has a total surface reflectance of at least 0.70 (70%) and has a minimum thermal emittance (the ability to release absorbed solar energy) of 0.75 (75%). White roofs, however, have been known to lose one-half of their ability to reflect light in their first 10 to 15 years, and a major portion of that in the first year and a half. Certain reflective coatings will slow down the rate of deterioration. This deterioration should be carefully checked prior to assuming full reflectance in the HVAC calculations. Dark roofs can tend to absorb solar energy and heat up to 170°F, while a reflective roof may not exceed 110°F. It should be noted, however, that all white or light colored roofing materials are not highly reflective and emissive.

While the individual roof elements have been discussed separately, as stated previously, the roof must be viewed as a complete compatible system—from deck, to fasteners, to underlayment, to the membrane, seams and adhesives, including penetrations and roof mounted equipment.

FUTURE TECHNOLOGIES

Newer technologies not yet in general commercial applications are photovoltaic cells buried in the wall to produce electricity, holographic glazing to refract up to 35%–40% of the light, and electrochromatic glazing (estimated to be market ready in 5–10 years) that change the optical density by applying a small amount of electricity (1 to 2 volts) to the thin coating (purportedly the optical density can shift from 10% to 90% light transmittance in less than one minute).

Integrated photovoltaics are enabling a variety of systems to be developed that can turn future walls, windows and roofs into solar energy collectors. Currently, there are investment tax credits and accelerated depreciation allowances available for building-integrated photovoltaic systems.

DECORATIVE LIGHTING AND BUILDING SIGNAGE

Subtle exterior accent lighting can enhance the geometry of the building's design, but bright, colored, or other garish lighting that creates a "look at me" attitude is usually a poor substitute for quality design.

Signage on a high-rise building should be discouraged, as it is an indication that the building design does not provide the unique identity that was intended. Low-rise buildings, particularly in suburban markets, frequently must offer building identity to attract major tenants. In such cases the architect should work closely with the tenant's designer so that the size, shape and color provide the desired identification—but coordinated well with the building, and within regulatory limits.

CASE STUDY

The detailed design of the fenestration proceeded from where it left off in the design studies in Chapter 15. It was now necessary to blend the desire for granite with the requirements of the Substantial Conformance Determination, the revised floor plate proportions, and the best features of Schemes 1A, 5, and 5A (Figure 15-7) with a relatively tight budget. A reasonable degree of character was desired for the building so that it will stand out from the other office buildings in the area, but it was necessary to simplify the details sufficiently to meet the budget objectives.

At one point it was proposed omitting the two balconies on the eighth floor to actually reduce the cost and gain rentable area, but the development department of the city declined to permit this change, as it was a specific requirement of the Carmel Valley Planning Board.

While studying the various design alternatives, parallel studies were initiated on the glazing, granite selection and the most efficient method of system design and erection.

Insulated glazing is not required in San Diego due to the temperate climate, as the benefit of this material is primarily during the heating cycle—which was verified in the energy analysis. Due to the location at the intersection of two major freeways, the potential for transmission of excessive highway noise needed to be tested. Plate glass ¼" thick seems to be providing satisfactory acoustical resistance in the Executive Center next door, however, those buildings are much shorter and have heat pumps in the tenant space that create a fairly high ambient noise level, which can mitigate noticing the highway noise.

An acoustical analysis was run at the site that resulted in a recommendation of providing at least ¼" laminated glazing, which incorporates two layers of 1/8" glass with a safety film in between, on the west and south faces. The laminated glazing for acoustical purposes was priced at both ¼" and 3/8" thickness. A structural analysis indicated that the ¼" glazing would not be satisfactory at the corners, so a premium of $19,000 was paid for the 3/8" glazing on the two sides.

The use of low-e glass that provides better natural light penetration was also priced even though it was believed the premium might be difficult to include in the budget. Low-e, which should be used in a laminated or insulated panel to protect the coating, had a premium of $180,000–190,000, which was rejected.

Four granites were considered, all polished—Carmen Red, Balmoral, Capro Bonita and Baltic Brown. The first three are attractive stones on a red tone with reasonably small-crystalline grain structure, and Baltic Brown is on a brown tone with very large grain structure. Baltic Brown is not really very attractive, and was not given too much consideration, but it was about the least expensive granite on the market in a darker tone that could be purchased in large quantities. There was a strong preference for Carmen Red that has a deep reddish brown color due to its blackish grain.

The initial pricing model was based on a unitized system as both the architect and the contractor preferred this approach due to better fabrication and installation control and faster installation. A budget cost, based on proposals from several window wall contractors, was $42.18 per sf of façade ($17.64 per gsf), including 40% granite with a unit price of $13, 40% tinted single-thickness glass and 20% spandrel glass. The cost would increase with the addition of either insulated or laminated glass.

An initial investigation of the alternate systems indicated that a unitized system would require a nine-month lead time and 12 weeks for erection—while a truss system would require eight months lead time and 20 weeks for erection. The weight of the various systems, which would have to be carried by the structural frame, would be 20 psf for a unitized or stick system, 30 psf for a steel truss, and 65 psf for a pre-cast concrete backing. A subsequent study by Swinerton & Walberg indicated that a $75,000 structural cost penalty must be allocated to any precast concrete backing system and, additionally, a precast concrete system might create some further issues in satisfying the seismic code. The steel truss systems would have a miscellaneous metal premium for brackets and attachments.

As different wall suppliers tend to prefer different systems, the economics of the various systems was uncertain, leading to taking preliminary pricing numbers on all three systems using the preferred design at that point. As a result of this exercise it became obvious that either a unitized or stick system would be the most economical solution. The analysis also verified that the selected design with 58% granite, which is normally too much to obtain reasonable pricing, with a series of 12" setbacks, would be significantly over budget.

The merits of the following design issues were evaluated: deep recessed glass features vs. shallow recesses, omitting some horizontal granite, omitting some vertical granite, spacing the first/second floor columns at 10' vs. 30' centers, changing some of the corner setbacks to primarily glass and alternating some glass spandrel panels with metal. Two of the many variations are shown as Figures 20-7 to 20-9. In order to reduce costs by reducing the amount of granite, five further alternative designs were evaluated that reduced the granite to between 32% and 40% of the fenestration surface, two examples of which are shown as Figures 20-10 and 20-11.

It was decided to proceed with the bidding in order to determine which type of system was appropriate, and then negotiate with the low bidder to obtain a solution that satisfied us, but first the modifications indicated below were incorporated. A long list of further alternatives was also included.

- Reduced the granite to about 50%
- Eliminated the 12" setbacks
- The first floor entrance doors were left with a seven-foot inset
- Eliminated the first floor colonnade that, since the building was rotated, no longer served its original purpose, and reduced costs while adding rentable area

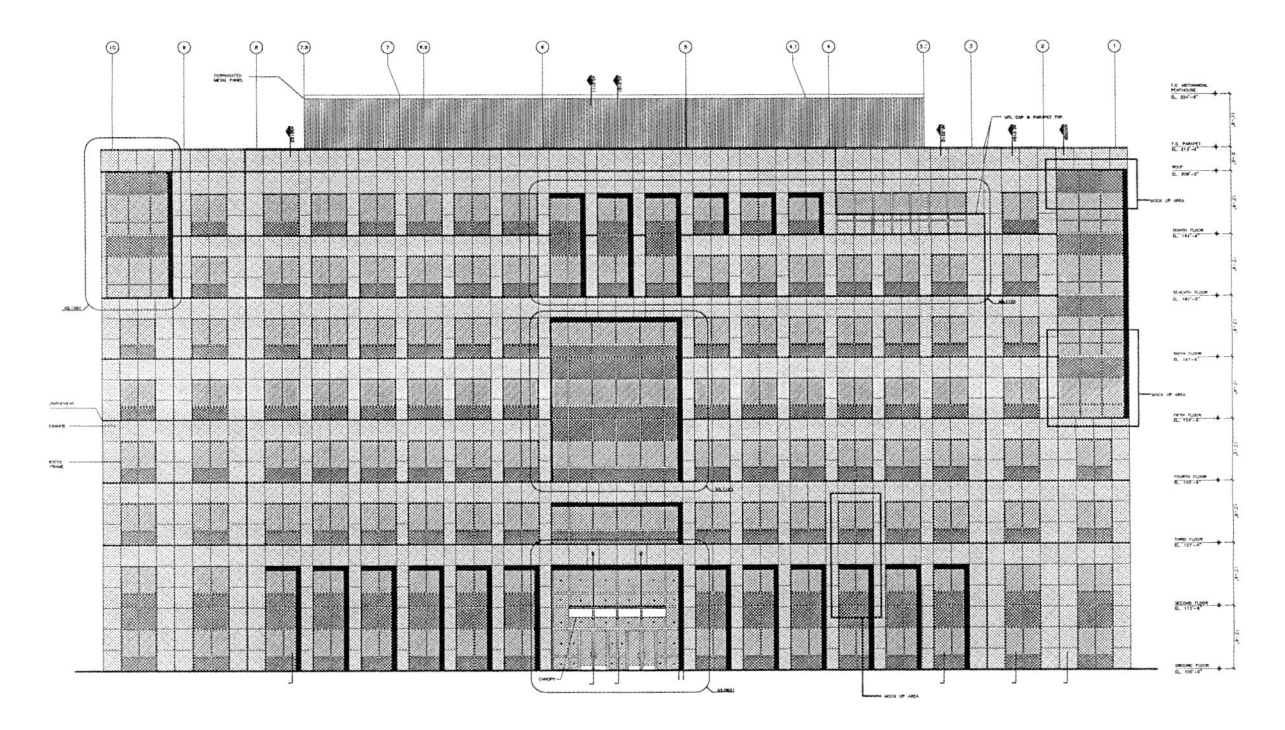

Figure 20-7

260   Office Development

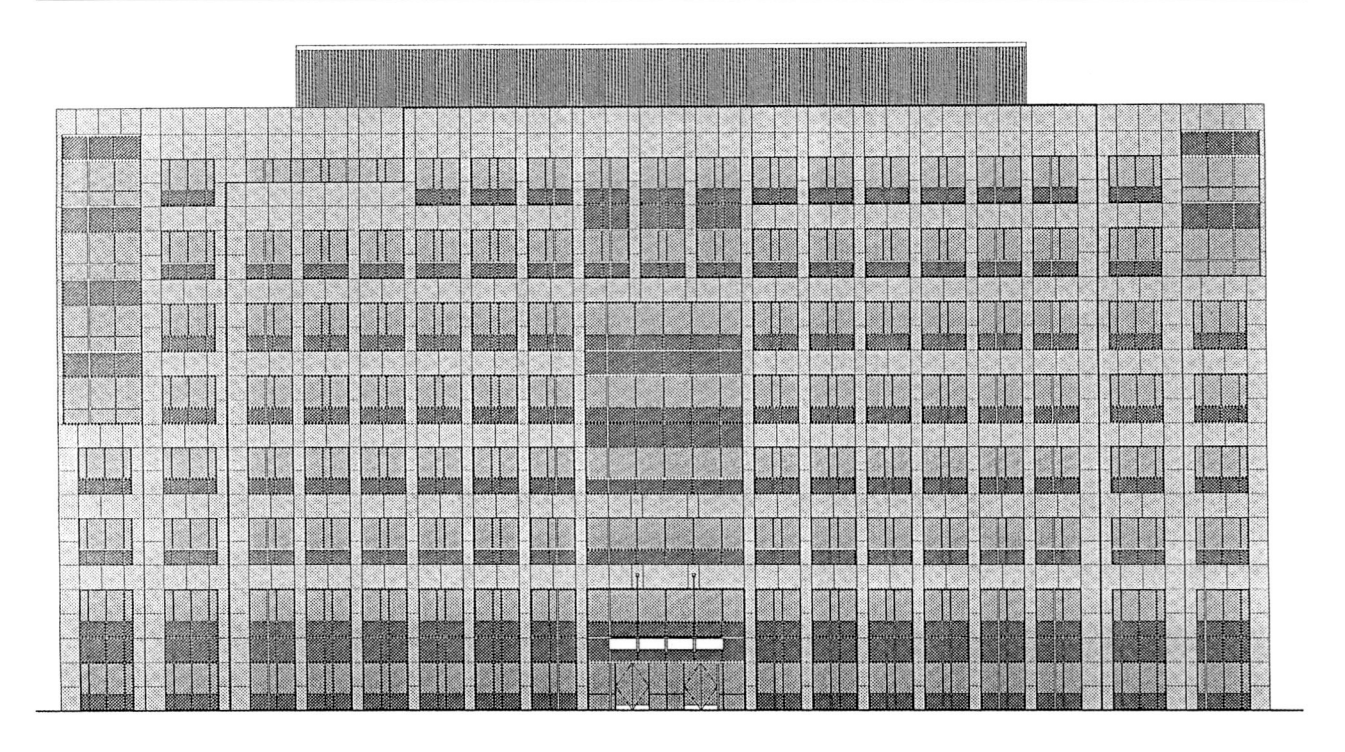

Figure 20-8

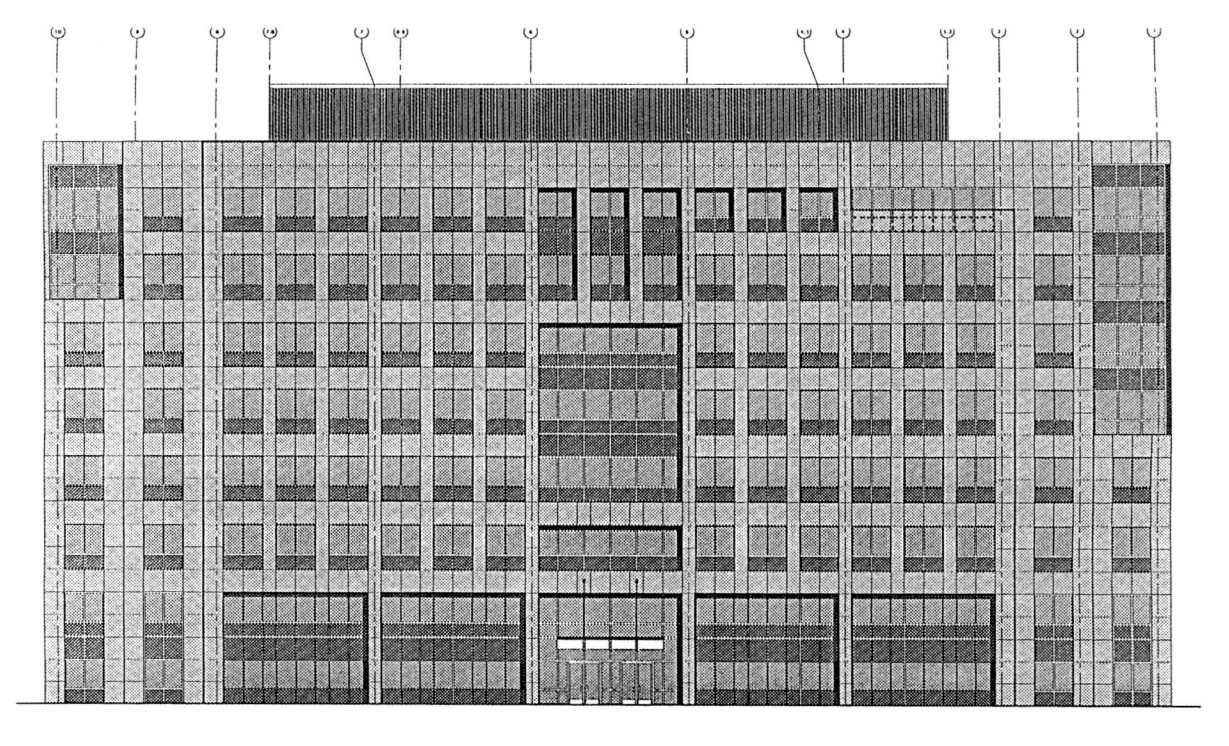

Figure 20-9

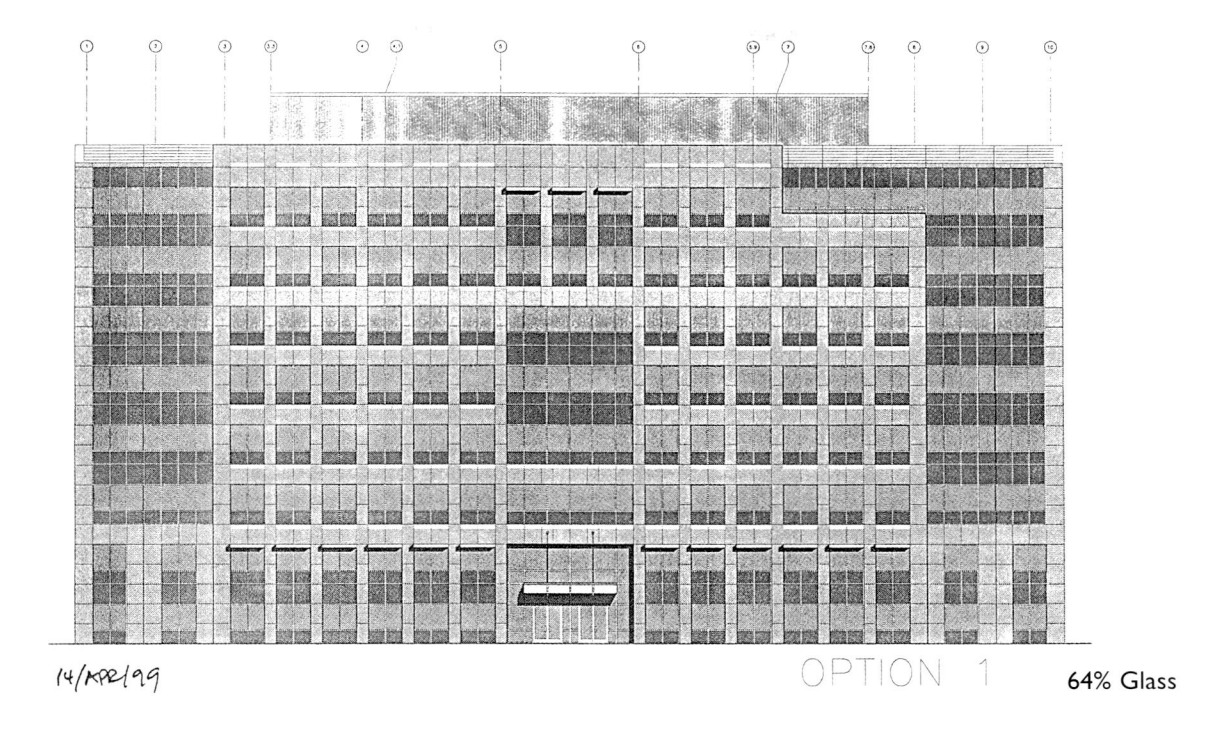

Figure 20-10

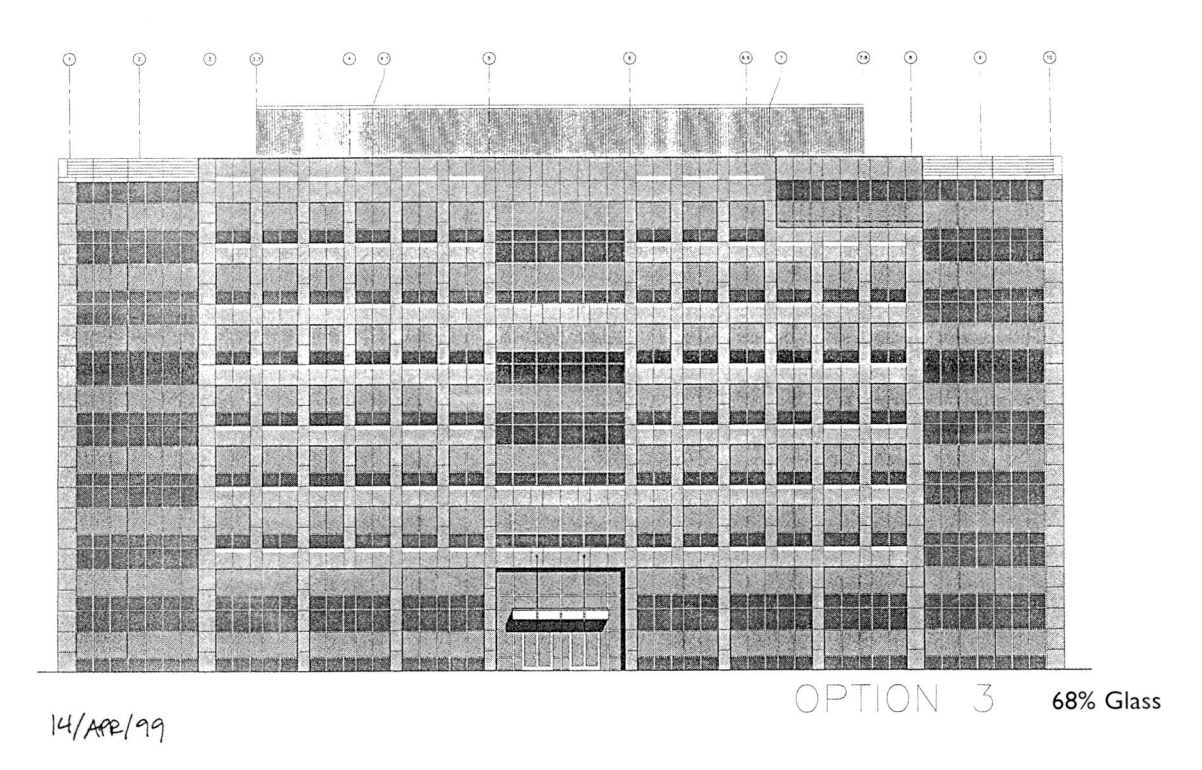

OPTION 1   64% Glass

Figure 20-11

OPTION 3   68% Glass

The low bidder, Walters & Wolfe, was significantly lower than any of the others. The bidder had a very attractive price for a high quality unitized system because the façade module was almost exactly identical to that used on a 20-story building currently being erected in Glendale. By minor shifting to use their dimensions, they were able to save on the engineering, testing and die costs, all of which they reflected in their bid price. Another favorable factor was that the façade was designed so that it required a minimum number of granite piece sizes.

Interestingly, the proposals to omit the granite on the corner setbacks and other changes to reduce the amount of granite would have added to the cost rather than reducing it. Those changes would have resulted in too many modified and added details. The curtain wall contractor was then requested to advise the cost impact of a design proposal on the corner setbacks that would simply replace the granite with spandrel glass without any major changing of details. This also would not save any money.

Walters & Wolfe was tentatively selected. The alternative bid items, as well as a determination as to what other modifications could be made inexpensively and yet add significantly to the character of the building, were reviewed at a detailed working meeting.

In order to add some further shadow lines and interest to the façade to replace the lost articulation, the architects requested quotations on:

- The typical glazing set back 3" from the granite face
- Back glazing, placing the glass 5" further back in the frame on the first and second floor and the central eighth floor windows
- Adding 18" sunshade fins, or "eyebrows," above the central second and eighth floor windows
- The addition of frit spandrels—spandrel glass with a small design—in lieu of standard glass spandrels in a portion of the façade area above the entrances
- The addition of 8" flamed finish stripes at the top of each of the granite spandrel pieces that were located directly below the spandrel glass on each façade

It was determined that longer clip-on mullion caps could be used at the first and second floors to achieve a recessed appearance. The longer clip-ons could be used for the horizontal window mullions in conjunction with much shorter mullion caps on the vertical mullions between glass lites to achieve a varied appearance. It reduced the eyebrow depth, but provides a satisfactory effect. The window mullion treatment was changed to a clear anodized aluminum—to reduce initial cost and provide a better long-term surface. After modifying the eyebrows, these additions were approved for a total add of almost $60,000.

The alternate bid premium for Carmen Red over Baltic Brown was only $38,000, so it was an easy decision. To complement the selected stone, a dark gray spandrel glass and solar gray vision glass with a shading coefficient of 0.66 was chosen. The impact of a glass with a shading coefficient of 0.60 was evaluated, but the premium couldn't be recovered and the tint of the glass did not complement the granite.

The final design is shown in Figures 20-12 and 20-13, and the final rendering for the project is shown in Figure 20-14. The final façade design ratio of the 76,500 square foot curtain wall was 50% granite, 12% spandrel glass and 38% vision glass.

A presentation board showing the exterior materials for the office building and the parking structure, as well the primary lobby finishes (mislabeled as Tenant Improvement Standards) is shown in Figure 20-15. Starting in the upper left hand corner and moving clockwise the material samples are:

Grouping consisting of the lobby wall paint, elevator doors, honed Carmen Red flooring, with the black and white granite floor accents beneath

- Spandrel glass with vision glass beneath
- Maple lobby and elevator wall panels
- Second floor lobby paint for canted panels
- Fabric panels for second floor elevator lobby
- Elevator cab rear wall, elevator ceiling, and parking structure elevator wall panels

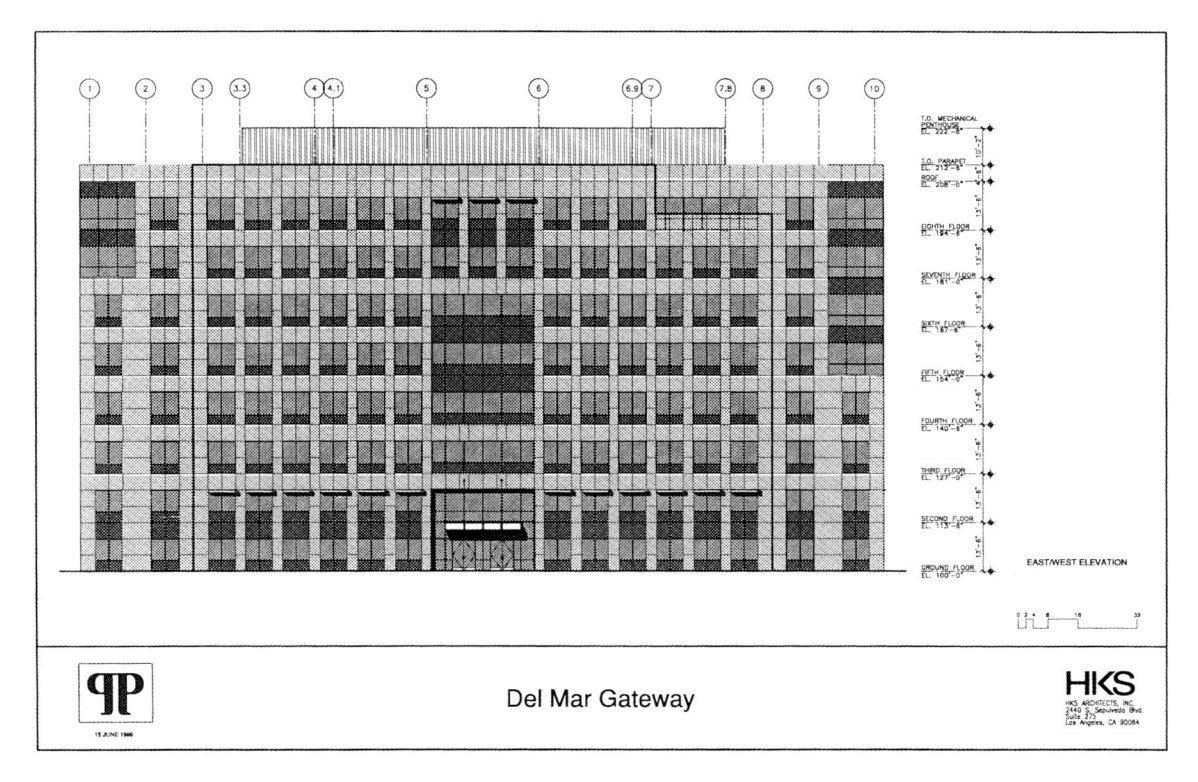

Figure 20-12

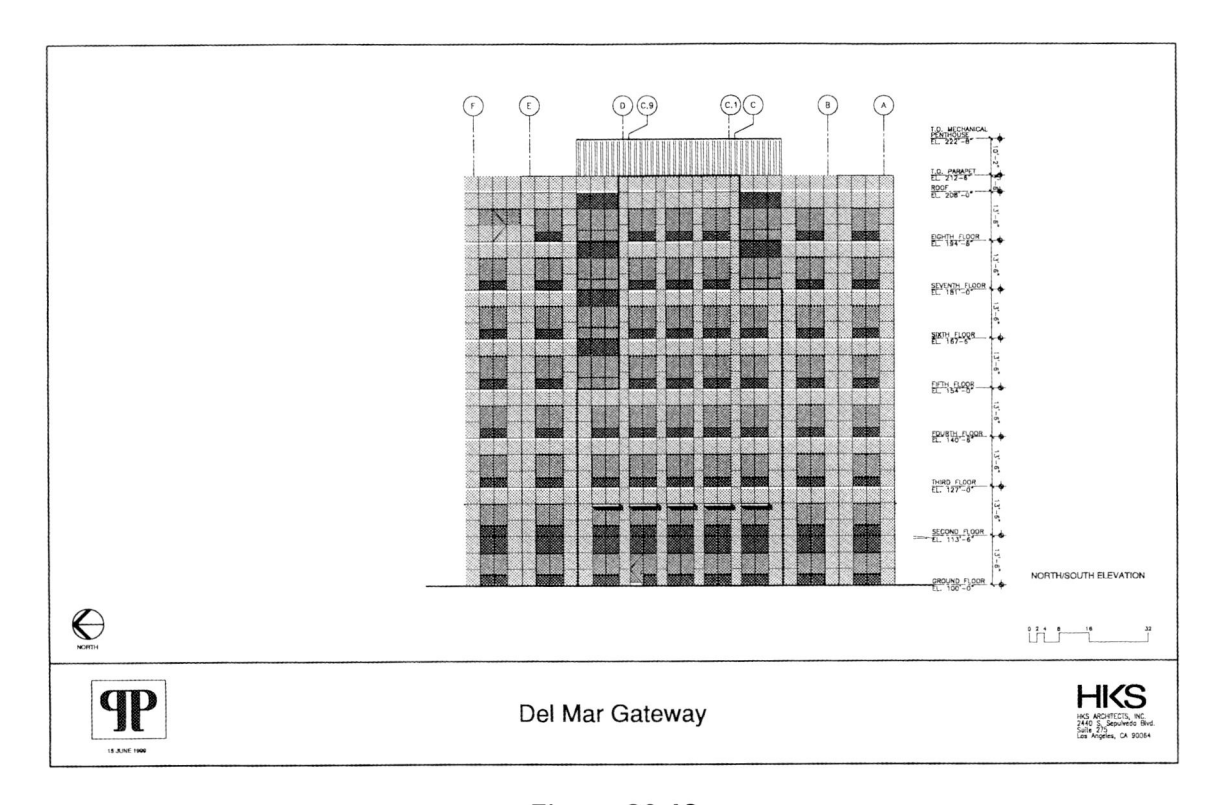

Figure 20-13

Figure 20-14

- Two colors of split face block for parking structure and service buildings
- Smooth block for parking structure and service buildings
- Geogrid retaining walls
- Tawny Pink paving with exposed aggregate
- Dark gray concrete benches
- French Gray paving with exposed aggregate

The wall design incorporates the typical nominal vertical dimensions of 4'7" of granite over the interstitial space, 2'7" of spandrel glass starting at the floor line and 6'4" of vision glass to the ceiling. Horizontally, the typical nominal wall dimensions are 2'6" of granite, two 3'9" frames of vision glass, and then 2'6" of granite again. This produces the repeating a nominal 5'0" interior planning module from the center of the granite to the mullion between the vision glass lites. In the central bay on the 3rd, 4th and 5th floors and on the two corners, where the vertical granite is omitted, the interior lites in the row of glazing are a nominal 5'0" to maintain the 5'0" module. The mullion faces, which are included in the nominal dimensions are 2½" wide. Where granite is at the corners, the horizontal dimension is 3'9" on each side.

Profiles of the vision head, jamb and frame, shown in Figures 20-16 through 20-18, are typical of the details used in the curtain wall construction.

The final cost of the curtain wall was $36.84 per surface square foot and $16.34/gsf, which was within the baseline budget and much lower than some of our earlier estimates.

The unitized system as proposed was factory assembled—granite installed, glazed and caulked—and installed in 7'6" x 13'6" sections. Due to the previous testing performed on the Glendale project it was not considered necessary to hire a curtain wall consultant or require testing.

In keeping with our energy budget, the insulation behind the stone and spandrel glass was R-13 batts, applied by others.

The structural frame design provided a 3/8" bent steel plate at the slab edge, welded to the beams and to 4-foot rebars on 12" centers, to support the

Figure 20-15

unitized system. This was later simplified after the curtain wall's final loads were determined.

The Land Purchase and Sale Agreement with Pardee gave them the right to approve the building design. A meeting was held with Pardee in August to obtain a final approval of the design, prior to obtaining the lot line split, executing the Brandes Lease, and closing on the land. They initially took the position that spandrel glass was not acceptable in their office park, and that the setbacks at the windows were not sufficiently deep. After presenting pictures that showed them several quality buildings utilizing spandrel glass, pointing out several buildings in their park that included it, and apparently convincing them that the setbacks would create a sufficiently strong shadow line, they ultimately appeared to agree that the design was acceptable. A letter was received prior to closing stating the designs were approved, except for the necessity of viewing the final color samples for the office building and the hotel together.

Several months later, with the deck being laid on the second floor of the building a meeting was scheduled for the purpose of approving the hotel design and final material colors. At that meeting Pardee's design representative said they would not approve the use of spandrel glass. This position was rejected outright, and they were advised that no portion of the façade design would be changed. A follow-up letter was received stating the use of spandrel glass was not approved.

Prentiss responded that Pardee had effectively approved spandrel glass in August, and, therefore, declined to change the design. Pardee's senior local officer apparently went over the head of the design committee and received authorization from senior management to approve the design and issue the necessary estoppel letters required by the lender, Société Générale.

A poured concrete deck was provided for the roof structure. A four-ply built-up roof was several dollars per sf less expensive than single-ply

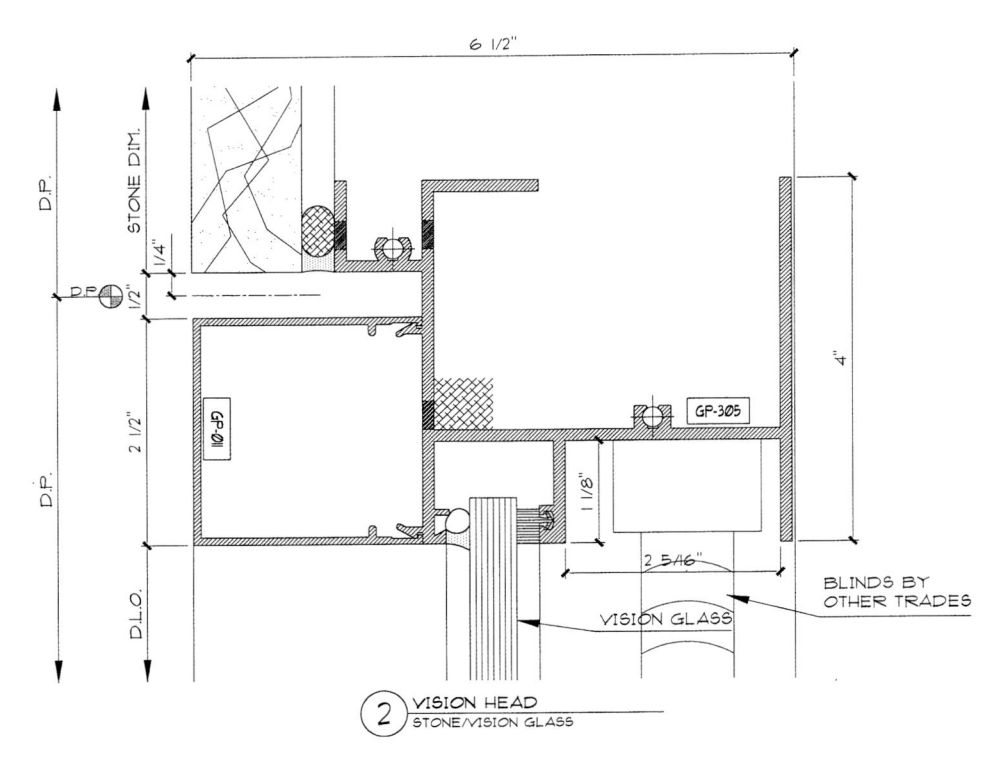

Figure 20-16

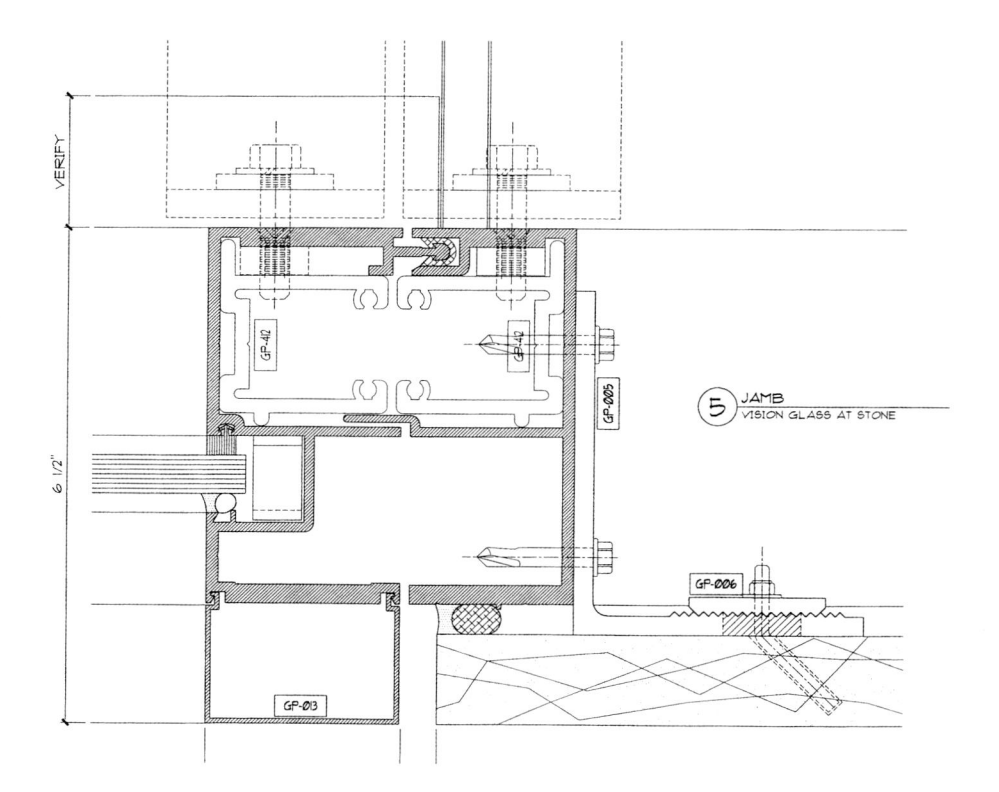

Figure 20-17

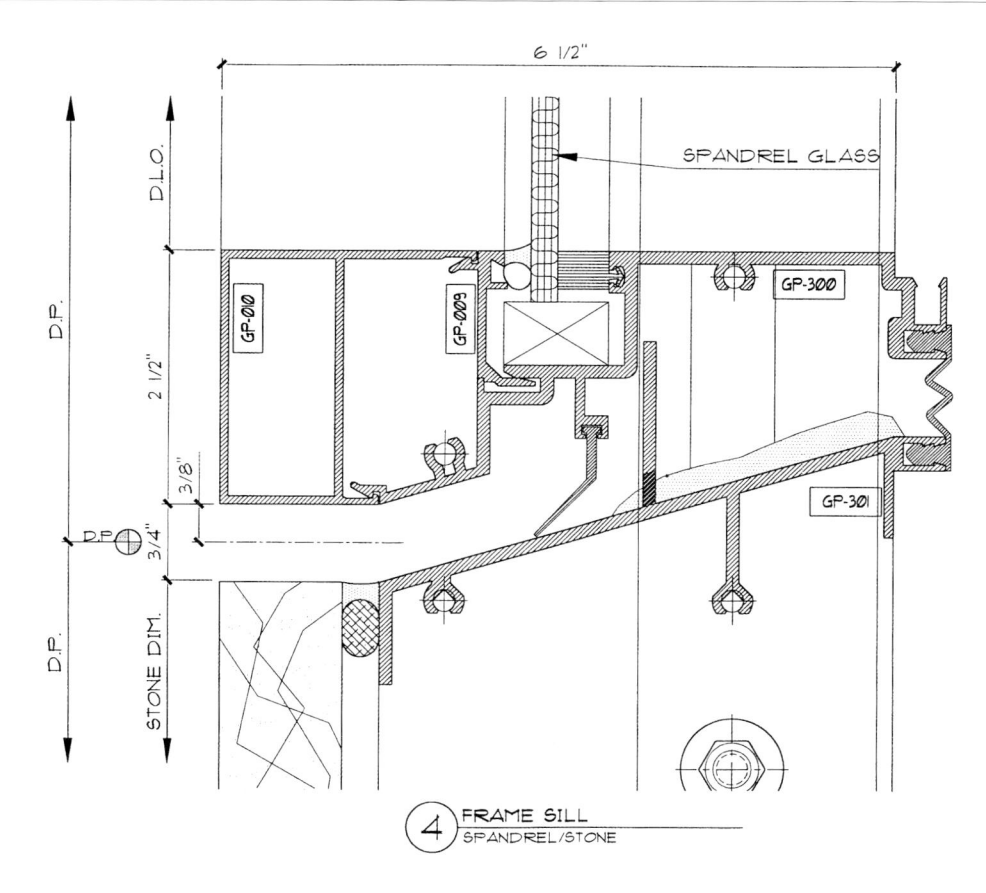

Figure 20-18

alternates, and was selected. Prentiss has had satisfactory service with this roofing in this and similar climates. An R-19 insulation, required by the energy analysis was used. Overflow roof drains discharge to internal drain lines independent of the primary roof drains. The overflow drain on the balconies is a scupper discharging to the open air. In addition:

- The original recommendation for window washing and maintenance servicing of the curtain wall was socket supports every 30 feet around the perimeter, with extra sockets at the step-back corners, one on each balcony, with davit sockets and davits provided. The recommendation was reviewed by Property Management and one of their local contractors, who both concurred.

- Precast concrete pavers were provided around the perimeter.

- Hose bibbs and convenience electrical outlets were provided around the perimeter.

- Four 4" roof jacks were installed for future communications cable, with conduit extensions to the communications room on the eighth floor.

The architect presented three penthouse enclosure options—corrugated metal, prefabricated aluminum louvers, painted galvanized metal up-turned blades. We selected the least expensive—the corrugated metal panels, which were painted to complement the granite.

01 SITE PLAN
NOT TO SCALE

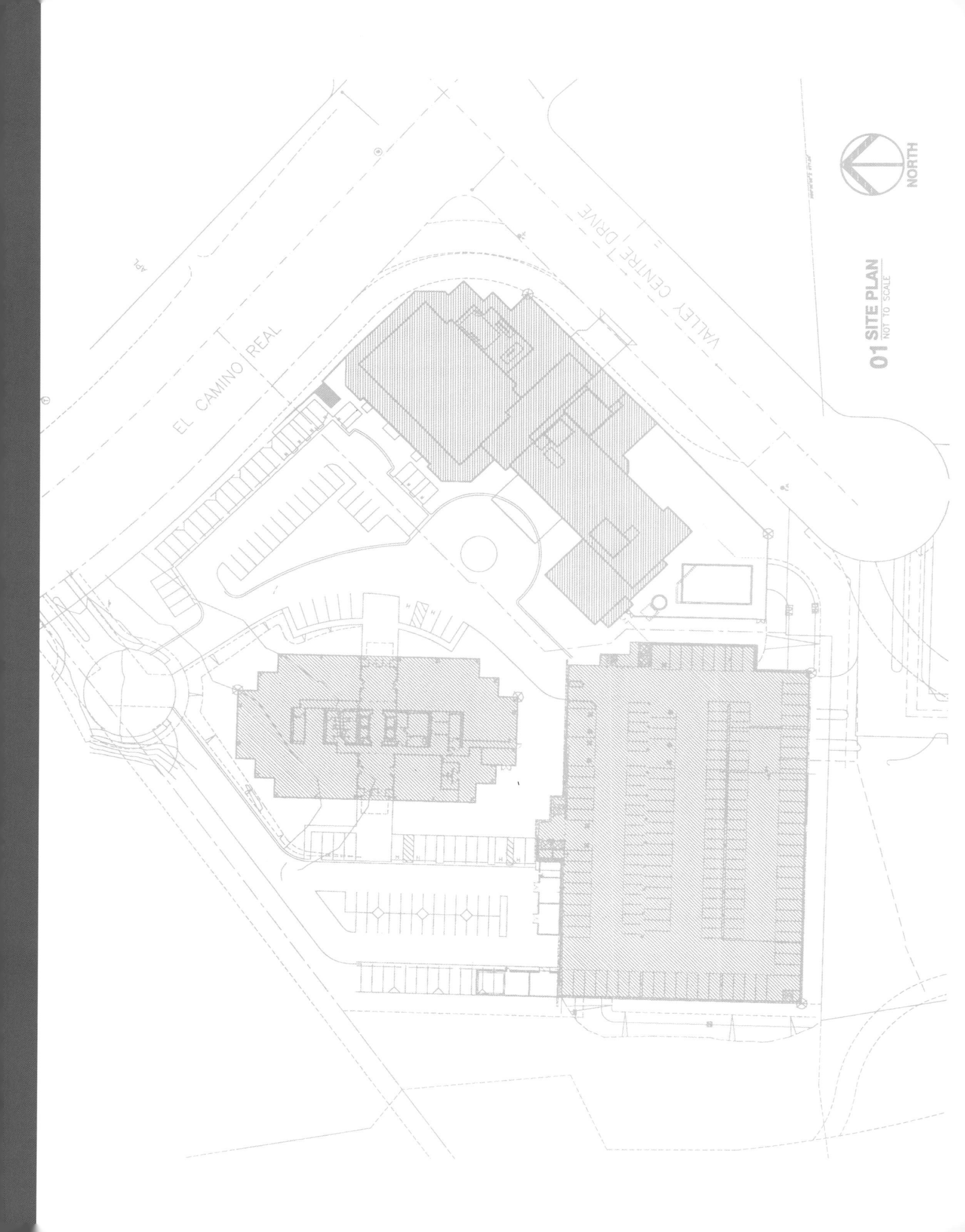

NORTH

EL CAMINO REAL

VALLEY CENTRE DRIVE

BUILDING LOBBY and ELEVATOR DESIGN

The building entry area, lobby and elevators provide the tenant or visitor with their first direct exposure to a building and, in the leasing period, can be a significant factor in the way your building is perceived. This chapter will discuss various features of the lobby design and the design criteria and components of the elevator system.

BUILDING LOBBY

The building lobby is one of the most important features in indicating building quality to tenants, as it sets the tone for their first approach to the building. It is important that it have a good circulation pattern, create an identity, and preferably accomplish a warm, comfortable feeling with sufficient natural light, rather than a stark but beautiful architectural solution. Some of the features are discussed below, but most projects will be limited in the number of quality features they can afford.

Perimeter Glazing

Clear glass is the most pleasing vision glazing at grade level, particularly if set back for sun control. Mullions of stainless steel or bronze are beautiful, but anodized aluminum is satisfactory in most circumstances. The clear glazing facilitates tying the lobby visually to the exterior landscaping, and they should be designed to complement each other.

Lobby Entrances

In most climates only enough swing doors are provided to meet the exit code and handicap access, as their use disrupts the interior environment (although some climates, such as coastal California may successfully use all swing doors). The taller the building, the more critical draft control becomes, as rising warm interior air leaking out of the top of the building can create a strong stack effect, resulting in cold air blowing across the lobby. Revolving doors should provide the normal ingress and egress. If swing doors are used in very cold climates, heated vestibules are necessary.

A standard 3'6" revolving door will handle 80–100 people in one direction in a five-minute period with one-way traffic, or 120–160 people both ways using two-way traffic. It has been stated that a 4'0" door leaf handles more traffic than a 3'6" leaf, but the author is not certain tests have ever verified that. The standard door height is 7'0". An 8'6" or 9'0" high door will have more aesthetic appeal, but it slows the door cycle, since speed is controlled by permissible kinetic energy, and they are considerably more costly.

The new ADA law and codes have made a major change in entrance doors. In many climates entrance doors had closers with a closing force in the range of 20 pounds in order for the doors to close against wind and building pressures. Now, low-force door closers are required—in the range of 4 to 5 pounds. In addition, there must be sufficient clear access to the side of the handle to accommodate a wheel-chair occupant.

To solve the dilemma of opening and closing forces and ADA requirements, power-assist and automatic openers have become the common answer. There are basically three types of automatic power-operated doors:

- Sliding doors—the cleanest looking and create the best passageway, handles two-way traffic, but they tend to stay open longer where a building may be impacted by a stack effect, and there may not be sufficient room for the doors to retract.

- Swing doors—can create the problem of possibly opening into someone, or make it difficult for a handicapped person unless there is a pair of doors to accommodate two-way traffic, each swinging in the direction of egress.

- Folding doors—a relatively new product which requires less installation width, handles two-way traffic, and offers less interference with the user than a single-swing door.

Power-assist doors may be of either the swing or revolving type and are actuated by the user, but an electric or hydraulic operator takes over and completes the action. Revolving doors may also be automatic, but their use is normally limited to retail or other high-usage public areas, and not justified on office buildings.

Small buildings with uncontrolled lobbies at night should have a night bell, card access, or a house telephone at the entrance. Provision is made on most entrance doors for automatic electrical locking and unlocking. During the locked period the door locks are released through use of the security card. Egress requires overrides to satisfy tenant convenience and exit code requirements.

Ceiling

Ceilings should be a minimum of 13 to 15 feet high, and within limits, the higher the better. The greater spatial feeling is important for tenant appeal. For small lobbies a partial raised area or atrium can create a similar positive impact. Some projects have used major atriums to separate two wings of the building. Most lobby ceilings are drywall or plaster, but some use fissured tile or metal pan. Only institutional buildings can afford integrated decorative lighting/ceiling systems. Note that if two-story lobbies or any type of atrium is used, clear interior glass walls cannot be used facing it, except in low-rise buildings, unless protected by a water curtain or deluge sprinkler system—water curtain usually being the most cost effective. Where atriums or the ceilings are unusually high, the design should be reviewed with Property Management to ensure there is provision to efficiently clean the glass and maintain the light fixtures.

Walls and Floors

Granite and marble are the highest quality floor finishes, with honed and flame finishes better than polished due to slippage problems, particularly when wet. There are sealers available that increase traction on all floor finishes, including polished stone surfaces. One caveat, where the stone is set in a setting bed, time for complete drying should be allowed, since if sealed too soon moisture can be trapped inside and it may never dry out.

Some stones can have a cold color tone, which diminishes their effect, as the author believes a warm feeling to the lobby appeals to most tenants. For many institutional buildings a monochromatic color scheme may be suitable, but for most buildings a patterned stone floor with a stone base is probably more effective. Marbles tend to have a warmer feel than many granites, while granites can be more visually dramatic. A common solution in the current market is a mixture of marble and granite.

Polished marble can be a more costly long-term maintenance problem, and its use should be reviewed with Property Management for an estimated annual cost premium. Frequently, however, the Development Officer will determine that the visual impact of the marble outweighs the increased operating costs. Brick, tile and terrazzo are also appropriate in certain settings.

Carpet can be used in the non-high-usage areas and inset in the elevator and building lobbies. Recessed carpet mats at the doors are highly recommended to remove soil and moisture from people's feet. It is important that carpet be somewhere on the traffic path to collect the dirt where maintenance can be controlled in a limited area, as one source has been quoted as saying that 90% of the dirt in office carpeting comes in on shoes.

Walls should be some attractive finish, which could be at least partially stone, wood, articulated drywall, or some other decorative finish to the

> The need for attention to good architectural detailing cannot be over estimated—it can change a routine space into a classic one. However, detailing can be overdone to the point that value is not obtained in relation to cost.
>
> Philip Johnson, one of my all-time favorite architects, designed a marble ceiling moulding for the high-ceilinged lobby at Momentum Place. The actual size was about 42" high and 30" deep. During our value engineering review we were debating whether to fabricate this section out of three or four thinner pieces, epoxied together and hung on a frame. Philip, who had been supportive throughout our VE analyses, put his foot down and absolutely refused to agree to anything but solid marble. Notwithstanding this, we fabricated the moulding in four pieces, saving over $200,000.
>
> At the grand opening reception, Philip had several bankers as an audience and, seeing me across the lobby, waved for me to join them. "I was just telling these gentlemen how I handle my developers. Remember when you wanted to fabricate that beautiful moulding in multiple pieces, and I refused? Look at it—I was right wasn't I?" I smiled at the group and said, "Yes, Philip, you were right." He couldn't tell the difference, but I wouldn't hurt his feelings for the world.
>
> The additional expense would have hardly been worth it.

extent the budget can handle it. If a significant proportion of the wall surface is painted drywall it frequently sets off the beauty of the more exotic materials.

Lobby Layout

There should be generous space for comfortable traffic flow, and all traffic should be routed past a central console, where one exists, or other control point for ease of surveillance. Security is becoming an increasing concern for many tenants. Where feasible to provide security personnel in the lobby, a control console should be provided. The console provides a visual focal point, and can include in one place the security control panel, elevator control panel, after hours mechanical and lighting control panels, tenant card reader to access the elevators after hours, and frequently a built-in directory. Small buildings with unattended lobbies should consider a closed circuit TV system, with card reader access.

Amenities

Amenities such as artwork, plants and trees, a piano, coffee/espresso kiosk, newsstand or other services should be considered for the lobby for both appearance and convenience.

Where practical, provision for multi-purpose use can be a positive factor.

The directory, which can also be free standing or wall-mounted, should contain a minimum of 1 line per 600 rsf and a maximum of 1 line per 400 rsf. Provide public telephones, postal and express letter/package facilities, preferably in an alcove.

Electrical outlets should be located for the convenience of floor maintenance as well as near the entrance for special holiday lighting or other displays.

Elevator Lobbies

More often than not the ceiling is dropped for a more comfortable feeling or to provide for a second-floor landing if the lobby is an atrium, but some buildings leave it full height—it can depend on the height of the main lobby ceiling. Elevator doors can be brushed, polished (this can show every ding or scratch) or preferably articulated stainless steel, or bronze, if economically feasible. Painted doors require extensive repetitive maintenance, and rarely look good after a period of use. The doors should, along with the elevator lobby design, provide a welcoming and warm feeling. The elevator lobby should be designed to be an integral part of the lobby design, with subtle variances to make it a separate space.

A lobby with eight elevators and two-way traffic should be a minimum of 11'0" wide, and a lobby with six elevators and two-way access should be a minimum of 10'0" wide. A lesser number of elevators, or one-way traffic, can be handled with 8'0" or 9'0" widths. If the traffic is heavy, two sets of call buttons on each side should be provided per bank when there six or more elevators. The call buttons, car indicators and any code-required or other signage must be carefully coordinated so it does not ultimately appear to be a series of uncoordinated add-ons. Unless it is a smoke-free building, provide recessed ash trays to protect the elevators.

ELEVATORS

The quality of the elevators is very important, second only to the lobby, to the perceived quality of the building, both aesthetically and for the quality of service. Quality service is important both initially and for the long-term viability of the building.

There are three basic types of elevators: gearless electric, geared electric and hydraulic. Gearless and geared elevators are also referred to as traction elevators.

Gearless are the smoothest, quietest, fastest and most expensive. They are normally used in all but the low-rise bank of high-rise buildings, since the primary benefit of speed occurs while bypassing a large number of floors. They generally operate at speeds of 700 to 1600 fpm.

Geared elevators are used most commonly for rises of from 4 or 5 to 10 or 11 floors, and don't have as smooth a ride as gearless elevators. They are often used in shorter rises by some owners who prefer them to hydraulic elevators as they are more dependable and less expensive to maintain, although significantly more expensive to purchase. They generally operate in a range of 300 to 700 fpm.

Hydraulic elevators have a maximum vertical travel distance of 60 feet, and probably should not be used over 50 feet. They are slow, operating at about 175 feet per minute. In a five-story building with 13 feet floor-to-floor height, the nonstop travel time is about 18 seconds, which can seem like a very long time.

Some traction elevators have the cable mechanism beneath the cab with the machinery located to the side of the shaft, as opposed to the standard orientation of the cable mechanism on top and the machinery in a penthouse above the hoistway. These are referred to as "under-slung" cabs. They are more expensive, but are often used where a penthouse would violate a height limit or be aesthetically unacceptable.

A newer alternative to the direct current drives that have been used for electric-driven elevators is the variable-frequency alternating-current drive. These drives take the building 480 volt line current, rectify it to DC, and then revert it back to a variable frequency AC current to run the AC motors. This procedure is necessary, as a direct 480-volt line current cannot provide the high torque, slow speed start-up required by elevators.

Elevator Cabs

Aesthetics are important in the cabs, and wood or some other decorative material is particularly desirable. It is important to have a comfortable, preferably warm, feeling in the cab. Partial mirrored walls can help to create a more spacious feeling, and well-detailed plastic laminate installations are a good low-cost substitute to more exotic materials. All elevator cabs must be equipped with hooks around the top of the walls and protective blankets that can be installed when hauling any materials, furniture or tools.

Carpet is probably the best practical floor material, since it gives a warm and comfortable feeling, and is easily cleanable, or replaceable, but many people prefer the appearance of stone. Stone is much heavier and has been known to crack during the required periodic elevator load tests.

Cab ceilings equal in height to the office floor ceiling height are visually preferable.

Lighting can be an integrated ceiling, cove lights, down lights, incandescent lamps through ceiling perforations, or strip lighting at the edges, as selected for budget and appearance. The lighting should be soft but sufficient—many cabs are too dark. In some cabs it is difficult to read the floor buttons.

All regulatory, emergency and operational graphics should be carefully designed to avoid a "cluttered" or "added-on" appearance. When legal to do so, graphics saying that the elevator inspection certificate is located at some specific place, such as the building office, is more attractive than the posted certificate. As the graphics are placed on the return panel supplied by the elevator manufacturer, all graphic information must be organized and detailed in the bid documents, even when the remainder of the cab finishes are to be bid separately. The author prefers not to permit the elevator company to advertise its name in the cab or on the sills.

Card readers, or their equivalent, should be provided for after-hours control. Care should be taken to insure they are flush mounted or recessed behind a glass plate in the cab return panel and coordinated with the design.

There should be an intercom and a two-way telephone to facilitate immediate access to help and to provide comfort to stranded passengers.

Handicap provisions should include railings, proper button heights, raised numbers and Braille.

The standard cab door height is 7'0". A full ceiling-height door, usually 9'0", is more attractive, and more expensive, but due to kinetic energy limitations, the door cycle time is increased by 0.2 seconds, which will increase the interval (see elevator analysis below) by 1.4 to 2.0 seconds. One common visual solution is to use the standard door height, but place a matching transom panel above it to simulate the appearance of a full height door.

The standard door width is 3'6". A 4'0" door theoretically improves passenger transfer time. Since kinetic energy limitation controls door speeds, these larger doors will add 0.3 seconds to cycle time. Though there is disagreement regarding transfer time saved by two persons passing through at the same time, a reasonable assumption is that possibly one-half of the added cycle time is saved, probably increasing the overall interval by possibly 1.0 to 1.5 seconds.

Special elevator cab features include:

- Anti-nuisance—cancels all car calls when the car has no load, or is under-loaded
- Automatic weighing—to permit early starts from terminal floor, or to bypass hall calls when 80% loaded
- Automatic two-way leveling—adjusts landing at all loads to be within $3/8$" size of the floor line
- Provide closed-circuit TV cable for future security, if not required initially
- Repeat the floor numbers on the hall door jambs

Cab Allowances

The elevators are frequently purchased before all of the details of the cab design are completed in order to comply with the construction schedule, so they are often purchased from the elevator contractor with an allowance for cab finishes. Many people purchase the elevators with the entire cab as an allowance, but this presents a problem since it is hard to know the value of the platform, frame and controls. It is more effective to have the complete cab structure, controls and finished return panels in the base bid, and carry the floor, wall and ceiling finishes as an allowance. Be sure, however, to carefully specify the shape, material, finish and graphics on the return panel. Any attempt to provide return panels separately can create coordination problems with the controls.

Performance Criteria

Proper elevator service is essential to the long-term acceptance of the building. While elevators are selected on very specific criteria and extensive calculations, for early planning purposes one can assume that each elevator might serve approximately 45,000 rsf, with never more than eight elevators in a bank, and a bank of elevators serving no more than fourteen floors, preferably twelve or thirteen.

> In my first major building, the First National Bank of Chicago, we made some very poor decisions with regard to the elevatoring in the bank portion of the building. We had elevators serving both up and down from the first floor, and we had a 22-floor rise.
>
> The result was some very serious elevator traffic conditions. We theoretically had a sufficient number of elevators, and the traffic calculations indicated that they would serve the bank properly, but they just didn't accomplish the objective. We decorated and carpeted the stairwells to encourage people to use them when going up one floor or down two floors and we made many control modifications to try to satisfy the traffic needs. Unfortunately, the results were never fully satisfactory.
>
> Because of this experience, I am adamant about never serving two directions from a lower terminal and I try never to have a rise of more than thirteen floors in an elevator bank.

The first step in the calculation of elevator performance is the population assumption, which is based on the useable area. Very densely populated buildings that are largely clerical are assumed to have 120–140 usf per person, with more common clerical staff densities of 150 to 160 usf per person. Higher-quality buildings aimed at professional users can usually be calculated using 180–200 usf per person in low and mid-rises, and 200 usf or more for corporate executive or high end professional space. The anticipated type of tenant is important in making these assumptions. Where the potential mix is not clear, one should err on the side of conservatism. Where the prospective tenants are likely to have unusually large populations, that fact must be included in any system analysis. Elevator service should be based on all of the following criteria:

PERFORMANCE CRITERIA

Interval—frequency of service. The interval is calculated by dividing the average round trip time by the number of elevators in the bank. Theoretically, if there were uniform traffic demands in the building, a car from each bank would pass any given floor once in an interval.

- 20–25 seconds—excellent service
- 25–30 seconds—very good service, and the desired range for first class downtown office buildings
- 30–35 seconds—fair service, and generally acceptable in most markets
- Over 40 seconds—unacceptable

Handling capacity (5-minute): The passenger carrying capacity is usually expressed as moving a certain percentage of the population of an elevator bank in a five-minute period. In most cases the number of elevators is determined by the requirements during the up-peak condition.

- Under 10%—unacceptable
- 1%–12%—good in mixed-use buildings with minimal multi-floor tenants and where large numbers of employees do not arrive by high-speed mass transit
- 4%–15%—good for very large tenants with high clerical mix, where the majority of the employees arrive by high-speed mass transit

Number of floors served:

10—excellent service
12—very good service
14—maximum number—service deterioration is evident

PERFORMANCE CRITERIA (Continued)

Method of calculation for elevator selection—Industry standard used to assume an 80% loading of each car, but more recent analysis indicates that 60% loading is more likely. The analyses are run with various car sizes and speeds to choose the acceptable interval and handling capacity—usually one or the other of these criteria will govern. Frequently the result is an imbalance between the two. An alternate analysis method is to make a preliminary assumption of the number of cars, car size and speed from the above analysis. A reanalysis is then made with the speed, interval and handling capacity as assumptions, and calculate for the number of cars and percent fill. Selection can then be made with a balanced service if the results appear logical.

Average waiting time—This is the actual average waiting time in building service. It is the measured average waiting time at the lower terminal in heavy up-peak (usually over a sixty-minute period). It usually runs about 60% of the computed interval. Actual waiting times are shown by wait increment. Good service is:

Waiting time	Percent of riders served in This waiting time period
20 seconds	65%
30 seconds	75%
40 seconds	90%
60 seconds	99%
90 seconds	100%

Probable stops—the most likely number of stops an elevator will make when filled to its normal capacity:

Number of floors served	Probable stops
15	10
12	8
10	7

Some recent enhancements (or the perception thereof) obtained through computerized programmable systems and artificial intelligence components that allow specialized dispatching, are:

- The ability to provide at least one car waiting at the first floor at all times.

- Predictive hall lanterns that immediately advise which elevator will pick you up as soon as the hall button has been pushed (this does not necessarily improve service, but may give the perception of doing so).

- Replacement of traditional up or down corridor buttons with digital pads on which a person enters the desired exit floor number. This permits the elevator system to make selective pickups to group riders to minimize multiple stops and improve service.

Lower Terminal Floors

Avoid dual lower terminals where both the ground floor and either a lower concourse or upper pedestrian way level act as lower terminals by accepting up-bound passengers, as this causes significant degradation of service. It is better to move the occupants to a single lower terminal by escalator.

Service should never be provided both up and down from the lower terminal, as this can also cause a serious degradation of service. Separate elevators should be provided for lower level service.

Transfer Floors

Any contemplated present or future transfer floors in high-rise buildings must be included in the calculations. If upward-bound passengers from the lower terminal are not permitted to discharge at transfer floors, service is only minimally affected. Certain very limited transfer floors such as key-operated access lobbies for executives will not dilute service at all.

Future transfer capabilities are frequently an attractive leasing tool to accommodate future tenant expansion, but require allocating space for the future lobby and the added cost of the additional stops, doors and mechanisms for the elevators serving that floor.

Parking Elevator Service

If the parking is integrated with the office structure, the parking elevators should be an independent service to the lobby to provide security and to avoid deterioration of the basic elevator service.

Handling capacity is calculated as 10% of 80% of the spaces x 1.5 persons per car.

Interval—40–45 seconds is acceptable, but varies with whether it services primarily tenant employees or transients.

Use either geared drive or hydraulic elevators in parking garages, depending on the rise and desired quality of service.

Freight Elevators

A dedicated freight car is required in any building of 400,000 rsf or larger (preferably in any building of 300,000 rsf or larger). Provision of a second freight should be considered in any building of 700,000 rsf or over, but a swing car may be used as the second freight up to 900,000 rsf, or so. A separate freight lobby is desirable when dedicated freight service is provided. Freight elevators should have a good, preferably direct, access to the loading area.

The minimum cab size should be 3,500 pounds, with a minimum door width of 48", and preferably 50". Door height should be the full standard floor height. Minimum cab height is 10'0", or the typical floor to ceiling height, whichever is greater. The ceiling should have a hinged section that opens for carrying long loads such as carpet rolls, pipe, conduit and lumber. A freight car should have steel checkered plate or woven wire walls to take the abuse to which it is subjected. Heavy vinyl is probably the best flooring material, although some recommend wood.

When no freight elevator is provided in a building, a designated "swing" car is recommended in any building of 100,000 rsf or larger. A swing car is one that is designed to be alternately for passenger and freight traffic. These "swing cars" should have at least a 3500-pound capacity, preferably a door height equal to the standard floor ceiling height, a clear ceiling height at least equal to the floor to ceiling height, an operable section in the ceiling that can swing away for transporting carpeting, pipe, etc., and provision of heavy protection for the walls while in such service. Reasonable access must be available for these cars. Swing cars are sometimes designed with doors at both the front and rear of the cab to service a separate freight lobby.

Note that any materials, equipment or furniture that cannot fit into the freight or swing car must be either cut or disassembled for transport to the floor, or provision must be made to hoist material through a window in a low-rise building. If window access will be required, it is essential that hoisting equipment will have access all around the building to avoid having to move through one tenant's space to reach another. In high-rise buildings where capacity is inadequate, hoisting is accomplished either externally by means of a crane or roof-based hoist, or through an elevator shaft with special rigging. Advice from Property Management is important in evaluating this issue.

Equipment Rooms, Shafts and Overrides

The equipment on a hydraulic elevator is normally located beside the shaft, but the equipment for an electric machine is, except under rare circumstances, directly over the shaft. Where the elevator machinery room is adjacent to occupied space, such as where the building has multi-elevator banks, acoustic treatment is required as specified for mechanical rooms, as discussed in Chapter 22. In those rare occasions where an elevator penthouse is not practical or feasible, the elevator can use underslung cabling, with the machinery room beside the shaft.

Elevator shafts are now required by 1997 UBC to be isolated from each other for the safety of maintenance workers and passengers attempting to escape from an elevator stranded in the shaft. The most common methods are framed wire mesh dividers or dry wall.

The speed of an elevator determines the necessary override required for safety, and the override plus the height of the cab in the highest elevator bank determines the height of the shaft below the penthouse. The pit beneath the shaft has a spring mechanism to ease the shock of a fall. In the relatively rare cases where occupied space is desired beneath an elevator pit, a counterweight safety and additional structural safety provisions are required.

Construction and Maintenance

On most projects it is important to obtain the use of at least one permanent elevator at the earliest possible time for use for personnel and material hoisting. Until one of these elevators is available, outside personnel and material hoists are necessary for buildings over two or three stories. As long as these temporary hoists are in service the building skin cannot be completed. More often than not, the permanent cab finishes are not installed until the rough construction usage is completed. This early availability requirement should be covered in the specifications, and the general contractor should include the projected availability date in their request for bids, and in the purchase contract.

The 1997 UBC code made it more difficult to obtain an operating permit for an elevator—the shaft must be complete and the division barriers must be in place, the machinery rooms locked and all controls tested. All elevators must be complete prior to the final testing of the emergency generator and the life safety systems.

It is very important to evaluate the proposed maintenance contract for the elevators prior to executing the purchase contract. Property Management should review and approve the scope and terms of the maintenance contract. It is quite common to purchase a one-, three- or five-year maintenance contract included in the construction purchase contract. You can separately allocate the maintenance portion of the cost to the annual operating costs. On a large building, or where the elevators are placed in service over a period of time, it is beneficial to negotiate a temporary monthly maintenance price per elevator to apply until the last elevator is placed in service. Then the warranty period and annual maintenance contract can all be tied to a single start date based on completion and acceptance of the last elevator.

Double-Deck Elevators

In a few, very rare high-rise buildings a double-deck elevator cab has been used to reduce the number of shafts. When the elevator is traveling up from the first floor, or downward at rush hour, one cab stops only at the odd floors and the other stops only at the even floors. For interfloor traffic one can get on at an odd floor and get off at an even floor.

Sky Lobbies

This is another rare concept for certain very tall buildings. In this scheme lobby elevators express the passengers part of the way up the building to an upper lobby where they change to local elevators to continue on to their floors. The solution reduces shaft space, since some upper rise elevators use the extension of the shaft space used by some of the lower rise elevators.

Horizontal/Vertical Elevators

Otis has recently offered a system called Odyssey, which can travel horizontally, then vertically, and then possibly horizontal again. One of its proposed uses is for transportation from a garage structure into a building.

Escalators

Width: 32" or 48"—the 32" width does not permit two abreast, or passing. The narrower escalator should not be used in high traffic areas.

Speed: normal speed is 90 fpm, maximum is 120 fpm.

Materials: Normally stainless steel or bronze frame, with balustrades of glass or metal.

CASE STUDY

The main building lobby is two stories high on the front and single story on the back side. The entrance doors are set back seven feet and each has two swing doors, one on each side has an automatic operator to meet handicap code. The architects proposed three lobby designs:

- Traditional—granite on floor, wood panels and back-lighted glass on walls, coffered ceiling, all based on the grid of the building exterior, using dark materials that equal or complement the exterior. Typical of an urban lobby, Figure 21-1.

- Transitional—granite on the floor in a carpet-like pattern, Galece (plaster-like material) on walls, ceiling element uniting the two lobbies and uses a combination of dark and light materials. A little more applicable to a suburban market, could complement urban fenestration, Figure 21-2. The reflected ceiling plan for this scheme is not available.

- Contemporary—asymmetrical in plan and elevation, granite on floors, glass and wood panels on walls, barrel ceiling and uses lighter materials. Very modern and suburban, Figure 21-3.

The traditional scheme was selected for further refinement. A pair of glass tenant entrance doors was requested in each lobby wall, the security desk was to be eliminated and the directory had an allowance of $10,000. The traditional scheme was refined somewhat and submitted to the contractor for preliminary pricing.

The preliminary estimate for the lobby was $140,000 over the baseline budget, and it was redesigned and simplified. Back-lighted glass and wood paneling were removed from the wall and substituted with a plain sliced maple veneer. Full height granite faux columns in black granite along the walls were reduced in the two-story lobby and changed to polished Carmen Red to relate more effectively to the exterior. The granite sizing was reduced from 24" pieces to 18" and the installation simplified—it was installed as an interior tile, rather than mechanically fastened. Drywall was substituted above the shortened granite faux columns. Faux columns under the second floor elevator lobby were eliminated.

The granite columns are 18" wide and 13'6" high in the two-story lobby, with a drywall continuation that cants out at a slight angle with a light fixture behind it to cast a glow on the ceiling. Between the columns is the wood veneer paneling.

The floor has a field of 18" square honed Carmen Red granite with strips of honed Chinese Black running from column to column. There are inset pieces of French Vanilla white marble, 7'0" wide by 6", down the center directing traffic toward the elevator lobby.

The ceiling remained coffered, with slightly bowed drywall beams crossing the lobby from one column to another. The ceiling in between is flat. The basic lighting is from CFL downlights, with additional lighting from sconces on the columns.

The first floor elevator lobby has a coffered ceiling with recessed lighting. The walls are polished Carmen Red granite. The floor has a border and cross strips on each side of each elevator door of the honed Chinese Black, inset with the honed Carmen Red.

The savings amounted to more than one-half of the overage as compared to the baseline budget.

The lease with Brandes required they be provided with a place for a security representative in the lobby. They later decided against that and will provide a security reception area on their seventh floor.

A picture of the lobby is shown in Figure 21-4, and the material board showing the stone and wood samples is Figure 20-15 in the prior chapter. A darker wood was originally selected, but after studying an early lobby rendering and obtaining the architect's opinion that it correctly represented the

Building Lobby and Elevator Design 279

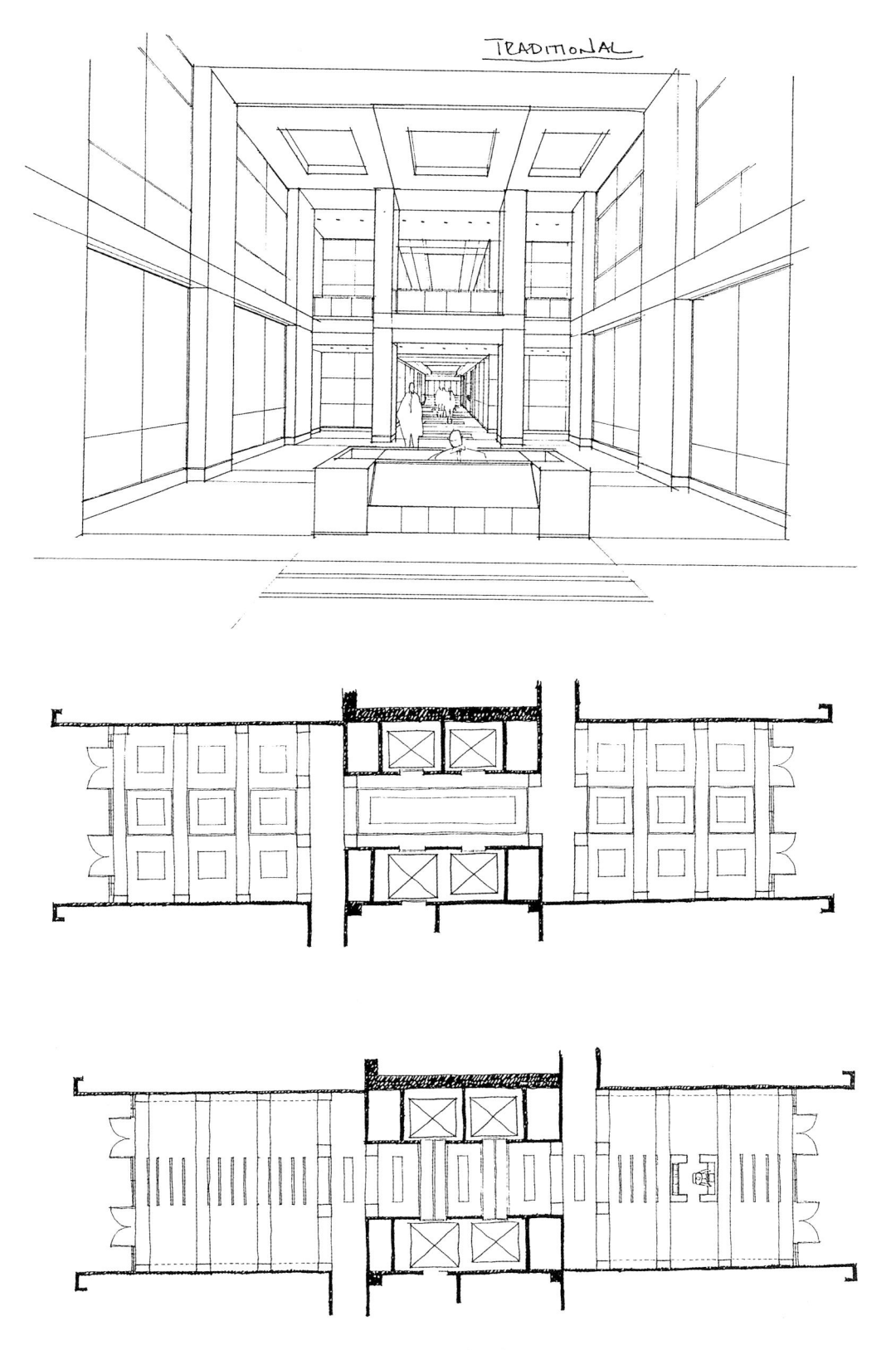

TRADITIONAL

Figure 21-1

280 *Office Development*

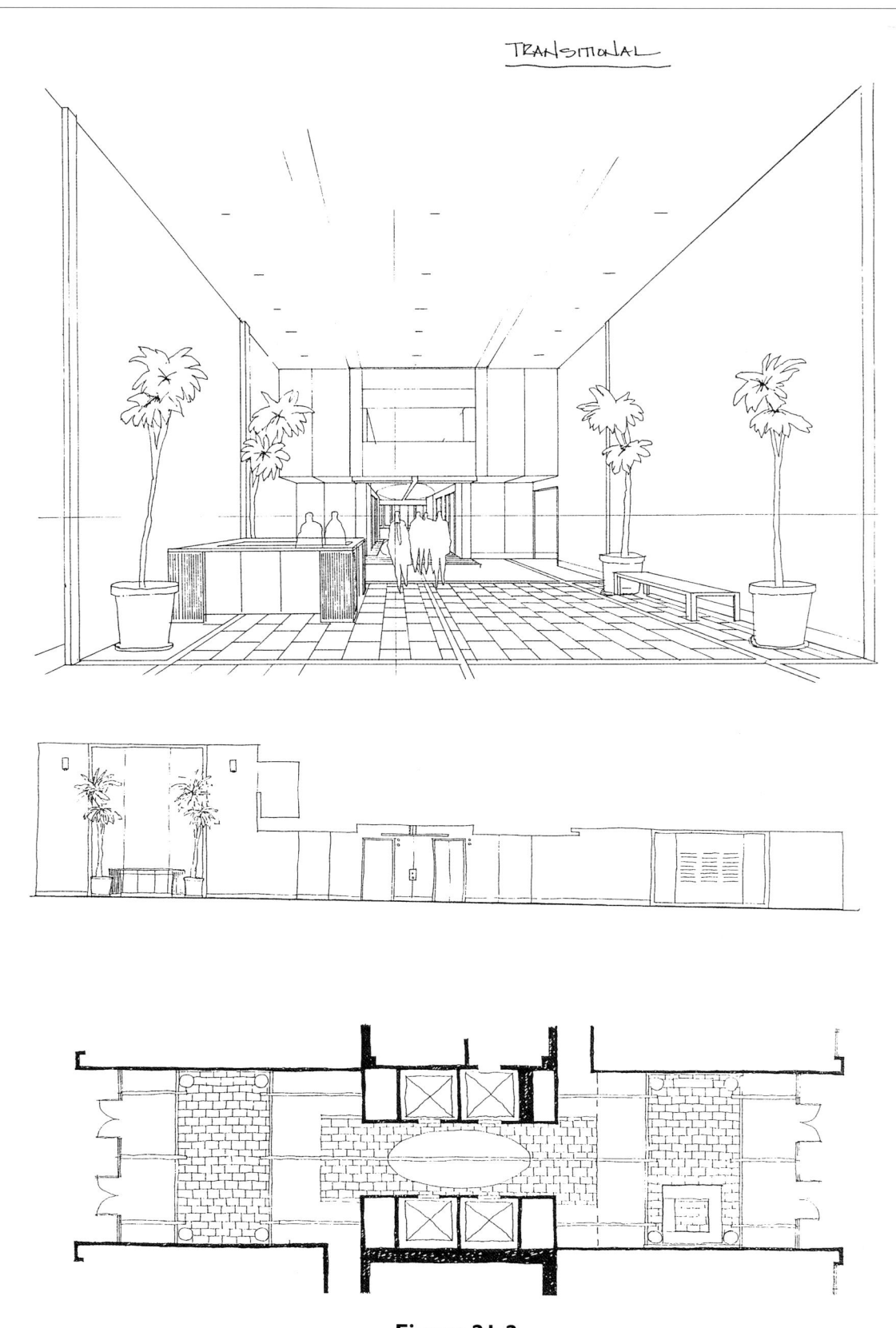

TRANSITIONAL

Figure 21-2

Building Lobby and Elevator Design

CONTEMPORARY

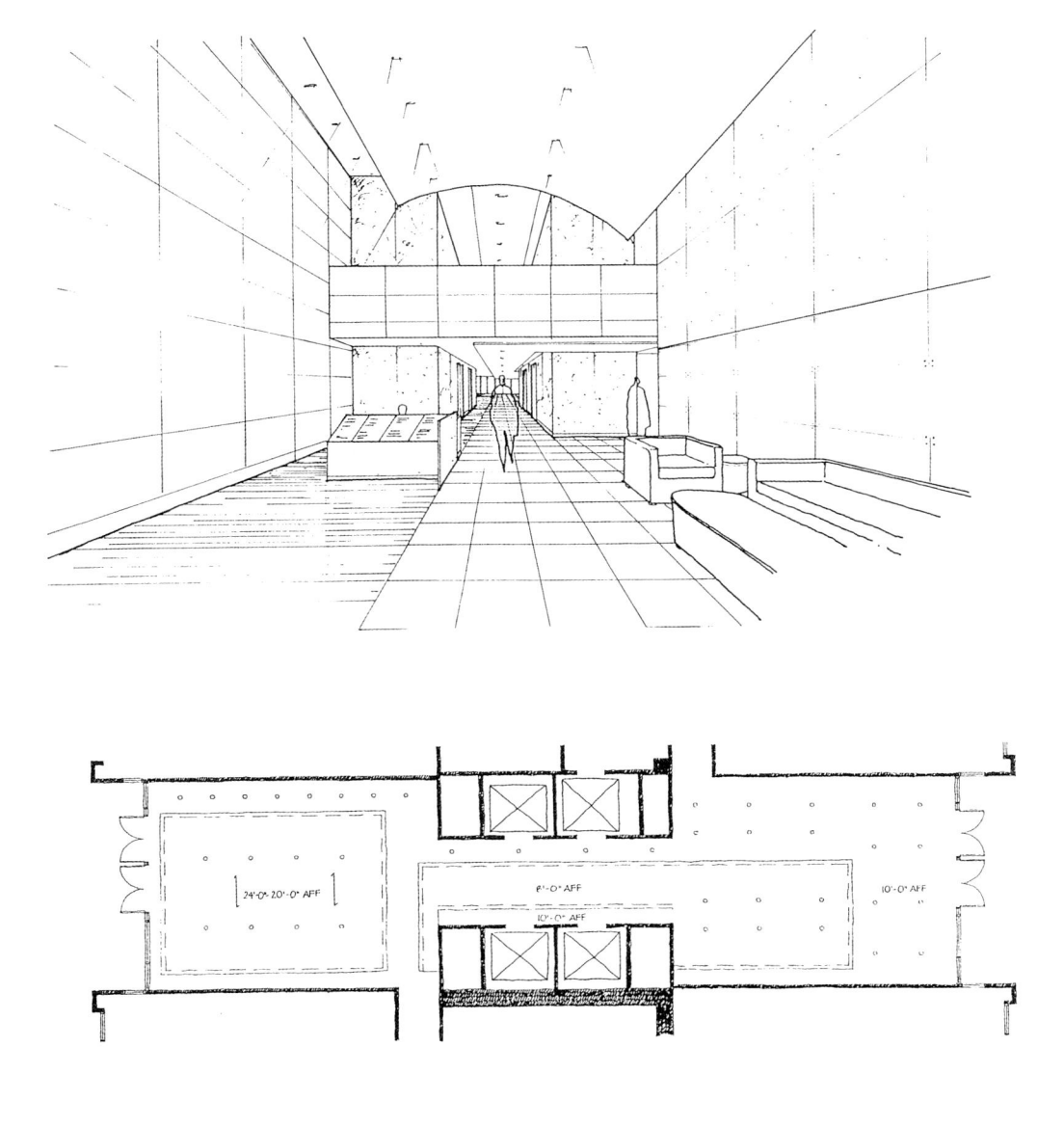

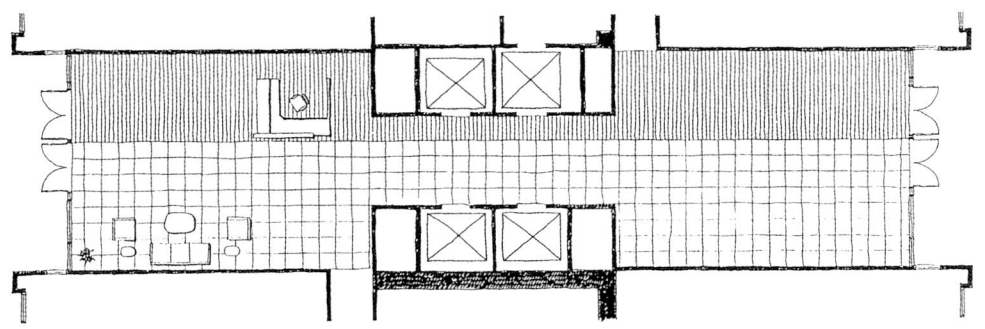

Figure 21-3

Figure 21-4

materials, it was decided to change the wood to plain sliced maple, a lighter-colored material, as currently shown. The directory is 4'0" wide by 4'9" high with a 9" wide recessed stainless steel shroud around a recessed blackout glass illuminated panel, shown in Figure 21-5.

To satisfy the city's interpretation of the exiting code with respect to the second floor side of the two-story lobby, the lobby tenant doors were changed from glass to sliced maple, and doors added to the exit corridors in order to obtain a one-hour rating for the lobby. Since the smoke proof doors had to swing two ways, they were made with wood veneer and the remainder of the exposed second floor face was covered with the same wood veneer to provide a balanced appearance.

In retrospect, there were two significant mistakes made with regard to the lobby design:

- There should have been a much greater effort made to obtain approval for an additional 4 to 5 feet in height for the building, so that the entire lobby could have been one and one-half stories. The additional rentable area would have more than paid for the added construction cost caused by increased building height, and the balanced lobby would have related better to the traffic patterns.

Figure 21-5

- The transitional design should have been selected. It would have been less expensive, would have a fresher appearance and would have been appropriate to this market.

  The elevator consultant used a population assumption of 190 rsf per person, and an assumed required handling capacity of 13% for purposes of evaluating the elevator system.

  The design criteria that some elevator consultants are now using in suburban markets are somewhat different from the long time standard assumptions included in the text. The interval criteria are a little less stringent than previously used on the excellent end, and more stringent on the unacceptable end. The stated reason is that a large portion of the suburban market is now made up of firms that have moved from downtown high-rise buildings, and are used to better service. The criteria our consultants used are:

Interval:	Under 28 seconds	Excellent
	28–29 seconds	Above average
	29–30 seconds	Average
	30–31 seconds	Below average
	Over 31 seconds	Unacceptable
Handling Capacity:	14%–16%	Single user
	13%–14%	Mixed, single + Diversified users
	12%–13%	Diversified users

- They computed the interval for both three-elevator and four-elevator schemes, with the calculated interval being:

Three elevators	33.6 seconds
Four elevators	25.2 seconds

- Our elevator selection was four elevators, with three being 3500-pound passenger cars, and with one being a 4000-pound swing car, all geared machines at 350 fpm. This not only provides excellent theoretical service, but would easily handle the traffic if there is a single tenant who occupies a major portion of the building. The doors are 7'0" high and 3'6" wide. The swing car has a rear door facing the freight lobby which will be 7'0" high by 4'0" wide.

  The swing elevator has pad hooks, a removable ceiling and an operable hatch in the top of the cab structure. There is a hatch above the freight lobby on the eighth floor to provide service to the roof and mechanical rooms.

  The cab finishes were installed in the field under separate contract, but the elevators were purchased with the complete cab structure, furnished with all controls and side (or return) panels. The architects completely detailed all finishes, security devices and signage required prior to bidding.

  The elevator cab design consists of stainless steel control panels on each side of the door, patterned stainless steel doors, plain sliced maple veneer wood paneling on each sidewall to match the building lobby. The rear of the cab has stainless steel panels on the sides with two 2-foot wide mirrors separated in the center with a reveal in between in order to avoid too much visual differentiation from the swing car, which will have a biparting service door in the rear of the cab. The floors are carpeted and the ceilings have removable stainless panels with a combination of downlights and indirect light around the ceiling as well as through two slots near the center.

  The elevators are provided with emergency electrical power that may be applied to each elevator, one at a time, through a transfer switch. This control may be actuated from the fireman's control room on the first floor.

  It was originally intended to install two hydraulic elevators in the parking structure, one near the office building entrance and one close to the hotel. The elevator consultant's analysis indicated this was insufficient. Their analysis was based on:

Population density:	1.4 persons per car (probably too high in this market)
Target interval:	35 to 40 seconds maximum
Peak traffic:	Morning arrival peak
Estimated demand:	11.0% of population in five minutes
Stair access:	50% of people accessing Floors 2 and B-1, 20% B-2

  The analysis shown in the following table compares two traction (geared) elevators to two and three hydraulic elevators, based on a central elevator bank.

INITIAL COMPARATIVE PARKING ELEVATOR ANALYSIS

Equipment	Elev. Qty.	Capacity	Speed (fpm)	Interval	Handling Cap.
Traction	2	3500	350	33.6 sec.	62
Hydraulic	3	3500	150	34.7 sec.	62
Hydraulic	2	3500	150	59.1 sec.	62

Agreement could not be reached with the hotel operator for a central elevator location, as either the office tenants or hotel occupants would have to cross a main entrance to the parking structure to reach their destination.

The elevator consultant believed that with separate elevator banks, each should have either three hydraulics or two traction elevators, and strongly recommended the traction. Since traction elevators should not have penthouses in parking structures for aesthetic reasons, the use of under-slung traction elevators would increase the cost to more than three times the cost of hydraulics.

Concerned with this issue, a second analysis was requested from Otis Elevator Company. They used a passenger ratio of 1.25 per car (1.1 per car is probably more accurate in this market), separately analyzed the parking analysis for the office and hotel, assumed 8% as an acceptable handling capacity in two-way traffic, and considered 40 to 60 seconds as an acceptable interval for a self-parking garage in two-way traffic. Car loading of 6 persons as opposed to the rated capacity of 12 persons was assumed, and the same stair usage assumptions as included in the original study. Otis also recommended a central elevator location, but made separate calculations as requested, as shown in the tables below.

After giving due consideration to the two studies, and recognizing the fact that hydraulic elevators have somewhat higher maintenance costs, the two hydraulic elevator scheme for each bank was selected as providing acceptable service at an affordable cost.

The design of the elevator cabs recalls the design of the office building cabs, but use vinyl flooring and plastic laminate on the walls. The side walls have a beige color vinyl with ridges and the back is a slate green.

The competitive bids were rather widely scattered and no manufacturer had even a reasonably competitive bid for both the traction elevators for the office building and the hydraulic elevators for the parking structure. It looked like there might have be two manufacturers, until the bids were received for the hotel. The contractor negotiated with several manufacturers for the entire project, and Otis finally proposed competitive pricing for the entire package.

Maintenance contracts for the equipment were reviewed and accepted by Property Management prior to purchase.

OFFICE BUILDING PARKING ELEVATOR BANK

Type	Elevator Quantity	Capacity (pounds)	Speed (fpm)	Interval (seconds)	Handling Cap. (%)	Rating
Hydraulic	1	3500	150	95.6	10.5	Poor
Hydraulic	2	3500	150	47.8	20.9	Good
Hydraulic	3	3500	150	31.9	31.4	Excellent
Traction	1	3500	350	73.2	13.7	Poor
Traction	2	3500	350	36.6	27.3	Excellent

HOTEL PARKING ELEVATOR BANK

Type	Elevator Quantity	Capacity (pounds)	Speed (fpm)	Interval (seconds)	Handling Cap. (%)	Rating
Hydraulic	1	3500	150	95.6	19.6	Poor
Hydraulic	2	3500	150	47.8	39.2	Good
Hydraulic	3	3500	150	31.9	58.8	Excellent
Traction	1	3500	350	73.2	25.6	Poor
Traction	2	3500	350	36.6	51.3	Excellent

ACOUSTICS

22

Acoustics are an extremely important element of the Interior Environmental Quality (IEQ), so necessary to the productive use of office space. This subject should be thoroughly understood by the Development Officer in order that proper precautions can be taken while designing the building, and for troubleshooting should a tenant encounter unsatisfactory conditions in the space. There is so much potential for unsatisfactory acoustical issues to occur that retention of an acoustical consultant is recommended.

Perceptible sound covers a wide spectrum of frequencies. The human ear can perceive sounds that have frequencies between 20 cycles per second (20 hertz) and 20,000 hertz. "Middle C" on the piano is 250 hertz.

The human hearing mechanism is not equally sensitive to sounds over the entire range. Our hearing is best for the important "speech" frequencies in the range of 500 to 4,000 hertz. Acoustical tests are carried out in a series of frequency bands because the performance of sound is different at different frequencies. In general, most sound-absorptive and sound-blocking elements are more effective at controlling high frequencies than they are low ones.

Although frequency band analysis is the realm of the acoustical expert, there are many situations—such as the ranking-ordering of product effectiveness—where it is useful to have a single number that describes how well a product performs in terms of acoustics. For most acoustical tests these single number figures of merit have been standardized and will be discussed below.

For discussion purposes the subject will be divided into three separate issues—Sources of Noise, Acoustical Transmission Control, and Issues for Mechanical, Electrical and Elevator Systems.

The subject is further divided into those that are the basic responsibility of the developer, and those that are the tenant's internal issues.

Sources of Noise

As a general rule, the developer will endeavor to provide the tenant with premises where the background noise level from external sources will not exceed Noise Criteria (NC) 40, and preferably NC 35. The primary noise sources external to the premises that are the developer's primary responsibility, and the general methods for control, are listed below. It should be remembered that the primary means of restricting sound transmission is through mass, elimination of openings, and vibration control.

- Outside noise—highways, trains and airport glide paths are the most common outside sources. The severity of these sources should be measured prior to the building design through an acoustical model. The remedies are insulated glazing with a greater than normal air space and/or laminated glass, additional insulation in the walls, and tight sealing for the windows and doors. Testing to gauge the effectiveness of façade construction to control such noise measures the Indoor-Outdoor Transmission Class (IOTC). An average value is 40.

- Noise external to the premises—demising walls separating the premises from public corridors and adjacent tenant spaces should be constructed to a Sound Transmission Class (STC) rating of at least 40. This is normally accomplished with two sheets of drywall on at least one side, drywall extended from slab to slab and sealed top and bottom, insulation in the cavity, and no back-to-back electrical outlets. For some curtain wall systems the gasket detail where a demising wall meets the perimeter must be carefully designed.

- Equipment—mechanical, electrical and elevator equipment should be mounted on high mass concrete bases, preferably supported by vibration isolators. Vibration isolation supports should be used for major pipes and ducts located near or through occupied space, as well as fans or other equipment hung from the structure. This issue will be discussed in more detail at the end of this chapter.

- Equipment room and shaft walls—should be designed in a similar manner to demising walls, with a possible additional layer of drywall. Any doors from equipment rooms must be equipped with acoustical seals. If noise transmission problems are found after completion, the two most common solutions are adding extra drywall sheets and applying sound absorbing materials to the inside of the room or shaft. All penetrations should be tightly sealed.

- Air noise—fan noise and air velocity noise are transmitted through the ducts into the space. The best solution is to internally insulate the ducts, but care must be taken to coat this insulation to avoid entraining fibers in the air stream. The most environmentally satisfactory solutions are to use sound traps after the fans, reduce the air velocity, and/or use insulation with an impervious casing. Air boots are often installed on the return outlets through the ceiling to reduce plenum noises. This will be discussed in more detail at the end of this chapter.

- A large number of acoustical issues in an occupied space are a function of how the space is used, open or closed office space, tenant partition design, the type and location of tenant equipment, occupant speech and circulation, and the degree of speech privacy desired.

Acoustical Issues, Measurement and Control

There are two basic factors in acoustical control—speech privacy and the environmental discomfort resulting from certain background noises, particularly those that are irregular in intensity and pitch. The common use of video conferencing systems,

---

We developed a building in Los Angeles that we believed had been appropriately evaluated acoustically. We leased several floors to a law firm whose partners had visited the empty floors several times during the negotiations. Shortly after the lease was signed the tenant advised us that the space was unsatisfactory due to the excessive noise from the elevators running through the shaft. We rechecked our acoustical analysis, listened to the sounds in the space, and concluded that it met normal standards. Nevertheless, we added some additional insulation in the wall cavity and one extra layer of drywall in an effort to satisfy the tenant.

The tenant proceeded to file a lawsuit, but during discovery it became clear that they had no cause for complaint and they dropped the suit. We concluded that the suit was nothing but an attempt to negotiate a reduction in the rental rate, but it does indicate this type of problem that could result from a lack of appropriate acoustical control.

---

speakerphones, and large printers and copiers have amplified problems with both speech privacy and background noise. Speech privacy is considered to be very important in certain uses where privacy and/or mental concentration is extremely important—executive offices, conference and boardrooms, lawyers offices, etc. Speech privacy is a product of both the background noises in a space and the amount of acoustical separation provided between

ACOUSTIC PRIVACY

PRIVACY RATING POTENTIAL	SPEECH PRIVACY	DESCRIPTION OF PRIVACY
Total Privacy	85	Shouting is barely audible.
Highly Confidential	80	Normal voice levels not audible. Raised voices barely audible but not intelligible.
Excellent	75	Normal voice levels barely audible. Raised voices are audible but largely unintelligible.
Good	70	Normal voices are audible but unintelligible most of the time. Raised voices are partially intelligible.
Fair	65	Normal voices audible and intelligible some of the time. Raised voices are intelligible.
Poor	60	Normal voices audible and intelligible most of the time.
None	Less than 60	No speech privacy.

two spaces. A table has been developed to indicate relative degrees of speech privacy from human voice, exclusive of voice amplification systems.

Noise Criteria is a measure of the background noise level in a given space, with the higher ratings being indicative of a noisier environment. A range of NC 35 to NC 40 is normally considered to be acceptable in most office spaces, as a certain amount of background noise can be useful in masking voice transmission between two spaces. Generally accepted background noise levels for different uses are shown below. It is frequently difficult (and some say unnecessary) to accomplish the NC 30 level.

Construction that attempts to reduce background noise and create voice privacy is accomplished by using materials and construction techniques that have higher Sound Transmission Class (STC) ratings. STC is the single number rating used to measure the ability of construction elements to block sound at speech frequencies, particularly the sound blocking value for a partition or ceiling. It measures transmission of speech and other sounds in a way the human ear perceives it. Typical values range from 30 to 55, the higher the rating the better. Office construction elements and approximate Sound Transmission Class ratings for various construction details are:

ACCEPTABLE BACKGROUND NOISE LEVELS

Boardroom, auditorium, and video/conference room	NC 30
Typical conference room	NC 35
Private office	NC 35-38
Open office plan	NC 38-40

SOUND TRANSMISSION CLASS RATINGS

Typical Demountable Partition — STC 20-30

Fixed Partition Construction
    Drywall partition with cavity insulation to acoustical ceiling line — STC 30
    Drywall partition with cavity insulation extending into ceiling plenum six inches above acoustical ceiling tile system — STC 35
    Drywall partition with cavity insulation, erected full height to the underside of slab above — STC 40-45
    Multi-layer drywall partition with insulation, erected full height to the underside of slab above — STC 50

Doors
    Non-gasketed doors — STC 20
    Gasketed doors — STC 30
    Acoustical doors — STC 40

Ceilings
    Fiberglass tile system — STC 22
    Mineral tile system — STC 35

To reduce background noise caused by noise leakage through the ceiling plenum from one occupied space to another—add insulated boots to the return air slots, or duct the return air. If cross sound leakage on the supply air side is a problem, separate the two spaces from sharing the same supply duct or internally insulate the ducts.

Sources of noise and voice transmission, as well as privacy issues, can create problems in open space office areas. Two of the best solutions in these cases are to use sound absorbing partial height partitions and to create a masking sound system, or "white noise." White noise systems consist of a series of speakers located within the ceiling plenum above an office space. The speakers are spaced evenly at intervals determined by the configuration of the office space below. When properly tuned, a masking sound system fills the ceiling plenum with a diffuse, constant noise source of roughly 48 decibels that then filters down evenly through the ceiling. At the proper volume, a masking system should produce a background noise that helps cover sounds in the workspace but is hardly noticeable to office workers. The level of background noise is given a Room Criterion (RC) rating, where RC-15 is considered inaudible and RC-30 to RC-35 are generally preferred in most office settings. Some users have provided uniform background music, but its reception varies with the type of work being performed.

While most acoustic testing is performed in the laboratory, there are two field tests used to determine the ability of construction elements to block sound. The first, Noise Isolation Class (NIC), measures the ability of materials to block speech frequencies along the combination of all sound paths, including walls, doors, ceiling and ductwork between rooms. NIC measures overall isolation between adjacent rooms separated by complete construction—it is not for open offices. A typical number is 40.

The second field test, Field Sound Transmission Class (FSTC), is calculated in a manner similar to the Sound Transmission Class, but is done on a site specific construction element, such as an operable wall. A typical value is 40.

There are several other measures, tests and terms used in acoustical analysis that are beneficial for the Development Officer to be aware of. They are explained below.

- The measure of the effectiveness of ceiling materials to block sound between rooms—called the Ceiling Attenuation Class (CAC)—is used when the dividing wall does not connect with the overhead construction. A typical value is 35.

- To measure the sound absorption of a material or assembly, a Noise Reduction Coefficient (NRC) has been developed to measure the efficiency of a material to absorb sound. It is based on the average of sound absorption coefficients at 250, 500, 1000, and 2000 hertz. A standardized laboratory test establishes the NRC coefficient, typically ranging from 0.50 to 0.95 for ceiling and wall panels. The higher the number, the more absorption.

- The Articulation Class (AC) measures how effectively ceilings, wall panels and furniture provide speech privacy in open offices. A typical value is 180. Consultants can use the AC data to model an open office in order to determine acoustic acceptability prior to construction. These tests measure sounds striking a ceiling at angles of incidence of 45 to 55 degrees, the angles at which sound most often bounces over cubicle walls. High performance units are frequently required in these areas—usually with an AC of 200 or above.

- Articulation Index (AI) is a measure of the degree of privacy between two locations in an open office environment, based on frequencies most intelligible to the human ear. The lower the AC number, the greater the degree of privacy. A typical value is 0.10.

Any special acoustical treatment is considered to be the tenant's responsibility, unless the problem was caused by an unusual building or external noise problem.

In addition to the many construction methods discussed herein, many of the acoustical problems can be at least partially mitigated by high NRC ceilings, heavier than normal carpeting, draperies, acoustically treated wall panels and sound masking.

Issues for Mechanical, Electrical and Elevator Systems

Improperly designed and/or installed HVAC or other mechanical, electrical and elevator systems can create a wide range of annoying noise.

Equipment vibration can be a significant source of noise transmitted through ducts, pipes and the structure. Mechanical, electrical and elevator equipment should be mounted on high mass concrete bases, preferably supported on vibration isolators. Thicker floor slabs are often required in addition to the proper bases.

Vibration isolation hangars should be used to support major pipes and ducts located near or through occupied spaces, as well as any fans or other equipment hung from the structure.

Air noise results primarily from the fan's rotation and air velocity noise that are transmitted through the ducts into the space. A good rule of thumb is for main duct velocities not to exceed 1500 feet per minute (fpm) on the floor and 1700 fpm in the shafts. While reducing air velocity is the most effective method of controlling this source of noise, it requires larger equipment and larger ducts.

One solution for air noise reduction is to internally insulate the ducts with open cell insulating material, but care must be taken to properly coat this insulation to avoid entrainment of fibers into the air stream. The coating of such materials require careful "buttering" of all cut edges, and addition of a coating to prevent the shedding that harms the air quality.

Currently, there are closed cell insulation materials with an impervious coating that effectively accomplishes sound reduction through the duct walls, as well as transmission into the space through the diffuser without permitting impurities to enter the air stream. Additional environmentally satisfactory solutions are to use sound traps after the fans and reduce the air velocity.

To reduce noise leakage through the ceiling plenum from one occupied space to another—add insulated boots to the return air slots, or duct the return air. If cross-sound leakage on the supply duct side is a problem, separate the two spaces from sharing the same supply duct.

Piping noise is usually a function of how the pipe is sized (i.e., the velocity of the liquid through the pipe in feet per second), how it is hung and guided (vibration isolators), and whether there are shock absorbers required to mitigate the impact of quick-closing valves. A rule of thumb is for the velocity through the pipe to be limited to 6 fps for cold water and 4 fps for hot water, with a friction loss of 1 pound per square inch (psi) head of water per 100 feet of pipe length.

Two field tests are used to measure the amount of background noise created by HVAC systems:

- Noise Criterion (NC) is being supplanted by newer tests that attempt to measure low frequency sounds that produce vibrations. If used, an acceptable value is NC 35.
- The newer test, Room Criterion (RC), not only measures the level of noise but whether the noise is a rumble (abbreviated with an R), a hiss (abbreviated with an H), or a vibration (abbreviated with a V). A neutral reading (abbreviated with a N) is always possible.

RC is not appropriate for rating HVAC components, such as air supply diffusers, because these devices typically do not produce sound across the entire audible spectrum. The RC method, by design, is used to evaluate the entire spectrum; for HVAC components, the NC can be used in conjunction with laboratory tests.

CASE STUDY

The acoustic mitigations were incorporated as recommended by the acoustical consultant. While most of these recommendations were applicable to various sections of the base building work, they are included here to remain consistent with the text.

An analysis of the freeway noise was made at the site. Based on the consultant's experience, they recommended the interior be limited to an Equivalent Sound Pressure Level of 43dBA. This would require glazing with a Sound Transmission Class Rating of 30 STC on the north and east faces and STC 35 on the south and west faces. STC 30 can be met with ¼" plate glass and STC 35 can be met with ¼" laminated glass. A ⅜" laminated glass was selected due to a concern about using two pieces of ⅛" glass laminated together. Since the recommendation is for a composite STC rating, the glazing system as a whole, including frames and seals, must meet this criteria, not just the glass. The curtain wall contractor conducted an acoustical test per the specifications.

The design criteria for the office areas is to be NC 40 adjacent to the core and NC 35 elsewhere. This requirement is to be met through the HVAC system by duct sizing, equipment selection, sound traps and duct lining, and structurally, as shown below.

The structural recommendations to control noise and vibration from major items of equipment are to provide 8"-thick reinforced concrete slabs beneath the chiller room and the cooling towers. Slabs 6" thick are recommended for pump and air handler rooms.

Mechanical noises were controlled by setting maximum velocities for water and airflow, and by the use of vibration isolators for all equipment, piping and ductwork.

The details of the various core walls are as shown below. All mechanical and electrical doors that open to occupied space or public corridors were acoustically sealed.

COREWALL DESIGN CRITERIA

Between all mechanical and electrical rooms and occupied spaces.	Original recommendation was for 8" concrete block filled with grout. After it was agreed to accept NC 40 adjacent to the core the recommendation was revised to 5 layers of ⅝" gypsum board, slab to slab, fiberglass batts and continuous acoustical sealant.
Between mechanical and/or electrical rooms.	⅝" gypsum board, fiberglass batts.
Between toilet rooms and freight lobby and occupied space, and public tenant corridors.	⅝" gypsum board, slab to slab with continuous acoustical sealant.
Between walls with brace framing and occupied spaces.	⅝" gypsum board, fiberglass batts, 1" air space, fiberglass batts, ⅝" gypsum board, slab to slab with continuous acoustical sealant.
Pipe chases.	Same as above, but air space sufficient for pipe.
Between elevator and pipe shafts and occupied spaces.	1" coreboard, fiberglass batts, two layers of ⅝" gypsum board, slab to slab with continuous acoustical sealant.

01 SITE PLAN
NOT TO SCALE

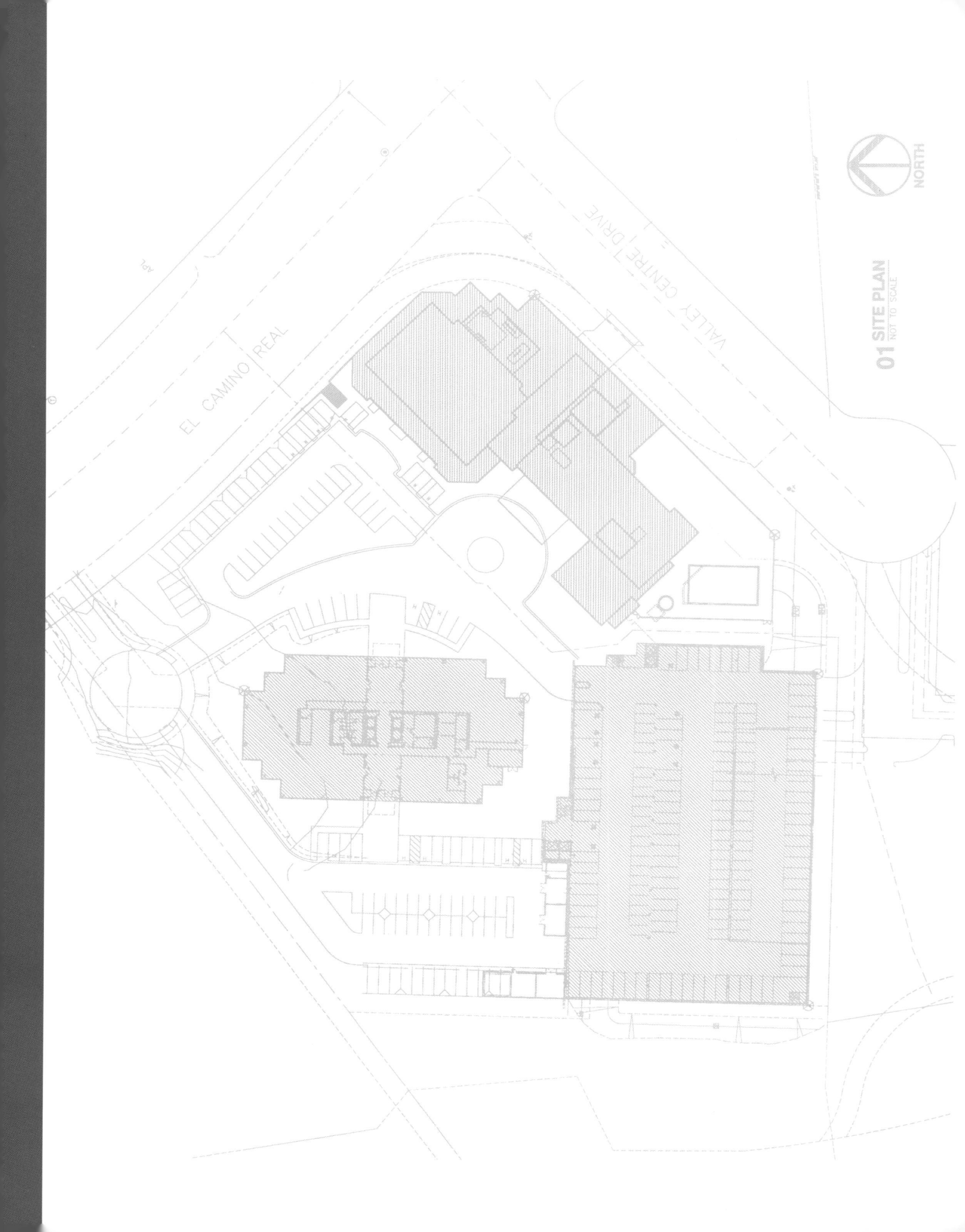

CORE AREA DESIGN

23

The layout of the core areas is very important to the ability to lease the floor, particularly efficiently fitting in the smaller tenants. The arrangement of some of these elements are covered in Chapter 16. In this chapter we discuss some details of these important facilities, with particular emphasis on the toilet rooms, which can be a major factor in successful leasing and tenant retention.

Efficient design of the core is essential. All of the areas in the core reduce the useable area. While all common areas are normally included in rentable area, when the "add on" factor (the amount by which the rentable/useable [R/U] ratio exceeds 100%) exceeds the norm in the market, this excess may not be recoverable and requires a downward adjustment in the effective rentable area.

Acoustical control, as discussed in Chapter 22, is important wherever occupied space abuts a mechanical room, electrical room, public corridor or a piping, air or elevator shaft. These walls must be floor to ceiling construction with components as recommended by the acoustic consultant. The mechanical and electrical equipment rooms will require acoustically sealed doors and may require extra thick structural slabs to dampen vibrations.

FLOOR ELEVATOR LOBBIES

A well-designed elevator lobby on each floor can be a positive leasing tool, particularly for less than full-floor tenants, as it is the gateway to their offices. Frequently, soffits and a reduction in the opening at the entrances provide a more personal feeling. Wall materials may vary with the budget, but those to consider are stone, wood, articulated drywall, fabric or vinyl. The floors may have a stone or wood border and base around the perimeter, with carpet inset. Usually this work will be postponed until it is determined that a floor will not be let to a full-floor tenant, who may wish to be responsible for this work subject to the owner's approval. On a divided floor this will always be a part of the shell and core construction.

The building graphics on each floor should be consistent with the specified standard for the building. Special graphics for full-floor tenants require owner approval. Graphics in these lobbies, including all directional and code-mandated life safety instructions, must be carefully detailed during the design phase to avoid the cluttered, "added-on" look that frequently occurs when not properly planned.

Most codes now require that there be 20-minute rated smoke actuated doors to close off the elevator lobby. The doors are held open magnetically in normal operation, and the magnets are released letting the doors close in an alarm condition. These regulations make a clean design more difficult. When a "Z" corridor is used for exiting, as discussed in Chapter 16, some jurisdictions require that the pair of doors at each end of the lobby be designed so that they swing in different directions, so that one always swings in the direction of egress, regardless which direction the occupants are traveling. (See Figure 23-1.) This is accomplished either by having the length of the entrance to the

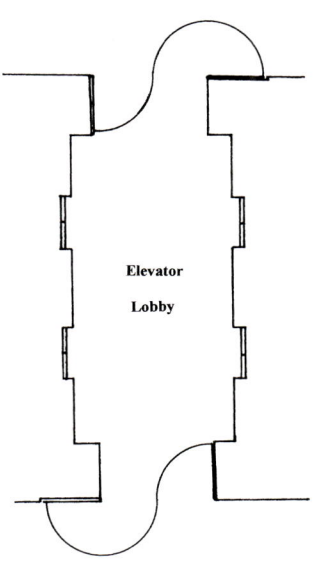

Figure 23-1

lobby slightly greater than the width so each door can fold back into the entrance wall, or placing the doors near the outer face of the lobby adjacent to the corridor. In the latter case, in its normal position the door that swings into the lobby is flush against, or recessed into, the lobby entrance wall. The outward swinging door would be located directly opposite, so that a smoke seal can be accomplished, but in its normal position it is swung 180° to recess into the corridor wall. For visual design purposes, it is common either to place dummy panels matching each door in the opposite position from the other door's open position, or to paint or cover the smoke barrier doors to match the corridor and elevator walls so they are not too obvious.

STAIRWELLS

The size of a stairwell is governed by code, and is based on the estimated population to be evacuated. The construction of the stairwells and the exit corridors from them to the outside must be of the fire resistance required of the structure, usually two hours, but in certain instances one-hour construction is permitted in buildings with limited fire resistance construction. Note that if a restaurant, auditorium or other large assembly facility is placed in the upper part of the building the stairwell width might have to be increased for the entire building height. Sometimes a stairwell must transfer to another shaft. In such case, the transfer corridor must be the width of the stairwell and of the same fireproof construction. There are at least two stairwells required for exiting, usually at least one-half the building diagonal apart. Frequently, leasing concerns dictate a third stairwell so that one-half of the floor or more may be leased to one tenant with multiple tenants on the remainder of the floor.

Stair treads can be reinforced concrete (usually only in the basement), pre-cast concrete, metal runners with the pan filled with concrete, or diamond plate. Some buildings have plastered soffits beneath the treads, but its marketing value is minimal to non-existent. Handrails should be kept simple, like a pipe rail. Brightly painted block walls are normally satisfactory, and floors and treads should be sealed or painted. Light fixtures can be surface mounted, but the lighting should be generous, and must be on the emergency power circuit. When leasing to multi-floor tenants there may be a benefit to upgrading the finishes to make interfloor traffic more attractive.

Stairwells must always be unlocked from the space side and should always be locked from the stairwell side to provide security to the tenants. Whenever a multi-floor tenant requests that the stairwell side be left unlocked to facilitate interfloor traffic, the request should not be honored unless the tenant signs a satisfactory security waiver. Stairwell doors must be electrically unlockable from a central point, usually the firemen's control panel, for fire department access.

Codes require many building stairwells to be pressurized by a fan at the top of the shaft actuated by a smoke detector. Some codes require a parallel exhaust air shaft beside the stairwell with smoke-operated dampers at each floor. The 1997 UBC requires a separate smoke-proof vestibule for high-rise construction, which is also mechanically pressurized, but at a lower pressure than the stairwell.

Normally there will be a manual fire alarm pull box by each stairwell. An exit light with emergency power will be above the stairwell door, as well as wherever needed throughout the floor to guide evacuees to the stair. There should also be intercoms periodically in the shaft, and the floor numbers should be painted on the door at each floor. Standpipes with a 2½" hose connection for the fire department are required, but a 1½" hose for building use that was formerly required in or near the stairwell at each floor level is no longer required under some codes in a sprinklered building.

PUBLIC CORRIDORS AND TENANT ENTRANCE DOORS

Public corridors should be a minimum of a nominal five feet wide, but a nominal six feet is better, and under most circumstances must be constructed to provide at least a one-hour fire rating. They should have a vinyl wall covering for appearance and durability, but a Zolatone or other paint finish is often used. Light fixtures are preferably Compact Fluorescent Lights (CFL) or 2' x 2' fluorescent fixtures. Some buildings use a gypsum board ceiling, but this creates excess expense when corridors are changed during the life of the project. The appearance of these corridors is enhanced if the entrance doors are an attractive wood or glass double doors, or doors with one or two glass sidelights. As mentioned in another chapter, door closers must have a very low closing force to satisfy ADA. Locks on entrance doors may be card or key actuated, depending on tenant desires and the type of security system, as discussed further under Security Systems in Chapter 27.

On divided tenant floors the public corridors and the elevator lobbies will be installed as part of the shell and core construction. The exact number is unknown initially, so the pro forma usually includes an assumed number of floors as an allowance, usually one-third.

TOILET ROOMS

The toilet rooms are one of the most important facilities in a building. They must not only be functional, but that same sense of design and quality that started in the building lobby must carry over into the toilet rooms. Their appearance, perceived cleanliness and germ free environment are a major tenant issue in the initial leasing and for the long-term.

Arrangement

Toilet rooms should be arranged to the greatest extent possible to permit the minimum number of straight plumbing chases. The most efficient arrangement, where it is not necessary to fit the toilet rooms between elevator shafts, is to locate them back to back, with all fixtures on one wall and both rooms backing up to the same chase. When fixtures are back to back there should be 1'10" from face of wall to face of wall. Where there are three or four elevators in a bank, toilet rooms may be arranged end to end—again it's beneficial if as much of the piping as possible is on one wall. In high-rise buildings with large cores, some users prefer toilet rooms with an entrance at each end to make it more convenient for employees, but it requires more space for a second vestibule and it does not fit with some elevator bank layouts. The piping manifolds are normally prefabricated and brought to the job site for installation.

Fixtures

To set the fixture count, it is first necessary to set the floor population count using the useable area of the floor. Historically, 100 usf per person was used in the codes, but current codes are more liberal, with the 1997 UBC allowing 200 usf per person. The normal code assumption of useable square feet is the area outside of the core. Fixture counts are usually determined by the 1997 UBC shown below, normally based on the assumption of 50% men and 50% women. All fixtures must be wall hung. The code fixture count is shown below.

The fixture counts per code have gone from being so excessive some years ago that many juris-

FIXTURE REQUIREMENTS

Water Closets	Lavatories		Drinking Fountains
No. of Persons / **No. of Fixtures***			
1–15 / 1		1 per 2 water closets	Over 30 persons, provide 1 for each 150 persons
16–35 / 2			
36–55 / 3			
1 fixture for each 50 additional persons			

* Wherever urinals are provided for men, one water closet less than the number specified may be provided for each urinal installed, except the number of water closets in such cases shall not be reduced to less than ½ of the minimum specified.

For large conference and assembly facilities, occupant load is counted at 1 person per 30 sf, but the author has never seen a normal tenant layout that has large meeting rooms affect the base building fixture allowance.

dictions partially waived some of the requirements, to where currently you must be careful that enough fixtures are provided for good service. If the count is marginal, it is better to add a fixture to ensure acceptable service.

Special consideration should be given to the fixture count in the women's restrooms, particularly if there is a likelihood of a preponderance of women on any floor. Women's time requirements are greater and some states have new "potty parity" rules added to the building codes, increasing the number of fixtures by as much as 50% above to the men's room requirements.

A continuous lavatory top should be provided as discussed later in this chapter.

In many jurisdictions showers must be provided either in each toilet room or in a central location for the benefit of bicyclists and joggers.

Layout

It is essential that the sight lines are visually blocked from external view. A single door is preferable where sight lines permit, otherwise a vestibule and a second door is required. Arranging the toilet rooms into separate compartments, one for the lavatories, and one for the water closets and urinals adds a perception of quality to the building, and the door between the two compartments can substitute for a vestibule door where sight lines require it. Current handicap requirements significantly affect the layout, as discussed below. It is important that the restroom avoid a crowded or cramped feeling—sufficient roominess for easy circulation is important.

Wall, Floor and Ceiling Construction

Tile is still the predominant material for a quality restroom, but some high profile buildings are using more granite and marble. At least the wet wall(s) and floor should be tile, with at least a 4" cove base on all walls (some cities require fully tiled toilet rooms). Other walls can be vinyl, but in some markets fully tiled toilet rooms are an important marketing feature. Floor tile (most commonly 2" x 2", but can be larger) should be non-glazed with dark grout, as it is almost impossible to keep light colored grout looking clean. Wall tile can be from 2" to 12" with different design approaches. The basic tile selection should be white or a light color that strongly indicates cleanliness. More frequently architects are including some color contrast or design into the tile installation for brightness and interest. Any tile design should be properly coordinated with the lavatory tops, urinals and accessories.

Drywall makes a better appearing ceiling unless too many access panels are required for equipment service, then it should be 12" x 12" or 24" x 24" fissured mineral tile.

Toilet Partitions

Toilet partitions should preferably be ceiling hung to promote cleanliness, and be stainless steel, granite, marble, plastic laminate, polyethylene, solid phenolic or porcelainized steel. The various plastic compartments are more maintenance-free over a period of years. Painted steel should be avoided because it tends to chip and does not wear well. Urinal vanity panels to match should be used with multiple urinals.

Lighting

Lighting is an important factor and should create a nice soft effect without compromising light quality. It should accentuate a good clean feeling in the space, and since the lighting is on longer than many other areas, it can be expensive. Toilet rooms should be light, but not bright, and fairly uniform—dark corners can make a room look dingy or not clean. Some extra light should be provided over the mirrors, and the fixtures should provide a good color-rendering index (CRI)—people look carefully at themselves in the mirrors. Energy efficient lighting fixtures can provide adequate lighting levels at around one watt per sf. Low wattage fluorescent fixtures, particularly the CFLs, have become an almost mandatory substitute for incandescent fixtures.

One good solution is a recessed continuous strip fluorescent light with louvers over the lavatories, water closets and urinals, with CFL fixtures over the traffic areas. This recessed strip lighting provides a nice soft effect without compromising light quality. An alternate approach gaining popularity is indirect lighting in an open cove in the same location. Some codes require buildings to use sensors to turn on the toilet room lights when someone enters, but it is preferred to leave them on and turn them off by computer in the evening, with the tenant able to override this with a card-actuated device or timed switch.

Faucets, Flush Valves and Hot Water

Hot water can be provided by a central system, or by small local electric heaters for one or several toilet rooms that are usually more cost effective. Tempered water only can be provided in lieu of hot and cold water, and is recommended as it saves piping and some energy.

Water conservation and the quality of valves and fittings are important factors in long-term cost control. In some areas water is scarce, and in virtually every area its costs are rapidly escalating due to the cost of availability and the replacement of deteriorating infrastructure.

Good quality faucets and flush valves should be used to minimize maintenance problems and tenant annoyance. Faucets are preferably touchless, sensor-operated automatic faucets with tempered water. Infrared technology is rapidly becoming the standard for automatic faucets. In addition to water savings, the perception and reality of sanitation is improved since no contact is required. Automatic water limiting faucets are required by some jurisdictions, but good judgment indicates their use in virtually all installations. Flow restrictors built into lavatory faucets can reduce flow rates from five gallons per minute to one gallon. Selection of the faucets should be made in conjunction with Property Management to insure current information on maintenance costs and other issues on the various types available.

Low-rate flush valves use less than two gallons of water compared to five to eight gallons on formerly standard toilets. Sensor-operated flush valves for urinals and water closets have long been essential in areas with heavy use by the general public, and the author now considers them essential in office floor toilet rooms due to the increased tenant desire for touchless fixtures and the increased perception of sanitary conditions.

There is a wide range in the quality of faucets and flush valves. While appearance is a judgment issue, the units should always be selected for top quality performance.

Note that each fixture should be isolated with shutoff valves, so that maintenance can work on one without shutting down the entire toilet room.

Lavatories

A continuous lavatory top is a virtual necessity in a building of any reasonable quality. The best product for cleanliness and reduced maintenance costs are those tops integrally molded with the lavatories. The most aesthetically appealing are granite and marble—granite is a little easier to maintain because it is not as porous. Stone lavatory tops provide the perception of high quality at very little extra cost. They should have underset bowls to provide easier cleaning. Back splashes should be 6" high.

A sleek design currently in vogue is to have the stone lavatory top pulled away from the wall about 2". It is most attractive, when clean, when the mirror runs past the top, however, good maintenance practice probably dictates that the wall tile run up 6" above the top.

A local soap source (liquid, flake, leaf or powder) should be provided. The author prefers bulk liquid soap with the source under the lavatory top and the spout through the top—extending far enough so any drippage is only into the bowl. Soap dispensers with push rather than pull mechanisms provide greater longevity.

Shower Rooms

It has become increasingly common to add shower rooms, at least one for each sex per building, to support bicyclists and those who run at noon. In some jurisdictions it is a requirement, and in others it can be a tenant amenity.

Accessories

Mirrors should be full-width above the lavatories up to about seven feet in height. Some recommend that mirrors preferably not be located over the lavatories in the women's room, as excessive time can be spent in front of a mirror. A shelf is required beneath any mirror not over a lavatory top.

Towel dispensers should be recessed brushed stainless steel for folded paper towels, with an integral waste receptacle below. Periodically there is an effort to encourage rolled cloth towels for cost and ecological reasons, but the dispenser requires a thicker wall construction and the towels are not as acceptable to most tenants as paper.

Ash trays (unless it's a smoke free building), hand bag shelves with utility hook below in women's stalls, double roll toilet paper holders, coat hooks, recessed toilet seat cover (optional), sanitary napkin disposal in each women's stall, and one napkin dispenser per room are normal requirements.

Brushed stainless steel is the normal standard for long-term service and cleanability of accessories, but solid phenolic surfaces provide even superior service. Accessories should be fully recessed wherever possible, and baked enamel or cheap accessories should be avoided.

Toilet Room Maintenance

Toilet rooms, the fixtures, faucets and supplies represent a significant annual maintenance cost. The design and materials should be reviewed thoroughly with property management. Hose bibbs should be located under the lavatories to fill buckets or for other maintenance purposes.

Ventilation

Toilet rooms should be well ventilated—a rule of thumb is that 12 air changes per hour will provide adequate ventilation.

Floor Drains

There are various opinions concerning the necessity for floor drains. Some conclude that they are necessary in the event of flooding from equipment or piping failure. Others feel that spills are remote, and a drain that is not constantly checked to insure that water is in the trap becomes a source of odors and insects. The author leans toward the latter view that the risk of water damage does not warrant the expense or problems.

Water Fountains

Water fountains should be located as close as possible to the plumbing shaft. Some buildings have used central chilled water systems, but local electrical water coolers are less expensive to install and operate. They should be recessed into a niche in the wall to avoid an impediment to traffic and to satisfy ADA requirements. Most buildings now provide a pair of fountains, one height for the handicapped and one at normal height.

Water Treatment

Some locations have high mineral content in the water that can stain the fixtures, even with the best of maintenance. This creates the appearance of a dirty toilet room. If this possibility exists, an appropriate filtration treatment system should be installed.

There are some concerns over tap water quality nationally, and an increasing desire by some occupants for bottled water. Bottled water should be avoided as a building responsibility because the supply procedure is a major hassle, and each dispenser should be sanitized at least every three months to avoid bacterial growth.

To satisfy the occupant's rightful desire for clean water, the local water supplier should be requested to provide a copy of the latest water quality report, which can be checked for any contaminants that are in excess of the Environmental Protection Agency's standards. Property Management should arrange to automatically receive these reports as they are issued.

Where any enhancement to the tap water is deemed or perceived to be required, or to minimize unpleasant odors or taste, there are many methods of treatment available. No single product or system is effective for all water issues. Some of the methods in current use are:

- Pre-Filtration—removes sediment and larger particles, extending the life of the filtration system. Can include lead reduction media.

- Carbon/GAC—Granular Activated Carbon (GAC) either absorbs or physically screens out a wide range of contaminants, including taste and odor, chlorine, sulfur, iron, manganese, and more serious contaminants such as lead, heavy metals (mercury, zinc or copper), radon, VOCs and trihalomethanes, biological pathogens and others.

- Carbon Block—compressed GAC into block form, known to have more surface area than GAC, and able to trap smaller contaminants in larger capacities.

- Reverse Osmosis (RO)—greater contaminant removal than carbon and comprised of a synthetic semi-permeable membrane through which water and contaminants are separated. Most RO systems have carbon pre- and post-filters for additional contaminant removal.

- Ultraviolet—eliminates various biological pathogens (bacteria / virus) by using ultraviolet light.

- Distillation—treated water produced by heating the source water into steam, then passing the steam through a condensation coil where it is cooled and condensed back into drinking water.

Any products selected for this purpose must have been tested by an independent agency, preferably the National Sanitation Foundation (NSF). Approval by NSF, a regulatory agency, is required in a few states and testing includes contaminant removal and filter life.

Treatment raises the issue of whether to treat all of the potable water at greater treatment cost or only the drinking water, which requires either localized treatment or extra piping.

ADA Requirements

The planning of toilet rooms has changed significantly with ADA. Successful compliance starts with the layout of routes leading to the toilet room. Corridors must be clear and level, with a minimum width of 36". Entrances are designed with easy access, with 32" clear door opening and 18" clear area to the side of the door handle. Thresholds are to be avoided and door closers require a maximum of five pounds to open. All passageways through the toilet room must be at least 36" wide and there must be a 60" clear turning diameter for wheelchairs.

One compartment must be sized with space for a turning diameter of 60" in front of the water closet. Horizontal grab bars must be provided behind the toilet and on the nearest wall. If there are six or more toilets, a 36" wide stall must be provided in addition to the primary handicap stall.

At least one lavatory must be a maximum height of 34" from the floor with a minimum of 27" of knee clearance. All exposed plumbing beneath the lavatory must be insulated, configured, or covered to avoid possible contact. All accessories must be located to satisfy the ADA code.

FAN ROOMS

In mid- and high-rise buildings the trend is to have a fan room on each floor, or one every other floor. The reasons are to use less expensive equipment, save on shaft space, and to make it easier and less expensive to provide after hours air conditioning to tenants who request it. In addition, floor fan rooms are normally considered to be rentable area. This concept is rarely if ever used in low-rise buildings. Fan rooms should be arranged to permit air to be returned from and distributed to both sides of the core where possible to reduce ductwork. If the core is too wide to be used exclusively by a fan room, the abutting room should be arranged so the ductwork may pass through it.

ELECTRICAL CLOSETS

One or two electric closets should be located on each floor to provide the panels from which electrical services are provided to the floor. Electrical distribution will be discussed in Chapter 27, but the service to the floor is normally 277/480 volts for lighting, with step-down transformers to 120/208 volts for receptacles and equipment. The step-down transformers are usually located in these closets, serving one or more floors. Panels are provided on the closet walls for the distribution at 277v for lighting, 120/208v for miscellaneous power and one for emergency power. Sometimes building distribution at 120/208 volts has been shown to be more economical for both lighting and power, but most commonly 277v is most economical. The electrical and communications rooms may be combined in some jurisdictions, as long as tradesmen pass through the communications compartment to reach the electrical compartment, and not vice versa.

COMMUNICATIONS ROOM

Like electrical closets, one or two are located on each floor. They provide access for the tenant's telephone, cable, ISDN, and other communication services, and also house the building's security, building management and emergency communications systems. Sufficient room must be provided for competing telephone and cable companies, as well as distribution for the roof-mounted satellite communications systems. The tenant's actual communication equipment will be located in his useable space. The owner normally provides fire resistant ¾" plywood attached to the walls, with a grounding system so the tenant communication panels can be installed.

JANITOR CLOSETS

A janitor closet should be installed on each floor, and should contain sufficient room for cleaning personnel carts and supplies. Convenient availability of supplies is the first step in toilet room cleanliness. Property Management usually requests a mop sink in each janitor closet, but the author has rarely been convinced as to the necessity for them.

DOORS, FRAMES AND HARDWARE

The doors and frames in the core are usually hollow metal (although wood doors can achieve fire ratings up to 90 minutes), and most have either a one- or two-hour fire rating, based on UL or equivalent testing. Technically, a rated door must have a fire rating equal to the fire resistance required for the wall in which it is installed. Newer codes are now adding provisions to require doors to have an "S" label, signifying a smoke rating. Hollow metal frames are less expensive than other types and are normally used in the core, but all hardware cutouts are normally made at the factory from shop drawings to accommodate the specific hardware. As mentioned in Chapter 22, mechanical and electrical room doors that exit directly into occupied space or public corridors must be acoustically sealed.

As with all of the other doors, these must meet ADA requirements—lever handles, door closers with low opening forces, and adequate room (18" minimum) to the side for wheelchair occupants.

Hardware is a very complicated subject and most architects and contractors use a hardware consultant. Some consultants perform this service for a fee, while others serve at no charge (theoretically) in return for the hardware contract based on unit prices. The fee approach is preferable.

The choice of locksets and keying system should be delegated to Property Management, as they will be responsible for initial keying and key control. It should be noted that during construction, any keying must be accomplished with construction keys and cylinders, which are discarded and replaced with permanent cylinders and keys when the owner assumes control.

Core Area Design

CASE STUDY

The core area of a typical floor and the first floor are shown on Figures 23-2 and 3. As mentioned in Chapters 16 and 30, the original core design was modified by moving each stairwell ten feet outboard and by widening the core by two feet. The result of these changes was a more efficient multi-tenant floor layout, better dimensions for a stairwell vestibule, better toilet room layout, and a more efficient provision for the brace-framing structural system.

The first floor differs from the typical floor in that the fire control room is located off the freight lobby below an area that contains a major airshaft. The main electrical room is located off of the drawing to the lower right (southwest), as it requires outside access for SDG&E. The north stair exits through the lobby and the south stair exits to the outside alongside the electrical room. The north exit was altered as discussed in Chapter 14 during the

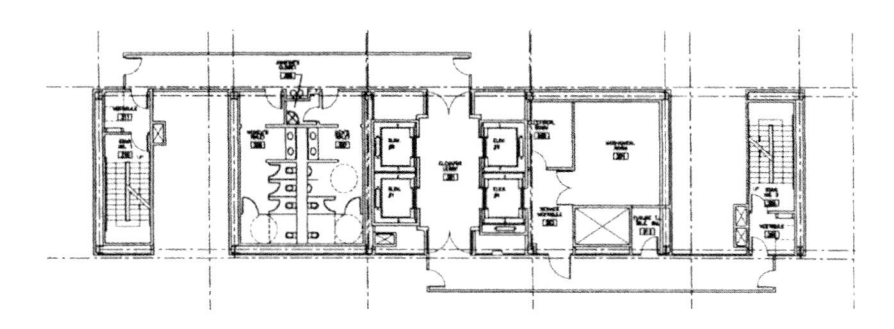

Typical Floor Lobby

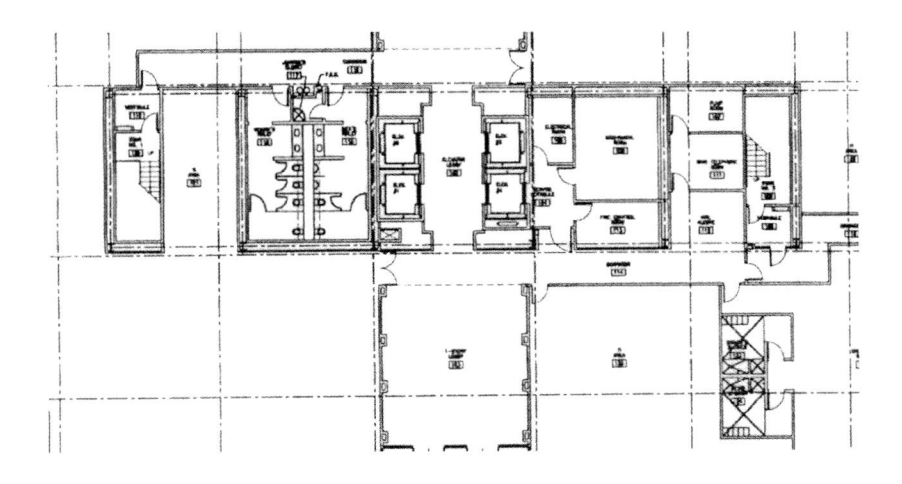

First Floor Lobby

Figure 23-2

permit review. The showers for the health club are shown in the lower right hand corner.

The core area walls were detailed as to thickness, sealants and insulation as recommended by the acoustical consultant based on NC 35 criteria, as modified. The original recommendation specified grout-filled masonry where electrical rooms and mechanical rooms abutted occupied or corridor space. After further consultation, the specifications were changed to five layers of gypsum board with sealants and insulation when it was agreed to accept NC 40 within five feet of those walls.

The mechanical system consists of a central chiller and cooling towers on the roof with a fan system in the mechanical room on each floor.

The multi-floor elevator lobbies have cove ceilings with indirect lighting and fabric-covered wallboard panels. The floor will have polished Carmen Red granite in the entrances, and as a border and base around the lobby, with an inset carpet.

Brandes elected to take a credit for the elevator lobby finishes on their floors and develop their own designs, subject to landlord approval, as described in Chapter 30.

The freight elevator lobby is arranged so that it is facing the back door of the swing elevator cab. It also provides access into the mechanical and electrical rooms. The telephone room is accessed from the corridor.

The electrical room on the divided floors will include the 480/277-volt bus duct with transformers from 480/277 to 120/208 volts and distribution panels. The Brandes floors will have only the bus duct taps. The telephone room on each floor contains six 4" risers with ¾" plywood backing on the walls.

The stairwells are pressurized and have smoke-control vestibules pressurized at a slightly lower pressure.

The toilet room layout is shown in Figure 23-3. The layout is clean and uncrowded, and the sight line control is excellent without the necessity of a vestibule door. The design included one more water closet (or urinal) in each room than required by code. Based on 50% usage by gender, each room was close to the maximum permitted population, and it was preferred to allow for a disproportionate ratio on any given floor without the possibility of being underserved. A reduced drawing of the toilet room plans and elevations is shown as Figure 23-4. The toilet room design incorporates:

- Ceramic tile (2" x 2") on the floor is off-white with major bands of beige and green. The walls have ceramic tile (6"x 6") up to 6'6" from the floor, with vinyl above. The tile wall is off-white with bands of green tile.

- Vestibules have carpeted floor and vinyl walls.

- Ceilings are drywall, with appropriate access panels.

- Tunas Green granite lavatory tops with under mounted lavatories and a 4" backsplash.

- A full-width mirror is located immediately above the splash plate, and extends about 6" above the top line of the wall tile.

- Toilet partitions and vanity panels are ceiling hung with an off-white porcelainized finish.

- Continuous recessed light fixture along the fixture wall with staggered 4' fluorescent lamps, supplemented by four CFL downlights in the ceiling.

- Stainless steel specialties, including an under-counter-mounted liquid soap dispenser with a spout length that insures any drip will be into the lavatory.

- Lavatories will have 0.5 gpm flow restrictors using self-actuating, metered infrared goose-neck faucets using tempered water. Circulating pumps from local heaters assure availability of the proper temperature at the faucet during periods of low usage.

- Wall-mounted water closets are water conserving 1.5-gallon flushometer type, with infra-red operation.

- Urinals will be wall hung with siphon jet, water-conserving one-gallon flushometer type with infrared operation.

Core Area Design

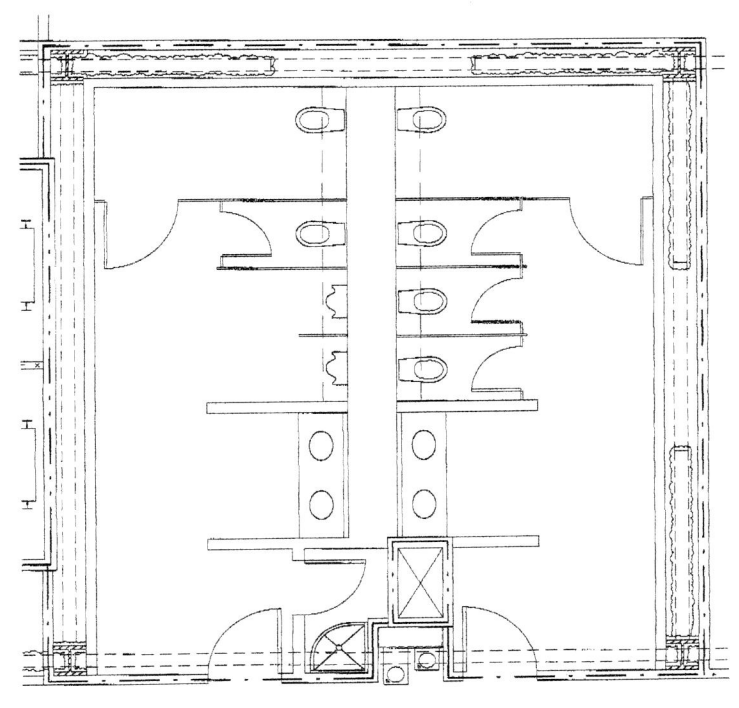

Figure 23-3

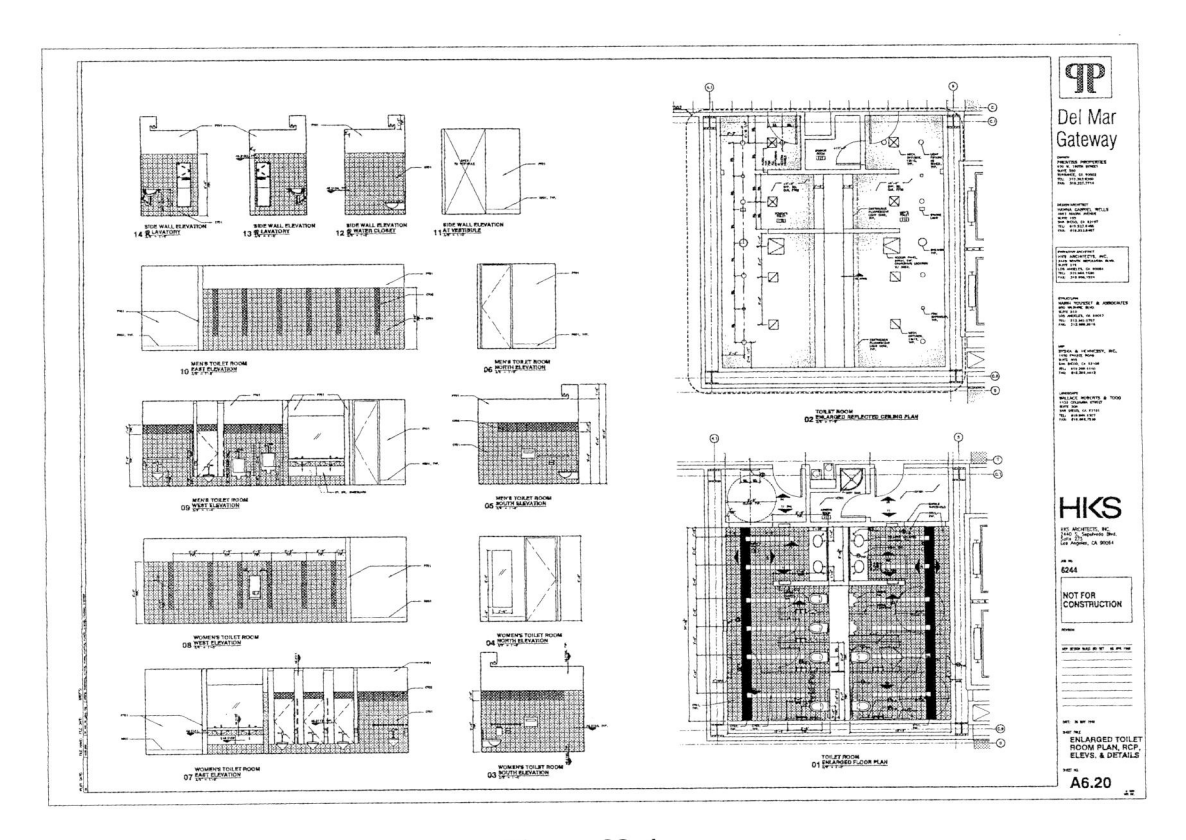

Figure 23-4

- Appropriate barrier-free fixtures are provided and the lavatory traps and hot water piping are insulated.

A pair of water fountains with integral chillers for drinking water, one standard and one handicap height, are located just outside the toilet rooms. Janitor closets are provided in the vestibule of the men's toilet rooms with floor sinks and storage shelves.

Selected toilet room fixtures and colors, along with other public area samples are shown in Figure 23-5 (mislabeled as TI Standards). Starting in the upper left hand corner and moving in a clockwise direction they are:

- Toilet room wall tile, beneath which are the wall paint, grout and floor tile
- Grouping consisting of a robe hook, shower room lockers, and towel dispenser with waste receptacle
- Mirror
- Faucet
- Sanitary napkin vendor
- Soap dispenser
- Lavatory bowl—the lavatory top and faucets are not correct
- Tunas green lavatory top
- Grouping consisting of toilet tissue dispenser, sanitary napkin disposal, coat hook and toilet seat cover dispenser
- Mop and broom holder
- Fire extinguisher cabinet

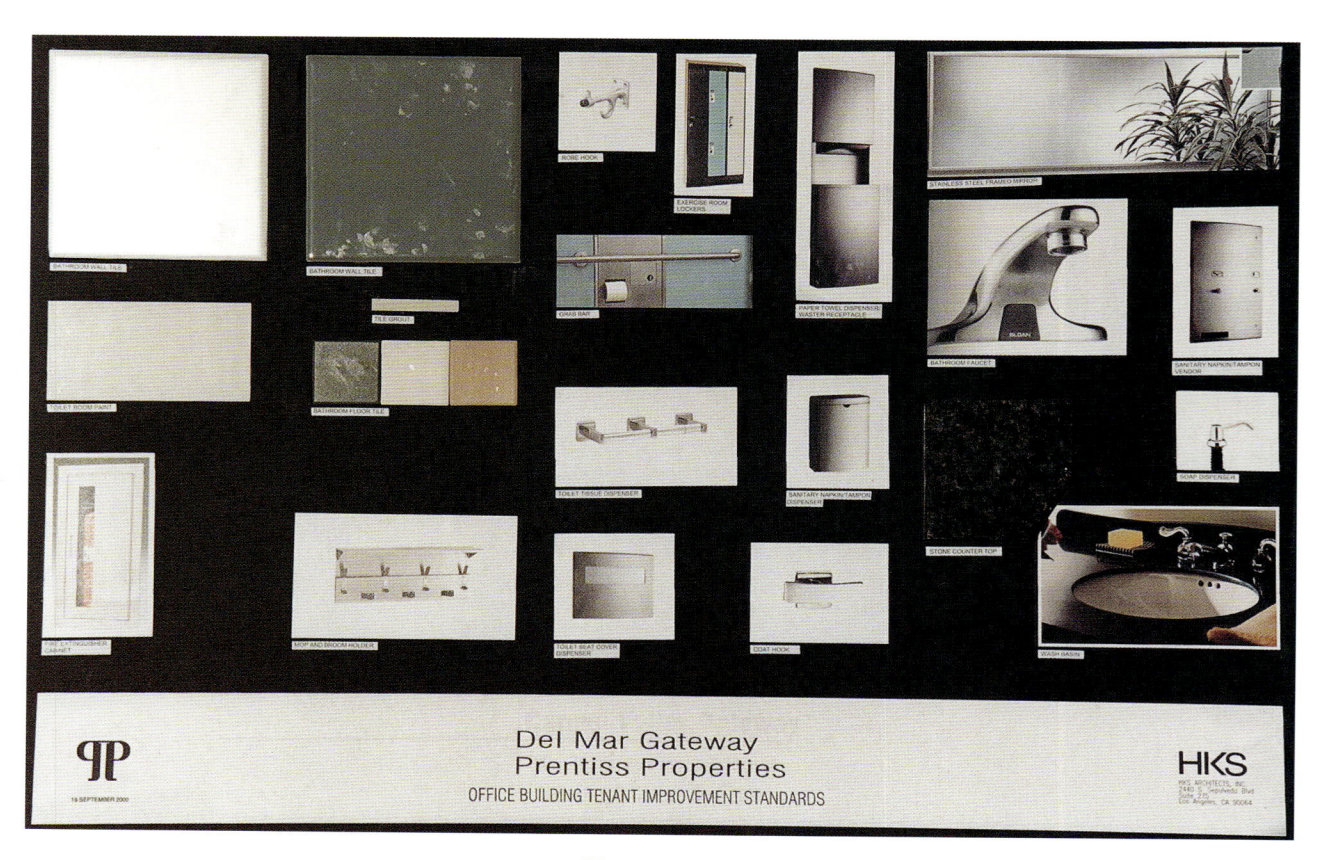

Figure 23-5

CENTRAL FACILITIES DESIGN 24

The central facilities are the functional heart of an office building. This chapter will discuss the location and design of the Main Mechanical Room, Electrical Distribution Room, Communications Room, Loading Dock and Trash Handling, Maintenance Storage and that very important and frequently expensive issue—Parking.

MAIN MECHANICAL ROOM

While the main mechanical room can be located anywhere, there are many reasons to locate it as low in the building as possible, preferably at grade or in a basement area. Some of the reasons are: great possibility of water leakage, reduction of electrical feeder line length and power loss, less structural column length that must carry the weight of this heavy floor, and lesser vibration problems due to the type of construction in the lower areas. There is one counter factor—the higher the top floor is above the chiller equipment, the higher the pressure that the machines and piping must be designed to accommodate, and the run of the condenser water lines is much longer. On a low- to mid-rise building, the last two issues are not a factor.

This room must have appropriate curbs and drainage to control water spillage. The layout must take into account sufficient room for maintenance, particularly for cleaning and pulling the chiller bundles. This room is normally the preferred location for the chief engineer's office, if any, and the Building Management System (BMS). The walls and doors of this room must be acoustically treated as per recommendations of the acoustic consultant, the floor slab will be thickened as recommended to damp any vibrations and vibration isolation pads are usually required.

On smaller buildings most of the equipment will be roof-mounted to reduce cost, simplify distribution, avoid excavation and not interfere with ground floor rentable space. This requires extra care in regards to acoustic and vibration treatment.

ELECTRICAL DISTRIBUTION ROOM

This room should be located for direct access to the incoming service, which is normally through the street, and is usually located on the first floor or in the basement level, as close to the point of incoming service as possible. Preferably this room will be located close to the main mechanical room to minimize electrical power losses. This room should be fully protected from the possibility of water leakage. This room contains the main switchgear and distribution bus. Distribution of the high-voltage power through the building can be either by bus duct or cable risers preferably through a straight vertical chase to the electrical rooms on each floor. Acoustical treatment such as that for the main mechanical room is required.

This area, or the main mechanical room, is a frequent location for any required emergency generator or diesel-driven fire pump, although remote locations are also common. The generator and pump must be located conveniently to a safe place for the fuel tank, and where an appropriate source of outside air and exhaust are available.

Suburban buildings often will be provided with an outside step-down transformer near the point of building entrance, in lieu of a central distribution room. This unit is usually shielded visually with landscaping. Where the transformers are provided within the building, provision must for be made for a separate transforming vault readily accessible to the utility company for maintenance and removal.

COMMUNICATIONS ROOM

This room is where the telephone and other communications enter from the street for distribution throughout the building. Sufficient room must be provided to satisfy the needs of competing telephone and cable companies, and special connections to the Internet. This room is located on the first floor or in a basement area with a chase space to extend sufficient empty conduits to the telephone closets on each floor.

LOADING DOCK AND TRASH HANDLING

The minimum off-street loading requirement is specified by code, which is more often than not excessive unless the building has unusually heavy requirements. Many cities now require that all truck maneuvering be completely on-site. The code breaks down the types of usage and their respective requirements by office, retail and services, commercial and industrial, hotel and motel, bar and restaurant, etc. (Except with special waivers, loading facilities must be provided on the same lot as the use.) Where possible the dock should have direct access from the street, and the truck berth itself may be largely outside of cover, where permitted. There is wide disagreement over the necessity of having dock levelers at the truck dock—the author's view is that most trucks that handle heavy items have their own leveling systems, and the extra costs of the raised dock and levelers are unnecessary.

If a ramp is required, the minimum width should be 10'0" if straight, and 12'0" wide with a minimum radius of 40'0". Two-way ramps should be double the single-ramp widths.

Generally the first berth, and 40% of the total required off-street berths, must be of a medium or large size (but never larger than the largest truck size permitted on the streets in the vicinity of the building during normal hours). Larger trucks can be scheduled at appropriate off-hours and access the building from the street in a manner approved by property management. Turning capacity must be provided for the largest size truck. Typical sizes of various truck berths are:

- Large space must be at least 11'0" wide, 55'0" long and 14'0" in height
- Medium space must be at least 11'0" wide, 35'0" long and 13'0" in height
- Small size spaces for vans and pickups must have a height of not less than 7'6", and either a length of not less than 25'0" with a width of not less than 8'0", or a length of not less than 20'0" with a width of not less than 10'0"

In some jurisdictions, buildings with a high number of required off-street spaces are permitted to provide anywhere from 15% to 40% of the requirement from the street.

A study performed in Dallas in the 1980s provided the following interesting actual activity for office building loading.

DALLAS LOADING DOCK STUDY

2.0 stops/day/10,000 rsf of office space
7.0 stops/day/10,000 rsf feet of retail and trade
1.2 stops/day/10,000 rsf feet of hotel

Peak hour demand = $\dfrac{\text{Daily demand} \times 1.25}{6}$

Average dwell time = 15 minutes

Number of berths actually needed for an office building:

Berths Actually Required =

$$\dfrac{2 \times 1.25}{6} \times \dfrac{\text{Net Rentable Area}}{10,000} \times \dfrac{1}{4}$$

Actual proportion of total usage was 60% by vans and pickups, the remainder by larger trucks

Adjacent storage areas are desirable for buildings with over 300,000 rsf.

Trash handling should be provided at the dock by either compaction or non-compacted containers based on estimated usage, frequency of pickup and requirements of the waste removal contractor. The contractor normally provides these containers as they match the hauling equipment. The containers should be convenient to the freight elevators, and have the availability of a drain and hose bibb. Some buildings with restaurant facilities provide sealed liquid containers, refrigerated garbage storage, and/or can-wash rooms, but these should not be necessary with daily trash pickup.

Security is a major issue at or near the truck dock. The entrance doors/gates should be lockable and observable, at least by closed circuit television. When the dock area is not supervised by an attendant or security officer, all doors from the dock into the building should be locked and observed from a central point. Larger buildings provide a small dock office with a dock manager who has visual control of the entire dock area.

Many smaller suburban buildings cannot justify an internal loading dock and just use a designated external area adjacent to building entrance for deliveries. In such cases the Development Officer should consult with Property Management to determine a satisfactory method of ingress and egress for materials, furniture and tools to facilitate their movement and minimize damage. Property Management should also advise as to the preferred location for a trash storage and recycle facility, and how the movement of the trash can be best accommodated. This area should be screened from normal viewing.

MAINTENANCE STORAGE

There must be a reasonable amount of space provided for the storage of maintenance and construction materials, supplies and tools. Where a loading dock is provided, that is most likely the best location. Otherwise, available space must be found in a penthouse, basement area, odd areas in the core, under the stairs at the lowest level, in the corners of the parking structure inaccessible by cars, or by enclosing one or two parking spaces on a lower parking deck.

PARKING

On-site parking is required for virtually all office buildings by code and, even more important, it is a major marketing requirement for a successful project. More often than not, the marketing requirements will govern, although some jurisdictions have a maximum ratio of spaces in order to promote public transportation.

Since the area required for parking is frequently greater than the building area (almost always so in suburban markets), it is essential that the Development Officer thoroughly review the requirements and the efficiency of the parking design to avoid excess costs.

The construction cost of the parking facility is a function of the square feet of parking structure, or paved surface area, required per car multiplied by the construction cost per square foot times the number of cars. The efficiency of a parking facility is normally the result of the length of the parking aisle, any columns that affect the layout efficiency, and the length of any access roads or ramps. In other words, the longer the service aisle, the higher the efficiency, and columns can interfere with efficiency by causing parking space dimensions to be less than optimal.

Many inefficient parking structures require over 400 sf/car, while very efficient layouts can require as little as 280 sf/car. A more common allocation in an efficient structure is 300 to 320 sf per car. When one recognizes that the unit cost of construction will not vary appreciably between efficient and inefficient structures, cost penalties for inefficiency become obvious. Parking areas beneath an office tower are always less efficient than in a free-standing facility, since the overall economics dictate that the column spacing must satisfy the office tower first, rather than the garage.

As discussed in Chapter 18, the results of the traffic study and requirements of the local jurisdiction set many constraints on the location and design of a parking facility, such as permissible curb cut locations, turning and stacking lanes, signalization, left turn prohibitions and other limitations.

The author recommends a parking consultant be used in the design of parking structures. There are so many variables it is better not to rely solely on the architect or structural engineer. Based on the number of stalls and site constraints, it is normal for a parking consultant to prepare three or four, and frequently five or six, alternative layouts from which the architect and Development Officer may select the features that best satisfy the project's objectives. The most basic alternative types, each of which has many variations, are:

- Flat deck structures accessed by external or internal straight speed ramps or an external circular access ramp.

- Structures several parking modules wide (see parking module diagram at the end of the chapter) with one module serving as a one-way ramp up and another a one-way ramp down. Note that ramps upon which cars are parked should not have a grade exceeding 6%, and preferably not exceeding 5%.

- Structures several parking modules wide with one module serving as a two-way ramp for up and down circulation with the other modules flat. The grade limitation above applies.

One-way entrance ramps, if straight, should be 12 feet wide if there are walls, and 10 feet wide without walls. Two-way ramps should be 24 feet wide with walls, and 22 feet wide if there are no walls. Straight speed ramps may have grades up to 15%, although some are steeper. For curved ramps, the minimum radius should be 30 feet to the inside of the ramp, the grade usually limited to 13%. For one-way traffic, the lane width should be 15 feet at the minimum radius. For two-way traffic with a separator, the inside lane should be 15 feet wide at the minimum radius and the outside can be 13 feet or 14 feet wide.

The two most commonly used structural types are flat slab and the post-tensioned slab. Precast "T's" have lost favor due to a tendency toward leakage, difficulty maintaining even cambers, being bulky to transport and not adaptable to special conditions.

In flat slab systems the columns must be located carefully in relation to the stall widths so as to incur the least amount of wasted space in order to maintain the area per stall at the lowest possible value, but it always causes some lost efficiency. In addition, in most cases two out of three parkers must park next to a column. When the layout involves both standard and compact spaces further inefficiency occurs, as repetitive column spacing will not efficiently accommodate both. This construction type does have the advantage of lower slab-to-slab heights and slightly narrower parking modules, which can reduce construction costs, particularly in subsurface locations. The recommended slab-to-slab height for flat slab is 9'0" to maintain the 7'0" clear height and good signage visibility for the typical deck and 10'2" for handicap vans. It is possible to reduce this to 8'6" on the typical, but signage becomes more difficult to place and in large structures it begins to have an uncomfortable feel.

The post-tensioned system creates a clear span across the parking module, increasing the space efficiency by having no impact on stall spacing, but frequently has a slightly higher unit construction cost. The post-tensioned structure permits unlimited striping changes between full size and compact cars over the years.

The slab-to-slab height for a post-tensioned parking structure is normally 10'0" or 10'2" for the typical deck to maintain 7'0" clear, and 11'4" on the entry floor in order to provide 8'2" clear access for handicap vans. When there is entry on more than one level, some jurisdictions require the handicap van clearance be maintained at each such level.

The location of the ingress/egress points must be carefully studied so they promote a smooth flow of traffic by providing turning and stacking room both internally and externally. In addition, their placement can affect the efficiency of parking space layout—usually the most efficient entry point is directly in line with a traffic aisle.

The number of ingress/egress points will directly affect the efficiency of traffic flow at the rush hours. In an office building parking structure the majority of parkers are tenants. When there is a charge for parking, the control system for tenants is usually actuated by the security cards (refer to Chapter 27) that are used for building access. Where more than one entry point is required, it is normal practice to provide only one cashier and to direct all exiting paying customers to that point while tenants can use any exit. It is frequently beneficial to have a third entry lane at the point served by the cashier that can be reversible for ingress during the morning rush hour, and out in the evening. In this manner tenants are not held up by payment transactions.

An emerging trend in the control of parking facilities is the automatic vehicle identification technology, which will be widely used in future parking applications. The AVI system uses radio frequency to detect a readable transponder attached to a vehicle as it passes by a system reader. These systems, which have been in use for some years on certain tollways, will greatly accelerate the ingress to and egress from the facility.

Stall sizes vary between a small car and a standard size car. Each jurisdiction has its own code requirement as to the minimum required and maximum permitted percentage of small cars, and frequently specifies the minimum size for each—preventing an efficient "one size fits all" solution. Remember, codes require the owner to stripe and label small car spaces, but only the owner is required to police the activity and there is rarely, if ever, any action taken for parking a standard car in a small space. The number of handicap spaces is always required by code and must be located at the most convenient point. Normally there must be one handicap van space for each eight handicap spaces. The number of required handicap spaces virtually always exceeds the usage.

The trend to small cars started after the oil shock in the 1970s and increased rapidly, until they reached a peak of 58% of car sales in 1986. Since then, oil became more plentiful and gasoline more reasonably priced, and the rate has settled back to well under 50% of annual sales. Small cars now constitute about 35% to 40% of the cars on the road, varying somewhat by community. There is now an accelerating reverse trend toward the purchase of utility vehicles, minivans and light trucks, but it has yet to have a significant impact on the design size of a large car stall, as the majority of these vehicles fit within that space. The main impact of this size reversal trend is to use less compact spaces where permitted.

While almost every jurisdiction has a requirement for a certain percentage of small cars, and it does cost the developer less to provide them, several factors lead us to recommend the use of "averaged sized" or "one size fits all" parking spaces, where permitted by code:

- Many drivers of small cars park in standard spaces
- Many drivers of large cars park in small car spaces
- Policing of the space usage is difficult and nonproductive
- Over 60% of the small cars sold are near the top of the small-car size range
- Over 50% of the large cars sold are near the bottom of the large-car size range

Practice has shown that the type of use significantly affects parking space design criteria. It is recommended that all-day parkers be provided with at least 20" for door opening clearance, normal visitors with somewhat more space and retail-type parkers with approximately 28" for door opening clearance.

The Parking Consultants Council of the National Parking Association has compiled data on vehicle sizes and prepared recommendations for various parking stall sizes as shown in the table below. While this data is professionally recommended and provides a basis for general planning, each city and county have their own requirements that must be followed.

The council has compiled the Parking Module Dimension diagram, Figure 24-1, for one-size-fits-all spaces for use where permitted by code. This diagram shows the interrelationship between many variables in module width for an assumed mix of 40% compact cars and 60% large cars. The stall sizes are calculated on the basis of the average car size being the 85th percentile, i.e., 84% of the cars in each category are smaller than the design car. LT stands for long-term parkers and ST is for short-

CAR AND PARKING STALL SIZES

Stall Width—Various Parkers

	Car Size	Retail	Visitor	All Day	Stall Length
Small Car	5'7" x 14'8"	8'0"	7'6"	7'4"	15'6"
Standard	6'6" x 18'0"	8'10"	8'6"	8'2"	18'8"
Combined (one size fits all)	NA	8'6"	8'2"	7'10"	17'4"

PARKING MODULE DIMENSIONS
FOR MINIMUM COMFORT STALLS
ONE SIZE FITS ALL - 40% COMPACT/60% STANDARD

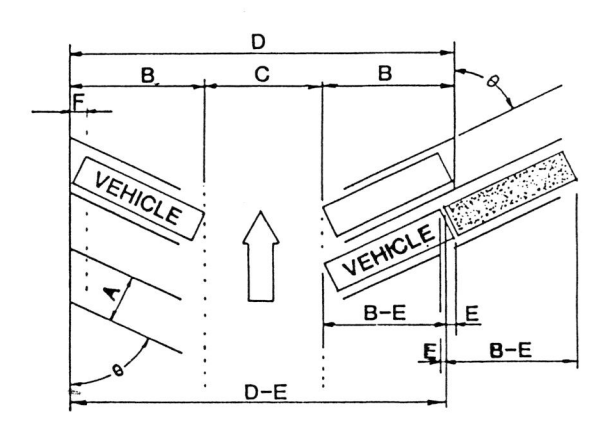

TABLE V-4
Parking Module Dimensions

Angle ⊖	Minimum Stall Width (A) LT	Minimum Stall Width (A) ST	Vehicle Projection (B)	Aisle (C)	Typical Module (D)	Interlock Reduction (E)	Overhang (F)
0°	7'-11"	8'-3"	7'-7"	10'-0"	25'-2"	–	2'-0"
45°	7'-11"	8'-3"	17'-0"	12'-1"	46'-1"	2'-0"	2'-0"
50°	7'-11"	8'-3"	17'-8"	12'-6"	47'-10"	1'-10"	2'-0"
55°	7'-11"	8'-3"	18'-3"	13'-0"	49'-6"	1'-7"	2'-1"
60°	7'-11"	8'-3"	18'-5"	14'-0"	50'-10"	1'-4"	2'-2"
65°	7'-11"	8'-3"	18'-8"	14'-11"	52'-3"	1'-2"	2'-3"
70°	7'-11"	8'-3"	18'-9"	15'-9"	53'-3"	0'-11"	2'-4"
75°	7'-11"	8'-3"	18'-8"	17'-3"	54'-7"	0'-8"	2'-5"
90°	7'-11"	8'-3"	17'-6"	22'-4"	57'-4"	–	2'-7"

NOTES:

Module width is based on the module being bounded by walls.

Module width may be reduced by the interlock adjustment factor if the module interlocks with the next module in both directions.

Module width may be reduced by the overhang adjustment if the cars may overhang on both sides and there is a restraint barrier.

Module width may be reduced by 3" for every 1" of additional stall width.

Column and light pole encroachments into the module may be ignored if the combined encroachment on both sides is 2'0" or less. The encroachment will occur in less than 30% of the spaces, and 84% of the cars will be shorter than the space.

For columns between stalls, or walls next to a stall, add 10" of width to that stall.

To provide greater parking comfort, you may add 4" to 6" to the stall width and add 2' to 3' to the module width.

Figure 24-1

term. In the 90° layout the aisle is sized for two-way traffic. Similar tables are available for different code requirements from the council, and from most local jurisdictions. This data can assist the Development Officer in roughly estimating dimensions required for a parking facility.

Many consultants recommend designing for 90° parking with two-way traffic and all full size spaces, where space permits, to obtain the most flexible structure over time. When this approach is used with clear span construction, spaces can be added when needed by re-striping. Some jurisdictions require oversized stalls of 9'0" or 10'0" width and oversized parking module widths of 65 feet.

Practice has shown that the parking facility should be sized for the desired (or required) number of spaces, with the estimated 15–30% float providing space for the daily parkers. Because reserved parking reduces this flexibility for oversell of the float, it should be minimized to the extent that marketing pressures permit. The remainder of the spaces may be offered to tenants as undesignated spaces, or licenses to use an undesignated space.

Separate visitor parking areas, exclusive of a few short-term spaces near the entrance, should be avoided as this eliminates the benefit of using the float to obtain revenue from unused spaces already allocated to tenants.

Where reserved spaces are requested and granted, the monthly fee, if any, should be a minimum of 25–35% greater than an undesignated space. Whenever the market permits, a parking facility should charge a market rate for parking. When charging for parking, or otherwise controlling the ingress and egress, the gates and ticket-booth islands should be carefully designed to minimize confusion and delays. The control system should be carefully coordinated with the building security system for control and ease of tenant access. The equipment pads, islands, power and communications conduit should be incorporated early in the planning rather than added later.

When designing a project at a time when the market does not permit charging for parking, it is wise to lay out lanes, islands and install the conduit to facilitate adding the equipment later when charging becomes feasible. This is consistent with the lease strategy of limiting free parking to the initial term only.

Clear and highly visible signage to the exits and other parking sections, and to the stairs and elevators in a parking structure can greatly improve the flow of vehicles and pedestrians. All graphics, or architectural signage, should be carefully planned and coordinated, as discussed in Chapter 30.

RECOMMENDED PARKING LIGHTING LEVELS (in foot-candles)

	Average	Minimum
Parking garage		
Entrance/exit/elevator areas	30	10
Ramps/aisles/corridors	5-10	3-4
Stairwells	20-50	7-15
Open parking lot	3	1

In some jurisdictions the minimum lighting level is 1½ foot-candles

Proper lighting is necessary in parking structures and parking lots. Recommended lighting levels in foot-candles are shown below.

In the relatively rare cases where it is not possible to build all of the necessary parking spaces, or where it is discovered in a completed project that there are too few spaces to satisfy tenant requirements, valet parking can be a solution. Depending upon the layout, aisle width and other factors, valet parking can increase the capacity by 15% to 25%, most often in the range of 20%.

Achieving this additional capacity adds significantly to the cost of operating the facility. Some of the additional cost factors, the unit cost of which will vary with location, are:

- One parking attendant is required for approximately every 25 cars.

- The extensive personnel requirement often requires a full-time manager.

- While a normal office building facility requires only one cashier, regardless of the number of ingress/egress points, for valet parking one cashier will normally be required for every 200 to 300 cars. Although a cashier can handle four transactions per minute (240 per hour), staffing must be higher to avoid excessive delays that can create dissatisfaction from the tenants due to the uneven flow that will occur during the peak hour when 60% of the exiting traffic occurs.

- Damage claims can be a significant increased cost. In a 237-car facility in Oakland this cost currently runs about $1500 per month.

Central Facilities Design

CASE STUDY

MAIN MECHANICAL ROOM

The chillers and cooling towers are located on the roof of the structure. While there is a basic preference for the chillers to be on grade, there is no basement and no reasonable location near the parking structure. The chemical treatment equipment and safety eye bubbler were located near the cooling towers. The water heater room is located in the first floor core, and the fan rooms are located on each floor.

ELECTRICAL DISTRIBUTION ROOM

The electric service is from the San Diego Gas and Electric main line in El Camino Real through their 12kv to 480/277-volt transformer located adjacent to the parking structure. From the transformer the service goes to the first floor main electrical room containing the meters and the 480/277v, 4,000 amp main switchboards that provide the building distribution. The room has outside access for SDG&E. The lighting and power panels are 480/277v with step-down transformers throughout the building for the 120/208v power.

COMMUNICATIONS ROOM

The communications room is located in the center core of the first floor. The conduits for cable and telephone risers extend upward from this room.

MAIL ALCOVE

The mail alcove is located in front of the communications room. It contains the tenant mailboxes, two pay telephones and outgoing mailboxes for the overnight couriers.

HEALTH CLUB

A 1,000 square foot health club is located on the first floor. It will incorporate shower rooms for both men and women, with two showers, a lavatory and lockers in each. The equipment has not yet been selected. The club is defined as common area, so that it is included in the rentable area.

LIFE SAFETY EQUIPMENT

The diesel-driven fire pump, with the fire water storage tank and the emergency generator are located at the west side of the office building surface parking area, near the parking structure. The fireman's control room with the Fire Alarm and Control Panel (FACP) is accessed through the freight elevator lobby on the first floor.

A late change was required during the city permit process to relocate the emergency transfer switch into a separate room away from the remainder of the electrical equipment. No one on the team has heard of such a requirement before.

At one point in the design it was intended to locate the emergency generator, fire pump and fire water reservoir in the parking structure—but they were moved out to the area along the north wall of the structure to conserve parking spaces and to reduce pipe and cabling runs to the building. They were relocated again to the area west of the office building surface parking, as their weight put too great a surcharge on the soil-nailed retaining wall.

LOADING DOCK

The loading dock area consists of two outside berths that are located at the northwest corner of the building, between the building and the surface parking, just before the parking control gates. It will have ready access to the west entrance of the building. Semi-trailers will have to be scheduled for after hours delivery, and will be required to turn around at the entrance circle adjacent to El Camino Real and back into the berths.

TRASH RETAINAGE

The trash and recycle facility with a combined area of 17' x 43' is located adjacent to the north wall of the parking structure adjacent to the SDG&E transformer room, facing the surface parking area.

MAINTENANCE STORAGE

A maintenance storage area will be constructed in the parking structure where the right angle rows of stalls meet and form a dead corner. Dead space beneath the first floor stairs will also be used.

PARKING

As is frequently the case, parking turned out to be a major issue—satisfying the market and code requirements as cost effectively as possible, while satisfying the seller's requirements, the city and two different shared uses.

The initial total parking requirement, based on the market-driven need for four stalls per 1,000 gsf for a 150,000 sf office building, one per room for 250 hotel rooms, less an estimated reduction for "shared parking" resulted in a little less than 800 spaces. As the opportunity occurred to increase the size of the office building, and it became obvious that the hotel would have banquet facilities, the requirement was adjusted upward to the range of 900 spaces. Subtracting the estimated potential of 100 surface parking spaces yielded a parking structure with about 800 spaces.

The only logical traffic access points are the existing shared entrance with Executive Center Del Mar on El Camino Real and in the lower southeast corner from Valley Centre Drive, which is 29 feet lower in elevation. As discussed in Chapter 18, it was deemed more efficient to bring primarily surface parking, some office users and hotel guest vehicles in from El Camino Real, and the bulk of the office traffic from Valley Centre Drive.

The entrance from El Camino Real behind the office building primarily serves the plaza level of the structure as well as the surface parking. The second entrance point on the plaza level between the office building and the hotel is to facilitate parking of hotel guests cars, valet parkers or office visitors who could not find a short-term parking space in front of the building.

The author normally prefers a parking structure with a "one size fits all" stall size based on an average of about 60% large cars. The city of San Diego does not recognize this approach, so the structure was designed for a target of about 40% small car spaces. The parking module is 61'6" based on the San Diego standards for two-way traffic for large cars. All of the surface spaces were designed for full-size cars.

The early siting studies had assumed the office building and the hotel would be at right angles to each other, and the parking structure would be a three-level garage on a more or less triangular site. The parking consultant's studies indicated that the parking efficiency with that approach would yield a structure requiring approximately 340 square feet per stall. He recommended rotating the office building about 22° one way or the other so that the parking structure could be rectangular, as shown in Figures 15-1 and 15-2 in Chapter 15. This change would require four levels, but would permit a structure requiring no more than 310 square feet per stall, and probably less. The scheme in Figure 15-2 was selected, not only because of the parking efficiency, but it was believed to actually enhance the siting composition. This design for the parking structure was "L"-shaped, with two levels below the surface parking located behind the office building. The B-1 level, shown as Figure 24-2, was typical of the proposed below grade levels.

The "L"-shaped structure had some cost penalties—there is more wall surface per stall, so the scheme was reanalyzed for improvements. It was determined that the best solution was to add another half deck on the main section of the structure.

This refinement of the parking structure omitted the subsurface right angle, or "L", portion and replaced it with surface parking and a partial fifth level. The additional level above grade was much less expensive than the former solution. There were two variations for the fifth level—one where it was lengthwise on the opposite side from the building, and the other was along the short side of the structure adjacent to the hotel. The latter scheme

OPTION 5   B-1 LEVEL
                  248 SPACES

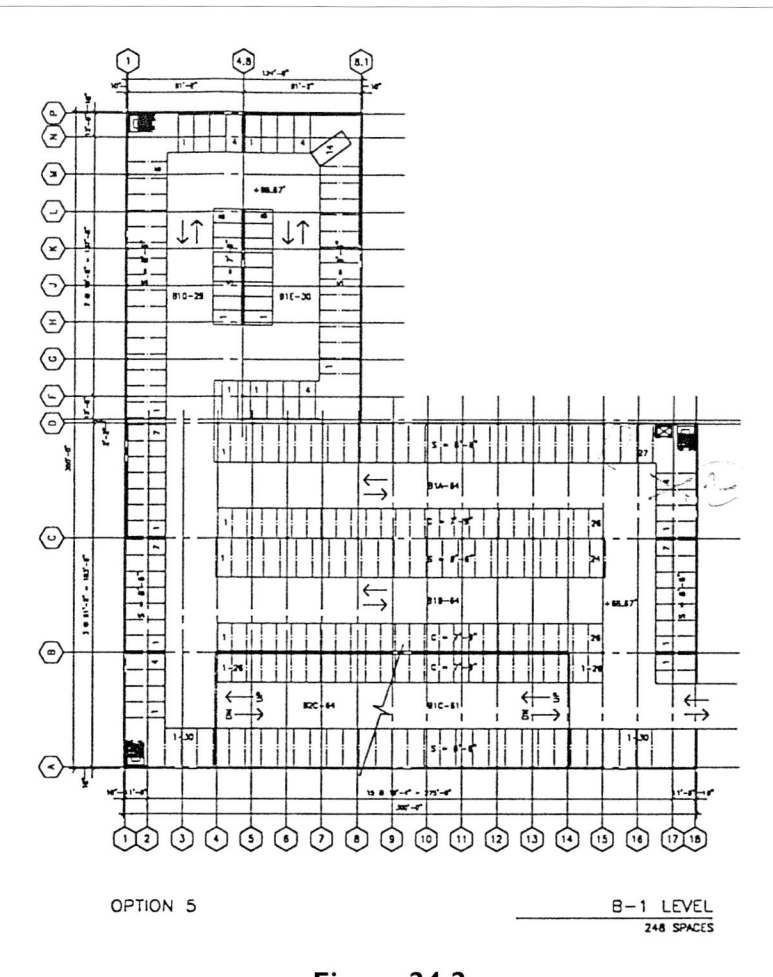

Figure 24-2

was selected, which yields 809 spaces at approximately 303 sf per stall.

The proposed fifth level adjacent to the hotel was almost the same height as the ballroom. It was intended to adjust the façade to read in a complementary manner. As discussed under Permitting in Chapter 7, responding to objections by Pardee and the Carmel Valley Planning Board concerning the amount of structure exposed to the highway, the second upper level was eliminated and three alternative below-grade solutions (see table below) to replace the spaces were evaluated, all at considerable extra cost.

A few extra spaces were needed, and as the hotel was still adding some rooms, the office building might grow a little more and there might be a requirement for some spaces for equipment and maintenance. The first scheme above was considered to provide insufficient spaces, and the other two were priced.

PARKING STRUCTURE ALTERNATIVES

	Structure	Surface	Surplus /(Shortfall)
One lower level in "L" shape	800	56	(29)
Two lower levels in "L" shape	869	56	40
No subsurface in "L", but new one-half floor at B-3 level	867	56	38

The scheme with the two floors in the "L" configuration, which had been evaluated before, appeared to be the least costly. After initially selecting it, a structural evaluation revealed some potential seismic issues with the design, and there was some difficulty obtaining the proper dimensions for the fire truck loop without constructing the deck to carry fire truck loading or building a very tall (up to about 18 feet) retaining wall on the west side of the surface parking area. The creation of a nearly full B-3 level then became the preferred solution.

After some fine tuning of the design, reducing the floor to floor height to 10'0" on the B-1 and B-3 levels (the plaza and B-2 levels must remain at 11'4" to satisfy the 8'2" clearance in the handicap code) and raising the overall site grade for the three structures by about two feet, the price of the preferred solution indicated a savings of about $80,000 less than the "L"-shaped scheme.

The final design consisted of three parking modules, or bays, running in an east-west direction. The northern and center bays were flat, and the southern bay was ramped. All parking was right-angle and the aisles were two-way. The layout is for about 40% small-cars, with small car rows opposite large-car rows to minimize structure size. The structure has two entrances and exits on the plaza level, one on the west side of the office building and one between the hotel and the office building, with another entrance at the B-2 level from Valley Centre Drive. All levels with entrances were 8'2" clear as mentioned above for handicap access.

The parking requirement was revised several times to accommodate changes in the office area and the hotel rooms, as well as the addition of, and size modifications to, banquet and dining facilities, but ended up at our early assumption of about 900 cars. There were two separate calculations as to the parking requirements using the shared parking. The final recommended capacity by the parking consultant based on shared parking was for 899 spaces.

The final shared parking calculation by the traffic consultant, which was based on four spaces per 1000 gross square foot of office building and the San Diego code requirements for hotels, adjusted to a shared-parking basis, at 10AM on a week day was for 916 spaces.

SHARED PARKING CALCULATIONS

Parking Consultant

Office building @ 172,500 gsf	172.5 x 4	=	690
Hotel: 284 guest rooms	284 x 0.45 x 0.70	=	89
Meeting rooms	9660 sf / 2 /35 @ 2 / car	=	69
Dining—3000 sf	170 seats x 0.85 x 0.40 / 2.25/car	=	26
Employees	50 @ 2 / car	=	25
Total spaces			899

Traffic Consultant

Office building @ 172,500 gsf	172.5 x 4	=	690
Hotel: 284 guest rooms	284 x 0.45	=	128
Banquet space	9660 / 80	=	98
Total spaces			916

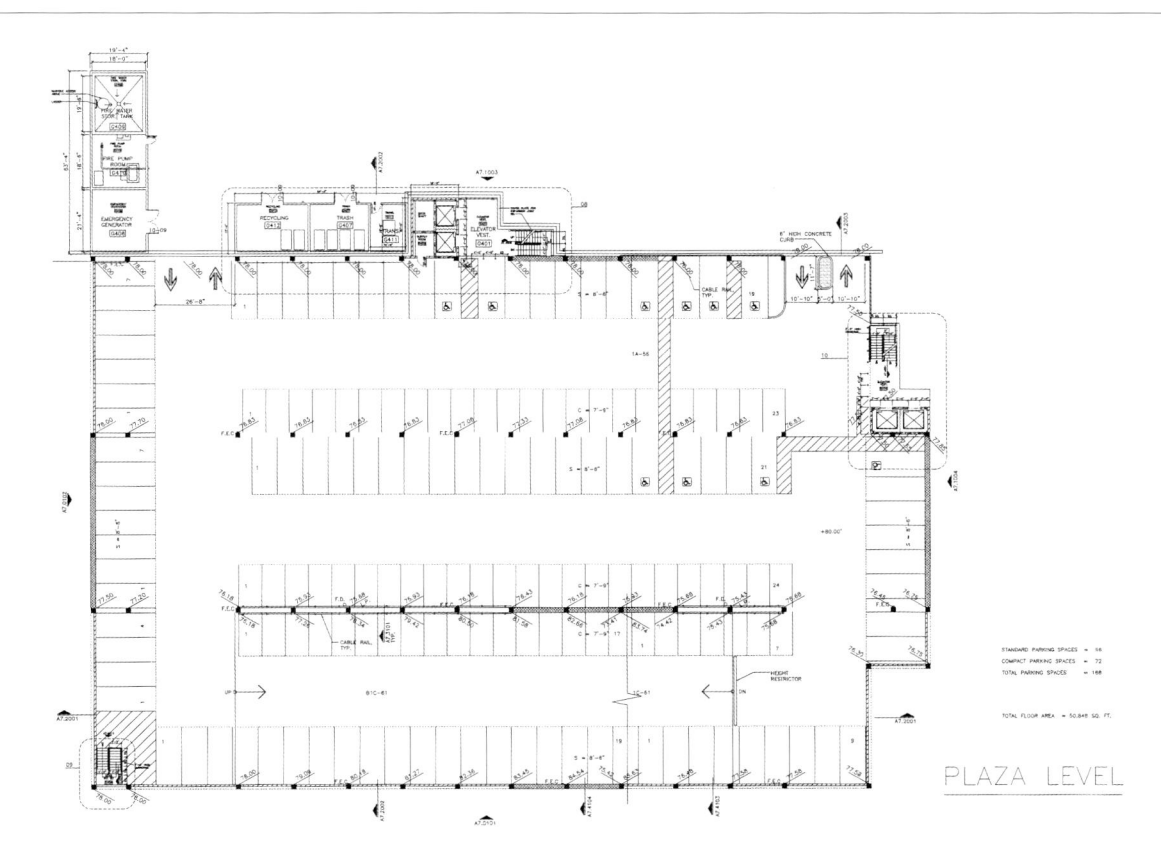

Figure 24-3

The number recommended by the parking consultant was accepted, but it was decided to try for 10 to 15 additional spaces for a higher comfort level.

Several new issues arose. The pool deck of the hotel was deemed to be too restrictive for Marriott's standards, and needed to be expanded. Additional space was provided by relocating the parking structure's Valley Centre Drive entrance from the east side to the south side. There was still insufficient space for their desired deck, and to achieve the required twenty-foot building separation. To accomplish this objective required eliminating one 18'6" bay from the length of the parking structure and extending B-3 to a full level to make up for those lost spaces. This increased the cost and decreased the parking efficiency slightly, as the aisles are shorter. Marriott still wanted additional space, so it was agreed they could extend their deck as far as they wished into the legal separation space. This did not cause a lot line issue because that portion of the deck was on grade and could be removed at any time.

Figure 24-3 shows the final design for the plaza level with its two entrance/exits (and also indicates the office building service areas). Figure 24-4 shows the B-1 level. The second floor, B-2 and B-3 levels are identical to B-1, except that B-2 has an entrance/exit in the upper right hand corner.

The lower levels of the parking structure are fully sprinklered and mechanically ventilated as required. The ventilation fans are actuated by CO_2 sensors. The plaza level has sufficient open area at the perimeter so that ventilation is not needed.

The lighting on the top deck of the structure consisted of eight double low-pressure sodium fixtures on 20-foot poles. Each fixture has two 90-watt lamps. Four poles were located along each structural line between the three parking bays and provide an average lighting level of 2+ foot-candles and a minimum of 0.2 foot-candles. (See Chapter 18 for further discussion.)

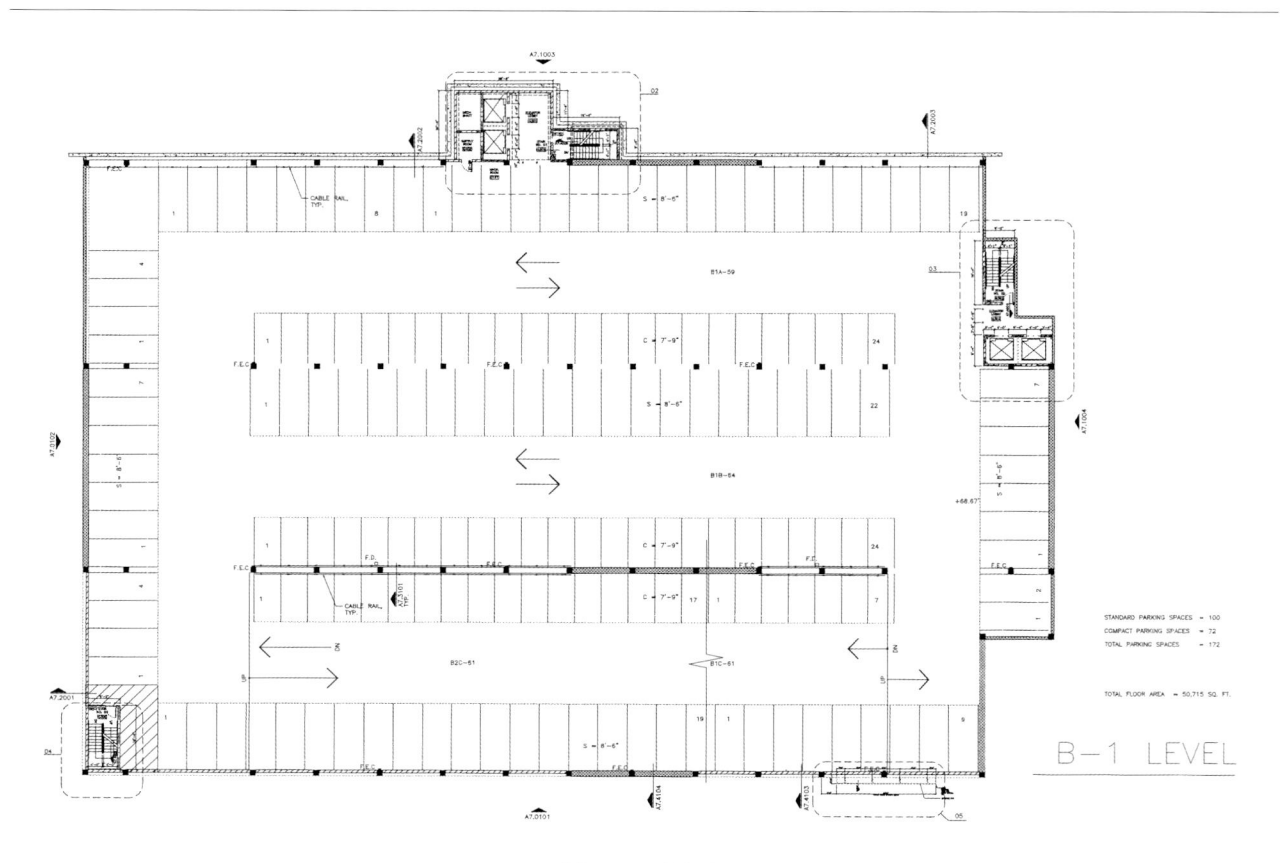

Figure 24-4

The typical lower levels of the structure have two 8-foot fixtures with four 4-foot fluorescent lamps in each structural bay, mounted on each side of the driving aisle. They provide an average of 8 foot-candles at the driving aisles and one foot-candle at the darkest point on the floor. Additional fixtures are installed at the ingress/egress points to obtain 25+/- foot-candles.

Thirteen-inch round 26-watt vandal proof CFL fixtures are installed in the ceilings of the elevator lobbies and in the stairwells.

The preliminary design incorporated a two hydraulic-elevator bank. Agreement could not be reached with the hotel upon a satisfactory location, since guests of one of the facilities or the other would have to cross traffic lanes of a main entrance to the parking structure in order to reach their destination. Two separate locations were finally agreed upon—one oriented toward the office building, and one toward the hotel. The elevator consultant established that this was inadequate and the service was increased to two hydraulic elevators in each bank, as more fully discussed in Chapter 21.

The CC&Rs, as well as the Substantial Conformance Determination required that all parking be offered free to tenants and guests. When the hotel developer's cost increases created a problem achieving an acceptable return, with Prentiss' concurrence, they initiated a request through Pardee to change the CC&Rs to permit paid parking. The CC&Rs were changed, and the city has been requested to modify the Substantial Conformance Determination to permit paid parking. Even if approved, Prentiss will not change its current policy with regard to free parking for office use during the initial term of the leases, but has reserved the right to charge for parking in the future. Since Prentiss would not be participating in the initial revenue, the hotel will pay all installation and operating costs relative to paid parking. All controls and procedures must be approved by Prentiss to avoid inconvenience to tenants and their guests.

Since the paid parking issue was not fully resolved prior to completion of the parking structure working drawings, it was decided to incorporate lanes and islands to permit efficient operation as a fee facility, and provide conduit to all potential booth and gate locations that will permit installation at a later date.

When going through the final parking layouts during the working drawings, satisfying the handicap requirements and the San Diego tree and landscape ordinance, several ways had to be investigated to retain the required number of spaces.

The ability to provide additional parking spaces was extremely limited. Adding an additional parking deck above grade was prohibited, as Pardee and the planning board would not approve it, and additional spaces further below grade would be into the water table and would be cost prohibitive. Expanding the structure in the east/west direction was not possible, since it had already been shortened by 18'6" to accommodate the hotel deck and the required building separation at the east end, and the west end abutted a city restricted drainage and freeway easement. There was no room to expand in the north/south direction except for the additional below grade right angle addition that, as discussed before, would be cost prohibitive due to the seismic and fire truck issues previously considered.

The San Diego tree ordinance requires trees "in the parking area" be planted so that no car is more than 30 feet from a tree, and each tree must be in a 40 square foot planting bed. In addition, there must be a minimum of 5% landscaped area per total vehicle use area (VUA) and the landscape and planting grids must align with the parking stall layout. In the surface parking areas the 30-foot condition could have easily been satisfied by planting trees immediately adjacent to the parking area, but the initial interpretation was the city would not consider them "in the parking area."

The designers initially attempted to satisfy the ordinance by creating four-foot-wide planting beds between parking spaces that caused a net loss of 12 spaces. Submission of a design where a diamond extension into the parking area with 6-foot sides would be created to meet the "in" requirement, while the adjacent planting beds would meet the requirement of 40-square-foot planting beds was suggested. Four spaces in the hotel area could be added back, but the 5% rule prevented doing so in the office surface area.

Upon review with the city landscape planners, they agreed to accept trees directly bordering the surface parking lots as meeting the "in the parking area" requirement. Additionally, where trees were required in the center of the surface lot behind the office building, the city accepted 6'3" square-sided planting beds, rotated 45°, between the adjacent rows of stalls, which resulted in not losing any spaces.

As mentioned earlier, the parking structure consisted of three parking bays running east and west. The southern bay was ramped and the other two were flat. The architectural design components for the parking structure consisted of:

- The retaining wall structure that encompassed the central portion of each side would be reinforced concrete

- The edges of the deck were pulled back from the column faces to permit the columns to appear free-standing as a major visual element

- Expanded metal was indicated on the open areas of the structure facing the office building and hotel to facilitate coverage by vegetation

- Cable rails were used as retainers for the cars

- The elevator and stair towers, as well as the support facilities for the office building that are located along the north wall of the structure, were two types of split block—one rough and one saw cut

- Trees and bushes surround the structure and trees were planted in 4-foot square pots on the top deck

Pardee had retained design approval rights for all structures under the Purchase and Sale Agreement, and were very displeased with the design presentation on the parking structure. They rejected the use of cable rails, objected to the corner of the upper deck that extended back over the ramp (which added 13 cars, but made the structure appear bulkier), believed that they had been promised that the B-2 level would be below grade (i.e., the earth bermed to that level), wanted the ramped bay to be in the middle or north side of the structure instead of on the south side, and requested generous use of granite panels. Basically, they did not want the parking structure to look like one.

The budget prohibited consideration of using granite on the parking structure. Prentiss declined to relocate the ramped bay. It could not be located on the north side as that would interfere with the elevator system. To locate the ramp in the middle would reduce the search efficiency of the garage and reduce the perception of safety, since the ramped middle bay would significantly reduce visibility. It would also create more complexity with the post-tensioned concrete decks.

After several meetings with the Pardee representatives, and there was no further time to negotiate, agreement was reached to modify the parking structure at a cost of about $150,000, as follows:

- Replace the cable rails with split face masonry at the outside ramp edges

- Berm the earth up 10 feet on the south side and partially on the sloping east and west sides, and plant them with Hopseed bushes that have a normal height of about 15 feet

- Remove the corner of the upper deck, and lose the 13 spaces

The resolution of the parking structure design was far more complicated and difficult than the office building. Its shape, size and design were constantly being determined by external factors—the hotel's needs, the city, Pardee and difficult structural issues.

The Land Purchase Agreement required that a minimum of the average number of spaces determined from the studies by the parking and traffic consultants be provided, or a total parking requirement of 908 spaces. At the time the land sale was ready to be closed the parking structure and site had not yet even submitted for a building permit, and the count could vary considerably based on city determinations involving handicap and landscape issues. A modification to the agreement was negotiated that changed our obligation to the provision of between 890 and 915 spaces.

The final count was 903 spaces—10 in front of the office building, 43 for the hotel, 51 behind the building and 799 in the parking structure. Broken down functionally—there were 485 full-size spaces, 388 compacts, 27 handicap stalls and 3 handicap van spaces. The final efficiency of the parking structure was 308 square feet per space.

MECHANICAL and BUILDING MANAGEMENT SYSTEMS

This chapter will try to demystify the seemingly complex subjects of Mechanical and Building Management Systems. A general discussion covers an overview of the HVAC systems and their importance to tenant satisfaction and the economics of the building. This is followed by specific discussion of the Design Criteria, Refrigeration Cycle Energy Savings, Air Distribution Systems, Interior Air Quality and Air Circulation, Humidification and Dehumidification, Filters, and Life Cycle Costing. Later in this chapter we discuss Plumbing Systems, Building Management Systems and Energy Budgets.

HEATING, VENTILATING AND AIR CONDITIONING SYSTEMS

The HVAC system is an extremely important part of the building from the standpoint of initial cost, operating expenses and tenant satisfaction. The Development Officer should pay close attention to the design criteria and the design of these systems. Among the reasons these systems deserve such close attention are:

- The system will amount to from 12% to 16% of the base building construction cost, depending on the scope of work installed as shell and core construction versus that included as TIs.

- The HVAC system can significantly impact the structural and architectural costs, and affect the building rentable/useable efficiency.

- HVAC systems represent as much as 40% to 50% of the annual operating and utility costs, and savings resulting from energy efficiency should drop directly to net income on re-leasing, even when not fully recovered initially.

- A good, well-controlled system is essential to personnel comfort, productivity and equipment operation—therefore, tenant satisfaction.

- Flexibility must be provided so that the office space may be adapted to various future uses.

- Sufficient outside air, even at minimal cooling conditions is important to addressing the perception, as well as the reality, of Indoor Air Quality (IAQ) and the sick building syndrome. Note, however, that providing additional air can create greater cooling and dehumidification requirements.

- Inadequate sound control can create a significant source of tenant dissatisfaction.

- The BOMA/ULI Office Tenant Survey Report, *What Office Tenants Want,* listed the desire for comfortable temperature, Indoor Air Quality, and noise control at the highest rating given in the survey. (Refer to Figure 4-3 in Chapter 4.)

It is a requirement in many jurisdictions, and good practice everywhere, to prepare an energy budget for every project. As described in detail at the end of this chapter, an energy budget correlates all of the factors that affect energy consumption and guides the necessary balanced judgments to be made early in the project regarding design conditions, building envelope thermal resistance, lighting, equipment and economizer cycles. In order to set an appropriate energy budget, it is necessary to have the engineers prepare a series of energy analyses during the schematic design phase, as initially recommended in Chapter 14. This assists in making the many first cost vs. operating cost decisions in relation to the market, the owner's desire with regard to long-term ownership benefits, and satisfying community concerns for ecologically sound sustainable design.

Some jurisdictions are now providing faster plan checks and lower permit fees for projects that are below the regulatory energy budget by a stipulated percentage.

The reader should recognize there is significant evidence that long-term energy shortages may well be a continuing problem over the next decade, and possibly longer. Electrical power plants are being shut down for failure to meet air quality standards, some hydroelectric dams are threatened by endangered species issues, and few new power plants have been constructed in the last decade, at least partially due to environmental and permitting issues. Continuing turbulence in the Mid-East and other oil-producing areas, combined with the growing energy consumption in developing countries, may well produce temporary, if not semi-permanent shortages of petroleum products that are increasingly used in newer power plants.

As energy consumption becomes more and more of a political and social issue, in addition to the long-term benefits determined through life-cycle cost analysis, all of the building's systems must be considered in greater depth—not just the mechanical and electrical systems. As you will see in this and other chapters, the overall systems analyses are extremely important.

Energy efficient design can start with the site planning where the solar orientation can be a significant factor. The building fenestration can be designed with appropriate shading to reduce solar load in the heat of the summer while introducing it during the colder months. Greater attention should be paid to the insulating value of the walls, glazing, and roof as well as solar heat gain coefficient of the glazing, as discussed in Chapter 20. In addition, as mentioned earlier, photovoltaic systems are being developed so that the fenestration surfaces may someday become solar energy collectors. Building mass may in certain circumstances become a factor in reducing peak loads through its energy storage, and motorized shading elements can insure the maximum reasonable amount of solar energy control. In other words, all of the building's components can work together to minimize energy consumption.

While the understanding of the long-range social and political goals is essential, the Development Officer is faced with a dilemma. Even though reduced operating costs may well dwarf initial cost premiums over a building's life, choosing long-range solutions whose costs cannot be fully recovered initially by projected operating savings will reduce the project's initial return. Some factors to keep in mind when addressing this issue are:

- If the initial leases are quoted on a gross basis, including all utilities, the initial benefit of operating cost savings may be taken into consideration, as they should positively affect the pro forma when balanced against the impact of the increased construction cost.

- When the operating costs are quoted separately, or if the utility costs are excluded from the gross rent, initial tenants are unlikely to give full, or even any, credence toward claims of energy savings in spite of engineering analyses, and thus the developer may obtain no benefit from the additional construction cost during the initial lease terms.

- As the leases turn over, and buildings compete on gross rental rates or proven operating costs, any benefit of reduced operating costs will accrue to the building owner.

The author's recommendation regarding this issue is, even when the full original cost benefit may not be recovered for the owner, to stay current with both the technology and political trends, and to **stretch as far as reasonably possible on the side of positive life-cycle costing** in order to have the most efficient building possible without excessively penalizing its initial economics.

There has been a trend toward designing the air conditioning systems in ways to provide tenants with more control over their interior environment for efficiency and for psychological reasons, such as:

- Smaller air distribution zones with convenient thermostats.

- Operable windows have become more in demand. While individual tenants may gain great satisfaction from this feature, the author has had no experience with how to control the central system efficiently with random window openings. It is believed there must be interlocking controls to shut off either a mixing box or diffuser when a window is opened.

Another concern of many tenants is convenience and ease of providing appropriate after hours or supplemental air conditioning. Some of the methods used are listed below.

- Local packaged air conditioning units located on each floor that can be controlled by an access card or a local control.

- Where there is a central system, localized fan rooms and one smaller, or "pony," chiller, which can be controlled by the tenant with an access card or other code, provides cooling on demand with appropriate charges, but without excessive cost.

- A central condenser water loop with individual small self-contained air conditioning units provided by the tenant can provide a great degree of flexibility, cost control and extra capacity where required.

- A variation is to use heat pumps that can be operated individually in conjunction with the condenser water loop.

There are seven objectives of a well-designed heating, ventilating and air conditioning system:

- Occupant comfort
- Provide fresh air and acceptable air movement
- Control humidity
- Remove internal heat load
- Counteract perimeter heating/cooling loads
- Provide flexibility and control
- Acceptable sound transmission

Air conditioning systems consist of several elements to provide the proper environmental systems for the building.

- Refrigeration system, which generates the chilled water that provides the cooling

- Condenser water system to remove the rejected heat from the chillers (except for air cooled units)

- Cooling tower system, which dissipates the heat from the condenser water into the atmosphere

- Central air distribution system, which provides the tempered air and/or outside air to the floors

- Floor air distribution system, which provides the proper amount of air at the right temperature to each controlled area

- Filtration units to remove particulate matter from the air

- Humidification (not normally provided in commercial office buildings) and dehumidification systems

- Individual floor or room controls and various types of mixing boxes and variable volume air valves

- Energy management system that controls the efficiency of the system operation

System Selection

System and equipment selection alternatives and their costs vary widely, and it is up to the Development Officer to ensure that all of the appropriate factors and assumptions are incorporated into the selection process. Only the Development Officer can determine the relative importance of the various factors that must be included in the analysis:

- Market expectations as to employee comfort and health
- First cost
- Flexibility
- Annual energy, operating and maintenance cost
- Political and social value of reduced energy consumption
- After-hour operating cost,
- Space utilization
- System life expectancy

As discussed in various chapters of this text, there are a wide range of systems, equipment and materials that are used with presumably acceptable results in some projects, and they result in a wide range of initial cost, operating cost, personal comfort, function and reliability. The alternatives for some of the various types of systems and equipment, rated from the lowest first cost to the highest, are:

- From packaged self-contained direct expansion (DX), air cooled rooftop units (usually limited to three stories in height), to packaged direct expansion units on each floor, to central centrifugal chillers
- Large zones for temperature control—to smaller flexible zones
- Electric reheat—to hydronic reheat—to double duct systems
- Minimum code outside air—to outside air economizers
- Maximum permitted air velocities—to lower air velocities, to minimize sound issues and provide for future load increases
- Minimum filtration—to the maximum reasonable filtration
- Dehumidification by passing air over the cooling coils—to desiccant dehumidification
- Standard motors and drives—to premium efficiency motors and variable frequency drives
- Single cooling tower cell and one set of pumps—to cells and pumps matched to each chiller
- Minimum acoustical treatment—to linings and sound traps to ensure a specified noise level
- From none to extensive heat recovery

The Development Officer, with a general knowledge of the systems, in conjunction with the mechanical engineer, will make the determination of the system selection and the quality to be designed into each element of the HVAC system in order to accomplish the project's objectives and requirements.

Design Criteria

Prior to the actual system selection, extensive engineering and economic analysis will consider the climate of the geographic location, utility competition and pricing schedules, the building orientation, energy codes, any unusual internal usage, building population, the estimated heat losses through the building envelope, and the energy efficiency objectives for the project. While there are many criteria for economic solutions, the criteria in the table on the next page are considered reasonably typical for mild climates. **The Development Officer should understand and be fully aware of all design criteria and assumptions used so that he can compare them with the assessment of the marketplace, the political values of the community, the project's overall long-term objectives and any commitments in the lease.**

Of particular concern are the building population, electrical loads and the air circulation assumptions. Some tenants are crowding up to ten persons per thousand square feet on a floor and are asking for 6 to 7 w/sf for power in addition to their lighting. If tenants require above normal loading, an analysis will be required to determine whether they can be accommodated. Even so, the operating expenses must be adjusted so that other tenants are not paying a premium for another tenant's costs.

With regard to the tenant lighting and power requirements, refer to the further detailed discussion on the assumptions to be used under the Tenant Miscellaneous Power Requirements in Chapter 26, and interrelationship with the lease under Services of Landlord in Chapter 32. In spite of the request for excessive electrical energy availability, the assumption of 3½ to 4 w/usf should be adequate for purposes of calculating the design HVAC load for a speculative building in most markets. (Where call centers or users with unusual electrical requirements are likely targets, special surveys of the requirements should be undertaken.) Excessive sizing of the HVAC system not only increases the initial cost, but the operating costs as well, as part-load operation is less efficient than full-load operation.

Although the following outline of typical design criteria may not be completely current, and will vary with climate, it is included herein primarily for scope and format. As pressures continue to reduce energy consumption, "U" values and gas and electrical consumption will be reduced. The current thinking in energy efficiency is spelled out in ASHRAE Standard 90.1, which is currently under a rolling revision process.

TYPICAL DESIGN CRITERIA

Normal design factors
Inside
    Summer — 75°F / 50° RH (or lower)
    Winter — 72°F / no humidity control
Outdoor conditions — Per ASHRAE recommendations

Air requirements
Outside air — 20 cfm/person or code, whichever is greater
Interior air circulation
    Design — 0.7–0.8 cfm/sf
    Minimum — N/A
Perimeter air circulation
    Design — 1.2–2.0 +/- cfm/sf
    Minimum — 30%, 50%, or 100% of design, depending on system (Not less than 0.3 cfm/sf)
Filtration — 85% efficiency cartridges

Noise criteria
NC 55—computer rooms
NC 40—open plan general purpose office
NC 35—executive offices
NC 35—private offices
NC 35—board and conference rooms
(some recommend NC 30, but the cost to achieve it should be a tenant cost, as the value is subject to debate)

Zoning requirements (temperature control)
Corner zoning — One zone at each corner
Perimeter zoning — One zone per each 60 to 80 lineal feet by 15 feet deep
Interior zone — 4 zones per floor, with a maximum of 2,000 to 2,500 sf per zone to limit VAV size and to control sound levels

Normal hours of operation for maintained conditions
Monday through Friday — 8 am to 6 pm (earlier, if necessary)
Saturday — 8 am to 1 pm

Building factors
Orientation — Known
Percentage glass — 40% +/-
"U" factors—will vary with location
    Glass — 0.35 to 0.75
        Many low-e glasses are available in 0.35 "U" factor in summer and 0.31 in winter
    Skin — 0.15

TYPICAL DESIGN CRITERIA (Continued)

	Roof	0.05 to 0.08, lower end for metal deck systems and upper end for concrete roof systems. Cooling load on metal deck system will peak closer to the time the rest of the building load peaks.
Solar heat gain coefficient—varies w/ location		0.4 to 0.55
Shading coefficient (w/o drapes)		0.20 to 0.30
If the coefficient is 0.20, draperies will not have much impact		

Lighting and misc. power assumptions
Building standard lighting	1 to 1.25 w/usf
Use 75% of heat from lights into space	
Tenant's power	2.75 to 3.5 w/usf
Combined electrical demand	3.5 to 4.0 w/usf, or 3.0 to 3.5 w/gsf

Population density
For calculating a room or a zone	120 sf / person
For calculating a floor	150 sf / person
For calculating chiller plant capacity	200 sf / person

Utilities and Utility Industry Deregulation

The restructuring of the utility industry, with its new impending competition, adds significant complexity and uncertainty to HVAC design. Trends in electric utility pricing—including seasonal and time-of-day rates and real-time pricing—indicate that the cost of electricity after deregulation may vary widely. Rates will continue to be relatively higher during peak demand and for high-demand, low-load-factor applications.

One trend that is likely to accelerate is "demand side management," with the almost certain advent of hourly pricing. With price changes potentially narrowed down to as small an increment as 15 minutes, the value of load shaping, and the controls necessary to accomplish it, will grow substantially. The building's load shape will be much more important than average pricing rates.

A reason for this demand-timed trend is that utilities operate their most efficient plants during the low-demand periods, which means that, in addition to their saving the cost of acquiring incrementally greater capacity, each unit of electricity used during these periods will require less energy to generate.

Trends also indicate that natural gas prices, while on a long-term rising trend due to the demand/supply ratio, will continue to be lower during the summer, when demand is generally lower, and that pipeline capacity to deliver gas will be available at discounted prices during those same periods. Taken together, these trends mean that building owners and design teams may want to consider designing facilities that are sufficiently flexible to use different sources of energy at their most economical times.

It is always wise to investigate the cost benefits of "interruptible" gas service, where the gas company can cut off your service on short notice in return for much lower rates throughout the year. To obtain this cost benefit, an alternative fuel source is required.

As deregulation of the utility industry expands nationally, the property owner will face many challenges in selecting suppliers. Before addressing alternate suppliers it will be essential to understand both your own facility and the current and projected market. Suppliers must be chosen carefully—not just for their current rate structure, but for their low-cost production record, proven performance, and stability. Additionally, during the early phases of this period it may prove wise to accept a small premium to obtain a relatively shorter-term contract, as the future trends may not be clear.

Refrigeration Systems

The refrigeration system provides the chilled water that is the cooling medium for the building. There are many types of refrigeration systems, some of which will be discussed here.

In a conventional or large system, the chillers are machines that chill the water used to cool the building. The chillers may be operated by electricity, gas or steam. In most locations the electric-driven centrifugal machines have historically been the most economical, although that may change. The preferred design for a large central chilled water system will be composed of three chillers, designed for 40%, 40% and 20% (some believe that three equal machines is better for downtime protection, but there is a penalty at low loads) of the load. This provides for reasonable 24-hour operation, permits the system to be operated close to its most efficient point at most operating conditions, and also minimizes problems when one machine is down for repairs. The chilled water pumps, and the cooling towers and condenser water system with their pump, should mirror the chiller sizing.

When smaller buildings cannot afford more than two machines, they should each provide 50% of the load for downtime protection. Either a small pony chiller or a condenser loop should be installed to provide for tenant's 24-hour and special incremental loads. The condenser loop permits the tenant to install a small unit for these loads.

Water treatment is normally required for the chilled and condenser water systems. A shower and eye bubbler should be located near where the chemicals are handled for personnel safety.

Future HVAC systems will need to maintain flexible operating schedules and maximize load factors in order to take advantage of pricing opportunities, and undoubtedly base its fuel selection on hourly or daily cost of energy. For example, a hybrid gas/electric plant might have a direct gas-fired absorption system or an engine-driven chiller combined with an electric chiller, with appropriate piping to allow preferential loading to reduce fuel costs.

Depending on the type and size of application, compressors may be reciprocating (up to 200 tons), screw-type (100 tons to 1,250 tons) or centrifugal (400 tons and up).

As shown in Figure 25-1, the compressor compresses the refrigerant vapor to a higher pressure, thereby increasing its condensing temperature. The high-pressure vapor is then condensed to liquid at this higher temperature and pressure. The heat released through the condensation process is rejected. The high-pressure liquid leaving the condenser then passes through a throttling valve that reduces its pressure prior to entering the evaporator. This low-pressure liquid is then vaporized in the evaporator at a temperature low enough to cool the chilled water, which in turn removes the heat from the conditioned air. The low-pressure vapor is then transferred back to the compressor, completing the cycle.

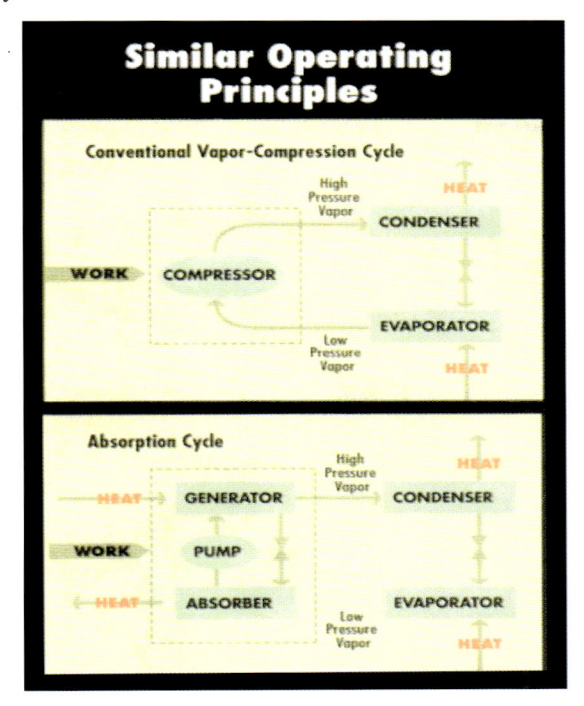

Figure 25-1

Special attention should be paid to the efficiency of the chillers, both at design load and at low partial loads. They should have solid-state starters, high-efficiency motors, and use variable frequency drives for chiller sizes that permit a positive return. A chiller efficiency of less than 0.60 kilowatts per ton should be a minimum target.

The absorption cycle is similar to the conventional vapor-compressor cycle above. The generator, pump and absorber, shown in the dotted section of the absorption cycle diagram, merely replace the function of the compressor in the conventional vapor-compressor cycle. A main difference between the two cycles is that large absorption refrigeration systems use distilled water as the refrigerant. An absorption cycle also requires the use of heat to separate the refrigerant from the absorbent (lithium bromide). In a single-effect absorption cycle, a recuperative heat exchanger is also included. The double-effect absorption cycle takes absorption to the next level by increasing the coefficient of performance (COP) by a factor of approximately two. Direct-fired absorption (DFA) chillers can generally require the same 3 gpm per ton of cooling tower flow rates as an electric chiller by using a higher temperature rise than normal for an electric chiller, and thus maintain the same cooling tower performance. Absorption systems can reduce building electric consumption and peak demand.

In a gas engine-driven system, a gas engine takes the place of an electric motor to drive the vapor-compression cycle, as shown in Figure 25-2. This system consists of an evaporator, compressor, condenser and expansion valve. Because a gas engine can operate on variable speed, it can maintain a much higher efficiency at part-load than an electric motor. This modulation of speed contributes to longer operating hours for a compressor, and more closely matches fuel consumption to operating hours. A gas engine-driven system increases the use of off-peak, low-cost gas in summer, and directly decreases the use of high-cost, on-peak electricity during that period.

The chiller diagrams and a significant amount of the information on chillers was taken from "Time to Take Another Look at Gas Cooling" by Milton Meckler in the August 1997 issue of *Building Operating Management*.

There are many alternate systems to the central chiller system, used primarily in buildings that are smaller than 150,000 to 200,000 square feet. Some of the most common types are:

- Packaged direct expansion (DX) systems with variable air volume (VAV) located on each floor. A cooling tower would be located on the roof and an outside air shaft provides the fresh air. These are usually the least expensive systems and provide the tenant on the floor (if it is a full-floor tenant) with full control over the system. Drawbacks are that unless designed with multiple chillers, if a unit is out for repairs there is no air conditioning at all, and there is minimum ability to have energy-saving economizers.

- Built-up DX air-cooled unit, normally located on the roof. Both conditioned and outside air must be ducted down a shaft from the roof to each floor. Solves the partial service problem during repairs. These units are complicated—you are at the mercy of the competence of the contractor, and maintenance can be difficult. There is limited energy savings capability, and they require excess non-rentable vertical shaft space.

- Multiple DX systems located on the roof. Both conditioned and outside air must be ducted down a shaft from the roof to each floor. Solves the problem of partial service during repairs, but takes up a lot of non-rentable vertical shaft space. Can have provision for economizer cycle, but energy-saving alternatives are limited. Sizing can be important, since standard units are limited to 70 tons or less.

- Water source heat pumps have a reversible refrigeration cycle that permits the changeover from cooling to heating on demand. They are

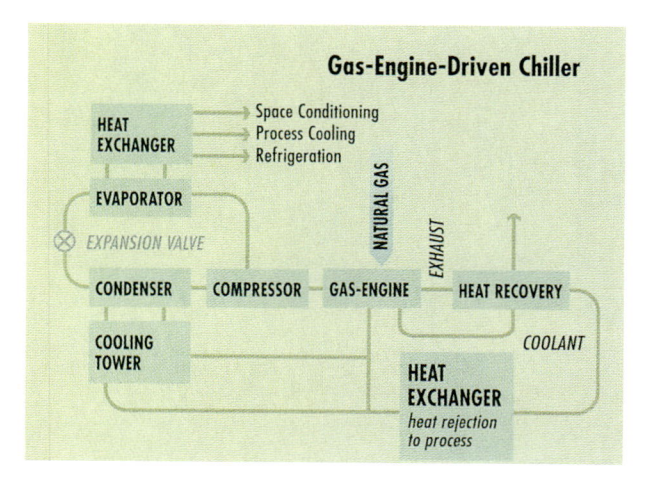

Figure 25-2

usually located above the ceiling in the tenant space. While this is a tenant expense, the TI allowance must normally be adjusted to cover this added tenant cost. Expenditure of funds is not made until tenant develops the space. Relatively efficient, it has a "free cooling" coil to utilize condenser water when appropriate, but it is not adaptable to many other energy reduction efforts. Requires a condenser loop to the machines and an outside air duct. Provides tenant with local control, but a unit may have to be replaced with another size if the tenant area is significantly modified. These units create a relatively high ambient noise level in the space.

- Other packaged alternative drive chillers now on the market are gas engine, steam turbine and direct gas-fired units.

The building type and size, budget, and the local climate tend to limit appropriate system selection.

Typically, all packaged units, water source heat pumps or built-up DX units, have somewhat higher maintenance and energy costs to balance their lower first costs.

For a building above about 150,000 to 200,000 sf, it is more likely that a central refrigeration plant will be the most efficient solution, and it certainly will be above 250,000 sf.

The former standard chlorofluorocarbon refrigerants, CFCs R-11 and R-12 are being completely removed from service due to their impact on the ozone layer. They have been replaced with hydrogenated CFCs or hydrochlorofluorocarbons (HCFCs), which are just as efficient in most equipment, but must also be phased out over the next 20 to 25 years because they have some impact on the ozone layer, even though less than the former refrigerants. Newer refrigerants that will have no ozone impact, but are less efficient, are now in use on some types of chillers, and will ultimately attain universal usage. Alternative refrigerants for newly designed refrigeration equipment are HCFC-22, HFC-410A, ammonia, lithium bromide/water and ammonia/water.

Refrigeration Cycle Energy Savings

A thermal energy storage system (TES), can create either chilled water or ice during the low demand nighttime period and store it for use during the daytime. An analysis of such a system is frequently wise when there is the possibility of a significant difference between normal and after hours energy rates. It should be noted that some former systems actually used more energy (but at a lower cost), however, newer design techniques, particularly for ice systems circulating 34°F water, are claimed to actually result in energy usage reductions. They achieve these reductions by using lower pumping rates due to the lower chilled water temperature and lower air circulation rates by cooling the supply air to as low as 45°F instead of the more common 55°F. Construction cost is saved by permitting smaller pipes, ducts and equipment. The cost of providing the space for the thermal storage must be included in the analysis.

There is frequently **not a guarantee** of long-term energy rate differential, however, the trend in electric rates is for the demand-related portion of the rate to increase at a faster pace than the consumption-related portion of the rate; and, of course, it is the demand-related portion that produces the primary cost savings from a thermal storage system. The change in the regulatory climate for electricity may make this and other analyses of this nature a little more difficult to project. As mentioned earlier in the text, however, both the utility's increased costs in providing additional demand capacity, and the fact that they will operate more efficient plants during off-hours may well increase cost effectiveness of these systems. Between 40% to 80% of the annual kilowatt-hours expended for air conditioning has shifted from daytime to nighttime periods, as reported by current users of TES systems in California.

Low temperature air distribution may also be analyzed as a possibility even when not incorporated into a thermal energy storage system discussed in the prior paragraph. The air is circulated at 46 to 48°F through the building in lieu of the more standard 55°F. Less air is required to cool the space so ductwork and fans can be smaller. To cool the air to this temperature the chilled water is cooled to as low as 38°F, thus reducing the size of the pumps and piping, but increasing the size of the chiller. Air at this temperature cannot be released directly into the room, as it would cause significant discomfort. To provide proper comfort the air must be mixed with return air, such as in a fan-powered mixing box, so that it enters the room at an acceptable temperature. The cost of the larger chiller and fan-powered mixing boxes may obviate any benefit from the smaller sizing of piping and ductwork.

Another energy-saving design is to use a heat recovery chiller to recover rejected heat that would otherwise be dissipated to the atmosphere and wasted, and to apply that heat to water heating, space heating or terminal reheating. Heat recovery chillers are conventional chillers with double-condensers or desuperheaters, and cost slightly more than a standard chiller. One way this approach has been efficiently used is to install one heat recovery chiller and one standard chiller. The heat recovery chiller will be the lead chiller in the heating season, supplying chilled water for the cooling load and hot water for space heating and terminal-reheat. In the cooling season, the standard chiller will be the lead chiller, as less recovered heat can be utilized.

Thermocycle, another form of "free" hydronic cooling, makes use of the centrifugal chiller itself as a heat exchanger by means of natural circulation (migration) of the refrigerant caused by the difference between the condenser water temperatures and the chilled water temperatures. Depending on conditions, about 20% of the chiller's normal capacity can be obtained without running the compressor, but the pumps and cooling tower must be operating. Generally, this approach will probably not be as effective as a standard heat exchange method.

Another alternate energy reduction approach are the Geoexchange systems. These systems are a variation of the residential geothermal heat pump systems. They circulate water or other liquids through underground pipes. In cold weather, the system transfers the earth's heat through the pipes into the circulating liquid, which transfers it into the building. In hot weather, the fluid in the system's pipes takes warmth from the building and transfers it to the earth.

Cooling Towers

All refrigeration units, other than the air-cooled units that can be used in some climates, require cooling towers. The condenser water is circulated through the cooling tower from top to bottom, dropping across baffles to increase the contact with the air, which cools the water. Towers should be designed to reduce drift, the entrained water droplets in the airflow that are carried out of the tower and are wasted. Low drift towers should be purchased to reduce water usage. A well-designed and maintained cooling tower should have a drift in the 0.1% to 0.2% range. In contrast, a poorly operating tower can lose between 1% and 2% of the water flowing through it. Another water saver is to put a meter on the tower make-up line, as make-up valves sometimes leak for a long time without being discovered.

The best practice dictates that the cells of the cooling tower, the condenser water pumps and the chilled water pumps all be designed to reflect the chiller sizing, so that downtime for any chiller unit will not affect the efficiency or performance of the others.

Equipment

All mechanical and electrical equipment must be provided with appropriate concrete bases and vibration isolators, and all penetrations properly treated, to minimize or eliminate the transmission of vibrations and noise to occupied spaces.

Every piece of equipment that handles water, or is subject to condensation, should have a drip pan with a generous two-way slope to a sufficiently sized drain line to avoid algae, mold and microbials.

As with cooling towers, all boiler make-up lines should have meters that are read at least weekly.

Solid state starters, high efficiency motors and variable frequency drives (VFDs) should be used where practical to maximize energy savings, but care should be taken to ensure they have proper electronic filters to eliminate or minimize harmonic distortions, as discussed further in Chapter 26.

Specifications are very difficult for anyone other than the design engineer to read and understand, as they consist largely of references to various industry standards and manufacturer's model numbers. Be certain that you understand the quality of the various items of equipment that are specified to ensure they will perform as you intend for many years. If the specifications are not clear to you, have the design engineer and the Property Management engineer explain the cost and service performance of the various alternatives.

Air Distribution Systems

There are several different types of air distribution systems (or hydronic variations that accomplish the same result) that direct the right amount of air to each space to provide for its comfort. An air distribution system consists of a fresh air intake fan and shaft, an exhaust or return air fan and shaft, and a distribution system that provides the conditioned air to the occupied spaces. The outside air and exhaust systems, through centrally controlled dampers, are commonly used for emergency smoke removal during a fire condition, as will be discussed under Life Safety Systems. The most common types of air distribution systems for office buildings are described below.

Variable air volume (VAV) single duct system, as shown in Figure 25-3, is the most common type of air distribution system in use in office buildings. The outside air is mixed with recirculated air through a modulating control damper near the inlet of the fan, and is then tempered by passing through a cooling/heating coil, filter and sound trap at the fan outlet. The tempered air is provided to the spaces, with the volume controlled by the mixing box to reach the correct temperature. Final control on the perimeter, and units located beneath the roof, is provided by an electric or hot water terminal reheat coil.

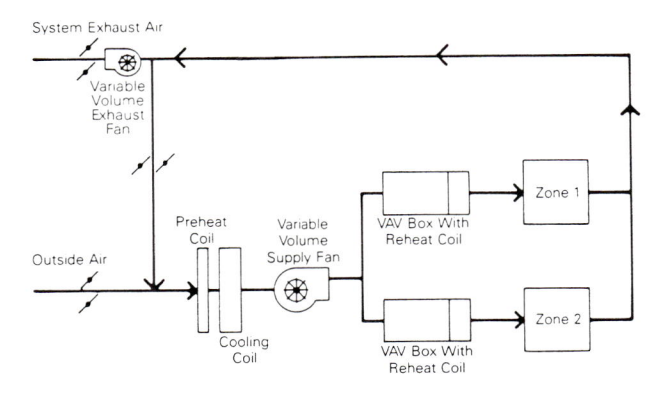

Figure 25-3

A VAV variation is the fan powered mixing box (Figure 25-4). In this system the return air is cycled directly into the box through a modulating valve, which has its own fan, to control the air temperature. As before, the thermostat that modulates the reheat coil controls the final temperature at the perimeter boxes.

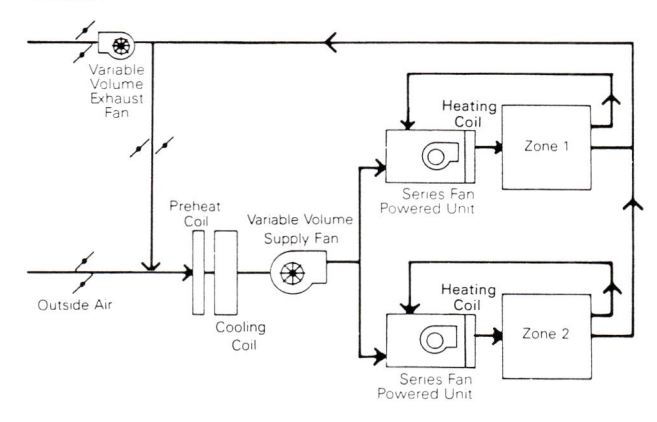

Figure 25-4

Dual duct VAV system (Figure 25-5) is similar to the single duct system, except it has a hot and a cold duct, which mix in the mixing box, instead of terminal reheat. This system provides excellent comfort but is more expensive, and only the VAV type is reasonably efficient.

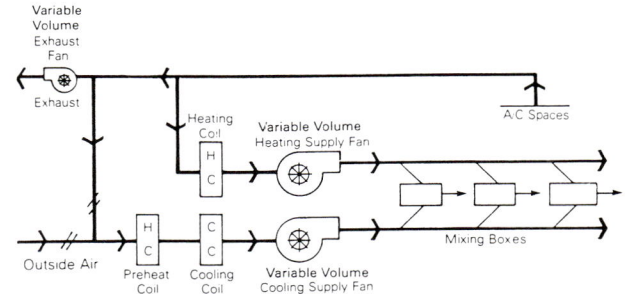

Figure 25-5

Multi-zone system (Figure 25-6) is where the air is mixed with recirculated air in front of the fan and is then heated and cooled as it passes over the coils. The air to each zone is then blended through mixing dampers as dictated by the thermostat in each zone served, and is then pumped by the fan into the occupied space.

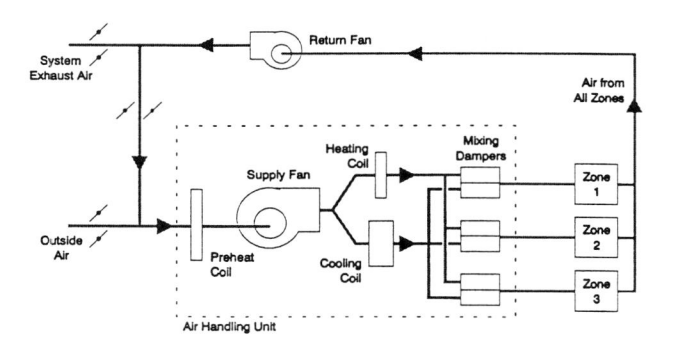

Figure 25-6

A fan coil system is a hydronic variation, shown in Figure 25-7. In a two-pipe system, tempered water is pumped to free-standing packaged fan coil units around the perimeter that bring in air, mixes it with return air and then tempers it with the water before it enters the room. The water is chilled in the cooling season and hot in the heating season. In a four-pipe system there are a supply and return pipes for both the chilled water and hot water system. They mix in the unit to provide the proper temperature to the space at any time. This type of system usually requires more maintenance due to the coils and filters being spread throughout the building.

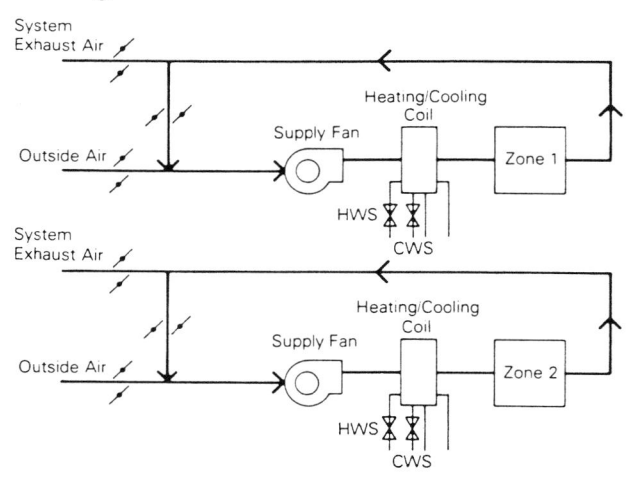

Figure 25-7

A further variation is a three-pipe fan coil system that uses a common return line.

In every type of the above systems there must be a limiting control so that the amount of outside air may not drop below a predetermined airflow in order to satisfy the IAQ requirements.

Although normally specified by the tenant, with VAV systems the perimeter is usually zoned with a zone in each corner and one for each 500 sf in between. Corner zones are recommended because they frequently house the most important clients, and at differing times of day the sun loads are from different directions. For interior zones, one zone for each 1200 sf is considered good practice, and they should not exceed one per 2000 sf.

The ducts for conditioned air must be insulated to avoid being heated in the plenum through which it passes, which would increase energy usage. For many years the standard practice was to insulate ducts on the inside where it could accomplish a double objective—reduce heat transfer and absorb air and equipment noise. This approach has become less attractive, since there is the possibility of the glass fibers from the insulation being entrained in the air. The result is that ducts are now more often being insulated on the outside, although specially coated interior insulations are still appropriate for use. The sound transmission issue is being addressed by the use of sound traps and by lining the inside of fan casings with a washable, metallic-coated foam insulation, which provides sound attenuation without affecting air quality.

Air handlers can be located either on the roof of low-rise buildings or on an occupied floor in mid- or high-rise buildings, and are served by fresh air and return air shafts. Like chiller systems, building size and climate affects building design. It should be noted that fan rooms on a floor are considered rentable area while shafts are not. Since fan rooms are not useable area, this advantage can be lost if the rentable/useable ratio becomes marginal or unfavorable.

A trend that was popular many years ago in major computer facilities that is again gaining prominence is delivering the air up through a raised floor, called displacement ventilation, also referred to by some as the Building Technology Platform. With displacement ventilation, air flows from a VAV box into a pressurized, 12" to 18" raised floor cavity (most often 16"), passes through a floor air terminal, heats up from people, lights and equipment in the room and rises to be exhausted through the ceiling. Stated HVAC benefits are that there are:

- Significant energy savings
- Pollutants are removed more effectively improving IAQ
- It is more efficient because the entire volume of air turns over rather than the partial short-circuiting that occurs in most systems
- Supply air is warmer and requires less static pressure
- Fans and motors are reduced in size
- Cool air can be directed past heat-producing equipment more accurately

It is very easy to relocate the air inlet terminal by relocating the floor tiles that contain these diffusers, or vary the air-flow quantity or direction by adjustments at the diffuser.

A major benefit for many users is the cavity of the raised floor system that is also used for modular electrical distribution and communication cable trays. Some who have used this system claim there is a $2 to $4 overall cost premium, and it would not have been justified without the benefit of electrical distribution savings and future flexibility. It has been stated that the overall floor-to-floor height need not be increased because the ceiling plenum can be reduced by the amount of the raised floor cavity, but that may not always be true. The flooring consists entirely of carpet tiles, filled for stability. As the entire building must be designed for the raised floor system, the author has not yet satisfied himself that use of this system is appropriate for a general-purpose speculative building.

Air Side Energy Saving Alternatives

The primary energy savings opportunities from the air distribution system is to either pre-warm or pre-cool the outside air to bring it closer to the design air temperature, or use free cooling through an economizer cycle. With the various systems there are several ways in which the outside air and/or the exhaust air can be used to reduce energy consumption.

The airside cooling economizer cycle consists of dampers and a properly sized air shaft capable of delivering up to 100% outside air to the space when directed by local controls. When the dry-bulb temperature sensor determines the outside air is cooler than the occupied space, the dampers let in as much outside air as required to take advantage of the free cooling. A wet-bulb sensor (measures both temperature and relative humidity) is sometimes used to control this type of system, but they are not always as accurate or reliable over time. The disadvantage of this approach is that it requires a much larger, non-rentable outside air shaft and special built-up air handling units with extra controls, which may make it uneconomical in many buildings. An alternative to larger central outside airshafts is to bring outside air in through louvers in the façade, duct it to a fan room and exhaust through another set of louvers.

Another economy method is to control the outside air with a CO_2 sensor, which serves as a proxy for the desired health and comfort conditions. If the outside air is warmer than the occupied space, it requires energy to cool the air and also possibly additional energy to dehumidify it and vice versa. If the CO_2 sensor recognizes a low level of impurities in the occupied space, it can operate a damper that reduces the amount of outside air delivered to the space, thus saving energy, without harming the air quality. Naturally, there would be a temperature override to prevent such outside air reduction if the outside was cooler. This approach is most productive in climates with extremes of heating and cooling conditions.

Several heat recovery strategies are used to transfer energy from the exhaust air to the outside air in order to reduce the energy required to condition the outside air during the heating season. There are three common methods by which the heat from the exhaust air is transferred—the rotary heat wheel, a plate-type heat exchanger, and a circulating pipe exchanger.

Perimeter Air Distribution

A major issue in perimeter air distribution and control, particularly in colder climates, is to prevent a "cold wall" or down draft effect. Down draft is where the room air is cooled by contact with the cold glass in the winter, and flows down and across the floor causing an uncomfortable draft. This is frequently resolved by placing a linear ceiling diffuser anywhere from 12" to 36" inches from the glass line, blowing toward the room at a calculated velocity based on the outside air temperature, to recirculate the return air across the glass and out an exhaust slot, which is located outboard of the diffuser and as close to the glass line as possible.

Air Testing and Balancing

The system design assumes a specific air quantity being delivered from each diffuser at design conditions. It may be difficult to maintain comfortable conditions for the tenant if the system is not properly balanced, i.e., design air quantity is not proven to be correctly delivered. To ensure that the system meets the design intent, the air system must be measured at the outlets and then rebalanced if it is out of conformance with the design drawings. At substantial completion finished floors can have a final balance, but unfinished floors can be only roughly balanced, as most if not all outlets are not in their finished position. As each tenant space is completed it can have a final balance.

The best practice is to have an independent air balancing company perform this work, as it provides a double check on the performance of the ventilation contractor.

Indoor Air Quality and Air Circulation

The reduction in, or elimination of, smoking has removed one major need for excessive air circulation, but Indoor-Air Quality (IAQ) has increased in importance, particularly as the "sick building syndrome" has increased both in perception and in reality. Poor IAQ is caused primarily by the sensation and/or actuality of low air circulation, and by airborne impurities, which primarily result from furnishings and construction materials such as adhesives, solvents and finishes. Special tenant operations, particularly printing, contribute impurities. Some of the most common of the 900 identified indoor air pollutants that may affect IAQ are:

- Carbon dioxide—while not a problem at normal levels, high levels may indicate an increased concentration of other pollutants, and that the air circulation system is not effective.

- Volatile organic compounds (VOCs)—low carbon compounds off-gassed from the surface of solvents, adhesives and finishes. Many satisfactory products with low VOCs are now available.

- Formaldehyde—a lighter carbon VOC with sensitizing and allergenic properties. Exposure to a high concentration at one time may later cause severe reactions to trace amounts.

- Microbials—molds, bacteria and viruses. Fungi, including molds and mildew, can grow on a variety of surfaces with sufficient moisture, and can cause allergies, infections and disease. Their most likely cause is condensation occurring without provision for acceptable drainage.

- Respirable particles—the most common category of dust found in buildings, representing 70% of airborne particulates in one recent study. Respirable particles are those small dust particles that can be inhaled deeply into the lungs, and are in the lung-damaging sub-micron size.

- Inhalable particles are larger in size. High dust levels may indicate malfunctioning filters or construction in the building that is not properly isolated.

- Nitrogen dioxide and carbon monoxide—usually the result of incomplete combustion.

The important factors in preventing poor air quality conditions are:

- Minimize the quantity of known pollutants under the developer's control.

- Provide appropriate filtration.

- Maintain a constant, or at least an acceptable minimum, rate of outside air delivery. Since nearly all air handling systems in these types of buildings are variable air volume, as the total air quantity diminishes below the design value during periods of reduced load, it is important to keep the absolute outside air CFM relatively constant (which means the percentage of outside air to total air supply increases as the total air supply decreases). The recommended minimum rate of outside air today is 20 cfm per person.

- Insure that the equipment and any related drip pans cannot collect water that can cause molds or mildew that can enter the air stream.
- Ensure that all air intake sources are located away from parking lots, loading docks, or other contaminant sources.
- Properly maintain the equipment.

Indoor Air Quality standards are covered in ASHRAE Standard 62–89, which is currently undergoing revision.

There are many impurities that may be found in the air in office buildings. A recent adaptation by the Trane Company of ASHRAE Tables 1 and 3, covering acceptable exposure levels for indoor air, is summarized below.

midification, but can be less effective when the dehumidification load is greater than the temperature-cooling load. In a cooling-based dehumidification system, the heat and moisture is removed directly by the cooling coil. In desiccant dehumidification (an alternate approach), moisture is drawn from the air by an area of low vapor pressure at the surface of the desiccant. Gas-fired or other desiccant cooling systems are more effective in reducing the humidity and are particularly attractive for buildings with high humidity potential.

Desiccants can be classified as either liquid or solid. If the moisture is collected on the surface of the desiccant, it is called an *adsorbent* and is usually solid. If the desiccant experiences a chemical or physical change during the process, it is called an

ACCEPTABLE INDOOR AIR EXPOSURE LEVELS

Contaminant	Long-Term Exposure (Time in years)	Short-Term Exposure (Time in hours)
Carbon dioxide	1,000 ppm / continuous	
Carbon monoxide		35 ppm / 1 hour
		9 ppm / 8 hours
Chlordane	0.0003 ppm / 1 year	
Nitrogen dioxide	0.055 ppm / 1 year	
Ozone	0.05 ppm / continuous	
Radon	4 parts Ci / liter for 1 year	
Sulfur dioxide	0.030 ppm / 1 year	0.14 ppm / 24 hours

Humidification and Dehumidification

The increased outside air quantities, due to IAQ concerns, often bring in much more moisture than previously encountered, which can greatly increase the cooling energy required for dehumidification.

For personnel comfort the air should be controlled to maintain between 30% and 60% relative humidity. When humidity is too low, it causes respiratory problems, particularly for people with allergies, sinus problems or asthma. If humidity is too high, in addition to physical discomfort, more places become breeding grounds for microbial growth. Night setbacks should be controlled so that relative humidity does not rise above 60%.

Conventional equipment normally provides cooling for both temperature reduction and dehu-

absorbent and can be either a liquid or a solid that becomes a liquid as it absorbs moisture. Desiccant materials attract and retain moisture from the air. The air is dried as it flows through the desiccant and is then cooled with a supplemental chiller. Once the desiccant material is saturated, it is heated to evaporate the moisture and prepare it for reuse. There are five typical equipment configurations now available for desiccant dehumidification applications:

- Liquid-spray-tower
- Solid-packed tower
- Rotating horizontal bed
- Multiple vertical bed
- Rotating honeycomb

Alternatively, under many conditions the excess outside air greatly reduces the humidity level below that satisfactory for personnel comfort and proper operation of some equipment. Humidification has not normally been used in general purpose office buildings, but it may become appropriate in some climates. There have been claims by some manufacturers of a two-year payback for their humidification systems. It may well be, but the author will remain somewhat dubious until he sees an analysis by a qualified consulting engineer.

Filters

Good filtration is an important factor in IAQ. There is a change underway in filter medium from fiberglass material to polymer-based fibers. Oxidizers are now being coated on some filter fibers to remove odors and gasses from the air. Fiber diameters are getting smaller, particularly to control air-borne microbials that are sometimes associated with the sick building syndrome. The minimum recommendation today is for a single 4" thick 60% filter.

In many urban areas a better solution is the use of high efficiency 85% cartridge filters, as outside air quality can vary from time to time during the day, with the seasons, or over a period of years. The 85% filters require a pre-filter and create a higher fan static pressure requiring more fan horsepower, and they need more frequent replacement.

Controls

Fully electronic Direct Digital Controls (DDC) are generally utilized in new buildings today. These systems are included in the Building Management System (BMS), as will be discussed later in this chapter.

Life Cycle Costing

A detailed life cycle economic analysis should be made to select the building's mechanical system. Factors that should be incorporated in the analysis are shown in the following table.

HVAC ECONOMIC ANALYSIS FACTORS

- Affect on the building's floor to floor height
- Affect on floor framing or any other aspect of the structural system
- Total area of fan rooms per floor, or in total
- Potentially rentable or useable space used for fan rooms
- Annual operating differences
    - BTU/sf/year
    - Operating costs at current levels
    - Operating costs at projected energy prices
    - Maintenance cost differentials
- Initial construction cost differentials
    - Mechanical system cost
    - Electrical system cost
    - Structural/architectural costs
- Owning operating analysis will assume
    - Rentable area at $ ——— /sf
    - Financing cost at —— %
    - Required rate of return of ——- %
- Method and cost of providing for individually-controlled zones
- Quality of systems
    - Air movement

HVAC ECONOMIC ANALYSIS FACTORS (Continued)

Smoke purging
Degree of control
Impact on down draft or cold wall
Damage, dirt or inconvenience caused by service access to occupied areas
Ease of provision for individual control
Ease of provision for special noise and temperature control and purging at special conference rooms
Energy budget

Acoustical Issues

This subject is covered in Chapter 22.

Development Officer Approvals

The Development Officer will normally have the benefit of a qualified consulting engineer, specialists such as an acoustical consultant and the engineering staff from the Property Management department to assist in the selection and design of the HVAC system. Notwithstanding the quality of support, the **Development Officer, alone, must make or specifically approve** the following decisions to ensure the system meets market demand, is coordinated with the lease, is appropriate for the intended life span and is cost effective.

- Population assumptions
- Tenant electrical load assumptions
- "U" factors of building envelope
- Energy conservation—alternate solutions, life-cycle costing
- Energy budget
- Cost/benefit of system selection
- IAQ provisions
- Noise criteria and control
- Efficiency of after hours usage for tenants
- Equipment room locations

Visual Approvals

As discussed earlier under other chapters, the Development Officer should visually approve samples of all diffusers, grills, thermostats and all other devices that have exposed finishes in the occupied and public spaces. Catalogue cuts do not sufficiently indicate the appearance and quality of these items.

Provisions for Maintenance

Every piece of equipment will require maintenance periodically, and often at the worst possible time. In addition to the normal operating hours, many buildings must run 24 hours a day, at least during some periods. To permit proper maintenance, it is necessary to isolate each piece of equipment with proper valves so that the maintenance work can proceed while the plant is operating.

This same approach must be applied to all water lines serving individual floors, as they must be isolated from time to time for maintenance work or modifications to meet a tenant's requirements. In addition, each line, riser and piece of equipment must have a drain valve at the low points adjacent to, or flowing toward a floor drain. Note that drain lines must never run along or above the floor, as they are a serious tripping hazard. The proper location of floor drains in each equipment room is very important.

In addition, the documents should require that all equipment rooms should be laid out in a manner that provides room for and facilitates maintenance of the equipment. Where it will be difficult to handle heavy equipment, monorails or hoisting davits should be provided.

These issues must be fully covered in the specifications, and Property Management engineers should review the working drawings carefully for compliance, whether the work is bid from the engineer's contract documents, or on a design-build basis.

It is necessary to determine by what manner equipment can be removed and replaced. If on the roof, there should be wear protection surfaces along the path from each equipment room to the point where it can be removed. Where equipment will not fit into the freight elevator, provision should be made for davits to lower it to the ground, unless it is within reach of a truck crane. Where the freight elevator does not travel to the roof, usually because of height limitations, a hatch must be provided through the roof for equipment access.

All of the above comments apply to all of the other MEP, elevator and life safety equipment and system design.

PLUMBING SYSTEMS

Plumbing systems include potable water, water heating, steam, sanitary drainage, storm drainage, gas, decorative water features and many special systems such as compressed air, oxygen, etc. Where the site work is not extensive, the connections to various water, sewer, storm and gas systems are considered plumbing; otherwise that which is beyond five feet from the building line is incorporated in the civil engineering work.

A major issue in the plumbing design is the conservation of water. Once thought of as limitless and inexpensive, water has become expensive and, in many locales, scarce. In recent years water rates have increased rapidly, doubling or tripling in many cases. The primary reasons for the rapid price increases are scarce supplies caused by increased demand and lower water tables, increased treatment of supply and waste, replacement and upgrading of aging infrastructures, environmental impediments to new supply and distribution, and reduction of funding of water and sewer projects by federal and state governments. The user is now paying the full cost. Where water is scarce there is an obligation to conserve, in addition to the economic benefit. The impact of various fixtures, make-up lines and irrigation are discussed in their respective chapters.

The potable water system provides for all personnel needs, make-up water for HVAC and boiler equipment, and for fire service where there is not a separate fire service system. Potable water should never be used for cooling, as it has been for small loads in the past. This system starts with the backflow preventor, to protect the integrity of the municipal water system, and the meter. Frequently the water meter and isolating valves must be installed above ground between the property line and the building. Preferably it should be located where it can be sufficiently screened with landscaping.

Pumping is necessary when the water main pressure might not reach the farthest fixture with sufficient pressure. In many high-rise buildings the water is pumped in series where the pump in the second zone is fed from the first zone pump, etc.

Water heating systems are usually small packaged remote electric water heaters, with each heater serving from two to four toilet rooms. In a relatively few buildings it has been determined that it is more satisfactory to have central systems which should have a recirculation loop to ensure hot water at all points at all times. Many buildings now provide only tempered water instead of both hot and cold water to the lavatories to reduce piping costs and energy. In rare instances it is advisable to provide water treatment to potable water, but only with approval of the local health department.

Water hammer shock absorbers are installed to prevent noise, vibration and damage in any water line that has quick shutoff valves. Further discussion of controlling mechanical system noises is covered in Chapter 22.

All plumbing fixtures and the necessary piping are supplied under the plumbing contract but for the purpose of this text they were discussed under Toilet Rooms in Chapter 23.

Sanitary drainage systems take all of the waste from the plumbing fixtures, mechanical equipment and condensate drains. The drains from each fixture must be trapped and vented, the vents ultimately discharging above the roof. The carrying capacity of a drainage pipe is measured in fixture units at a specified pitch (slope) in the horizontal runs. The standard pitch is ¼" per foot of pipe for pipe sizes 3" or smaller, but codes allow slopes as low as ⅛" for piping 4" and over. The shallower slope is usually necessary in buildings to avoid interference problems. When the lesser pitch is used, the drain must either be larger, or carry waste from a lesser number of fixtures.

The awkwardness of running horizontal drain piping for any great distance in a ceiling plenum is the reason many buildings add wet columns (extra drain and vent piping) away from the core to facilitate adding private toilet rooms, kitchens or other water-consuming fixtures for tenants. Kitchens require grease traps for all waste lines and floor drains.

Storm drainage takes the water from the roof down through roof drain piping and away from the building line. Overflow drains set 2" higher than the basic roof drains carry excess water down through separate drain piping. Some codes will accept scuppers through the building parapet in lieu of overflow drains. Some taller building designs provide for storage of a specified volume of water on the roof during intense storms and letting it gradually run off over time, in order to reduce the size of the storm drain piping. Storm piping is also preferably set at a pitch of ¼" to one foot of pipe, but frequently must be run at ⅛" per foot slope within the building.

Sump pumps in elevator pits and any foundation drain systems pump water into the drainage system. Storm water from the building and site catch basins is carried to a local sewer or is handled by the site water management system. (See Chapter 18.)

As discussed earlier under the architectural and HVAC chapters, the Development Officer should visually approve samples of all fixtures, faucets, flush valves, soap and towel dispensers and any other devices that have exposed finishes in the occupied and public spaces. Catalogue cuts do not sufficiently indicate the appearance and quality of these items.

BUILDING MANAGEMENT SYSTEM

The building management system will control and report on every facet of the building's operation, as determined by the requirements of the project. The mechanical/electrical control can be combined with security, preventive maintenance, and the accounting for chargeable after hours usage of electricity and air conditioning by the tenants. Analysis frequently shows, however, that currently separate systems for mechanical/electrical and security can be more economical than a combined system that handles all requirements. Each project should be carefully analyzed to determine the best solution.

Some of the features that can be built into the system(s) are listed in the following table. The proposed system should be reviewed carefully with Property Management to determine how the size, location, design and proposed staffing of the building will affect the BMS.

While this discussion covers extensive control and management points and issues, the best approach is usually to keep the systems as simple as possible to accomplish the necessary functions efficiently. The engineers in the Property Management department can normally give a clear statement as to the degree of complexity that is effective in the actual building operation.

TYPICAL BMS CONTROLS

Security controls
- Discussed in Chapter 27

Energy management
- Duty cycling
- Chiller optimization
- Power demand control and load shedding
- Optimum start/stop
- Enthalpy control
- Load reset
- Temperature reset
- Night cycle
- Zero energy band

TYPICAL BMS CONTROLS (Continued)

- Night purge
- Card or keypad control of night lighting
- Card or keypad after hours control of air handling systems

Central command and control
- Start/stop programs
- Event-initiated programs
- Colorgraphics
- Change alarm limits
- Automatic control device
- Trend log modifications
- Temporary scheduler
- Extended service programs
- Run-time programs
- Automatic alarm enable/disable
- Set point adjustment for all field controllers

Logs and reports
- All point log
- Status summary log
- Single group log
- Alarm summary log
- Trend log
- Access control log
- Energy management log
- Time and event initiated log
- Data file logs
- Temperature, flow and pressure readings wherever required
- KW and BTU readouts
- Run time totalizers

Environmental control
- Air flow measurement
- Analog variable control
- Boiler control
- Electrical energy control
- Chiller control
- Energy reporting
- Solar energy usage

Management
- Monitor status of all emergency equipment
- High, low and off alarms
- Run failure alarms
- Affirmative operator acknowledgment of each alarm
- Feedback of all commands
- Equipment maintenance scheduling and records
- Training mode for new operators
- Intercom to all major equipment and to security
- Duplicate controls in the engineer's office and either the security console in the lobby, the fire control station in the lobby, or the management office

Life-safety
- Discussed in Chapter 27

The future of building automation, accelerated by advances in computers and microprocessors, is "interoperability", or the capacity for different systems and equipment, designed and made by different manufacturers to perform different tasks, to operate together and to share communications, data and command capabilities. Clearly, in the near future advanced integrated systems will link nearly all building functions, including HVAC, security, lighting, fire alarm, elevators and power monitoring and load shedding. Building management systems will be fully integrated with telecommunications to control systems to satisfy tenant needs. There are two approaches to accomplishing this result, which are not yet fully mutually compatible.

LonMark, utilizing LonWorks technology by Echelon Corporation, has most successfully marketed their proprietary communications protocols to the building automation industry through the LonMark Interoperability Association. LonMark is a specific technology that permits individual control devices from different manufacturers to effectively communicate with each other in a seamless system when designed to fit with this protocol.

The LonMark Association has initiated a testing and certification program to place a LonMark stamp on products that have been designed in accordance with interoperability guidelines to ensure they can reliably be installed into a LonWorks system as specified.

BACnet is basically a set of rules developed by an ASHRAE committee and set forth in ANSI/ASHRAE Standard 135-1995. It has become the standard for a universal open software protocol for building automation that provides a set of guidelines to govern the exchange of data over computer networks operating at speeds up to 10–100 million bits per second (bps) using the Ethernet protocol. These open standards permit all manufacturers to develop products that can be integrated with all others. The ultimate end result will be a "plug and play" standard to which all manufacturers of related equipment can comply.

The above notwithstanding, while today there are many integrated systems being purchased or tied together with software, for smaller buildings it is probably still most economical in the immediate future to use packaged stand alone systems for BMS and security.

Where the building size and/or location does not justify an on-site operating engineer or manager, duplicate data should be transmitted to a central office for ease of evaluation. All emergency indicators should be directed to a 24-hour answering service.

ENERGY BUDGET

An energy budget is also known as Building Energy Performance Standards (BEPS). There are ASHRAE recommendations (ASHRAE 90.1-1989 Energy Efficient Design of New Buildings Except Low-Rise Residential Buildings) and Federal (Department of Energy) and State requirements. California's Title 24 is the most stringent that I am aware of. An energy budget is an organized estimate of the energy requirements of a building, based upon specific assumptions.

Under Title 24, and other such standards, there are prescriptive designs that are very specific, or performance standards that permit the engineers leeway in designing an efficient building to meet a specified end result. Under any BEPS the operating condition and time assumptions are specified to permit comparisons between buildings. For example, under Title 24 the specified operating hours for computation purposes are:

• Lighting	Monday through Friday	90% on—9 AM to 6 PM 50% on—6 AM to 8 PM Off thereafter
	Saturday	90% on—9 AM to 1 PM 50% on—1 PM to 3 PM Off thereafter
• Thermostat control	Monday through Friday	6 AM to 7 PM
	Saturday	6 AM to 2 PM

Override controls turn the central system on when temperature drops below 55°F in the heating season and above 95°F in the cooling season.

An office building complying with Title 24 would use about 17 kilowatt-hours of energy annually per gross square foot in coastal California, and a greater amount in more severe climates. A well-designed office building attempting maximum reasonable energy efficiency could achieve 60% or less of that number. New regulations for Title 24, effective in 1999, will reduce the lighting levels by 20% to 25%, which is really in line with current design. Note that their definition of area is conditioned space measured to the outside of the outside wall, or slightly more than the standard definition of a rentable square foot.

Some engineers consider it to be good practice to set a minimum goal to exceed ASHRAE 90.1-1989 by at least 30%, while exceeding it by 50% can be achievable. The developer of speculative office buildings has somewhat less control over this process than an owner/builder—the specific requirements of unknown tenants cannot be accurately predicted, and you don't want to exclude any more potential tenants than necessary.

There are different energy source weighting factors to penalize the least efficient energy sources. For example, the energy source rating for electricity used for heating is approximately 3.0, where gas is about 1.1. This results in a significant penalty for using electric heat. The reason is that about two-thirds of the energy input to the power plant is lost through plant inefficiency and transmission losses, while the only losses for gas consumed on-site is the 90% efficiency factor of the boiler or heater. The reverse will occur for cooling loads due to the relative inefficiency of gas-fired absorption chillers. Current regulations and budget tables should be obtained.

An energy budget should be prepared at the initiation of each project. It should be noted that when the tenants pay utilities separately, the owner may be faced with increased first costs in creating an energy efficient building, without sharing in the savings. The following is an energy budget outline, which like the typical design criteria discussed previously, may not be completely current, and is included basically for scope and format. As pressures continue to reduce energy consumption the specified values will change.

ENERGY BUDGET

Basic Building Parameters
 Orientation
 Other nearby structures
 Shape
 Surface to volume ratio

Building Design
 Roof—U Values   Varies with climate
 Walls—U Values   Varies with climate
 Separations between occupied spaces and
 unoccupied spaces (i.e., parking and dock)
 Varies with climate
 Glass   Insulated   U Values
                    0.35 to 0.75, varies with climate
                    Low-e glass is available with "U" factors of
                    0.35 in summer and 0.31 in winter
                    Tint and heat absorption are additional factors.
      Reflectivity   0.23–0.25 shading coefficient is desirable
      % Vision glass   40% maximum in less temperate climates

External Shading Features
 Vertical protrusions
 Horizontal protrusions

ENERGY BUDGET (Continued)

Window setbacks
Other shapes

Internal Shading Features
Draperies
Blinds

Infiltration
Revolving doors or vestibules
Caulking and sealing
Duct construction—SMACNA or ASHRAE standards (testing required)

Design Criteria (see also air conditioning section)
Use ASHRAE for interior and exterior standards
Verify population loading
Electrical

	General lighting	1 to 1.25 w/sf is normal range plus (w/sf for special lighting
	Miscellaneous power	3.0 w/sf is normal
Minimum outside air		Greater of 20 cfm/person, or code
Minimum air circulation		N/A

Systems (Special Savings Methods)

Free cooling	Outside air
Free hydronic cooling	Plate frame heat exchanger between condenser water and chilled water circuits
Thermocycle	Similar to free hydronic cooling, except it makes use of the centrifugal chiller as a heat exchanger by means of the natural circulation caused by the differential between the condenser and chilled—water temperatures. About 20% of the chiller capacity can be obtained without running the compressor.
Load shaving	Reduce peak electric load thru use of emergency generator, but generator must be upgraded in quality.
Thermal storage	Store cooling medium at night for daytime use the following day
Heat recovery	Double bundle heat recovery for: Normal heating Hot water generation Start-up heat Temper outside air
Heat pump systems	
Heat exchange wheels	

Building Management Systems (BMS)   (see separate section)
Equipment
    Chillers   Extra chiller surface
                   Double bundle
                   High efficiency motors

ENERGY BUDGET (Continued)

	Coefficient of performance
	KW/ton
	Number of units and size for operating efficiency
	Condenser and chilled water pumps coordinated with chillers
Fans	Low pressure rather than high pressure where possible
	Variable inlet vane
	Variable pitch axial flow
	Variable speed drives
	Variable frequency drives
	High efficiency motors
Cooling towers	Variable air volume
Air terminal unit	Fan powered mixing box
Miscellaneous	Duct construction and testing
	High quality outside air dampers—neoprene edged
Pipe and duct insulation	

Lighting
Task lighting where feasible
General lighting
    High efficiency
    Control unit area covered
    1.0 w/sf is a minimum, 1.5 w/sf is a maximum
Miscellaneous power
    0.25–0.5 w/sf is normal for normal space
    Electronic equipment and other power consuming equipment can require an additional 2.5 w/sf

Lighting Fixtures
    High efficiency fixture, i.e., parabolic
    High efficiency, energy saving T8 lamps
    High efficiency electronic ballasts

Lighting Controls
    Perimeter
        Can be controlled by solar sensor
    Central
        Reduced for cleaning operations
        Cores controlled
        Office lighting time controlled
    Local
        Individual office—two-level control or movement control

CASE STUDY

Because of the decision to let the mechanical contracts on design/build contracts, the system selection and design criteria were evaluated and resolved early in the design development phase. The building engineer was included in this process to have the benefit of his operating knowledge.

HEATING, VENTILATING AND AIR CONDITIONING SYSTEM

The adjacent Executive Center Del Mar buildings, and most other buildings in the office park, were designed to use a water source heat pump HVAC system with the heat pumps and floor ductwork installed by the tenant. The condenser water loop and fresh air and exhaust shafts were installed as part of the base building. The tenant was also responsible for the electric service from his own meter at the ground level.

For a larger eight-story building it was believed that a more centralized system with VAV air distribution was more appropriate, particularly with its opportunity for various energy efficiencies. Additionally, in a high-rise building the heat pump system would create some additional code-related issues.

Syska & Hennessy proposed four central HVAC systems for consideration and comparison to the heat pump concept. They were:

- Self-contained direct expansion (DX) VAV air handling units located on each floor. Considered the least expensive, prior to the request to consider an outside air economizer. Required a room on each floor of about 15' x 20'. Mechanical rooms are considered rentable area, while shafts are not. It has the advantage of tenant control by a full-floor user, but the disadvantage of no backup if the compressor is down for repairs, unless the units are purchased with multiple compressors.

- Built-up DX unit with supply and return fans on the roof. More efficient than the individual DX systems, but requires more non-rentable shaft area. Can be complex to design and build and difficult to maintain.

- Multiple packaged DX units on the roof with air handling units (14' x 14') on each floor. The building would require four units of at least 110 tons each, while factory standard units are normally 70 tons or less.

- Central chiller plant. Two centrifugal chillers on the roof or at grade level with VAV air handlers on each floor. This was considered the best and most efficient system, but the most costly.

The self-contained DX system located on each floor was initially selected for incorporation into the baseline budget. With fans and a conditioned air loop on each floor, and electric service provided by bus duct to an electrical room on each floor as part of the base building, it would add approximately $4.00/gsf to the shell cost. To make a decision of this magnitude, it was necessary to evaluate all of the factors involved.

The TIs with the centralized system would be reduced by about 80¢/usf for electrical work and about $3.20/usf for HVAC, or a total of $4.00/usf. If tenants would accept this lesser allowance for their TI work as an even exchange, this would result in an approximate equivalent base building construction savings of $3.40/gsf, reducing the premium to about $100,000 with the benefit of energy savings.

To accomplish these changes it was deemed necessary to include the cost of electricity in the rental rate. Tenants in the area were paying for their electricity separately at an average cost of approximately $1.44 annually. The Development Officer and the brokers agreed they could successfully handle both issues—the reduction in TI allowance and an additional 15¢ per month in the base rent to include all energy costs. The changes were incorporated in the baseline budget and the pro forma, which coincided with the timing of the negotiation of the Brandes Lease.

An owning and operating analysis study was then undertaken to compare the DX system with a central chiller system. In both cases a VAV air system with hot water reheat at the perimeter boxes was included. The analysis indicated a cost premium of $300,000 for the central chiller system with a minimum annual operating savings of $60,000 (38¢ per rsf). In addition, the maintenance costs were projected be lower and the dependability greater over the years. The offset between the additional base building cost and the electrical energy savings made this upgrade financially attractive, and it was accepted.

The final chiller calculated tonnage was 450 tons. It was decided to use two 250-ton McQuay centrifugal chillers, since that was a natural equipment breakpoint. The centrifugal chillers have a minimum efficiency of 0.55 kw per ton.

An evaluation was made as to whether to utilize a small chiller or a condenser water loop to provide for tenant's 24-hour requirements. A 95-ton, four-compressor reciprocating chiller, with a minimum efficiency of 0.83 kw per ton at full load, was selected because of the potential for additional operational savings at low daytime cooling loads, and the initial costs were approximately even. The higher kw per ton for these units is offset by using the chillers in increments that balance with the load. The large chillers have pumps and cooling tower cells to match, and the smaller chiller will utilize the existing tower with its own pumps.

DESIGN CRITERIA FOR THE HVAC SYSTEM

Climate
    Summer: 88°F dry bulb; 72°F wet bulb (equiv. to 47% RH)
    Winter: 42°F dry bulb;

Space Conditions
    Summer: 72°F dry bulb;
    Winter 70°F dry bulb;

Envelope
    Roof R-19
    Walls and spandrels R-13
    Glass Shading coefficient 0.66

Ventilation Rates
    Occupied areas per ASHRAE Standard 62-198
    General office area
        Total circulation 1.5 cfm/usf average (10 air changes / hour)
        Minimum outside air 20 cfm/person (0.1 cfm/usf)
    Toilet rooms, janitor closets, etc.— 12 air changes per hour
    Store rooms, electric rooms, etc.— 4 air changes per hour

Tenant Electrical Load—office equipment and lighting—3½ watts per gsf

Design Occupancy
        Office space—150 usf per person
        Lobbies and public areas—50 usf per person
        Conference rooms—20 usf per person

There had been some concern as to the electrical load required by Brandes, but their requirements were within the design allowance.

Several means of additional energy savings were evaluated. Low temperature air and water distribution for cooling is not really applicable in this climate, nor is an interior CO_2 outside air reset system to draw in less outside air when the interior air has minimal impurities, usually more beneficial under extreme temperature conditions.

The possibility of an outside air economizer was studied, bringing in excess outside air when it is cooler than the interior air, to reduce operating costs. There was computed to be approximately a $20,000 annual savings. With fan rooms on each floor, there was not sufficient space for the fans and the required area for outside air ducts, and the façade design did not lend itself to louvers that would bring in outside air. Putting either two or four air handlers on the roof was then evaluated. This solution would add $200,000 to $250,000, plus massively increasing the penthouse, so the idea was dropped. Incidentally, the larger airshaft would have been excluded from the rentable area, while the fan rooms on each floor included. The opportunity for the economizer was reluctantly dropped.

The maximum main duct velocities do not exceed 1500 fpm on the floors and 1700 fpm in the shafts. The tenants will provide perimeter zones served with a single central air duct using variable air volume (VAV) terminal air units complete with hot water heating coil and lined discharge plenums, with an assumed allowance of 500 square feet per zone. The tenants will also provide interior zones, estimated at 1200 square feet per zone, with single duct VAV terminal air units set to limit the reduction of air volume to minimum acceptable ventilation requirements.

After review of the building height and the ambient air quality at this location, it was determined that 60% washable outdoor air filters would be satisfactory. There would be both an initial and ongoing energy savings over the use of 85% filters, at no real disadvantage to the occupants.

Sound attenuation for the air distribution system is primarily through sound traps on the return air, interior duct insulation that is covered with a non-microbial coating to prevent particles of the liner from entering the air stream on the main supply duct, and the limitation of duct velocities. The air distribution ducts for the floor distribution are insulated outside with fiberglass with foil backing, as the foregoing installations should satisfy the air noise issues.

There is a nominal 500-ton stainless steel, induced-draft, cross-flow, two-cell cooling tower, with a constant speed 750-gpm condenser water pump provided for each chiller. Water treatment and filtration systems are provided.

Variable speed drives are provided on the cooling tower fans. Such drives on the chillers were too expensive to obtain a sufficient return.

The heating hot water system is provided from two low NOx, 1500 btu/hour input capacity gas-fired water-tube hot water boilers with 80% minimum efficiency. Two constant speed hot water distribution pumps are provided. Heating is accomplished through two-row hydronic heating coils at the exterior (perimeter and top floor) terminal reheat VAV boxes.

Stairwell and vestibule pressurization are provided. Each stairwell has a pressurization fan, and a motorized damper will control the pressurization for its vestibules. All air systems are equipped with smoke dampers and smoke detectors (duct mounted or area detectors) to record smoke from the fire floor. These systems are discussed more thoroughly in Chapter 27.

San Diego Gas and Electric Company will provide a cash rebate of approximately $40,000 for the calculated energy savings designed into the system.

PLUMBING SYSTEM

The plumbing systems consist of the storm, sanitary, domestic water, gas, fuel oil and irrigation systems.

Storm Water Drainage System

The roof and eighth floor patios are drained by gravity from roof drains through inside leaders, house drains and house sewers to the site storm sewers. Overflow drains are set 2" higher than the roof drains and have a separate set of house leaders and drains to the site storm sewers. Subsoil drainage is provided as required by the soil engineer's report.

Sanitary Drainage and Vent Systems

Plumbing fixtures are drained by gravity through soil, waste and house drains and house sewers to site sanitary sewers. Vent stacks were installed extending through the roof as per code. A duplex sewage ejector pump is provided in the parking structure's lowest level for drainage with a discharge connection into gravity sanitary lines.

Domestic Water Supply System

Metered water service for the 4" domestic water is extended from street mains to the building and parking structure through reduced-type backflow preventors. Water is distributed from the first to fourth floors at city main pressure through a pressure reducing station (PRV) and the valved mains, risers, and branches to plumbing fixtures and equipment, providing a minimum of 30 psi at the highest fixture. Operating pressure on the riser serving the fifth through the eighth floors will be augmented by a triplex booster pumping system, provided with a pressure reducing station at the fifth floor to limit pressure to a maximum of 80 psi at any fixture or equipment. Shock arrestors are provided at the top of risers to avoid water hammer conditions. Domestic tempered water for the faucets in the toilet rooms is provided by localized electrical instant water heaters with re-circulating pumps.

Gas System

Gas is brought in from the street main and distributed through a gas meter and regulator provided by San Diego Gas and Electric with valved mains, riser, and branches to the space heating gas-fired boiler and any kitchen appliances requiring gas.

Fuel Oil System

Fuel oil systems are provided for the emergency generator and the diesel driven fire pump incorporating double walled supply and return piping, a transfer oil pump and double-walled fuel tanks in two-hour enclosures. The generator utilizes a 200-gallon tank, and the fire pump has a 140-gallon tank. Monitoring devices include overfill protection annunciation, remote fill, overflow shutoff solenoid and alarms, and leak detection monitoring and alarm, all with remote monitoring and signaling devices.

Landscape Irrigation

An irrigation system is provided throughout the site, controlled by zoned timers. The water is sub-metered so that the cost can be prorated one half to the hotel and one half to the office building.

BUILDING MANAGEMENT SYSTEM

The energy portion of the building management system (BMS) is a distributed direct digital control (DDC) system that monitors and controls the various set points of the HVAC system and controls the equipment from its central location. It is a Johnson Controls Metasys system that can connect to BACnet networks and can monitor LonWorks controllers, allowing communication with the control language of various equipment manufacturers. The system utilizes an N1 Ethernet/IP Network, and is certified to the ISO 9000 Quality System Standard. It provides standalone control, supervisory control and information management, and it is fully expandable. While each application specific controller is completely independent, its operation can be dictated by a higher level controller through the network. There is a touchtone telephone interface, with appropriate password protection, to permit the building engineer to provide or change instructions.

Tenant requests for after hours climate control for a specific area from approved tenant representatives, with a valid password, is by a telephone interface through a program that guides them with voice prompts. All prompts must be answered, including the time for the termination of service, prior to the system accepting a request for initiation.

The system automatically generates a detailed, custom work order and subsequent invoice, with split billing for multiple tenants using the same system simultaneously, if desired. If a tenant desires ongoing service, the automatic start and termination of the service can be programmed up to a year in advance. When a tenant is in default, their password can be disabled until they become current.

There is an automatic paging system to notify the building engineer in the event of a critical alarm (non-critical alarms are saved in the operator work station for later review). It supports dedicated or commercial paging services and cell phones, and can be programmed to contact multiple engineers at differing times of day.

The operator workstation, which need not be in the same building, permits ready reference to all alarm and set points, as well as permitting programming and implementing various control strategies. Due to the sensitivity of its impact on the systems, the password system has five levels of protection. There are graphical displays of each floor and each system. Trend graphs, history logs, custom programs and schedules can be obtained at the touch of a button. For example, customized reports can be prepared that contain up-to-the-minute consumption and operating costs, which can be linked to spreadsheets, word processor or database programs.

A thermostat in each zone controls a variable air volume box that varies the flow of cooled air to the space by modulating an internal damper. The damper has a minimum position to ensure sufficient airflow to maintain appropriate IAQ. Variable volume boxes that serve the perimeter and top floor of the building also have hot water coils with the flow controlled by the thermostat to provide heating when necessary. Alarms indicate a stalled damper, a starved box, flow and other points.

Each thermostat in the occupied spaces has visual readouts and allows adjustments through the touch of a button. The range of adjustment set points is programmable through the BMS system, and is normally 1°F down and 1°F up from the building design temperature.

The BMS system has parallel annunciation and controls with the fire and life safety system.

In addition to the programmed set points, start up and shutdown sequences, the efficiency of the operating system is controlled by:

- Optimal start—uses outdoor and indoor temperature sensors to determine the optimal time to start the air-handling units and chillers.

- Dry bulb economizer—when the outdoor air temperature is greater than a predetermined setting on an economizer switch, the outdoor air damper is decreased toward the minimum position, and when it is below the set point, the damper is modulated toward full open to provide the maximum available free cooling.

There is no electrical demand control or load shedding programmed into the system, but it is capable of handling these functions in the future with the addition of the appropriate CTs.

ALARM AND/OR CONTROL POINTS:

Air Handling Unit Control
    Outside temperature
    Return temperature
Filter pressure drop
Chilled water coil supply/return
Fans—status/speed/start/stop
Supply air temperature
Supply air smoke detector
Supply air static pressure
Pressure differential across filters
Chilled water valve position
Fans—status/start/stop/speed
Variable Air Volume Boxes
    Zone temperature
    Zone set point
    Sideloop (humidity, dew point)
Supply air temperature to space
Damper actuator
Velocity pressure sensor
Reheat valves (perimeter and top floor only)—status
Reheat water temperature
Velocity pressure
On/off
Heating Hot Water System
    Pumps—status/on/off
    Boiler—alarm/on/off
    Hot water supply/return- temperature and valve position
Chillers and Chilled Water System
    Pumps—status/start/stop/on/off
    Temperature—supply/return
Valve status—supply/return/bypass
    Chillers—status/start/stop
    Chiller temperature flow—supply return
    Chiller flow—supply/return
    Chiller load—amps/ton-hours
    Lead/lag capability
    Load trend lines
    Oil pressure
    Refrigerant pressure
    Chiller room refrigerant sensor
    Chiller room exhaust fan—status/start/stop

ALARM AND/OR CONTROL POINTS (Continued)

Condenser Water System
    Fans—status/start/stop/speed
    Condenser water valves—supply/return/bypass/status/open/close
Tower water level
Stairwell / Vestibule Pressurization Control
    Supply fans—status/start/stop
Supply air damper actuator
    Vent damper actuator
    Stairwell static pressure
    Vestibule static pressure
Lighting Control
    On/off/after-hour sweeps
    Reduce parking and landscape levels at specified times
Fire Fighter's Smoke Control (mirrors Main Fireman's Panel)
    Stairway pressurization fans—off/on/auto
    Building supply and exhaust fans—off/on/auto
    Exhaust smoke dampers (by floor)—open/fault/close
    Wondoors (Brandes stairway)—open/fault/close
Parking structure
    Exhaust fans—status/start/stop
    Carbon monoxide sensor
    Elevator equipment room fans—TS control
Life Safety
    Mirrors central Life Safety panel

ELECTRICAL and COMMUNICATIONS SYSTEMS 26

The Electrical Systems portion of this chapter discusses Building Power Distribution, Tenant Miscellaneous Power Requirements, Tenant Power and Distribution, and Equipment Energy Efficiency, and there is a special emphasis on the important field of Lighting Selection. Under Communications we will discuss some of the current needs of tenants in a rapidly changing world of communication.

ELECTRICAL SYSTEMS

The electrical systems are among the most important, and frequently the least discussed, of the building systems. Many Development Officers just assume the correct decisions will be made, but the author believes it is necessary to review these systems in depth.

Building Power Distribution

Depending on the location, electrical power may be available from the source at as high as 25 KV, 13KV or 4160 volts, or as low as 208 volts. When sizing the building incoming power requirements, a reasonable practice is to size the transformers, switchboard, and incoming service for (a) the amount required for base building lighting and equipment, plus (b) 6 to 8 w/usf for tenant lighting and power. Riser design is based on the load served. The allowance for tenant power is discussed in detail in the next subsection. The transformers, which are most often provided by the utility, are then sized based on the above, but using a reasonable diversity for the tenant power load.

The power source enters the building in a protected vault, where it connects to the building system through the primary transformer (or in smaller suburban buildings is served from an outside transformer close to the service entry point of the building) and the building's switchgear. The power is then distributed at high voltage (the higher the transmission voltage, the lower the power losses) to the various load centers, such as the mechanical, elevator, other equipment rooms, and the electrical rooms on each floor. The starters for major equipment are located in motor control centers (MCC) near the equipment served. This distribution may be either by cable or bus duct risers.

It is always beneficial if the source of power is available from two different sources (preferably different substations) to minimize the possibility of a power outage. In most suburban areas power is not available from two different substations, but in downtown settings, there is frequently a hard grid system with multiple sources of power.

In some markets the practice, where service is available at lower voltages (primarily at 120/208 volts), is for direct metering of tenant electricity by the utility. This requires a meter room with a sufficient number of meters for the unknown tenant mix to be located at the ground level with 24-hour access by the utility.

An analysis is required to ascertain the most cost effective electrical distribution system for each building. Normally, power at the highest available voltage, up to 4160 volts, would be distributed directly to the chillers with step-down transformers at various locations throughout the building. The voltage from 4160-volt incoming power is reduced through the step-down transformers to 277/480 volts for serving air conditioning system motors (cooling towers, pumps, air handling unit fans), vertical transportation, and fluorescent lighting. 120/208-volt step-down transformers would provide power for incandescent lighting, tenant workstation power, receptacles, and numerous small loads. In some instances, it has been considered economical for 120/208-volt power to also serve the fluorescent lighting, instead of 277/480 volt, but this is becoming less frequent as incandescent lamps are replaced with CFLs.

Tenant Miscellaneous Power Requirements

An important issue for the Development Officer to understand is the design building electrical load, as it is a balance between satisfying the National Electric Code, building construction cost, lease language and tenant requirements. An understanding of this issue is complicated because the code is both unreasonable in regard to lighting and is somewhat ambiguous, tenant power requests are frequently unreasonable, and there is confusion as to what constitutes a square foot.

Simplistically, the code requires the building electrical service to provide for the entire electrical load of the base building equipment and machinery without considering diversity. It specifies a minimum of 3 w/sf for lighting and 2 w/sf for tenant power. The strange facts regarding the code are that the building equipment clearly has some diversity, no office space needs, or can reasonably use, 3 w/sf for lighting, and virtually all tenants desire, and usually need, the availability of more than 2 w/sf of connected power load. The code does not indicate whether a sf is a gross sf, a rentable sf, or a useable sf. Most engineers assume the code means per gross square foot, but some engineers justify it as meaning per rentable square foot since nonrentable areas are shaft penetrations requiring very little lighting or power.

The code does not permit the use of any excess lighting electrical capacity for tenant miscellaneous power until after one year. For a multi-tenant building it does not clarify whether the year starts at Certificate of Occupancy or when substantially occupied—certainly an acceptable assumption is at the Certificate of Occupancy.

For purposes of discussing tenant lighting loads, an assumption of using rentable square feet is reasonable, since the core lighting is included in calculating the power assigned to lighting. Tenant miscellaneous power is best discussed in terms of usable area, since tenant equipment is placed only in useable areas.

To further complicate this issue, very few tenants really know their electrical power needs, and are frequently goaded by brokers who recommend very high numbers they have heard discussed, such as 6 to 8 w/sf, for miscellaneous power to ensure their client is never short of power. Interestingly, the author has never discussed this issue with a broker who knew whether they were talking about connected load or consumption, or whether they meant gross, rentable or useable square feet. It is almost a certainty they mean connected load and useable square feet, whether they realize it or not. Over the years, the author has rarely received a definitive answer to these questions, or justification for the magnitude of an apparently excessive request. In spite of the questionable justification, however, it can become a marketing issue that the Development Officer must handle as best he can.

One reason for this detailed discussion is to provide the Development Officer with the background to understand the calculations that the engineer uses to size the electrical service, which can significantly affect the project cost. There are certain incremental increases of electrical service equipment size that cause large increases in cost, sometimes with no benefit to the project. The other reason is so the Development Officer will understand what he can agree to in the lease negotiations, and the impact on the calculation of the air conditioning load.

It is essential both for discussion purposes and in the lease, to understand and spell out the difference between connected load and consumption, or demand. (Demand, as used in this section must not be confused with the utility's demand charge, which represents the charge for the peak usage of electricity during a billing period. Demand control, when discussed in Chapter 25, will mean peak electrical loads.) Connected load is the sum of the electrical requirements of each and every light, device and 20-amp receptacle circuit installed. There is a maximum connected load permitted on each circuit or riser based on the size of the circuit breaker that protects that circuit or riser. If the installation follows the reasonable practice of 6 to 8 receptacles per circuit, and about one receptacle per 170 usf, the connected receptacle load alone is about 1w/usf. Therefore, a total connected load of 3w/usf, or even 4w/usf for a tenant's connected power load is normally reasonable.

Consumption, or demand, is the actual usage of electricity, and reflects the diversity of use from all connected electrical loads, including the many unused or lightly used receptacle circuits, and may vary throughout the day and from time to time. Demand directly affects the cost of electricity and the heat load transmitted into the space, which must not exceed that assumed by the engineers in calculating the size of the HVAC system, if satisfactory comfort is to be maintained. A reasonably safe assumption of combined demand for HVAC purposes is 3 w/gsf, with 4 w/gsf a maximum except in very unusual circumstances. This normally translates to a normal design of 3 to 3½ w/usf. Most office buildings actually operate in the 2w to 3w/usf range. Any demand above the 3½ w/usf should create a tenant charge for increased HVAC system capacity, and additional energy charges for HVAC and electricity.

An interesting calculation is to compute the tenant lighting and miscellaneous power load according to the code, which presumably totals 5w/gsf. Since a normal ratio is about 85 useable square feet to 100 gross square feet, one could conclude that the code required 5.88 w/usf for the tenant load. Given that the tenant lighting will require 1¼ to 1½ w/usf, 4.38 to 4.63 w/usf remains available to assign to tenant miscellaneous power. Conversely, if a tenant insists on 6 w/sf, you can reasonably assume that it means per useable square foot, resulting in an allowance of only 5.1 w/gsf for that load. The useable square foot (usf) definition should be carefully spelled out in the lease.

As discussed in Chapters 25, 31, and 32, if an excessive amount of tenant power availability is agreed to under the lease, the tenant may have a right to assume that their HVAC system will perform properly if they use that full amount of power, unless a lesser demand allowance is included in the lease for HVAC calculation purposes and electrical charges. Otherwise, by approving an excessive amount of allowable tenant power you may be paying a triple premium—in the cost of the building electrical service, the cost of increased HVAC capacity, and increased electricity cost. All or some of those costs may have no real benefit to anyone.

Another factor to consider is the possibility of a construction cost penalty in the sizing of the electrical distribution. The increased cost of extra electrical availability is relatively minor unless the size of the system reaches a costly break point, such as when the service exceeds 4000 amps. At such break points, there is a very large jump in construction cost.

Tenant Power Distribution

Miscellaneous power is distributed to the tenant space from electrical closets on the floor. The step-down transformers, where required for miscellaneous power, are usually located in the electric closets, along with the distribution panels. The discussion of the computation of tenant miscellaneous power is covered in detail above and under Services of Landlord in Chapter 32.

Miscellaneous power is provided for equipment and special lamps through wall or floor mounted duplex receptacles and, in the case of some large clerical floors, through ceiling power poles. Wall-mounted receptacles at a height of 15" above the finished floor are the most common to include in the building's work letter. Floor outlets, or wall outlets mounted immediately above or in the base are more expensive, and are normally excluded from the landlord's cost in a work letter.

Where floor mounted outlets are required, the conduit is run from a panel on the floor to be served, down into the ceiling plenum of the floor below, across to the desired location and up through a hole drilled in the floor. The source panel must always be on the same floor as an outlet served from it.

There are some users who desire under floor duct systems (i.e., electrical duct systems that are part of the floor system), sometimes referred to as an electrified floor. The rationale is that wires can be pulled through these ducts, and then a shallow hole is drilled through to set a floor-mounted receptacle. There are separate ducts for power and communications. There is no credible evidence available to the author that in a normal office building there is any life-cycle-cost benefit.

The modern day solution for ease of electrical and communication distribution, as well as the ability to provide service at any point on the floor, is the raised floor system that has become very popular and was discussed under Air Distribution Systems in Chapter 25. The cable trays and power distribution can be efficiently organized and can be accessed at any point by removal of the normally 2' x 2' floor sections. There is a significant additional initial cost that must be recovered through a combination of electrical and HVAC advantages.

It was formerly common to install a power grid above the ceiling with one box per bay, or one per 1,000 sf, but varying tenant requirements now dictate that circuits be run in accordance with tenant's plans. While codes permit more, it is good practice to install only 6 to 8 outlets per circuit to permit future changes and additions. Eight outlets are usually sufficient for 1,000 to 1300 usf.

Equipment Energy Efficiency

The passage of the Energy Policy Act of 1992 (EPACT) helped to accelerate the development of new products that are much more energy efficient. NEMA Standard 12-6c was incorporated into EPACT and specifies minimum operating efficiencies for motors. Manufacturers who produce motors with significantly higher efficiencies than required, market them as "premium efficiency" motors. While the cost of these premium efficiency motors are typically 30% to 35% higher than standard efficiency motors, their increased first cost can generally be recovered within two to three years. Upgrading to variable speed drives with high efficiency motors can achieve further savings.

Most motors start at their full operating voltage. With standard motors the initial current draw is typically six times the normal full load operating current. This can accelerate the breakdown of the motor's insulation, cause increased wear on the drive connection and can cause a voltage sag that is significant enough to disrupt the operation of voltage-sensitive computers and control systems. Solid-state reduced voltage starters for chillers eliminate, or significantly reduce, these problems by controlling the motor's voltage during the acceleration phase.

A wide range of variable frequency drives (VFD) have recently demonstrated their effectiveness in fan and pump applications, particularly in systems that operate for extended periods of time at partial load. While widely accepted for their energy savings, their use has created some problems within the electrical distribution system due the generation of harmonic distortions. These distortions can cause problems for computers and other sensitive electronic equipment. Newer VFDs are being developed to filter out and limit the amount of harmonic distortion, and any proposed equipment should be reviewed carefully to ensure that adequate filtering is incorporated.

Other Power Distribution Issues

When emergency generators are required to provide electricity for the building's emergency power requirements, a review should be made as to whether or not a slightly larger generator would be an attractive tenant amenity by offering limited connection to the emergency power as long as no additional liability is undertaken. In addition, some utilities will enter into an agreement that if you will run your generator when directed by them at their peak demand, the utility will reduce your full year's cost for electricity based on your contractual agreement with them. In such a circumstance, the generator equipment should be upgraded to a quality rating better than "standby," and it should be recognized that there will be some additional electrical construction cost related to controls for "switching over" from utility company to your own power for a particular load.

In addition, utilities have many incentive rebate programs if you install energy efficient equipment or construct an energy efficient building to reduce electrical capacity, particularly their system-wide demand. The availability of these incentives may go through a period of uncertainty as the country converts to competitive electrical supply

The use of "K-rated" transformers and electronic grade panels to provide "clean" circuits for tenants is discussed in Chapter 30.

All electrical equipment must be provided with appropriate concrete bases and mounting isolators, and all floor and wall penetrations must be properly sealed, to minimize or eliminate the transmission of vibration and sound to occupied spaces.

Lighting Selection

Lighting selection is very important for the Development Officer to understand and to focus his attention toward. Some of the reasons this effort is necessary are:

- Depending upon where the cost responsibility lies, lighting systems and their controls represent a rather significant cost—either to the base building or to the tenant through their TI costs.

- The quality of lighting can have a major impact on user comfort and future leasability.

- The type of lighting required can affect the building's ceiling height.

- The lighting energy designed and used in the space impacts both the initial installation cost and the operating costs of the HVAC system.

- Lighting design greatly impacts long-term energy usage and operating costs—one life-cycle-cost analysis showed that of the total cost over the system's life, 8–9% was initial cost, 1–2% was maintenance, and 90% was energy cost.

- While energy efficient lighting savings may not necessarily be recognized by the market on initial leasing, operating cost savings relative to your competition drop directly to the bottom line upon re-leasing when an accurate record of your costs is available.

Lighting, which is also discussed in Chapter 30, is a very important design issue; the Development Officer, in attempting to satisfy the visual comfort and effectiveness of the office worker, must take into consideration many often-conflicting factors.

- Quantity—the amount of light available at the task, is usually in the range of 60 to 65 footcandles at the desktop, but the requirement can be higher or lower depending on the intensity of light required and the duration of the task. Lighting must be appropriate to the task—too much light wastes energy, and too little can reduce productivity.

- Efficacy—measured in lumens per watt, or the rate in which the fixture is able to convert electrical input (watts) into light output (expressed in lumens). The overall energy efficiency of the lighting system is the efficacy applied to the lighting level required in footcandles.

- Comfort—Visual Comfort Probability (VCP) is the measure of the percentage of persons who would find the overall lighting comfortable. A major factor in visual comfort is glare. While glare has always been a visual issue, its importance has increased with the extensive use of CRTs. Glare is controlled through the choice of reflectors and/or lenses, or through the installation of indirect or direct/indirect lighting fixtures.

- Color temperature—called Correlated Color Temperature, is the warmth or coolness of the light as expressed in degrees Kelvin. Warm is in the 3000K range and provides a personal, intimate atmosphere; neutral is in the 3500K range and is friendly and inviting; and cool is in the 4100K range and tends to create a clean, neat and efficient atmosphere. All three of these ranges are applicable to various office functions, with the warm range most applicable to executive offices, conference rooms and lobbies. The daylight range of about 5000K is for bright exacting sight, more applicable to galleries and medical examination areas than to offices.

- Color rendition—measured on a Color Rendition Index (CRI), it represents the ability of a light source to represent colors in objects. A higher CRI is considered a higher quality of light because people and objects are more natural and visual clarity is increased.

- Maintenance—the long-term maintenance cost is a function of the initial ballast and lamp cost versus the lamp life and replacement cost. Due to these maintenance costs, as well as energy efficiency, the short-lived incandescent lamp is rapidly disappearing from office buildings. It should be noted that fluorescent lamps have a life of up to 24,000 hours compared to the 500 to 2,000-hour life of incandescent lamps.

Lighting Fixtures

Standard office space fixtures have typically been 12", 20", or 24"-wide fluorescent fixtures that are 48" long. They were normally lay-in fixtures with 12-foot long flexible wiring tail (usually gives one or two feet of slack with a normal layout—with a 15- to 17-foot tail, lights can be placed anywhere) that are installed in a ceiling grid and wired to an electrical conduit grid above the ceiling. The fixtures must be coordinated with the ceiling tile size to provide a neat ceiling appearance. The author has historically preferred the 24" x 48" fixture with 12" x 12" fissured ceiling tile, but as the 24" x 24" tile with a semi concealed spline has rapidly increased in popularity it has become the standard for most office installations. This change has tended to increase the popularity of four-foot and six-foot modules. An option to satisfy a five-foot module is to use 20" x 20" tile with a 20" wide fixture.

Fixtures are frequently provided with modular plug-in connections such that the fixtures plug into each other, in a "daisy chain" manner thereby eliminating most of the "hard wiring" requirements.

Light fixtures must not only provide sufficient light for general office work, generally agreed to be between 50 and 75 foot-candles at the desk level, but to do so without excessive contrast ratios and glare. It should also provide a visual comfort probability, the percentage of people who would find the fixture acceptable, of 70 or greater. The most popular office space fixture over the last two decades has been the parabolic reflector type that provided the best combination of lumen efficiency and quality of light. Three lamp parabolic reflector fixtures at about 1/80 sf provide quality lighting of about 65 foot-candles at the desktop at 1.2w/usf. Other fixtures use acrylic and Para wedge lenses, but acrylic lenses tend to look very inexpensive and Para wedge lenses appear quite dark.

Indirect lighting has become an increasingly important requirement for some users, partially to improve visual acuity when using computer monitors, and partially due to the perception of a more comfortable, uniform and glare-free light. Indirect lighting fixtures are either hung from the ceiling, where the fixture design requires either a 9'6" or 10'0" ceiling height for quality lighting, or they can be mounted on top of the cubicle enclosures.

A recent development that may seriously challenge the parabolic reflector type of fixture and satisfy the indirect lighting requirements is the recessed direct/indirect fixture. These fixtures can be either 24" x 24" or 24" x 48", with the 24" x 24" being the most popular when that size ceiling tiles are used. The square fixture has either two or three "U"-shaped lamps that are rated at 38 watts, located near the centerline of the fixture with a semi-circular perforated deflector beneath them. The deflector lets some of the light through the perforations (generally 30%) and directs the remainder (generally 70%) back onto the reflector and then into the space. Glare is minimized and the fixture purports to provide an even and more comfortable light for general office work, with about the same light output as the parabolic reflector fixture when using the same number of lamps, and more satisfactory for working with CRTs. It provides equal or better color rendition index and visual comfort probability. In addition, for those users who had demanded indirect lighting, it can be provided without requiring greater ceiling height to accommodate pendent hung fixtures. These fixtures are more expensive, and the lamps are about three times the price of the T8s, but this will probably tend to equalize with time. The major advantage of these fixtures is the ability to provide partial indirect lighting effectively with 9'0" ceiling heights.

A type of fixture preferred by many users is an air troffer fixture—actually it is a linear air diffuser that is coordinated with and fits into the light fixture. The diffuser is placed in the air slot in the light fixture and the air comes in through a reveal around the fixture's perimeter, and provides a better appearance than separate air diffusers in the ceiling. It is also common to have a slot in the fixture reveal to provide for the return air in lieu of 2' x 2' square return air grilles that can be provided. The use of this type of air troffer, while aesthetically more attractive, generally increases the cost since a greater quantity of air devices is required.

Heat extraction fixtures, so called because return air is drawn through the fixture itself over and cooling the lamps and then into the ceiling plenum, have frequently been used because the air passes over the lamps and ballasts preventing some of the heat from entering the office space. The author believes this is of primary importance in very high lighting wattage installations, but much less important in the current lower wattage installations. This type of fixture should not be confused with a fixture that permits return air to pass through slots around the fixture that was discussed previously.

Note that light fixtures and other equipment supported by a ceiling grid must have a secondary support, such as chains, in seismic zones to prevent injury if one should fall during an earthquake.

Ballasts

Electronic ballasts have become the industry standard and, when used in conjunction with the T8 fluorescent lamps, can provide the same lighting levels formerly achieved by magnetic ballasts and T12 lamps while using up to 40% less energy. They also offer better color rendition—a color rendition index in the high 70s to low 80s, compared to the 60s for the older T12 lamps. Incidentally, while on the subject of CRI, there is much new research into the effect of color on human response, which should be followed as the information becomes known.

Dimmable electronic ballasts are now the state of the art due to their high efficiency and their ability to control the light through a wide range of light levels, down to 20% or less of the lamps rated light output. Special dimmable ballasts can reduce the levels even further. An electronic ballast can operate two to four fluorescent lamps, and the same ballast can operate 26, 32 and 42-watt lamps. It is important for the fixture to be wired in parallel so that when a lamp burns out, only that one lamp goes dark.

Aside from reducing energy consumption, electronic ballasts offer other advantages, such as an operating frequency of 20,000 to 50,000 kilohertz as compared to 60 hertz for magnetic ballasts. This higher frequency virtually eliminates the flicker associated with magnetic ballasts. Electronic ballasts operate more quietly than their predecessor.

Lamps

The T8 lamp is currently the standard in this country because it can be retrofitted into the fixtures formerly designed for T12 lamps. The next major improvement in fluorescent lighting is the T5 lamp, which at 28 watts compared to the 32-watt T8 lamp, offers more light with less energy, with an output of 104 vs. 88 lumens per watt. These T5 lamps are currently in use in Europe, and a newer version is being developed that is even brighter. T5s cannot be used in a simple retrofit, as they are ⅝" diameter as compared to the 1" diameter for the T8 lamps, and require new fixtures designed to optimize the light output and control glare.

Compact fluorescent lamps (CFLs) have now been developed so that a 15-watt CFL emits as much light as a 60-watt incandescent lamp, with good color rendition, and has a rated life nearly ten times as long. CFLs are now available with dimming electronic ballasts and as replacements for standard 75, 100, and 150-watt incandescent lamps. The CFLs should always be used where incandescent lamps were formerly specified.

Some manufacturers are ensuring their lamps pass the Toxic Characteristic Leaching Procedure (TCLP) hazardous test for disposal by producing lamps of low or reduced mercury content. Some of these new low-mercury fluorescent lamps have about 80% less mercury with no reported loss in lamp performance. Even though more expensive, low toxicity of this product can save considerable money in disposal costs.

There are many future improvements in lighting that are in the development stage, of which the Development Officer should be aware. These improvements are driven by the joint objectives of energy reduction (for both cost and environmental reasons), light quality and reduced fixture sizes.

There will be much wider usage of high intensity discharge (HID) lamps, especially metal halide. Metal halides the size of a thumb can produce 80-90 lumens per watt—the amount a four-foot T8 supplies. The newer developments will mean lower wattages, 100% dimmability, and achieving efficacies similar to high-pressure sodium lamps, with much better color rendition. New metal halides using ceramic discharge technology are proving even more efficient than the current quartz technology, and will have rated lives of 6,000 to 9,000 hours.

New developments in electronic technology have paved the way for electrode-less lamps. They can use either an induction coil to create a magnetic field or microwaves to excite the mercury in a lamp in order to create ultraviolet energy that in turn excites a phosphor coating on the inside of the lamp, which then emits light. These induction lamps can offer good color and longer life—some claim a lamp life of from 10,000 to 100,000 hours. Because the lamp has no filament it won't fail from sputtering, breakage by shock or other electrode-related phenomena. Their primary initial applications will be outdoor lighting.

Another new technology is fiber optic remote source lighting. Light will travel from an illuminator through hollow light guides of plastic or glass fibers to mini-fixtures called emitters. The guides can emit light at the end, along their sides, or both. There could be one light source for multiple fixtures.

Further in the future is sulfur light. It will be able to provide an incredibly bright and energy efficient light source with a lamp life in the neighborhood of 100,000 hours.

Lighting Controls

Lighting controls have become almost as important as the fixtures and lamps in the control of energy consumption and the ability to provide the proper lighting level to the task. Many newer energy codes have strong requirements on lighting control to reduce energy consumption. The common means of lighting controls are:

- On/off switching—the old standby, has moved to double switching in recent years where, with a three lamp fixture, lighting can be provided at $1/3$, $2/3$, and full lighting levels. For private offices, or other relatively small controlled zones, dual switching can provide very effective control with disciplined employees.

- Photo sensors—reduce the fixture light levels in an office or perimeter zone through dimming ballasts to compensate for the solar light impact. The location of photo sensors can be important—focusing on a white or black object can distort the reading and, if located behind the drapes, the occupant can negate the benefit by closing the drapes.

- Timer controls—control a lighting zone by turning the lights off at pre-selected times, with a manual or card controlled override if employees are working in the area. The timer will then normally turn the lights back off after a predetermined interval. Public areas such as corridors, lobbies and toilet rooms are normally timer controlled.

- Occupancy sensors—usually by motion detectors. They have frequently been plagued with false "ons" and "offs" in general work areas —drapery movement could incorrectly indicate occupancy and a relatively inactive employee might not be sensed; the latter issue is normally solved with multiple sensors per zone. Most current sensors now employ either infrared or ultrasonic technology and some use both, referred to as dual-technology sensors. Another technology incorporates a micro phonic sensor that listens for minute sounds, even the turning of a page.

- Dimming—is most effective in perimeter zones, particularly when controlled by a photo sensor. Dimming of larger areas can create personnel issues due to a potential lack of agreement as to the proper light level. Individual work area dimmers can be effective, as employees tend to want more control over their work area, but it is not certain that energy consumption would be less than with dual switching.

- Dedicated intelligent controllers, often called "smart panels," use microprocessors to control the lighting within the facility. The microprocessors collect data from such sources as occupancy sensors, photo sensors, energy use monitors, occupancy schedules and switches, and use it to perform control functions including dimming, on-off operation and demand limiting. These microprocessors can be programmed to the specifics of each building. Note that automatic lighting controls should always have a local override capability during off-hours, usually using an access card, telephone dial-up or manual switches.

Tenant Lighting Layout

The lighting layout is normally determined by the tenants to provide for the efficient use of their space. Fixtures are normally located to provide maximum light over desks and workstations. Efficient general office lighting today should require from 0.9 to 1.25 w/sf, although with supplemental use of task lighting, however, acceptable lighting has been provided using from 0.75 to 0.85 w/sf. The current GSA requirement is 1.1 w/sf. The developer has no direct control over the tenant's lighting layout, however, under appropriate market conditions, you can control the overall wattage per square foot for lighting.

The electrical load that is most commonly assumed by the developer for general office lighting is 1 to 1½ w/sf plus another ¼ to ½ w/sf for specialty lighting. Power to the lighting fixtures is at either 277 volts or 120 volts, based on an overall economic analysis by the electrical engineer.

Building Service Lighting

The building service lighting is subject to the same rigorous energy use evaluations as the office space. Public corridors, toilet rooms, and other service areas should be equipped with fixtures with electronic ballasts, and can be operated on-off by motion sensors, usually subject to a normal workday override, or by timers with a manual override. Required "night lighting" in corridors, toilet rooms, and other required areas are excluded from this automatic light extinguishment.

The use of compact fluorescent light fixtures for exit lights, which operate 24 hours per day and 365 days per year, have reduced their energy use by 75% and extended lamp life from the 1,000 to 3,000 hours for incandescent lamps to upwards of 10,000 hours. More recently, exit lights have been produced that use light emitting diodes (LED) requiring only two or three watts per fixture, consuming approximately 5% of the energy of the incandescent lamps, and have a rated life of 25 years.

Specifications and Visual Approval

Specifications are very difficult for anyone other than the design engineer to read and understand, as they consist largely of references to various industry standards and manufacturer's model numbers. Be certain that you understand the quality of the various items of equipment that are specified to ensure they will perform as you intend for many years. If the specifications are not clear to you, have the engineer and the property management specialist discuss with you the cost and service performance of the various alternatives.

As discussed earlier under architectural and mechanical chapters, the Development Officer should visually approve samples of all fixtures, outlet and switch plates, and any other devices that have exposed finishes in the occupied and public spaces. Catalogue cuts do not sufficiently indicate the appearance and quality of these items.

COMMUNICATIONS

Communications will undoubtedly develop into one of the most important tenant issues over the next decade. The availability of fiber optic telephone and cable lines, Integrated Service Digital Network (ISDN) lines, Asymmetric Digital Subscriber Line (ADSL), Digital Subscriber Lines (DSL), Satellite Data Service (SDS), and cable connections directly through the Ethernet to an Internet provider, can vary widely between communications providers and specific geographic areas. To indicate the relative importance of these systems that connect to the Internet, the fastest modem today that connects through standard telephone lines is 56 thousand bits per second (kbs), and even that is only the download speed. ISDN lines require special equipment and transmit at 128 kbs, while DSL lines can transmit at 1.54 million bits per second (mbs), ADSL lines can transmit at from 1 to 6 mbs and the direct cable connection transmits downloads at 8 mbs and uploads at 2 mbs. Current efforts are underway to improve all of these speeds.

It should be noted, however, that DSL speeds can vary with the distance from a central station and cable speeds vary with the number of users actively on a service line. The current status of these services and the needs of different types of tenants will be an important source of knowledge. Locations that are served better than others with communications may draw tenants in the same way that transportation nodes did in a different era. While presumably the recent deregulation of communication systems providers may ultimately provide competitive and equal services to all locations, it might take more than a decade to accomplish that. In the meanwhile, those areas with better service options or lower pricing will have an advantage. This may change drastically in the near future when wireless access is likely to become the primary Internet access.

The technology in this field is changing so rapidly that at the inception of each project the Development Officer, or his designate, should talk to the primary local telephone company, alternate telephone service providers and cable companies to ascertain the availability of both copper and fiber local cabling and the availability of high speed data lines that can be provided to tenants. This is not only important in the building planning, but in preparing information to provide to prospective tenants.

Another facet of this rapidly evolving field is the development of electronic technology that impacts the speed with which data can be transmitted through copper cable. At present, many of the data transmission methods discussed above can be provided through copper. There are some who predict that in the near future the speed of data transmission through copper could even exceed that through fiber.

An important issue in this era of rapid communications change will be for the owner not only to provide, but also to control the access, communications rooms, risers and rooftops to the greatest extent possible. They are not only a tenant amenity, but will become a major source of revenue. Property Management should incorporate a riser management system into their operations, and some have entered into a national contract with companies that specialize in that work to manage rooftop commercial systems for rental income.

During this transition period in data transmission many local telephone companies may have both copper and fiber in the street in the vicinity of your site. Alternative telephone companies will most likely have fiber. Present policy for the primary local telephone companies and the public utility commissions who regulate them is to provide copper service to the building. The telephone company will also bring in fiber, if available, but there will be a charge for this installation unless a specific tenant has a requirement for that service.

Telephone and data transmission equipment are designed for either copper or fiber service, since a laser light is used for the optical signal required for fiber and data is transmitted through copper as electrical signals. Wherever an interconnection is required between the two types of signals it must be through a multiplexer that changes the signals from one type to the other.

Provision of extra incoming conduit and communication room space to accommodate several cable and telephone companies will provide tenants with a competitive opportunity to choose the communication services that best satisfy their needs. To maintain maximum flexibility in your service conduit, and permit as many vendors as possible, require the communication companies to pull their cable in through an intercable (a small plastic tube that protects individual cables within a conduit).

As satellite sources of communications increase in importance, building owners may find that while some receivers and their distribution throughout the building may be expensive, at least it is under the building owner's control. They are an important requirement of some tenants, and a revenue opportunity for the building. As a minimum, bases and jacks (sleeves through the roof) for future receivers should be provided before the roofing is installed.

Standard practice in speculative buildings is to provide communications closet access by the tenant for connections to both telephone and tenant communication requirements. Communications closets best service the tenant's cabling needs when they are located fairly centrally to the work areas. The communication closet is provided with ¾" plywood panels for installation of communication racks. Tenant's equipment is then usually located in their premises. Building low voltage systems are also located in these closets.

For build-to-suit projects it is frequently better to provide separate telephone and communications closets. They should be about 70 to 100 sf to provide room for both access and equipment, and should have 24-hour air conditioning, slightly pressurized to prevent entrance of dust.

Where ceiling plenums are used for return air (almost always) there are really two basic options for low voltage cabling, including telephone and communications wiring. One is to enclose it in conduit. The other is to use a more expensive "plenum rated" cable, having low flame spread and smoke generation properties, without conduit. Plenum smoke detectors are not usually required in either case.

The tenant usually installs telephone and communications wiring in their space. The standard approach is for the developer to install the outlet in a partition with only a fish wire to the plenum. Many users with extensive communications and power cabling are utilizing raised floor systems, usually 12" to 18" high, as discussed in Chapter 25.

In many buildings with heavy communications requirements (where raised floor systems are not used) cable trays are being installed above the ceiling of each floor, in a loop configuration around the core (generally located about midway between the core and the perimeter wall) with an extension to the voice/data closet. This provides a means of organizing the main runs of the tenant's cabling systems. This does, however, introduce physical space problems as the cable tray is usually about 4" deep, and it requires probably 6" of clear space above it in order to be able to lay in new cables and pull out old ones. Frequently this can be coordinated with the ductwork such that no additional ceiling plenum space is required.

The availability of fiber optic cable installed from the street to the building, and in the risers to the communications rooms is an advantage for many tenants at this time, although for some years to come fiber will function in parallel with copper in office buildings to serve varying needs. Category 5 (four pair of twisted cable enclosed in a single jacket) or other shielded cable can be used for distribution to the desktop. Another common communications cable is the T-1 line, with a bandwidth of 1.5 megabits per second. The new EIA/TIA Standards developed by the electronic and communications associations define the design of the infrastructure, cabling pathways and spaces for high-speed data communications.

The coming trend is for the building owner to provide a complete structured cabling system through the building to carry voice, data, image, etc. The system starts with an entrance room, where the various carriers cabling is terminated and then into the building's main communications room. Backbone cabling, normally fiber, runs from the main communication room to the communications closets on each floor, where it is connected to the horizontal cabling on each floor. The horizontal cabling is normally copper, and delivers the cabling to each workstation. It is essential not to undersize the backbone cable. With structured cabling systems the building essentially becomes a data provision intermediary.

CASE STUDY

As in the case of the mechanical systems, the important electrical and communications decisions were made early in the process to facilitate letting the electrical contract on a design/build basis.

Electric Service

12 KV electrical service from the street is stepped down to 480/277-volt three-phase building power in a transformer located in an enclosure west of the surface parking area near the parking structure. (See Figure 24-2.) The main switchboard is 4,000 amps, 480/277-volt, and will be located in the main electrical room on the first floor with outside access for SDG&E.

The tenant electrical load was recommended as 3.0 w/gsf for lighting (required by code) and 4 w/gsf for power, for a total of 7.0 w/gsf available in the building for tenant lighting and power connected loads. In addition, the building will have an estimated equipment load of 8 w/gsf. Actual lighting loads were estimated to be approximately 1.25 watts per useable square foot. Many tenants are asking for six to seven w/sf for power and more than 1.5 for lighting, which we consider excessive, and will rarely, if ever, be used. Note in Chapter 25 the HVAC load assumptions include only 3½ w/gsf electrical demand load (about 4 w/usf) for tenant lighting and power.

A 300kw, 480/277-volt diesel-driven emergency generator with an automatic transfer switch is provided to satisfy the fire/life-safety requirements of a high rise building. The city required the automatic transfer switch to be located in a separate room away from other electrical equipment, a requirement that no one on the team had encountered before. The lease with Brandes required offering to include a 150kw load to serve their equipment at their cost. The generator will serve the following building functions:

- Smoke control fans and motorized dampers
- Fuel oil pumps, controls and alarms for generator
- Stairwell and vestibule pressurization
- Fuel oil tank monitoring alarms
- Sump sewage ejector pumps
- Elevators—switched to operate one at a time
- Fire alarm system
- Fire sprinkler water reserve monitoring
  Egress lighting and exit signs
- Selected Brandes equipment

Lighting

General office lighting was specified to be either 34-watt 2' x 2' or 64-watt 2' x 4' direct/indirect fixtures, at Brandes' option, with T-8 lamps and electronic ballasts with less than 10% total harmonic distortion. Brandes selected the 2' x 2' fixture, that became standard for all tenant areas, and their final lighting load was 1.34 w/usf. Control of the office and conference room lighting is through occupancy sensors and timers. There will be timer controls on all lighting, which will be swept about every two hours after normal hours, is through the BMS system. Tenant after-hours control is further discussed in Chapter 27.

Toilet room lighting consists of staggered 4-foot fluorescent tube fixtures recessed in an architectural cove along the fixture wall. In addition, CFL downlights are included in the center of the room and in the vestibules.

Pendant-hung strip fluorescent fixtures with acrylic lenses are provided in mechanical, electrical, telephone and janitor rooms.

The exit lamps are LED fixtures provided at each stairway door and along each path of egress toward the stairway.

The site and parking structure lighting are described in Chapters 18 and 24, respectively. This lighting is reduced to one-third of the normal level during specified hours through a timer. The top deck of the parking structure and the surface parking are controlled by photocells in addition to timers.

Lighting in the main building lobby is primarily downlights with uplights above the granite columns. The floor elevator lobbies will have staggered 4-foot fluorescent lamps recessed in a ceiling cove.

Lighting controls consist of a microprocessor with programmable relay panels to control time clock scheduling, overrides and local motion sensors, interfaced with the building management system.

Electrical rooms on each undivided floor are provided with bus taps for tenant lighting and power. On divided floors a step-down transformer and switches are provided along with 480/277-volt panels for lighting and 120/208-volt panels for miscellaneous power.

Communications System

Six 4" conduits with radius bends suitable for fiber service are provided from the services in the street to the minimum point of presence (MPOP) in the main telephone room. An empty conduit system consisting of six 4" conduits are provided to the wiring closets on each floor, with appropriate sleeves through the floor.

There is communications system competition, as both Pacific Bell and Time-Warner have telephone service in El Camino Real and Time-Warner has cable service.

Fire-rated telephone mounting boards, ¾" thick minimum, are provided on all walls in each telephone room, with a copper grounding bond at each mounting board.

01 SITE PLAN
NOT TO SCALE

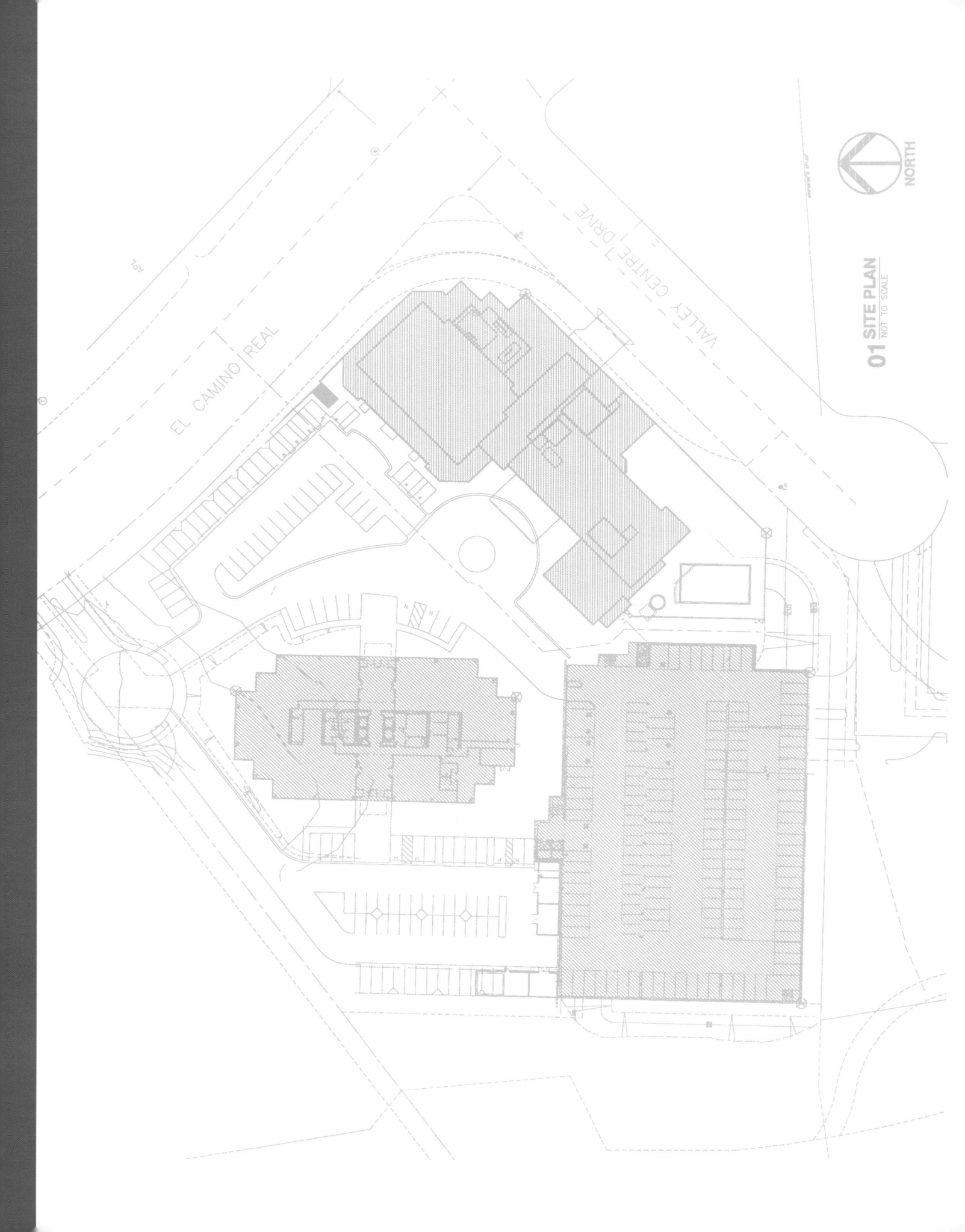

NORTH

EL CAMINO REAL

VALLEY CENTRE DRIVE

LIFE SAFETY and SECURITY SYSTEMS

27

Office buildings are the safest type of structures, but the life safety codes governing them are continually becoming more stringent, to the point where rarely does a building provide life safety features in excess of the prevailing code. An example of this trend is that when the codes changed to require fully sprinklered buildings, most of the codes kept in place many requirements that had been deemed necessary in a non-sprinklered building. A discussion of alarms, exiting, suppression, smoke removal/control, emergency power and fireman's facilities follows.

Almost all life safety codes are totally prescriptive. There is movement toward the potential conversion in many jurisdictions to performance-based codes shortly after the year 2000. The International Code Council (ICC) and the National Fire Protection Association (NFPA) are both well along in the development of performance based codes. Until then the concentration will be on the existing prescriptive codes.

Security systems are normally a function of the determination by property management of the degree of security necessary to satisfy conditions in the market area. A discussion of various levels of security is included.

LIFE SAFETY SYSTEMS

Life safety systems are covered in local codes, and are based on the requirements of the national building codes, National Fire Protection Association (NFPA), and the state insurance boards. The main elements are notification (alarms), exiting, suppression, smoke removal/control, emergency services (emergency power) and firemen's facilities.

Alarms

Smoke or heat detectors—detect products of combustion (POC), actual temperature, or rate of heat rise (ROR). Normal locations are:

- Mechanical and storage rooms
- Ceiling mounted in office areas
- Ceiling mounted in elevator lobbies and corridors
- POC detectors in return air ducts at return air shaft
- POC detectors in main supply ducts
- POC detectors in return air ducts to each air handling system

Sprinkler system alarms are:

- Water flow indicators
- Tampering devices
- Valve closed
- Pull stations on floors
- Fire dampers (shutters)
- Between floors and vertical risers
- In ducts across demising walls

In some situations alarms automatically initiate action, such as activating voice alarms, and activating air exhaust and pressurization systems. Elevator lobby detectors might activate an elevator bypass circuit and send all elevators to the lobby, as well as prevent any elevator from opening its doors at the floor of incidence.

Each alarm is transmitted to the engineer's BMS, the security console and/or the 24-hour security service, and to the fire alarm and control panel (FACP). These indicate the type of alarm (i.e., pull station, POC indicator, flow alarm, or tamper switch), and are zoned by floor, or portions of a floor where feasible. The circuits are supervised by the security panel and the FACP for grounding, open circuit and/or removal of device. The console normally has the ability to manually reset alarms, and to selectively communicate throughout the building (office areas by floor, stairways, elevators, elevator lobbies, and corridors).

Exiting

The basic element for exiting is the stairwells. There are exit signs on emergency power at each stairwell and at appropriate points on the egress paths to the stairwell. Emergency vision lighting is provided in corridors and exit paths to the stairwell. Stairwell doors are electrically unlocked either automatically or from the security console or fireman's station under alarm conditions for fireman's access. There are voice speakers in the stairwells and usually house telephones every five floors connected to the security console and to the fireman's station. The stairwells are pressurized in tall buildings to minimize smoke infiltration and the floor numbers are prominently located on the inside of each stairwell door.

In certain tall buildings, there are emergency plans to evacuate occupants to a lower floor, say three floors below the fire floor, until instructions are received from the fire department or security. In some tall buildings, and for mid-rise buildings in some jurisdictions, some floors are evacuated upward to a helipad on the roof.

Elevators are not to be used for evacuation, and signs are located appropriately to so inform the occupants. Elevators are brought to the lowest terminal, either automatically or from the fireman's station, depending on the type of alarm, and remain there during the emergency unless required for use by the fire department. Emergency power must be provided to permit operation of a minimum number of elevators in certain mid-rise and all high-rise buildings to bring elevators to the ground floor or to assist the firemen. After the emergency is under control, one elevator per bank may be used for evacuation under the supervision of the fire department or security.

At least one exit stairwell, and sometimes two, must exit directly to the outside at the ground level, without passing through any non-fire rated space.

Suppression

The primary form of suppression is a wet pipe building sprinkler system. Sprinkler heads are positioned by code at not more than 7'6" from any wall. NFPA allows certain leniency as to head spacing, maximum distance from walls, etc. for rooms 800 sf and smaller. There may be not less than one head per 225 sf in any case.

The sprinkler loop and major runouts are normally installed on initial shell and core installation. The heads are either not installed until the tenant layout is received or until required for the early occupancy permits on other floors. These heads are usually turned upward in unfinished space, and then later positioned and turned downward as part of the development of the tenant spaces.

The layout of sprinkler heads will vary with the tenant space layout due to code requirements for the number and location of heads in any area, and limitations on how far a head can be from a wall or obstruction. The remaining runouts and heads are then installed to comply with the layout. If heads must be installed prior to tenant layout, sprinkler heads may either be installed at 1/150 sf to 1/180 sf on the assumption that a minimum number of heads will have to be relocated, or at 1/225 sf to meet the minimum requirement for unfinished space with a greater number of heads added and/or relocated.

Pumps are provided if the required pressure to reach the farthest floor served cannot be counted on to be available from the water main pressure. Any pumps will be either diesel or, if electric motor driven, on emergency power as noted later. There is a shutoff valve for the loops at each floor to permit work from time to time, but each valve is "supervised", meaning that an alarm is sent to the engineer's BMS and security consoles or panels showing when any valve is closed.

Standpipes

There are standpipes in or adjacent to each stairwell, and no more than 150 feet from any location on the floor, with a connection and hose for both a 2½" hose for the fire department and a 1½" hose for building personnel, although some jurisdictions no longer require the smaller hoses. Some jurisdictions permit a single riser to serve both the sprinkler and hose standpipes, and others require they be separate.

Fire Extinguishers

Local fire extinguishers are located as required in the core and in tenant spaces.

Special

Special suppression systems such as CO_2 and Halon may be required for cooking or for special equipment, and will not be covered here.

Smoke Removal/Control

Smoke exhaust on a floor is normally provided by a mechanical exhaust system under current codes. The mechanical smoke removal/control is frequently accomplished by reversing controls on the existing air handling system. The dampers that control the air return to the risers are motorized so that the floor can be properly isolated when smoke is detected. The capacity requirement for smoke removal frequently governs the duct sizes. A common approach is to exhaust from the fire floor and pressurize the floor above and the floor below to prevent the spread of the fire.

Formerly, and possibly still on low-rise buildings in some jurisdictions, smoke removal was provided by tempered glass windows no more that 50 feet apart around the perimeter that can be identified and safely broken to relieve the smoke.

Stairwells and sometimes the elevator shafts are pressurized in tall buildings, but some have questioned the value of the latter. Some stairwells in high-rise buildings are required to have a smoke removal shaft that parallels it and removes the smoke from stairwell vestibules at various intervals.

Other codes require the vestibule to be pressurized, but at a lower pressure than the stairwell.

All fans used for pressurization or smoke removal must be on emergency power.

Newer codes are now requiring "positive pressure" fire tests, which require that applicable doors have an "S" label, signifying a smoke rating, in addition to the standard fire resistance rating.

The 1997 UBC has greatly increased the requirements for life safety testing, particularly smoke control. The local jurisdictions are now testing every variation of emergency condition to ensure that the systems all work as intended. The testing has become sufficiently complex and has given rise to a new function by the life safety engineering firms. When they have been through a complete test and given approval, receiving the local jurisdiction approval for a TCO is simplified. This type of testing is lengthening the construction period by several weeks.

Emergency Power

An emergency generator is required to provide emergency power to all life safety equipment in all high-rise and some mid-rise buildings. The load transfer to the generator through automatic transfer switches should occur within 60 seconds. Emergency power should provide for:

- Fire alarm system
- Exit and emergency lighting
- Stairwell lighting
- One elevator for exclusive fire department use (normally the freight) and one elevator per bank
- Voice communication
- Fire pumps, if not diesel
- Fire water storage tank instruments
- Fuel oil system for emergency generator and fire pump
- Emergency sensors, controls and door locks
- Stairwell and vestibule pressurization
- Fans used for smoke removal/control
- Sewage ejectors

While the fire pumps can be motor driven with power provided from the emergency generator, in most instances a diesel driven fire pump will be more economical. Some high-rise codes require a diesel driven fire pump and an electric driven pump which is backed up by an emergency generator.

In certain low-rise buildings where no major equipment is required to be operated on emergency power, emergency and exit lighting may be battery powered.

Fireman's Station

A fireman's station is required adjacent to or in the building lobby with convenient access for firemen. This station contains the fire alarm and control panel (FACP) that includes all life safety alarms, central telephone set, voice communication controls, stairwell door lock release, fire pump control panel, emergency control panel, elevator control panel, and an air handling system control panel. Portable handsets are stored here for firemen's use in the remote jacks located in each stairwell landing, each elevator lobby and in other zones as required. This becomes a command center during fire emergencies to control communications and all life-safety devices and equipment.

Miscellaneous

As discussed earlier under architectural and mechanical chapters, the Development Officer should visually approve samples of all fixtures, outlet and switch plates, and any other devices that have exposed finishes in the occupied and public spaces. Catalogue cuts do not sufficiently indicate the appearance and quality of these items.

SECURITY

Security is a major factor in a building for both personnel and property security. A good security system is a combination of a well-thought-out access system and a protection system consisting of surveillance, audible and visual alarms, voice communication, recordation of all nonstandard activities, and response capabilities. These are all centered in a security console located in the lobby, if available, or in the engineering or manager's office, as well as at the 24-hour security service.

The analysis of the type and scope of a security system is usually made by Property Management and is based on the security conditions in the area, the estimated number and type of tenants, and the level of control desired to meet company standards. As a general rule, individual tenants with unusually tight security requirements provide their own system in their premises, subject to landlord approval.

Access Control

There are four methods of access control, and all security systems are based on one or a combination of them: personal recognition, unique possession, unique knowledge, and biomedics. Personal recognition and biomedics (iris, voice, face and fingerprints) are not currently applicable to a normal office building security system. Unique knowledge (usually numerical codes for touch pads) are effective in certain special circumstances, but since the knowledge of a code cannot be taken back, and in consideration of typical office personnel turnover, it is normally impractical due to frequently required code changes.

Unique possession (keys and cards) is the normal procedure for commercial office buildings. Keys, combined with some form of sign-in/out sheet and identification, have been the basic historic means of access control, but clearly the trend is to access through the use of card systems. Various card systems can not only limit access by specified areas, but also record the time of access, maintain a constant audit trail of access through every controlled door, and a card can be canceled on a moment's notice. The best systems will use the same card, with its unique codes, for access to parking, building ingress, elevator floor access, and even for turning on building equipment after hours and instigating an appropriate charge. Information on various card systems are shown below. The one currently favored by most property managers is the proximity card. Some of the available systems are:

CARD SECURITY SYSTEMS

Type	Description	Advantages	Disadvantages
Magnetic Stripe	A film strip on a plastic card, similar to a credit card. Card is passed over a magnetic head that records information. Normally stored information reflects a site code and ID number.	Most widely used due its lowest cost and ease of re-programming. Damaged cards are readily replaced.	Less durable due to wear on cards and more maintenance necessary on reader heads. Requires protection from dirt and freezing rain if outdoors. Readily duplicated, altered or counterfeited.
Proximity Device	A smart card is one that has the processing capability inside the card. Can be either an intelligent card with read/write capability to revise information, or a memory card with stored information only.	Hands free operation inside wallets or clothing and holds a large amount of data. Can be read from several feet away and is faster than the magnetic stripe. Durable and difficult to duplicate. Easier to use by persons with some disabilities.	Certain electromagnetic fields may affect read distance and performance.
Bar Code	A vertical band of black bars and spaces scanned by an optical reader.	Least cost technology. Can be added to another technology card to add other functions.	Easily damaged and duplicated.
Smart Cards	Access card is held near reader that contains an antenna to read the site, ID and other information from the chip in the card.	Can store large amounts of data. Effective for remote locations.	Lack of database control at the reader—problems occur in denying access to former employees still in possession of their cards.

The author believes that tenant ingress card control should be expanded to include tenant space access where a tenant desires it, but the policy of some management firms precludes this practice due to a liability concern. It is hard to believe that the issue could not be treated with proper waivers, and turned into a tenant amenity.

Various alternative systems are being marketed to compete with card systems that operate in basically a similar manner. Some have a device that resembles a standard key, but operate electronically. Information can be stored in the "key" or provided to the operating system through a read mechanism. The key is inserted in the reader in the same manner as in a standard lock.

Another possible solution is combining a card with a pin number to eliminate the greatest drawback of the keypad system. The card and PIN number can provide a rather secure system.

Most buildings will find it practical to connect directly to an outside security service.

Surveillance

In addition to access control, it is frequently deemed necessary to provide surveillance systems for the protection of personnel and property. The need varies with the location of the property, the hours worked by the employees and the configuration of the building and its appurtenant structures. Closed circuit television (CCTV), monitored and/or recorded is the most effective surveillance method for areas such as parking structures, loading docks, isolated passageways, elevators, emergency building exits and, in some cases, sidewalks and plaza areas. It is frequently necessary to supplement CCTV coverage with audio and emergency call button alarms.

In addition to the ability of surveillance to spot a crime or physical attack, it can record it for later purposes of evidence. CCTV is considered a deterrent, as the perpetrator is never sure how effective the prevention system may be, even during periods that the monitors are unattended.

In addition to any CCTV surveillance installation, every facility should be equipped with security tour stations that must be activated at predetermined intervals by a security officer on scheduled tours.

Alarms

A checklist of the types of alarms and prevention devices that are frequently required for proper security control are listed below. These should be reviewed in detail with Property Management to evaluate how the building size, location, design and proposed management procedures will affect the security system requirements.

Many years ago we encountered a rash of defacements to the wood panels in the elevators in a specific elevator bank. In an attempt to eliminate this vandalism we installed a rotating TV camera in the corner of each cab near the ceiling. The effectiveness of these cameras as a deterrent was immediately obvious—all vandalism stopped—except in the corner directly beneath the camera where it was out of range.

TYPICAL SECURITY POINTS

Perimeter protection
- Exterior lighting
- Exterior TV surveillance (not too common)
- Two-way communication to each entrance
- Alarms on unobservable doors
- Alarm and TV to lockable loading dock entrance
- TV or visual control inside loading dock
- Sensors in loading dock access ramp to alert security after hours
- Alarm and locked doors between loading dock and building space
- Locked grilles, alarms, TV, and sometimes motion detectors on any tunnel entrances
- Alarm, locked doors, and TV at access from parking structure
- Alarm, motion detectors, TV and possibly dead man controls on locked door for stairwell
- Exitways that bypass security control

Elevators
- Normal hours
  - Annunciation of location
  - Status
  - Lockout control

TYPICAL SECURITY POINTS (Continued)

- > Return to lobby control
- > Two-way voice control
- Control after hours
  - > Lock out all elevators from all floors
  - > If manual control, the security guard, after verification of identification, releases one elevator with ability to stop at the approved floor only
  - > If automatic, a card reader or key pad actuates an elevator car and provides the ability to stop at approved floor only
  - > In either case, no other car calls will be answered on the up ride
  - > On the down ride, cars will respond only to down corridor calls, and no car calls
  - > Freight cars will be similarly controlled by security

Equipment alarms
- All life safety alarms outlined elsewhere will be recorded at the security console, as well as certain alarms from the building management system (BMS), as agreed upon with Property Management.

Interior security
- Stairwells
  - > Locked from stair side (emergency unlocking for firemen is covered elsewhere)
  - > Two-way voice control
  - > House telephone every five floors
- Core rooms
  - > Locks and alarms on electrical, telephone, security equipment and mechanical rooms

Security tour stations
In properties without a resident manager, it may be desired to have duplicate alarm printout at a remote central office for ease of review and evaluation. All critical alarms should be transmitted to a 24-hour answering service for response.

CASE STUDY

The life safety was dictated by the code and the preferred procedures of the fire department, while the security system was jointly determined with property management.

LIFE SAFETY SYSTEM

The life safety system was included in the design/build MEP systems.

Alarm and Control System

An addressable fire alarm and control panel (FACP) has been provided in the fireman's control room located off the main building lobby. The system includes:

- An evacuation paging system, including public address speakers and strobes in all areas of the building
- Sprinkler flow and supervision alarms with annunciation
- Fireman's intercom system
- Fan status and control of supply, exhaust and stairwell pressurization fans
- Floor damper status and control
- Emergency generator status and control
- Fire pump status and control
- Emergency fuel system status
- Emergency elevator status, capture, recall and independent operating control

Fire and life safety alarms cause automatic notification to the cell phone and/or pager to a preset personnel list. The list will always include the building engineer, the property manager and the 24-hour security-monitoring firm through a hard wire system. The security firm will immediately notify the fire department if it is a fire alarm.

Fire Protection

A fire suppression system is provided that includes the city fire line connection, an on-site 26,000-gallon (20,000-gallon useable) water storage reservoir, a supervised automatic wet sprinkler system and wet type standpipes.

The system pressure is provided by an automatic 750 gpm at 3000-rpm diesel-driven fire pump and jockey pump. A diesel-driven pump was considerably less expensive than an electric-driven pump backed up by a larger emergency generator. The diesel engine has a double wall 140-gallon tank in a two-hour rated enclosure. The fire pump and water storage reservoir are located at the west side of the surface parking area behind the office building. (See Figure 24-2.) The water reservoir is a concrete tank.

There is a combined 4" standpipe in each vestibule for the automatic wet sprinkler system and 2-2½" outlets for fire department use in each stairwell extended to siamese roof outlets. The wet pipe sprinkler system is provided with automatic sprinklers, control valve, water flow switches, tamper switches, drain valve and alarm panel.

Emergency Generator

The 300kw emergency generator is located in a room adjacent to the diesel driven fire pump. It has a 200-gallon double-wall fuel oil tank. See Chapter 26 for further discussion.

Smoke Control System

The approach to smoke control during a fire condition is different in San Diego from experience in other jurisdictions, and it has a reasonable logic. The only action initiated by a smoke detector alarm in the return air system is to shut down the air handler for that floor, close the outdoor air damper and annunciate a floor alarm. A smoke detector in an elevator lobby will return all elevators to the first floor.

When the water flow switch for any floor indicates the sprinklers on that floor have been activated, it will shut down the air handler for that floor, stop all outside air fans, stop the toilet exhaust fans, initiate smoke removal and initiate the stairwell pressurization. Only the electrical room ventilation will remain operating.

When smoke removal is initiated, the smoke exhaust damper on the fire floor opens and, when a sensor verifies it as open, the VFD-driven smoke exhaust fan starts. The firemen, at their discretion may put the fire floor on exhaust mode and control the other fan systems from the fire control station.

A separate fan system pressurizes each stairwell under fire or smoke removal conditions and automatic dampers are provided from each stairwell to pressurize its vestibule to keep them free from smoke. The stairwells will be pressurized at 0.1" of water, and the vestibules at 0.05" of water.

The only location from which a general alarm may be initiated is the fire control station. There are no local fire pull stations on any floor.

The city required utilizing either Rolf Jensen Associates or Schirmer Engineering to test and inspect the smoke removal system when applying for the temporary Certificate of Occupancy, prior to city inspection. Schirmer was chosen because they were local and several of its consultants formerly worked for the city. A requirement to require inspection consultants prior to city inspection had never encountered before, but apparently many cities are taking this approach since the newer codes require increasingly complex testing for smoke control. In spite of the original concern, Schirmer was very helpful in organizing the necessary testing and completing it within the time requirements.

Life Safety/ Fire Alarm System

- Duct smoke detectors in return air paths
- Addressable area smoke detectors are provided in public corridors, electrical, and mechanical rooms
- Fire extinguishers are provided at stairwells and as otherwise required by code

SECURITY SYSTEM

The security system controls ingress to the building, access to specific floors from each elevator and, in the future, ingress and egress to the parking structure using proximity cards. The system utilizes proximity cards that must only be held within a few inches of the card reader to actuate it

The system is based on LonWorks technology, which is an open system of network communication and protocol, providing a dependable, high speed and low cost network supported by many suppliers. It utilizes independent controllers, which insure reliable operation. It has a Pentium II processor, 64 MB of RAM, 4GB hard drive, SVGA 15" monitor, 40X CD-ROM, 56K internal modem, Windows 98, network interface and access software. The software is used only when maintaining the system—changing access, scheduling, etc.

The software permits easy and quick activation of tenant proximity cards with appropriate access on a seven-day-per-week, 365-days-a-year basis, with automatic daylight savings and leap year updates, and it automatically updates each affected controller. Each cardholder will be logged into (or removed from) the system as to the approved times of entry and approved access to specific elevator floors. Approved times may be set on a daily basis to the nearest minute, and can be adjusted for up to 20 holidays. The system will store the following information associated with each card:

- Name of cardholder
- Name of tenant
- Areas of access
- Areas not accessible
- Handicap access Y/N
- Activate / Deactivate
- Photo of cardholder (optional)
- Signature of cardholder (optional)

Access points may be scheduled as locked, unlocked, or card access only. A log can be maintained of all events, including cards that try to gain unauthorized access.

After-hours ingress to the building will be through card-operated door controllers, one in each lobby when the building is in security mode. Egress will be by sensors mounted above the doors. The door controller will activate a 24-volt door lock and will accept up to two card readers. An alarm will activate if a door is held or forced open.

There will be a card reader in each of the four elevators. The elevator controller will have relay outputs to control each of the eight floors individually at specified times. It will automatically log each access during those periods and, additionally, all cards that try to gain unauthorized access. The system can be expanded to control access to individual tenant spaces, if desired.

In addition to the logging of each event, all breaches, or attempted breaches of security, are immediately transmitted to a Property Management office and the 24-hour security contractor.

After reviewing the safety records, as well as the perception of safety at the adjacent complex and the remainder of San Diego Corporate Center, it was determined there was no basis for a CCTV installation in the parking structure or elsewhere. Conduit was provided in the event it was required in the future. Pull stations for touring security officers were installed.

If the city of San Diego approves the hotel proposal for paid parking, additional card readers will be installed by the hotel developer as specified by Prentiss to permit full card ingress/egress by authorized tenant personnel.

LEASING TEAM

28

Leasing is a full-time job that must be carried out with a great intensity. The leasing team must be committed to finding a way to successfully lease the building without giving away enough concessions to harm its value. Not only is it critical to attain the required stabilized occupancy, but to accomplish that while achieving the necessary net rental rate (the rental rate exclusive of operating and utility costs), at a pace that provides the rental income within the time schedule assumed in the pro forma. Constant comparison of the leasing success with the pro forma will provide monitoring of the project's ultimate financial success.

The leasing team—whether in-house or external—needs to have been involved from the beginning, participating in obtaining the market data and agreeing to the market criteria and strategy, so that they "buy into" the pro forma requirements as to lease-up timing and effective rental rates. If possible, the team should have contributed to the pro forma so as to be under self-imposed pressure to perform as promised. For best results the Development Officer's continuous leadership must be provided throughout the project.

Brokerage Team

The first step in the process is determining whether to use in-house leasing personnel, an outside broker, or a combination where in-house personnel direct the brokers. The Development Officer must select the team, be involved in all decision making, and be fully responsible for the success of the program. The factors to consider in determining the selection of the leasing team are:

- The quality and size of any existing in-house marketing team in the immediate market area.

- The size of the project and the estimated number of tenants required to achieve full occupancy.

- The size of the market and the degree of effort required to effectively reach all office brokers in the market.

- Whether you and your firm are well known and respected in that market, understand the market, and are considered a leader in the office market. If you are new or not a significant factor in the market, an outside broker would normally be essential.

- If one or more brokers control a disproportionate share of the market, their retention might result in your project being shown to a large number of tenants as soon as possible.

- In some markets, certain brokers are reluctant to show space under their control to other brokers, preferring to retain it for themselves. In that case, retaining a broker will result in the building not being fully shown.

- Current market conditions—a surplus or shortage of space relative to demand.

- The brokerage commission structure in the market. If there is a general commission level, and all brokers respect it and split the commission between the leasing and procuring broker, then in theory there is no additional cost to retaining an office broker.

- In a difficult market, or one in which the leasing broker retains his one half of the commission and the procuring broker insists on a full commission, there is a major cost to retaining an office broker.

Most marketing directors strongly recommend using an in-house team because of their total commitment to the project and their ability to reach all brokers in the market area. The author generally agrees, but has serious reservations about creating an untested staff from scratch to handle an important project.

Whatever the decision as to leasing responsibility, the in-house leasing personnel and/or the outside broker should be brought in at the beginning so as to participate through the design process. Their knowledge of the current practices in the office market, such as the definition of rentable area, definition of shell and core construction, and the features deemed most cost effective to attracting tenants in the current marketplace is invaluable.

If an in-house team is used, the contacts with outside brokers and prospective tenants should be carefully maintained in computer databases and this information should be reviewed regularly.

If an outside brokerage is selected, full formal reports of activity should be required on a monthly basis in addition to daily or weekly monitoring.

Selecting the Broker

It is wise to interview the primary office brokers as soon as reasonably practical, as it provides an opportunity to meet many brokers, and also gives them the opportunity to meet you and learn about your company as well as the proposed project.

You might want to invite several brokers early to "focus group" lunches to discuss the project and get feedback. Some brokers will seem more enthused than others and that may help in the selection. If you have a PR firm, they can coordinate this effort.

Selection should be based on the size and influence of the broker, the scope of services they offer, the key individual proposed to be their lead broker, their apparent level of interest and enthusiasm, the likelihood of any conflict of interest with other projects represented by the broker, their ability to work cooperatively with other brokers and the chemistry you feel with them. Agree on the services to be provided, such as:

- Provide, or assist in the preparation of brochures, web sites and other materials

- Maintain and share lists of all tenants in the marketplace, with the details of their leases, structured by termination date

- Method of reaching all other brokers in the market—personal contact, mailings, broker parties, etc.

- Maintain their personnel in the marketing center, if any

- Provide their own space planner to assist in preparation of lease proposals and control the layouts on divided floors

Commission Agreement

Negotiation of the brokerage agreement, which is normally an exclusive agreement, should clearly outline the duties and responsibilities of the broker and the owner. In addition, the broker should warrant that he is a licensed real estate broker in the state, and will put forth diligent efforts to lease the building in a timely manner and within the required rental rate range. Broker will agree to hold owner harmless from any and all entities claiming a commission under a lease for which the broker earns a commission.

The agreement must have a specific commencement and termination date. In addition, owner reserves the right to terminate the brokerage agreement at any time, but broker will be paid a commission for any fully consummated leases, as defined below, and for any lease for which broker was responsible which is executed within a stipulated period (usually 90 days) after termination.

The owner must have the unqualified right to reject any proposed lease for any reason whatsoever at any time prior to unconditional execution, and no commission shall be payable for any such lease. Any rights of broker under the commission agreement may be enforced only against the estate in the premises.

The brokerage agreement should specify that broker will share the commission with any procuring broker, and the commissions will be calculated as follows:

- **Commission:** Commission rates must be spelled out for various term lengths and various premises sizes, if applicable. Commissions shall be payable at the agreed upon commission rate(s) multiplied by the stipulated rental rate(s) over the term in question (exclusive of parking, Tenant Improvement allowances, over-standard services, any increases to cover operating costs or other expenses, or any other inducements paid to tenant to enter into the lease) multiplied by the net rentable area, and multiplied by the term.

  In a seller's market, it is frequently possible to limit any commission payable to no more that ten years from the lease commencement, regardless of the term of the lease or renewal options. This can rarely be accomplished, and when not feasible, try to limit any commissions payable to fifteen years with the last five years limited to one-half of a commission. Where the commission is payable for a portion of a term greater than ten years, try to defer payment until the end of the tenth year.

- **Initial Term:** Fifty percent of the commission for the initial term will be paid when the lease has been fully executed unconditionally and delivered by all parties, including any consents and required non-disturbance agreements with holders of superior leases or superior mortgages. The remainder of the commission will be paid when the term of the lease has commenced, tenant occupies the space and pays the first month's rent (frequently the broker will demand only occupancy as a criteria, which is dangerous for the owner if there is a period requiring extensive free rent).

- **Expansion Space:** Providing the tenant is not then in default, and the lease expansion agreement is fully executed and delivered, at the start of the expansion term a commission will be paid.

- **Renewal Term:** Providing the tenant is not then in default, and the lease renewal agreement is fully executed and delivered, at the start of the renewal term a commission will be paid. This commission should be limited to 2% or one-half of the standard commission.

- **Additional Agreement with Tenant:** There shall be no commission payable to broker for any expansion, renewal, or increased rental payments agreed to with tenant without the benefit of broker's services under this agreement.

While you should always try to limit any expense, it is important not to limit commissions to the point where the brokers will not recommend your project. In addition, one of the best ways to ensure broker support is to establish a reputation for fair commissions and immediate payment.

Every developer should have a standard lease commission agreement—to be modified as necessary to suit the individual circumstances.

Leasing Space Planning

A space planner, retained by the broker or the owner, is a key participant in the overall leasing process. A highly qualified planner is important for their analysis and advice during the building planning as discussed in Chapter 16, efficiently placing tenants in the building, and through the quality and presentation of each proposed plan, serve as an effective sales representative for the project.

When preparing to submit a proposal to a tenant for less than a full floor, it is necessary to carefully consider the specific location to be proposed. Codes have very limiting requirements—dead end corridors are normally limited to 20 or 30 feet in length, tenant spaces over 3,000 sf (under UBC) require two exits, which must be separated by at least one-half of the longest diagonal of the space, and from each exit there must be two directions of travel to reach a stairwell as discussed in Chapter 16. Each tenant has its own desires concerning its space, such as the number of offices, the visual orientation, the amount of window exposure, the size and type of interior space, and how close the tenant will be to the elevator lobby and the toilet rooms.

If the tenant requires expansion space, that space (or several potential spaces) must be identified and tested to determine if that additional space will create any code issues for either that or adjacent tenants. An accurate leasing floor plan (stacking plan) must be carefully maintained for each floor showing all leased areas, all expansions, all renewal spaces, and all other rights, to ensure that there are no future code issues, no overlapping obligations (the worst thing that can happen in real estate) and no future relatively unleaseable spaces.

To accomplish the above objectives without leaving any space that is difficult or impossible to lease is a giant jigsaw puzzle. It is a function that is very difficult to accomplish properly and, in the author's opinion, is the most underrated function in the development of an office building. Errors can be very costly in both the short- and long-term. In addition to the planner's ability to be accurate, he must respond quickly and have the ability to make the plan look attractive so it is an effective leasing tool. The space planner must also be personable and a good salesperson—the ability to sell the tenant on the space plan and the building often helps to close a lease negotiation.

It is highly advisable to have the tenant space planner committed early so as to participate in the design process and early decisions on proposed floor layouts, as well as advising on leasing issues. A reasonable range for this service would be 10¢ to 15¢ per sf for an initial space plan, and $1 to $1.50 per sf for working drawings using building standard items.

Attorney

When distance or the availability of time precludes the use of in-house counsel for participation in lease negotiations, a clear understanding and control of the effort must be agreed upon with the selected outside counsel, so that you are handling all of the business issues and the attorney is handling the legal and liability issues. It is important to have an attorney who is experienced in lease negotiation and who understands your standard lease as well as your objectives. Otherwise the cost for legal services can become excessive.

CASE STUDY

The choice of the basic leasing team was a very easy decision. There were no in-house leasing personnel in the Del Mar area, and the project was not of sufficient size to consider setting up such a group. An outside brokerage firm would be required.

Business Real Estate Brokerage (BRE), with offices in Carlsbad and University Town Center (UTC), was the logical choice. BRE represented Pardee in the sale of both the Executive Center and Gateway sites, and it was believed they were helpful in recommending that Pardee sell to Prentiss, even though Prentiss was not the high bidder. In addition, they did an outstanding job in leasing the Executive Center, which reached 100% occupancy in less than four months from completion with rates 10% in excess of pro forma.

Allen, Matkin, Leck, Gamble & Mallory LLP was selected as the legal support, as they have been handling the legal work for the Prentiss acquisition and leasing efforts in Southern California for more than ten years.

Smith Consulting Architects was selected to do the tenant space planning based on the quality of their performance with several tenants in the Executive Center in which they are a tenant.

01 SITE PLAN
NOT TO SCALE

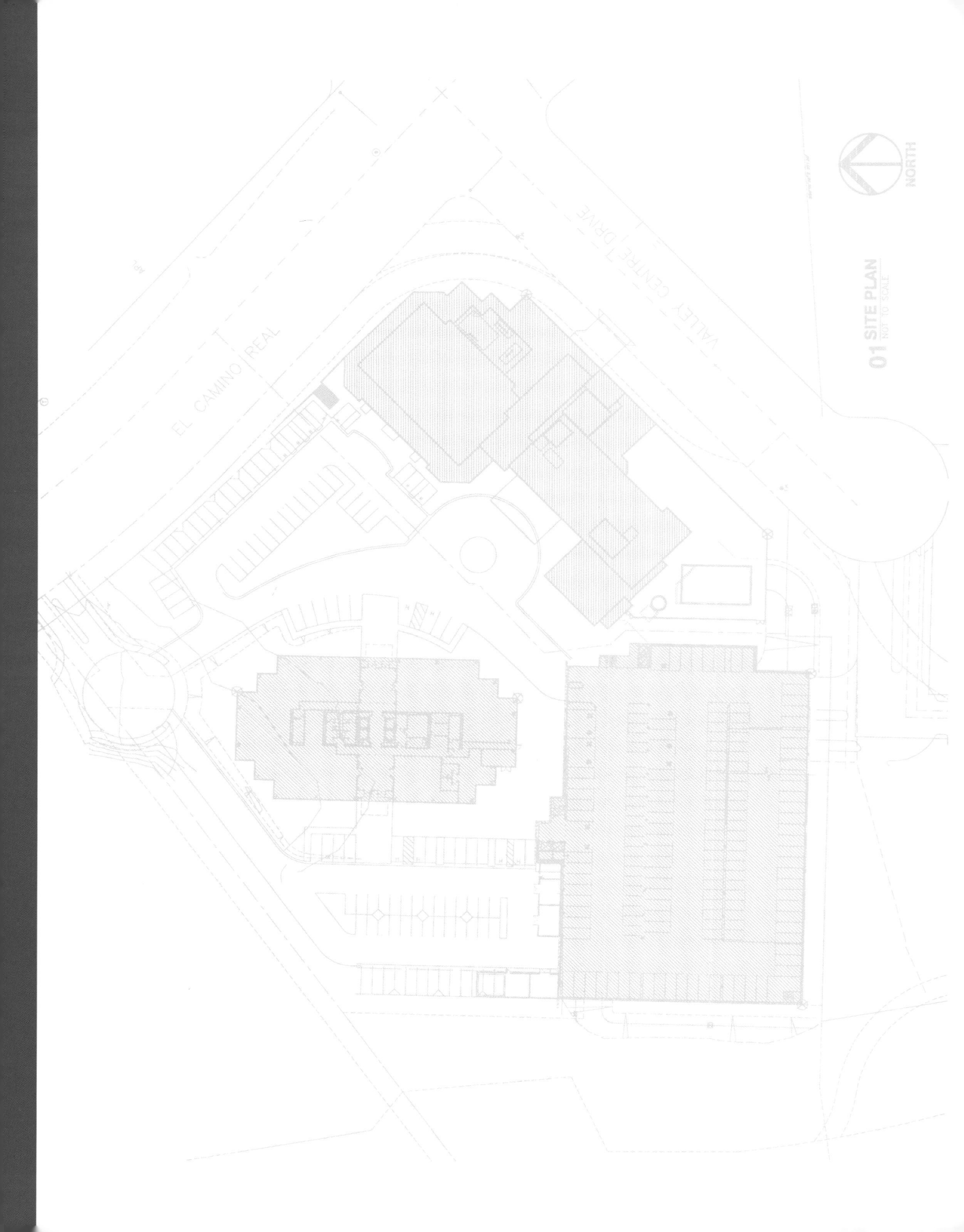

LEASING STRATEGIES   29

You have spent a great deal of time determining the right location for the building to attract tenants. You have evaluated countless design issues trying to create a building that would satisfy the assumed functional needs as well as provide an appropriate and aesthetically attractive facility, all for the sole purpose of inducing prospective tenants to make your project their new home. You must now find a way to communicate the benefits of your project and consummate the leases.

An effective leasing program builds upon the marketing program. The Development Officer must recognize that effective leasing is without a doubt the most important effort in the development process. There is no feature of the building, or anything you have done to date, that can overcome unsuccessful leasing.

Survey, "What Office Tenants Want", the summary of which is shown as Figure 4-4 in Chapter 4. In addition to the summary, the study is broken down by geographical area and by tenant type. The author is surprised at, and unsure of the validity of some of the ranking of various issues, but it is a source of information that should be taken into consideration.

A clearly understood and coherent leasing strategy, based on the Market Study, as modified from time to time based on current market conditions, must be prepared under the direction of the Development Officer, with the participation of every member of the leasing team, so that the team has fully "bought in" to its objectives. The strategy should include an effort to incorporate the support of the company's nationwide tenant relationships.

> Trammell Crow, one of the most productive developers of the last century, upon being questioned by a reporter for a Dallas newspaper about architectural design, reportedly said, "I've never seen a beautiful empty building, and I've never seen an ugly full building."

A poor investment will result if there is enough equity to retain ownership, and the building may be lost completely if the value of a partially leased building sinks below the value of the loans. Throughout the entire Feasibility Analysis and design periods the requirements of the most likely prospective tenants have been uppermost in your mind, as **successful leasing is the only acceptable end result**—the final examination, as it were.

In developing a marketing strategy, it is of interest to note the 1999 BOMA/ULI Office Tenant

A well-thought-out leasing strategy will be based on the current reading of the market, judgment and discipline, and will include:

- Types of target tenants

- Importance of, and strategy to find, a lead tenant

- Net rental rate, including periodic fixed or percentage increases over the term for a lead tenant, and any special concession allowances

- Net rental rate for speculative tenants including fixed or percentage increases (the rental rate is adjusted upward from the average pro forma rate to compensate for lower rates for encumbered and lower quality spaces)
- Building Standard Tenant Improvements that satisfy both the market and the building's long-term objectives
- Types and amount of TI allowance and other concessions
- Policy toward expansions—market rates, maximum percentage of tenant's original space, and the refurbishing allowance, if any
- Policy toward number and terms of lease renewals, market rates and refurbishment allowance, if any
- Charges for parking and limits on reserved parking
- Minimum size tenant for top-of-building or monument signage, if made available, and charges for this or other special signage
- Amenities provided
- Operating and utility costs, and calculation method for periodic adjustments
- Separate taxes from operating expense where they cannot be accurately projected
- Policy toward endeavoring to lease the most difficult spaces first
- Signage and elevator lobby exposure
- Avoidance of most leases expiring in the same time period
- Required credit worthiness
- Printed lease, including all exhibits and riders, to minimize changes

The first issue in implementing any leasing strategy is the necessity for, and size of, any major prelease tenant(s) prior to the commencement of construction. Preleasing in many markets has been difficult in recent years, unlike in the 70s and 80s, but as the available space has tightened it has started to return. A real credibility problem occurred during the late 80s and early 90s, as too many developers had floated too many projects that never became a reality, or were developed in a much later time frame than promised.

Nevertheless, the preleasing policy is determined by management policy, availability of financing for a speculative building, or a judgment based upon an assessment of market conditions. To find a potential prelease tenant(s) may require aggressive action on the part of the leasing team, including:

- Analyzing all lease records in the market area for leases of the appropriate size which expire within 12 to 24 months of the earliest potential completion of your project
- Staying in constant touch with the local and/or regional economic development agencies
- Keeping your project in front of all office building brokers in the region with appropriate marketing presentations
- Staying alert for potential mergers, firms in buildings with a less than satisfactory image, firms in more than one building or fragmented within a building, and rapidly growing firms who may outgrow their presently leased space
- Implementing an aggressive effort toward all identified target tenants

It is not unusual that a successful prelease is accomplished with a tenant who had not yet taken steps to address its future space requirements.

As important as a major prelease tenant(s) may be to the commencement of a project, it is essential that not too much be given away in the form of rate, inducement concessions, or excessive expansion rights that would make it difficult to accomplish the required project return.

Most pro formas tend to show 25% to 35% of the space leased with rental income in the first month after completion. Such lease(s) must be signed either prior to the commencement of construction in the event of a required prelease or at least six to eight months prior to rent commencement if the building started on a speculative basis. This raises the age-old question: Is the lead tenant offered an incentive for an early lease, or charged a premium if they want to encumber too much space with expansion options? There is no clear answer—only good judgment exercised with an understanding all of the circumstances at the time.

It is important that the average rental rate used in the pro forma not be the top rate achievable in the marketplace. If it is, problems will occur in meeting the overall project returns, as lower rents are likely in the spaces encumbered by expansion options and other less desirable space in the building. If one assumes that 15% to 20% of the rentable space will be encumbered or less desirable, and that a reduction of 10% of the net rental rate will be required to lease it in a timely manner, then all other leases must achieve a net rental rate 2% to 3% above the average pro forma rate in order to satisfy the objective. In addition, if the option on any encumbered space is for less than five years, it may not be leasable at all in some markets. Based on your own assumptions as to the amount of encumbered or inferior space, and the rate reduction required to lease it, you can make your own calculation of the rate premium required for the remainder of the space.

TIs on expansion and renewal spaces, if necessary to provide at all, should be limited to refurbishment, where possible—basically carpet replacement and painting—or a dollar amount that recognizes the value of most of the work in place. When a short-term "must take" expansion option is included, it is common to provide the standard TI allowance where the space has not been improved, and a minor allowance if it has been improved.

As the project progresses it is essential to maintain a current reading as to all circumstances and all changes in the market. As market changes (up or down) occur, **it is essential to modify the strategy**. The important issue in this regard is to have the discipline to change the strategy on a rational and considered basis, rather than to make ad hoc or "seat of the pants" adjustments.

> It is difficult to fully understand real estate markets until you have experienced the full spectrum from red hot, to good, to stabilized normality, to bad.
>
> A person would have difficulty understanding the depths to which a market can sink unless they had the misfortune to operate in Houston in the mid-1980s. There was so much space and so few viable tenants that the market was a virtual disaster.
>
> There were instances where tenants with marginal credit were improving their economic position by moving into Class A buildings with their space built-to-suit, their old lease picked up, and some free rent added in. Did it make sense? No, but it did occur out of desperation in trying to reach some acceptable level of occupancy.

Throughout the project your "old friend" the market cycle, discussed in the Market Study, should be carefully monitored. If you are still well below the peak of the absorption cycle curve, vacancy is flat to downward and rates have a slight upward bias —you can probably successfully raise your rate target and hold back a little, waiting for more attractive deal opportunities. Conversely, if you believe you are at the peak of the absorption cycle or slightly on the downward side, vacancy is rising and rates are more heavily negotiated – it may be time to bite the bullet and drop the rates a little and/or increase the concessions to lease-up before the market worsens.

Other issues for consideration in preparing and implementing your leasing strategy are:

- When weighing rental rate reductions, concession increases, and/or onerous expansion requirements that will cause greater than anticipated income reduction as opposed to a slower lease-up (i.e., greater concessions versus greater vacancy)— a flat rate equivalent model or a full pro forma analysis should be used to assist in the difficult judgment.

- Acceptable credit-worthiness. When there is a credit issue, a deposit of sufficient size to at least cover the commission and TIs necessary to re-lease the space should be required as an absolute minimum. Cash is preferred, as there can sometimes be a problem collecting on a letter of credit.

- It is frequently beneficial to hold open the building or monument signage until later in the leasing program unless required for a prelease tenant. Signage of a company in a particular industry may well preclude others in that industry from considering your building. Additionally, many tenants who ask for signage don't expect their request to be honored, and there is always the possibility of a larger tenant coming along at a later date.

- Holding the elevator exposure open until later in the leasing cycle frequently justifies a higher rate for that space. Ground floor space can be an enigma. This space is attractive to many service industries but negative to others because it is broken up by the exit corridors and lobby and does not have the feeling of privacy for many clients.

- Try to avoid payment for tenant's excess TI costs, even when recovered through increased rent. You may have a superior use for that additional equity.

- Parking charges, if applicable, should be adjusted to market, but not downward, annually. Where there is no charge for parking, the lease should specify it is free for the initial term only.

- Where there are charges for parking, evaluate requiring the tenant to take and pay for all requested spaces so that any non-revenue spaces can be allocated to other tenants.

- If tenants have heavy population densities (some have up to 10 persons per one thousand square feet) or heavy electrical loads (up to 6 watts per square foot plus lighting) special analyses must be made of the elevator and HVAC systems to ensure the requirements can be properly satisfied.

- If necessary and prudent to provide a tenant with a termination right, there should be a penalty to cover TI and brokerage costs that have not been recovered, and termination must be due only to a valid specific issue, never open ended.

One of the best strategies of all is to remember what keeps the brokers enthusiastic with a positive attitude toward your project—good commissions, quick deals and fast pay.

Most important of all is to identify and prioritize all possible tenants, and pursue them aggressively in a disciplined manner. Of all of the issues addressed in leasing strategies, the essential one is to **close the deal**.

CASE STUDY

In Chapter 17 the positive marketing elements for this project were listed. The leasing strategy was to build on those advantages. The initial target tenants were the larger (20,000 sf and up)—legal, investment and smaller corporate tenants, largely from UTC and the many expanding tenants in Del Mar. The 20,000 sf floor could efficiently accommodate these larger tenants and the relative lack of traffic congestion in Del Mar vs. UTC was a significant benefit.

The building was further positioned for larger tenants, as it is the tallest building (with the best visual exposure) north of UTC, and with the granite curtain wall and overall quality, was perceived as the highest quality building in the market area. The adjacent Marriott was an additional plus factor for tenants of this type.

The 20,000 sf floor is configured so that it can be assured of efficiently satisfying the many small tenants in this market that were required to fill up the expansion option spaces.

The initial rental rate assumption used in the earliest pro formas was $2.15 /rsf, exclusive of electricity. Based on continued study of the market, the rate was revised upward to $2.25, plus 15¢ for electricity that was included in the operating costs to permit justification of an upgraded and more efficient HVAC system. That made the proposed gross rental rate $2.40, with 3% annual increases.

The TI allowance was set at $31.25 /usf, which was based on the current market, plus an inflation factor, less the excess TI cost of heat pump systems used elsewhere in Del Mar, as discussed more fully in Chapter 4. For various reasons this rate was not strictly adhered to in practice.

Expansions were to be controlled to no more than 20–25% of the original premises, with minimum refurbishments, and rental rates at fair market value.

Renewals were limited to one five-year term, except for tenants in excess of 40,000 sf who could receive up to two five-year terms, all at fair market value.

There was no initial specific policy with regard to leasing any specific space first for larger tenants, but it was planned to do so with the smaller tenants in the option spaces.

The top of the building signage was very dramatic in this location, the tallest building in the area and visible from two major freeways. The sign was intended for use in attracting a major tenant to the project.

Parking was a major positive factor, as at 4/1,000 gsf it was as high as any competitive product, and higher than most. Parking was offered at no charge in keeping with the CC&Rs for the San Diego Corporate Center, and free tenant parking was also included as a condition of the Substantial Conformance Determination. The hotel developer obtained a change in the CC&Rs and is discussing approval for paid parking with the city. They will charge for parking if they receive this approval. The office leases provide for free parking in the initial term, as paid parking is not currently acceptable in the market, but did not exclude charging for parking in subsequent terms.

Before initiating serious marketing efforts a 100,000 sf tenant surfaced interested in this area. Even though the building was still in the schematic design phase, and in the process of the Substantial Conformance Review, a satisfactory Letter of Intent was entered into with Brandes Investment Partners, L.P. without giving away the top of building signage.

The agreement with Brandes significantly changed the direction with regard to leasing the remainder of the building. With the signage still available efforts turned to searching for a one to two floor tenant who could significantly benefit from the signage—financial, real estate, or other entity requiring public awareness. The signage was considered to be worth $3-4000 per month above the pro forma rate for the space.

The search was successful, also before completion of the Substantial Conformance Review, when Scripps Bank agreed to take most of the first floor and all of the second for their headquarters, a total of almost 30,000 rsf. Scripps is an attractive amenity for the remainder of the leasing, in addition to the upscale Marriott and the health club required under the Brandes Lease.

The remaining issue that now required marketing attention was to lease 20,000 rsf of small tenant space for terms of four years or less, due to the Brandes option to lease the third floor at the end of the 48th month. The approach was to sell the benefits of the hotel along with the building quality, and to offer renewal options subject to the Brandes' option.

The concern regarding leasing this short-term space was eased when the brokers brought a 8,500 rsf user while the site grading was still in progress, who entered into a lease in the option space. This lease changed the approach to marketing the remainder of the space. It was originally believed it was unlikely to attract the small tenants until the building was almost complete, but the market was such that it permitted aggressively leasing virtually the entire building prior to completion of construction.

TENANT SPACE DEVELOPMENT

30

The completed tenant space provides the working environment for the tenant's employees—their satisfaction can be a major factor in tenant retention. This satisfaction of the employees with their workspace is a shared responsibility with the tenant, through space planning and material, color selection and other amenities, and the landlord through the quality of the base building systems and the Building Standard Tenant Improvements.

It should be noted that as the market more frequently dictates that the Tenant Improvements be performed by the tenant based on an allowance, it becomes more difficult to require tenants to use standard materials, and even more important to have the building standards incorporated into the lease. It can be even more difficult to require the installation of materials and systems to achieve energy savings—such as photo sensors and dimming ballasts on the perimeter—when the tenant may not share in the savings, or when their lease does not have a sufficiently long term in which to return their investment. In spite of potential objections, the author believes it is important to structure the lease and standards so as to require appropriate energy conservation.

This chapter will discuss the factors in Interior Environmental Quality (IEQ), the market-driven definition of Base Building vs. Tenant Improvements, and details of the material components of these improvements.

INTERIOR ENVIRONMENTAL QUALITY

The primary purpose of office space is to provide an environment in which employees can perform their necessary functions successfully in an atmosphere that promotes efficiency and productivity, while minimizing absenteeism. We call this atmosphere the Interior Environmental Quality (IEQ).

Some of the factors in achieving a satisfactory IEQ are under the control of the developer, some are under the control of the tenant, and many are jointly impacted by both the developer and the tenant. In either case, however, it is important that the Development Officer fully understand these issues—both while directing the base building design and coordinating with the tenant. The primary factors in IEQ, and the chapters in which they are discussed in detail, are listed below.

- Temperature control (Chapter 25)
- Humidity control (Chapter 25)
- IAQ—flow and quality of the air (this chapter and Chapter 25)
- Sound control—acoustics (Chapter 22)
- Daylight—reports have indicated employee health complaints increase as the distance from the exterior windows increases, and the impact of daylight decreases (Chapter 20)
- Lighting (this chapter and Chapter 26)
- Cleanliness—a function of design for cleanability (toilet rooms in Chapter 23, air filtration in Chapter 25, and landlord's maintenance procedures)
- Interior aesthetics (Building Standard Tenant Improvements in this chapter, and tenant's own design standards)

- Ergonomics (a tenant issue)
- Workplace relationship efficiencies (an impact from size and layout in Chapter 16, but primarily the layout design and priorities of tenant)

TENANT IMPROVEMENT DEVELOPMENT

The development of the tenant space is a major cost to the project—the owner's Tenant Improvement (TI) cost can amount to 30% to 50% or more of the shell and core construction cost. It can also amount to a large additional cost to the tenant.

It is very important for the Development Officer to properly evaluate the market in general, and the target tenants in particular, in order to determine the quality of each component of the Building Standard Tenant Improvements. In addition to meeting initial acceptable standards, one must consider materials that will not have early deterioration or obsolescence in order to minimize future re-leasing costs.

The first step in approaching the TI cost, as well as to set the parameters for the base building construction cost, is to determine the generally accepted definition in each market as to which are the shell and core construction, and which are TIs. The definition can vary widely in various markets and under various market conditions, and was determined from the Market Study in Chapter 4. The following is the range of typical shell and core definitions for each of many components:

SHELL AND CORE VS. TENANT IMPROVEMENT DEFINITION

Perimeter columns or walls: from complete drywall installation, to none at all.

Core walls or tenant side of corridor walls: from complete dry wall installation, to studs on tenant side exposed for tenant installation.

Demising walls: from complete dry wall installation, to studs on each tenant's side exposed for tenant installation.

Tenant's entrance door: from complete installation to tenant responsibility.

Ceiling grid: from complete grid installation, to nothing installed but the hanger rods.

Ceiling tiles: from tiles stacked on the deck, to not provided.

Electrical lighting grid above ceiling: from complete grid installation with outlet boxes every 400 sf +/-, to providing power at an electrical panel only (in some cases power is provided only to the tenant meter at the ground level). Where service is provided from the electrical room, the 120/277v transformers are sometimes provided, and sometimes not.

Electrical miscellaneous power: sometimes included with a lighting grid if lighting is at 120 volts, if provided, to providing power at an electrical panel only (or to meters, as above).

Lighting fixtures: from fixtures tied into the outlet boxes with 12' +/- long lighting tails and laid in the ceiling grid, to fixtures delivered to the floor, or to none provided.

Chilled water system: from a complete central chiller system, to small package chillers, fan coil units or heat pumps installed by the tenant.

Condenser water loop: provided by owner to service self-contained, water-cooled air conditioning units, if used as above.

Air distribution: from air ducted to fixed mixing boxes at the perimeter and to interior mixing boxes in a standard distribution pattern, to providing only the fresh air and exhaust risers and the main air loop with stub outs.

Sprinklers: from a complete riser and water loop with runouts and heads installed upturned at 180 to 225 usf per head on the unfinished floors, to riser and water loop only (if runouts and heads must be installed for Certificate of Occupancy on other parts of the building, tenant is charged for this cost as a preinstalled item).

Relocation of sprinkler heads per space plan: from complete relocation, to tenant responsibility.

Smoke detectors and voice communication: from complete installation on standard pattern, to no installation (if detectors and speakers must be installed for Certificate of Occupancy on other parts of the building, they are installed and tenant is charged as a preinstalled item).

Tenant floor elevator lobby and public corridors: from completely finished on all floors, to finished only on divided floors (note that when these areas are finished as base building work, the area is subtracted from the useable area for calculation of the Tenant Improvement allowance).

Window treatment: from complete installation by owner, to installation by tenant, or to installation by owner with a charge to tenant as a preinstalled item.

Public corridor graphics: from owner cost, to tenant charge.

Tenant space development and/or working drawings: from owner providing two layouts and working drawings for building standard items only, to layouts and working drawings by tenant. Owner contribution to the tenant nonstandard working drawings, if any, is usually a stipulated dollar amount.

After defining the demarcation between the shell and core construction and the Tenant Improvement work, there are three basic ways to structure the financial responsibility for TIs, the selection of which is determined by market competition. They are listed in the order they are most likely to occur, from the strongest landlord market to the weakest.

- Provide tenant with a work letter in which tenant is provided with the installation of a specific number of each building standard items on a per square foot basis, i.e., one light fixture per 80 usf; or one linear foot of partition per 12 usf. Costs above the work letter are the tenant's responsibility.

- Provide tenant with a specific dollar allowance per useable square foot (usf) with which to accomplish the work, and require tenant to use the building contractors

- Provide tenant with a dollar allowance, agree on dates for base building completion for start of TI work, a date for rent commencement and let tenant take full responsibility

- Provide tenant with a complete build-to-suit installation with building standard items only.

When a dollar allowance for Tenant Improvement work is provided, it is reasonable for a tenant to assume that if they use only building standard materials in reasonable quantities, they will be able to build out a normal space layout within that allowance, including the 5% cost included to cover landlord's coordination and supervision costs. (In some very strong markets landlords have successfully charged 15% for coordination.)

Each firm should develop their own standard form of Tenant Work Agreement, as well as General and Supplementary Conditions, modified from the AIA form to suit those issues deemed to be important. See Chapter 33 for specific contractual terms an owner should include.

TENANT FINISHES

Tenant finishes are a function of the market as to their quality and quantity, however, the quality should be kept high enough to enhance the future as well as current leasing. Regardless of the method of providing the tenant with a TI allowance, a Building Standard Material List should be developed to clearly designate the quality (if not the quantity) of building standard tenant finishes. Even when the tenant is responsible for all of the TI work, the utilization of building standard components should be strongly encouraged as it simplifies maintenance and adds to the value of the building when leases roll over. Unit prices should be obtained for each item, particularly for the benefit of the smaller tenants.

An issue regarding TIs that is not too widely discussed is the depreciable life of the various components. Moveable fixtures are personal property rather than real estate. Modular lighting, moveable partitions, removable ceilings, raised flooring, supplementary cooling units, carpet that is not glued down, and even walls or cabinetry that are hung on clips rather than rigidly fastened to the structure and many other improvements can be considered personal property for tax purposes.

The base building subcontractors are frequently directed to order a minimum number of each building standard item with a potentially long delivery with the understanding that more will be required. This ensures that the materials will be available without delaying the space development, and the loss of rental income. While the following discussion covers material preferences and installation procedures, the financial agreement between owner and tenant is usually governed by the market factors discussed above. A typical Building Standard Material List for a Class A project, which must be competitive in its market, might include:

Ceilings

Ceiling heights in a first-class office building are 9'0". In some localities, other than for professional firms or those with significant computer usage, 8'6" or 8'9" can be acceptable. In some suburban markets as little as 8'0" have been deemed acceptable, but this should be very carefully evaluated before making such a decision. The recent trend to offices with heavy usage of CRTs and electronic equipment has tended to increase the need for higher ceilings for some users to allow for indirect lighting, usually 9'6" to 10'0". The ceiling height requirement may be further increased where the user has excessive cabling requirements that require a raised floor, unless the entire building is designed with a raised floor system as discussed in Chapters 25 and 26.

Accessible fissured ceiling tile is considered the normal material for office area ceilings. For some years there was a preference for the 12" x 12" concealed spline fissured tile, but in recent years the 24" x 24" tiles have become more popular as the semi-concealed support splines have become more attractive—they are less costly and easier to access. Where a five-foot module is respected, 20" wide ceiling tiles are frequently used. 12" x 48" and 24" x 48" are not commonly used in quality office space. Some concealed spline ceilings are fully accessible, while others are progressive (i.e., one tile in sixteen is removable, and then you work across to the desired location). The fully accessible ceiling receives less damage over its lifetime. The ceiling grid should be coordinated with the window mullions.

Tiles that do not have a trim can be chamfered or butt, ⅝" or ¾" thick, with coarse or subtle texture, and with either a directional or non-directional pattern. The author tends to prefer a ¾" chamfered tile with non-directional pattern and subtle texture.

When it is the owner's responsibility, the ceiling grid is frequently installed as the rough construction finish of the floor is accomplished, and the ceiling tile is stacked on the floor to await the tenant layout and completion of all mechanical and electrical work above the ceiling. As stated under the module reference in Chapter 16, a properly designed ceiling grid can provide for the efficient installation of partitions and fixtures.

The electrical and mechanical equipment above the ceiling requires convenient access. (Note that frequently, property management places small colored tacks in the ceiling to locate different equipment without having to access by trial and error.)

Special areas such as kitchens, dining rooms, conference rooms and elevator lobbies normally use drywall, metal pan or other materials due to the special usage, aesthetics, acoustics and code-mandated requirements.

Where tenants prefer to use floor to ceiling movable partitions, bolt slot grids are utilized. A typical configuration is ⁹⁄₁₆" wide with a screw slot to attach the head track of the wall system. Grids are available in a rolled metal version that utilizes a T-nut in the slot to anchor the screw. An extruded aluminum version includes a threaded slot for a machine bolt to attach the head track.

Light Fixtures

High quality, energy-efficient lighting at a reasonable cost is essential for the benefit of the tenant since, one way or the other, they are paying for it. (It also benefits the owner through the opportunity to obtain higher net rental income on future leases if the costs are less than competitive buildings.) I believe that the best fixtures used in recent years for combined quality of light and cost efficiency in office spaces have been either the 24" x 48" three lamp, or the 24" x 24" four-lamp, parabolic fixtures. A 20'-wide fixture is commonly used when trying to respect the five-foot module in the ceiling layout.

Many tenants currently prefer pendant-hung indirect lighting fixtures in the general office areas to provide better light for using CRTs, as well as a more uniform indirect light. A much newer fixture that can accomplish many of the same results as either of the above fixture types is the recessed direct/indirect fixture. They are available in either 24" x 24" or 24" x 48" recessed lay-in fixtures. These fixtures are currently more expensive, but future competition will certainly bring them in line with other fixtures in a few years.

The goal for most office purposes is to provide an acceptable overall lighting level of 60 to 65 foot-candles (higher on the workstation), with minimal glare, and with minimum wattage per square foot. This can be accomplished with one 3-lamp parabolic fixture per 80 sf, which will require 1.2 w/sf of electrical energy. When lighting is more task-oriented less fixtures can be used resulting in less energy consumption.

A technical discussion of the current standards and trends in fixtures, ballasts, lamps and controllers is found in Chapter 26.

Most current codes require positive energy-saving lighting controls. Rooms and office areas over 500 sf are often required to be controlled on and off by motion sensors (infrared or ultrasonic) and many users are putting these sensors in all offices as well. Larger areas require several sensors to ensure that each person registers on a sensor.

Many jurisdictions also require photo sensors to dim the perimeter lighting when daylight is available to supplement the lighting system and developers should promote this practice when not required. Lighting can also be controlled by low voltage double switches that provide three different lighting levels. General floor area lighting is usually divided into segments, not exceeding 3,000 to 4,000 sf per control.

Lighting fixtures may be served at either 277 volts or 120 volts. There can be more than twice the number of fixtures per circuit when using 277-volt service, but 120v is sometimes used to avoid running a separate grid for miscellaneous power. One formerly common method of wiring the fixtures was to install a conduit grid above the ceiling with junction boxes at specified locations for connection to the fixtures. Since the lighting will be located in accordance each tenant's space layout, the specified number of fixtures can be provided loosely installed on the ceiling grid with 12' or 16' long wiring tails when that is the practice in the area. When the lighting layout is received, the lights are relocated to the specified location in the ceiling grid.

Currently, a frequently used alternative fixture wiring method is to bring the lighting circuits out of the panel to a single location above the tenant area ceiling, close to the lighting panel, and from that point on all of the wiring to the fixtures is "modular" plug-in type, wherein the fixtures are "daisy chained." Twelve-foot long plug-in "whips" are normally used.

Power and Communication

An owner normally commits in the lease to provide a specified amount of electricity from the building's system available for the tenant's use under defined circumstances—frequently on the order of 5 to 6 w/usf. A normal connected load would be 1 to 1½ w/usf for lighting and 3 to 4 w/usf for power. Some tenants request much more power availability. Careful coordination must be made between the stated requirements of the tenant, the actual connected load, the design assumptions used in the air conditioning load calculations for electrical demand and the lease language.

The design of the air conditioning system includes an assumption of the actual electricity usage, or demand, and a reasonable number is 3 w/gsf, which equates to approximately 3½ w/usf. If usage exceeds the design assumption, the air conditioning system must be increased at significant cost, and in a full-service building the tenant will not be paying enough to cover the cost of electricity. The subject of tenant lighting and miscellaneous power is discussed in much more detail under Building Power Distribution in Chapter 26 and under Services of Landlord in Chapter 32.

Most 120/208-volt miscellaneous power wiring is installed above the ceiling to provide power to the partitions on each floor. Power other than at 120/208 volts is considered a special installation. To provide floor outlets (which are not normally provided in a work letter), the conduit would be run from the panel on the floor on which the outlets are to be located, down through the ceiling plenum of the floor below, then horizontally to the location where they are "poked through" the floor. This ensures that all outlets on a given floor are served from a panel located on that floor.

Good practice limits the number of outlets to six to eight per circuit to provide for changes and additions. The same conduit grid can be used for both power and lighting when the lighting fixtures are designed for 120 volts. A reasonable tenant allowance is to provide one wall-mounted duplex outlet per 170 useable square feet, and one telephone wall outlet with pull string for every 200 useable square feet for normal office work. The tenant installs the telephone cable. Many special uses, such as call centers and other heavy users of electronic and communications equipment, require much denser layouts of electrical and telephone/data outlets.

More and more tenants are requiring two types of 120 volt branch circuits for their electronic workstation equipment—"normal" circuits for non-critical loads such as task lighting and miscellaneous loads such as desk lamps, radios, pencil sharpeners, copiers, printers, etc., and "clean" circuits for critical loads such as computers. "Clean" circuits originate from "K-rated" transformers (designed to properly filter the harmonics generated by today's electronic equipment technology), and generally are run from electronic-grade branch circuit panels (with 200% neutral capacity, isolated ground bus, and a transient voltage suppression system). The K-rated transformers and electronic grade panels are totally separate from the "normal" transformers and panels serving non-critical loads. The method of providing for this in the base building design is dependent upon the owner's view as to how much of the premium cost should be at the owner's expense versus the tenant's expense. (The author has never heard this issue raised during leasing.)

Life Safety

The main sprinkler floor loop is installed with the building construction, usually along with major runouts and sufficient upturned heads (charged to the tenant where custom and practice permits as pre-installed items) so that other floors can obtain their early occupancy permits. Additional heads are installed later to fit the pattern of the tenant layout and all heads are turned downward to their final position. Most codes require that one or more entire floors below an occupied tenant floor be fully actively sprinklered, and sometimes a floor above before an Occupancy Certificate can be issued. In some jurisdictions all floors must be sprinklered prior to any occupancy. Additional discussion of the sprinkler system is provided in Chapter 27. Smoke detectors will be installed in the ceiling plenum or air return, voice communication speakers installed, fire extinguishers provided per code, exit signs, and exit and path lighting provided with emergency power.

Partitions

Most often the tenants are provided floor to ceiling drywall partitions with one sheet of ⅝" drywall board on each side (some buildings use 1/2) with 2⅝" metal studs (3⅝" if 10' high or more), 24" on center. Partitions that extend above the ceiling line create greatly increased costs during relocations. The least expensive ceiling connection is a channel cap; higher quality installations can have revealed connectors. To provide sound privacy, batt insulation is usually provided in the wall cavity, electrical and telephone outlets placed so they are not back-to-back or sealed for sound control, and a neoprene gasket should be provided between the partition cap and the ceiling as well as at the window mullions. Special treatment can be provided where a noise problem is anticipated, as discussed in Chapter 22, Acoustics.

A reasonable tenant allowance is one linear foot of partition per 12 useable square feet (usf). Extruded aluminum frames are normally used with tenant office doors, because the hardware can be installed on the job site without fabrication delays.

Corridor partitions, demising walls and special acoustically treated areas extend to the slab above and should have two layers of drywall on one side and one layer on the other.

Wall Covering

Tenant walls are usually painted with two coats of flat acrylic paint, with semi-gloss paint in toilet rooms and service areas. Public corridors should preferably have vinyl wall covering to resist wear. Vinyls are readily cleanable and are now created in designs and textures that can mimic almost anything. When specifying the installation of vinyl coverings, low or no VOC adhesives should be used to reduce indoor air impurities.

Special effect panels such as Zolatone (3–5 color pigments suspended in a base paint that do not mix when sprayed on, creating a multi-colored stipple appearance and texture) have been used in corridors in some cases.

Doors and Hardware

Full height, 36" wide, 1¾" thick solid core doors with plain sliced, premium grade, book matched, pre-finished hardwood veneer are normally provided (although painted doors are sometimes used), with extruded anodized aluminum frames and high-quality hardware—1½ or 2 pair butts, door stop, and lever handle latch sets (which are virtually required by ADA). (Note that full height means about 1½ to 2½" or so less than the ceiling height to allow the frame to be exposed and for some tolerance on the ceiling height.) A reasonable tenant allowance is one door with latch set per 30 linear feet of partition.

Door frames built up of aluminum sections provide the best appearance and simplify the hardware installation. Hollow metal frames are less expensive than other types of frames, but since all hardware, cutouts were normally made at the factory from shop drawings to accommodate specific hardware they were historically not used for tenant construction. Currently knock-down steel frames are made that permit the hardware to be installed on site to avoid the problem of coordinating hardware with steel hollow metal frames at the factory, but they are visually less attractive.

A lockset is provided at the entrance door, and can be either key or card operated, see further discussion under Security Systems in Chapter 27. Entrance doors require a closer with low opening forces that satisfy ADA. Temporary construction cylinder cores and keys are used during the construction period and then new cores with permanent keys are installed when the space is delivered to the tenant.

The hardware can either be stainless steel or bronze, with polished, satin or brushed finish as selected for design purposes. The tenant hardware must be coordinated with the base building hardware. A common trend that is effective and has become quite common is to retain an architectural hardware consultant to make the rather complex hardware recommendations and schedules. The consultant is either paid a fee, or is given the hardware contract for the services based on a unit price schedule.

Window Covering

Light colored, horizontal, 1" mini blinds are the most common and least expensive window treatment, but some markets prefer vertical blinds or Mecho Shades (a roller shade product with degrees of translucency when in the lowered position), which cost significantly more. Mecho shades have increased in popularity, and can be either manually or automatically operated. A standard perimeter window treatment should be required in all tenant spaces for visual uniformity. Decorative drapes are the tenant's responsibility, and may be installed, with owner approval, inboard of the building standard treatment, and in a manner not to disrupt the perimeter air distribution.

Carpet

A high-quality carpet should be used throughout and selected for appearance, cleanability and wearability. Good carpet will normally not physically wear out, but can deteriorate in appearance—so the basic goal is "appearance retention" over at least a ten-year period. There are a wide range of materials—wool, olefin and nylon (including the Antrons). Face fibers of Antron or other nylons have a particularly good resistance to crushing, abrasion and scratching of the fibers. The resistance to scratching prevents soil from bonding to the fiber and makes it easier to clean. The weight can vary from 28 to 48 oz./sf.

One drawback to nylon is an inability to satisfactorily dissipate static electricity. Untreated nylon carpets can readily generate static charges in excess of 12,000 volts, well above the threshold of human sensitivity and the recommended limits for sensitive electronic equipment. To improve performance, either a carbonized fiber is added to the yarn, or a conductive coating is added to the fiber's surface to dissipate static charges.

The fiber may be Beck dyed or solution dyed. Beck dyeing adds the color to the fiber after fabrication and provides a wide variety of colors. In the solution, stock and yarn dyed process, the color is added prior to construction of the carpet, and has much greater color fastness, but a smaller choice of colors.

Olefin (also known as polypropylene) is a synthetic polymer from a petroleum base and is less expensive, but the fibers are not as hard and lack nylon's resiliency. Once crushed the pile cannot be lifted. Olefin fibers are not dyable, therefore, must be solution dyed. They do resist moisture and can be used outdoors.

Wool, which is considered the fiber of elegance, is the only feasible natural carpet fiber, and the most expensive choice. It has a luxurious look and feel and a high resistance to crushing, matting and wear. The use of wool in commercial buildings is usually limited to executive areas, conference rooms and other special areas.

Commercial carpet construction is either woven or tufted. Weaving is performed on a loom in a traditional manner, while in tufted construction the yarn is pulled through a backing material. Most carpet used in office buildings is tufted.

There are many pile types—cut, cut and uncut, loop, cut and loop, twisted, and high/low pile, which are selected mostly on appearance. Among the many different textures used, the most common are the:

- Single-level loop—loops of yarn of equal height. Very durable construction. When subjected to load the piles flex and then return to their previous position, making them well-suited for heavy traffic areas.

- Multi-level loop—consists of loops of yarn with two or three levels, which form a random sculptured surface. Also hold up well in high traffic areas.

- Cut pile—consists of yarn cut at the surface rather than looped back to the carpet backing. Yarn tufts are usually densely packed to present a smooth soft surface. The yarn has a tendency to lay over and does not hold up as well as loop pile.

Loop pile is good in commercial applications because of its resistance to wear, while cut pile usually has a more luxurious look initially—a combination of cut and loop combines the merits of both.

A carpet with 32 oz. weight, Dupont Antron XL (or equal), cut and uncut texture, 1/8" gauge, 7800 denier (a unit of fiber fineness), 0.260" pile height, yarn (solution) dyed, with woven polypropylene primary and secondary backings, anti-static treatment, with a ten-year wear guarantee, and glued to the floor has proven satisfactory as a basic standard carpet for commercial buildings. A multi-toned color, not too light, will generally be more easily cleaned. Either a 2½" or 4" rubber or vinyl straight base, or a 4" carpet base should be provided. Naturally, special areas such as lobbies, elevator lobbies and elevator cabs may have special weaves, materials and colors.

Backing can be a major factor in carpet performance and appearance retention. The carpet is constructed with loops of yarn stitched through a backing fabric and locked into place. The primary functions of the backing are providing strength and stability (changes of less than 0.1% are acceptable), binding the yarns to the carpet (recommended minimum tuft binding in most applications is 10 pounds), and moisture protection. When moisture penetrates the backing, it can wick back and imbed in the fibers and contribute to the growth of bacteria and mold. There are several commonly used backings:

- Styrene butadiene latex (SBR)—the most widely used commercial backing. It has only fair to good dimensional stability and does not serve as a moisture barrier.

- Polyurethane—has enhanced physical properties—higher tuft bind, excellent dimensional stability and improved moisture resistance. Stands up well in heavy traffic areas.

- Vinyl composites—high-performance backing with excellent dimensional stability, high tuft bind and is essentially waterproof. Excellent in heavy traffic areas.

- Polypropylene—strong, durable, resists mildew and well-suited to humid or damp locations. It is permeable, making it easier to vacuum because it allows more air to pass through the material.

- Jute—strong, resilient and durable, but can mildew in damp applications. It is permeable like the polypropylene.

- Foam backing—not as strong as polypropylene or jute, it eliminates any need for a carpet underpad, and allows the carpet to be readily glued to the floor. Foam backing is not permeable, but makes it easier to clean up liquid spills typically found in restaurants and cafeterias.

The guaranty should cover backing delamination, unraveling and tuft bind. Some people recommend installing carpet cushion between the carpet and the floor to extend life, increase sound absorption, add ergonomic benefits and provide a more luxurious feel, but it has a tendency to look uneven when installed in corridors with heavy traffic.

Carpet installation is either a stretch-in or glue-down type, the choice dependent upon the type of carpet, the particulars of the application and the environmental concerns.

- Stretch-in—the carpet is installed, frequently over a separate cushioning pad, and held in place with either tack or tackless strips around the edge of the room. In a variation of this method, a hook tape is applied to the floor around the perimeter of the room and at the seams, carpet with loop backing is then installed over the tape creating a mechanical bond.

- Glue-down—the most common installation method for both carpet and carpet tiles. This method must be used when using foam-backed carpet. Glue-down is particularly well-suited for applications where carpet is exposed to rolling equipment and heavy traffic. A major negative has been the fumes and VOCs from the adhesives, however, low VOC adhesives have recently come on the market.

Modular Carpet Tiles

Some users are requiring raised flooring, anywhere from 6" or 18" high to accommodate extensive cabling between workstations. This normally requires greater floor slab to ceiling height to maintain a good visual height to the finished ceiling unless the entire building is designed for this purpose as discussed in Chapters 25 and 26. Raised flooring panels are normally 24" x 24", covered with carpet tile, to provide for access. Newer floor panels are filled to provide the feeling of a solid floor.

The demand for modular carpet tiles is also increasing by some tenants who prefer it due to the need to frequently relocate floor-mounted electrical outlets, for access to underfloor ducts, or just to minimize replacement when wear tends to occur in localized areas.

Tiles are now available in 36" x 36" tiles, as well as the 24" x 24" and 18" x 18" tiles. There are now more choices of carpet surface, and the most commonly used backing system is PVC backing that has been modified to reduce smoke emissions and toxicity. At least one manufacturer reinforces its

PVC backing with fiberglass, using a closed-cell structure for cushioning.

The concerns of off gassing of volatile organic compounds (VOCs) from adhesives are being met as pre-applied adhesives, or "peel and stick" type, are gaining in popularity. These glue-free adhesives virtually eliminate VOCs from being introduced into the building environment.

The carpet tile industry is working toward a closed loop carpet tile—recycling old carpet into new carpet tile that contains no virgin materials. One manufacturer is producing its standard backing from 100% recycled carpet tiles.

In spite of the benefits to some tenants through the use of modular carpet tiles, it does not appear reasonable for the developer to offer this product as a standard TI, since recent pricing has shown cost premiums of up to 60% over standard carpet installations.

Core, Perimeter Walls and Columns

Finish furring of core and perimeter walls and columns is increasingly performed as a part of the tenant work. As mentioned in the Chapter 20, the window frames should have provision to receive the perimeter drywall in a neat and clean manner. No penetrations, such as electrical outlets, should be placed in the perimeter wall if the façade is of rain screen construction.

The use of a new low-emissivity latex-like paint called Radiance on the inside surfaces of perimeter walls can reduce energy consumption by reflecting radiant energy—keeping the heat inside in the winter and outside during the summer.

Graphics

Architectural signage, or graphics, is an important factor in creating the appropriate character and image in the workplace. It consists of a combination of written language, pictograms, symbols and Braille graphics. All of its elements—shape, color, font, symbols, materials and texture should combine to form a clear common language and a visual consistency.

Signage functions fall into four basic categories—identification, direction, restriction and information. An effective signage program should be designed to be clear to first-time visitors, and repeat the message any time the visitor reaches a decision point such as a crossroad (corridor) or unpredictable turn, provide reinforcement if there is a great distance between signs, or awareness of some architectural feature that may require further directions or explanation.

Building standard directional signs in the elevator lobbies, and standard entrance signs are specified for uniformity with the other tenant floor graphics, as well as the building directory listings.

Air Conditioning

The air conditioning duct loop is most often a base building cost and is usually installed on each floor as construction proceeds. Floor distribution ductwork, mixing boxes, flexible ducts and diffusers are installed from the tenant layout drawings. One thermostat is provided per mixing box. Additional information is provided under HVAC in Chapter 25.

Where design details provide for perimeter ceiling soffits with perimeter air diffusers they can most effectively be installed with the flow of the building construction and are not affected by the future tenant layouts. Gypsum board ceiling soffits usually have upgraded diffusers. In such case they would normally be a preinstalled tenant cost.

In some locales small chillers, fan coil units, or heat pumps are included as part of the TI work, with the building providing the condenser water and air loops.

Tenant Space Working Drawings

The working drawings for the tenant's space, based on using building standard components, are frequently provided by the owner. These drawings are prepared by the building mechanical and electrical engineers and a preselected interior design firm. Use of the building engineers provides better control of the building systems.

A common approach is to provide one preliminary and one final space layout, and working drawings utilizing building standard components only. Extra layouts, or detailing nonstandard components would be an extra charge.

The trend today, however, is away from this approach, as the landlord position becomes stronger most tenants select their own architect. The owner makes available the building interior designer, charged as part of the TIs, for those tenants who prefer not to go through the selection process. The landlord should insist that the tenant retain the building mechanical and electrical engineers.

Preinstalled Work

Many times construction expediency dictates that certain items of TI construction that is a tenant responsibility, such as life safety equipment, be installed with the flow of the base building work. The tenant should be advised during the lease negotiations that in such instances they will be charged for this preinstalled work at predetermined rates out of the TI allowance.

TENANT IMPROVEMENT CONSTRUCTION

Until the building general contractor completes the majority of his work, it is advantageous to have him to perform all TI construction. He has the advantage of competitively bid unit prices, and avoids the problems concerning provision of hoisting, access and general conditions services. The developer should endeavor to require the tenant to use the building mechanical, electrical, and fire protection contractors to ensure the integrity of the building operating systems. This subject is discussed in greater depth in Chapter 32, Lease Negotiation.

For the majority of the Tenant Improvements, which usually occur after the basic completion of the general contractor's work, it is normally beneficial to require the use of one or more approved contractors who specialize in such work. On a small project it is normal to have one such TI contractor but, when requested by the tenant, permit an approved tenant-selected contractor to bid against him. On large projects it is common to select three TI contractors to bid on each tenant contract.

It is essential that the developer provide competent personnel to oversee the TI contractors and provide all necessary coordination between the tenant, his contractor, the building general contractor, building standard materials and procedures and Property Management.

The fee for this service can range from 3% to 15% varying by market regions and/or market conditions, and whether it is an initial lease or re-lease project. The most common fee is 5% and it is charged against the TI allowance.

It is important to prepare a Tenant Procedure Manual and Reference Book prior to negotiating any leases. To assist the tenant in making a smooth transition from the lease through the design of the space, the construction, and ultimately the move-in and occupancy, it is beneficial to present to the tenant a clear description of all of the issues he will face. Many factors become non-issues when presented in a proper and timely manner, but can become major issues if they surface in the middle of the process. The Tenant Procedure Manual is designed to be a communication guide to assist in this purpose, particularly for the benefit of the tenant's project manager and their designers. It can be the first step in building a good relationship with the tenant.

While the lease should be clear about the dividing line between the developer's responsibility on the shell and core and the Tenant Improvement work, it should be clarified here, pointing out exactly how the tenant work integrates with the shell and core.

Each building standard item for use in the tenant work should be clearly spelled out using descriptions, type and manufacturer's numbers, sketches and/or specifications. Details of how these items connect to the base building are very helpful, and can simplify the preparation of the TI drawings.

Where you have a requirement that certain tenant drawings (frequently all of the engineering disciplines) be prepared by the building's engineers, the reasons therefor should be explained. If, for some valid reason, the tenant insists on using other engineers, it must be explained that they will have to pay for the building engineers to review the design work. Building systems are integrated and the installation of one tenant's work must not interfere with proper operation and maintenance of other tenants or the base building systems.

Design control for the elevator lobbies and public corridors must be clearly described, indicating potential variations, if any, and the necessity for the developer to approve any variation.

The tenant should be provided with a clear description of the structural frame, its average floor load capability, locations on the floor where heavier loads can be placed (usually in the core), and where and how the floor structure can be modified to handle very heavy loads. Multi-floor tenants should be advised where it is feasible to accommodate an interior stairwell, and how the framing can be modified. Sketches of typical attachments should be included.

The tenant should be presented with the model numbers of the selected building standard lighting fixtures and the most common other fixtures added for unique tenant requirements. A typical fixture layout should be provided, showing the recommended average wattage per useable square foot, and a description of the proposed lighting controls. Developers should increasingly insist on motion detectors and on photo-cells in perimeter zones. Any limits on connected electrical load should be clearly explained.

The HVAC system should be clearly described including the acceptable equipment, installation specifications, design loads, maximum electrical demand, permissible velocities in ducts and piping, and final testing and balancing. The life safety systems should be described in the same manner.

The security system should be explained in detail, including construction keys, issuance of operational keys and/or cards, control of after hour lighting and HVAC systems, and ingress and egress after hours.

If there are requirements to use any of the building contractors, the reasons should be clearly explained. If the tenant uses his own contractors, the developer should clearly explain that his approval is required for each selected contractor, permissible hours of work, noise, proper isolation of the work area, use of temporary filters, scheduling of hoisting, specific procedures for handling oversize or overweight loads, and the contractor's responsibility for security and personal hygiene facilities for the workmen. In addition, the manual should list approved adhesives, paints, solvents and thinners to minimize VOCs and other contaminants in the space. The right of inspections by owner or owner's representatives must be clarified.

A description should be provided of any common areas and/or amenities available for the tenant's use. The allowable number and procedure for the tenant's identification on the directory board(s) should be provided.

An operations guide prepared by property management could be provided in this manual, or provided separately at a later time.

Once the first Tenant Procedure Manual is completed and reviewed, it should be distributed to all Development Officers and construction managers. It should be relatively easy task to tailor a manual for each project using the initial manual as a guide.

CASE STUDY

The base building design successfully addresses many of the features that positively affect the Interior Environmental Quality (IEQ)—an efficient central chiller system, good temperature control system, sufficient well-filtered outside air to provide good IAQ, good acoustical control, and toilet rooms designed for cleanability and neatness. High-quality lighting with motion detection and timer controls are included in the building standard for Tenant Improvements.

It should be noted that a building cannot always force the tenant to install higher cost and quality features, particularly if the cost should exceed the allowance and tenant must install these with his own funds, but inclusion in the standards will promote this effort.

The division of the work between that installed as part of the base building, and that to be Tenant Improvements was determined during the Market Study, and was shown in Chapter 4. Also detailed in that section was an analysis of the appropriate TI allowance. It was derived by taking the allowance in use at Del Mar Executive Center, adding for a two-year difference, and then adjusting for the provision of a central chiller system and electricity brought to the floor closets, rather than the tenant providing water source heat pumps and electricity from their meter in the main electrical room on the first floor. The result was an allowance of $31.50/usf, which was not adhered to very faithfully for various reasons.

The tenants had the responsibility of designing their space, subject to landlord approval, and subject to the building standard for Tenant Improvements. These building standards for Del Mar Gateway, including all general construction materials and specifications, are shown at the end of this chapter. They were reviewed with the brokers and Property Management before issuance. The material board shown in Figure 30-1 (mislabeled as Core and Shell Standards) illustrates the most common TI standard materials. From the upper left hand corner, moving clockwise they are:

- Plain sliced white maple doors with corridor and support area wall covering
- Non-directional fissured and beveled regular 24" x 24" ceiling tile alternates, with exposed ceiling grid beneath.
- Corridor paint sample and typical door lever handle beneath ceiling tiles
- Louver blind
- Kitchen grouping consisting of a microwave, dishwasher, trash compactor, faucet, cabinet handle and double sink
- Support area VCT
- VCT rubber base
- Aluminum doorframe
- Carpet rubber base
- Corridor carpet
- Elevator lobby carpet
- Elevator lobby stone base
- Alternate elevator carpet

A specification was prepared for all MEP and fire protection work, but it was too lengthy to include in this study. In essence the MEP specifications spell out the calculations, sizing, applicable standards, installation, supports, acoustic requirements, inspection and testing for all ductwork, piping, raceways, electric feeders and equipment. Each item of equipment was specified by its type and manufacturer. Installation will meet all fire and life safety codes. A brief outline of the MEP work is covered in the following paragraphs.

The tenant will install all VAV boxes, ductwork, hot water supply and returns to the reheat coils, diffusers, return grills and controls for the HVAC

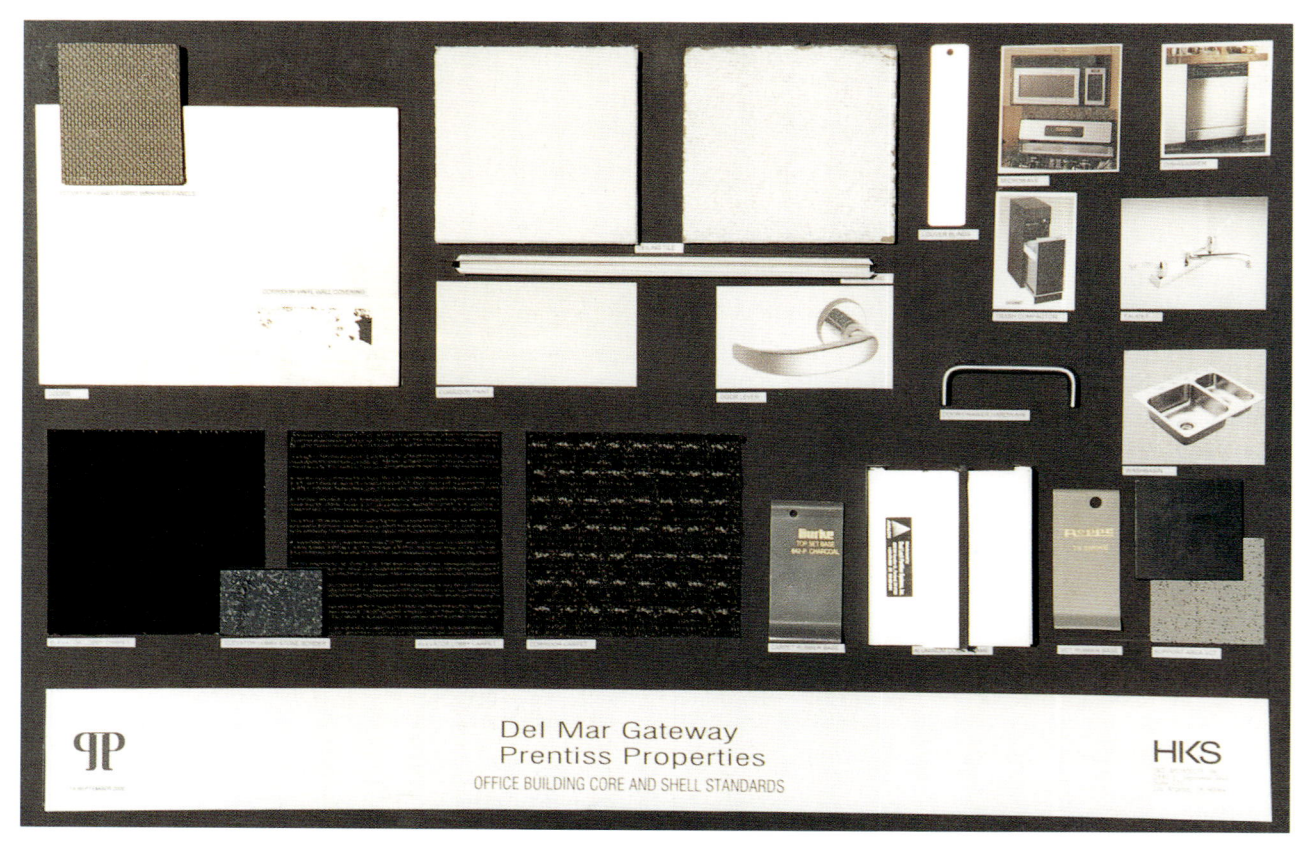

Figure 30-1

system from the cooled-air supply loop around the core and from the hot water supply and return risers. All smoke sensors and damper controls whose installation is required in the floor distribution system will be by tenant.

Tenant will be responsible for any modifications or extensions required to the standard sprinkler head layout that was installed under the base building contract, but charged to the tenant as a preinstalled TI (except in the case of Brandes, where it was included in the base building). Tenant will also install any alarms and fire extinguishers required by the space layout.

Both the 34-watt 2' x 2' and 64-watt 2' x 4' Lithonia direct/indirect lighting fixtures were specified, with the understanding that Brandes could select the fixture they prefer and that would become the standard for the remaining tenants. They selected the preferred 2' x 2' fixtures, and Scripps was pleased, as that was their preference also.

Occupancy sensors with timer controls were specified for all spaces. Downlights will be 18-watt CFLs. Tenant will install all path-of-egress and LED exit lights required by their layout. Electrical power is obtained from the electrical room on the floor, and any communications service is obtained from the main communications room.

The lease provided Brandes a choice of using either Syska & Hennessy or the engineers for the build-to-suit mechanical and electrical contractors, whom they selected, to perform their electrical and mechanical design.

The Brandes Lease required bids to be taken from five pre-approved general contractors but their TI consultant with encouragement from Prentiss convinced them to select a general contractor through bidding the fee and General Conditions. Everyone was pleased that Swinerton & Walberg was selected, as it greatly decreased the potential for conflicts during the construction. You will note from the schedule in Chapter 34 that the base building and TI work are very closely interrelated.

Due to the long lead time required for light fixtures and mixing boxes, plus the tightly integrated schedule for rough ductwork and smoke control, bids were taken for the MEP trades for the Brandes work as soon as the design development drawings and specifications were complete. It was highly beneficial to the project that all of the base building MEP contractors were the low bidders, and accepted by Brandes.

Brandes had specified or later requested several changes to the base building, all at their cost. They included:

- A security station in or off the first floor lobby—later they decided against this and visitors will go directly to the seventh floor reception area.

- Connecting stairs between the sixth, seventh and eighth floors. As soon as authorized to proceed, based on the location and dimensions of the opening, the structural steel framing was revised. As a condition of permitting this stairway, it was required that all applicable fire and smoke permits be included in their building permit (which is a critical date in their schedule of responsibility) and that they restore upon vacating the premises. It was later agreed that they would not be required to restore if they remained in occupancy for 16 years.

- They had the option to add their 150kw emergency electrical load to the building's emergency generator at their expense, which they elected to do.

- They requested that they be able to redesign the finishes for their floor elevator lobbies, subject to landlord approval. They changed the floor to have a 12" x 12" Tunas Green granite border with limestone accent bands and olive green carpet inlays. The walls are a combination of olive green fabric wrapped panels and natural maple millwork. On the executive floor, the 7th, they used wood paneling on the walls, a 12" x 12" limestone infill on the floor, and ran the granite out through the reception area.

- They requested to interchange the women's and men's toilet rooms on the 7th floor so they could add a five stall men's shower/locker room connecting to the men's toilet room, which was approved. They built a similar woman's shower/locker room connected to the woman's toilet room on the eighth floor.

- They requested a change of the accent tile on the toilet room walls to green and to green and beige on the floor, which was not only approved but changed on the other floors as well.

- They requested relocation of the doors to the eighth floor patios, which was accomplished at very little cost to them when they agreed to the limited locations acceptable to Walters & Wolfe.

- They requested substituting perforated clear 1" aluminum mini-blinds, which we agreed to and made it the building standard. They have proved to be unsatisfactory, as the sun shining through the perforations is too bright.

Brandes submitted their design development and construction drawings on schedule, and approvals were prompt, but subject to a few noted conditions. They were late, however, by 21 days in obtaining their building permits, which was recorded as tenant delay. They did not accept the tenant delay, as they had released a large amount of their work without the permits being received, and resolution was reserved until later as it might become moot.

Brandes was unable to obtain their Certificate of Occupancy when the building received its Temporary Certificate of Occupancy (TCO) because they were in the process of connecting the electrical wiring in their modular furniture. They resolved this issue by stopping all work, terminating the wiring at its present location until the C of O was received, and then completing the electrical installation. As the building TCO had been received in conformance with the lease the rent commenced on schedule.

Scripps Bank was required by the lease to use the building's TI designer, Smith Consulting Architects, and the general contractor. Scripps required a separate entrance with an eyebrow sign above it. It was originally agreed to be a shared-cost modification to the base building storefront. Later, when they requested to sublease the entire second floor, as discussed in Chapter 32, the entire cost reverted to them. They were several months late with their contract documents, but their rental payments commenced on September 1, per the lease. As discussed in Chapter 32, they later decided to sublease the majority of their space rather than occupying it.

All other tenants were required to use Swinerton & Walberg and the building's MEP contractors. The remainder of the other tenant Improvement work was completed on schedule and with no unusual issues.

Prentiss Properties
DEL MAR GATEWAY

BUILDING STANDARDS FOR TENANT IMPROVEMENTS

August 9, 1999

PARTITIONS

A. DEMISING PARTITIONS & CORRIDOR WALLS
   1. 2-½"—20 gauge metal studs 24" on center maximum to underside or structure above (16" o.c. when supporting wall mounted cabinets or equipment).
   2. ⅝" gypsum wallboard one layer each side of studs (or as required for specific fire rating).
   3. Seismic bracing per code.
   4. Two rows of continuous acoustical sealant—top and bottom tracks.
   5. R-11 halt type fiberglass insulation between studs.
   6. Cables taped smooth and sanded to receive paint or wall covering.
   7. No back-to-back electric or data outlets.

B. TYPICAL INTERIOR PARTITION (non-rated)
   1. 2-1/2"gauge metal studs 24" on center maximum terminating at suspended ceiling (16" o.c. when supporting wall mounted cabinets or equipment).
   2. ⅝" gypsum wallboard one layer each side of studs.
   3. Height from floor to ceiling grid—approximately 9'-0"at all floors (interior partitions shall not typically penetrate the suspended ceiling).
   4. Seismic bracing per code.
   5. Partition taped smooth and sanded to receive point or wall covering.
   6. All exterior corners van corner beads.

C. PERIMETER DRYWALL (where required)
   1. ⅝" gypsum wallboard, one layer on existing framing per plans. Batt insulation to remain.
   2. Height-floor slab to 6" above ceiling grid where occurs.
   3. Lap onto window mullions ½" all around or lap under horizontal mullion cap extension. Seal with caulk.
   4 "L" metal at all exposed edges of gypsum wallboard.
   5. Gypsum wallboard taped smooth and sanded to receive paint or wall covering.

D. COLUMN FURRING
   1. ⅝" gypsum wallboard, one layer on 2-½"—25 Ga. metal studs (minimum).
   2. Height—floor slab to 6" above ceiling grid.
   3. Gypsum wallboard taped smooth and sanded to receive paint or wall covering.
   4. Provide all exterior corners with corner beads.
   5. Option ¾" MDO painted over ¾" hat channels.

INSULATION
   1. Partition acoustic insulation demising partitions rated walls and where required by code.

F. PARTITIONS AT EXTERIOR WINDOWS

BUILDING STANDARDS FOR TENANT IMPROVEMENTS (Continued)

1. Partitions abutting window mullions to receive continuous metal end cap to match window interior finish all exposed edge. Provide 1/8" neoprene gasket and silicone sealant between partition edge and mullion. No mechanical connection to mullion. Where necessary, provide false mullion to match existing, where partition walls abuts shorefront/curtain wall system. SEE ATTACHED DETAILS. Under no circumstances may wall abut glass where mullions do not occur.

DOORS, FRAMES AND HARDWARE

A. ALUMINUM DOOR FRAMES

Manufacturer:	Dual Lock Partition Systems, Inc. (or equal)
Product:	Eagle series dual lock partition system
Color:	Clear aluminum
Note:	To be non-rated
Location:	Tenant
Contact:	Rick Carlton
	800-678-0566

Manufacturer:	Dual Lock Partition Systems, Inc. (or equal)
Product:	Eagle series dual lock partition system
Color:	Clear aluminum
Note:	20 min. rated
Location:	Corridor
Contact:	Rick Carlton
	800-678-0566

Manufacturer:	Alumax or equal
Product:	Eagle series dual lock partition system 1 PC029-9
Color:	Clear aluminum
Glazing:	¼" tempered safety glass where required per code
Note:	Return gypsum board into opening at both sides, provide metal corner bead all around opening. Finish to match wall. Provide two 20 Ga. metal fastened at 12" o.c. back-to-back at jambs and head (minimum) as per detail. Seismic brace per code.
Location:	Sidelights
Contact:	800-678-0566

B. FLUSH WOOD DOORS

Manufacturer:	Weyerhauser (or equal)
Product:	California
Wood:	premium grade plain-sliced white maple
Finish:	pre-finished Autumn 32-95
Note:	Flush hardwood, solid core 3'-0" x 8'-10-¾" full height x 1-¾" doors to conform to AWI standards and have a lifetime guarantee. Certification of applicable labels and warranties to be provided. Doors shall match existing core doors in finish, material and appearance. Undercut doors 1/2" and finish all edges. Stainless steel hinges.
Rating:	DFP-20
Location:	Corridor
Contact:	Bill Schmid
	650-579-5829

Manufacturer:	Weyerhauser (or equal)
Product:	California
Wood:	premium grade plain-sliced white maple
Finish:	pre-finished Autumn 32-95

BUILDING STANDARDS FOR TENANT IMPROVEMENTS (Continued)

Note:	Flush hardwood, solid core 3'-0" x 8'-10-¾" full height x 1-¾" doors to conform to AWI standards and have a lifetime guarantee. Certification of applicable labels and warranties to be provided. Doors shall match existing core doors in finish, material and appearance. Undercut doors ½" and finish all edges. Stainless steel hinges.
Rating:	DPC-1
Location:	Tenant
Contact:	Bill Schmid
	650-579-5829

C. DOOR HARDWARE

FOR CORRIDOR DOORS (FIRE RATED)

SINGLE DOOR

Qty.	Subtype	Item Description
4	Butts	Hager BB1279 4-½" x 4-½"—652
1	Stop	Quality W302T—630
1	Closer	Norton 8501 689
1	Smoke Seal	Pemco
1	Lockset	Schlage L Series 17 Satin Chromium Plated 626

PAIR OF DOORS

Qty.	Subtype	Item Description
8	Butts	Hager BB1279 4-½" X 4-½—652
1	Lockset	Yale CRR8747 FL 626
2	Closers	Norton 8501 689
1	Auto Flush Bolts	Door Controls 942—626
1	Dust Proof Strike	Door Controls 80—626
1	Coordinator	Door Controls 672—600
1	Astrigal	Pemco 355AV x door height 355CS
2	Stops	Quality W302T—630
2	Smoke Seal	Pemco, furnished by frame manufacturer

FOR INTERIOR TENANT DOOR

SINGLE DOOR

Qty.	Subtype	Item Description
4	Butts	Hager BB1279 4-½" x 4-½"—652
1	Latchset	Yale CRR8701 FL 626
1	Stop	Quality W302PT 630

PAIR OF DOORS

Qty.	Subtype	Item Description
8	Butts	Hager BB1279 4-½' x 4'½—652
1	Latchset	Yale CRR 8701 FL 626
1	Semi-Auto FB	Door Controls 945—626
1	Dust Proof Strike	Door Controls 80-626
2	Stops	Quality W302T—630

INTERIOR GLAZING
  A. ¼" thick clear glass in non-rated, prefinished aluminum frames by Alumax or equal similar to: Eagle series dual lock partition system 1PC029-9. Color shall be Clear Aluminum.
  B. ¼" thick tempered safety glass where required per code.
  C. Return gypsum board into opening at both sides, provide metal corner bead all around opening. Finish to match wall.

BUILDING STANDARDS FOR TENANT IMPROVEMENTS (Continued)

D. Provide two 20 Ga. metal studs fastened at 12" o.c. back-to-back at jambs and head (minimum) as per detail. Seismic brace per code.

SUSPENDED ACOUSTICAL CEILING
- Manufacturer: Armstrong
- Product: Silhouette XL 9/16", Bolt System 1/4" Reveal
- Grid Dimension: 24" x 24"
- Color: Dunn Edwards, Swiss Coffee SP 836
- Note: Seismic bracing per code. Ceiling Grid Hanger Wires and Seismic wires for lighting and electrical to be provided by Acoustical Ceiling Contractor.
- Location: Typical
- Note: 9'-0" AFF at all locations
- Contact: Linda Ruse
  800-356-9301 ext. 8136

- Manufacturer: Armstrong
- Product: Ultima Beveled Tegular
- Grid Dimension: 24" x 24" x 3/4"
- Color: Dunn Edwards, Swiss Coffee SP 836
- Note: Seismic bracing per code. Ceiling Grid Hanger Wires and Seismic wires for lighting and electrical to be provided by Acoustical Ceiling Contractor.
- Location: Typical
- Note: 9'-0" AFF at all locations
- Contact: Linda Ruse
  800-356-9301 ext. 8136

ALTERNATE
- Manufacturer: Armstrong
- Product: Cirrus Beveled Tegular
- Grid Dimension: 24" x 24" x ¾"
- Color: Dunn Edwards, Swiss Coffee SP 836
- Note: Seismic bracing per code. Ceiling Grid Hanger Wires and Seismic wires for lighting and electrical to be provided by Acoustical Ceiling Contractor.
- Location: Typical
- Note: 9'-0" AFF at all locations
- Contact: Linda Ruse
  800-356-9301 ext. 8136

FLOOR COVERING

A. RESILIENT TILE FLOORING
- Manufacturer: Armstrong
- Product: Premium Excelon Tile Stonetex
- Color: 52125 Granite Gray
- Dimension: 12" x 12" x 1/8"
  - Location: Telephone room and janitor closet
  - Note: Float floors with floor leveling compound
  - Contact: Laura Hubbard
    1-800-292-6308 ext. 8993

ALTERNATE
- Manufacturer: Armstrong
- Product: Excelon Imperial Texture VCT

BUILDING STANDARDS FOR TENANT IMPROVEMENTS (Continued)

    Color: Varies from tenant to tenant
    Dimension: 12" x 12" x 1/8"
    Adhesive: As recommended by Manufacturer (no asbestos containing adhesives are permitted)
    Location: Telephone room and janitor closet
    Contact: Laura Hubbard
        1-800-292-6308 ext. 8993

B. RESILIENT BASE AND ACCESSORIES
    Manufacturer: Burke Flooring Products
    Product: Top Set Base
    Color: Charcoal 642-P
    Location: Typical at Carpet
    Note: 2-½" straight base at carpet
    Contact: Jayne Mapes
        800-669-7010 ext. 557

    Manufacturer: Roppe
    Product: Rubber Cove Base
    Color: Smoke 74
    Location: Typical at VCT
    Note: 4" rubber cove base at resilient flooring
    Contact: Lil Talley
        800-526-5845 ext. 724

C. CARPET
  1. TENANT AREAS CARPET
    Manufacturer: Shaw
    Product: Time and Space, Turning Point BL
    Color: Legume 71320
    Fiber Content: Monsanto LXI-SD BCF Nylon-6, 6
    Width: 12'
    Pattern Repeat: 26/32" X 23/32"
    Location: Option as TI carpet
    Contact: Rebecca Snider
        800-424-7429 ext. 8426

  2. SHELL CARPET (CORRIDORS)
    Manufacturer: Shaw
    Product: Time and Space, Turning Point BL
    Color: Legume 71320
    Fiber Content: Monsanto -XI-SD BCF Nylon-6, 6
    Width: 12'
    Pattern Repeat: 26/32" X 23/32"
    Location: 1st and 3rd floor corridors
    Contact: Rebecca Snider
        800-424-7429 ext. 8426

  3. SHELL CARPET (ELEVATOR LOBBIES)
    Manufacturer: Fortune Contract
    Product: Talisman
    Color: Black
    Fiber Content: TBD
    Width: TBD

BUILDING STANDARDS FOR TENANT IMPROVEMENTS (Continued)

    Pattern Repeat: TBD
    Location: 2nd thru 8th floor elevator lobbies
    Contact: Fortune Contract
    706-279-3669

PAINT
    Manufacturer: Dunn Edwards Paints
    Color: Swiss Coffee SP 836
    Finish: Eggshell
    Contact: Pam Esparza
    800-537-4098 ext. 7574

HORIZONTAL LOUVER BLINDS
    Manufacturer: Levelor (or equal)
    Product: Riviera 1 Dustguard
    Size: 7/8" slats metal blinds, inside mounting
    Color: 34 Brushed Aluminum
    Installation: Mounted within curtain wall head track
    Note: Window blinds at exterior glass will be provided by building owner at a tenant cost of $.50/usf.
    Contact: Nils Anderson, CSI
    800-828-8799

RESIDENTIAL APPLIANCES
    Manufacturer: General Electric
    Model: Microwave JVM1460S
    Finish: Stainless Steel

    Manufacturer: General Electric
    Model: Dishwasher GSD4940
    Finish: Stainless Steel

    Manufacturer: General Electric
    Model: Trash Compactor
    Finish: Stainless Steel

    Manufacturer: General Electric
    Model: Garbage Disposal GFC705

CUSTOM CABINETS
    Manufacturer: TBD
    Finish: Plastic laminate or hardwood veneer horizontal and vertical surfaces
    Counter: Plastic laminate, stone or tile countertops
    Color: Varies by tenant
    Cabinetry Construction: Designation ¾" high pressure particle board. Plastic laminate or hardwood veneer finish, countertops and splashes shall be constructed in accordance with WIC Manual of Millwork, 'Premium' grade.
    Hardware:
    HINGES—self-closing type, fully concealed when the doors are closed designed to open at least 175 degrees. Hinges shall have independence vertical, horizontal and depth adjustment. Hinges shall be steel with nickel plated finish.
    Manufacturer: Brass America, Inc. No. 1200/1201
        Julius Blum, Inc. No 91.650
        Stanley Hardware Nos. 1511-2/1511-8x or equal.

BUILDING STANDARDS FOR TENANT IMPROVEMENTS (Continued)

PULLS
Manufacturer: Hafele (or equal)
Size: $^5/_{16}$" diameter wire pulls with 4" c. to c. spacing
Product: 116.39.464
Finish: Brass wire handle, chrome plated matt
Location: Coffee Room and Copy Room cabinets
Contact: Greg Trejo
800-423-3531 ext. 122

ADJUSTABLE SHELF STANDARD—Aluminum standards and zinc plated steel shelf supports designed to provide adjustments at 1/2" centers.
Manufacturer: Grant Hardware Company Nos. 120/121
Knapp & Vogt Nos. 255A/258
Stanley Hardware No. 180/CD 1806 or equal.

DRAWERS—Provide heavy duty full extension drawer slides
Manufacturer: Hafele, Blum or equal

FASTENERS AND ANCHORAGES: Provide nails, screws or other anchoring devices of type, size material and finish suitable for intended use and required to provide secure attachment, concealed where possible.

CASEWORK
(1) Drawer Boxes: Provide sub-front and applied finish fronts securely fastened with square corners and self-edges. Provide drawers with metal studs and full height boxes.
(2) Doors: Flush overlay type, hinges toseing flat against the face of adjoining cabinet or the side of the cabinet ends or divisions to received hinges. Provide clear plastic bumpers.
(3) Shelves: ¾" thick for spans up to 35" and 1" thick for spans over 35" up to 48", and adjustable to 1" centers. Do not recess metal shelf standards into the end panels; notch shelving to clear standards.

PLUMBING FIXTURES
Manufacturer: Moen
Product: Sani-stream, 8798 8" centers
Note: Commercial washerless ceramic cartridge
Contact: Security Plumbing
310-473-1107

Manufacturer: Moen
Product: Sani-sink, 22116, CSR-2522-2
Finish: Steel
Contact: Security Plumbing
310-473-1107

MISCELLANEOUS NOTES
1. Building standard ground floor directory tenant identification/suite number strip to be provided by building owner.
2. Building standard tenant identification/suite number or sign adjacent to suite entry door to be provided by building owner.
3. The building shell is constructed to bear a 60 psi live load and a 20 psi partition load (see loading diagram).

LEASE PROPOSALS 31

The proposal is the first real step in the leasing process. The purpose of a proposal is to be sufficiently attractive to the potential tenant to **induce him/her to seriously consider your building** and enter into further negotiations with you, and it should be carefully thought through to insure this result. Proposing excessive inducements or terms at this time makes future negotiations difficult. The key factors in the planning for and preparation of lease proposals are discussed in this chapter.

> An important trait in a leasing program is to never give up as long as there is the slightest chance of landing a targeted tenant. Two examples from a major building in Dallas illustrate this point.
>
> There was a large independent oil company located in a Class B building with a lease due to expire in the next year-and-a-half. Our outside broker and our internal leasing personnel had called on their chief financial officer several times, but were repeatedly told there was no interest whatsoever in relocating. As a last resort, I made a personal appointment with him to attempt one final time to interest them in our building. A few hours before I arrived, a small cooling tower located on a roof adjacent to their chairman's office had leaked badly causing him to vacate his office. They were receptive to our presentation, we believe, largely due to the disruption caused by the leak, and within several weeks we negotiated a lease for 175,000 square feet. No other developer ever got to look at that opportunity.
>
> In a similar case, both our outside brokers and our internal leasing personnel had tried repeatedly without any success to reach the managing partner of a major law firm who were rumored to be interested in another project. I started calling for an appointment and had no greater success. I finally found out that a friend had this gentleman as his personal attorney. At my request he tried to arrange a meeting for me, and within a few weeks I had an appointment for 5 PM on a Friday evening. When I arrived shortly before 5 PM he was not there and did not return until well after 6 PM. When he did arrive, he had an unpleasant frown on his face and walked straight into his office without saying a word. When his secretary invited me to go in, I thought to myself, "This is a terrible time to make a sales presentation." As it turned out, he had returned from an all-afternoon meeting at which he had expected to execute a letter of intent with another developer, but believed they had reneged on their previous agreements. Within two weeks, on a Saturday morning in the family room of one of their partners, we executed a letter of intent.
>
> The foregoing experiences can be considered as pure luck, but the good fortune would not have occurred without our refusal to give up as long as these potentially viable tenants were in the market.

An effective leasing effort is a well-planned proactive effort, wherein you make every effort to ensure that your representatives put a proposal in front of every potential tenant that your research has indicated is a viable prospect.

In a stable to upward market, the developer can adhere fairly strictly to the pro forma rates and conditions, and review periodically for possible upward revision. Where the market is soft or has a downward bias, a computerized program for lease analysis should be set up, insuring that parties—lenders, owners, brokers, etc.—agree with the method used so that a quick determination of lease feasibility and flexibility can be made before a lease proposal is written.

A sample lease proposal should be prepared at the beginning of the project outlining all of the basic information to be included in a proposal, as well as any attachments or exhibits to incorporate issues frequently addressed in proposals, but which the owner prefers to avoid if at all possible. It should be organized on the computer so that it can be prepared on very short notice.

Frequently a proposal is based on the discussions with a prospective tenant or a broker representing one, but it often results from a formal request for a proposal based on specific requirements spelled out by the tenant. When submitting a proposal without specific requirements, all rates should be those from the current lease strategy and renewals or expansions should not be proposed. Both renewals and expansions can hurt the economics of the project because they are one-way streets—the owner takes on an obligation that may hurt in leasing the remaining space, in return for the right of a tenant to choose at a later date. To minimize the impact of expansions, if they cannot be avoided, place that obligation during the sixth year of the year of the lease term, which provides some extra leasing time to find a five-year tenant for that space. For renewals, as well as expansions, place the tenant's option exercise date as far in advance as possible, preferably a year.

When responding to requests for proposals submitted by a prospective tenant, you must decide whether you will initially agree to provide the extent of expansions or renewals requested, and on what terms. Expansions should be limited to no more than one-third of the original space, and renewals should be limited to one five-year extension. Any extensions or expansions must be qualified that they are effective only if, at the time of notice, tenant is not in default under the lease, and is occupying at least a stipulated percentage of their currently leased space (say 80% or 85%).

In the current market proposals have become less formal—many transmitted back and forth via e-mail. Remember that e-mails can be edited, and consideration should be given to the use of encryption systems.

The practice of negotiating detailed letters of intent has been abandoned in most markets, unless it is a very large lease. It takes almost as much time and effort to negotiate a letter of intent as a lease—and when converting the L/I to a lease, it just gives the tenant another opportunity to raise new issues or re-address old ones. It is usually better to go directly to the lease as soon as the basic economic issues are agreed upon.

Certain onerous requests, particularly those that may be frivolous, are best ignored in the initial proposal phase rather than rejected outright. If brought up again in a counter proposal or discussion, endeavor to have the tenant justify why such a request is reasonable and important.

It is initially assumed that all lease proposals will be structured to meet the pro forma, but market conditions may modify that positively or negatively. When considering proposals or counter offers for space that are significantly different from the pro forma, a flat rate equivalent model should be used to compute the true present value variance of the proposal from the base assumptions.

A very common situation that must be addressed is when a major tenant is considering your project during the early stages, but insists on excessive concessions. An alternate pro forma run, which includes the cost impact of all the concessions, should be made and analyzed. Frequently, the reduced interest expense resulting from a large tenant paying rent early will offset part of the increased costs, and the value of the certainty of a tenant will offset some amount of reduced return by reducing risk. An important caveat is to **never** increase other income projections or reduce unrelated costs in order to obtain an acceptable return in such an analysis. If other income or projections have changed, discipline and the integrity of the analysis dictate that the pro forma should be rerun with the new data prior to the run with the prospective tenant. Following that policy will insure that you are defining the true impact of the proposed lease.

Key factors in the Lease Proposal are:

Proposal Preparer: Should preferably be sent by an agent for the owning entity, either the broker or another entity affiliated with the owner.

Entities: The owner's entity should be a unique entity that owns only the premises. The tenant entity should be an entity with significant net worth (as determined later through a credit check) to meet the obligations of the lease.

Leased Premises: The premises should be spelled out as a specific portion of the stated floor in the identified project supported, if possible, by a leasing space plan. The definition of the rentable area should be included as an attachment. Alternate approaches to measurement of the premises are discussed in the Lease Negotiation chapter.

Initial Term: The term should be a stipulated number of years from the commencement date. Note that if the building is not yet completed, an estimated commencement date and firm termination date should be provided.

Base Rental Rate: The initial rental rate that may be either a net rental rate (exclusive of any operating costs) or a gross rental rate (including operating expenses and sometimes utilities) for the premises. In a proposal this is initially set by the pro forma, but may be modified to accommodate changed market conditions. As discussed in the prior chapter, a premium might be required for a tenant encumbering too much additional space, and a reduced rental rate might be offered a tenant to lease encumbered or less desirable space.

Base Rental Rate Adjustments: Spell out any step rents or adjustments in the base rental rate based on the CPI or other well understood index, or in fixed dollar terms.

Operating Expenses: Whether quoting a net or gross lease, the operating and/or utility costs are stipulated here with an estimate of the base year cost. In a gross rental rate proposal it will be the tenant's obligation to pay a proportional increase of actual operating costs above the base each year. In a net lease the tenant will pay the operating costs as they occur. In either case the base year and the current year must be adjusted to reflect what the costs would be if the building were 95% occupied for the full year in question. The estimate of operating expenses should be prepared by Property Management for the costs anticipated to occur in the first full year (calendar, or other year) of operation. When utilities are specified separately, another similar section should be included.

Remember, in a gross lease if you underestimate the actual operating expenses the difference will come out of the net rental rate, and hurt the performance with respect to the pro forma. Conversely, if the estimate is too high it might make the building less economically attractive to prospective tenants.

Real estate taxes during the first year are frequently based on less than a full assessment due to the timing of the tax appraisal or the incomplete status of tenant construction, but must be adjusted to the value that will occur when fully occupied.

HVAC: The hours of operation should spelled out as the normal hours, with the statement that after hours service, or excessive requirements over the design load, may be obtained at tenant's expense. Sometimes a maximum hourly rate is specified for excess or after hours air conditioning.

Electrical Consumption: The maximum electrical consumption (or connected load, which is easier to verify in advance) must be accurately specified in the lease to match the design electrical capacity, and the demand, or usage, must not exceed the assumptions used in the HVAC design and assumed in the operating cost projections.

When it is a full-service lease, with utilities included, it should clearly state that any excess usage during normal business hours over the design demand will be a reimbursable charge, and after hours electricity usage will be charged to tenant unless nominal. One common method of charging for after hours electricity consumption is to include it in the after hours HVAC charge.

When responding to a tenant request for what appears to be excessive miscellaneous electrical power, the initial proposal should include the design amount that is a reasonable level, and it should be presented in terms as watts per useable square feet. For more detailed discussion of this subject refer to Miscellaneous Tenant Power Requirements in Chapter 26. Any excess demand will trigger the tenant to pay for additional cost for additional HVAC or electrical service.

Rental Abatement: If the current market requires rent abatement (heaven forbid!) it should be clearly stated as to whether only net rent is abated or net rent plus operating expenses.

Lease Renewals: When necessary to include lease renewals, they should be limited to no more than five years, unless it is a very large lead tenant, and then only if tenant is not then in default, and is in occupancy of at least 80% to 85% of their premises. The rental should be at either a fixed rental rate or at the fair market rate, but not less than tenant's then current rental rate. If a refurbishing allowance is provided it should be limited to the value of carpet and painting.

Lease Expansions: When necessary to include expansions, they should be limited to one-third of the original premises, and preferably less, and then only if tenant is not then in default and is in occupancy of at least 80% to 85% of their premises. The expansion term should commence in not less than five years, and preferably should commence during the sixth year of the term as determined by landlord. The rental rate should be set at either a fixed rental rate or the fair market rental rate. If a refurbishing allowance is provided it should be limited to the value of carpet and painting, if the space has previously been built out.

If it should ever be necessary to offer an expansion for a term commencing in less than five years, it should be on a "must take" basis. A standard TI allowance can be offered if the space has never been built out for another purpose.

Fair Market Rental Rate: The fair market rental rate should be that rate then being obtained in arms-length transactions for comparable buildings within a stipulated market area. This should be the net rental rate plus the operating expenses being charged, without any adjustments for lease commissions, TIs or any other costs or concessions. (You have already paid them).

Right of First Refusal: A one-time right to acquire a specified area adjacent to the premises might be offered initially in lieu of an expansion option. Tenant shall, if not in default and in occupancy of a stipulated percentage of the leased premises, be provided three business days to match a bona fide offer for the space received by owner.

Right of First Opportunity: Another potential substitute for an expansion option, it should spell out that it is a one-time right to acquire a specified amount of adjacent space at the termination of an existing lease, if tenant is not in default and is in occupancy of a stipulated percentage of their space. Tenant will be given a stipulated number of days after notice of availability to take the space "as is" at fair market rental rate, but not less than the rent tenant is paying on the leased premises. If the tenant declines, landlord will have a stipulated period, usually six months to a year to lease the space to others under any terms desired. This is the least onerous of the commitments to provide space to tenant.

Assignment and Subletting: This right should never be offered in a proposal unless tenant has made clear this is an important issue. The offer should provide certain rights to sublease up to a stipulated percentage of the leased premises, if not in default and then occupying a stipulated percentage of the leased premises, subject to landlord's certain recapture rights, right to approve the subtenant, and to participate in any gross rents or other payments to tenant in excess of the gross rents under the lease. Assignment will be at landlord's sole option unless to a credit worthy affiliate of tenant.

Non-disturbance: Landlord will either use reasonable efforts to obtain a commercially reasonable non-disturbance agreement, or will agree to obtain such agreement from lender within a specified number of days from the execution of the lease, or otherwise the lease will be voidable

Tenant Improvement Allowance: Based upon the current market policies, landlord may offer tenant in a new building either:

- A fixed dollar amount per useable square foot (usf) for Tenant Improvements, or
- The number of units of building standard improvement items as specified in a detailed work letter, or
- Provide at landlord's expense the work shown on an attached set of plans and specifications or,
- Provide tenant with a build-to-suit, normally using building standard components only.

In the current market the fixed dollar allowance is pretty much standard, but as markets turn more tenant friendly, other measures come into play. A 5% developer's coordination fee should be included in the TI cost when using the fixed dollar allowance, and 5% added to the over-standard work when providing units from a work letter.

Note that when providing a specific dollar allowance, tenant has a reasonable right to expect that they can build out a normal space when using only a normal amount of building standard items within the allowance, including the 5% coordination fee.

Condition of the Leased Premises: For an initial lease the condition will be the base building condition, the contemplated shell and core construction, as spelled out in an attached exhibit. Where applicable, if some of the work that is tenant's responsibility, such as sprinklers, life safety alarms or features, or perimeter window covering, called the preinstalled items, are installed by landlord, the amount of the allowance that must be applied to this work must be specified. With regard to renewals, expansions, and rights of first opportunity, condition shall be specified as in "as is" condition.

Refurbishment Allowance: Whenever it is agreed to provide an allowance for expansion or renewal space, it should be limited to carpet and painting.

Moving Allowance: An inducement to make the lease, only if absolutely necessary.

Current Lease Reimbursement: Used only when the proposed lease is of extreme importance to the project, and the reimbursement must be limited by a maximum number of dollars payable by landlord, with detailed conditions on the negotiations with the prior landlord.

Termination Right: A one-time right to terminate at a specified time for a specified penalty on a specified notice is never offered without an indication that the issue is an absolute requirement of the tenant. Try to determine why it is so important, and maybe it can be tied to some issue or event they are concerned about. The termination payment should cover at least the unamortized costs of the TIs and lease commission, plus some allowance for downtime.

Parking: Should be spelled out as a specified number of unreserved spaces in the parking lot or structure at the specified current rate, if applicable. The rate should be adjustable upward from time to time to match the prevailing rate in the area for similar spaces. The reason for specifying unreserved spaces (sometimes called licenses) is to be able to utilize the float (temporary absences, that can amount to from 15% to 30%) for the use of transients. Reserved spaces should be avoided where possible, and if required, kept to a minimum. The charged for reserved spaces should be at a premium of 30% to 35% to make up for lost transient revenue.

Exculpatory Clause: Proposal may be withdrawn at any time for any reason, is non-binding, and conditioned upon the negotiation and unconditional execution of a definitive lease.

CASE STUDY

While still in the schematic design phase and in the process of attempting to satisfy the Substantial Conformance Review, the brokers brought in a request for proposal from Brandes Investment Partners, L.P., a potential 100,000 rsf lease. They were located in two different buildings in the same office park, and had just broken off renewal negotiations with their current landlord, who refused to build an additional parking deck considered necessary to relieve their current parking shortage.

They were very interested in the project due to the location, sufficient availability of parking, perception of high quality, adjacent hotel, and there were only two other planned buildings that could satisfy their requirements.

A lease of this nature was very attractive because, as mentioned earlier, this was a period in which the REITs were in disfavor in the investment community, making acquiring new funds difficult, and it appeared necessary to sell a half interest in this building and the adjacent Executive Center in order to finance the project. With this extensive pre-leasing the project could be financed normally while retaining full ownership.

Three key issues for Brandes were sufficient parking, a front-end payment to at least partially defray the cost of buying out the remaining term of the existing staggered-term leases, and a comfort level that the building would be constructed in time to satisfy their requirements. The response to Brandes' Request for Proposal indicated a desire to make the deal. The proposal is shown below with tenant's RFP requirements shown in parentheses.

LEASE PROPOSAL TO BRANDES INVESTMENT PARTNERS, LP

Premises:	Five floors, approximately 100,000 rsf.
Term:	11 years (11 years for ease of comparison with present location).
Rental Rate:	$2.25 /rsf, plus electricity, increasing annually at 5¢ /mo.
Lease Commencement:	Delivery of the space by August 1, 2000, with 30 days for cabling, equipment and furniture installation, etc.
Landlord Delay:	Landlord will pay Tenant's holdover rent based on certain established milestone dates and prompt lease execution. (Landlord to assume the lease obligation).
Operating Expense:	Standard (7% cap on controllable expenses and Proposition 13 protection).
TI Allowance:	$33 /usf, plus sprinkler installation and $50,000 for UPS system ($35 / usf plus the UPS).
Moving Allowance:	$1.50 / usf ($1.50).
Refurbishment Allowance:	$5 / usf in 7th year (Same).
Signing Bonus:	$8.50 /rsf to partially offset termination penalties ($1 million plus 6 months free rent).
Expansion:	One full floor in the 49th month, original TIs if not built out, otherwise $10 /usf (Same).

Renewal:	Two 5-year terms @ prevailing FMV, with $3 /usf refurbishing allowance (Same).
Assignment and Subletting:	Normal.
Parking:	5 spaces /1,000 usf, with 20% reserved (Same).
Health Club:	1,000 sf on the First Floor if hotel facility is not available to tenant's employees (Same).
Signage:	None.
Letter of Credit:	$3 million decreasing over time.

Due to the location of the building at a major freeway interchange, and being the tallest office building between UTC and Orange County, it was very desirable for top of the building identification. While still negotiating the Brandes Lease (which excluded top of building signage) the brokers identified three prospective tenants who were very interested in the first and second floors. The local Scripps Bank was selected for initial negotiation. The initial proposal responded to their request for proposal, whose requested terms are shown in parentheses:

LEASE PROPOSAL TO SCRIPPS BANK

Premises:	25,000 rsf comprising portions of the first and second floors (Same).
Term:	Ten years (Same).
Commencement Date:	At completion of the premises.
Renewal Options:	Not addressed (Two five renewals).
Rental Rate:	$2.60 / rsf including electricity. Base rental increasing at 3% annually.
Operating Expenses:	Tenant shall pay increases over 2000 base year pro rata (Requested 5% cap on increases).
Tenant Improvements:	TI allowance of $32 / usf plus an additional $8 / usf allowance amortized at 10.5% over the initial term ($50 for the first floor and $40 for the second floor).
Parking:	4 spaces / 1000 usf, 20% reserved (20 reserved spaces for visitors near entrance and an agreed upon number for employees).
Signage:	Top of the building signage at a rate of $3,500 per month (Top of building signage plus eyebrow signage above their banking facility and illuminated monument signage).

The remaining leases were small and will not be discussed further in this chapter. The proposals were basically in conformance with the leasing strategy, but there was some play in the negotiations in order to make these short-term leases. They are discussed in Chapter 32.

EL CAMINO REAL

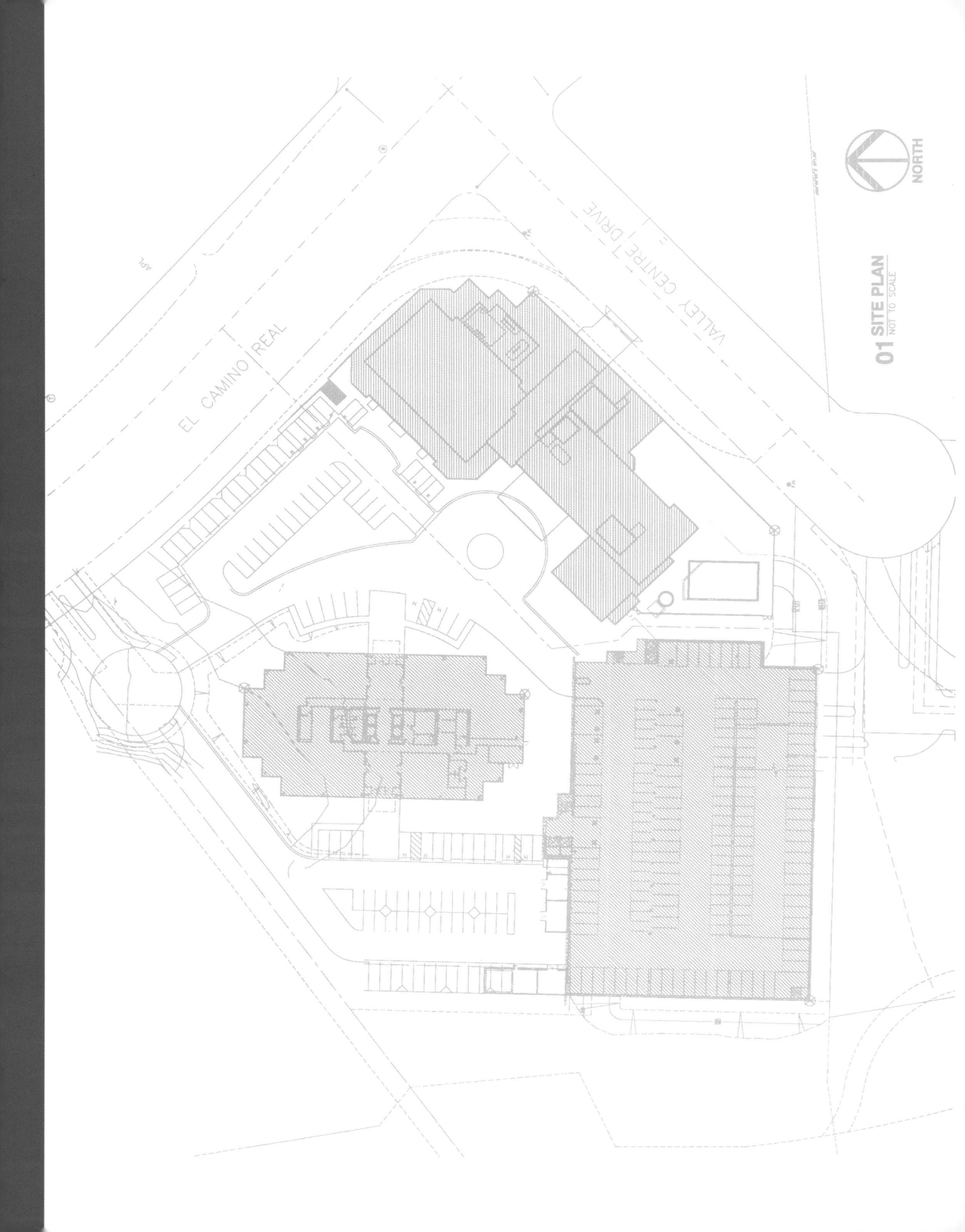

VALLEY CENTRE DRIVE

01 SITE PLAN
NOT TO SCALE

NORTH

LEASE NEGOTIATION   32

When a tenant selects your building, based generally on your proposal, you now have the opportunity to enter into a lease that reasonably satisfies everyone—the tenant, the lender and the owner. The negotiating strength of the parties is obviously affected by whether the market is tight, balanced or overbuilt.

As soon as a meeting of the minds has generally been reached through discussion of your lease proposal or through a letter of intent, a proposed lease should be presented to the tenant. It should be the standard printed lease, discussed in Chapter 29, modified only by those terms already agreed upon.

This is the stage where you make or break the deal—you concede those terms and inducements necessary to satisfy the tenant that your building is their appropriate choice, without giving away so much that the necessary pro forma return, as determined from your current leasing strategy, cannot be met. Many times a tenant can be guided back to more reasonable positions. In a worse case scenario, it is sometimes necessary to walk away from a deal that is too expensive.

It is important to remember that delay in reaching an agreement places a deal at risk—requirements and opportunities can change—resulting in the loss of a lease that could have been consummated. Over-negotiating on points that are not really essential can create unnecessary delays and annoy the tenant's negotiators. Use your creativity to find compromise solutions to the tenant's issues. **Make the deal—that was the purpose of initiating the development project.**

On a new building that is not yet fully leased, some prospective tenants, spurred on by their brokers, are likely to ask for anything they can think of, on the basis that you will be anxious to lease the building up as quickly as possible. On the other hand you are constrained by your lender, short-term pro forma requirements, and the long-term objectives for the building.

It is important to continually ask questions to try to understand why each request is important to the tenant's needs, so as to determine which requests are really important to them and which are just efforts to get something additional. At the same time, to be effective, you must articulate why it is not possible or appropriate to grant certain of their requests.

It is difficult to hold the line where necessary while maintaining a positive and often conciliatory approach with the tenant. Do not be afraid to counter new requests with, ". . . if you really need this, then we can't afford that." As a general rule the larger tenants are much more demanding. Smaller tenants who are quite interested in your building tend to more quickly accept issues you say you cannot accommodate.

It is important to remember that, as in any other negotiation, no issue is fully agreed upon until the last issue is resolved. When faced with what appears to be a very serious demand that exceeds your willingness to comply, you can often successfully propose agreement conditioned on trading that issue off against a tentatively agreed-upon issue.

The opportunity is there to thread your way through a maze of legal, lender and economic issues to achieve a satisfactory result for all parties.

The discussion of individual issues follows the outline of a standard office lease the author has used for a long period of time. Comments are primarily addressed to issues found to be highly negotiated in practice.

Parties to the Agreement

The entity who owns the building and the tenant are the parties. At this point it should be made clear that the landlord will accept no financial obligations of any kind beyond the building. The tenant must be carefully evaluated to ensure that it is sufficiently credit worthy to meet its obligations under the lease. If necessary a parent corporation, a personal guarantee or a significant security deposit is required.

Premises

Clearly define the suite with the floor number and location, and provide an attached plan as an exhibit.

Building

Clearly identify the building by name and street address, and refer to the parcels of the land on which it is situated, as shown in an exhibit.

Commencement Date

The commencement date should be a date certain, if possible. If the space is to be taken "as is" or if all work is to be performed by tenant, it may be a date certain. If the Tenant Improvements are to be performed by landlord, the date will be a date certain, or the date the space is judged as substantially complete by the building architect, and receives a Certificate of Occupancy, whichever is later, plus an agreed upon (say three days) notice to tenant. If tenant will perform the work while base building work is still in progress, be certain to warrant only that base building work will be sufficiently complete so as to permit commencement of tenant's work.

If the tenant intends to enter the premises to finish special work, after completion of work by landlord, the commencement date should be the date the tenant's contractor could enter the space, or an agreed upon number of business days thereafter. When the scope of the Tenant Improvement work greatly exceeds the scope of building standard work, an effort should be made to require the commencement date to be a negotiated number of weeks prior to the actual issuance of the Certificate of Occupancy. These last two assumptions can be highly contested, and are frequently resolved by compromise. Notwithstanding the above, if a tenant delay caused a delay in occupancy, as discussed in the Leasehold Improvements Exhibit, the lease will be assumed to have commenced as if the tenant delay had not occurred.

When a landlord delay occurs, and the tenant is required to holdover in their current space, landlord's damages should be limited to the difference between the holdover rent and the rent in the new building. No penalty would accrue in the event the delay was caused by *force majeure*. It is important to incorporate in the definition of *force majeure* that not only weather, strikes and acts of God, etc., are included, but also shortage of materials.

Termination Date

Should preferably be a date certain. Issues can arise when the commencement date must be somewhat flexible due to the uncertain date for completion of the Tenant Improvement work, sometimes resulting in slightly less than the agreed-upon term.

Term

Usually specified as a fixed number of years, but if a flexible commencement date is necessary, it should be an approximate number of years, with the termination date preferably fixed.

Rentable Area of the Premises and Building

The premises should a fixed area, tied down by the plan attached as an exhibit. If the premises are measured according to The Building Owners and Managers Association, International (American National Standards ANSI/BOMA Z65.1-1996), this should be stated in the lease; if not, or if the standard is modified, this should be clear to avoid future problems. Any alternative definition of rentable area should be attached as an exhibit. The rentable areas are computed by the architect in conformance with the that definition. The tenant's share is the percent of the building occupied by tenant, the rentable area of the premises divided by the building rentable area. There should not normally be too much of an issue with these measurements, as long as it is accepted in the brokerage community that the definition used is the market definition. Note that amenities for the sole use of tenants, such as a health club, should be deemed as common area and, thus, be included pro rata in the rentable area. In some cases, there are sufficient unknowns that there should be an adjustment when the tenant completes their space plans. There are, however, tenants who will contest the rentable area and request an adjustment, usually without a reasonable basis.

Another school of thought regarding this issue is merely to stipulate the rentable area without providing a checkable definition. This method probably permits an easier resolution whenever the area is contested, but the author does not believe it builds credibility between the landlord and the tenant.

A different approach that is apparently used in some markets is to calculate and specify the useable area and the add-on factor to compute the rentable area. This add-on factor, which is market-related, may or may not be verifiable. While the author does not really recommend this approach, it is probably all right if it is the prevalent practice.

Tenant's Occupancy

Usually occupancy confirms that the space and common areas are complete and free of defects, exclusive of Tenant Improvement work punch lists, and complies with the terms of the lease commencement. This is not too much of an issue, except for the issue of responsibility for latent defects, which bother some tenants. Latent defects on the base building work can frequently be resolved by a clear definition and landlord's acceptance of responsibility for those defects that occur prior to the expiration of contractor's warranties on such work. This is normally one year after substantial completion of the base building work, the period usually covered by warranties and insurance. However, some subcontractors try to have their warranties start prior to the building's substantial completion. Every effort should be made to have lease obligations mirror contractor's liability. Latent defects in the Tenant Improvement work, if performed by landlord, should be tied to substantial completion of that work. See further discussion of latent defects in Chapter 33.

Rent

Defined as Base Rent and Additional Rent. Rent is the money paid to the landlord for any and all purposes and is defined in many different ways in different markets. Some of the most common rental rates that rent is based upon are:

- Net Rental Rate Plus Operating Expenses: The net rental rate is the return to the landlord to pay the debt service on the loans, recover the investment and make a profit. The operating expenses are paid directly to the landlord as they occur or, in a triple net lease, paid directly by the tenant.

- Gross Rental Rental Rate: This combines the net rental rate and operating expenses into one rental rate.

- Gross Rental Rate Plus Utilities: As above, but utilities are excluded and paid separately by the tenant, either by meter or engineering analysis, or both.

If properly structured, and expenses correctly estimated, the total occupancy cost paid by the tenant will be the same. The adjustments as discussed below should be identical if the enabling clauses are properly drafted.

The author believes it is always better to structure the rental calculations in accordance with current practice in the market to avoid confusion and/or suspicion. The foregoing would not apply when your local position is sufficient to influence a change in market practice.

Rent commencement should coincide with the commencement of the term. Under poor market conditions, many tenants request free rent for a period of months. This is obviously something that the landlord resists as strenuously as possible, but you can avoid current market terms only to a small degree. When providing free rent, at least make an effort to recover operating costs. Some large tenants frequently are able to negotiate from two weeks to a month for installation of their specialized or furniture systems even in a market that does not demand free rent.

Base Rent

The base rent is the initial rental rate, adjusted by any fixed or percentage periodic increases that will increase the owner's return over time.

Additional Rent

Additional rent includes operating costs and utility costs (if separate), parking, operating and utility expense increases, charges for services, periodic payment and interest on excess TI work, costs of any site association and any other valid charges to tenant by landlord.

A primary issue in a new building is the validity of the estimated operating expense and utility costs. When quoted separately from the net rent, the tenant is frequently suspicious that the estimate is a low-ball figure, and his total rental will be higher than contemplated. This is not a major issue if most leases in the area are quoted as a net rent plus operating expense because they can basically compare both figures, but if some buildings quote a gross rental rate, the comparisons are not clear. One way to solve this issue is to cap the operating cost, such that any overage in the base year effectively results in a permanent reduction in the net rent to the building.

Frequently, one year of maintenance is purchased for building equipment as part of the construction contract. The amount should be identified and added to the first year operating expense, in other than a straight gross rental lease, so that the cost may be recovered.

Operating Expense and Adjustments

Where the operating costs are included in the rental rate, a similar issue to that above arises, in that the tenant may suspect the quoted operating expense for adjustment purposes is low-balled so as to get a greater increase in future years. Again, the base year can be pegged, but only if necessary.

The definition of operating costs should include every cost that occurs in the operation of a building, including all employee related costs. Some of the issues that are most frequently a concern of tenants are:

- Amortization of improvements "... to enhance the property for the benefit of all tenants" is a little difficult to sell, but is normally reasonable.

- Amortization of the replacement of any building equipment considered necessary to operate the building at the same level of service are reasonably considered as capital improvements by most tenants, rather than operating costs.

- When new equipment is added for the purpose of increasing operational efficiency and reduction of utility cost, it is reasonable to include the amortization of that equipment, up to the monthly amount of utility cost or other operational savings.

- Another issue is the gross up of operating expense to 95% occupancy. This is hard for some tenants to understand, but is perfectly valid. Try to explain that a major portion of expense, such as janitorial service, is a function of space occupied, and the gross up merely has every tenant paying the costs of supporting their own tenancy.

- Where real estate taxes are included within the rent, the treatment for purposes of comparison can be a point of contention. In the initial year the building's taxes are based on a partial assessment, normally based on the cost expended at the time the assessment is made and, therefore, are significantly below the stabilized assessment. The correct amount of the stabilized assessment is difficult to establish, since some jurisdictions switch their assessment basis from cost to income producing value after the project is complete and occupied. One solution is to use the assessment for the first full calendar year after initial occupancy of the building.

- Many tenants rightfully object to paying for the cost of complying with ADA if their lease was subsequent to the enactment of the law, however, if they were responsible for the design of their space they should accept that portion of the liability.

- Tenants also rightfully object to the cost of converting the CFCs to a new approved refrigerant in the chiller system.
- Some tenants object to inclusion of costs of education, travel, entertainment and association dues, such as BOMA, for management personnel. The author believes these objections are unreasonable, as they are small and a normal part of providing qualified management.

Currently many tenant attorneys are insisting on a complete listing of operating expenses to be included and excluded. This only highlights the growing trend of tenants to question and sometimes sue to recover increases billed to them. It is important that the Property Management team review any nonstandard clauses as they will be responsible for implementation in future years.

Latent Defects

When tenants object to the exclusion of latent defects, the best solution is to clearly define them and try to limit them to one year from substantial completion, when the work should be covered by warranties and insurance.

Parking

Landlord grants to tenant a license to use a stated number of parking spaces, usually his proportionate share of unreserved parking spaces in the parking structure or lot. Insist on unreserved to the greatest extent possible, because the float of 15% to 30% can be used for visitor and transient parking. Reserved parking makes the parking area inefficiently utilized. When the market permits charging for parking, the owner should reserve the right from time to time to increase the rate to equal the market rate in the designated competitive area. Reserved spaces should bear a 30% to 35% premium rate.

Where parking charges are in effect, many developers have been successful in insisting that a tenant must agree to take and pay for his allotment initially, or the allotment will be reduced to the amount they are willing to pay for. The reason for this is if a tenant insists on the right for a large number of spaces but doesn't use and pay for them, they are not really available to satisfy the actual needs of some other tenant.

Where parking is free, the lease should make it clear that this commitment is for the initial term only. A legal description of the parking facility should be provided in an exhibit unless included in the description of the building and/or the land.

Services of Landlord

This section describes the scope of services provided by the landlord, and defines the level above which additional services required by tenant must be performed at the tenant's cost. The most important issue in this section is the limitation of the electrical requirements of the tenant—both as to availability of connected load, normally in the range of 4‰ w to 5‰ w/usf for the sum of electricity for lighting and power, and the maximum electrical demand, or consumption, in the range of 3 to 4 w/usf, with 3‰ w/usf being the most common, which determines the sizing of the HVAC system and the cost of electricity used. The lease must require the tenant to pay for the increased electrical consumption, as determined by survey or meter, above the stipulated amount. In addition, while the tenant must pay for the cost of providing additional electricity to the space, there must be a provision for increasing the capacity of the HVAC system to handle the additional heat load at tenant's expense. The lease and the HVAC and electrical system design must be carefully coordinated so that limitations on the consumption of electricity by the tenant are tied directly to the criteria incorporated in the design of the building systems.

With regard to responding to requests for what appears to be excessive tenant miscellaneous power, an effort should be made to negotiate the request down to a more reasonable number. Remember, if you agree to a level considerably above the average, without also specifying a maximum demand, with a provision to provide additional construction and/or operating costs at tenant's expense, in the event they actually use that much power, you may be responsible to provide sufficient HVAC to satisfy that load at your expense. For further discussion of this issue, see Tenant Miscellaneous Power Requirements in Chapter 26.

There are several real potential penalties to the developer resulting from excessive requests for electricity, or the actual excess usage of electricity:

- If the leases are on a gross basis, any excess, or unplanned electricity charges, and the resulting use of additional HVAC energy, accrue to landlord and serve to reduce the net income
- Landlord will incur a serious liability if, within the terms of the lease, tenant's uses of excess electricity energy exceeds the capability of the HVAC system to satisfy acceptable conditions in the space, unless there is a protective caveat regarding this issue
- The request for excessive electrical requirements, later unused, dictates over-sizing the HVAC system at significant cost, for no benefit to anyone
- If the request for excessive electrical connected load increases the sizing of the switchgear above a significant cost breakpoint

It is also important that the operating expenses whose base year is fixed in the lease correctly includes the utility cost reasonably permitted under the lease.

The denial of landlord responsibility for rebate of rent or damages for any stoppage of services is an essential requirement that not only protects the landlord, but is usually a lender required clause.

Assignment

As a general rule the landlord should reserve the right to reject any proposed assignment for any legal reasons, except where the assignment is proposed to an affiliate who controls or is controlled by tenant, and only then if the assignee has at least the credit worthiness that tenant had when the initial lease was executed.

Subletting

This is resisted as much as possible as you do not want any tenant to be in the real estate business in your building. Notwithstanding this, tenant will need reasonable flexibility to operate his business that may have varying space requirements over time. On request, subleasing is normally permitted up to some reasonable amount (say 30%) of the space for a period less than the remaining term of the lease. Other than above, you should stand firm for landlord's right upon receiving a sublease request to (a) terminate the space in question, (b) approve the sublease but reserve to landlord 50% of the amount by which the rent exceeds the current rent under the lease, or (c) reject the request. Action (b) above is fraught with issues, such as how to treat any expenses of tenant in preparing for or inducing subtenant to enter the sublease. It's important to require that those expenses not be permitted in the calculation. The principle in subleasing is to keep complete control of the building and not let others make a profit on your investment.

Repairs

Normally require all repairs that are tenant's responsibility to be performed by landlord or landlord's contractors so as to permit landlord to properly control the condition of and access to the building. If this is contested, it is not uncommon to permit work on other than structure or central building systems by tenant, providing landlord approves the contractors in advance, they carry all required insurance and follow the building rules. It is normal to request a landlord fee of 15% on all repairs or additional services; whether you can get it or not is a function of the marketplace.

Alterations

Standard language properly requires approval of all drawings and specifications for any work proposed by the tenant, and that any work performed on the structure or the building central systems must be performed under the landlord's control to protect the integrity of the building. The normally requested 15% fees are clearly negotiable, but there is a real cost for landlord to properly coordinate and inspect the work for conformance with the approved documents.

Default and Remedies

These are written to fully protect the landlord and lender and generally cover failure to pay rent, abandonment of premises, failure to maintain insurance in force, any act that places landlord's insurance at risk of cancellation, insolvency or any petition filed under the bankruptcy code, and failure to perform other terms of this lease.

Remedies generally are to take possession of the premises and terminate the lease, or take possession without terminating the lease and either maintaining or re-letting the space. In either case tenant will hold landlord harmless for any costs or loss of rental income.

Tenants will usually insist on landlord using best efforts to mitigate the loss. Aside from this, these provisions must not be modified without the approval of the lender, which is difficult to obtain.

Right of Offset

Never give the tenant the right to offset any claims against the rent. If the tenant wins at arbitration, landlord will pay the adjudicated claim plus interest.

Insurance

Insurance carried by the landlord covers the building and all appurtenances for all insurable occurrences for the full replacement cost, and includes coverage for loss in rental income from all circumstances. The insurance requirements are not usually readily negotiable since they tie into landlord's overall insurance program and also the requirements of the lender. It should be made clear whether the landlord or tenant is responsible for insuring Tenant Improvements, regardless of who installed or paid for them. It makes sense for them to be insured by landlord, as the coverage is an operating expense. The tenant will insure his own contents, including art and cash.

Damage by Fire or Other Cause

Generally these provisions require that, in the event of damage by fire or other casualty, if the premises cannot be restored within a specified period of time, or if the insurance proceeds are insufficient for restoration, landlord may terminate the lease. For partial damage, the lease will remain in force and repairs will be completed as soon as reasonably possible, with rent abated during reconstruction.

Tenants usually negotiate for a shorter period for restoration, and then an equal right to terminate.

This type of clause is usually eminently fair, and is normally required by the lender to be left unmodified. Some large tenants dispute the number of days in some of the decision periods.

Condemnation

Upon condemnation, the term will cease and landlord will receive all compensation paid. Many tenants insist on recovering any of their unamortized investment in the premises, but lenders are not sympathetic to this claim.

Partial condemnation is more complex, involving when the tenant has the right to terminate the lease. The author always had difficulty in negotiations on this point, as it had such little basis in reality, and lenders are usually quite rigid.

Indemnification

This section limits each party's liability to their insurance coverage. It is also an issue important to the lender.

Subordination and Estoppel Certificates

The lease is subordinate to any underlying leases, deeds of trust or other financing instruments, and prior leases, including future changes thereto. This section is pretty boilerplate, except some tenants take exception to permitting future changes in superior leases and loans they are required to suborn to. Tenant is required upon request to provide estoppel certificates confirming that the lease is unmodified and in effect. These certificates should be routine.

Surrender of the Premises

This section covers the condition of the premises at the end of the term, requires the repair of any damage, and requires the premises to be restored to the condition at the beginning of the term, subject to reasonable use and wear. Frequently, the removal of special items, such an internal stairway, is required as a result of the original approval for its installation. Removal of building standard items is not required. These requirements are reasonable and rarely subject to too much discussion unless the space was originally leased "as is." Removal of all of tenant's personal property and business equipment are both permitted and required.

Rental in case of holdover by tenant is usually defined as twice the greater of the current rental rate or the fair market value, whichever is greater, plus indemnification of landlord for any damages resulting from failure to deliver the space to another tenant.

Landlord's Right to Inspect

Landlord requires the right to inspect the premises at any reasonable time. tenants frequently insist on the right to notice prior to inspection unless there is an emergency, or there is a need to access the space for repairs.

Credit Risk and Security Deposit

Most credit tenants, and many others, object to a security deposit, and many are waived with lender's approval, except when there is a real question as to the ability and willingness of the tenant to pay all obligations under the lease. One should always endeavor to obtain at least several months deposit from any tenant, other than those with a top credit rating, frequently with a planned reduction after two or three years. Cash is much preferable to a letter of credit, as the L/Cs have an expiration date on which they must be rolled over, and are sometimes difficult to collect upon.

Many high technology tenants in today's marketplace have difficulty providing an income statement and balance sheet that gives the landlord much comfort, but it is not necessarily prudent to reject that market. This is an area where some creative thinking may be necessary to make a deal and satisfy your lender. If a letter of credit doesn't seem to fit, try prepaid rent. The primary objective is to at least recover the leasing commission and TI cost in event of a default.

Brokerage

Representation that neither party has dealt with any broker in the transaction other than those listed in the agreement, and each will indemnify the other party from any claims to the contrary. This is routine.

Observance of Rules and Regulations

The rules are basically routine, except major tenants sometimes object to landlord's absolute right to modify rules, and some comfort language is then added, since the tenant also benefits from the rules.

Notices

Usually specified as delivered to tenant when placed in the U.S. mail, certified, return receipt requested, or with a courier service. A few major tenants obtain agreement to actual receipt.

Miscellaneous

This a series of minor issues, including severability, non-merger, landlord's liability, *force majeure*, successors and assigns, landlord representations, entire agreement, tenant's authority, governing law, tenant's use of building name, changes to project by landlord, time of essence, landlord acceptance of lease, performance by tenant, landlord's right to change name and address, and financial statements.

These issues are pretty straightforward except for the changes to the project by landlord. Many tenants will want more comfort language regarding access and convenience during such changes, and the language can usually be worked out easily. The right to change the name or address may bring forth the reasonable request for landlord to reimburse tenant for costs of replacing stationary, signage, etc.

Substitution Space

This is landlord's right to relocate tenant to a reasonably equivalent space, at landlord's expense, to facilitating re-leasing space in the building. It is applicable only to rather small tenants, as larger tenants will never agree. Tenants will usually rightfully ask for reimbursement for letterheads and other costs associated with relocation from the original suite and added language to insure that landlord pays all costs of relocation and that the new Tenant Improvements include all existing improvements regardless of when or by whom they where installed.

Other Definitions

Covers any definitions necessary to clarify the intent of the lease. These are usually not too much of an issue.

Arbitration

Arbitration is a frequent issue. The author has negotiated the form of arbitration hundreds of times, and never participated in arbitration, so he has no idea which form is the best. His belief is that you should qualify the experience of the arbitrators as to knowledge of office buildings and their operations in a defined market area where the building is located, if possible. Also limit the flexibility the arbitrator has to go beyond the language and intent of the lease. Many people have a preference for the "baseball" type arbitration. This seems logical, as it should tend to keep the positions of both parties within a reasonable range.

Execution

Execution by the owner is normally conditioned upon approval by the lender and, in some instances, upon approval by a major tenant.

EXHIBITS and RIDERS

Floor Plan(s) of the Premises

A complete floor plan(s), or a portion of the floor plan, with the premises clearly indicated must be provided, so that it leaves no doubt as to the specific premises.

The Land

The legal description of the parcel(s) of land on which the building and parking is located.

Leasehold Improvements

This is an issue that can be the most difficult to negotiate, for the benefit of both parties. The landlord's objectives are to spend the least amount of money that is reasonable, have the earliest possible commencement of rent, use as many building standard items as feasible for ease of future changeovers, and to protect the building's central systems and structure. The latter issue is the reason it is important to require the use of the building's mechanical, electrical and structural engineers, for the design of that portion of all TIs and preferably also use the building's mechanical and electrical contractors, for any work that is part of the central systems.

Frequently, a tenant does not wish to come out of pocket for their over-standard TI cost and requests landlord to finance these costs as additional rent. This request is often accommodated, providing it is amortized over the term at an interest rate equal to or exceeding the desired project return, the tenant is sufficiently credit worthy, there is either enough room under the interim and/or permanent loans, and the landlord is willing to provide the additional equity at that rate. As a general rule, however, landlord has opportunities for greater return on his equity than financing TIs and this financing should be resisted. When providing such financing the security deposit becomes even more important.

There are four basic ways in which development of the TI work can be performed. First, provide tenant with a dollar allowance, agree on a commencement date, and let tenant take responsibility for the design, construction and on-time delivery. This will provide landlord with the most direct cost control, but gives up a certain amount of control of the building.

In a second approach, landlord provides tenant with a fixed dollar amount for the work but requires the work to be performed by the building contractor or a selected interior contractor. This satisfies the control of the building issue and landlord's cost of the work, but landlord assumes responsibility for the rent commencement, except for tenant delays, discussed below, and frequently leads to an issue of the appropriateness of the cost of the work.

Third, landlord offers to build out the space for tenant in accordance with a specific number of units of each item in the work letter (discussed in Chapter 30) such as one lighting fixture per 80 usf and 1 linear foot of partitions per 12 usf, etc. Tenant then pays for all costs above the work letter, unless an additional allowance is negotiated. Again, the landlord is pretty well covered, but at risk for the rent commencement, except for tenant delay, and there is room for some disagreement on the cost of the above standard work.

Lastly, in a really bad market, tenants are frequently able to negotiate for landlord to completely build their space to satisfy their needs. In such case, a space plan and detail of finishes are required so that landlord can fully evaluate the request.

Tenant delay is probably one of the most difficult issues to resolve with many tenants. At the lease negotiation, both parties sincerely intend to complete the design and construction as quickly and properly as possible. In spite of good intentions, tenant delays occur frequently, particularly because of a lack of understanding of the process and decision-makers who were not a party to the original intent.

The primary sources of potential delays are delayed completion of the design of the tenant space due to lack of decisions or repeated changes, lack of approval of the bids or cost of the work, changes to the space during construction, and the specification of long lead time items that delay completion. These issues must all be addressed in the lease.

When tenant uses his own architect or space planner, the lease should require him to submit his completed plans and specifications to landlord for approval at specified stages of completion by specified dates, allowing a specified number of days for the building's engineers to complete their work. After landlord's approval of tenant's plans, (many lenders also require plan approval) landlord will obtain bids where applicable and submit a cost estimate for approval by tenant. Tenant will usually have five days to accept the cost proposal and direct the work to proceed. Any delay in submitting the completed documents, approving the bids, or redesign to reduce the cost are all treated as tenant delay and used to accelerate the date of rent commencement. It has been found beneficial to include a detailed schedule showing the number of days for each step, including landlord and tenant approvals. When tenant uses the landlord's space, designer care must be taken to set up a design schedule, specifying the number of times the space plans are to be prepared or revised before approval to start the working drawings, and the number of days the tenant has to approve each submittal, etc.

When the TI work is designed and/or constructed by tenant it is important that, notwithstanding any approvals by landlord or his architect, any code, ADA, or other regulatory requirements are the responsibility of tenant. It is also important that landlord's review of the plans verify that tenant's connected electrical load and estimated demand are within the limits set in the lease, and within the building standards.

Base Building Condition

The base building condition is a detailed description of the shell and core construction required of landlord prior the start of the Tenant Improvement work. This is the definition determined by market practice through the Market Study and incorporated in the lease. This issue is discussed in the Tenant Space Development portion of Chapter 30. Landlord will provide those items specified and leave the floors broom clean. All other work will be part of the Tenant Improvements. This can be an attachment to the Leasehold Improvement Exhibit, rather than a separate exhibit.

In the case of a large tenant whose anticipated occupancy will approximate the time of receipt of the base building Certificate of Occupancy, the TI work will often need to commence prior to completion of the shell and core work on those floors. This is a primary reason why the use of the same general contractor is recommended in Chapter 35.

Preinstalled Items

This is a detailed list, normally priced, that indicates all work and materials that are not base building condition, but for the sake of construction efficiency or to satisfy a code or regulation, were installed prior to the start of the Tenant Improvement work, and are to be charged against such work. This can be an attachment to the Leasehold Improvement Exhibit, rather than a separate exhibit. The most common of these are window treatment and sprinkler runouts with code-required sprinkler heads, other life safety equipment or alarms, and exterior soffits.

Building Standard Improvements

A detailed list of the quality of materials, finishes and workmanship specified by landlord as the building standard for use in the Tenant Improvements. This list, when the appropriate number of units of each item is added, becomes the work letter sometimes used in TI work. This can be an attachment to the Leasehold Improvement Exhibit, rather than a separate exhibit. The Building Standards were set early in the design stage and should be made available to the tenant at the initiation of negotiations.

Tenant's Current Lease

A clause covering this issue would be included if landlord is taking any responsibility for any provision of tenant's existing lease obligation. It should never be open ended—enough information must be included to ensure that there is a known maximum dollar expenditure by landlord, than can be justified in making the lease.

Definition of Rentable Area

This is the definition of rentable area that is used to compute the rentable area of the premises and of the building. This will normally be the BOMA Floor Area Measurement or a variation accepted in the local market.

Definition of Useable Area

Normally all space outside the core and code-required corridor, plus area within the core that is useable by tenant. Where tenant is responsible for construction of the corridor and elevator lobby they become considered useable area. This value is primarily used for calculating the TI allowance.

Extension Option

The major issues in any renewal option are the term of the option(s), the rental rate, and any refurbishment allowance. The numbers of options should not exceed the greater of five years or 50% of the initial term. The most preferable rental rate is fair market rental rate, but not less than the rental rate the tenant is then paying. Major refurbishment should be resisted, endeavoring to settle for carpet and painting as a maximum expense.

The definition of fair market rental rate must be very clear and is frequently highly negotiated by larger tenants. Some want it to reflect full market TIs and real estate commissions, which must absolutely be resisted. It is not unusual for tenant to want a cap on the fair market rental rate, but if willing to grant it, a corresponding minimum rate should be negotiated. In any case, the specific comparison area and type of building and other requirements should be clearly spelled out, and a dispute in agreeing to the fair market rental rate should be resolved by arbitration. A less attractive alternative is to fix the rental rate at a specific dollar value(s) for the option period, since if it turns out to be above market rates, tenant may renegotiate or leave, while if it is below market he receives a bargain rate.

Notice of acceptance of the renewal should be required at least one year in advance of the renewal date to permit landlord time to effectively lease the space if the option is not exercised.

Expansion Space

The primary issue with regard to expansion options is the impact on the ability of landlord to effectively lease the space prior to the option period. In most markets a lease of less than five years will require a significant discount, if rentable at all. The most effective terms are, if the option is exercised by tenant, for landlord to be able to convey the space to tenant during the sixth year (or the eleventh year in some cases) of the term, at landlord's discretion. This allows a reasonable opportunity to find and lease to an initial tenant who may require a full five-year term.

Expansion space should be provided to tenant "as is" with the argument that the building has already developed it once. This can be an issue requiring considerable discussion, and is usually settled for at least a refurbishment allowance. The rental rate should be the greater of the then current rental rate and the fair market rental rate. Notice of acceptance of the expansion should be a year prior to the assumed commencement date for the expansion.

When tenant insists on an option in less than five years, if you are willing to grant it, it is usually wise to make the period as short as possible, and make it a "must take" space. If the space has been built out, the tenant should take the space "as is." If the space has never been built out, the original TIs should be provided.

Right of First Refusal

This right is an attempt to compromise and offer tenant an option of sorts for additional or renewal space, while preserving landlord's flexibility in the leasing program. The only problem is you must search out and consummate a tentative lease agreement before requiring tenant to commit. Tenant's right to exercise the right should be limited to either three or five business days after the offer is extended. If the tenant passes, and the proposed lease is not consummated, it is preferable if tenant's right is terminated. Failing this, landlord should be free to enter into a lease on any reasonable terms for a period of six months to a year. Some tenants try to limit any such lease to the exact terms, but this is unreasonable, as there are so many issues in each lease proposal.

Right of First Opportunity

This is another effort to combine some flexibility for tenant as well as facilitate the landlord's leasing program. Any adjacent space that comes available will be offered to tenant. If tenant rejects the space, landlord is free to lease the space to anyone else under any terms during the specified time period, usually six months to a year. Avoid restricting your rights to lease the space to the same terms offered to the tenant.

Guarantee of Lease

Where the financial strength of tenant is considered insufficient to satisfy all of the obligations under the lease, a personal or corporate guarantee is required. It requires the guarantor to fulfill any financial responsibility of tenant under the lease.

Form of Commencement Notice

An agreed upon form that will be issued at the time of commencement of the lease.

Rules and Regulations

A copy of the rules and regulations referred to in the lease.

Non-disturbance and Recognition Agreement

This is an agreement between the mortgagee and the tenant, with the landlord basically a middle man. It provides for the obligations of the parties in the event of landlord default, and mortgagee's succession into landlord's position. Where possible, try to avoid being required to obtain nondisturbance agreements.

Tenant Retention

Sincere effort should be made throughout the negotiations, even when they are difficult, to use that period to build a relationship of trust and the start of a long and satisfactory relationship. Although your responsibility for the project will end when occupancy is stabilized, many tenants will be in occupancy before that occurs. It is important that the Development Officer, leasing team and Property Management work together to carefully nurture those tenants from lease to occupancy and beyond.

CASE STUDY

The negotiations with Brandes from the initial proposal on December 30, 1998 until the Letter of Intent was executed on February 23, 1999 were quite extensive. The Letter of Intent was finally agreed to upon the following terms:

BRANDES INVESTMENT PARTNERS, L.P. LETTER OF INTENT

Premises:	Five floors, approximately 107,000 rsf.
Term:	11 years.
Rental Rate Per Month:	$2.41 /rsf, including electricity, increasing annually at 5¢.
Lease Commencement:	Thirty days after delivery of the space, estimated to be August 1, 2000. There were a series of construction schedule milestones which if not met would permit Brandes to terminate the lease, recognizing their concern with a building not yet permitted. There were penalties representing Brandes' increased occupancy costs if the space was not delivered by 8/1/00, and $10,000 per day penalties if not delivered by 1/1/01.
Operating Expense:	Standard, but controllable expenses capped cumulatively at 7% per year cumulatively. Base year to be 2000, unless commencement is after 10/1/00, then it will be 2001.
TI Allowance:	$35 /usf ($1 paid through reduction in brokerage fee), plus $50,000 for UPS system, plus $7 refurbishing allowance in 7th year.
Space Planning:	$1.50 /usf.
Moving Allowance:	$1.50 /usf.
Signing Bonus:	$10 /rsf, not to exceed $1,025,000, to partially offset existing lease termination penalties. Initially provided as a Letter of Credit which tenant could draw upon to pay any lease termination costs, or liquidated damages in the event landlord fails to meet any construction milestone, or on 8/1/00.
Expansion:	One full floor in the 49th month, original TIs if not built out, otherwise $10 /usf, at then current rental rate, with 12 months notice.
Right of First Negotiation:	On any available space, with at least 4 years remaining in Term.
Renewal:	Two 5-year terms @ 95% of prevailing FMV, with $3 /usf refurbishing allowance.
Parking:	5 spaces /1,000 usf, with 20% reserved.
Health Club:	1,000 sf on the first floor for the benefit of all tenants, included as common area.
Signage:	Monument at entrance only, no rights to top of the building.
Assignment/ Subletting:	Right to assign to related entity. Approved subleases of 36 months or more, split premium with landlord. Right to recapture a full floor sublease space with a Term of 36 months or longer.
Security Deposit:	One month's rent.
Work Letter:	Too complicated. Discussed later in text.

The deal was very expensive, but it was offset by a reduction in vacancy cost and permitted elimination of $600,000 in lease-up contingency, as a result of the perceived reduction in lease-up risk. Analysis indicates this deal reduced the initial cash on cash return by 21 basis points and increased the IRR by 10 basis points, permitting normal financing for the project. Initial concerns were the unknown potential cost relative to how effectively the third floor could be leased with only four-year terms available and the cost of any penalties, but the leasing concern evaporated at an early date.

When the lease draft was submitted to Brandes based on the Letter of Intent and Prentiss' standard lease language, their lawyer and broker-driven response was to completely rewrite about one half of the draft with many requests for significant additional issues that were well outside the Letter of Intent, some quite onerous.

The response to these comments was a new draft that ignored most of their redrafting, but included those requests believed to be reasonable. The Prentiss position was that the negotiations be based on their standard lease language, but specific changes would be reasonably negotiated.

The lease negotiations were lengthy, difficult, and entailed a great deal of language changes, in addition to the normal fleshing out of the various lease terms. The most important changes from the Letter of Intent to the final lease were:

- The dates at which landlord delay penalties would apply were extended by 15 days because of delays in the negotiations, but no *force majeure* would apply.

- The potential for penalties was too great with no *force majeure*, so the penalties were restructured so as to provide an acceptable cap. If, due to a landlord delay, any employees were required to relocate, Prentiss would pay a one-time penalty of $40,000. In addition, starting on August 15, 2000, and each month thereafter Prentiss would pay penalties of $45,000 the first month, $50,000 the next month, and then $55,000 per month until the total reached $410,000.

- The parking spaces available for their expansion space would be reduced to 4.25 per 1000 usf for the third floor option and to 4 per 1000 usf for the first and second floor options. This limitation was necessary to satisfy the agreement with the hotel that limited the tenant parking permits to 690, the number of spaces designated for the office building.

- Approval for tenant to request expansion of the building emergency electrical generator system to satisfy their emergency requirements, at their expense.

- The Work Letter Exhibit was totally rewritten. The Letter of Intent assumed performance of the TI working drawings by landlord and the revised lease gave control of the TI working drawings and building permit to tenant. There were a series of key dates from the submission of the building plans through submission of final plans for bidding, receipt of the building permit, and tenant's approval of the bids and authorization of the work. A list of approved contractors to bid on the work was carried over from the L/I. Any dates missed by the tenant would be considered tenant delay days with respect to the Prentiss penalties and rent commencement.

- The Letter of Credit from tenant to satisfy any financial obligations of tenant was $1,500,000 in the first year, reducing by $150,000 per annum through the ninth year, at which time the requirement is terminated.

- The health club is included in the definition of common area so this space will be incorporated into the rentable area.

- After extensive discussion it was finally agreed that the tenant will pay for over-standard electricity usage, if applicable, but will not pay for after hours electricity.

The negotiations reached such a point of near stalemate that management approval was obtained not to go forward with the lease and proceed on a speculative basis if a satisfactory conclusion could not be reached. Shortly after that the final issues were resolved. The lease was finally executed September 8, 1999, just prior to closing on the land, and prior to receiving the grading permit. Happily, as discussed in detail in other chapters, the TCO was received on August 14, 2000, negating the potential for any landlord delay penalty and permitted rent commencement on September 15.

The Scripps lease negotiation was relatively smooth, with most open issues settled by compromise. The issue over their objection to paying for the top-of-building signage was resolved by increasing the rental rate by 5¢ per rsf per month. They objected to paying a 3% annual increase in the rental rate in addition to the operating expense pass through, so it was agreed to adjust the annual base rental rate by 5¢ per rsf per month.

The Letter of Intent for Scripps Bank, subject to approval of their board and the state and federal banking regulators, was:

SCRIPPS BANK LETTER OF INTENT

Premises:	Approximately 27,700 nrsf, comprising approximately 7,700 nrsf on the first floor and approximately 20,000 rsf on the second floor.
Term:	Ten years.
Commencement Date:	At completion of the premises, or September 1, 2000, subject to landlord delay.
Renewal Options:	One five-year renewal option, at prevailing market rates.
Rental Rate:	$2.65 / rsf, including electricity. Base rental increasing by 5¢ / rsf / month on the anniversary date of term commencement.
Operating Expenses:	Tenant shall pay increases over 2000 base year pro rata. Controllable expenses (exclusive of real estate property taxes, insurance premiums and utility costs) will be capped at 7% per annum.
Tenant Improvements:	TI allowance of $35 / usf plus an additional $5 / usf allowance amortized at 10.5% over the initial term for the first floor only.
Parking:	4 spaces / 1000 usf, with 25 reserved, 15 in the structure and 10 on the surface lot.
Signage:	Top of the building signage plus eyebrow signage above any exterior entrance created by tenant.
Right of First Negotiation:	Tenant shall have a second right (Brandes has the first) of negotiation for the entire third floor.
Exclusivity:	Only bank, savings and loan or thrift offering retail banking services at this location.
After-Hours	landlord provides tenant HVAC services at no additional charge from 7:30 AM to 6:00 PM Monday through Friday, and 9:00 AM to 1:00 PM on Saturday. Any "after hours" charges incurred will be billed to tenant at cost.

Only two serious issues occurred in negotiating a lease with Scripps.

- There was a clear indication that the CC&Rs might prevent adding their name above a main entrance, and they objected to paying for a new entrance that would cost at least $10,000. The issue was resolved through agreement to use best efforts to put their name on one of the main entrances, and failing that, to split the cost of the new entrance.

- A plan check reviewer at the city initially took the position that the second stairway exit could not be through the lobby, even though permitted under UBC. This was discussed further with the reviewer who finally waived this requirement, as discussed in Chapter 14, as a corridor through the bank floor would have undoubtedly caused Scripps to forego entering into the lease.

After the regulators had approved the Scripps Lease, and it was executed, the bank came back to renegotiate it. They apparently had some severe losses, and the board did not want to undertake the significant increase in occupancy costs. They wanted to either give back or sublease the entire second floor, and retain only a branch bank. This was not acceptable as it would create competition for the remaining four-year lease space, and it was felt an 8,000 sf tenant should not, on principal, have a sign on the top of the building. The issue was resolved by:

- Scripps would retain the entire space, at the agreed-upon rent, and the rent would start on September 1 as required by the lease
- They were precluded from leasing less than 10,000 sf to any subtenant prior to landlord leasing the remainder of the third floor space
- The cost of the separate bank entrance would be solely the tenant's
- They could not have the sign at the top of the building, but the rent would remain the same

While still grading the site, the brokers brought a potential 8,500 rsf tenant, Heritage Golf Group, who was interested in Brandes' four-year option space on the third floor. The lease was negotiated with $2.65/rsf rental rate with occupancy on September 1, but it was necessary to provide $37/usf in TIs. The TIs were excessive, but since the end of the available term was fixed, the TI overage would be less than the lost revenue from a two-month delay in occupancy of the space, and the rental rate was above pro forma. An option for a five-year extension was provided, subject to Brandes not exercising their expansion option.

As construction proceeded, six additional leases were signed with rental rates increasing up to $2.85/rsf, making the building 100% leased.

As of September 15, 2000, only 30 days after receipt of the TCO, rental income was being received on 91% of the space, with the net income more than covering the debt service.

CONSTRUCTION CONTRACTOR

33

A good general contractor is an important contributor to a successful project. In this chapter we will discuss the forms of contracts, understanding the GMP, selection of the contractor, important contract provisions, subcontractors, insurance and bonding.

Form of General Construction Contract

A highly qualified and reputable general contractor is an important and essential member of a development team. Not only must they be able provide valuable estimating, material evaluation and scheduling resources in the preconstruction period, but also must have the necessary project management skills and the ability to attract a wide range of quality subcontractors and material suppliers in order to construct the project in an efficient and proper manner.

A frequent project issue is whether to have a general construction contractor with a negotiated Guaranteed Maximum Price (GMP) contract, a construction manager, or a lump sum bid general construction contract.

A GMP contract is a detailed estimate of the cost of the work that is developed by the contractor retained at the start of the project as the design work progresses from the initial baseline budget until such time as both parties agree that the work is sufficiently defined that they are willing to enter a contract based on that estimate. The contractor agrees that the total cost of construction will not exceed that specific amount, except as qualified therein. The GMP protects the owner as to the cost of the work that the contractor could reasonably infer from the contract documents and any other information provided by the owner. The cost of work beyond that scope is the responsibility of the owner. It should be understood that when the GMP is executed based on incomplete plans, agreed upon allowances are required for the unknown or not clearly detailed work—and the intended scope of these items should be delineated as clearly as possible in the explanatory portion of the agreement. The Guaranteed Maximum Price is for the shell and core construction, but may include unit prices to be used in pricing the tenant work.

The author strongly believes in the negotiated GMP form of contract. Its only negative is the perception (and it is only a perception) of leaving some premium on the table, while its advantages are:

- Fees run from 2–5%, with 2½–3% the norm, so there can be little or no fee premium

- Normally about 75–95% of work is bid—so there is reasonably full competition (and some contractors willingly bid against themselves on all self-performed work, except some of the general conditions work)

- The benefit of contractor's estimating ability during the predevelopment and design period—i.e., continuous value engineering, rather than the issue of cutting costs at the end when the bids come in over budget

- The benefit of contractor's scheduling ability throughout the predevelopment period

- More specific information on materials and construction processes

- A team approach throughout the process

- Normally reduced chance of premiums on change orders

- Permitting the start of construction with partially complete drawings, frequently at 40–65% completion of the working drawings—saves construction time by starting about 4 to 6 weeks or more prior to completion of the working drawings instead of at least 4 to 8 weeks after their completion—i.e., fast tracking

- Site work, excavation and subsurface construction starting prior to full permitting

- Permitting preordering of materials or letting certain subcontracts before the rest of the work is ready to bid—long lead time materials such as steel, elevators and stone

- Reassessing the remaining work in order to recoup the funds or time when an unexpected cost overrun or project delay occurs

Some people believe the construction manager approach is the best of the alternatives, while others (like the author) believe it is the worst. The construction manager does provide estimating and scheduling services during the predevelopment and design phases, and under some circumstances can direct the early bidding of certain subcontracts to gain cost or schedule advantages. However, their fee structure usually is not all that much less than that of a general contractor, and they do no work on their own and take no responsibility at all for costs. The author believes there is much less protection on change orders.

The lump sum bid process provides no up-front cost or schedule estimating ability (architects are notoriously poor at cost information). If you find a cost problem at the end of the design process it is very difficult to correct in a satisfactory and balanced manner, and there is a high likelihood of paying excessively on the unavoidable change orders. The few stated advantages are:

- The contract sum is known before committing to construction

- There may not be qualified contractors experienced in negotiated work available due to project size or location

- It is possible that the general conditions and/or the work the contractor does with his own forces could be performed more competitively than with the negotiated general

An alternative method that has gained favor in recent years for selecting a contractor for a negotiated contract is to select several qualified contractors and then have them bid their fee and general conditions along with the presentation of their personnel and qualifications. The author has no experience with this approach, and has some concerns that there may be no real benefit. You might be influenced by unrealizable savings and choose other than the best contractor, unless there is at a minimum:

- A clear definition and criteria as to what is included in the general conditions

- A clear policy as to charge-backs and those requirements delegated to the subcontractors

- A detailed personnel projection for comparison

Different contractors use different definitions as to which cost items are charged to general conditions, and which are direct job cost items—which can create wide apparent variances.

The largest component of the general conditions is the supervision. A lesser number, or lesser quality, of site supervision may yield a lower general conditions cost, but may result in a lower quality of job performance. The author's preference will remain for using a detailed estimate of personnel and other general conditions line items as a guide, but selecting the contractor you believe to be the best for your specific project at that point in time.

A newer compromise solution recommended by some is to request GMP bids from several contractors at the completion of the schematic design. This approach concerns me even more. First, you have been through a critical part of the development process without the benefit of a knowledgeable contractor. Further, if the contractor is held to the GMP, you are essentially delegating all of the systems selection and detailing to the contractor, which is a questionable practice. Alternatively, if the accepted GMP is merely used as a guide and adjusted up and down with various design decisions, then the purported benefit has probably disappeared. This approach can create some conflicts between the contractor and owner that are not normally present with a negotiated contract.

General Contractor Selection

When evaluating contractors for negotiated contracts, if you have not had prior experience with your preferred choice or choices, it is important to investigate thoroughly, as there are many otherwise reputable and responsible contractors who are not experienced in conceptual estimating and negotiated work.

The best way to approach the selection is to narrow down potential candidates, based upon recommendations, to those who have successfully completed negotiated projects of similar size and complexity in the locality under consideration. For those selected for consideration and interviews, a Request For Proposal (RFP) or letter requesting information on the important criteria to be evaluated, will permit the interview to effectively bring forth the desired information in order to make an intelligent selection. Factors to consider are:

- Integrity
- Performance on projects of a similar type, a similar or greater scope and with similar complexity on a negotiated basis
- Chief estimator, project managers, superintendents, engineers proposed for the project with a description of comparable projects they actually worked on
- Reputation with subcontractors and architects, as well as owners
- Skill in conceptual estimating, rather than just detail estimating
- Current workload in the area
- Open shop vs. union shop, signatory to which union contracts—open shop usually results in lower costs in locations where practical
- Cost control systems
- Schedule control systems
- Quality control systems
- Safety program and record
- Technical skills in HVAC and electrical fields
- Subcontractor relationships
- Fee shall include all officers and personnel not full time on project site
- Estimate of general conditions, including estimate of each type of service included
- List of items included in general conditions that are subject to charge-backs from the subcontractors
- Markups, if any, on change orders
- Fee proposal

The author tends to give a little extra credit to contractors who are capable of providing work with their own forces, such as general labor, rough carpentry, shoring and excavation, minor demolition, formwork, concrete placement and finishing, and furnishing rebar placement. There should be an understanding as to whether, and how successfully, they bid against themselves for such work when requested to do so by the owner. The allocated overhead and fee for self-performed work should be agreed upon. Additionally, it is often a plus factor if the contractor performs some hard bid work occasionally, as long as it is a relatively small portion of their total work.

It is important to have a clear understanding as to what is covered in the contractor's fee. It should normally cover all of the contractor's officers and services performed by those personnel not located full time at the job site, including all front-end estimating and planning. In many smaller projects where the project manager, and possibly some other personnel, are not full time at the site, it may be reasonable to include their applicable time spent on site in the cost of the work, but this must be clearly spelled out in the proposal and the contract. Some contractors, not unreasonably, want a fee to be allocated to the front-end preconstruction work to protect them against the job not proceeding or being hard bid. This is usually negotiable.

The list of chargeable items should be reviewed carefully to ensure that no home office items are included, chargeable employees are billed at local market rates and benefits, no bonuses are included, company owned trucks and equipment are charged at local fair market rental rates and only for the period they are required, and that you understand the charge-backs and general conditions requirements delegated to the subs.

The general conditions include such items as the contractor's field supervision, employee expenses, temporary offices with equipment and supplies, safety services, fencing and security, weather protection, temporary roads and parking, approved travel, hoisting, clean up and disposal, printing and as-builts, communications, water and toilet facilities, dust control and noise abatement, insurance and temporary utilities. Clean up and hoisting are frequently charged back to the applicable subcontractors, although many contractors limit subcontractor clean up to bringing all waste to a central point on each floor for removal and disposal.

General Construction Contract

Each company should have a standard GMP contract form, as well as the General and Supplementary Conditions. For those who have not yet developed one, the best source of various well-drafted forms of Contracts for Construction and the General and Supplementary Conditions, are those prepared by and available from the American Institute of Architects. (See References, Appendix A.) As well drafted as they are, it is important to modify them to suit those issues deemed to be important to the owner. If other than in-house counsel is used in contract negotiations, all business matters should be handled directly by the Development Officer and/or the construction manager. Outside counsel should be utilized only for legal and liability issues to avoid unnecessary legal fees. Some of the contract issues the author deems important are listed below.

- In all documents, the owner, not the architect, is the judge of disputed issues
- Contract is assignable by owner
- Contract is assignable to any lender
- Contract is not assignable by the contractor
- Subcontracts and major material supply contracts are assignable to owner upon default of contractor
- Errors and omissions insurance in approved form and amounts
- Indemnity agreement
- Approved report formats
- Inventory control procedures
- Equipment price lists
- Equal opportunity clause

In addition to the above, the contract must include any obligations imposed on the owner by the interim or permanent lender, or in some cases a major prelease tenant, including executing, delivering and/or acknowledging any and all instruments agreements and documents required by owner or any lender. Contractor must usually also subordinate any rights, interests and claims under the contract to the liens, benefits and privileges of any lender, consistent with the agreement.

An issue to be addressed in every contract is contingency. There must be an allowance for unforeseen changes—from foreseeable but underestimated issues to accelerating the schedule to respond to delays to contradictions in the contract documents. The contingency can be carried in the GMP, or may be carried separately by the owner. In either case the contingency should be limited to no more than 2% of the GMP, and preferably 1%. Contractor must notify owner before spending these sums, unless it is an emergency field condition. Design changes, exceedingly the allowance for work not designed at the time of the GMP and work not reasonably foreseeable by the contractor are owner's changes not included in the contingency.

It is important to have an understanding as to any charges applicable to change orders, as every project will have many. In addition to all direct charges, the contractor is entitled to the fee, but it should be included for both additions and deductions. Most contractors want a stipulated percentage for general conditions, which should be carefully discussed. If the allowance for general conditions on the project is based on a pure percentage, this may or may not be reasonable. If they are based on specific staffing and other fixed expenses, no addition may be justified, as you may be charged twice for the same expense. In any case, it should be agreed to as part of the initial negotiation.

Another frequent issue is to make the contractor financially responsible for timely completion of the project. It's best to both discuss this with your attorney and evaluate the necessity before addressing this issue. The author has been advised that some states will not enforce contract penalties unless there were corresponding bonus payments. Where there are important potential cost penalties to the owner it may be important to incorporate liquidated or consequential damages into the contract. When proposing such damages, recognize that the contractor will protect himself through higher general conditions charges, contingency and/or fee, as well as imposing the damage potential on the major subcontractors who will provide a cushion in their bids to cover the risk. Be certain that these actual indirect costs are worth the additional protection you seek. Sometimes the best schedule protection comes from the quality of the contractor and major subcontractors, and from the quality of your own project control.

Recognize that the contractor undertakes certain risks when entering into an agreement with a developer. It is prudent (not impudent) for a contractor to request verification of site ownership and approve the lending agreements and your financial stability.

Subcontractors

The owner should always retain the right of reasonable approval of all subcontractors. The best way to exercise this right is to review and approve a proposed list of recommended subcontractors prior to the bidding, rather than after the bids are received. A good contractor will already have limited the list to those believed to be competent for the subject work.

As mentioned briefly in Chapter 14, the mechanical and electrical contractors are frequently selected on a design-build basis. Some of the benefits are early lock-in on the costs, advance order of equipment, and improved coordination and time saved by not waiting for the contract drawings to be redrawn as shop drawings. There are three basic ways to accomplish this approach.

- The mechanical and electrical engineers would prepare the design criteria, select major systems, locate and size the major equipment and distribution systems, and prepare design development drawings and a specification. A review of the contractor-prepared final engineering documents and a few site visits should be included. The design fees for these engineering services would be about 50% of a full-service design.

- The mechanical and electrical engineers provide initial system analyses, develop design criteria, and prepare an outline specification.

- Negotiate the mechanical and electrical construction work on a full design-build basis with a typical GMP contract, if appropriately qualified firms are available.

It is sometimes appropriate to have other negotiated or design-build contracts for selected subtrades—particularly when it is necessary to maintain the project schedule, they have an unusual skill, it is advantageous to preorder material, or the subcontractor has invaluable front-end knowledge that will assist in the design phase. While many subcontractors can very competently construct competitively bid work, only certain subcontractors have the conceptual estimating experience and planning capabilities to properly perform negotiated or design/build work. Frequent candidates in addition to the MEP contractors discussed above are curtain wall, steel, precast concrete, foundation or retaining wall, or special equipment contractors.

There is a growing trend toward letting more subcontracts that are competitively bid on a performance basis, where all of the owner's requirements are clearly spelled out, giving the subcontractor the freedom to choose how to accomplish the stated objectives. It is important to note, however, that the performance requirement must be very carefully thought out and carefully specified in advance, and the subcontractor's plans thoroughly reviewed and approved by the architect and consulting engineers.

Insurance

The general contractor and each subcontractor must carry the insurance called for in the general conditions, usually General Liability, Comprehensive Bodily Injury and Property Damage from both automotive and construction operations and Workman's Compensation Insurance, in the amounts specified. A satisfactory Errors and Omissions insurance policy should be included with agreed upon coverage, as discussed under the architect's contract. A certificate of each policy must be provided to the owner, with the owner as an additional insured, and with a requirement to notify owner at least thirty (30) days prior to cancellation. A waiver of subrogation is normally required by the owner's insurance carrier and, frequently by the lender. The owner's representative must maintain an accurate record of all policies and termination dates to ensure there are no policy lapses throughout the entire construction period.

The insurance coverage notwithstanding, the general contractor and each subcontractor must sign an indemnity agreement prior to entering on the site.

Contractor's Warranties

Contractor's warranties are usually specified as one year from completion, but the definition of completion must be carefully resolved. While substantial completion is most often used, it should never be prior to the final Certificate of Occupancy, of the base building and TI work respectively so that it can be properly tied to any obligation landlord undertakes under latent defects under the primary leases. For protection of both contractor and owner the subcontractor agreements should carry the same obligation. This can be a significant issue, as certain subcontractors such as elevator, curtain wall, mechanical, electrical, plumbing, etc., want their warranty to commence when their work is finished, tested and turned over to others for utilization. Permitting an accelerated warranty leaves the contractor and/or the owner in a vulnerable position, as it would be difficult to include such a schedule in a lease.

Elevator companies can be the most obstinate in refusing to cooperate in warranty commencement, but that issue can usually be overcome if a maintenance contract is entered into with the supplier, or if they are paid a specified sum per elevator per month to cover maintenance during the interim period prior to the Certificate of Occupancy.

Payment and Performance Bonds

Bonds are normally recommended to protect against the risk of loss through a default, most often a bankruptcy filing or insolvency, by the general contractor or any subcontractor. This can provide very important cost protection, but in the author's opinion, the protection is not always as clear-cut or as complete as often assumed. The bonding company will normally fully cover all direct costs, but may delay replacing the defaulted contractor while endeavoring to minimize their own costs. Upon default the surety is entitled to any and all rights or defenses the contractor might have held. Typical bonds are:

- Completion or performance bonds—guarantee that the work will be completed as per the contract at the specified price.

- Payment bonds—assures that the surety will pay all claims arising from the work of his client.

- Warranty bonds—warrant that the work will perform as specified for a stipulated period of years, such as a roofing bond. They are important where there is no reasonable certainty that the responsible contractor will be able to honor the obligation over a long period, however the surety must have the ability to perform.

The author leans toward selective bonding (exclusive of warranty bonding on selected trades), consistent with carefully weighing the various risks and costs—contractor's financial condition, bonding cost, potential cost risk through a default, and potential schedule risk through default—in conjunction with proper procedures and safeguards.

Frequently, the general contractor and/or the lender have policies that require bonding of all subcontractors. Many general contractors will not accept responsibility within the GMP for subcontractor default when bonding is omitted. In such case, the owner may proceed with omission of the bond, but make it contractually clear that you are only accepting financial responsibility that would have been covered by the bond, and that the contractor is not waiving the indirect obligations from any resulting delay to the project.

A compromise may be omitting bonding only on very creditworthy contractors or for those contracts wherein the delay issue is most crucial.

Where schedule is the primary concern, it may be necessary to convince the lender—and it makes a difference whether all, part or none of the loan is non-recourse—that there is a greater relative risk in project delay as opposed to the cost of retaining a replacement contractor in event of a default.

In determining a policy toward bonding it is necessary to evaluate the risks resulting from a default—and which of these risks is most important to a particular project. There is a significant savings in construction cost through total or partial elimination of bonding, but this theoretical savings must be weighed against the risks. Exclusive of special warranty bonds, the primary risks faced through a contractor default are:

- The cost of replacing the (sub)contractor, and responsibility for unpaid obligations for work in place

- The cost of project delay resulting from a default

- The cost of contractual guarantees and warranties

On any given project, one of the above risks may outweigh the other. If time is not the major factor, cost protection may be most important. But if project delay carries the greater risk—through commitments to tenants, market conditions, or other reasons—then minimizing the delay risk becomes paramount. Almost any contractor default will create some project delay, therefore, when schedule is most important, the issue is how to best mitigate such delay.

Unless a bond is very carefully negotiated with a cooperative bonding company, upon default the surety can determine what recovery efforts it will make prior to resolving payment of the loss, including performing the work themselves. In the meantime, materials may be tied up and the contractor cannot be replaced, resulting in project delays that can dwarf the cost of replacing the defaulting contractor and proceeding without the impediment of dealing with a surety whose objectives are opposite to yours. It should be noted that, in addition, a project delay will increase the cost of the general conditions and may increase the price of certain labor and materials. These increases can create an obligation to the many subcontractors whose work is delayed, which may or may not be fully covered under the bond or the GMP.

It is true that a performance bond normally requires completion of the work within the contract period specified, but since no project flows smoothly throughout, there are often issues that may be raised by the bonding company to reasonably justify delays in performance. The most successful way to minimize project delay is to be in complete control of the process—in other words, not subject to the actions of a bonding company.

Selecting a general contractor whose history or financial condition indicates a need for bonding should be avoided. Nevertheless, the contract should include the right to terminate upon specified defaults, and require that all subcontractors and major material purchases be assignable to the owner upon default, and owner's construction manager should thoroughly check the reasonableness of all progress billings and the completeness of the partial waivers of lien.

To protect against, and minimize the risk occurring through subcontractor defaults, the following procedures should be followed—whether they are bonded or not.

- Evaluate the strength as well as the bid price of each subcontractor—don't gamble on high-risk subcontractors unless they can be readily replaced without disruption to the project schedule

- Include the right to terminate each contract due to specific defaults

- Require that each subcontractor require that sub-subcontractor and material contracts be assignable to the general contractor and/or the owner

- Require the general contractor accept the costs of project delay resulting from a default
- Carefully review all schedules of value used for progress payments
- Carefully review all progress payments and partial waivers of lien for accuracy and completeness.

CASE STUDY

It was decided early in the project that, because the construction site would be rather congested, and the parking and site work were to be jointly used by the hotel and the office building, there was an overwhelming benefit to using the same general contractor for the entire project. The office building, parking and site work would be under contract to Prentiss and the hotel under contract to Waterford. The two contracts would have relatively equal dollar amounts.

It had been the original intent to use Ninteman Construction, the general contractor on the Executive Center Del Mar project. Unfortunately, Ninteman lost control of that project in the last three months, causing several unanticipated and unnecessary delays. This loss of control caused the decision to interview several of the other leading contractors operating in San Diego. Those considered were Turner Construction, Swinerton & Walberg, DPR, and McCarthy Construction, in addition to Ninteman. All of the contractors operate open shop in San Diego County.

Each contractor was asked to provide a description of the projects they had recently completed that provided some reasonable relationship to the proposed project, and to bring the key preconstruction and construction personnel they proposed to assign to the project to the interview. They were jointly interviewed by Prentiss and Waterford and asked many questions about their cost control, scheduling systems, skills in HVAC and electrical work—work they performed with their own forces, their workload in San Diego, and which projects were negotiated with a GMP, and their estimates of General Conditions and fee. In addition to the joint evaluations, references were sought from architects and other owners.

Turner and Ninteman were dropped from consideration early—Turner made a weak presentation and the proposed personnel were not impressive, and Ninteman did nothing to alleviate the prior concerns. DPR had some very impressive people and excellent office building experience, but was finally dropped from consideration because their experience in hotels was limited. Swinerton was finally selected over McCarthy because they had a better combination of office and hotel experience, showed greater interest in tailoring their available personnel to the project's needs, had a lower fee, and had a lower overhead burden on site personnel.

The fee was 3%, which was intended to include the preconstruction effort, and the standard Prentiss construction contract was to be used. They requested $45,000 for preconstruction work to protect against the project not proceeding. One of the Prentiss representatives later converted that protection into a fee that was in addition to the 3% fee.

There was a general understanding as to the likelihood of certain personnel being assigned to the project, but a delay in the anticipated starting date, and some organizational changes by the contractor negated those understandings.

It was the early intention to bid the mechanical and electrical work on a design-build basis to selected contractors at the end of the design development phase. Where quality contractors are available in a market that qualify for this approach, it is believed that good pricing is achieved and the working drawings become the finished product. This often avoids conflicts as the work proceeds. The bidding would be based on specifications and drawings prepared by the engineers. It was also assumed that, due to long lead times, a structural steel mill order would be committed to prior to completion of design documents and obtaining a building permit.

The general construction contract and General Conditions and Supplementary General Conditions were basically the Prentiss standard documents. There was not a savings sharing clause, as common practice now in Southern California is that all savings go the owner. There was quite a delay in reaching an executed contract for three reasons—it was just not addressed it in a timely manner, there was considerable disagreement regarding bonding and there was a belated added requirement for liquidated damages.

Prentiss did not wish to bond certain subcontractors because time was the most critical factor and it was believed that a defaulting contractor could be replaced much more quickly without having to deal with a bonding company. The penalty exposure would likely exceed the cost of replacing the defaulting contractor. Contract language was added requiring that each subcontractor, sub-subcontractor and major material suppliers contracts be assignable to the general contractor and/or owner, but the contractor still was resistant, wanting total cost responsibility for any default to rest with Prentiss. The issue was finally resolved when Swinerton converted to an umbrella bonding program corporate-wide, which provided cost protection as well as freedom to replace the defaulting contractor through their own procedures and judgment.

There was some concern by management about the penalty exposure in the Brandes Lease, and it was desired that the contractor share that obligation. There were two problems with this—one was that the Brandes penalties had no relief through *force majeure*, and the other was that the contract was priced and negotiated without knowledge of this requirement. An agreement was finally worked out, but the delay prior to the contractor's obligation becoming effective was four months beyond the anticipated construction completion, and the likelihood of exposure was little or none. The only thing accomplished was to provide some home office personnel with peace of mind since the contract had a liquidated damages clause.

PROJECT SCHEDULE 34

Every type of project requires a good, detailed schedule to facilitate planning, monitoring and control. Development is an extreme example of the essential requirement for accurate scheduling. In this chapter we will discuss types of schedules, and the extent to which the project success depends on scheduling of non-construction activities—such as entitlements, financing, marketing, leasing and other factors. The Development Officer must participate actively in the preparation and monitoring of the schedule—providing all non-construction information and working with the contractors to ensure they understand all project issues, including the value of premium time, if any, and to ensure you understand the contractor's complete thought process.

The best project schedules use a true Critical Path Method (CPM), or some similar dynamic approach, which identifies the one specific chain of activities that limit the earliest project completion, **in accordance with the specific schedule analysis that has been input to the program.** Note that when the resulting schedule does not meet your requirements, it is necessary to re-analyze each of the critical activities to determine alternate ways to plan the project in order to accomplish your objectives. This type of scheduling tool enhances the "what if" analyses that permits finding an acceptable solution. Every time a portion of the project slips, and **it will happen several times on every project,** the logic and schedule must be reassessed to regain the desired schedule.

In a true CPM analysis, every single activity is specifically defined, not just as "dig the pipe trench," but "dig the northerly 400 feet of the pipe trench." Through a network analysis then, CPM not only enables a scheduler to make more detailed analyses, but also permits every other party involved in the project to understand the thought process and assumptions.

Many large, quality general contractors have personnel skilled in CPM. One common misconception regarding CPM is that specially trained CPM technicians create the schedules—they are really just a resource, as it is essential that the person(s) directly in charge of the project must actually prepare and update the schedule. Frequently the results of the CPM analysis are printed out in both bar chart and "early start" tabular forms for ease of communication.

Currently, most if not all contractors have foregone a full CPM network analysis for commercial programs, such as *Primavera, SureTrak Program Manager*, and *Microsoft Project*. These programs perform similar calculations to those of CPM, but study the activities in bar chart or data form rather than in network form. When activities are studied in bar graph form, several activities are frequently lumped together, and succeeding bars are overlapped by using specified lead and lag times, without a clear delineation as to how they interrelate. This produces a much less precise analysis and does not have the same value in team problem solving.

SureTrak is currently the most commonly used by contractors, and can handle up to 10,000 activities. *Primavera,* the parent of *SureTrak* is much more expensive and performs about the same way—but can handle many more activities. *Primavera* is frequently used as a master schedule to incorporate many projects that are individually scheduled with *SureTrak*. *Microsoft Project* is considered easier to use initially, but more difficult to update.

An example of the bar chart based CPM type analysis prepared using *SureTrak* is shown in the

> A thoroughly prepared schedule, in great detail, is an essential tool in properly managing a project.
>
> A projected completion date, over a month later than we required, was solved at First City Center through our ability to analyze a very well-prepared critical path schedule.
>
> We found that the personnel hoist was designed to be attached to the building in such a manner that, when the internal freight elevators were operational so as to be available for construction work, the temporary hoist would be removed to permit installation of a 20-foot-wide section of the building skin for 50 floors. Two bays of glazing, granite spandrels and column covers could not be installed prior to its removal.
>
> The supporting connections were modified so that an "L" shaped structural bracket was attached to the perimeter beam, aligned in the center of a window line so it only penetrated the wall line through the location of the glazing opening on every third floor. With this seemingly minor change, at nominal cost, the contractor was able to install all of the granite, all of the window framing and all the glazing except for one lite on every third floor. On the floors where these glass lites were temporarily left out, a neatly painted barricade was built that covered the opening, extended into the space only about two feet, and did not interfere with the interior construction work.
>
> The result was that we met our schedule obligation and collected well over one-half million dollars of rental income that much sooner.

Case Study that follows this chapter. The project is for the development of an eight-story office building and a ten-story hotel. The hotel is being developed by another developer, using the same general contractor, but a with different architect. Each sheet of the schedule encompasses the entire project period and it is intended they be arranged vertically for review. The estimated duration, early start and early finish dates are shown for each activity.

Because these schedules do not have the rigorous analysis that can be so important in a successful project, they must be supplemented with detail schedules, which the Development Officer must also clearly understand. One major detail schedule is the shop drawing schedule and log, which covers submittal, review and approval, and requirement dates for each shop drawing, and ensures that any affected trade see and review each drawing. Another detail schedule tracks the purchase, fabrication and delivery of all important materials. Delivery schedules become even more important with the trend to fabricate more materials off-site.

In addition to the master schedule, the general contractor must prepare either two-week or four-week "look ahead" schedules which, in much more detail, describe the work to be performed by each trade during that period, and indicate the interrelationship between the work of one trade to another.

While you may have preferences as to the form of schedule, it is best to let each contractor utilize their normal systems and procedures rather than induce them to change to a system of your choice. But the less rigorous the contractor's system, the more thoroughly the Development Officer must review and query those schedules. The use of CPM is less critical on smaller projects because it is easier to mentally grasp the various activity interrelationships.

For the Development Officer to gain satisfactory control of a project it is necessary to continually question the contractor, or other team member, responsible for a particular activity, as to the limiting conditions to the start of each activity. When not satisfied, an analysis of alternatives should be initiated. The schedule should be reviewed in detail each week.

A major misconception is that the construction work is the only complicated and essential formal schedule required. This is incorrect as many other project functions are critical to the start of construction, the leasing and occupancy.

It is important to estimate as accurately as possible the elapsed time required by the local jurisdiction for each of their approval steps, from initial development request submissions to final development approval and subdivision approval, if applicable. This period is not only affected by the number of approval steps, their procedures, the number of scheduled public meetings involved, but also by their current workload caused by the level of development activity.

Building permit approval time, for everything from separate grading permits to full working drawings, can vary widely by jurisdiction and current activity. The author has obtained full working drawing approval for a 50-story building in less than four weeks, and it has taken three-and-a-half months for a very small project in another city. Some jurisdictions have set up priority approval schedules involving staff overtime for a premium payment, but in periods of heavy activity every developer requests it, resulting in little or no schedule improvement.

A typical predevelopment period schedule is shown in Figures 34-1 and 34-2, the first two sheets of an early schedule for the Case Study project. This predevelopment period is rather detailed due to the joint entitlement process. This schedule should have had the critical path in red.

The start of construction is normally dependent on **all** of the following activities being completed:

- Land purchase or ground lease closings
- Completion of all political, zoning and code approvals, that cannot be properly obtained at a later date
- Completion of certain site work that is outside the general contract, if any
- Proper site plat or subdivision map
- In some states, placement of a Deed of Trust is required prior to loan closing or start of any work
- Completing the buy-sell agreement between lenders
- Closing the interim loan
- Closing of the permanent loan commitment
- Completion of regulatory mitigation upon which the project is conditioned
- Initial foundation or building permit
- Owner acceptance of the guaranteed maximum price and issuance of the notice to proceed

In addition, where applicable, demolition and its approval chain, existing tenant/occupant relocations, or a major tenant lease commitment may be required prior to the start of construction.

All major marketing events and requirements—models, renderings, brochures and marketing centers—should be incorporated into the schedule as they are closely integrated with various design steps and with each other.

It frequently requires a thorough, preferably network, analysis of the various preconstruction activities to insure that there will not be any surprise delays to the start of construction, as it is not always clear early in the process where the critical path for preconstruction will lie. For example, the critical path could lie on any of these types of paths:

- Documentation of the interim loan, documentation of the permanent loan commitment, acceptable buy/sell between the two lenders, lender approval of the pro forma, plans and preleasing, interim loan closing and the permanent loan commitment.

- Close on land purchase, relocate tenants, relocate utilities, demolition, subdivision map and resolution of any hazardous waste or wetlands type of issues.

- Find, negotiate, and execute leases with a sufficient number of lead tenants to satisfy owner and lenders as to the project's viability.

- Approval of the EIR/EIS, resolution of citizen group challenges, zoning variances or waivers, resolution of mitigations, execution of a development agreement, and issuance of initial building or foundation permits. Court challenges to EIR/EIS and governmental rulings are becoming more common.

Office Development

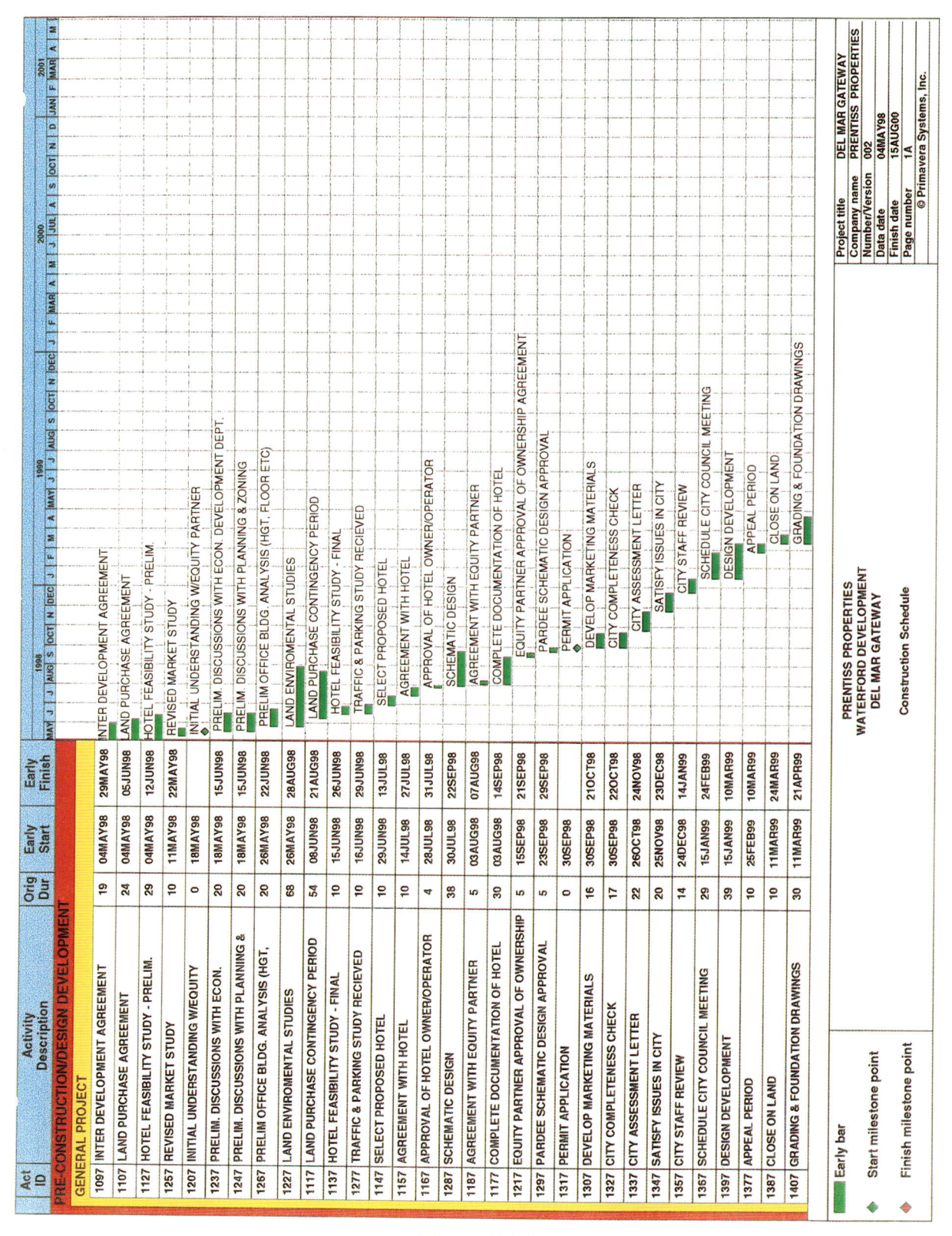

Act ID	Activity Description	Orig Dur	Early Start	Early Finish
	PRE-CONSTRUCTION/DESIGN DEVELOPMENT			
	GENERAL PROJECT			
1097	INTER DEVELOPMENT AGREEMENT	19	04MAY98	29MAY98
1107	LAND PURCHASE AGREEMENT	24	04MAY98	05JUN98
1127	HOTEL FEASIBILITY STUDY - PRELIM.	29	04MAY98	12JUN98
1257	REVISED MARKET STUDY	10	11MAY98	22MAY98
1207	INITIAL UNDERSTANDING W/EQUITY	0	18MAY98	
1237	PRELIM. DISCUSSIONS WITH ECON.	20	18MAY98	15JUN98
1247	PRELIM. DISCUSSIONS WITH PLANNING &	20	18MAY98	15JUN98
1267	PRELIM OFFICE BLDG. ANALYSIS (HGT,	20	26MAY98	22JUN98
1227	LAND ENVIROMENTAL STUDIES	68	26MAY98	28AUG98
1117	LAND PURCHASE CONTINGENCY PERIOD	54	08JUN98	21AUG98
1137	HOTEL FEASIBILITY STUDY - FINAL	10	15JUN98	26JUN98
1277	TRAFFIC & PARKING STUDY RECIEVED	10	16JUN98	29JUN98
1147	SELECT PROPOSED HOTEL	10	29JUN98	13JUL98
1157	AGREEMENT WITH HOTEL	10	14JUL98	27JUL98
1167	APPROVAL OF HOTEL OWNER/OPERATOR	4	28JUL98	31JUL98
1287	SCHEMATIC DESIGN	38	30JUL98	22SEP98
1187	AGREEMENT WITH EQUITY PARTNER	5	03AUG98	07AUG98
1177	COMPLETE DOCUMENTATION OF HOTEL	30	03AUG98	14SEP98
1217	EQUITY PARTNER APPROVAL OF OWNERSHIP	5	15SEP98	21SEP98
1297	PARDEE SCHEMATIC DESIGN APPROVAL	5	23SEP98	29SEP98
1317	PERMIT APPLICATION	0	30SEP98	
1307	DEVELOP MARKETING MATERIALS	16	30SEP98	21OCT98
1327	CITY COMPLETENESS CHECK	17	30SEP98	22OCT98
1337	CITY ASSESSMENT LETTER	22	26OCT98	24NOV98
1347	SATISFY ISSUES IN CITY	20	25NOV98	23DEC98
1357	CITY STAFF REVIEW	14	24DEC98	14JAN99
1367	SCHEDULE CITY COUNCIL MEETING	29	15JAN99	24FEB99
1397	DESIGN DEVELOPMENT	39	15JAN99	10MAR99
1377	APPEAL PERIOD	10	25FEB99	10MAR99
1387	CLOSE ON LAND	10	11MAR99	24MAR99
1407	GRADING & FOUNDATION DRAWINGS	30	11MAR99	21APR99

PRENTISS PROPERTIES
WATERFORD DEVELOPMENT
DEL MAR GATEWAY

Construction Schedule

Project title: DEL MAR GATEWAY
Company name: PRENTISS PROPERTIES
Number/Version: 002
Data date: 04MAY98
Finish date: 15AUG00
Page number: 1A

© Primavera Systems, Inc.

Legend:
- Early bar
- Start milestone point
- Finish milestone point

Figure 34-1

Project Schedule

Act ID	Activity Description	Orig Dur	Early Start	Early Finish
1417	HOTEL/OFFICE BUILDING WORKING	50	11MAR99	19MAY99
1418	FOUNDATION & GRADING PERMIT	0		21APR99
1439	NOTICE TO PROCEED - GRADING/FDNS	0	22APR99	
1428	BUILDING PERMIT PROCESS	40	22APR99	16JUN99
1438	ESTABLISH GMP	21	20MAY99	17JUN99
1429	BUILDING PERMIT - PARKING STRUCTURE	0	17JUN99	
1430	BUILDING PERMIT - HOTEL	0	17JUN99	
1431	BUILDING PERMIT - OFFICE BUILDING	0	17JUN99	
1449	NOTICE TO PROCEED - HOTEL/OFFICE	0	18JUN99	
PROCUREMENT				
1527	BID - PLUMBING - DESIGN/BUILD	15	18NOV98	09DEC98
1627	BID - HVAC - DESIGN/BUILD	15	18NOV98	09DEC98
1635	BID - ELECTRICAL - DESIGN/BUILD	15	18NOV98	09DEC98
1537	AWARD - PLUMBING	5	10DEC98	16DEC98
1549	AWARD - HVAC SYSTEM	5	10DEC98	16DEC98
1637	AWARD - ELECTRICAL	5	10DEC98	16DEC98
1477	PLUMBING - DESIGN DRWGS	40	17DEC98	12FEB99
1577	HVAC - DESIGN DRWGS	40	17DEC98	12FEB99
1677	ELECTRICAL - DESIGN DRWGS	50	17DEC98	26FEB99
1427	BID - STRUCTURAL STEEL	15	11MAR99	31MAR99
1459	BID ELEVATOR PACKAGE	15	11MAR99	31MAR99
1509	BID - CURTAIN WALL SYSTEM	15	11MAR99	31MAR99
1437	AWARD - STRUCTURAL STEEL	5	01APR99	07APR99
1469	AWARD - ELEVATOR PACKAGE	5	01APR99	07APR99
1519	AWARD - CURTAIN WALL SYSTEM	5	01APR99	07APR99
1447	STRUCTURAL STEEL - SHOP DRWGS.	20	08APR99	05MAY99
1479	ELEVATORS - DESIGN/SHOP DWGS	20	08APR99	05MAY99
1497	PLUMBING - SHOP DRWGS	30	08APR99	19MAY99
1597	ELECTRICAL - SHOP DRWGS	30	08APR99	19MAY99
1547	HVAC- SHOP DRWGS.	40	08APR99	02JUN99
1529	CURTAIN WALL SYSTEM - FAB/DELIVER	260	08APR99	06APR00
1467	STRUCTURAL STEEL - SHOP DRWGS	10	06MAY99	19MAY99
1499	ELEVATORS - SHOP DWGS APPROVAL	10	06MAY99	19MAY99

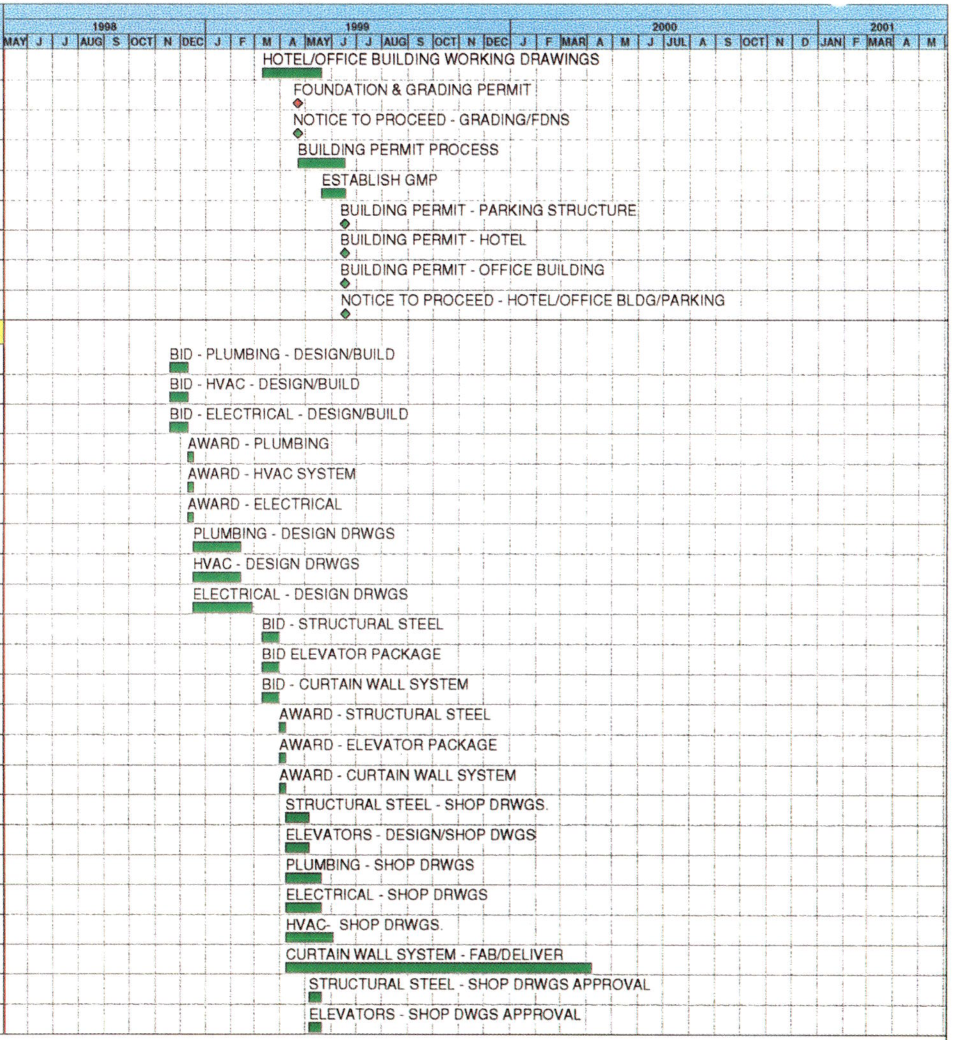

PRENTISS PROPERTIES
WATERFORD DEVELOPMENT
DEL MAR GATEWAY

Construction Schedule

Project title: DEL MAR GATEWAY
Company name: PRENTISS PROPERTIES
Number/Version: 002
Data date: 04MAY98
Finish date: 15AUG00
Page number: 2A

© Primavera Systems, Inc.

- Early bar
- Start milestone point
- Finish milestone point

Figure 34-2

CASE STUDY

The initial schedule was developed at the very beginning of the project to insure complete evaluation of the various interrelated factors that had to be monitored and controlled in order to properly perform the work and to reasonably predict a completion schedule. It was essential that each party was aware of the front-end issues. Some of the early complications that needed to be monitored and controlled were:

- Pardee's Land Purchase Agreement documentation and approval process
- Land Sale Agreement and documentation between Prentiss and Waterford
- Two developers with different architects designing a single site
- Environmental and site testing studies
- Hotel feasibility study
- Selection, approval and documentation of a hotel operator
- Waterford's documentation of a financial partner
- Mutually approved site plan and conceptual design
- Approval of Carmel Valley Association, the local planning board
- Substantial Conformance Determination by city of San Diego
- COREA agreement between Prentiss and Waterford
- Lot split
- The unusually long time required to process plans through the city

There were many early delays. Pardee was many months late with the documentation for the Land Purchase Agreement. At the same time, Waterford, after receiving a positive hotel feasibility report, selected Patriot American's Wyndham chain to be the operator, only to have them back out when the REIT had some financial setbacks. They were replaced with Marriott.

Approval by the Carmel Valley Association had been projected to take no more than two months and occur simultaneously with the city's Substantial Conformance Review. It actually took four months for the association, and another month for the final determination by the city.

Prior to receiving the Substantial Conformance Determination from the city, a Letter of Intent was entered into with Brandes Financial to lease five floors, with an occupancy date of August 1, 2000. With the SCD not received until April 4, 1999 and the schematic design not fully resolved, the schedule was very tight. There was some delay in executing the lease, and the occupancy date was changed to August 15, 2000. There was a 30-day fitting out period with the rent commencing on September 15.

To accomplish the most favorable schedule possible, it was necessary to expedite portions of the design, and to separately let contracts for mechanical and electrical, plumbing, fire protection, curtain wall, structural steel, elevators, concrete, soil-nailing, grading and foundations, as discussed in Chapter 35.

The project schedule is shown in Figures 34-3 through 34-12, with the hotel portion omitted for simplicity. The front-end delays discussed above, which are not shown on this issue of the schedule, delayed the certified pad by four months from the original target date. This schedule was prepared at the time the contractor was still projecting the TCO would be received on September 15, or one month later than was believed to be achievable, and one month beyond the obligations under Brandes Lease.

The contractor did break the elements of the project down in more detail than normal at the

Development Officer's request. This form of schedule, however, still misses, showing many of the trade interrelationships, making detailed four-week look-ahead schedules essential for job site communication.

The contractor also broke out the design development, site work and general project sections separately instead of letting all activities flow along in their natural order. It is workable in this manner once you get used to it, but it takes a little more effort to understand it.

The schedule presented with the GMP indicated the parking structure receiving the TCO almost a week prior to our occupancy obligation, but the office tower would be one month late.

Most of the final GMP schedule, shown on the following pages, was accepted as reasonable, but the eight weeks allocated to the commissioning, testing, inspecting and approval of the mechanical, electrical and fire protection systems was not accepted. It was decided to wait a month or so, until all contracting issues were resolved and all equipment was purchased, and then meet with the contractors as frequently as necessary until mutually agreed upon procedures and timing targets were reached. This is discussed further in the next chapter.

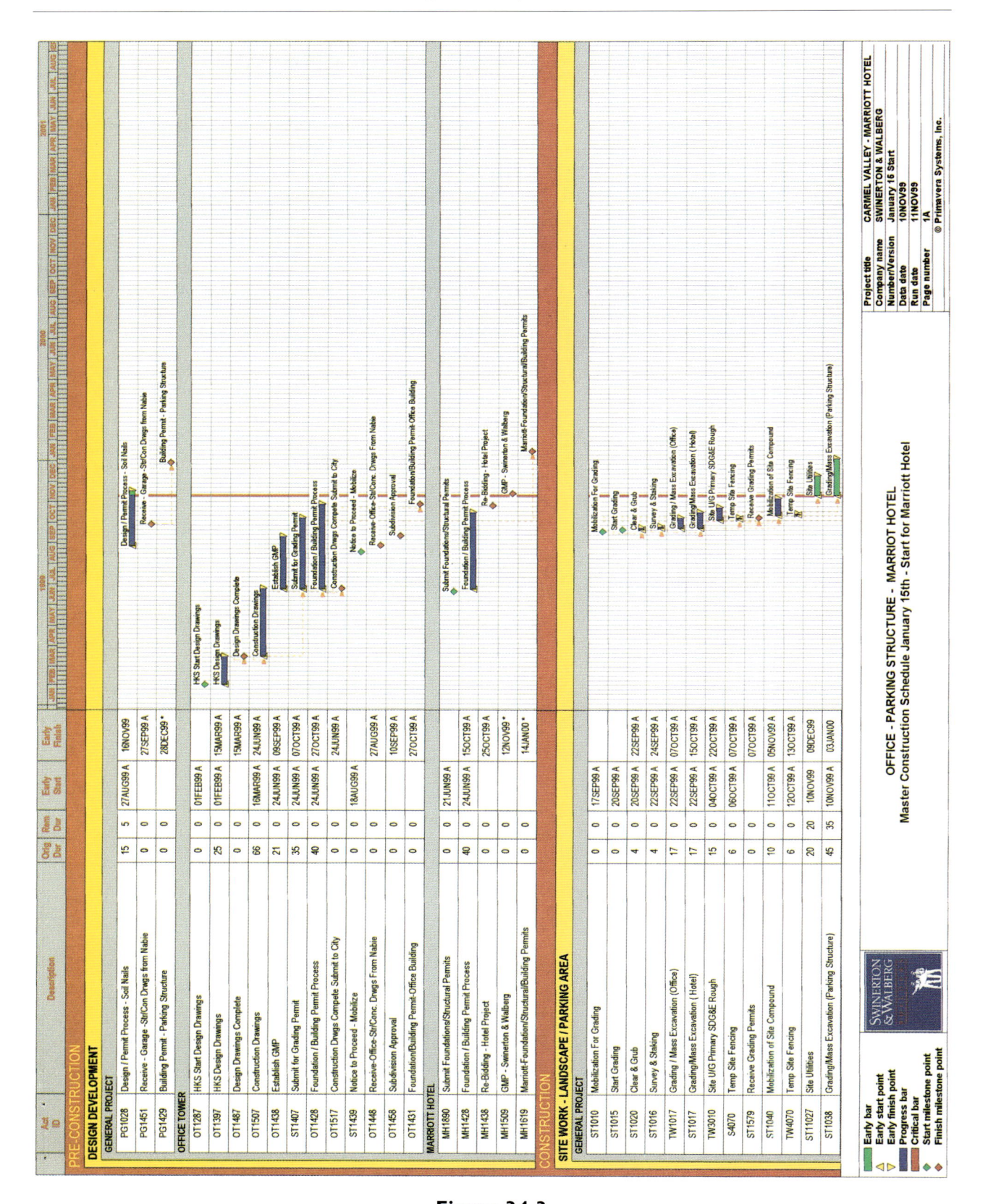

Figure 34-3

Project Schedule

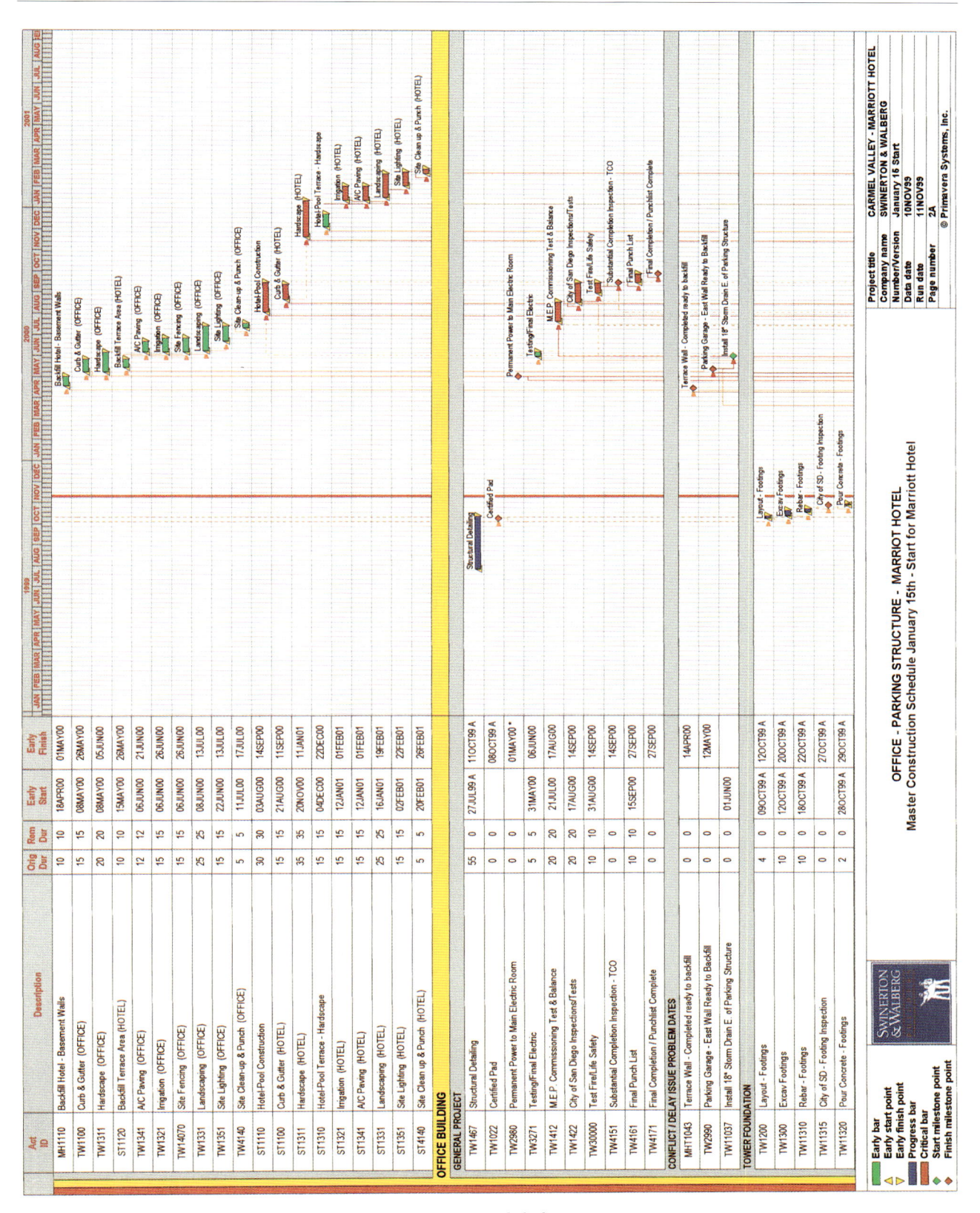

Figure 34-4

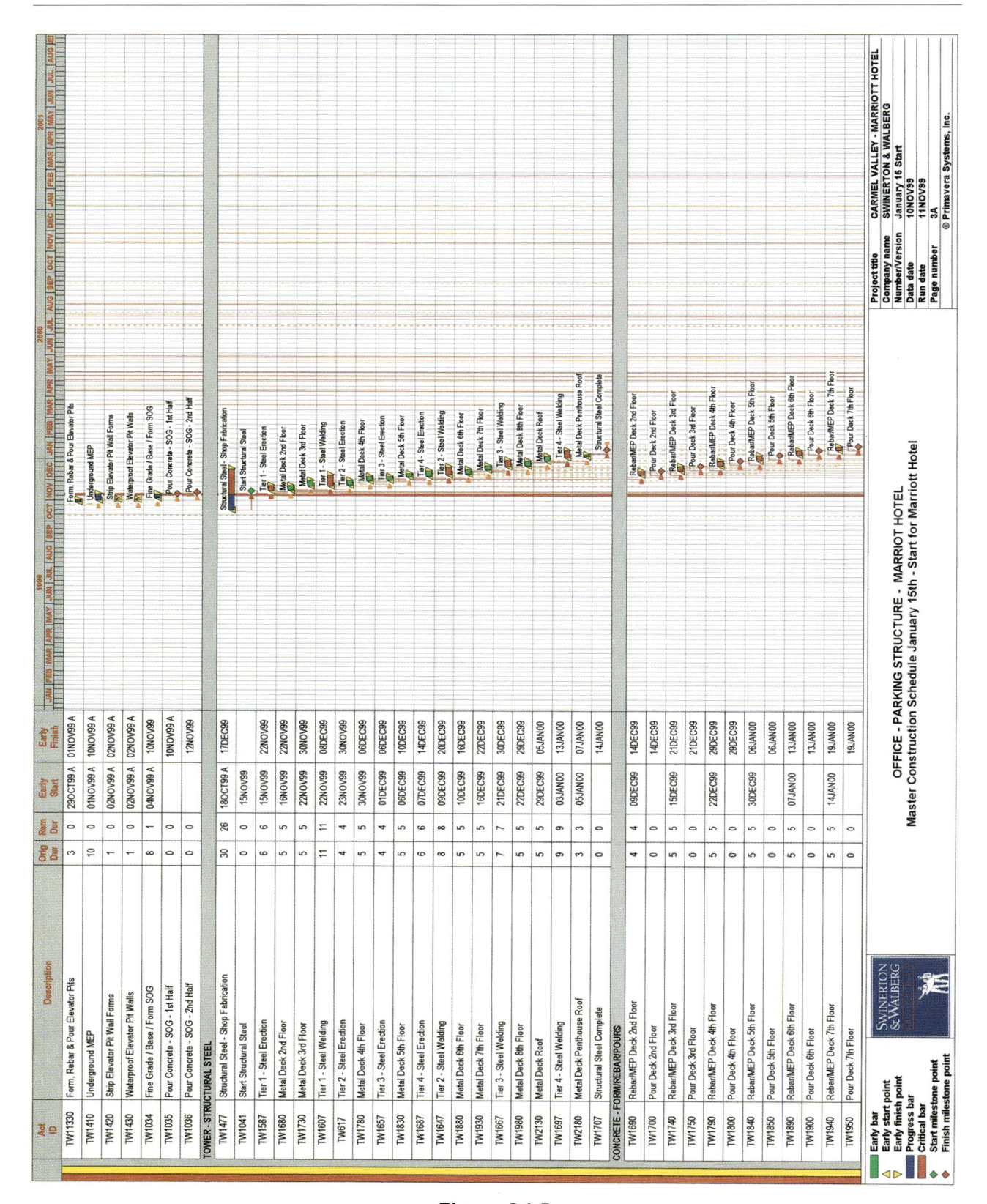

Figure 34-5

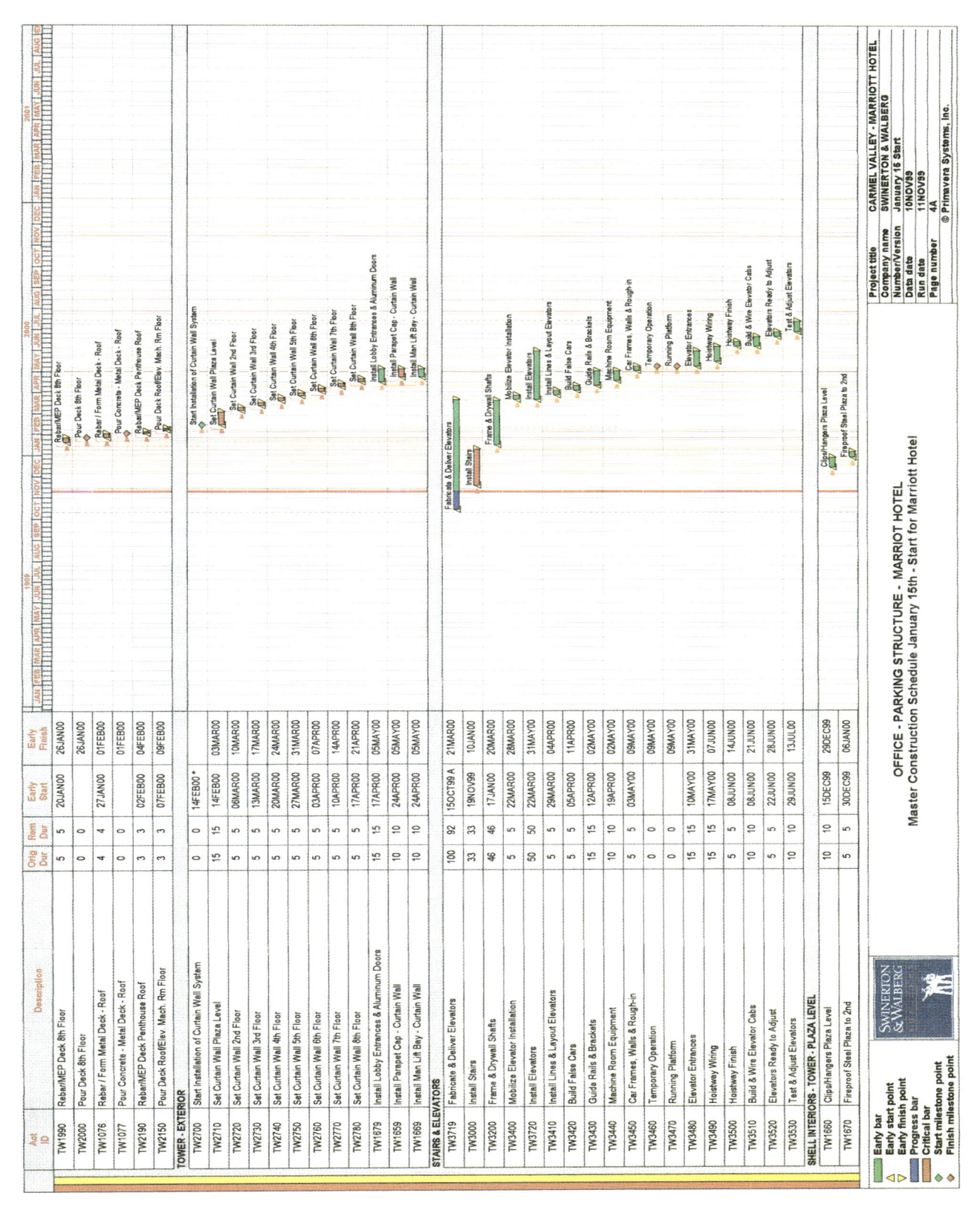

Figure 34-6

Office Development

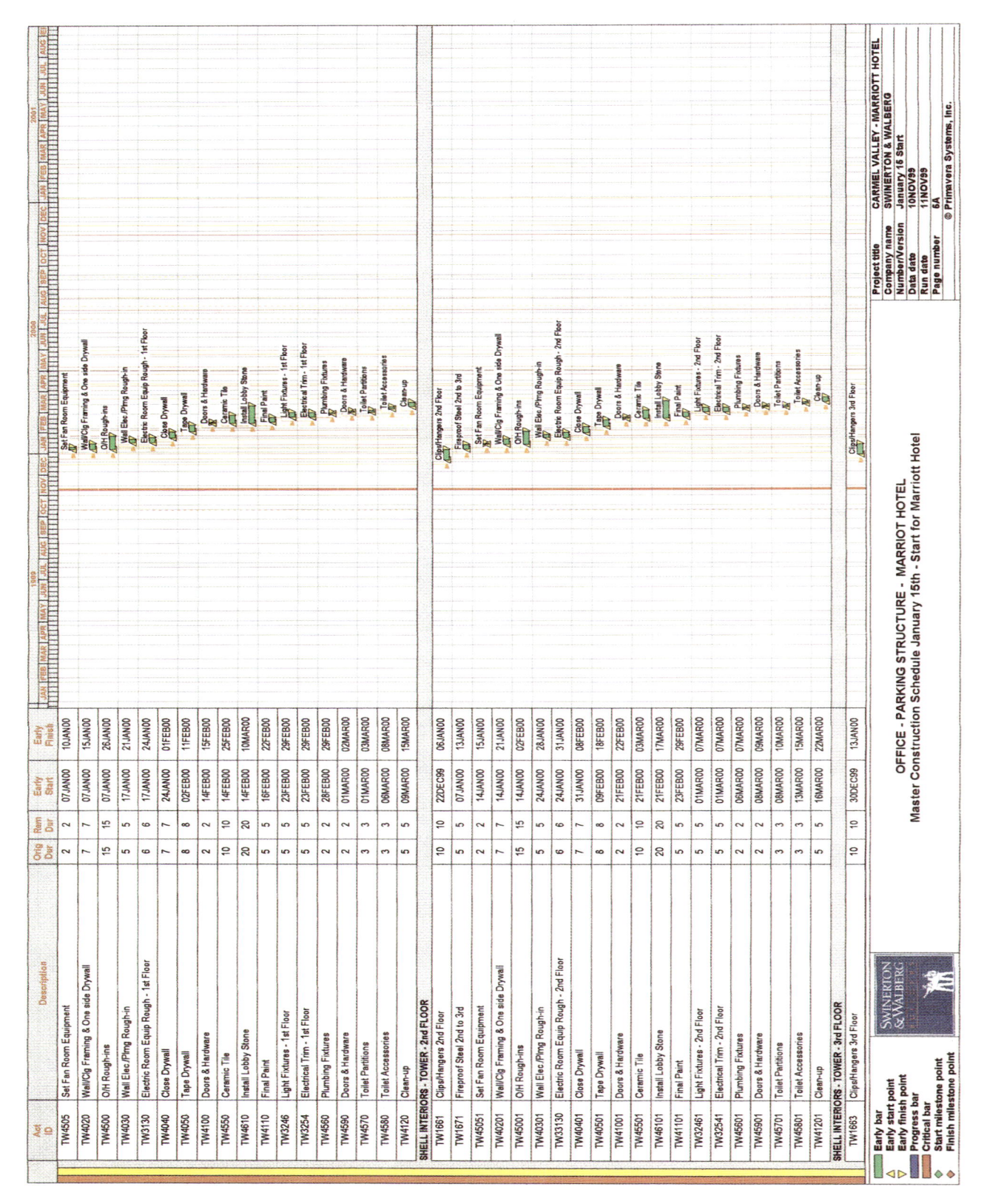

Act ID	Description	Orig Dur	Rem Dur	Early Start	Early Finish
TW4505	Set Fan Room Equipment	2	2	07JAN00	10JAN00
TW4020	Wall/Clg Framing & One side Drywall	7	7	07JAN00	15JAN00
TW4500	O/H Rough-ins	15	15	07JAN00	26JAN00
TW4030	Wall Elec./Plmg Rough-in	5	5	17JAN00	21JAN00
TW3130	Electric Room Equip Rough - 1st Floor	6	6	17JAN00	24JAN00
TW4040	Close Drywall	7	7	24JAN00	01FEB00
TW4050	Tape Drywall	8	8	02FEB00	11FEB00
TW4100	Doors & Hardware	2	2	14FEB00	15FEB00
TW4550	Ceramic Tile	10	10	14FEB00	25FEB00
TW4610	Install Lobby Stone	20	20	14FEB00	10MAR00
TW4110	Final Paint	5	5	16FEB00	22FEB00
TW3246	Light Fixtures - 1st Floor	5	5	23FEB00	29FEB00
TW3254	Electrical Trim - 1st Floor	5	5	23FEB00	29FEB00
TW4560	Plumbing Fixtures	2	2	28FEB00	29FEB00
TW4590	Doors & Hardware	2	2	01MAR00	02MAR00
TW4570	Toilet Partitions	3	3	01MAR00	03MAR00
TW4580	Toilet Accessories	3	3	06MAR00	08MAR00
TW4120	Clean-up	5	5	09MAR00	15MAR00
SHELL INTERIORS - TOWER - 2nd FLOOR					
TW1661	Clips/Hangers 2nd Floor	10	10	22DEC99	06JAN00
TW1671	Fireproof Steel 2nd to 3rd	5	5	07JAN00	13JAN00
TW45051	Set Fan Room Equipment	2	2	14JAN00	15JAN00
TW40201	Wall/Clg Framing & One side Drywall	7	7	14JAN00	21JAN00
TW45001	O/H Rough-ins	15	15	14JAN00	02FEB00
TW40301	Wall Elec./Plmg Rough-in	5	5	24JAN00	28JAN00
TW33130	Electric Room Equip Rough - 2nd Floor	6	6	24JAN00	31JAN00
TW40401	Close Drywall	7	7	31JAN00	08FEB00
TW40501	Tape Drywall	8	8	09FEB00	18FEB00
TW41001	Doors & Hardware	2	2	21FEB00	22FEB00
TW45501	Ceramic Tile	10	10	21FEB00	03MAR00
TW46101	Install Lobby Stone	20	20	21FEB00	17MAR00
TW41101	Final Paint	5	5	23FEB00	29FEB00
TW32461	Light Fixtures - 2nd Floor	5	5	01MAR00	07MAR00
TW32541	Electrical Trim - 2nd Floor	5	5	01MAR00	07MAR00
TW45601	Plumbing Fixtures	2	2	06MAR00	07MAR00
TW45901	Doors & Hardware	2	2	08MAR00	09MAR00
TW45701	Toilet Partitions	3	3	08MAR00	10MAR00
TW45801	Toilet Accessories	3	3	13MAR00	15MAR00
TW41201	Clean-up	5	5	16MAR00	22MAR00
SHELL INTERIORS - TOWER - 3rd FLOOR					
TW1663	Clips/Hangers 3rd Floor	10	10	30DEC99	13JAN00

OFFICE - PARKING STRUCTURE - MARRIOT HOTEL
Master Construction Schedule January 15th - Start for Marriott Hotel

Project title	CARMEL VALLEY - MARRIOTT HOTEL
Company name	SWINERTON & WALBERG
Number/Version	January 15 Start
Data date	10NOV99
Run date	11NOV99
Page number	6A
	© Primavera Systems, Inc.

Legend:
- Early bar
- Early start point
- Early finish point
- Progress bar
- Critical bar
- Start milestone point
- Finish milestone point

Figure 34-7

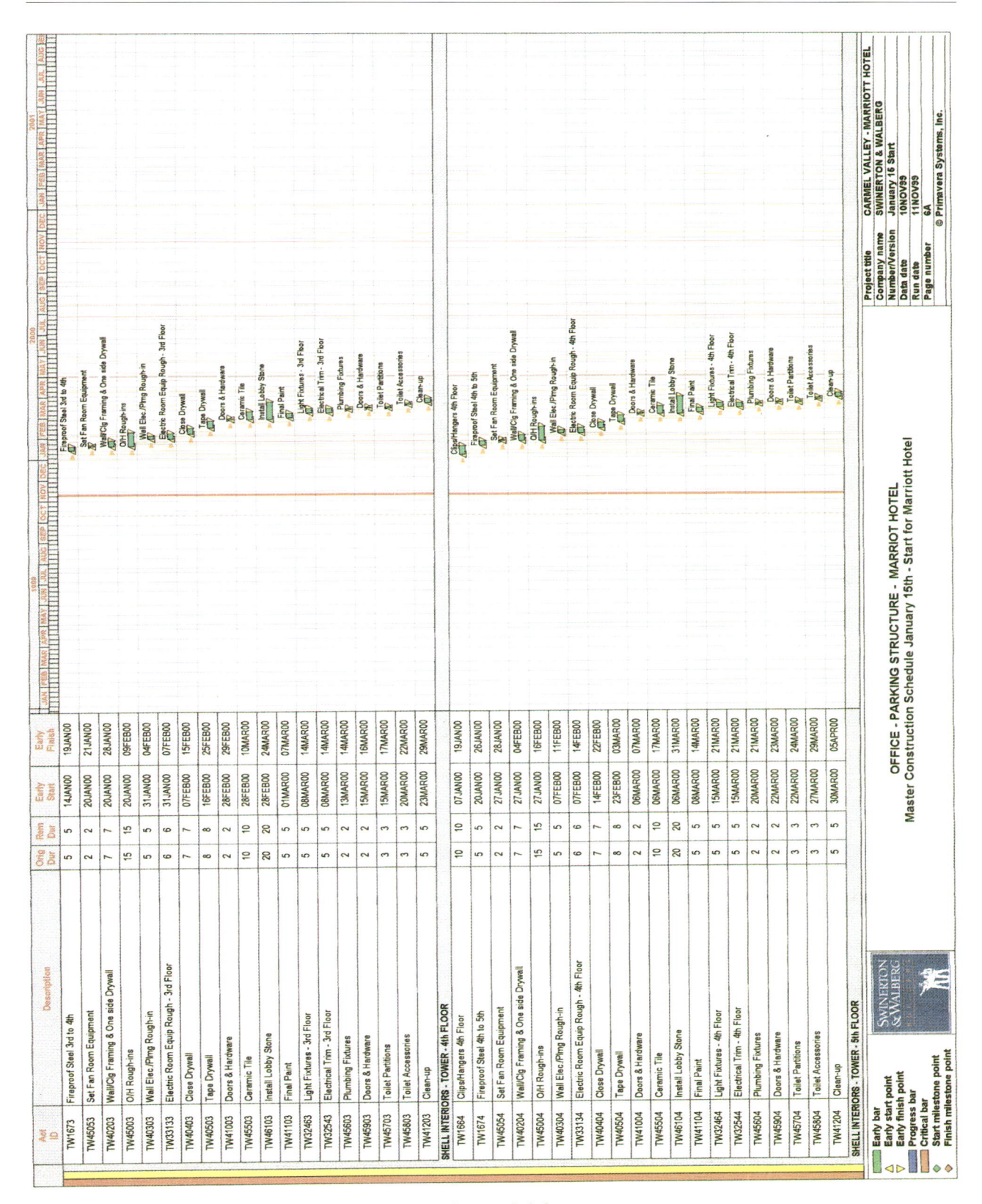

Figure 34-8

Office Development

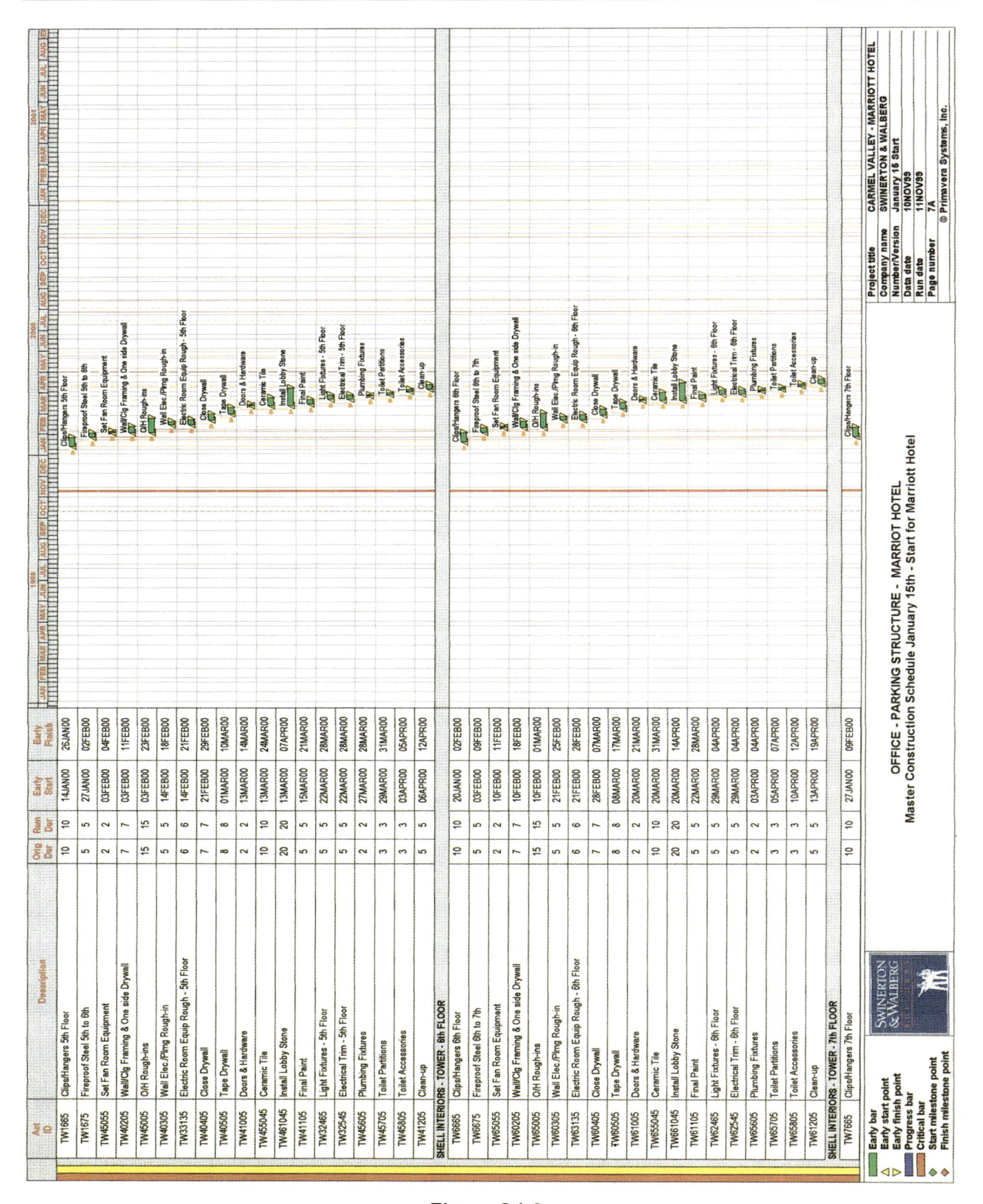

Act ID	Description	Orig Dur	Rem Dur	Early Start	Early Finish
TW1665	Clips/Hangers 5th Floor	10	10	14JAN00	26JAN00
TW1675	Fireproof Steel 5th to 6th	5	5	27JAN00	02FEB00
TW45055	Set Fan Room Equipment	2	2	03FEB00	04FEB00
TW40205	Wall/Clg Framing & One side Drywall	7	7	03FEB00	11FEB00
TW45005	O/H Rough-ins	15	15	03FEB00	23FEB00
TW40305	Wall Elec./Plmg Rough-in	5	5	14FEB00	18FEB00
TW33135	Electric Room Equip Rough - 5th Floor	6	6	14FEB00	21FEB00
TW40405	Close Drywall	7	7	21FEB00	29FEB00
TW40505	Tape Drywall	8	8	01MAR00	10MAR00
TW41005	Doors & Hardware	2	2	13MAR00	14MAR00
TW455045	Ceramic Tile	10	10	13MAR00	24MAR00
TW461045	Install Lobby Stone	20	20	13MAR00	07APR00
TW41105	Final Paint	5	5	15MAR00	21MAR00
TW32465	Light Fixtures - 5th Floor	5	5	22MAR00	28FEB00
TW32545	Electrical Trim - 5th Floor	5	5	22MAR00	28MAR00
TW45605	Plumbing Fixtures	2	2	27MAR00	28MAR00
TW45705	Toilet Partitions	3	3	29MAR00	31MAR00
TW45805	Toilet Accessories	3	3	03APR00	05APR00
TW41205	Clean-up	5	5	06APR00	12APR00
SHELL INTERIORS - TOWER - 6th FLOOR					
TW6665	Clips/Hangers 6th Floor	10	10	20JAN00	02FEB00
TW65075	Fireproof Steel 6th to 7th	5	5	03FEB00	09FEB00
TW60055	Set Fan Room Equipment	2	2	10FEB00	11FEB00
TW60205	Wall/Clg Framing & One side Drywall	7	7	10FEB00	18FEB00
TW65005	O/H Rough-ins	15	15	10FEB00	01MAR00
TW60305	Wall Elec./Plmg Rough-in	5	5	21FEB00	25FEB00
TW53135	Electric Room Equip Rough - 6th Floor	6	6	21FEB00	28FEB00
TW60405	Close Drywall	7	7	28FEB00	07MAR00
TW60505	Tape Drywall	8	8	08MAR00	17MAR00
TW61005	Doors & Hardware	2	2	20MAR00	21MAR00
TW655045	Ceramic Tile	10	10	20MAR00	31MAR00
TW661045	Install Lobby Stone	20	20	20MAR00	14APR00
TW61105	Final Paint	5	5	22MAR00	28MAR00
TW62465	Light Fixtures - 6th Floor	5	5	29MAR00	04APR00
TW62545	Electrical Trim - 6th Floor	5	5	29MAR00	04APR00
TW65605	Plumbing Fixtures	2	2	03APR00	04APR00
TW65705	Toilet Partitions	3	3	05APR00	07APR00
TW65805	Toilet Accessories	3	3	10APR00	12APR00
TW61205	Clean-up	5	5	13APR00	19APR00
SHELL INTERIORS - TOWER - 7th FLOOR					
TW7665	Clips/Hangers 7th Floor	10	10	27JAN00	09FEB00

OFFICE - PARKING STRUCTURE - MARRIOT HOTEL
Master Construction Schedule January 15th - Start for Marriott Hotel

Project title: CARMEL VALLEY - MARRIOTT HOTEL
Company name: SWINERTON & WALBERG
Number/Version: January 15 Start
Data date: 10NOV99
Run date: 11NOV99
Page number: 7A
© Primavera Systems, Inc.

Legend:
- Early bar
- Early start point
- Early finish point
- Progress bar
- Critical bar
- Start milestone point
- Finish milestone point

Figure 34-9

Project Schedule

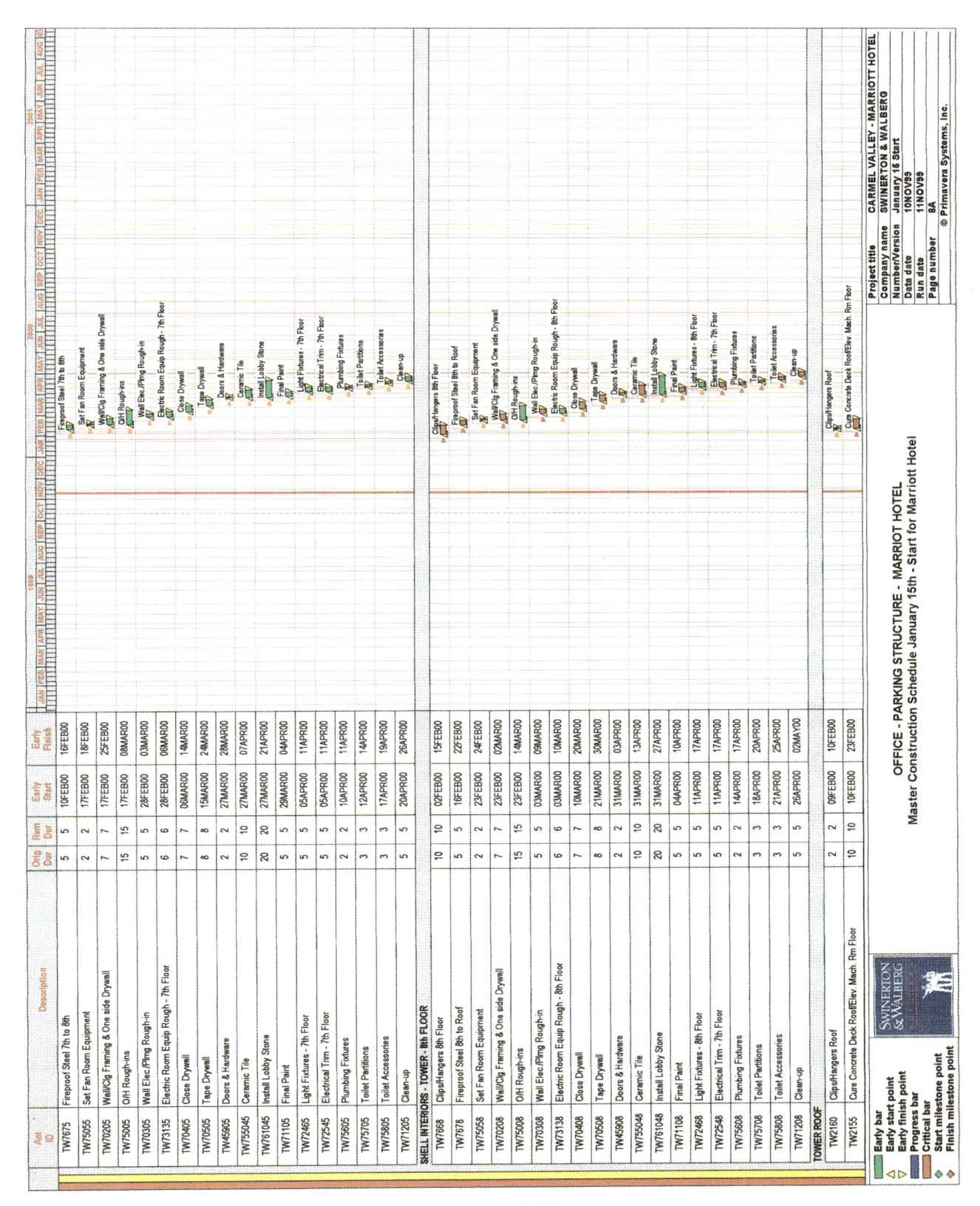

Act ID	Description	Orig Dur	Rem Dur	Early Start	Early Finish
TW7675	Fireproof Steel 7th to 8th	5	5	10FEB00	16FEB00
TW75055	Set Fan Room Equipment	2	2	17FEB00	18FEB00
TW70205	Wall/Clg Framing & One side Drywall	7	7	17FEB00	25FEB00
TW75005	O/H Rough-ins	15	15	17FEB00	08MAR00
TW70305	Wall Elec./Plmg Rough-in	5	5	28FEB00	03MAR00
TW73135	Electric Room Equip Rough - 7th Floor	6	6	28FEB00	06MAR00
TW70405	Close Drywall	7	7	06MAR00	14MAR00
TW70505	Tape Drywall	8	8	15MAR00	24MAR00
TW45905	Doors & Hardware	2	2	27MAR00	28MAR00
TW75045	Ceramic Tile	10	10	27MAR00	07APR00
TW761045	Install Lobby Stone	20	20	27MAR00	21APR00
TW71105	Final Paint	5	5	29MAR00	04APR00
TW72465	Light Fixtures - 7th Floor	5	5	05APR00	11APR00
TW72545	Electrical Trim - 7th Floor	5	5	05APR00	11APR00
TW75605	Plumbing Fixtures	2	2	10APR00	11APR00
TW75705	Toilet Partitions	3	3	12APR00	14APR00
TW75805	Toilet Accessories	3	3	17APR00	19APR00
TW71205	Clean-up	5	5	20APR00	26APR00
SHELL INTERIORS - TOWER - 8th FLOOR					
TW7668	Clips/Hangers 8th Floor	10	10	02FEB00	15FEB00
TW7678	Fireproof Steel 8th to Roof	5	5	16FEB00	22FEB00
TW75058	Set Fan Room Equipment	2	2	23FEB00	24FEB00
TW70208	Wall/Clg Framing & One side Drywall	7	7	23FEB00	02MAR00
TW75008	O/H Rough-ins	15	15	23FEB00	14MAR00
TW70308	Wall Elec./Plmg Rough-in	5	5	03MAR00	09MAR00
TW73138	Electric Room Equip Rough - 8th Floor	6	6	03MAR00	10MAR00
TW70408	Close Drywall	7	7	10MAR00	20MAR00
TW70508	Tape Drywall	8	8	21MAR00	30MAR00
TW46908	Doors & Hardware	2	2	31MAR00	03APR00
TW75048	Ceramic Tile	10	10	31MAR00	13APR00
TW761048	Install Lobby Stone	20	20	31MAR00	27APR00
TW71108	Final Paint	5	5	04APR00	10APR00
TW72468	Light Fixtures - 8th Floor	5	5	11APR00	17APR00
TW72548	Electrical Trim - 7th Floor	5	5	11APR00	17APR00
TW75608	Plumbing Fixtures	2	2	14APR00	17APR00
TW75708	Toilet Partitions	3	3	18APR00	20APR00
TW75808	Toilet Accessories	3	3	21APR00	25APR00
TW71208	Clean-up	5	5	26APR00	02MAY00
TOWER ROOF					
TW2160	Clips/Hangers Roof	2	2	09FEB00	10FEB00
TW2155	Cure Concrete Deck Roof/Elev. Mech. Rm Floor	10	10	10FEB00	23FEB00

OFFICE - PARKING STRUCTURE - MARRIOT HOTEL
Master Construction Schedule January 15th - Start for Marriott Hotel

Project title: CARMEL VALLEY - MARRIOTT HOTEL
Company name: SWINERTON & WALBERG
Number/Version: January 16 Start
Data date: 10NOV99
Run date: 11NOV99
Page number: 8A
© Primavera Systems, Inc.

Legend:
- Early bar
- Early start point
- Early finish point
- Progress bar
- Critical bar
- Start milestone point
- Finish milestone point

Figure 34-10

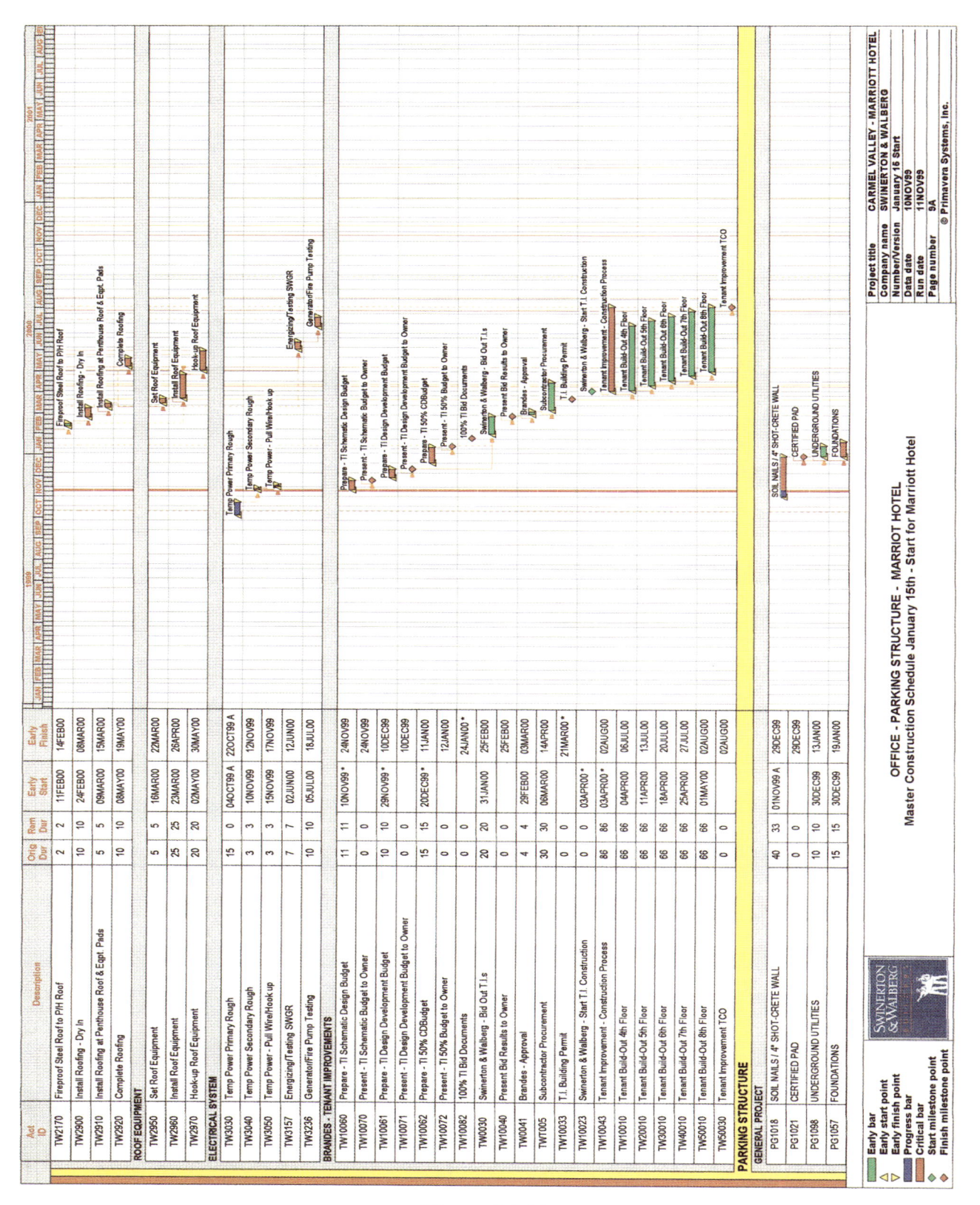

Figure 34-11

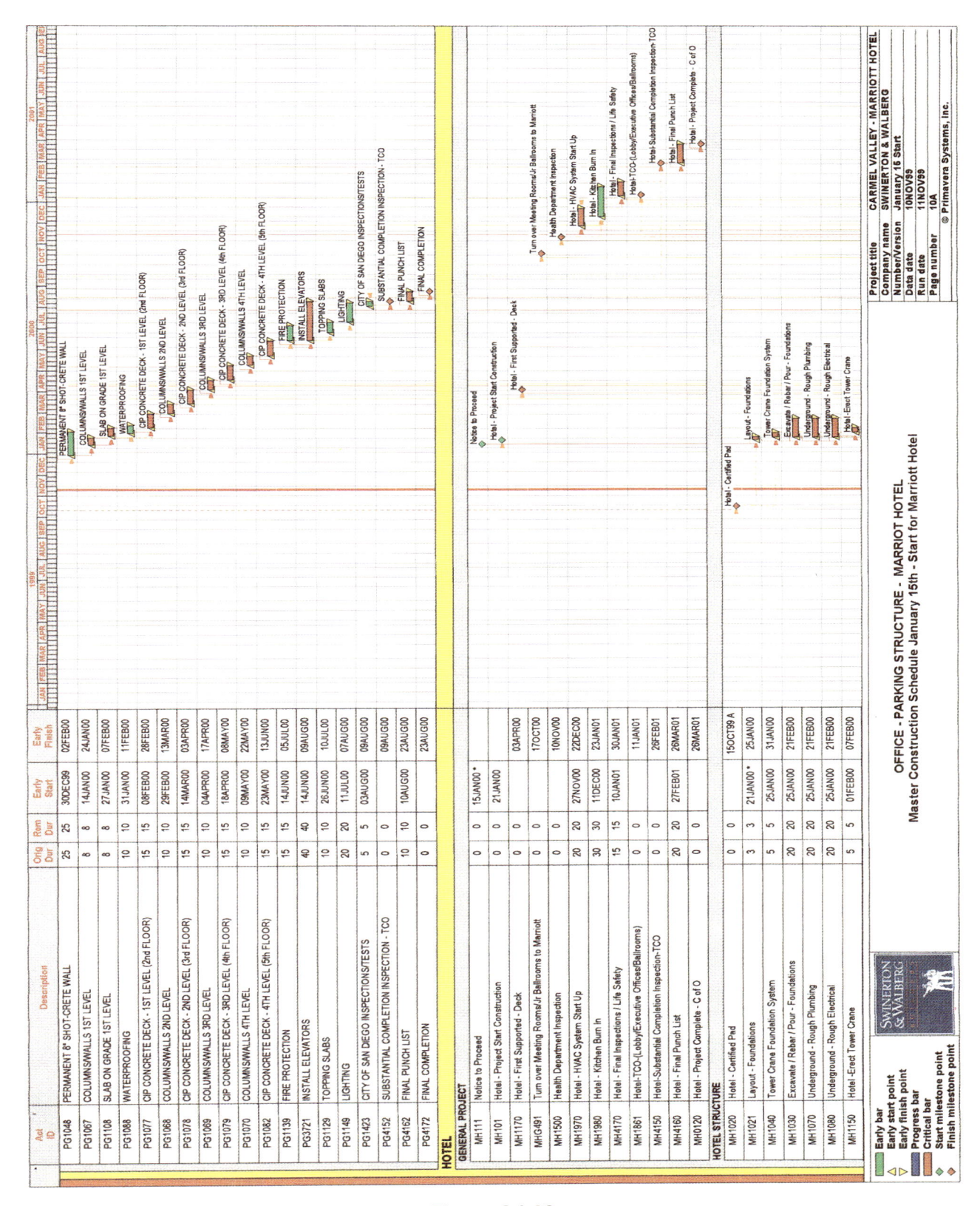

Figure 34-12

01 SITE PLAN
NOT TO SCALE

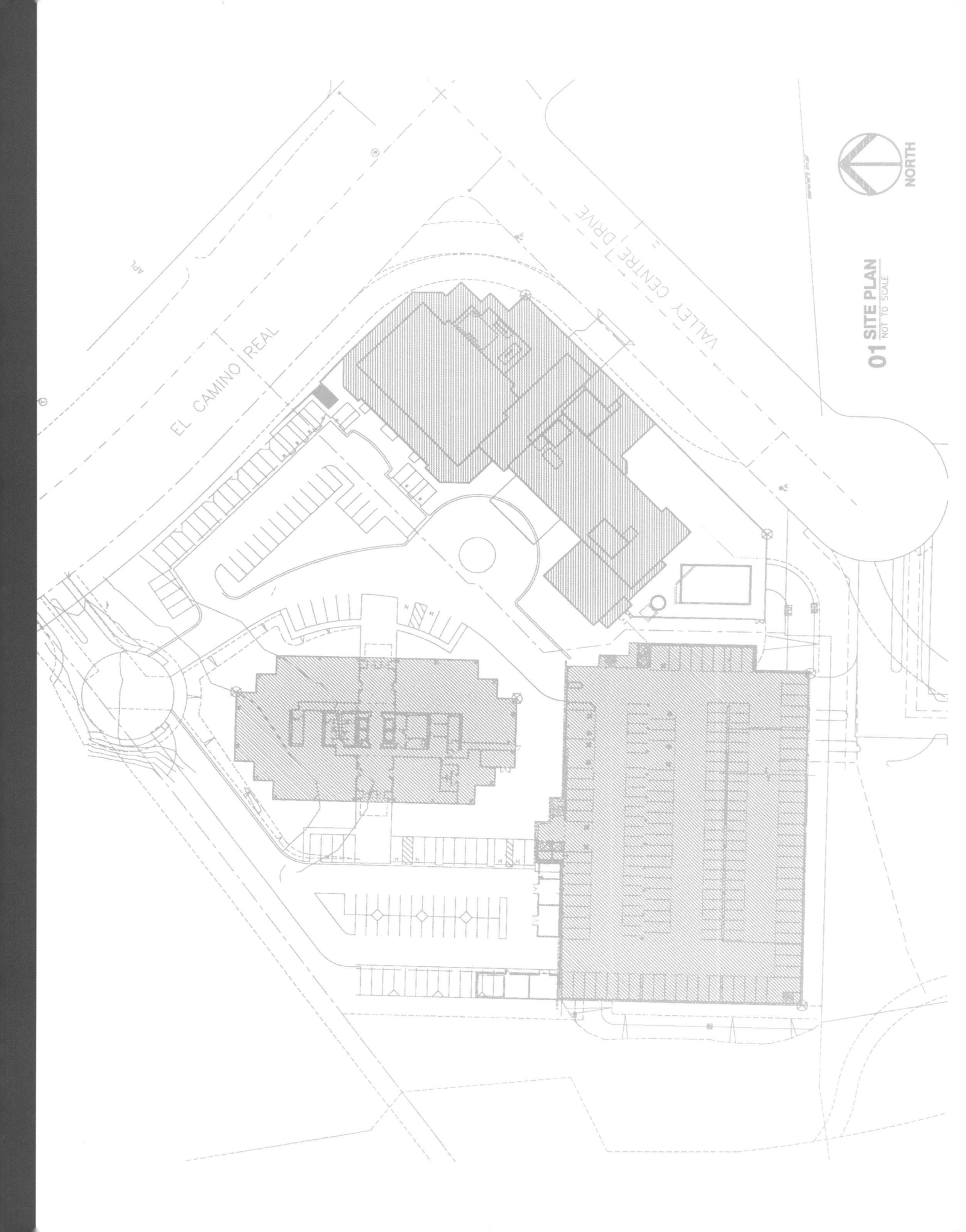

THE CONSTRUCTION PROCESS

35

Construction of a building is a complex management task, frequently involving scores of subcontractors and major material suppliers and the on-site work of hundreds (sometimes thousands) of tradesmen. In addition, there are many sub-subcontractors and material suppliers to each subcontractor and many more persons fabricating special materials at off-site locations. It requires appropriate staging and storage areas and the efficient transfer of materials and personnel to the point of use. It represents a very large coordination and monitoring effort.

The full scope of construction management is an extensive text of its own, and beyond the scope of this one. This discussion will be limited to the control and testing activities for which the Development Officer should take primary responsibility.

The construction process really contains two distinct functions—the construction of the base building, the shell and core, which most of this text has addressed—and the installation of the Tenant Improvements. The shell and core represents the entire enclosed structure, public areas, completely finished core areas on each floor, and basic central mechanical, electrical and life safety systems. The detailed discussion of the breakpoint between the shell and core work and the Tenant Improvement work was determined during the Market Study and is covered in the Tenant Improvement portion of Chapter 30.

The base building development process is market-driven and most decisions are based on the Development Officer's interpretation of that market. The Tenant Improvement construction is the implementation of the contractual agreements negotiated in the leases.

A recent practice, becoming almost mandatory, is to control the project information flow through an Internet-based Project Management System as discussed in Chapter 14. The inclusion of web cameras continually monitoring the site is an important part of this effort to keep team members as fully informed as possible as the work progresses.

Base Building Construction

This section discusses the Notice to Proceed, cost control, schedule control, shop drawings and testing, paperwork flow, substantial completion, and generally the Development Officer's role through this period. It is normally found that with the importance of the leasing program, and the likelihood of the Development Officer initiating investigations on potential new projects, the construction project is usually best controlled by a construction manager reporting directly to the Development Officer.

The general contractor has been involved in the project for months through the design, estimating and planning phases. At an agreed upon time a proposed Guaranteed Maximum Price, a detailed statement of total base building construction cost prepared by the contractor, is submitted to the owner for approval. There should be no cost surprises at this time since the GMP has gradually evolved and been refined throughout the design process, and been tentatively approved at each step.

When the owner accepts the GMP, the construction process normally starts with a detailed

Notice to Proceed (NTP) from the owner to the contractor. Based on the agreement between owner and contractor, the General Conditions and Supplementary Conditions are executed along with the Notice To Proceed. The Notice To Proceed for the Guaranteed Maximum Price contract includes the following elements:

- The Guaranteed Maximum Price with the detailed project estimate.

- Agreement between the owner and contractor, which has been previously agreed to as to form, and is executed as part of this Notice to Proceed.

- General and Supplementary Conditions, which have previously been agreed to as to form.

- The contract documents, listing every drawing, specification or sketch, or other information, and applicable revision numbers and dates, on which the Guaranteed Maximum Price was based.

- The proposed start date and a detailed project schedule, usually in bar chart form, with the "early start" dates in tabular form.

- Any special design details that could not be estimated at that time, indicating an allowance and the basis therefore. These allowances should be resolved as expeditiously as possible to ensure sufficient time for redesign, if necessary, to remain within the allowance.

- Staffing levels and specified key individuals.

- A specific list of issues to which the contractor takes exception and states are not included in the estimate.

- Any qualifications the contractor believes necessary to protect him from major losses, subject to owner acceptance.

- Normally includes a detailed list of unit prices, most commonly for use in tenant work, to protect the owner and/or tenant from excess cost, particularly by mechanical and electrical subcontractors.

- Procedure for approval and use of the contingency funds.

- Terms of the profit sharing agreement, if any, relative to savings from the GMP.

- Vendor agreements or specialty contractors under contract to owner.

- Penalty or bonus provisions, if any.

The most common formula for profit sharing has typically been 75% to the owner and 25% to the contractor, usually with a maximum on the contractor's participation—such as up to a specified percentage of his base fee. Many contractors today, however, do not request any cost saving participation, returning all savings to the owner. All remaining contingency funds are returned to owner.

While it is stated above that the Notice to Proceed normally starts the construction process, it is not unusual for construction work to be authorized earlier so as to preorder or contract for long-lead-time materials or services, or to perform preliminary work at the site. In such case it is necessary to enter into a short form contract to financially protect the contractor and owner, and to insure that all necessary insurance is in place. It may be necessary to obtain approval from the construction lender in some cases. In the event of work on-site when the loan is not already in place, in states where this process is legal, a dummy Deed of Trust should be placed on the property for future assignment to the lender, in order to avoid the mechanics liens having priority over the construction loan.

Cost control does not end with the Notice to Proceed. Most GMPs contain a certain allowance for work that was not completely designed and priced at the time it was necessary to enter into the GMP. This is because the construction timing is frequently dictated by the requirements of the market or of a major tenant rather than final completion of the contract documents. The most common items carried as allowances are lobbies, elevator cabs, signage, retail or amenity areas where applicable, or other specially detailed areas. The Development Officer must exercise close control over the allowances to ensure the architect designs within the allowance, and that the contractor carefully evaluates the proposed design to accomplish that result.

The construction contingency, to some agreed upon limit, is to protect the contractor and covers issues that were presumably covered in the GMP, whose impact was not fully anticipated by the contractor. The contingency is sometimes carried within the contract, and sometimes is carried separately by the owner. In either case, the Development Officer must exercise joint control with the contractor over the contingency to ensure that it is used properly. It is important for the developer to carry a further construction contingency to cover unanticipated changes in scope.

The buyout period, wherein the contractor lets the various subcontracts that were not let before the Notice to Proceed is a period that requires close cooperation between the owner and contractor. Because of the financial obligation undertaken by the contractor under the GMP, they have the basic right to let each subcontract to the lowest qualified bidder. Notwithstanding the above, the contractor should advise the owner in each case, in the event the owner has a valid reason to object or prefers another subcontractor. If the owner prefers a subcontractor whose price exceeds the lowest-qualified bidder, the premium should be treated as a change order and the GMP increased. Conversely, if the contractor strongly believes the selected bidder will perform better and be more dependable as to the schedule, the owner should accept that advice. It is also important for the owner to be aware of the cost and details of each subcontract so as to continually be able to judge the potential of possible savings—there may be a desirable use for those funds.

The early weeks after the Notice to Proceed hold the most risk for the timing and smooth control of the project, and the Development Officer should monitor this period very carefully. This is the period in which the contractor's field personnel review the contract documents thoroughly and will normally find many details that are missing, in conflict or appear difficult to construct. At the same time, the subcontracts are being let and the subcontractors are reviewing the documents in the same manner, both identifying conflicts and also suggesting modifications to accelerate construction, reduce cost or improve the project schedule. In addition, for contracts let prior to final permit approvals, there are likely to be changes resulting from the permit process.

It is very important that all submissions to the architect are thoroughly reviewed by the general contractor and that suggestions regarding constructability are included in a constructive manner, along with the description of the issue. Alternatively, the architect must, rather than trying to defend his work, promptly review each submission as to its reasonableness and return the response that is in the best interests of the project. In the absence of full cooperation between all parties, this is the period in the project schedule that provides the greatest likelihood of schedule delays.

At the same time, the general and subcontractors are submitting their shop (or fabrication) drawings and information on all prefabricated and purchased materials for approval. The architect and the engineers will review these shop drawings and samples submitted by the contractor, subcontractors, and suppliers. Any modifications or rejections by the architect or engineers must be corrected and resubmitted for approval prior to fabrication or installation. Minor changes should be marked "approved as noted," with resubmission waived. In addition, catalogue cuts, wiring diagrams and other technical data must be submitted for approval prior to the purchase of equipment. The Development Officer must advise the architect that all samples of materials that are visible in any spaces are also to be personally reviewed. Equipment submittals are additionally to be reviewed by the construction manager and/or the Property Management representative.

At the same time the architect or engineer reviews for technical acceptance, the general contractor reviews each submission for timeliness, conformance with the subcontract, and proper coordination with other trades. These submissions and reviews can become a major timing issue and seriously impact the project schedule if not initiated, reviewed and coordinated promptly. At the start of construction, the general contractor must develop and maintain a submittal log of all anticipated submissions, indicating their required and actual dates, and the approval status.

It is not uncommon for both the contractor and the architect to posture somewhat during this period, providing submissions and answers that are not fully thought out, delaying responses due to not having provided sufficient qualified staff for these reviews, or appear to have some particular agenda. If such a situation should occur, it is up to the Development Officer to step in and clearly direct the offending parties to modify their approach to suit the best interests of the project. Full enthusiastic cooperation is essential to a successful project. Delays in submittals and approvals at this stage may result in lost time that cannot be recaptured at a later date.

Close cost control is required in reviewing and processing change orders for the many minor changes or issues that arise. These changes result from exceeding the allowances discussed above, changes requested by the owner, those mandated by the reviewing authority during the permit process, conflicts or errors in the architectural details that the contractor could not have reasonably anticipated, tenant required changes, or *force majeure* issues in accordance with the contract. Some contractors try to claim changes for every detail on the drawings that is not clear or missing, but a well-drawn contract requires that any work that is clearly inferred from the contract documents is included in the GMP. It is important to have a general contractor who feels he is a full team member, and protects the owner from any unnecessary costs for required changes.

A major concern and responsibility of the Development Officer is to ensure the project maintains its schedule. Where issues occur that cause a delay, **and they will,** the schedule must be reanalyzed to determine how to make up for that delay. Schedule delays can greatly increase project costs through additional interest carry costs, increased general conditions, lost rental income and potential tenant penalties. In addition to the prompt processing of contractor submittals, discussed previously, delayed material deliveries can place the schedule at risk.

In-house, or contract, construction managers serve as the Development Officer's key representative throughout the construction process. Their experience and construction expertise is invaluable in properly supervising this work. The construction manager provides the necessary day-to-day oversight, and has primary responsibility for the administration of the construction contract.

Normally the Development Officer spells out the schedule requirements, monitors progress and leaves the detailed administration to the construction manager and contractor. But in unusual

---

The author has strong feelings about physically checking the status of material whose delivery is critical to the job schedule. It is not uncommon for suppliers to tell you what you want to hear rather than provide an accurate status. A trip to the factory or fabrication plant can frequently pay dividends, and is recommended as good practice for critical delivery items.

Toward the end of the construction of the First National Bank of Chicago, the delivery of a significant amount of bronze material was starting to become critical. The contractor was calling almost daily and getting what appeared to be satisfactory status reports but some of the information seemed inconsistent. One day, the contractor's project manager and I decided to fly to Minneapolis to personally view the status and determine its impact on the project. We arrived at the plant shortly after 4 PM and, when they took us out into the fabrication area, we found that no one was working and all of our bronze stock was still in its crates, just as it had been received. They were so embarrassed that before we left that night they had called some workers in to uncrate the material so that work could start the following morning. They also guaranteed that they would work two shifts until the work was finished and shipped. Several additional visits verified the schedule, and the last piece was installed on the day before our grand opening.

circumstances, he must step in and direct the activities in more detail in order to accomplish a necessary result. The case below was one of those instances.

The site must be maintained in a clean and safe manner for the protection of the tradesmen working on the project. In addition, the site should be kept as presentable as possible to assist in showing the building to brokers and prospective tenants.

While it is important to obtain the most highly qualified general contractor available, choosing good subcontractors (not necessarily the lowest bidder), and having a good set of well-coordinated drawings and specifications, and good inspection and testing are essential to a successful project.

The architect will provide job site inspection (or observation) on a part-time or full-time basis, depending on the scope of the project and the terms of their agreement. Their role is to make periodic inspections of the work (with legal waivers of responsibility as to any improper work) to verify conformance with the contract documents, provide supplemental details where the intent of the drawings is not clear, resolve technical disputes on intent between subcontract trades, approve partial and final payments, and review and approve field

> Virtually every tenant lease has a clause in which a rent commencement date is set forth based on the performance of the parties. If the landlord is late in making the space available, the rent is waived until such time as this obligation is satisfied. At the same time, if the space is otherwise available, the tenant must meet his obligations so that the space will be ready for their occupancy or pay rent as if they had not delayed their work. More often than not, those parties fulfill their obligations and the issue becomes moot. Other times, one party may miss their obligations by a few weeks to their financial detriment. We encountered an extreme case regarding this issue in a building in Dallas some years ago with a 350,000 square foot lease to a major bank.
>
> The tenant had negotiated extreme conditions as a test for whether the landlord met his obligations regarding completion of the base building—even to the point where every flower had to be planted and the building completed almost to perfection—far beyond the normal requirements. We agreed to these conditions because we anticipated the tenant would be as anxious to move in as we were to receive the rent. In this particular case the tenant had drastically changed their design plans at a late date and was not prepared to occupy the space for more than four months after the contractual rent commencement date.
>
> Anticipating they would hold us to the letter of the lease regarding landlord's obligations, and recognizing that our obligations were abnormal in the eyes of any contractor personnel, I described our requirements to the superintendents about two months prior to the rent commencement date. Since they obviously did not fully accept my stated requirements, I started weekly tours where I would point out the types of details that had to be completed. I knew they were rolling their eyes and chuckling to themselves, as buildings are rarely completed to that extent at the Certificate of Occupancy. We continued the tours every week until finally they either became convinced of the requirement, or they just decided to humor me. On the rent commencement date, after a tour with the chief financial officer of the bank, we received the rent check for in excess of one-half million dollars. It took unusual pressure to convince these very good superintendents what was required, but the results were worth it. Without demanding special performance, we would never have received the first month's rent on time. Sometimes the Development Officer must step out of his normal role during construction and do whatever is required.

and laboratory tests. In addition, the architect processes the job clarification notices, change order requests and change orders. The engineers will supplement this effort within their specialties.

Field inspection, testing laboratories and review of material certification are an important part of the construction process, and essential to effective quality control. Some of the more important of these are:

- Footing and soil inspection—verification by a geotechnical and/or structural engineer that the bearing and condition of the soil are in accordance with that assumed from the soil borings.
- Forms and rebars—inspected prior to concrete pours to verify proper form design and for the correct number, size, spacing and cover of the rebars.
- Concrete—the concrete from the batch plants are controlled by several tests, and records are kept of each pour.
  - Design mixes for each class of concrete are submitted for approval, specifying the type and ratio of cement, aggregate and water, including the use of plasticizers or other admixtures.
  - Certification by the batch plant as to the conformance of each batch with the specific design mix.
  - Time stamp as to the time the ready mix truck was loaded, as too long a stay in the truck may be cause for rejection.
  - Site (and batch plant) testing for slump—usually between 3" and 5" is acceptable, depending on the pour conditions.
  - Compression strength tests for both a preliminary strength determined by a break test at 7 days, and a final break test at 28 days.
- Fabricated structural steel testing requires:
  - Mill certification as to the chemical composition of the steel,
  - X-ray inspection of thick rolled sections, and
  - Welding inspection and certification.
- Curtain wall—anchoring fasteners and structural deflection are verified, usually in a wind tunnel test.
- Stone—anchors and sample epoxy joints are tested.
- Air balance and other mechanical, electrical and fire protection tests are covered later in this chapter and in Chapters 25 through 27.

Contracts with testing laboratories should be directly with the owner to insure independence from the contractor and the architect.

Two examples of the importance of thorough construction testing programs are illustrated by the occurrences at two different project sites.

At First City Center in Dallas some de-lamination occurred in the steel plate in several of the built-up main columns. (A de-lamination is when the steel splits longitudinally and if it completely de-laminates it is the equivalent of having two pieces of steel trying to do the work of one thick piece of steel.) This problem was uncovered by a thorough field inspection program, and we immediately retained one of the foremost authorities in the country to help us evaluate and correct the problem. It was finally solved by installing dowel-like pins through the steel, welded at each side, so as to hold the two pieces rigidly together While the repairs were being made the remainder of the work was rescheduled in such a manner that we were able to maintain the end date on our construction schedule.

In contrast, a building in Chicago was using concrete caissons as the foundation. The steel shells, which served as the form during the concrete pour, were designed to be removed as

> concrete placement progressed. While pulling the steel casings, the concrete on quite a few of the caissons apparently bridged across the opening, leaving some voids. When the steel columns were placed on the caissons, several of them sunk several inches under the weight, indicating a serious problem. The void areas in the caissons were verified by core drilling. Testing was then required on every caisson and extensive repairs made to all of those where voids were found. A proper field inspection would have measured the amount of concrete in each pour and verified that amount against the height of the concrete in the caisson after the pour. This procedure should have indicated the potential void in time to correct the problem immediately. The developer filed for bankruptcy before the building was completed, and it was reported that his financial problems resulted from the costs resulting from the repairs and delay.

The owner should have the construction manager on the job site as frequently as the size of the project justifies to evaluate the performance of all parties and be aware of any problems or issues that occur, hopefully before they become serious or difficult to correct. Property Management personnel should be part of the owner's inspection team, particularly to inspect and test the mechanical and electrical equipment and the building management and security systems.

It is not unusual for an owner's or tenant's representative to believe that some portion of the work that has been covered up with finish material was installed improperly and not in accordance with the contract documents. The fairest resolution to this issue is to require the owner (or tenant) to pay for the cost of uncovering and replacing the finish material if the work in question had been installed properly. If it was incorrect, the (sub)contractor is responsible for the cost.

The paperwork required to properly control and document a construction project is extensive. A partial list of the project paperwork includes:

- Contractors daily logs
- Architect/engineer inspection report and/or daily logs
- Owner's construction manager inspection reports
- Monthly progress reports
- Job meeting minutes
- Shop drawing, sample and equipment drawing control logs
- Job clarifications
- Supplemental details
- Submittal logs
- Project control notice and record
- Request for information
- Request for information log
- Request for proposal
- Change order requests
- Change orders
- Laboratory and field test reports
- Progress payment requests
- Partial waiver of liens
- Insurance updates
- Mechanical and electrical 72-hour operating tests
- Punch lists
- Guarantees/warranties
- Substantial completion notice
- Final payment request
- Final waivers of liens
- Repetition of many of these for the tenant installation work

Regular meetings should be held throughout the construction period, usually weekly, with responsible members of the construction team as necessary—contractors, major subcontractors, major material suppliers, architect, applicable engineers, and owner's representatives. Any conflicts or drawing clarifications must be addressed—indecision among team members always results in lost time. The status of tests, shop drawings, samples and technical data is of major importance, particularly in the early stages of the project, since it is common for one's trade work to affect that of several other trades. Current adherence to schedule and projections over the next month is reviewed. **There never was a construction project that went smoothly from beginning to end. Constant monitoring to maintain the schedule requires constant reassessment and fine-tuning.**

The Development Officer must know the status of every important issue at all times—he can delegate major portions of the work, but he cannot delegate the ultimate responsibility. The Development Officer is the only one who understands all of the issues in the lending documents, each lease or prospective lease, the pro forma, building design and the construction schedule. He should participate in project meetings whenever possible, even though the in-house construction manager should normally chair the regular project meetings.

Progress billings are made monthly subject to the contractual retainer, and are reviewed for accuracy by the architect and the construction manager, and approved by the Development Officer as to the amount of work in place before being processed for payment. The normal retainer is 10% of each payment amount, but the retainer is not normally increased after the work of each subcontractor reaches 50% if the work is being performed satisfactorily. A progress payment should be made only upon receipt of a proper partial waiver of lien from each contractor, subcontractor and major material supplier requesting payment. If payment is made without a proper waiver of lien, claims can be made later by a creditor, such as a material supplier, even though payment was actually made to the contractor or subcontractor. Sometimes lender approval can delay the actual payment to the contractor as the lender formally approves each loan request prior to funding the loan draw from which the payment is made.

It is often agreed that partial payment be made for material stored at the jobsite, or at an approved off-site location, to ensure that it is available when required. Material purchased overseas is normally paid for by a letter of credit prior to loading on board a ship, which is why prior inspection at the point of origin is recommended.

The key target date on the construction schedule is the Temporary Certificate of Occupancy. This is the time when all code required issues and life safety systems have been completed, inspected and/or tested to the satisfaction of the applicable local agencies. Based on this certificate, tenant occupancy is then dependent on the satisfactory completion and inspection of each individual tenant area and issuance of their Certificate of Occupancy. Obtaining this certificate can be extremely important in meeting obligations to tenants and the commencement of rental income.

Timely receipt of a Temporary Certificate of Occupancy requires working closely with the various inspectors representing different departments in the local jurisdiction. In many locales the field inspector can override the approved plan check information, creating a rush to comply, as there is rarely time to appeal the decision. In other cases, particularly when there is significant construction activity, it may take several days to reschedule an inspector, even to approve a minor correction. With the new smoke control regulations, several inspectors must be scheduled simultaneously, creating the potential for delay. It is becoming prudent to allocate additional time in the construction schedule to cover these inspections.

Contractors must demonstrate the proper performance of all mechanical, electrical and other operating equipment to the owner's personnel. In addition, all such equipment and controls should be subjected to a 72-hour operating test, following an approved checklist procedure, to the satisfaction of the architect, engineer and the owner prior to substantial completion and the start of warranties.

The rough air balance from the HVAC system, and the final balance on each floor where tenant space development has been finished, should be completed by this time. The final air balance for the remaining tenant spaces should be completed as part of the TI work.

Substantial completion triggers the closeout of most cost and construction issues. It is generally defined as that time when virtually all construction work has been completed, leaving only warranty work, defined punch list items, and work mutually deferred by the owner and contractor.

Punch lists are a detailed list of specified work that is deemed to have been omitted, installed incorrectly or otherwise does not satisfy the intent of the contract documents, but which should not reasonably hold up the substantial completion of the shell and core construction, or the occupancy of any tenant space. The architect, consulting engineers, construction manager, and/or the tenant's interior designer may prepare punch lists. Sufficient funds are held back to cover the incomplete work and every effort should be made to complete the work as quickly as possible.

At final payment, final waivers of lien are required, as discussed above. For certain contractors, such as a caisson contractor, whose work is completed early in the construction period, it is reasonable for final payment along with the appropriate waiver to be processed prior to overall construction completion.

At project completion the design team will prepare a complete checklist to insure the completeness of all information and turn over all documents, including permit sets, permits, as-built drawings, as-built specifications, calculations, shop drawings, catalogue cuts and/or equipment drawings, maintenance catalogues and parts lists, wiring diagrams, change orders, clarifications, laboratory reports, inspection reports, spare parts, warranties, all related correspondence, etc. to the owner. This data will normally be indexed and filed for use and reference by Property Management, along with the remainder of the development files.

As discussed in the next chapter, the Property Management department provides invaluable assistance in proper completion and smooth initial operation of the building.

Tenant Improvement Construction

The tenant work is in many ways more difficult to manage and control than the base building construction. This is because there are frequently so many separate TI installations at various stages of completion, and the tenant finish is normally on a much higher order of quality and variety. Where there are a large number of tenants, particularly when a great deal of the TI work will be under construction prior to completion of the base building, it is usually beneficially to have a tenant construction coordinator to assist, or even be independent of, the construction manager.

The TI construction may be performed either by the base building contractor, a TI contractor under the direction of the owner, or a TI contractor under the direction of the tenant, in accordance with the respective leases. When there is a major tenant whose lease is intended to commence at the approximate time of the Certificate of Occupancy for the base building, it is exceedingly important to have negotiated a requirement that the tenant utilize the base building general contractor to construct the TI work. There will be a high degree of interrelationship of the work, and conflicts over temporary utilities, staging and storage areas, hoisting and personnel lifts. Each contractor will tend to blame any of their shortcomings and delays on the other contractor, creating disputes. It is further beneficial to endeavor that the tenant use the same MEP subcontractors and/or engineers to ensure a continuous flow of the work and unit responsibility for these important systems.

A Tenant Information Manual should have been prepared early in the design process to advise the tenant and their designers as to required material and system specifications, standard details, any physical limitations, and outline necessary construction information to help facilitate the smooth development of tenant's space plans.

Each tenant's space development is a project of its own, and must be treated as such—it has most of the elements of a large project. Usually, for a tenant space development project of any significant size, a separate schedule is developed and integrated into the master project schedule. Usually it is important for the construction manager or the tenant construction coordinator to develop a TI preconstruction schedule for the Development Officer as discussed in Chapter 34, including all submissions and tenant written approvals, to insure that there will be no holdups in starting the construction or the receipt of rentals.

In accordance with the lease, the design of a tenant's space may be performed by an interior design firm selected and under the direction of the owner, initial space planning by the owner's designer with detailed finish design by the tenant's architect, or designed entirely by the tenant's architect. When the design is by the tenant's designer, the owner's responsibility is to track the design progress and thoroughly review the design documents to ensure the design complies with the tenant standards and energy usage limitations, and is completed within the schedule, or else is subject to tenant delay provisions.

When design is under the direction of the owner, there is responsibility for a design that satisfies the tenant, is completed within the agreed upon cost and meets the required schedule. A space planning authorization form should be used to ensure the tenant agrees to the cost for the basic service and any tenant changes that would increase the design cost.

When the cost of the TIs for each tenant have been prepared, it is essential to immediately have a tenant expenditure authorization prepared and executed by the tenant, indicating the party financially responsible for all costs. As the work progresses, each tenant change must be immediately documented by a tenant change order request and a tenant change order. Many tenants are relatively inexperienced in this type of work and, therefore, many opportunities exist for miscommunication. It is not unusual for a tenant to insist they absolutely require a certain change, and then change their mind when they learn the cost. If you have been too cooperative and commenced the work prior to a written authorization, a major dispute can occur.

As important as it is to control the costs of Tenant Improvements, it is just as important to closely monitor and control the schedules. Delayed rental income due to improperly documenting tenant delays throughout the process can be very expensive. This control, however, must be performed in a positive and cooperative manner to assist in establishing a positive long-term relationship with the tenant.

As the work progresses, the interior architect performs the role played by the architect for the base building.

It is essential that all tenant design drawings be carefully reviewed for adherence to building standards and for any negative impact on the base building.

At the Del Mar Executive Center in San Diego we had one tenant whose electrical load for equipment was significantly higher than the allowance in the HVAC design, and this was indicated clearly on the tenant's design submission. This was completely missed by the individuals responsible for checking the tenant drawings, and the problem was not discovered until there was difficulty encountered in controlling the heat load in the summer.

Even though our lease required the tenant be responsible for changes resulting from an electrical load that exceeded the lease provisions, the corrections cost considerably more after the fact than if they had been caught originally. For that reason we ended up splitting the costs of correcting the problem, which we would not have been obligated to do if we had caught the issue at the appropriate time.

CASE STUDY

The general contractor set up their field organization with a very senior executive scheduled to spend the majority of his time at the job site (not charged to General Conditions) to oversee both the office building and the hotel construction. He was supported by a senior project manager, field engineer, superintendent and clerk for each project. Other personnel were supplied on a part-time basis.

Meetings were held at the site each week from the beginning of grading through final completion with the Prentiss construction manager and Development Officer, the architect's project administrator, applicable consultants and the contractor project team. All issues from permits, design questions and/or conflicts, shop drawing status, and other open issues affecting the schedule were discussed each week.

The delays in completing the Land Purchase Agreement, Substantial Conformance Determination, lot line adjustment, grading permit and building permit, combined with the early lease to Brandes for five floors with an early occupancy date of August 15, 2000 created a very tight schedule, and basically drove the timing and many of the decisions. As a matter of fact, at the time construction commenced the schedule indicated completion would be more than a month and one-half late and that two months of penalties would be incurred under the lease, and almost $400,000 of rental income would be deferred.

It was necessary to take advantage of every possible opportunity to expedite the construction process so as to reduce the penalties and accelerate the rental income. This ultimately required letting separate contracts for the curtain wall, structural steel, elevators, concrete, grading, foundation, rebars and soil-nailing, in addition to the MEP contractors, prior to obtaining building permits, having a GMP, or even having an executed construction contract. Most of these contracts were bid on scope, or incomplete contract documents.

Actually, 70% of the office building cost and 50% of Prentiss' total construction cost was let in advance of obtaining the necessary permits. This is not a recommended procedure as it clearly added cost control risk, and required monitoring every issue very closely. This procedure was necessary in order to minimize the impact of the penalties and delayed rental income under the Brandes Lease.

The curtain wall contract was really bid on a scope basis as a design-build type contract based on the architect's elevations and details, with most of the details worked out after selecting Walters & Wolfe. This was easier than normal in this situation, because Walters & Wolfe was proposing to utilize most of the basic components from a project then under construction. The process went smoothly, and everyone was pleased with the result.

The soil-nailing contract for the retaining wall at the parking structure was also bid on a design-build basis, based on criteria set by the structural engineer. Design-build is frequently the best method for letting this type of work, as the subcontractor designs it, subject to the engineer's approval, and takes full responsibility. The contractor was Schnabel Foundation Company, well-known for difficult subsurface construction.

Approval was received from Pardee to permit entering upon the site two weeks prior to closing in order to perform the grading survey, staking, place trailers and start installation of the temporary utilities in return for holding them harmless.

It was planned to commence grading immediately after closing on the land on September 10. When the grading permit was delayed, the grading was started without it on September 20, and the office portion of the work was virtually complete before the permit was received on October 27.

The contractor advised that the first official inspection made by the city inspectors would be to inspect the rebars and excavation prior to the first concrete pour for the foundation. The city does not approve the certified pad, relying on the owner's testing agency. The city at first indicated a willingness to grant one or two gratuitous inspections prior to permit issuance, but later advised they had terminated that practice.

A decision was made to complete the work as far as possible. The pad was certified on October 7, and excavation for the entire office building foundation proceeded immediately. Installation of the rebar was completed on October 26, ready for inspection by the testing agency. The building permit was received about noon the next day, the city inspectors approved the work late that afternoon, and the first pour was started at 7 AM the following morning.

In order to complete the excavation for the parking structure and not interfere with the start of the office building, it was necessary to install the soil-nailed retaining wall almost immediately. Difficulty was encountered getting the permit for the wall released by the structural permit section, even though the wall was designed by a reputable foundation contractor, approved by the structural engineer and reviewed by the geotechnical engineer. They finally requested an analysis of the wall's ability to resist seismic loads without benefit of the resistance of the tendrels. When this analysis was positive, and approved, the retaining wall permit was obtained. In the meantime the Development Officer took advantage of the fact that the soil nailed wall is installed in two operations, a 4" initial wall to retain the soil, and the 8" reinforced concrete final retaining wall section, as discussed in depth in Chapter 18. It was rationalized that the 4" wall section was temporary shoring and did not require a permit. Construction of the soil-nailing was started and completed to the fourth level, or more than one-half of the wall, prior to receiving the permit. The building permit for the parking structure was not received until January 7, 2000.

In spite of all of the delays and concerns, the first floor slab of the building was completely poured prior to the time the structural steel was scheduled for release from the shop. The first day that steel erection started using a 150-ton mobile crane, the first significant construction problem was encountered—the anchor bolts were too short. A week was lost, but the problem solved by designing a coupler, having it approved by the structural engineer and tested, chipping out clearance around the existing bolts, cutting off the existing bolts, then installing and grouting the coupler. The concrete contractor who made the mistake worked through the Thanksgiving weekend to correct the situation and be ready for steel erection on Monday morning.

The steel erection went reasonably well, even though one day was lost to a strike by the crane operator, who objected to the nonunion man-hoist operator, and almost a week due to changes to the steel members on the roof. Most of the time was made up by the simpler edge angle condition discussed in Chapter 19. The rain delayed concrete pour on the eighth floor and roof decks delayed the start of the curtain wall erection by one week. The steel contractor claimed what was considered to be excessive payment requests due to the roof changes and some changes required by the city permit review. Resolution of this and other change orders is discussed later in this chapter.

Even though Otis was the low bidder for the elevators, there was extensive negotiation before the contract was agreed upon to insure that at least one elevator would be operational prior to completion of the curtain wall. This was important in order to remove the temporary hoist and install the missing sections of the wall while the tradesmen were still on the job, so as to not hold up the Tenant Improvement work. They missed the date by a week-and-a-half, but the curtain wall was completed in time to avoid affecting the tenant work. Property Management reviewed and approved the proposed maintenance contract prior to award.

Once the MEP work reached the point that all of the shop drawings and submittals were approved, all major material ordered, and all risers under construction a series of meetings was scheduled to review the commissioning and testing of those systems. It was essential to reduce the originally requested time by over a month in order to meet the schedule obligations. All MEP subcontractors, BMS and control contractor, the general contractor, Prentiss operating engineers and Schirmer Engineering participated in a detailed review of the process. As a result of these meetings, a schedule was developed that indicated obtaining the Temporary C of O about one week prior to the completion date under the Brandes Lease (discussed in Chapter 32), irrespective of any potential tenant delay. The progress toward this result was followed several times a week to ensure the preparatory work was completed, and daily once testing had started.

Because of the schedule concerns, primarily due to the life safety and smoke control tests, which could not commence until all systems were finished, the contractors were pressed to have the permanent electrical power available by mid-June and the major pieces of equipment installed by late June. This left three weeks for the hookup, installation and calibration of all controls, and four weeks for initial testing of all equipment and controls, corrections, and final testing for the city and fire department inspectors. The inspectors witnessed the tripping of every alarm device that could indicate a fire condition, and verified the proper response of all controls and equipment.

The Brandes space development was as critical as the base building, as landlord was responsible for its completion and the Certificate of Occupancy. Brandes was responsible for the design, approval of the contractor's cost estimate and Notice to Proceed, and receipt of the building permit in accordance with a rigid schedule. The design submissions were received as scheduled, but the permit was received 21 days late, however, they had released some of their work prior to receiving the permit and objected to the claim of a tenant delay.

Brandes had many special design issues as discussed in Chapter 30. The most important of these was the stairway connecting the 6th, 7th and 8th floors. Their stairway design was not completed in time to provide the framed structural opening as erection progressed, but the opening was blocked out so the deck would not be poured in that area. The steel was changed at a later date, and the floors were finished. A second issue regarding the stair was that the smoke control requirements were integrated with the base building for test and Certificate of Occupancy purposes. Approval of the stairway was conditioned upon its not delaying the base building C of O, and that Brandes would be responsible for the cost of restoring the floor at the end of their tenancy unless they renewed their lease through the 16th year.

The Brandes MEP contracts were bid prior to submitting the TI for permit review, because:

- The light fixtures, mixing boxes and some of the other materials were potential long lead purchase items
- By the time the building permits were issued the floors would be ready for the mechanical and electrical rough-in

All of the base building MEP contractors were low bidders and were awarded the contracts for this work, which greatly facilitated the coordination, scheduling and completion.

As project completion approached, Brandes requested permission to commence installing their modular furniture and equipment approximately ten days prior to the agreement date. While this had the potential for delaying some of the TI work, it was agreed to in order to facilitate their occupancy, but in return they agreed to a ten-day grace period on any potential landlord delay penalty.

The Temporary C of O on the base building was received on August 14, and the base building portion of the Certificate of Occupancy for the Brandes space was approved at the same time. Brandes was prevented from receiving the C of O for its floors because the electrical wiring in its modular furniture was in progress. This problem was solved by temporarily terminating all incomplete wiring at junction boxes, and then completing the installation after the certificate was received. Brandes obtained their C of O on August 22 and made their initial move-in, along with Heritage Golf on August 25.

The parking structure had its own set of schedule issues. The schedule was extremely tight even before realizing everyone had missed a note on the structural drawings requiring a 75-day delay after post-tensioning each slab prior to completing the pour strip left open for the post-tensioning operation. As the schedule was very tight in order to obtain the C of O for the parking structure by the time the C of O was required for the building, a delay in approval of the parking could trigger the completion penalty under the Brandes Lease. After extensive discussion with the structural engineer, the waiting period after the last pour was reduced to 45 days, based on a willingness to accept some minor surface cracking. The city inspector agreed that the top deck could be barricaded off until that pour strip was completed without affecting our Certificate of Occupancy, if necessary, since the hotel was a year away from completion and the full parking structure was not required until then.

A further issue on the parking structure was that after completing the concrete pours and stripping away all of the form work, the necessary masonry enclosures for elevator shafts and equipment rooms had to be constructed, the elevators installed and the electrical, ventilation, plumbing and life safety systems completed. The inspector agreed that only the two elevators serving the office building had to complete in order to satisfy the C of O. The parking structure actually received its C of O for the plaza level on August 14, and the remainder was approved on August 31.

The hotel was delayed considerably as discussed in Chapter 7. They finally started construction on July 17, 2000. The surface area adjacent to the hotel and most of the landscaping between the main driveway and El Camino Real are required for staging area during construction of the hotel. Under a revised agreement with the hotel developer, work in these areas has been deferred to suit their schedule, but they will assume full responsibility for any additional costs incurred.

JMI, the new hotel owner, installed the necessary well-detailed painted fence to separate their construction from our building area as agreed. All internal roadways for the project have been installed, as well as most of the landscaping outside of the construction fence. JMI and the contractor have agreed to move the temporary construction offices at their expense, as the structures would have too much impact on the office building's appearance to remain for a year. This work was delayed until after the receipt of the office building C of O so as to not impact its issuance.

Because the site work had been under contract to Prentiss, and since the work inside the construction fence would be delayed at least a year, an arrangement was worked out with JMI to assume the remainder of the work, with the costs allocated appropriately.

The hotel footing excavation was barely underway when they found a seam of clay that appeared to be unable to provide the 6,000 psf bearing required to support the footings. After further soil testing it was determined the bearing was satisfactory.

The current schedule for hotel completion of the hotel as this book goes to press is October 15, 2001.

There were a large number of change order requests, on the office building and parking structure, many determined to be invalid. Many of these requests were passed on from the subcontractors without any evaluation being made as to their validity under the contract documents. Toward the end of the project there were almost $400,000 of unresolved change order requests—almost one-half from the steel fabricator for claimed changes and delays—which were felt to be largely invalid. They were all settled, including a $25,000 bonus for completion prior to the penalty date and Prentiss' waiver of the benefit of any GMP savings, for approximately $100,000. It was believed that Swinerton could best resolve the steel claim if it was their own money, since Herrick was a frequently used subcontractor. It was later discovered that most of the potential savings the contractor had counted upon to cover other costs never materialized.

As examples of the paperwork flow, Figure 35-1 is one page of a typical submittal log, which is prepared early in the project to serve both as a checklist of required information and as a record of the submittals and approvals. In preparing this log the contractor tries to anticipate every submittal so as to be able to determine when submittals are late. Each one is tracked until returned to the subcontractor for purchase and/or installation.

One page of an RFI, a chronological list of requests for information, and their disposition, is shown as Figure 35-2. The current open items are shown in the open RFI list that is reviewed at each project meeting in order to focus on the open issues as shown in Figure 35-3. (Item 35 that appears to be over a month late is misleading; the expedited portion had been completed, but one follow-up issue remains.)

Figure 35-4 is the Project Reference Log (a nice expression for an open change order log). It is kept open until a change order is written to the contract.

SWINERTON & WALBERG
Del Mar Gateway Office Building, Parking Structure & Landscape/Sitework
S&W Job #9954-22

SUBMITTAL LOG

Print date: 3/15/00

Status:
P=Pending
A=Approved
RS=Resubmit

SUBMITTAL #	JOB	SUB	DESCRIPTION	Rec'd from Subcontractor	To Architect	Requested Return Date	Rec'd from Architect	Returned To Sub	Status
02300-01	SITE	SMI-site	Site Utilities product data, specifications & material submittal	12/20/99	1/17/00	2/11/00	2/14/00	2/14/00	RS
02300-01.1	SITE	SMI-site	Pipe, valve, fire hydrant & water assembly resubmittal	2/15/00	2/17/00	2/25/00	2/29/00	3/1/00	A
02520	SITE		Site Concrete paving finishes						
02621	SITE		Foundation drainage system						
02764	SITE		Pavement joint sealants						
02810	SITE		Irrigation						
02840	SITE		Parking Accessories						
02844	PS/SITE		Cable guardrail system						
02860	SITE		Site furnishings						
02900	SITE		Landscaping						
03100	SITE		Concrete formwork						
03150	SITE		Concrete accessories						
03200-01	OB	PCS	Foundation & metal deck rebar shop drawings - (A1,A2,B1-B3)	10/12/99	10/14/99	10/29/99	11/16/99	11/16/99	A
03200-02	PS	PCS	PS: Foundation, decks & columns shop drawings - (A1, B1-B10, C1-C6)	1/12/00	1/27/00	2/8/00	2/9/00	2/10/00	A
03200-03	PS	PCS	PS: PT slab shop drawings & calculations (PT1 - PT11)	2/10/00	2/14/00	2/22/00	2/29/00	3/1/00	A
03200-04	PS	PCS	PS: Rebar shop drawing - East shear wall (C7)	2/10/00	2/14/00	2/17/00	2/29/00	3/1/00	A
03300-01	OB	JR	Concrete design mix for columns, wall, structural slabs & beams	10/1/99	10/1/99	10/9/99	10/9/99	10/9/99	A
03300-02	OB	JR	Concrete design mix for footings, grade beams & fill on metal deck	10/1/99	10/1/99	10/9/99	10/9/99	10/9/99	A
03300-03	OB	JR	Concrete design mix for fill at metal deck	10/1/99	10/1/99	10/9/99	10/9/99	10/9/99	A
03300-04	OB	JR	Concrete design mix for slab on grade	11/4/99	11/8/99	11/8/99	11/8/99	11/8/99	A
03300-05	OB	JR	Control joints at slab on grade						
03300-06	OB	JR	Curing compound at slab on grade and metal decks	11/7/99	11/7/99	11/8/99	11/8/99	11/8/99	A
03300-07	OB	JR	Grout specification for under columns	11/10/99	11/10/99	11/12/99	12/3/99	12/3/99	A
03300-08	OB	JR	Alternate concrete design mix and accelerating admixture specifications	12/20/99	12/20/99	12/23/99	12/23/99	12/27/99	A
04200-01	SITE	Geogrid	Geogrid site walls approved by City						
04220	OB	Lyons	CMU						
04402	OB		Stone countertops at RR						A
04851	OB	W&W	Exterior stone cladding (see 08920 - W&W submittal)						A
05065	OB	JD2	Welded stud connectors (see 05300-01 - JD2 submittal)						A
05120-01	OB	THC	Erection drawings (E1-E10, E12, E13) - (THC subm #2)	8/12/99	8/16/99	8/25/99	9/1/99	9/8/99	A
05120-02	OB	THC	Anchor bolts, miscellaneous, standards (AB3, D4, S4 - S21) - (THC subm #3)	8/31/99	9/1/99	9/13/99	9/10/99	10/1/99	A
05120-02A	OB	THC	Templates, anchor bolts, AB setting plan (D1, D2, AB1, AB2) - (THC subm #1)	8/5/99	8/6/99	8/18/99	8/13/99	8/20/99	A
05120-03	OB	THC	Columns and standards (S22, S25, S26, S30, D1-D8, D10-D27) - (THC subm #4)	9/13/99	9/21/99	9/24/99	10/12/99	10/15/99	A
05120-04	OB	THC	Bracing and standards (D6-D14, S4, S12, S27-S29, S31, S32) - (THC subm #5)	9/27/99	9/22/99	10/4/99	10/4/99	10/15/99	A
05120-05	OB	THC	Columns (D28-D43, D50-D59) - (THC subm #7)	9/27/99	10/1/99	10/8/99	11/11/99	11/11/99	A
05120-06	OB	THC	Erection beams (E1-E7, E12, E13, D1-D40, D57-D59) - (THC subm #6)	9/21/99	10/1/99	10/4/99	10/25/99	10/25/99	A

Figure 35-1

SWINERTON & WALBERG
Del Mar Gateway Office Building, Parking Garage & Site
S&W Job #9954-22

RFI LOG

DATE: 11/10/99

RFI #	STATUS	SUBCONTRACTOR & RFI Reference	DESCRIPTION	To Architect	Response Required By	Rec'd from Architect	Returned To Sub
16	C	Herrick #16	Ref: Beam relocation	8/16/99	8/20/99	8/23/99	8/24/99
17	C	Herrick #17	Ref: Davit Location	8/16/99	8/20/99	8/24/99	8/24/99
18	C	Herrick #18	Ref: TS Brace size clarification	8/16/99	8/20/99	8/24/99	8/24/99
19	C	Herrick #19	Ref: Deck Support	8/16/99	8/20/99	8/24/99	8/24/99
20	C	Herrick #20	Ref: Seismic column to base weld clarification	8/16/99	8/20/99	8/24/99	8/24/99
21	C	Herrick #21	Ref: Top of grade beam & top of plate clarification	8/16/99	8/20/99	8/24/99	8/24/99
22	C	Herrick #22	Ref: Top of Steel Elevation	8/26/99	9/3/99	8/27/99	8/27/99
23	C	Herrick #23	Ref: Gussett Layout	8/31/99	9/2/99	9/3/99	9/7/99
24	C	Herrick #24	Ref: Screen wall Post/Brace	9/7/99	9/8/99	9/10/99	9/10/99
25	C	Schnabel (S&W request)	Ref: Loading of soil nail wall	9/7/99	9/8/99	9/9/99	9/9/99
26	C	Herrick #25	Ref: Deck Angle Support	9/8/99	9/9/99	9/8/99	9/8/99
27	C	Naton (S&W request)	Ref: Backfill material	9/7/99	9/9/99	9/9/99	9/9/99
28	C	S&W	Ref: Elevation at top of soil nail wall	9/16/99	9/27/99	10/1/99	10/1/99
29	C	W&W (S&W request)	Ref: Electric hardware required for aluminum and glass doors	9/24/99	10/1/99	10/1/99	10/1/99
30	C	W&W #1	Ref: Which leaf of which set of doors recieves the power actuation	9/24/99	10/1/99	9/30/99	10/1/99

Figure 35-2

SWINERTON & WALBERG

Del Mar Gateway Office Building, Parking Structure & Landscape/Sitework

S&W Job #9954-22

OPEN RFI LOG

DATE: 3/15/00

RFI #	JOB	REF#	STATUS	TRADE AFFECTED	DESCRIPTION	To Architect	Response Required By	Rec'd from Architect	Returned To Sub
80	Site		C revisit 4/10/00	S&W	Ref: grading plan 9-D, 10-D & 11-D, A 1.10 18" s d line conflict due to sequencing/no construction at Hotel	11/30/99	12/10/99		
155	Office	96-OFC	O re-design	S&W M&L, Brady	Ref: ASI #5, A 2.01 03-01 Door type clarification off of Lobby entrance per ASI #5 & Permit Set	1/17/00	1/18/00		
185	Office	96-OFC	O re-design	S&W M&L	Ref: ASI #5, A 2.01 Connection of inside corners of exterior window system to walls at east & west lobbies	2/2/00	2/4/00		
186	Office	96-OFC	O re-design	S&W M&L	Ref: ASI #5, A 2.01 Door type & finish for new 3'6"x8'6" door loc btwnn East lobby & exit corr from stair #1	2/2/00	2/4/00		
227	Office		O	S&W Int'l Iron	Ref: submittal #05500-01 Revised canopy connection to bldg weld dtl due to conflict with W&W vert mullions	3/6/00	3/7/00		
231	Office		O	S&W THC, Int'l Iron	Ref: A 2.60, 1/A 2.61, S 2.05, 5/S 4.01, 4,10,13,14/S 3.01, RFI #181 & 05120-19 Penthouse TS required at top of screenwall at "K" brace locations	3/9/00	3/13/00		

Figure 35-3

```
CMB544.1                                    AS OF: 02-16-00
PAGE:   6                               PRINTED: 02-16-00 08:20
*************************************************************
                    SWINERTON & WALBERG CO.
                    PROJECT REFERENCE LOG
*************************************************************
                                            FLG: * = UPDATE COST ACCOUNTING
JOB: 995422    CARMEL VALLEY GATEWAY OFFICE      O = ORIGINAL BUDGET
                                                                          F
                REF.                  SUBMIT  COR                     OCO APPROVED L
REF. NO.        TYPE  REF DATE        DATE    NO.  PENDING  SUBMITTED APPROVED NO. DATE G
```

REF. NO.	DESCRIPTION	REF. TYPE	REF DATE	SUBMIT DATE	COR NO.	PENDING	SUBMITTED	APPROVED	OCO NO.	APPROVED DATE
0086-OFC	ADD ALT #4: FURNISH & INSTALL FIRE SPRINKLER RUN OUT LOOP FOR FUTURE T.I. WORK AT ALL FLOORS PER GMP ADD ALTERNATE #4 DATED 11/10/99.	CTO	02-09-00	02-09-00	0012		57,503.00			
0088-OFC	BRADY: PROVIDE UNFINISHED 1/4 SLICED MAPLE VENEER AT 7TH FLOOR TOTAL-DOORS.	CTO	02-09-00	02-16-00	0013		2,057.00			
0080-OFC	BRADY: CUT DOWN TOTAL DOOR FRAMES AT ALL FLOORS FROM 9'0" HIGH TO 8'6" HIGH PER HKS ASI #7 DATED 1/31/00.	CTO	01-27-00	02-16-00	0014		1,476.00			
0089-OFC	BRADY: UPGRADE ALL WOOD DOORS FROM BIRCH TO MAPLE FINISH.	CTO	02-10-00	02-16-00	0015		9,445.00			
0090-OFC	BRADY: PROVIDE POSITIVE PRESSURE WOOD DOORS PER UBC 97 REQUIREMENTS.	CTO	02-10-00	02-16-00	0016		8,974.00			
0091-OFC	BRADY: FURNISH & INSTALL POSITIVE PRESSURE TOTAL-DOORS PER UBC 97 REQUIREMENTS.	CTO	02-10-00	02-16-00	0017		1,574.00			
0093-OFC	BRADY: CHANGE TO DUAL EGRESS AT ALL TOTAL-DOORS FLOORS 2 THROUGH 8 REQUIRED BY CITY OF SAN DIEGO BUILDING DEPARTMENT.	CTO	02-11-00	02-16-00	0020		2,990.00			

```
42 REFERENCES           TOTALS:              1,762.00   360,547.00    0.00
```

Figure 35-4

ASSET and PROPERTY MANAGEMENT

36

There will be no attempt in this work to cover the extensive fields of asset management and Property Management, rather to merely summarize the way they integrate into the development process.

It should be noted, however, that the 1999 BOMA/ULI Office Tenant Survey, *What Office Tenants Want,* gave the following categories the highest rating in the survey along with air conditioning comfort:

- Building management's responsiveness
- Effectiveness of communications with building management
- Building management's ability to meet your needs
- Quality of building maintenance work

The asset managers play an important role in helping provide initial information for the Market Study, and in providing ongoing competitive and market data throughout the process.

When there are existing operations in an area considered for a development, both asset managers and Property Management personnel are of great value in providing critical information concerning area measurement, the accepted definition of shell and core construction and the preferred local market method as to the inclusion of operating costs and utilities in the quoted rental rates. The property managers are also responsible for preparing the initial and the detailed final operating expense estimate, including a breakdown of all operating costs, utilities and taxes for the pro forma.

As the project proceeds through the design phase, Property Management provides continuous information to the Development Officer as to the wearability, cleanability and maintenance issues of various materials, and the efficiency and dependability of the mechanical, electrical, plumbing, building management, security and many other systems and materials.

During the construction phase, Property Management should assist in the inspection and the testing of all mechanical, electrical and other operating equipment, including the final 72-hour operating tests and those required for fire department or other governmental approval. Property Management is also responsible for the receipt, organizing and proper filing of all leases, contracts, permits, drawings, specifications, test reports, catalogues, wiring diagrams, calculations, reports, warranties, parts lists, etc., so as to maintain a complete record of the building as completed.

The Development Officer should ensure that the Property Management department has a satisfactory and complete building inspection, commissioning, opening and startup checklist through which they will assist the Development Officer in proper completion and initial operation of the building. It must not only provide for a complete final inspection and testing, and train all personnel and contractors who will operate and maintain the building, but develop and implement detailed procedures for each facet of operations and tenant relations. Provision must be made for all supplies, equipment and spare parts necessary for proper and successful operation.

In locations where your company has insufficient properties to support highly qualified operating engineers, provision should be made to borrow the appropriate personnel from another area or region to assist in both the design review and the inspection and testing of the various systems.

During the period from initial occupancy through stabilized occupancy (definitions discussed elsewhere), the asset manager and Property Management, under the direction of the Development Officer, assume responsibility for the building operations and tenant relationships. Prior to initial occupancy, the asset and property managers must familiarize themselves with stacking plan being developed by the leasing space planner, and take full responsibility for it at stabilized occupancy. The accurate and timely maintenance of the stacking plan, along with a successful tenant retention program, is essential to the long-term profitability of the building.

At stabilized occupancy, there is a final resolution of the financial results of the completed project to the official pro forma—the Development Officer's final report card. At this point the asset manager assumes the primary responsibility for the long-term profitability of the building and the property manager assumes full responsibility for all aspects of the operation and leasing. The Development Officer should remain in an advisory role, and be available as required.

From this point forward the most important issue facing the asset manager and Property Management is tenant retention.

CONCLUSIONS

37

The foregoing text and discussion have provided the necessary information relative to the development of office buildings to promote an understanding of the process, the role of the Development Officer in that process, and the decision-making required to achieve a successful project. It has provided an understanding of the extensive skills required from the many professionals who are essential to the accomplishment of that success. In this sense, the scope should be somewhat humbling.

It has discussed the many different studies and functional elements involved in an office development project and indicated the repetitive and interdependent relationships that exist. A successful project depends on the effective use of these studies throughout the process. In review:

- The Market Study not only determines the economic potential of a proposed project, it is also an essential part of the decision-making in site selection and acquisition, determining the quality and type of design necessary to satisfy the defined market, and determining the leasing strategy. It should be reviewed for market changes prior to the decision to commence construction.

- The Site Study and political analyses determine the limitations placed on the development, many of the cost factors, and additional design issues that may be required to satisfy community desires and market acceptability.

- The pro forma is an essential tool utilized from preliminary project evaluation through site selection and acquisition, committing to close on the land, determining allowable project costs, preparing various sensitivity analyses, committing to commencement of construction, and developing alternate leasing strategies in a deteriorating market. It is the ultimate measure of project performance.

- Financing must be obtained that satisfies the owner's requirements, and the various studies and pro forma analyses must satisfy the lender's current internal criteria.

- The design of the site is impacted by satisfying all of the various limitations defined in the Site Study, and the building form and parking requirements are dictated by both the Market and Site Studies.

- The overall building size, shape, materials and design concept is developed to satisfy the requirements of the Market Study, as limited by the restrictions of the Site Studies and political analyses, and the required return as determined through the pro forma.

- The various components of the building(s) are evaluated and selected to accomplish the owners financial objectives, satisfy the visual and functional requirements from the Market Study, meet all codes and life safety requirements, reasonably minimize energy costs, maintain a compatibility between components, and maintain a uniformity of quality, all within cost limits dictated by the pro forma.

- The leasing strategies and their implementation are based on the Market Study, and its periodic updating throughout the project development phase, and various lender requirements. Successful leasing is the final indication of the accuracy and judgment applied in these studies.

- The construction process is the implementation of the design resulting from all of the various studies and analyses, and must be performed in a manner that accomplishes the schedule and cost requirements, while minimizing risk.

- Implementation by a high quality development team, with a full understanding of the project objectives as defined in these studies and interpreted by the Development Officer, significantly increases the potential of a successful project.

The text has indicated that for a project to be truly successful, both initially and for the long-term it must fit in with and satisfy the broad community interests, not only as to location and design, but in the manner in which it addresses sustainability issues and, more specifically, energy conservation. As with other issues discussed, it is essential to stay current with, and preferably be ahead of, the trend of public consensus.

The text has concentrated on many details in order to provide you with the confidence to interface with and question the various professionals involved in the project. This provides an awareness of the necessity to recognize, understand and address each of the thousands of details that must be successfully accomplished in a timely manner for your project to be successful.

As important as the details are, and overlooking a few can badly harm a project, you must never become so bogged down in details that you lose sight of the overall objectives, as previously stated in the Introduction:

- Set clear objectives for the project
- Determine the market feasibility and, if feasible, define the limitations
- Determine the political feasibility and regulatory issues, and define the strategy to overcome them
- Ascertain and manage the degree of risk
- Execute the plan by coordinating the design of a product that will satisfy the identified market at a price that will produce an acceptable yield
- Develop and implement a strategy to market and lease the building effectively
- Accomplish the result in a timely manner, and within all economic constraints

This text has not provided specific directives or solutions to the various issues you will face. It has provided a background to recognize and address issues as they arise, and the thought processes to guide you to reasonable solutions. It has repeated various themes throughout, some over and over again, which are essential in meeting the overall objectives stated above. These themes are:

- A quality Feasibility Analysis
- Understanding the issues
- Getting the most effective effort from your project team
- An effective leasing program
- Discipline and focus
- Control of the process

It is sincerely hoped that this text has been helpful and that it will be the start of developing a body of knowledge expanded by your positive and negative experiences resulting from future projects.

Superior performance requires that the Development Officer continually master and utilize all applicable technological innovations in managing the process, as well as the new systems, materials and procedures incorporated into the project. Learning is a lifelong process, and he or she must maintain their knowledge of all current trends in the field.

Some of the publications of value in obtaining current information, most of which are free for persons in the business, include *Urban Land, Buildings, National Real Estate Investor, Building Operating Management, Institutional Investor, Building Design & Construction, Corporate Design & Realty* and *Energy Decisions* and *Environmental Building News*. **But primarily you will learn by your experiences, your mistakes and most of all from your development team members.**

CASE STUDY

This has been an extremely interesting project, containing a very large number of unusual issues for one of this size. Decision-making was shared or impacted, in various degrees, with the hotel developer, Marriott, the seller, the city and the lead tenant. Some of these issues that had to be addressed were:

- Resolving the differences in objectives and proposed solutions resulting from two developers with two types of projects on a single site with a single entitlement process
- Justifying using fifteen-year-old approval rights for a 500-room hotel for a smaller hotel and an office building
- Proceeding through a unique community process
- After satisfying the community and the development and planning department as to the Substantial Conformance Determination, a legal basis was developed for their decision to provide them with political cover
- Finding a way to legally subdivide the property without opening up the process to the discretionary approval of the planning and coastal commissions
- Difficulty tying down a COREA because the hotel developer had difficulty obtaining firm requirements from the hotel and financing partner
- Satisfying the open-ended design approval rights of the seller
- Completing the design of a parking structure by satisfying the demands of the office building, hotel developer, Marriott and the seller, while meeting code and seismic issues
- Resolving issues created by having a 20-foot SDG&E easement along the two street frontages and a freeway and drainage easement on another
- The early lease of 62% of the space to a tenant with tight occupancy requirements, and with onerous penalty provisions
- Maintaining the schedule for the start of construction despite a very difficult and slow permitting process
- Letting contracts for 50% of total project construction cost prior to issuance of a building permit, execution of a construction contract or agreeing on a GMP
- Dealing with a hotel developer who was a pawn in dealings between their banker, financing partner and Marriott, who was unable to close as scheduled, and ultimately lost their interest to their lender, who in turn sold the interest in the project to another developer
- Providing a very high quality unitized granite curtain wall within the budget
- Incorporating an upgraded central centrifugal chiller without impacting the pro forma returns
- Using excessive optimism in setting the construction costs in the pro forma substantially below the then current baseline budget
- Using a relatively unusual soil-nailing procedure to create a retaining wall on one side of the parking structure to most effectively satisfy the seismic and retaining stresses, while expediting construction on the site

In spite of extensive issues and difficulties during the permitting process, the inability of the hotel developer to close on the land in a timely manner and resolve design and other issues with Marriott, the difficult schedule required to avoid penalties under the Brandes Lease, and a tight budget, the project was an unqualified success. A photograph of the building taken immediately after Substantial Completion is shown as Figure 37-1.

Figure 37-1

The constant application of pressure by the Development Officer, combined with some creativity during the permitting and construction phases succeeded in meeting the very difficult completion schedule to avoid a penalty under the Brandes Lease.

While there were overruns in many categories of the budget, in large measure caused by permitting issues and some loss of timing control resulting from the Brandes occupancy requirement, the project was completed with a total project cost per rentable square foot slightly less than the approved and adjusted pro formas, and a cash-on-cash return that was higher. The very successful lease-up reduced the effective interest cost sufficiently to cover the overages, and the higher rental rate produced the higher return. The building was 100% leased prior to completion of construction, and rental income fully covered debt service 15 days after receiving the Temporary Certificate of Occupancy.

The resultant building is of a very high quality that should satisfy the tenant's and the owner's investment return for a very long time.

The project was unique in that it encountered so many relatively unusual issues and obstacles for its size. It provided a valuable learning experience for the project personnel and will do so for the reader who studies its process.

REFERENCES   A

The following is a brief list of books and other information sources that were helpful in preparing this work and should be of interest to Development Officers. The books on development approach the subject somewhat differently than the author, so it might be an interesting contrast. Other books have useful data and interesting discussions.

American Institute of Architects
1735 New York Avenue, N.W.
Washington, D.C. 20006
(202) 626-7300

Building Construction Handbook
Frederick S. Merritt, Editor-in-Chief
1982 (Out of print, but available from McGraw-Hill)
McGraw-Hill, Inc.
New York, NY

Building Owners and Managers Association International
1201 New York Avenue, N.W., Suite 300
Washington, D.C. 20005
(202) 408-2662

Dictionary of Architecture & Construction
Edited by Cyril M. Harris
Second edition, 1995
McGraw-Hill, Inc.
New York, NY

Environmental Issues & Obligations
Continuous Education in Real Estate
1995
Anthony Schools Corporation
Oakland, CA

Feng Shui Companion, The
George Birdsall
1997
Destiny Books
Rochester, VT

Leadership in Energy and Environmental Design
Green Building Rating System
U.S. Green Building Council
90 New Montgomery Street, Suite 1001
San Francisco, CA 94105
(415) 543-3001

Office Development Handbook
W. Paul O'Mara
Community Builders Handbook Series, 1982
Urban Land Institute
New York, NY

Office Development Handbook
Second Edition
ULI Handbook Series, 1998
Urban Land Institute
New York, NY

Professional Real Estate Development – the ULI Guide to the Business
Richard B. Peiser
1992
Dearborn Financial Publishing Inc. and the Urban Land Institute
Washington, DC

Real Estate Development Principles and Process
Third Edition, 1999
Mike E. Miles, Richard L. Haney, Jr., and Gayle Berens
Urban Land Institute
New York, NY

Real Estate Development Workbook and Manual
Howard A. Zuckerman and George D. Blevins
1991
Prentice Hall, Inc.
Paramus, NJ

Skyscraper, The Making of a Building
Karl Sabbagh
1989
Penguin Books
New York, NY

Time Saver Standards
A Handbook of Architectural Design
John H. Callender, Editor-in-Chief
1982
McGraw-Hill Inc.
New York, NY

What is Feng Shui?
Dr. Evelyn Lip
1997
Academy Group Limited,
London, England

What Office Tenants Want
1999 BOMA/ULI Office Tenant Survey Report
Building Owners and Managers Association (BOMA)
International and the
Urban Land Institute
Washington, DC

NOTES ON FENG SHUI   B

NOTES ON FENG SHUI

The author has had no experience with the art of *feng shui*, or the geomancers who practice the art. The art is quite complex and these notes are somewhat simplistic. They are based on reading relevant material in order to gain some knowledge, since the growing commercial activity with China will undoubtedly make it advantageous to understand this art. It is suggested that an effort be initiated to obtain a greater understanding of this subject. (Note that definitions of words in italics are listed at the end of this Appendix.)

Feng shui is an ancient Chinese system of rules, concepts and principles that endeavors to explain the impact of placement, layout and design on peoples' lives. It dates back almost to 3000 B.C. and purports to create a living and working environment that is balanced and harmonious. Many examples of ancient as well as newer palaces, temples and burial sites were designed using the art of *feng shui*.

Feng means wind and *shui* means water. Wind provides the movement or flow of universal energy, called *qi* (or *chi*), and water provides the container or receiver of *qi*. It is the art of placement in harmony with nature and surrounding man-made elements—the art of siting, the skill of design with reference to the physical land form, climatic conditions, geographical location, and so on. It uses symmetry, balance, hierarchy of height, wall enclosures, and auspicious orientation.

Eastern philosophy refers to *qi* as the flow of energy within a place—a building, a room or a defined outdoor area. If *qi* flows gently, good fortune will come your way. It is not too dissimilar to the flow of *qi* in the human body on which acupuncture is based.

There are two distinct schools of *feng shui*—the classical school and the intuitive school. The classical school is deeply rooted in Chinese cosmology. The Minggua of the owner of the building, or the user of the space, is determined by analyzing the birth date, the Element of Birth and sex of the person, as well as the era (varying by twenty-year periods) of the building construction. These factors are evaluated by the geomancer along with the topography and other features of the site. There are extensive tables called the Feixing Magic Diagrams that numerically show auspicious and inauspicious influences on a building and determine various locational requirements.

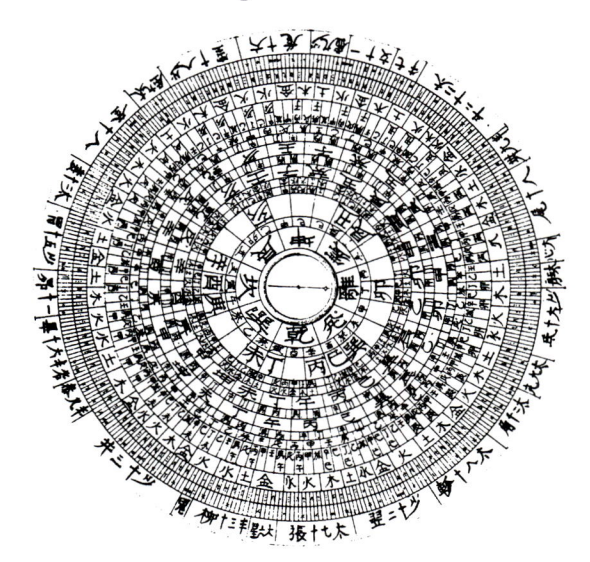

Figure B-1

The geomancer uses a compass-like diagram called a *luopan* (shown above), which has many variations. Usually the first ring of a *luopan* refers to the Eight Trigrams, which reflect the cosmic movements of the universe, and are used to assess

487

the course of underground water. The second ring refers to Later Heaven Trigrams which, when compared with the first, determine if there is a balance in terms of yin and yang (particularly with regard to color). Subsequent rings may be related to the twenty-eight Asterisms or Constellations, the twenty-four directions derived from the Ten Heavenly Stems and the Twelve Earthly Branches of the Later heavens, and are used to assess the *qi* of the earth and to determine the portents of the twenty-four stars. These readings are used to find the favorable locations and orientations of a building or space.

The lupanchi, or geomancer's ruler, contains eight divisions, some auspicious, and some not. Some auspicious dimensions rounded from centimeters to the nearest full inch are:

Doors—34", 35", 42" (main doors 43" and 49")

Corridors—43" or 57"

Ceilings—9'10" and 10'6"

Room width—9'10", 10'6", 12', 12'10", 13'5", 14', 14'8", 15'4", 16'3"

The second, or intuitive, school of *feng shui* is based on observation, intuition and feeling, and on basic rules that have been formulated by thousands of years of observation. *feng shui* involves the "right brain" approach of intuition and feelings, and is based on observation, reflection and common sense.

Ancient Chinese expressed their intuitive feelings about a place in terms of what we refer to as geomancy. Geo means earth and mancy means the divination or messages from the earth. This is not surprising since all early cultures had to "read" the land for water, weather conditions, the movement of animals and where to find food, in other words, to facilitate their survival.

Geomancy is a science or system to adjust universal energies, or *qi*, to allow human habitats to then be in balance or harmony with the visible and invisible world.

The energetic balance caused by the external shape of a place is defined in *feng shui* terms of the bagua (pictured below). The bagua is an octagonal shaped image that is a fundamental tool of *feng shui* and represents virtually every aspect of life. It is

Figure B-2

arranged more simply in a block diagram (below), which then represents the place being studied.

The front door of a place—whether land, home, office or room—determines the direction in which the bagua is applied. In *feng shui* the front door is seen as the source of the *qi* of that place. When a place has a void area it is considered a negative space, and must be "cured." For example, if there is a negative space, (such as a toilet room or void area) in the far left-hand corner, your wealth will dissipate. These issues can be solved by one of nine cures: crystals in the window, mirrors on the wall, living objects, moving objects, heavy objects, electrical objects, symbolic objects, colors and others. These "cures" either provide for a transference of energy (*qi*) to the negative space, or to symbolically square off that negative space.

With respect to the design of structures, it appears that objectives of *feng shui* do not vary significantly from good architectural practice. The site, the surrounding environment, the interior environment, the planning, the design and finish are all equally important in the assessment of *feng shui*. In fact, the first step in a geomancer evaluating a site is to observe the influence of the larger (built or natural) environment of a place—and then consider the source and amount of energy flow on the land being assessed. Some aspects of energy (or *qi*) are:

Hills are associated with *qi*.

WEALTH	FAME	RELATIONSHIPS
FAMILY/ HEALTH	TAI CHI	CREATIVE/ CHILDREN/ PROJECTS
INNER KNOWLEDGE/ INTUITION	CAREER	HELPFUL PEOPLE/ TRAVEL

⇧
Entrance

Figure B-3

Calm or gently flowing water retains *qi*, while rapidly flowing water, shallow sea or the wind will disperse *qi*.

Qi should approach a site in a curved path—a site or room at the end of a "T" corridor or intersection, or a river flowing toward the site exerts too much energy, like a dagger, and produces a direct and uncomfortably high *qi*.

A tall structure next to the site would overpower your site with *shaqi*.

Where negative *qi* affects your site, it can frequently be corrected by inserting some object (natural or built), or energy directing curves, between the site and the direction of flow of *qi*.

As with current design practice, the structure must be sound and built on good soil, the façade and room layouts must be in a reasonable balance, there must be good ventilation, good and glare-free lighting, noise control, good spatial composition, accessibility, good internal and external circulation, proper protection from the elements, and the design must be closely related to economic considerations of the project.

Every individual, workplace and nation needs to have *auspicious feng shui* for peace of mind, success and prosperity. In other words, a place where you spend your time should be pleasing, if not you wish to escape. The *qi* (energy) and magnetism of the earth, the symbolism of shapes with reference to the Five Elements, and the nature of the site must be in harmony with nature for the users to reap the benefits of *auspicious feng shui*.

Some specific design issues associated with *feng shui* are:

- The art of placement is about keeping control and feeling comfortable and that energy should not flow in straight lines.

- Doors and furniture must be well thought out to channel good energy into the interior of the building. For example, a bed should not be directly in line with the door.

- The *qi* is intuitive and intangible, while the *xue* is the form or the built environment. The *qi* would be in the outside or the courtyard.

- Landscape is a combination of *yin* and *yang* elements—rocks or hills and water, covered and uncovered space, light and shade, and high and low land. Bridges link *qi* and should be curved or zigzag to reduce *shaqi*.

- Colors are *yin* (cool colors) and *yang* (warm colors). There should be a balance of the *yin* and *yang* colors in a space, and they must be compatible with the user's Birth Element.
- When using the Minggua method, the location of important areas such as the front door, master bedroom and the kitchen are determined by the compatibility of the Birth Elements of the owner.
- The shapes of the elements should be carefully considered—for example, triangular (fire) shapes should not be combined with a circle (gold), as fire melts gold. The acceptable combination of shapes is governed by the compatibility of the elements shown in a table, below.
- If the ground floor of a building is too low, the *qi* is stifled. Main entrances should be generously sized.
- Front and rear doors should not be in line, and stairs and escalators should not face the door—both permit *qi*, and also money, to readily leave. The main door and entrance should be designed and placed with regard to their ceremonial importance.
- Toilet rooms should not be placed in the north, and the doors to male and female toilet rooms should not be located too near to one another.
- An executive's back should always be to a solid wall, never to a door, and his sitting position should be in harmony with the magnetism of the earth. Chairs should be at right angles to each other to inspire conversation and promote the flow of *qi*. Office and conference rooms should be subdued to promote harmonious dialogue.
- Structural beams or ceiling structure should not be too heavy, or should be hidden with a hung ceiling. Beams are believed to create a cutting action toward anyone below them and can block the flow of energy. However, the higher the beams above the floor, the less the impact. Interior columns should be round rather than square, as sharp corners cause *shaqi*.
- Artworks (as long it does not use any unacceptable graphic symbolism) and interior plants are a positive attribute of an interior design.
- A mirror or highly reflective surface should never be placed directly opposite a window, as it confuses the spirits.
- A mirror over or facing the front door, or toward an adjacent annoyance, will reflect negative energy.
- Doors should not be too small or *qi* can not easily enter.

Following are some additional factors used in *feng shui* that result from early Chinese philosophy and the practice of *feng shui* over the ages. In particular, they show the relationship between the Five Elements and show their impact on color and spatial arrangements.

- The five areas of influence in Chinese culture:

  Destiny
  Lucky and unlucky eras
  Art of placement (*feng shui*)
  Virtue
  Inheritance, background, education, experience, exposure

- The Five Elements:

Wood	east	green	wind	elongated or rectangular
Fire	south	red	heat	triangular
Earth	center	yellow	moisture	square
Gold	west	white	drought	round
Water	north	black	cold	free form or zigzag

- Compatible elements and shapes:

Gold with Water	round with free form
Water with Wood	free form with rectangular
Wood with Fire	rectangular with triangular
Fire with Earth	triangular with square
Earth with Gold	square with round

- Incompatible elements and shapes:

Earth with Water	square with free form
Water with Fire	free form with triangular
Fire with Gold	triangular with round
Gold with Wood	round with rectangular
Wood with Earth	rectangular with square

Appendix B: Notes on Feng Shui

Certain definitions used in discussion of *feng shui* are:

Auspicious—good or positive factors.

Bagua—a diagram from early philosophy utilizing the eight trigrams plus a *yin/yang* symbol, which serves as a tool in *feng shui*.

Inauspicious—negative factors.

Geomancer—a practitioner of the art of *feng shui*.

Luopan—a geomancer's compass—a magnetic needle surrounded by rings of information.

Lupanchi—a geomancer's ruler—used to assess measurements of doors, spaces and furniture.

Minggua—affect of a place based on the sex and birth signs of the owner/user.

Qi (or *chi*)—energy of the earth.

Shaqi (or *sa chi*)– the dispersion or outflow of energy.

Trigrams—factors in human life that are represented in a bagua.

Yin/yang—opposites, ancient Chinese believed that everything in nature could be classified under these two elements. The balance between yin and yang are important.

Yin—feminine, moon, night, valleys, relatively passive.

Yang—masculine, sun, day, hills, relatively active.

Xue—the built environment.

EL CAMINO REAL

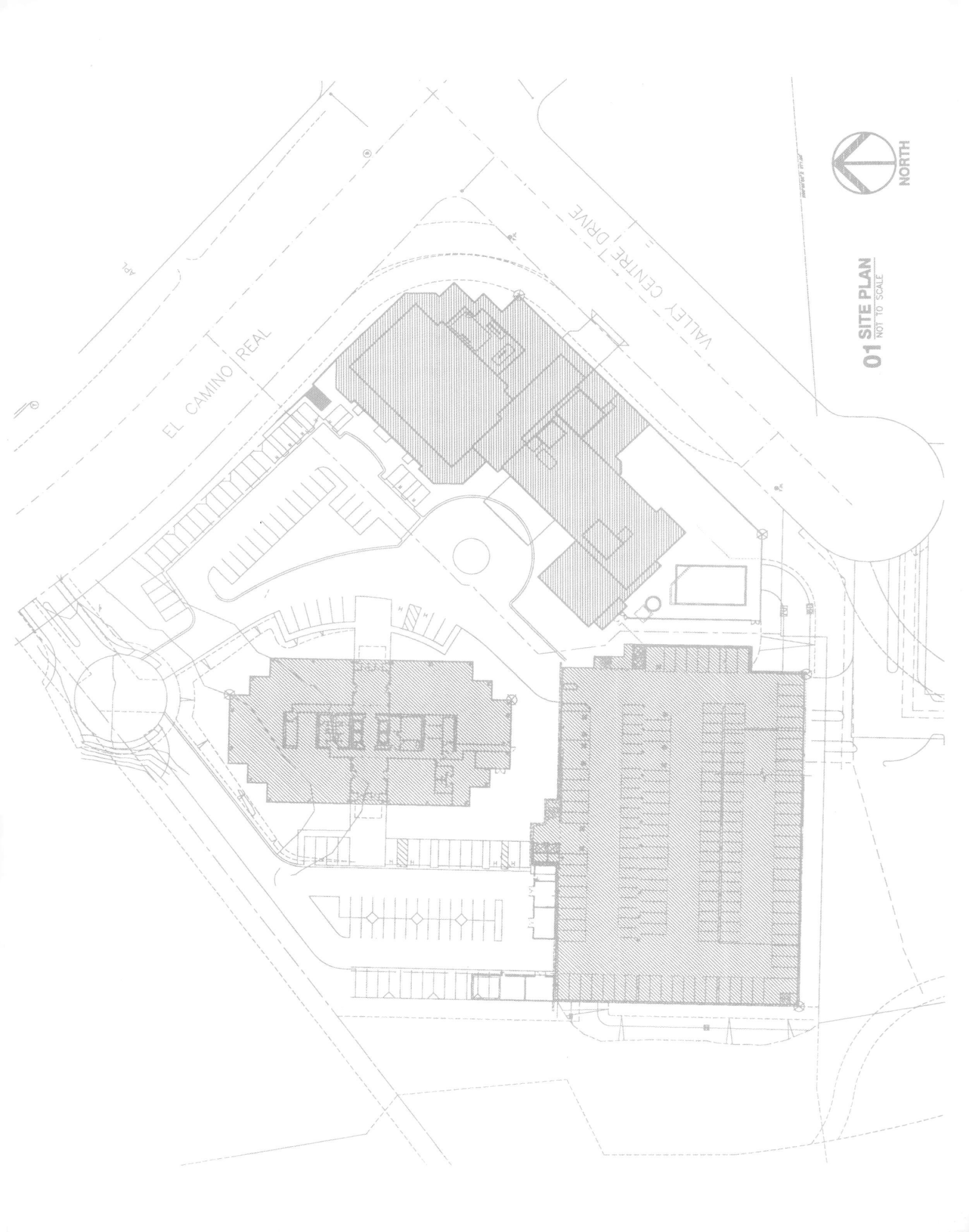

VALLEY CENTRE DRIVE

01 SITE PLAN
NOT TO SCALE

NORTH

HOW GREEN IS MY BUILDING?

HOW GREEN IS MY BUILDING?

The Introduction of this book discussed the necessity for the Development Officer to stay current with present and future trends, among them were the social and political issues and beliefs of the community.

In Chapter 13 under General Design Comments it was further stated that architecture will, among other things, reflect the environmental issues and serious social concerns of the day—the built form will in the long run tend to reflect the values of society. One of those values gaining momentum is the desire for ecologically sound development. Among these social concerns becoming more obvious today are:

- General environmental concerns
- Energy efficiency
- Recycling
- Natural light and air
- Sustainability
- Healthier buildings
- Personal comfort and control

Social trends affect the attitude of the community at large and, of specific importance to you, regulatory agencies, prospective tenants, employees, and the customers of tenants. It is essential to recognize these trends and implement those actions and decisions as may be appropriate and economically feasible at any point in time.

There are many serious social concerns that are held today by a wide percentage of our population and by many federal, state and local regulatory agencies. Even when there are personal doubts as to the technical validity of some of these issues, as the author has in some cases, the fact that the concerns exist and are believed by many people make them a real issue that must be addressed. A few of the more serious specific current issues are:

- Air pollution—federal and state agencies are currently tightening regulations governing products of combustion and particulate matter based on insufficient progress in meeting their standards in many locales.

- Ozone layer—these concerns have already changed the refrigerants used in air conditioning systems, and will change them further, and are changing the compositions of adhesives, solvents and finishes, and various spray propulsion media.

- Global warming—may be a far greater factor in forcing a reduction in the use of carbon-based fuels than the concern for air pollution. The recent protocol in Kyoto is potentially very far reaching. These concerns will not only affect the direct consumption of energy, but also indirect consumption resulting from the manufacture of products required by the building industry, and increasing the use of recycled products.

- De-forestation—growing concerns about forests on a worldwide scale will undoubtedly impact the availability of many species of wood.

- Water availability and quality—while the amount of water on earth is relatively constant, use is increasing, availability in many locales is becoming more restricted, and the quality is becoming more difficult to maintain.

- Recycling and Sustainability—creating new useable products from what was formerly waste, and the use of replaceable raw materials, both methods to insure the absence of depletion of the earth's resources.

These political, social and regulatory concerns will increase as more people become aware that the building industry consumes an estimated 16% of the water, 35–40% of the energy, 25% of the virgin wood, 40% of the raw stone, gravel and sand; it produces 30% of the carbon dioxide emissions, and 20–30% of municipal solid waste.

As a result of these and other concerns, we see a gradual but significant movement toward "green" development of commercial buildings. "Green" development is a young, evolving way to look at the built environment, and is generally defined as the integration of commercial development into an ecosystem that benefits both people and nature—with a positive effect on the land, on the people who work in it, and on the community around it. The trend will grow because of dual pressures—the increasing concern for the environment and the pressure to reduce building costs, particularly over the building life. But, it will only become a major trend when developers visualize the increased value of a "green" building in terms of return on investment, market demand and lower operating costs.

While there are many issues that individually make up a "green" or environmentally sensitive building, the response to them must be accomplished in a synergistically systems approach in accordance with predetermined objectives.

There is anecdotal evidence that employee morale, reduced absenteeism and productivity increases result from improved lighting quality, increased daylighting, air quality, personal temperature comfort, noise control, and the psychological benefit of knowing that the building was environmentally friendly. The economics of a building satisfying these conditions can improve significantly through higher net rental rates, earlier stabilized occupancy, higher level of stabilized occupancy and tenant retention. We discussed this issue as Interior Environmental Quality (IEQ) at the start of Chapter 30.

It has been estimated that a "green" building can be developed for an increase of 2% to 3% of total project cost. This may turn out to be good business if tenants accept that the buildings will have significantly lower operating cost, and improve employee efficiency, and that their customers and the community will applaud the product. In addition, the development may get more favorable regulatory treatment.

Throughout the design and construction chapters of the text many current and/or future solutions relative to (a) reducing life-cycle costs, (b) protecting the environment and (c) promoting personal comfort in the workspace have been discussed. These issues are categorized and listed below, along with many other issues not discussed. There are obviously many more that could have been added. The categories used below are arbitrary, as many issues can properly belong in more that one category. Some of the enhancements are mutually exclusive, but many are additive.

Air pollution (exclusive of direct energy reduction)
Avoid excessive grading
Minimize disturbance of soil outside the construction footprint
Hauling construction materials from shortest distances possible
Minimize construction dust
Omit or reduce sandblasted finishes

Ozone layer
Use non-ozone depleting refrigerants
Omit CFCs in insulation, carpet pad and foaming agents
Omit or reduce spray propulsion systems that affect the ozone layer

Noise pollution
Traffic noise
Airport glide path
Muffle pile drivers
Time of day work limitations to avoid disturbance

Global warming
Any reduction of use of fossil fuels
Reduction of production of CO_2, such as partial replacement of Portland cement with fly ash

Water conservation and quality
Becoming more important to developers as costs are increasing rapidly due to the cost of obtaining sufficient supplies and replacing aging or undersized infrastructure.

Low-water consuming indigenous plants (xeriscaping)
Drip systems, where irrigation is required
Low flow plumbing fixtures
Flow control faucets—electronic or mechanical
Automatic flush valves
Point of use water heaters (no tank losses)
Tempered potable water
Delimiters on cooling towers—reduce drift and evaporation
Meters on cooling tower makeup lines
Water quality—lead, etc.
Extra treatment or filtration, where warranted
Water recovery system for non-sewage waste
Reclaimed water for irrigation
Storm water retention
Oil grit separators or water quality ponds as run-off pretreatment
Pervious paving materials

Solid waste disposal
Nontoxic or low mercury fluorescent lamps
Non-recyclable materials
Construction waste equals almost one-third of municipal solid waste

Recycled products
Crushed concrete (aggregate base)
Tires (blacktop)
Fiberboard
Roofing membrane
Carpet, carpet tiles and their backing
Ceramic tile (recycled glass)
Power plant fly ash as a cement substitute

Recyclable materials
Bituminous roofing, coated roofing felts
Wood
Glass
Cardboard
Carpet and carpet tiles
Ceiling tile, fiberboard, gypsum board
Foam insulation
Steel
Aluminum
Copper
On-site construction recycling, where feasible
Operating recycling equipment and program
Salvaged or refurbished materials or equipment

Sustainable products
Wood—only valid when the lumber is certified as coming from a sustainably harvested forest (there are now 15 million acres worldwide), with provision as to chain-of-custody.
Non-fuel energy—discussed elsewhere

Transportation and miscellaneous energy reduction
Material selection—(example, concrete requires less energy than steel to fabricate)
Reduce transportation of construction materials
Locate project site close to mass transportation
Linkage to mass transportation and car pooling
Traffic management programs for tenants
Bike security
Shower facilities
Refueling for alternative fuel vehicles—electric, ethanol, natural gas

Alternative energy sources
Wind
Solar—fuel cells, photo-voltaic system, solar recovery farms
Hydro-power
Geothermal
Industry deregulation permits purchase of "green" energy
Biomass-fueled power
Nuclear

Passive energy reductions
Building orientation
Building partially protected by a hillside
Solar shading—vertical or horizontal
Shading with trees
Operable windows
Building mass

Building envelope (exclusive of vision glass)
Ratio of envelope to floor area
"U" value of wall
"U" value of roof
High reflectivity, high emissivity of roof
Low-emissivity paint on interior of exterior walls
Photo-voltaic cells
Tightly sealed windows and doors

Vision glass
Double or triple glazed
Inert gasses between lites

Thermal break mullions
Reflective glass
Tinted glass
Heat absorbing glass
Low-emissivity glass
Chromogenic glazing (changes with light)
Blinds or draperies
Automatic blinds

Electrical drives
Variable frequency drives (VFDs)
High efficiency motors—90% efficient
Solid state reduced low voltage starters
Emergency generators—used for utility load shaving
Optimized transformer size (reduce standby losses)

Lighting energy
Dimmable electronic ballasts
T8 or T5 lamps
Compact fluorescent lamps (CFLs)
Light emitting diodes (LEDs)
Heat extraction fixtures
Task (desk or workstation) lamps
High intensity discharge (HID) lamps
Metal halides
Metal halides with ceramic discharge technology
Electrodeless lamps
Fiber-optic remote source lamps
Sulfur light

Lighting controls
On/off switching
Double switching
Photo sensors—perimeter light control
Timer control
Occupancy sensors
Dimming
Intelligent controllers

Interior light quality
Indirect fixtures
Direct/indirect fixtures
Visual comfort probability (VCP)
Correlated color temperature
Coloring index (CRI)
Natural daylight
    Low-emissivity vision glass
    Atriums or skylights

Electronic ballasts—reduce flickering, greater dimming potential
More individual control
Reduced bay depths
Partial glass interior partitions

Telecommunications
High speed Internet access
Cable competition
Telephone competition
Satellite access and delivery

HVAC system
Avoid or minimize terminal reheat
After hours control
Load shaping
Multiple fuel—gas with interruptible service
Thermal energy storage systems
Heat recovery chillers
Geoexchange, geothermal systems
Thermocycle
Four pipe fan coil secondary systems
High efficiency boilers
Outside air economizer cooling
CO_2 controllers for outside air
Desiccant dehumidification
Waste heat recovery from exhaust air
DDC load control and operational timing systems
Interoperability control systems
More individual comfort control
Raised flooring—more efficient air distribution and reduced energy consumption

Indoor Air Quality (IAQ)
Minimum outside air—20 cfm per person
Minimum air circulation
Humidification, where needed
Low or no volatile organic compounds (VOCs)—adhesives, solvents, paint, thinners, sealants
High efficiency cartridge filters—85% in many cases
Electrostatic filters, where reasonable
Ducts, externally insulated, or internally with protective coatings to prevent entrainment
Reduced air noise levels—sound traps, lower air velocity
Good temperature control—personal comfort
Non-toxic pest control products
Smoking ban
Interior plants

Interior air monitoring system—CO_2, etc.
Architectural entryways to catch and hold dirt
Install 85% temporary filters when return air system used during construction

Miscellaneous
Movable wall systems
Light color and high reflectance on hard surface areas—reduce heat islands
Erosion and sediment control

Energy Star Program

One governmental program geared to environmental enhancement, though heavily weighted to energy reduction, is the Energy Star Buildings program of the Atmospheric Pollution Prevention Division of the EPA. In essence, the building owner enters into a partnership memorandum of understanding (MOU) with the EPA, agreeing to improve the overall energy efficiency of their facilities through the implementation of a comprehensive set of profitable upgrades. EPA assists participants by providing technical and administrative assistance to ensure maximum energy savings while satisfying cost-effective criteria. A brief outline of the partnership MOU is shown below.

Building Partner Responsibilities

- Survey and implement all profitable upgrades in one pilot building within two years.

- Complete full building upgrades where profitable in at least 50% of remaining qualifying space and lighting upgrades in remaining 40% within seven years (qualifying space is conditioned space that is owned or financially controlled by partner).

- Maintain or improve indoor air quality in upgraded Energy Star Buildings.

- Partners are encouraged to follow EPA Energy Star Buildings staged approach to upgrades, or at a minimum account for intersystem effects.

- Adhere to Energy Star energy-efficiency and profitability criteria when replacing failed or retired equipment during the term of the MOU.

- Annually report progress to EPA.

- Develop an employee outreach program entailing the Energy Star Buildings program goals and results, and your pollution prevention accomplishments.

- Allow EPA to use your results to promote EPA pollution prevention programs.

EPA Responsibilities

- Provide technical support, including written materials and guides, and a technical hotline.

- Provide software tools to aid in estimating energy savings and environmental benefits from specific upgrades (i.e., variable speed drives, fan systems).

- Advise and assist partners in planning and implementing the upgrades.

- Provide marketing resources, such as posters and fact sheets, to help partners communicate the Energy Star Buildings program within their organizations.

- Create an ally program of equipment manufacturers and distributors, contractors, utility companies, and building technical experts.

- Publicly recognize partners for their participation and publicize their successes.

- Provide special recognition for those buildings that achieve the greatest energy-use reductions.

- Allow partners to use EPA's Energy Star logo to publicize their participation in the program.

Additional information on the Energy Star Buildings program may be obtained from:

Manager
Energy Star Buildings Program
U.S. EPA Atmospheric Pollution Prevention Division
401 M Street, SW (6202J)
Washington, DC 20460
Tel. (202) 775-6650   FAX (202) 565-2134
Toll Free (888) STARYES
http://www.epa.gov/appdstar/buildings
or noferi.mark@epamail.epa.gov

Leadership in Energy and Environmental Design Program

A much more comprehensive system has been set up by the private U.S. Green Building Council to evaluate and recognize the environmental efficiency of buildings. The program is called *Leadership in Energy and Environmental Design,* and known as LEED™. The program was developed to promote the understanding, development, and accelerated implementation of Green Building policies. A more detailed document is the Green Building Rating System, Final Working Draft, August 13, 1997, available from the Green Building Council.

Plaques are awarded to buildings that meet stipulated accomplishments through a rating system that is based on accepted energy and environmental principles, and strikes a reasonable balance between known effective practices and emerging concepts.

To achieve a designation under the LEED™ program, a building must meet the rating body's minimum requirements under each of the ten following areas.

Asbestos
Building Commissioning
Energy Efficiency
Indoor Air Quality
Ozone depletion / CFCs
Smoking Ban
Storage and Collection of Recyclables
Thermal Comfort
Water Conservation
Water Quality (Lead)

There are 14 categories where credits are awarded for meeting various specified requirements. There are a total of 44 credits and four bonus credits. The categories, which may be explained in more detail by contacting the council, are:

Building materials
Construction Waste Management
Energy
Existing Building Rehabilitation
Indoor Air Quality
Landscaping / Exterior Design
LEED™-Certified Designer
Occupant Recycling
Operations and Maintenance Facilities
Ozone Depletion / CFCs
Siting
Transportation
Water Conservation
Water Quality

They award plaques, based on accomplishing a percentage of the base building rating credits, are awarded in the following four categories.

- LEED™ Building Platinum—buildings that earn 81% or more of the credits
- LEED™ Building Gold—buildings that earn 71–80% or more of the credits
- LEED™ Building Silver—buildings that earn 61–70% or more of the credits
- LEED™ Building Bronze—buildings that earn 50–60% or more of the credits

It should be recognized that this program is relatively new, and has been directed more toward owner-user buildings and rehabilitations. There is a committee currently studying the adaptation of this program to apply more specifically to speculative office buildings, where the developer has only limited control over the needs of the prospective tenants.

Whether the time is right to address a formal program of this nature, and attempt to implement broad environmental enhancements is subject to a variety of opinions. What the author does believe, however, is the certainty that the objectives of this and other programs are beneficial to society and will gradually become accepted practice. Ascertaining the timing when recognition of these issues will be an important factor in the competitive rental market and increase the profitability of each project will mean keeping our antennas tuned in each market in which we operate.

An effective method of staying in touch with the latest technical thinking would be to join the U.S. Green Building Council and have one or more Development Officers become active on various committees. The best contact is:

Kristin Raiff Douglas
Managing Director
U. S. Green Building Council
1015 18th Street, NW, Suite 805
Washington DC 20036
Telephone (202) 828-7422
FAX (415) 828-5110
kar@usgbc.org
www.usgbc.org

LAND DEVELOPMENT

LAND DEVELOPMENT

Land development for purposes of this discussion consists of a large tract of land virtually devoid of infrastructure, except for a nearby highway system. A site that would provide relatively few development pads with nearby infrastructure will not be considered herein as a land development. This Appendix will provide an overview of land development, describing the main issues and risks.

Land development is the riskiest of all forms of development due to its greater political and planning issues, the high cost of infrastructure, the long term required for sufficient land sales in order to recover the land and infrastructure cost with interest. It is further exacerbated by the fact that it will progress through more than one, sometimes many, market cycles. The fact that land developments are large will normally result in a high community profile and will almost certainly involve land use and zoning changes, increasing the concern for limiting "at risk" money in the purchase contract as discussed in the Site Acquisition portion of Chapter 7. Early political and community input and involvement can avoid more serious problems later on.

Prior to spending the time and legal fees to tie up a site, it is recommended that the political climate be studied to determine its impact on zoning use, density, infrastructure cost and development in general. If the property requires annexation, the negotiating leverage gained (if the community sees the project as beneficial from a fiscal impact standpoint) is extremely relevant to total projected infrastructure costs. A pre-acquisition meeting with the local or adjacent governmental officials/trustees is important to assess the level of cooperation to be expected in the predevelopment stages and if infrastructure subsidies can be obtained.

As with any other development, initiation should be based on a clear and valid set of objectives. A thorough Feasibility Analysis of the market, site and political environment issues, as discussed in various chapters of this work, for each of the intended end uses is a critically important prerequisite. The environmental reviews are often more important in land development than individual projects with the occurrence of wetlands and habitat issues, along with the normal environmental testing. The Feasibility Analysis must not only indicate the feasibility of the overall project, but must project the absorption by time increments for each intended product through to the final site sales, usually a minimum of seven to ten years.

After verifying the feasibility and gaining control of the site, governmental jurisdiction should be the first issue resolved. If the site is in an unincorporated area the political climate and pre-acquisition discussions should be evaluated to determine whether it is more beneficial to remain in the unincorporated area, apply for incorporation into an adjacent town or, if large enough, to create an incorporated entity of its own. In addressing this issue, factors such as the following must be evaluated:

- Political environment in each possible entity
- Time required to establish a new jurisdiction
- Ease of gaining acceptance of the general plan or Planned Unit Development (PUD), the time required, and the duration of the PUD
- Variation in tax rates
- Availability of utilities—long-term capacity, cost and whose burden the cost will be

- Availability of state of the art communications
- Exaction or impact fee costs
- Existing regulations and proposed changes
- Police and fire service

After determining the appropriate jurisdiction, a negotiating process should be agreed upon that all parties are able to live with comfortably.

The initial project team will be built around the land planner, civil engineer, land use attorney and a public relations firm that thoroughly understands the local political climate.

A preliminary budget including all costs and sales income should be prepared prior to closing on the site, including estimated political and environmental mitigation, financial costs, expense inflation and market price variations over the full assumed term.

A comprehensive master plan, general plan or PUD will be required that will satisfy not only the economic needs of the development, but also the requirements of the jurisdiction in which it is located. The master planning will be impacted by how many end uses are planned—office, industrial, residential, lodging and/or major retail—and the need for full community support services. The planning will include the complete infrastructure of the road system, all utilities, emergency and support services, and should recognize the need for extensive green space, complete with walking trails, parks and recreational facilities as separations between the various major end uses.

The most important and difficult determinate of project success, after an accurate Feasibility Analysis, is the phasing of the development. The critical cost issue is that the development should be planned so as to permit the minimum installation of the costly infrastructure initially, and to increase the infrastructure in optimum increments consistent with the projected land sales, as adjusted, over time. In addition to the construction cost, the initially installed infrastructure will incur maintenance and taxes; some communities require a bond to cover many years of maintenance, and a letter of credit is frequently required as security throughout the development period to insure the remainder of the necessary infrastructure is installed.

On the other hand, it is necessary to install sufficient infrastructure to differentiate the development from competitive parks and to define the ultimate project in such a way as to properly convey its image to attract the necessary developers and users. This is often a Catch 22 issue. In addition, consideration must be given to the fact that the future additions to the infrastructure can be disruptive to existing tenants.

An important part of the master planning is to establish CC&Rs with design, use, maintenance, and operating guidelines compatible with the long-term objectives of the development. The CC&Rs must address many marketing and strategic control issues; among the most critical are:

- Uniformity of maintenance of the front setbacks of the various lots as the project is sold or developed
- Sufficient approval and disapproval rights for the developer with flexibility to modify standards over time (a difficult balance)

The land development strategy varies with the size of the project, the variety of end uses and whether the developer is basically a land banker or intends to develop one or more end uses for its own account. If the developer intends to develop none, or only a few, of the end use products for his own account, it is frequently wise to bring in proposed developers for each of the other end uses early to obtain their expertise in their areas of specialty during the study and planning phases. Frequently, these other developers agree in advance to acquire all or a portion of the land planned for their specialty at the closing of the land purchase contract, at a pre-agreed upon price, which includes their proportionate share of the infrastructure cost.

For the developer's own projects, many developers recommend the land should be placed into development at a 10–15% discount to maintain a competitive advantage as the project is developed. To assure this discount it is important to obtain the approval of any financial partners in advance.

It must be clear, however, that the land development is a project unto itself, and must satisfy its pro forma through the land sales, regardless of the percentage of the project undertaken by the project developer. Not only is this appropriate from the standpoint of fiscal control, but it is necessary to satisfy the lender. A corollary is that each individual development undertaken by the developer must also stand on its own merit.

The proposed master plan will lay out the location of the area for each use, lot sizes, the circulation plan, the infrastructure and the final grades throughout the site.

The residential areas should be laid out so that they are isolated as much as possible from other uses. The residential streets, pedestrian ways and direct routes to schools and other residential related activities should be separated from the busy business ingress and egress routes. Protecting playground and recreation areas from street traffic is a very positive amenity. The type and price of the residential units would, hopefully, be those that would best support the primary activities in the development.

The timing of residential sales impacts the flexibility of the developers of commercial properties. Typically, new residents have a stake in preserving their environment from additional traffic congestion, building densities or building height variations. It is important that residential areas be well-screened from the commercial areas and all the new residents should be well-informed of the future development potential nearby. The zoning, CC&Rs and other regulatory issues should be sufficiently locked in so that the new population is not able to restrict the planned development necessary to meet the financial objectives.

Retail of any significant size and lodging facilities should be located along a major highway wherever possible and the back, or service, side of the retail should be visually shielded from the remainder of the development by berms, elevation differentials, heavy landscaping or walls. If properly laid out, lodging facilities can be developed so as to share with office buildings the use of parking lots or structures due to their off-hours parking use versus the prime-time office parking.

Industrial facilities should be restricted to clean light industry and should include loading area screening and truck maneuvering areas located to the side or rear of the facilities to minimize visual pollution. There are additional land usage and site costs to the user resulting from this restriction. If the park is predominately an industrial park, this additional screening and off-street loading requirement should be carefully assessed to avoid a noncompetitive situation with other parks.

The most extensive infrastructure work is usually the roadway system. Frequently one or more freeway interchanges will be required, as well as connections to feeder roads from the population or business centers. Once the initial points of a roadway design and contribution negotiation is reached with the local jurisdiction, a written long-term agreement should be executed that limits your expenditures regardless of the ultimate traffic volume. This agreement must be well-documented and recorded to protect the long-term project economics.

From the ingress/egress points an internal roadway system is laid out providing the proper sizing for future development sites, and integrating properly with pedestrian trails and green spaces. The initial road installation must not only serve the first phase efficiently, but also satisfactorily provide access for all emergency services. Those initial sections of built-out roadway should be constructed for their ultimate size requirement, rather than being enlarged as the project expands.

The water management system must be carefully thought out. Most jurisdictions, and good practice, will normally require ponds or depressions for interim water detention to reduce the maximum outflow, and may also require permanent retention ponds. The ultimate outflow may be either to an approved waterway in accordance with the drainage plan for that drainage basin or to an adjacent storm drainage system. Any retention areas can be converted to attractive lakes or ponds, while the detention areas and any flood plains may double as green belt or recreational areas for most of the year in many geographical areas. See Site Design in Chapter 18 for a more detailed discussion. The long-term detention/retention and flood plain improvements should be negotiated and documented in the PUD or similar agreement, as these requirements tend to become more restrictive over time, particularly if the project is successful.

The potable water supply will preferably be obtained from a nearby water district, but in a few cases a complete new water source, treatment plant and distribution system must be developed. If the water mains are insufficiently sized, or if the pressure is not consistently sufficient, approved fire water storage may be required. In some cases the fire department will require a separate distribution system for fire service.

If a tie-in to a local sanitary district is not available a complete sewage treatment plant would be required, designed to meet local environmental regulations. It is frequently advantageous, when a plant or holding area is required, to consider a reclaimed water system to irrigate the green spaces and landscaping. It has been stated that when reclaimed water systems are utilized some lenders require higher cover ratios and additional bonding. Any treatment plant must be located where it can be fully shielded from other areas and operated in a manner to preclude odors.

Electricity and gas will be provided by the local utilities. "Will Serve" letters to provide service for the ultimate build-out will be essential. The electric utility may have to construct one or more substations to satisfy the loads. All electricity should be underground and a complete loop should ultimately be installed, preferably receiving power from more than one substation, to provide a continuity of service if there is a cable failure or substation outage. The installation costs are usually negotiable. Utility installations typically require the developer to spend initial funds to install the conduits in the setback areas along the roadways. This up-front expenditure will minimize future trenching and landscape destruction. Over time, these costs will be recovered by way of a recapture agreement as the sites are developed. This cost must be anticipated in the initial infrastructure budget.

Telephone and cable installations should be planned to permit competition for both services and to provide the latest in communications technology. A Synchronous Optical Network (SONET) ring should be installed to provide two-way distribution of voice, video and data service to assure a continuation of service even with a cable outage. Communications access may frequently be provided by the service providers at no charge. A further discussion of communication services is included in Chapter 26.

Police, fire and emergency services will normally be obtained from a local jurisdiction. Local stations and equipment may be required, usually at the developer's cost.

Where public transportation exists in nearby cities, population centers or transportation nodes, an effort should be made to obtain a commitment for extended service to the development. It may be necessary to subsidize the operation through an association created to provide various services, until the ridership reaches a predetermined level. This can be a very expensive proposition. If public transportation does not exist, the possibility of potential labor shortages can occur, especially in areas of high growth with low unemployment. The potential for labor shortages can severely hamper sales efforts.

Attractive entranceways to the development are essential. Aesthetically pleasing green spaces, complete with water features, outdoor sculpture, landscaping, pedestrian trails and well-located recreational facilities will be a major attraction for the development. Where lodging, food service, health clubs, day care centers and other convenience services are not readily available, a major effort should be made to include them in the development if it can be accomplished within reasonable cost limits. Any health club and day care service should be included under the tenant's association.

Even when the land developer intends to develop one or more of the products for his own account, consideration should be given to selling off a portion of those parcels to other developers to assist in building an acceptable product mass, as well as to help cover the land and infrastructure cost of each phase. When selling such parcels it is preferable to limit those sales to build-to-suit users, with only a limited amount for speculative development to protect your own market.

The three most important factors in land development are:

- An accurate long-term Feasibility Analysis for all proposed products

- Sufficient equity for staying power through a long development period

- Phasing the project in appropriately designed and sized increments consistent with market absorption, so as to recover the land and infrastructure cost in a reasonable period of time

One rule of thumb is that a successful land development project will have recovered all land, planning, infrastructure, management and financing costs by the time two-thirds to three-fourths of the land has been sold or transferred into development.

An excellent example of a well-planned and well-executed land development is Prentiss' Continental Executive Parke in the village of Vernon Hills, Illinois. This 500-acre park includes office, industrial, retail and residence areas.

As shown in the Development Standards plan, Figure 1 on the prior page, the basic plan was:

- Office buildings with a maximum height of eight stories (yellow) along Milwaukee Avenue, the major north-south thoroughfare.

- Offices with a maximum height of five stories and other uses with a three-story limit (green) were located west of the primary office sites.

- Offices with a four-story maximum height and other uses with a three-story limit (purple) were located further west.

- Two-story office and one-story industrial (orange) were located adjacent to the western landscape buffer, which was just across a waterway from an existing residential area.

- Retail, hotel and office (blue) were located at the northern portion of the site along Town Line Road, the major east-west traffic artery.

- A residential area (white) was located in the southwest corner of the site, with access to another road to the south, and was sold to a residential developer at closing of the land.

The Master Plan, Figure 2, shows the phasing of the development.

- The first phase (brown) constituted the entire northern portion of the site, and about halfway down Milwaukee Avenue, and included retail, hotel, office and industrial sites.

- The second phase (yellow) encompassed most of the center of the park for both office and industrial sites.

- The third phase (pink) was composed of a few miscellaneous parcels, and

- The fourth phase (blue) was the lower southeast corner of the project.

This project, over a ten-year period, met its original financial objectives with almost unbelievable accuracy.

It is highly unlikely that most readers will undertake any large land development, but it was believed that a discussion of this subject would be helpful in broadening your overall knowledge of the real estate development process.

Office Development

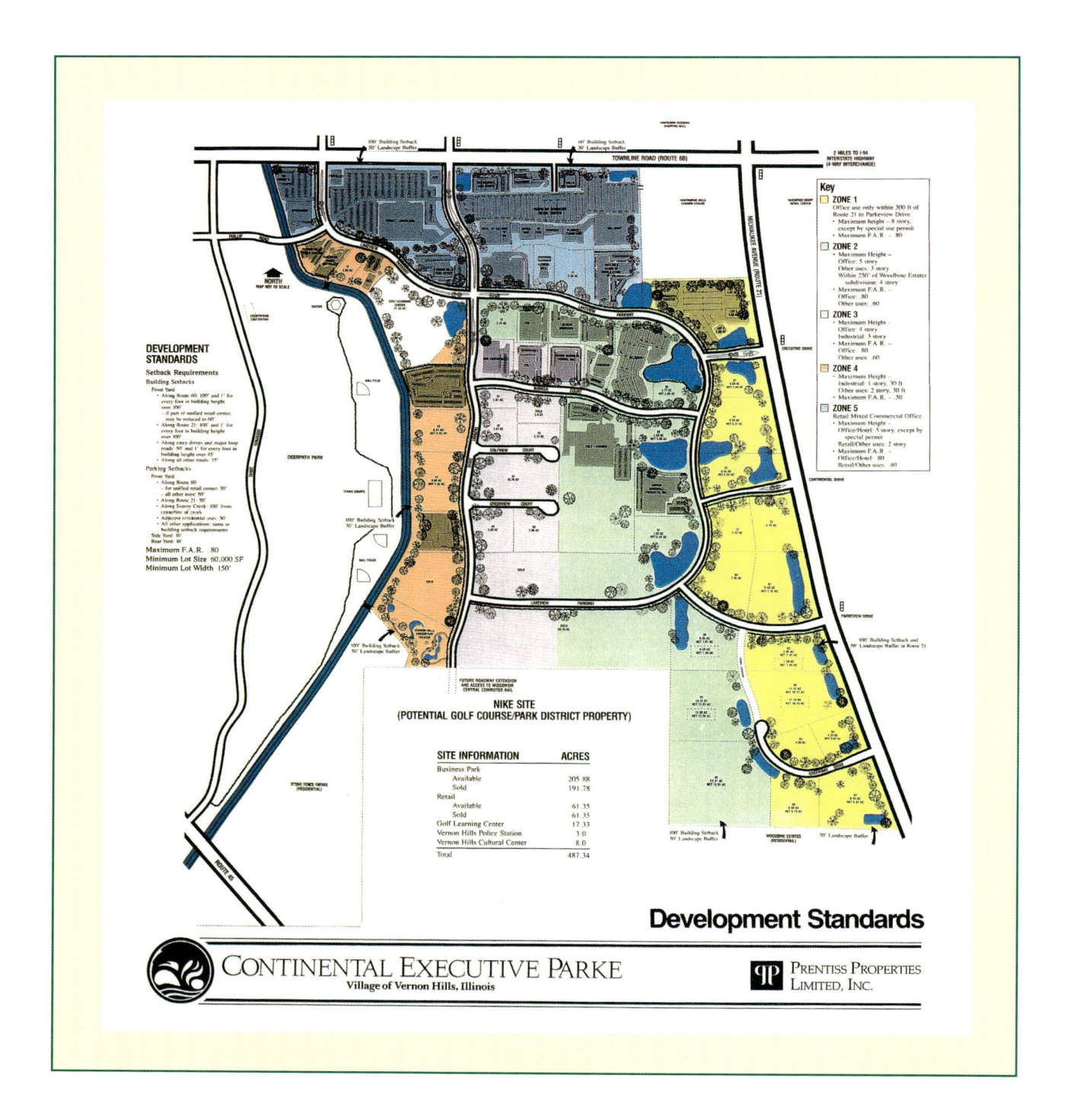

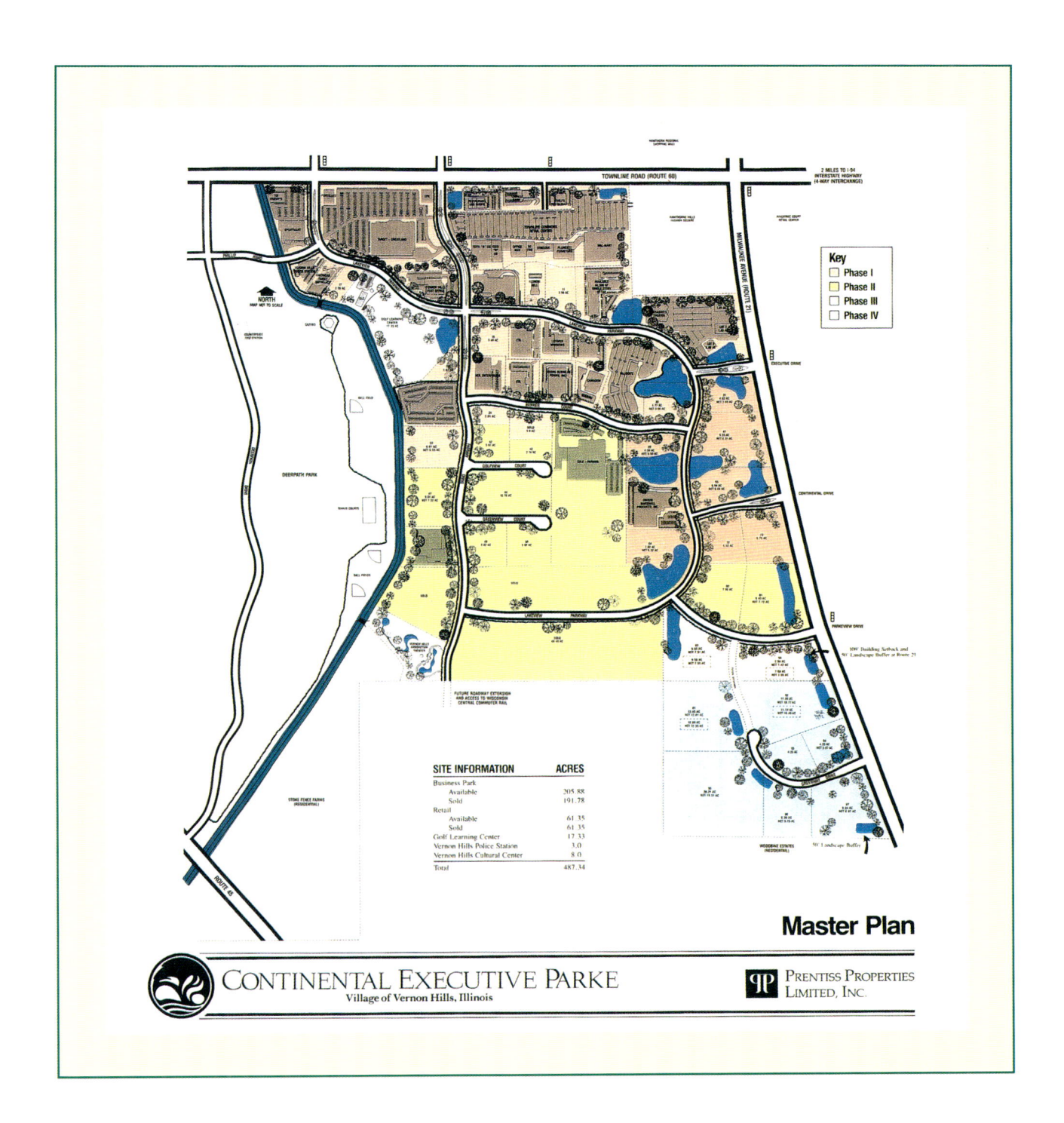

Appendix D: Land Development

EL CAMINO REAL

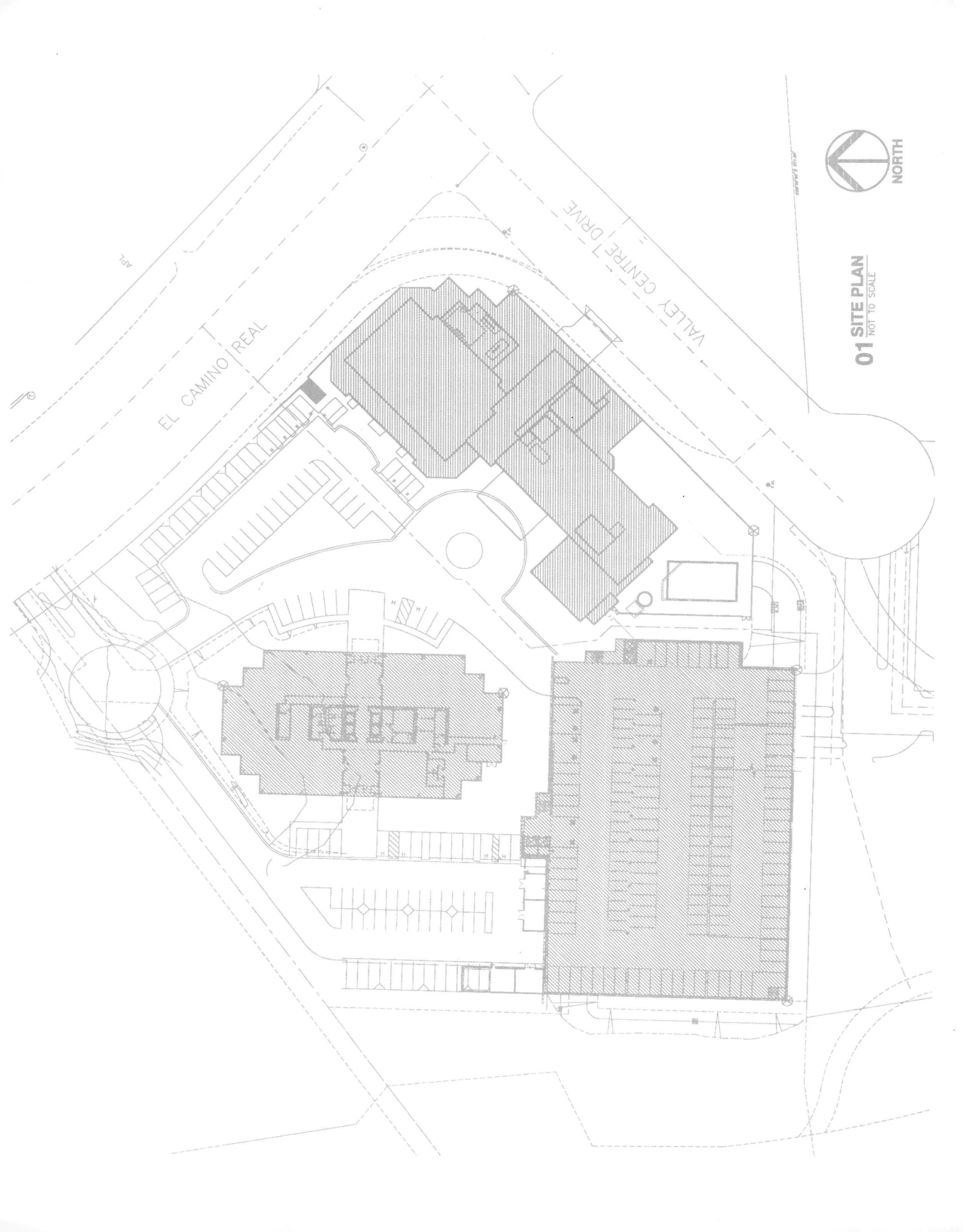

VALLEY CENTRE DRIVE

01 SITE PLAN
NOT TO SCALE

NORTH

GLOSSARY

The terms in this Glossary that may have multiple meanings are defined in the manner in which they are used in this text.

A

"As is" condition. Premises accepted in the condition as of the time of making the lease.

Absorption. The rate at which the available space will be or has been leased during a predetermined period of time.

Absorption cycle. Similar to a conventional vapor-compressor refrigeration cycle, but the generator and absorber replace the compressor.

Acceleration clause. Lender's right to accelerate the unpaid balance of a loan in the event of a default.

Acoustics. The study of sound and its affect on humans.

ADA. Americans with Disabilities Act.

Add on factor. See rentable/useable (R/U) ratio.

ADSL. See Asymmetrical Digital Subscriber Line.

Aggregate. Gravel or crushed stone used in a concrete mixture. See also lightweight aggregate.

Aggregate base. Crushed stone used as a base for paving.

AIA. American Institute of Architects.

Air change. Total replacement of the air in a space within sixty minutes.

Air distribution. Network of ducts delivering air from an air-handling unit to conditioned space.

Air distribution zone. An area of office space served by a supply duct and controlled by a thermostat.

Air handling unit. A fan and refrigeration coil in a housing that delivers conditioned air to a space.

Amenities. Retail and convenience type services considered desirable to tenants.

Americans with Disabilities Act. Federal legislation intended to ensure that those with disabilities have full reasonable access to all buildings.

Amperes. Unit of electrical current.

Appraisal. Estimate and opinion of value placed on real property by a qualified professional.

Articulation. Variation from a flat surface, either recessed or extended.

Articulation Class. Acoustical measurement of how effectively the ceilings, wall panels and furniture provide speech privacy in open offices.

Articulation Index. Ratio of the area of a curtain wall including its articulation, to the flat surface without articulation.

As-built. Completed project as it was actually constructed.

Assignment. Transfer of property, or rights to property, between parties.

Asymmetrical Digital Subscriber Line. High-speed line for Internet access where the upload and download speeds are different.

B

Backfill. Replacement of earth against a constructed element after the work is completed.

Backflow preventor. Form of a check valve that ensures that water will not flow backward into a municipal water system.

Background noise levels. General noise levels that are annoying or interfere with effective communication.

BACnet. Set of rules for a universal open protocol to govern the exchange of data over computer networks.

Balancing. Adjusting dampers and/or valves to deliver proper quantities of fluid to desired location.

Ballast. Weight to accomplish an objective, as to hold down a roofing membrane.

Ballasts. Devices in a lighting fixture that controls the fluorescent lamp.

BANANA. Build absolutely nothing anywhere near anything.

Base building. Constructed improvement prior to the start of any Tenant Improvements.

Base building condition. Condition of the base building when it is ready to receive Tenant Improvements.

Baseline budget. Maximum amount the owner wishes to spend for base building construction broken down by line items that are based upon the contractor's best judgment.

Basis point. 1/100 of 1% of interest.

Bay. Distance between rows of columns.

Bay depth. Distance from a core wall to the outside wall between a set of columns.

Beams. Horizontal structural members.

Bearing capacity. Amount of weight that the soil or rock will safely support.

Berms. Mound of earth created for structural, retention or aesthetic purposes.

Bgsf. *See* builders gross area.

Bitumens. Asphalt or coal tar pitch.

BMS. *See* building management system.

Boiler. Electric or gas fired equipment to produce hot water or steam.

Bollard. Post, usually to contain lighting or control traffic.

BOCA. Basic National Building Code.

BOMA. Building Owners and Managers Association International.

Bonds. Commitment by a third party to be financially responsible for certain obligations undertaken by another.

Brace frame. Structural design to resist overturning or seismic loads by stiffening a building with added members in the direction of stress.

Break-even cash flow. Rental income that covers all taxes, operating costs and debt service.

Break test. Cone of concrete is broken after a stipulated time to determine if it is as strong as the design specified.

Btu. British thermal unit, the quantity of heat required to raise the temperature of one pound of water 1° F.

BTU meter. Device that calculates the amount of heating or cooling delivered to a space.

Builder's gross area. *See* contractors gross building area.

Builder's Risk. Insurance carried by the owner to cover the value of materials installed in the project, or otherwise the financial responsibility of owner.

Building code. Set of laws and regulations governing the construction of buildings.

Building common areas. Central areas for the use or benefit of all tenants including lobbies, atrium spaces at the level of the finished floor, health clubs, conference rooms, lounges or vending areas, locker and shower facilities, mail rooms, fire control rooms, fully enclosed mechanical and equipment rooms, and loading dock space within the building envelope.

Building gross area. *See* Gross Measured Area.

Building management system. System to control the operation of the various building systems, and frequently includes security and accounting.

Building separation. Minimum legal distance permitted between two structures.

Building skin. Vertical cover of the building, also called façade or fenestration.

Building Standards. Approved materials that may be installed in the building.

Building Technology Platform. One term for an integrated raised floor system.

Build-to-suit. Construction of a building or a leased space to a tenant's specifications.

Built-up roofing. Roofing installed in layers.

Built-up sections. Structural steel sections fabricated for specific conditions rather than a rolled section from the mill.

Bulk. Area of the larger floors of a building, usually determined in relation to the site.

Bus duct. Copper or aluminum conducting bar that carries heavy electrical current through a building.

C

C of O. *See* Certificate of Occupancy.

CAD. Computer aided drafting.

Caissons. Subsurface structural support whose bottom can be inspected prior to installation.

Camber. Slight convex curve in a beam to allow for some settling under load.

Cantilever. Structural beam that extends beyond its supporting column.

Cap rate. *See* capitalization rate.

Capacitance. The ability to retain heat.

Capitalization rate. Value of an income producing property determined by dividing its net income by a market interest rate.

Capital reserve. Money set aside for future repairs or improvements.

Capture rate. Ratio of the leases entered into, or projected to be entered into, to the total available demand in the submarket.

Card readers. Security device that will read an approved card and provide access.

Cash flow. Funds from operations available for other purposes.

Caulking. Sealant to weatherproof a building.

CBD. Central Business District.

CC&Rs. Recorded covenants, conditions and restrictions that limit the use of real property.

CCTV. Closed circuit television.

Centrifugal chiller. Equipment with a centrifugal type compressor that produces chilled water for air conditioning a building.

Certificate of Completion. Certificate, usually prepared by the architect, stating that the construction of a building is completed in accordance with the contract documents.

Certificate of Occupancy. Authorization by the governing jurisdiction that the building may be occupied.

Certification. Process for establishing through testing that a product meets a particular specification.

CFL. Compact fluorescent lamp.

Cfm. Cubic feet per minute.

Change order. Approved directive to add or delete work from a contract at an agreed upon price.

Channels. Rolled structural steel member with a shallow "U" shape.

Chase. Vertical path up through a building for piping or electrical service.

Check valve. Valve with a flapper that permits the fluid to flow in only one direction.

Chilled water. Water, usually at about 55° F, circulated through coils to cool the air that is delivered to a space.

Chilled water pump. Pump that circulates chilled water.

Coefficient of friction. Resistance of a conduit to the fluid flowing through it.

Coefficient of performance. Ratio of the net heat removal to the rate of total energy input.

Cofferdam. Vertical sheeting with internal bracing at various depths.

Coil. Series of tubes with fins, through which air is cooled by passing on the outside while chilled water circulates inside.

Color rendition. Ability of a light source to represent colors in objects.

Color temperature. Warmth or coolness of light expressed in degrees Kelvin.

Column caps. Base for a column usually located over a caisson or piling.

Columns. Vertical member that supports the beam building loads.

Commissions. Fee paid to a real estate broker for procuring a tenant.

Commitment fee. Fee paid to a lender for committing to make a loan on the property.

Common areas. *See* floor common areas and building common areas.

Compact Fluorescent Lamps. Efficient lamp with good color rendition that is replacing incandescent lighting.

Comparables. Recorded sales of property similar in size, use, quality and age, usually located in the same sub-market.

Conceptual estimating. Construction cost estimate based on a general understanding of the design intent rather than on detailed Contract Documents.

Concessions. Cash value in the form of excess TIs, rent abatement or other payment to induce a tenant to enter into a lease.

Concrete. Mixture of Portland cement, aggregate, sand, water and admixtures to form a structural element.

Condemnation. Process of a governmental taking of private property without the owners consent.

Condensation. Physical process by which liquid is removed from a vapor.

Condenser. Apparatus used in refrigeration to condense hot refrigeration vapor to a liquid.

Condenser water. Circulating water that removes heat from the chillers.

Condenser water system. Pumps, piping and controls that circulate water between the condenser on a chiller and the cooling tower.

Construction loan. Floating rate loan against a property to cover expenditures during the construction period.

Contingency. Provision of funds in an estimate to protect against errors and/or unforeseen conditions.

Contract documents. Working drawings, specifications and general and special conditions that govern the construction of a project.

Contractors gross building area. Gross building area calculated from the outside extremities plus overhangs, covered walkways, etc. It is greater than the gross area calculated by the architect.

Convection. Heat transfer by fluid or air motion.

Conveyance. Transfer of title.

Cooling load. Amount of heat generated in or transmitted into a space that must be removed to maintain a desired condition.

Cooling tower. Device in the condenser water circuit that rejects heat to the atmosphere.

Core. Central portion of a floor in a structure containing the elevators, stairs, toilet rooms and other service and support areas.

COREA. Construction, Operation and Reciprocal Easement Agreement.

Core-to-glass. Distance from a core wall to the glass line of a building.

Cove lighting. Lighting placed in a recess with the lamp hidden by a louver or sight lines.

CPM. Critical path method.

CRI. Color rendition index.

Critical path method. Method of scheduling a project by organizing all activities into a network to determine the chain of activities that determine project completion in accordance with the current planning process.

CRTs. Cathode-ray tube, used as a monitor for computers and other devices.

CTs. *See* current transducers.

Cubicles. Small office area constructed from less than ceiling height movable walls or furniture.

Current transducers. Doughnut-like device that surrounds an electrical wire to measure the current.

Curtain wall. Non-load bearing wall that encloses a structure.

D

Damper. Series of metal volume controlling blades operated by mechanical linkage.

Daylight. Light from the atmosphere within the building.

Dead load. Vertical load carried by the building structure, basically its own weight, before allowing for partitions, furniture, equipment and people.

Deed. Instrument to convey the transfer of real property.

Deed of Trust. Deed to real property held in trust to be delivered to a lender upon the occurrence of specified defaults.

Deed restrictions. Any permitted legal restrictions on the use of real property that is recorded.

Default. Failure to timely perform a task or pay an obligation.

Dehumidification. System for removing moisture from the air.

Demand. (1) Actual use of electricity and one component of utility bill for electricity usage. (2) For office space, the estimated requirement for office in a submarket.

Demising walls. Walls that separate one tenant space from another and from the public corridors.

Demographics. Characteristics of a population.

Density. Amount of construction permitted on a given amount of property.

Design conditions. Maximum outdoor wet bulb and dry bulb temperature for cooling, minimum outdoor wet bulb and dry bulb temperature for heating, and the desired indoor wet bulb and dry bulb temperatures.

Design criteria. Set of requirements by the owner to govern the design of an improvement.

Design development. Phase in design of a structure when all of the building systems are defined.

Design-build. Process wherein a single entity is involved with both the design and construction of a structure, or a part thereof.

Detention pond. Area for temporarily storing storm water prior to releasing it at an acceptable rate.

Developer's markup. Number of basis points of return a developer requires above the loan rate to consider a project sufficiently profitable.

Developer's return. Overall net income as a percentage of project cost that the developer requires.

Development Officer. Individual directly responsible for the planning and execution of a development project.

Digital subscriber lines. High-speed telephone service for Internet access.

Direct expansion coil. Cooling coils that receive refrigerant directly from a compressor, and through an expansion process produces the refrigeration to lower the air temperature as required.

Dock levelers. Device that adjusts the loading dock height to match the tailgates of different trucks.

Drivit. Trade name for Exterior Insulation and Finish Systems.

Dry bulb temperature. Temperature of air indicated by a thermometer after correction for radiation.

DSL. *See* digital subscriber line.

DX. *See* direct expansion coil.

E

Easements. Right to use the property of another created by grant, agreement, reservation, prescription or implication.

Economizer cycle. Drawing in of 100% outdoor air for cooling whenever the outdoor enthalpy is less than the return air enthalpy.

Effective rent. Rental achieved by landlord over the term of the lease after adjusting for the value of concessions.

Efficacy. Rate at which a fixture is able to convert electrical input (watts) into light output (lumens).

EIFS. Exterior Insulation and Finish Systems.

EIR. *See* Environmental Impact Report.

EIS. *See* Environmental Impact Statement.

Electrical panel. Series of circuit breakers within a metal enclosure for distribution to lighting and power circuits on a floor.

Electrical vault. Normally a below-grade enclosure housing a power company transformer.

Electrochromatic glazing. Method of changing the optical density through application of electrical current to a film on the glazing panel.

Electronic grade panels. Electrical panels with provisions to protect against harmonics that might harm sensitive equipment.

Emissivity. Ability to reflect heat.

EMS. *See* Energy Management System.

Encroachment. Where a structure extends impermissibly over a property line, easement or setback.

Encryption. Sophisticated encoding system to protect the privacy of email.

Encumbrance. Claim, lien, or other liability attached to and binding real property.

Energy Management System. System for controlling the operating systems, with specific regard to reduction of energy use.

Enthalpy. Total heat content of air.

Entitlement. Right to use real property in a specific manner, such as development of a building.

Environmental Impact Report. A report prepared by an independent professional citing the probable environmental effect of a development on the surrounding area, and listing potential mitigations.

Environmental Impact Statement. Synonymous with EIR.

Equity. Value of one's interest in a property.

Errors and omissions. Insurance policy by professionals and contractors to cover errors in their performance.

Escalation. General increase in costs from which an owner is protected in a lease by an Escalation Clause.

Escrow. Property held by a third party in accordance with an agreement.

Estoppel. Statement concerning the status of an agreement and the performance of the parties to date that can be relied upon by a third party.

Ethernet. Widely integrated local area network for communication.

Exactions. Payment for the privilege for developing a project that is not directly related to the mitigation of any problem created by that project.

Exculpatory clause. To free a party from blame from an event.

Exhibit. An attachment to a lease that provides clarifying and/or legal information and descriptions relative to the lease.

Exit corridor. Safe egress path in the event of a fire or other occurrence.

Expansion space. Additional leased space available as an option to a tenant at a specified time.

Export soil. Excess soil from a project that must be disposed of off-site.

Exterior Insulation and Finish System. Integrated wall cladding system combining weatherproofing, insulation and finish.

F

Façade. The face of a building. Sometimes considered synonymous with curtain wall or building skin.

Face rental rate. Rental rate stated by landlord.

FACP. *See* fire alarm and control panel.

Fair Market Value. Cash price that would most likely be negotiated between a willing purchaser and a seller for a property.

Fan coil unit. Self-contained cabinet housing a small centrifugal fan with a cooling and/or a heating coil.

FAR. *See* floor area ratio.

Fast track. Commencing some portions of a construction project before other portions are fully designed.

Feasibility. Likelihood of a project meeting the developer's financial expectations.

Feasibility Analysis. Studies that determine economic feasibility.

Fee simple. Estate in real property where the owner has unrestricted right to dispose of the property.

Fenestration. The arrangement of windows and doors in a building. Often used interchangeably with façade and curtain wall.

Feng Shui. Ancient Chinese system of rules and principles that explain the impact of placement on people's lives.

FF&E. Furniture, fixtures and equipment.

Filter. Media in the supply air stream to remove dirt and impurities.

Filtration. Process of removal of dirt and impurities.

Financing rate. Effective interest rate charged on a loan.

Fire alarm and control panel. Complete emergency control center provided near the lobby of a building for ready access by the firemen.

Fire resistance. Tested ability of material or a structure to resist fire over a stipulated period of time.

Fireproofing. A fire resistive material, frequently cementitious or plaster based, to protect members from fire damage.

Flamed. Creation of a textured surface on stone by passing controlled flame across it.

Flame-spread. Extent and rapidity with which flames spread over a surface under test conditions.

Flashing. Material that directs weather elements away from a potential open joint in the building envelope.

Float. (1) Use of money for an interim period until transfer of funds has been completed. (2) In parking areas, it is the use of allocated spaces not currently in use for transients.

Floating rate. Borrowed funds whose interest rate will vary with market conditions.

Flood plain. Land adjoining a river that would flood if the river overflowed its banks.

Floor area ratio. Ratio of the permissible total floor area of a project to the size of the land.

Floor common areas. Areas shared by tenants on a floor, including washrooms, janitor closets, electrical and telephone rooms, mechanical rooms, elevator lobbies and public corridors.

Floor load. The load a floor of a structure is designed to carry.

Fly ash. Byproduct of coal burning power plants that is sometimes used in concrete in lieu of some of the Portland cement.

Foot-candles. Amount of direct light thrown by a source of one candle on a surface one foot away from the source.

Force majeure. Force or event that cannot be controlled or resisted, beyond the control of the parties.

Foreclosure. A proceeding to extinguish the rights of the owner in order to sell the property to satisfy a lien.

Foundation. Base on which a structure rests.

Fpm. Feet per minute.

Fps. Feet per second.

Frequencies. Periodic vibrations, oscillations, cycles or waves, expressed in hertz—applies to sound and electricity.

Furring. Application of lath to studs, columns or walls to attach finish material. Frequently refers to the entire process of enclosing stud walls or columns.

G

Gasket. Material that serves as a seal between two elements.

General Conditions. Document that supplements the specifications and generally spells out the general and business terms of the contract.

General contractor. Party who contracts for the construction of a project.

Geographic Information System. Computer system that through use of satellite generated data records, stores and analyzes the terrain for mapping and surveying.

Geo-piers. Alternate layers of aggregate and slurry placed in drilled holes to serve as a foundation.

Geotechnical. Engineering practice of studying the subsurface to determine the problems that may affect design of a proposed structure.

GFRC. *See* Glass Fiber Reinforced Concrete.

GIS. *See* Geographic Information System.

Glass Fiber Reinforced Concrete. A cement-based composite with glass fibers randomly dispersed throughout for strength.

GMP. *See* Guaranteed Maximum Price.

Gph. Gallons per hour.

Gpm. Gallons per minute.

Grade beams. Reinforced concrete beam on soil, often called a footing.

Grading plan. Plan with a complete survey, topography, rights of way, easements, building locations and utilities, frequently required to be approved prior to submission of any plans for a structure for a building permit.

Graphics. All signage or other visual directional information.

Gross area. *See* Gross Measured Area.

Gross building area. *See* Gross Measured Area.

Gross Measured Area. Above grade floor areas calculated from the inside faces of the outside lites and below grade areas calculated from the inside faces of the structural walls, less parking areas.

Gsf. Gross area of a building in square feet.

Guaranteed Maximum Price. The maximum price the contractor will charge for constructing a building under specified conditions.

H

"H" sections. A rolled structural steel section resembling the letter "H".

Handling capacity. Number of passengers an elevator bank will handle in a five-minute period under up-peak conditions.

Hard bid. Contractor's price to construct a project based on a complete set of Contract Documents.

Hardscape. Paved surfaces in a landscape plan.

Hazardous materials. Material whose presence is hazardous to personnel and whose removal requires special equipment and procedures.

Heat of hydration. Heat produced by the chemical reaction in concrete while it cures.

Heat pump. Device for cooling or warming an enclosed space by removing heat from interior air and transferring it out, or from a hot water source and transferring it in.

Heat recovery. Recovery of normally wasted heat for a useful purpose, usually condenser heat.

Heat transfer. Act of exchanging heat from one system to another.

Hertz. Unit of frequency in cycles per second.

HID. High intensity discharge.

High-intensity discharge. Small lamps that produce large amounts of light, usually of metal halide or high-pressure sodium type.

High-rise. Normally determined by code designation, the top occupied floor over 75 feet above grade under most codes.

Hollow metal. Factory formed metal doors and frames.

Honed. Smooth finish of a stone, but less than polished.

Horsepower. Unit for measuring power equal to 746 watts, or the force required to lift 33,000 pounds at the rate of one foot per minute.

Humidification. Process of adding moisture to interior air.

Humidity. *See* relative humidity.

HVAC. The system for heating, ventilating and air conditioning a building or space.

Hydraulic. A method of actuating a device by fluid pressure.

Hydraulic elevator. Elevator whose operation is by a large vertical hydraulic cylinder.

Hydronic. Means of heating or cooling by the circulation of liquids.

I

"I" sections. A rolled structural steel section resembling the letter "I".

IAQ. *See* Indoor Air Quality.

IEQ. *See* Interior Environmental Quality.

Impact fees. Fees paid to mitigate an environmental impact caused by the development of a project.

Import soil. Soil that is purchased and brought onto the site in the process of constructing a project.

Improvements. Any construction placed upon a parcel of land.

Indoor Air Quality. Measure of amount of air flow and presence of airborne impurities in a space.

Indirect lighting. Light that is reflected off of another surface before being directed into the space.

Infiltration. Ambient air leakage into a conditioned space.

Initial occupancy. First occupancy of a building by a tenant. Also used as start of a lease for any tenant.

Insolation. Rate of delivery of solar radiation per unit of surface area.

Insulation. Material used to delay the heat transfer process.

Interim loan. *See* construction loan.

Integrated Service Digital Network. Special telephone system for Internet access.

Interior Environmental Quality. Measure of the overall quality of a space to promote efficiency and productivity.

Internal rate of return. The overall rate of return of a project over a specified period of time with all surplus funds reinvested at the same rate.

Interval. The average frequency with which an elevator in an elevator bank passes a given point.

Inventory. Total amount of office space existing in a specified market area.

IREM. Institute of Real Estate Management.

IRR. *See* internal rate of return.

ISDN. *See* Integrated Service Digital Network.

J

Jockey pump. Small pump usually to start up a system or to keep a small amount of liquid circulating.

K

Kilowatt. 1,000 watts.

Kips. 1,000 pounds.

K-rated transformers. Transformer designed to minimize harmonic vibrations that might harm sensitive equipment.

Kw. Kilowatt.

L

Lagging. Lumber placed between vertical members to retain the soil surrounding an excavation.

Land development. Developing raw land with streets, utilities, etc. and subdividing in order to sell lots for individual development.

Latent defects. Deficiency in a completed improvement that cannot be readily determined by inspection when the work is completed.

Leader. Connection from a drain line to a sewer.

Lease. Agreement whereby the owner of real property gives another a right of possession for a specified period of time for a specified consideration.

Lease-up period. Length of time between substantial completion of a building until it reaches stabilized occupancy.

Led. Light-emitting diode

Letter of credit. Pledge by a financial institution to honor demands for payment based on compliance with specified conditions.

Letter of Intent. Non-binding expression of intent conditioned upon further documentation.

Leverage. Potential increased profits (or losses) resulting from the use of borrowed funds.

LIBOR. London Interbank Offering Rate.

Lien. Monetary encumbrance against a property for money.

Lien waiver. Waiver of mechanic's or material supplier's lien rights.

Life cycle costing. Sum of all initial operating and maintenance costs of a system or equipment over a stipulated period.

Light-emitting diode. Semiconductor diode that emits light when voltage is applied.

Lightweight aggregate. Products of blast furnace slag, shale, slate, and shale and clay. Permits lighter weight concrete for floors, etc.

Linear diffuser. Slot diffuser normally located at or near the perimeter of a building.

Lite. Section of window glazing.

Live load. Structural allowance for the weight of partitions, furniture, equipment and people.

Lock-in clause. Prevents a loan from being prepaid prior to a specified time.

LonMark. Proprietary communications protocol to permit devices from different manufacturers to communicate seamlessly.

Loop. Distribution circuit on a floor, as for conditioned air, hot water, or sprinkler water.

Lot. Parcel of land that is part of a subdivision that is created and shown by a plat.

Lot line adjustment. Revision to the boundaries between lots.

LULU. Locally unwanted land use.

Lumen. Unit for the flow of light equal to the flow from a unit point source of one foot-candle.

M

Macro. An overview evaluation.

Market cycle. Periodic increase and decrease in market demand in relation to supply and economic potential.

Market saturation. Existing office supply fully satisfies the demand.

Market Study. Forecast of the demand for office space, the requirements of potential tenants and the economic potential.

Market value. Most probable price that a property, or rental rate for a space for lease, would bring on an open market between knowledgeable and motivated buyers and sellers.

Mat. Thick heavily reinforced concrete slab over the entire footprint to serve as a building foundation.

MCC. Motor control center.

Mechanic's lien. Encumbrance created by statute filed against a property by a contractor or material supplier to ensure payment.

Mecho shade. Roller window covering with various degrees of translucency in the lowered position.

MEP. Mechanical, electrical and plumbing.

Metal halides. Small high-powered lamps with a high lumen output, most commonly used out of doors.

Metes and bounds. Boundaries of a property described by its terminal points and angles.

Micro. Very detailed analysis of a subject.

Microbials. Molds, bacteria and viruses.

Mini-perm. Short-term mortgage on a property that is an extension of the construction or interim loan.

Mitigate. Action to minimize an impact on an area by a development project.

Mixing box. A device for mixing two temperatures of air to achieve a desired space temperature.

Modular. Units of a standardized size, design, etc. that can be arranged or fitted together in a variety of ways.

Module. Standardized unit. In an office building it is a repetitive square unit of floor area. In a parking structure it is a drive path bounded by parking spaces—also called a ramp.

Moment frame. Structural resistance to overturning or seismic forces achieved through the design of the connections between the columns and beams.

Mortgage. Instrument created to serve as security for the performance or repayment of a loan.

Motor control center. Organized rack where various motor starters are placed.

Mullions. Vertical members in a façade or curtain wall.

N

Net absorption. Net amount of office space leased over a specific period of time in a market area, taking into consideration space vacated or not yet occupied.

Net rental income. Funds received as rental income less taxes and operating expenses.

NIMBY. Not in my backyard.

NIMTOO. Not in my term of office.

Noise Criterion. Field test to measure the amount of background noise.

Noise Reduction Coefficient. Efficiency of a material to absorb noise.

Noncombustible. Not capable of burning under specified conditions.

Non-recourse. Loan in which the borrower is not personally liable, i.e., the loan must be recovered exclusively against the property.

Notice to Proceed. Formal authorization to commence construction.

O

Office inventory. Amount of office space existing in a market or submarket.

Office space supply. The amount of office space available, or planned to be available, to lease in a market or submarket.

Office stock. *See* office inventory.

Operating expenses. All costs necessary to manage and operate an income producing property.

P

Parapet. Low wall, as around a balcony or roof.

Parking stall. Designated space to park one automobile.

Percolation test. Test to determine the ability of the soil to absorb water.

Permanent loan. Loan against real property for a period of years.

Permits. Authorization by a governing jurisdiction to construct an improvement in accordance with approved plans.

Permitting. Process of obtaining a permit.

Photovoltaic. System that can permit walls, windows and roofs to become solar energy collectors.

Pier. Concrete column bedded in rock.

Piling. Structural support whose bottom cannot be visually inspected prior to installation.

Planned Unit Development. Approval granted for a multi-building project that will be developed over a period of years. Individual permits are required but the general requirements are set.

Plat. Map dividing a parcel into lots, as in a subdivision.

Platting. Process of preparing a plat map.

Plenum. Enclosed space for delivering air. When no return air ducts are provided, and the air flows back between the ceiling and slab above, the entire space is a plenum.

POC. Products of combustion.

Pony chiller. Small refrigeration chiller to use under very light loads.

Post-tensioned. Non-bonded steel tendons threaded through conduits within the structural slab are stretched to create a stress after the concrete has reached its design strength to counteract tensile stresses.

Potable. Water that is fit to drink.

Power assist doors. Mechanism that provides part of the energy required to open a door when initiated by a manual effort.

Precast concrete. Concrete that is formed and poured off-site and later installed on an improvement.

Preconstruction. All efforts to develop an improvement that occur prior to commencement of construction.

Preinstalled items. Materials installed in the course of the base building construction that are later billed to the tenant as part of the TI allowance.

Prelease. Lease executed prior to the commencement of construction.

Premises. Property defined in a lease, deed or other conveyance.

Pressure drop. Loss due to friction when a fluid passes through a conduit or equipment, usually expressed in feet of water or inches of water gauge.

Pre-stressed. Steel tendons placed in a form and are stressed prior to pouring the concrete to counteract tensile stresses.

Privacy rating. Measure of acoustical privacy.

Pro forma. Analysis of a project's entire financial structure to determine total project cost and the predicted returns.

Promissory note. Written promise to pay a certain sum of money on demand or at a specified time.

Proximity device. Device that reads an access card placed close to it.

Psf. Pounds per square foot.

Psi. Pounds per square inch.

PUD. Planned Unit Development.

Punch list. Itemized list of incomplete or unsatisfactory work that must be corrected, but most often does not delay occupancy.

R

Radiation. Process in which energy in the form of rays of light, heat, etc. are sent through space.

Raft. Form of foundation, *see* mat.

Rain screen. Form of curtain wall where the pressure across the wall is equalized.

Raised floor. Modular floor sections mounted on posts above the floor slab to facilitate electrical and air distribution.

Ramp. Sloped surface. In a parking structure is often synonymous with a parking module.

Rate of return. Percentage return on an investment.

Real Estate Investment Trust. Trust that invests in real estate.

Rebars. *See* reinforcing bars.

Recourse. Right of a lender or holder of a note secured by a mortgage to look to other assets of a borrower for payment to satisfy a loan.

Redevelopment agency. Governmental agency charged with promoting and/or controlling development in a specific area to accomplish stated public purposes.

Reflectance. Ratio of the intensity of the total radiation of light reflected from a surface to the total incident on the surface.

Reflectivity. Capacity to reflect or divert light or solar heat.

Refrigeration. Act of producing the chilled water.

Refrigeration system. System that produces the chilled water, dissipates the excess heat and cools the air in an air conditioning system.

Reinforcing bars. Deformed steel bars placed in concrete to provide tensile strength.

REIT. Real Estate Investment Trust.

Relative humidity. Ratio of the amount of water vapor in the air at a specific temperature to the maximum capacity of the air at that temperature.

Renderings. Artist's picture to convey the appearance of a proposed building or portion thereof.

Renewal Term. Right in the lease for a tenant to elect to remain in the space for an additional period of time.

Rent. Sum of all payments due from a tenant in accordance with the lease.

Rentable area. Normally all floor area in an office building measured from the inside face of the outside lite on all sides, less the area of vertical penetrations, plus common areas.

Rentable/useable (R/U) ratio. The rentable area divided by the useable area, expressed as a percent. The amount the ratio exceeds 100% is called the "add on" factor.

Respirable particles. Small dust particles that can be inhaled deeply and are in the lung-damaging size.

Retaining walls. Structural wall that resists the forces of the earth behind it.

Retention ponds. Area that impounds storm water until it percolates into the ground or evaporates.

RFP. Request for Proposal.

RH. *See* relative humidity.

Riders. Appendage to a lease covering negotiated special conditions not included in the printed lease form.

Right of redemption. Certain rights to recover a property after foreclosure.

Riser. Vertical pipe, duct, bus duct or electrical cable serving higher floors.

Risk. Exposure to loss.

Rock anchors. Anchor drilled into rock to support sheeting or other retaining wall.

Room Criterion. Measure of background noise that also notes whether it is a rumble, hiss or vibration.

Rpm. Revolutions per minute.

Rsf. Rentable square foot.

R/U ratio. *See* rentable/useable ratio.

R-value. Reciprocal of the U-value.

S

Sanitary waste. Any waste other than storm runoff.

Schedule of values. Cost of a construction contract broken down by categories and units to facilitate a system for determining a fair amount to pay to the contractor each month.

Schematic design. First phase of a design in which the basic character and design of an improvement is determined.

Scuppers. Opening in a building to let water run off of a roof or balcony.

SDG&E. San Diego Gas and Electric.

Seismic. Having to do with, or caused by earthquakes.

Sensitivity analysis. Analyses that test various possible alternatives against the potential result, as in a pro forma.

Service areas. Areas on a floor that benefit the tenant, such as toilet rooms, elevator lobbies, mechanical and electrical rooms.

Setbacks. Minimum distance from the edge of a structure to a property line as required by zoning or other ordinance.

Sf. Square feet.

Shading coefficient. Percentage of insolation allowed to pass through glass.

Sheet piling. Heavy corrugated steel sections driven around the perimeter of an excavation on a site to retain the earth.

Shell and core construction. Extent of the base building construction before the start of the Tenant Improvements.

Site coverage. Percentage of a site on which improvements are constructed.

Sky lobby. Elevator transfer floor used in very tall buildings.

Slab. Floor in an improvement.

Slab-to-slab. Distance from the surface of one floor to the surface of the next one.

Slump test. Stiffness test for the amount of liquid in concrete.

Slurry walls. A low slump mixture of concrete and chemically treated soil pumped into a trench or drilled holes to retain soil and limit water intrusion.

Smart cards. A card that has processing capability used for security and access purposes.

Soffits. Plaster or drywall construction that extends from the exterior wall to the building standard ceiling.

Soil borings. Holes drilled into the earth to determine the type, quality and bearing capacity of the soil and the depth of the water table.

Soil-nailed. Steel tendrels inserted into drilled holes and tied to a reinforced wall to retain the adjacent soil.

Solar orientation. Direction a building faces with relation to maximizing solar heat in winter and minimizing solar energy intake in summer.

Soldier beams. Usually "H" beams driven or drilled into the ground that retain the soil when lagging is placed between them.

Sound transmission class. The single number rating used to measure the ability of construction elements to block sound at speech frequencies.

Space plan. Office and furniture layout to determine how well a tenant's functions could be satisfied in a specific space.

Span. The length of a beam between two supporting columns.

Spandrel. Horizontal element between glazing sections in a building façade.

Spandrel glass. Spandrel of glass.

Specifications. Written description of materials and workmanship that supplements the working drawings in describing the desired construction.

Speculative space. Amount of rentable area above the amount of space that was preleased.

Spread footing. Reinforced concrete beam resting on soil, also called grade beams.

Sprinkler head. Device with a fusible link that sprays water over a predetermined area when the link is melted.

Stabilized occupancy. Planned occupancy at which the building is projected to be sufficiently profitable.

Standpipe. Vertical water pipe for sprinkler and fire protection purposes.

Storm sewer. Sewer to handle storm water runoff.

Subcontractor. Contractor under contract to a general contractor.

Subdivision. Division of a parcel of land into two or more lots.

Subdivision map. Survey describing the subdivision.

Sublet. A tenant transfers his right to occupy space to another, normally with landlord's permission.

Subordination. Agreement in which one party agrees under certain conditions to yield its priority to another.

Substantial completion. When work under a construction is complete except for the punch list.

Substrate. Supportive material on which finished exterior wall surfaces are placed.

Sump pumps. Pumps for water that may collect from or beneath the floor slab.

Support areas. *See* service areas.

Survey. Measurement of the boundaries of a parcel of land, any encumbrances of record, utilities, and frequently the topography.

Sustainability. Use of materials and systems to promote energy efficiency and recycling.

Swing car. Elevator car used alternatively for passenger and freight service.

Switchgear. Organized assembly of the main switches for the major components in a building.

T

T12 lamp. 1¼" diameter fluorescent lamp consuming 40w.

T5 lamp. ⅝" diameter fluorescent lamp, currently used primarily in Europe, consuming 28w.

T8. 1" diameter fluorescent lamp most commonly used in this country today, consuming 32w.

TCO. Temporary Certificate of Occupancy.

Temporary Certificate of Occupancy. Governmental certification that the base building construction is sufficiently complete that a tenant can occupy their space when the TI worked is accepted.

Tenant Improvements. Improvements beyond the base building construction that meets the needs of tenants.

Term. Period of time for which a right in real property is granted or conveyed.

TES. *See* thermal energy storage.

Thermal break. Insulating material between the exterior and interior surfaces of a window frame.

Thermal energy storage. Chilled water or ice created in off-peak hours to be used at peak energy cost hours.

Thermocycle. Using the centrifugal chiller as a heat exchanger by means of natural circulation of the refrigerant caused by the temperature difference between the condenser and chilled water.

Thermoplastic. Plastic membranes that can be readily seamed by welding with a hot air gun or solvents.

Thermosets. Rubber polymer membranes bonded by liquid contact or tape adhesives.

Thermostat. Device capable of sensing the temperature in a space and causing the system to maintain a set temperature.

Tie backs. Anchors placed in a drilled hole that are filled with concrete to retain an element.

Tie-back sheeting. Sheeting reinforced with tiebacks.

TIs. Tenant Improvements.

Title. Legal evidence of a right to ownership of property.

Title companies. A company that searches all recorded documents to determine any encumbrances to a clear title and provides escrow and title insurance.

Title insurance. Insurance against loss resulting from defects of title to real property.

Tombstone. A form of advertising for financings and leases that generally resembles a tombstone.

Ton. 2,000 pounds of weight, or 12,000 BTUs per hour of refrigeration.

Topographical. Plotting of the site elevations on a survey.

Total Project Cost. Overall cost of a project including the cost of interest and vacancy.

Traction. Type of elevator using a motor and pulleys.

Transformers. Device that reduces the voltage of electrical service to a lower voltage.

Trust Deed. *See* Deed of Trust

U

UCC. Unified Commercial Code.

U-value. Overall coefficient of heat transmission for any section of a building shell. Units are btu per square foot of section per hour per degree F temperature difference between inside air and outside air.

Uniform Commercial Code. A codification of commercial laws designed to provide uniformity between states.

Useable area. Rentable area less service/support areas. For divided floors the corridors and elevator lobbies are also excluded.

Usf. Useable square feet.

V

V. Volts.

Vacancy. Space not leased or occupied.

Vacancy rate. Vacant space divided by total space in the subject market area.

Value engineering. Process of evaluating a design to determine if the project objectives can be met with less expensive systems materials or equipment.

Variable frequency drive. Electric motor wherein the frequency is varied to minimize starting current and to adjust for partial load operation.

Variable air volume system. System capable of delivering only the air quantity necessary to obtain the desired space conditions responding to instantaneous load requirements.

Variance. Permit that grants a property owner relief from certain provisions of a zoning ordinance.

VAV. Variable air volume system.

VCT. Vinyl composition tile.

Velocity. Rate at which a fluid is conducted through a pipe or duct, usually expressed in feet per minute.

Ventilation. Process taking outside air to condition a normally unconditioned space.

Vestibule. Enclosed entrance space between a stairwell and a corridor or occupied space.

VFD. *See* variable frequency drive.

Vinyl composition tile. Resilient material used for flooring in some service areas and as a base for vinyl tile and carpet installations.

Vision glass. Portion of a building enclosure that is transparent.

Visual comfort probability. Measure of the percentage of persons who would find the overall lighting in a space comfortable.

Visual light transmission. The percentage of visible light that enters a space.

VLT. Visual light transmission.

VOCs. Volatile organic compounds.

Volatile organic compounds. Low carbon compounds off-gassed from the surface of solvents, adhesives and finishes.

Voltage. Difference in potential between two points in an electric field that moves electrical current.

W

W. Watt.

Waiver of liens. Release of a monetary encumbrance, normally in return for receiving payment.

Warranty. Binding promise made at time of sale whereby seller gives buyer certain assurances as to the condition of property.

Water treatment. Chemical treatment process used to prevent scaling algae formations and other undesirable growth in water that inhibit heat transfer, or leads to corrosion.

Watt. Unit of electrical power developed by a current of one ampere flowing through a potential difference of one volt.

Wet bulb temperature. Temperature at which water evaporating into air can bring the air to saturation.

Wetlands. Geographic area with characteristics of both dry land and bodies of water, where the water surface is at or near the land surface, which permits growth adapted to wet conditions. Habitat for many endangered species.

White noise. Noise, usually air, injected into a space to promote speech privacy.

"Will Serve" letters. Utility company letter promising to provide services to a proposed project.

Wind tunnel. Tube in which a model of an improvement is tested at various rotation angles and various wind speeds.

Window wall. Curtain wall manufactured and field assembled in stick fashion.

Work letter. Statement that a developer will provide a tenant offering stipulated units of specific materials and systems in order to build out the space.

Working drawings. The architect's plans from which the contractor will construct the improvements.

Workstations. A furniture grouping with equipment for one or more employees.

Z

"Z" corridor. Public corridor that passes through the elevator lobby and connects to at least two exit stairwells.

Zones. In air conditioning, an area that is controlled by a single thermostat.

Zoning. Classification and regulation of land by local governments according to use categories, density and other factors.

INDEX

A

780 Third Avenue, 198
Absorption, 30, 33, 35, 37–39, 41, 72
Acceleration clause, 148
Access control, 368
Acoustic privacy, 287
Acoustics, 285
  analysis, 258
Additional rent, 420
Add on factor, 108, 200, 293
Advertising, 211
Aggregate base, *see* site
Air distribution, system, 329, 331, 333
  air handling unit, 331, 332
  dual duct, 331
  fan coil unit, 332
  mixing boxes, 331,332
  outside air economizer, *see* HVAC
  multi–zone, 331
  VAV system, 331
  zones, 332
Air pollution, during construction, 494
Alarms, 365, **372**
Amenities/services, 31, 33, 39, 40, 44, 45, 47, 382
American Institute of Architects (AIA), 155, 157, 164, 436
Americans with Disabilities Act (ADA), 155, 299
American National Standards Institute (ANSI), 156
Appraisal, 145, 147, 148
Architect, 33, 44, 66, 71, **81**, 107, 112, 113, 120, **122**, 126, 157, 158, 161, 163, 165, 166, 169–171, **173**, **174**, **179**, 184, 209
  construction administration, 418, 434, 438, 462–464, 468, 469, 158, 161, 163, 166, 169–174, 179, 182–185, 20/8, 209
  contract, 164
  selection, 161, **173**
Architecture, 153–155, 182–185, 208
Architectural metal, 248
ARCO, 58
Articulation, *see* facade
  Class, 289
  Index, 289
As-built drawings and specifications, 436, 469
"As is" condition, 413
Asset management, 29, 120, 159, 479, 480
Assignment, 412, 422
Asymmetrical Digital Subscriber Line (ADSL), 359
Attitude, 24

B

Background noise levels, 286, 288
BACnet, 341 **348**
Bagua, 488
Ballast, 255
Ballasts, 357
BANANA, 67
Bank of Nova Scotia, 146
Base, *see* structural base
  building, 426
  building condition, 413, 426
Baseline budget, 170, **174**, **175**, **191**
Bay depth, 198, **203**
  size, **234**
Bearing capacity, 226
Berms, 215
BMS, *see* building management system
BOCA, 156, 200, 231
BOMA, 33, 34, 37, 107, 321, 381, 479
Bonds, 111, **117**, **175**, 438, **442**
Brace frame, *see* structure
Bradley & Bradley, 76, 77

Brandes Investment Partners, **84**, **116**, **139**, **150**, **175**, **213**, **302**, **362**, **385**, **400**, **414**, **424**, **442**, **448**, **471**, **473**, **483**
Break-even, cash flow ratio, 109,
  point, 108
Brochures, 210
Brokers, 211, 375, 376, 424
  commission agreement, 376, 377
Brick, 248
Builder's gross area, 108
Builder's Risk, 114
Building class, 36
  codes, 155, 156, 265, 245
  envelope, *see* façade and roof
  management system, (BMS), 339, **348**, 365
  permits, *see* permits
  signage, 256, 257, 382, **385**, **386**, **415**, **431**, **432**
  shapes, 183
  skin, *see* facade.
  Standards, 382, 390, **402**, 427
  Technology Platform, 332, 361
Build-to-suit, 13, 33, 35, 47, 162, 166–168, 185, 212
Built-up roofing, *see* roof
Bulk, 31, 56, 160
Bus duct, 351
Buskuhl, Joe, 8
Business Real Estate Brokers (BRE), **122**, **379**
Buy-sell agreement, 146, 445

C

CAD, *see* computer aided drafting
Caissons, 226
Capital reserve, 138
Capitalization rate (cap rate), 109, 147
Capture rate, 40
Card readers, 368

The numbers indicated in bold refer to the Case Study.

Carmel Valley Planning Board, **69**, **89**, **95**, **96**, **192**, **418**
Carpet, 394
  carpet tiles, 395
Cash flow, 109, 143–145, 147
  analysis, 125–127
Cash-on-cash returns, *see* rate of return
Cathode ray tubes, 356, 391
Caulking, *see* façade, sealants
CCTV, *see* security
CC&Rs, 74, 84, **385**, **431**, 500, 501
Ceiling, 390
Centrifugal chiller, **191**, 327, 330, **345**
Certificate of Occupancy (C of O), **48**, **117**, **151**, 352, **401**, 418, 465, 468, **473**
Certification (of standards), 158
Change orders, 464, 467, **474**
Chilled water system, *see* HVAC
Codes and regulations, 155
Coefficient of performance (COP), 328, 344
Cofferdam, 226
Color Rendition Index (CRI), 355, 356
Columns, 199, 231
  caps, 227
  covers, 240
  footings, 226
Commencement date, *see* lease
Commissions, *see* brokers commission agreement
Commitment fee, 47
Common areas, 107, 293, 419
Communications, systems, 359, 363
  closets, 366
  rooms, 300, 305. **313**
  satellite, 360
Compact fluorescent lamps (CFLs), 357, **362**
Comparable (comparative) sales, 73
Computer Aided Drafting (CAD), 156, 208
Conceptual, design, 181, 184
  estimating, 171
Concessions, 383
Concrete, 227, 228
  cast-in-place, 248
  fly ash, 217, 218, 494, 495
  lightweight, 228
  post-tensioned, 236
  precast, 247

prestressed, 328
reinforced, 228–231, 236, 237, 239, 248
testing, *see* testing, field
see also reinforcing bars (rebars)
Condemnation, 423
Condensation, 242
Condenser water system, *see* HVAC
ConDoc Index, 157
Consultant selection, 163
Construction, process, 461
  administration, 169, 463, 464, **471**
  risk, 113
  (interim) loan, 113, 144, 445
  Specification Institute (CSI), 157
Contingency, 113, 115, 125, 129, **140**, **141**, 144, 147, **175**, **430**, 436, 437, 462, 463
Contract documents, 157, 169.
Controls, *see* building management system
Cooling load, *see* HVAC
Cooling towers, 330
Core, 199–201, **203**, **234**, 293, **301**
COREA, **83**, **84**, **104**, **448**, **483**
Corridors, loop, 200
  "Z", 200, **203**, 293
  see also exiting
Cost estimating, 170, 171
Couvillion, John, 8
Creditworthiness, 384, 424
Critical Path Method (CPM), 443–445, **448**, **449**
Crocker Bank, 66, 75, 170
Cross-default, 149
CRTs, *see* cathode ray tubes
Curtain wall, *see* facade
Cushman III, John C.

D

Dallas Athletic Club, 60
Daylight (natural daylight), 243, 387
Debt service, 109, 143
  coverage, 145
Deed of Trust, **117**, 146, **150**, 445
Default, 149, 422
Dehumidification, 335
Demand, office space, 35, 37
  electrical, 352, 353
Demising walls, 393
Demographics, 67
Demolition, 59, 60, 74, 445
Density, building population, 274, **283**, 384

see also floor area ratio (FAR)
Design Conditions, *see* HVAC systems
Design criteria, *see* project design criteria
HVAC, *see* HVAC
Design development, 168, **449**
Design-build, 37, 38, 163, 437
Detention ponds, 216, 501
Developer's markup, 108
  return, 108
Development team, 24, 119, **122**
Digital subscriber lines (DSL), 359.
Direct expansion coil (DX), *see* HVAC
Direct mail, 210
Discipline, 16, 126
Discretionary regulations, 56
Domestic water, 338, **348**, 501
Doors and hardware, 300, 393
Drivit, 249
Dry bulb temperature, **346**, **349**
Dual duct, *see* air distribution

E

Ecology/ecological issues, *see* social issues *See also* sustainable design
Economizer cycle, *see* HVAC
Economical potential, 39
Eddie Bauer, 75
Effective rent, 40, 41, 375
Efficacy, 355
Electrical, clean power, 354
  closets, 299, **302**
  consumption, 411
  distribution rooms, 305, **313**
  electronic grade panels, 354, 392
  equipment efficiency, 354
  K-rated transformers
  power distribution, 351, **362**
  tenant power requirements, 324, 352, 356, **362**, 391
  transformers, 299, 302, 305, 313, 351–354, 392
  switchgear, 305, 351
  vault, 305.
Electrochromatic glazing, 256
Elevators, 269, 272
  cabs, 272, 273
  construction, 277
  freight, 276
  hydraulic, 272, **283**, **284**
  lobbies, 271, 293, **302**
  maintenance, 277

The numbers indicated in bold refer to the Case Study.

parking structure, 276, **284**
performance criteria, 273, 274, **283**
swing car, 276, **283**
transfer floors, 275
Emergency power, 221, **313**, **362**, 367, **372**
Emissivity, 241
Encumbered space, 383
Energy budget, 321, 341
Energy efficient design, *see* electrical, HVAC and sustainable design
Energy Management System (EMS), 323
see also building management system
Engineer selection, *see* consultants
Entitlements, 79
Environmental Impact Report (Statement) (EIR, EIS), 57, **62**, **88**, 445
Environmental site assessment, 57, **64**, 74
Equity, 144
Ernst, Mike, 8
Errors and omissions, 112, 113, 115, 145, 148, 165
Ethernet, 359
Exactions, 56, 500
Excavation, 225
Exculpatory clause, 149
Exiting, 199, 282, 293, 294, 366
Expansion space, 412, 427
Extension term, *see* renewal
Exterior Insulation and Finish System (EIFS), 249.

F

Façade, 183, 239, **258**, 495
articulation (factor), 239, 240
curtain wall, 240, **258**, **264**, **471**, **472**
mockups, 249
rain screen, 249, 250
sealants, 250
testing, *see* testing, façade
thermal break, *see* glazing
vision glass, *see* glazing
window wall, 240
Fair market rental rate, 412
Fan, systems, *see* air distribution rooms, 299
Fast track, 164, 169
Feasibility (Analysis), 29, **80**, 111, 499, 500

Fenestration, *see* curtain wall
Feng Shui, 184, 488
FF&E, 129
Filter, 366
Financial Reporting, Inc., 126.
Financial returns, *see* rate of return
Financing, rate, 108
sources of, 143
packages, 144
Fire alarm and control panel (FACP), 366, 368, **372**
Fire lane, 216, **220**
Fire, protection, 232, 365–367, **372**
resistance, 231.
fireproofing, 232
pump, 313
First City Bank/First City Center, 78, 209, 444, 466
First National Bank of Chicago, 60, 197, 219, 252, 253
Flame-spread, 232
Flashing, 255, 249
Flat rate equivalent, 410
Float, *see* parking
Floating interest rate, 113, 144, 145
Flood plain, 58, 501
Floor area ratio (FAR), 31, 56, 73, 74, 166
Floor, layout, 184, 193, 197, 201, **203**
core-to-glass, 198
load, 231
size, 197
structure, 230, 231
see also modules
see also test floor plans
Fluorescent light fixtures, 356
Flush valves, *see* plumbing fixtures
Force majeure, 418, 424, 430, 442
Foundations, *see* structure
Freight elevators, *see* elevators

G

General Conditions, 157, 397, **400**, 433–439, **441**, 462, 464
General contractor, 112, 113, 120, 161–163, 169, 171, 433, 435, 436, 441, 462, 464
contract, 436, 437
selection, 436
Geographic Information System (GIS), 55, 72
Geomancer, 487, 488, 491
Geotechnical, 58, 119
Glass Fiber Reinforced Concrete

(GFRC), 248
Glazing (vision glass), 239, 241–244, 291, **258**
shading coefficient, 241
thermal break, 242
Grade beams, 226,
Grading, 215, 217, **220**, **238**
permit, *see* permits, grading
Granite, 244–247, **258**, **262**
Graphics, 396
Green building, 493
see also sustainable design
Gross area, 107
Guaranteed Maximum Price (GMP), 111, 171, 175, 433, 434, 441, 445, 449, 461, 471, 474, 483

H

Habib, David, 8
Hanna Gabriel Wells, **122**, **173**, **174**
Hard bid, 171
Hardscape, 218
Harris, Barbara S., 8
Hazardous materials, 58
Heat pump (water source), 328
Heat recovery, chiller, 330
air side, 333
High-intensity discharge (HID), 217, 357
High-rise, 182
HKS Architects, 8, **89**, **122**, 163, **173**, **174**
Humidification, 335
HVAC systems, 174, 321, 345, 396, 398, 411
chilled water system, 327, 329
condenser water system, 305, 323, 327, 329, 330, **345–347**, **350**
design criteria, 324, **346**, 352, 353, **362**
direct expansion coil (DX), **174**, **191**, 328, **345**
economic analysis, 337
outside air economizer cycle, 333, 347
energy reduction, 329, 330, 333, 496
selection, 323
refrigeration, 327
tenant electrical load, 324, 352, 353, 356, **362**, 391
thermal energy storage (TES), 329, 496
thermocycle, 330

The numbers indicated in bold refer to the Case Study.

thermostat, **349**
Hydraulic elevator, *see* elevators
Hydronic, 330, 332
   see also air distribution, fan coil units

I

IBM, 168, 245
Impact fees, 56, **63**, 500
Indemnification/indemnity, 165, 423, 436
Indirect lighting, 356, 391
Indoor Air Quality (IAQ), 321, 332–334, 387, **399**, 496
Inspection reports, 467
Insulation, 244, 255
Insurance, 111, 114, 423, 438
Integrated Service Digital Network (ISDN), 359
Integrity, 26
Interbank-Brenner, **86**, **87**
Interim loan, *see* construction loan
Interior Environmental Quality (IEQ), 168, 387, **399**, 492
Internal rate of return (IRR), 125, 127, **139**
Internet site, *see* web-based management
   see also marketing
Inventory, office space, 35, 38, 39, 41

J

Janitor closets, 300
Job meetings, *see* project meetings
Johnson, Philip, 154, 163
JMI, **87**, **474**

L

Laboratory reports, *see* testing
Lagging, 225
Land development, 499
   Purchase Agreement, **83**, **89**, **99**, **116**, **265**, **320**, **448**, **471**
   Sales Agreement, **81**, **83**, **86**, **88**, **101**, **151**, **448**
Landlord delay, **117**
Landscaping, 217, **221**, **348**
Latent defects, 115, 419, 421, 438
Lavatories, *see* plumbing fixtures
Lease, 409, 417
   commencement date, **116**, 411, 418
   commission, *see* broker
   negoptiation, 417
   proposals, 409, 410

Lease-up rate, 35
   period, 114, 126, 130
Leasing strategies, 381
Light-emitting diode (LED), 359, 362, 400
Letter of credit, 424, **430**
Letter of Intent, **385**, 410
Liability Insurance, 114, 165, 438
LIBOR, **116**, 145
Lien waiver, *see* waiver of liens
Life cycle costing, 13, 322, 336
Life safety, 365, **372**, 392
Lighting, controls, 358, 496
   design, **400**
   energy reduction, 354, 357, 358, 496
   fixtures, 356, 357, 362, 391
   layout, 359
   levels, 355, 356
   maintenance, 355
   parking, 311, **318**
   selection, 355, **362**
   site, 217, **224**
Limestone, 244, 247
Live load, *see* structure
Loading dock, 306, **313**
Lobby, 269, 271, **278**
   amenities, 271
   entrances, 269
   layout, 271
Lock-in clause, 148
LonMark, 341, **348**
LonWorks, **373**
Loop corridor, *see* corridor
Lot line adjustment, **84**, **85**, **98**, **176**, **471**
Low-emissivity (low-e), 243
LULU, 67
Luopan, 482

M

Maintenance, exterior, 251
   HVAC, 387
   storage, 307
Marble, 244, 247
Market, cycle, 40, 383
   data, 44
   equilibrium point, 41
   rental rates, 40
   saturation, 41
   Study, 29, 30, 33, 147, 183, 184, **188**, 197, 207, 383, **399**
   trends, 36.
   value, 147

Marketing, 207, **213**
   center, 209
   events, 211
   web site, 211, **213**
Marriott, **16**, **54**, **80**, **84–87**, **176**, **186**, **191**, **195**, **483**
Material boards, 210, **262**, **304**, **400**
Mechanic's lien, 146, **150**, 463
Mercantile Bank/Mbank, 76, 154
Merger of design phases, 169
Metal halides, 357
Meyer, David, 8
Microbials, 334
Mini-perm, 145
Mixing box, *see* air distribution
Mockups, *see* facade
Models, **190**, 208, 445
Modular, carpet, 395
   raised floor, 333
Module(s), planning, 199, **203**, 390
   see also floor layout
   see also parking
Moment frame, *see* structure
Momentum Place, 154, 163, 230, 246, 253, 271
Morrison Hotel, 60
Motor Control Center (MCC), 351
Multi-site assemblies, 76

N

Nabih Youssef & Associates, 8, 122
National Fire Protection Association, 365
Net income, 44, 47, 128
Net rental rate, 108
NIMBY, 67
NIMTOO, 67
Noise, Criterion, 285, 287, 289, **302**
   sources of, 285
   Reduction Coefficient, 289
Noncombustible, 232
Non-disturbance, 413, 418
Non-recourse loan, 143
Notice to Proceed, 171, 445, 462

O

Office inventory, *see* inventory, office space.
Office space supply, 33, 36, 39, 40
Office stock, *see* inventory, office space
Operating expense, 108, **140**, 411, 412, 419–422
   ratio, 109

The numbers indicated in bold refer to the Case Study.

Index

Orix, **85–87**
OSHA, 252
Outside air economizer, *see* HVAC

P

Pardee Homes, **15**, **16**, **80–89**, 175, 191, **265**, **319**, **320**
Parking, 184, 185, **186**, **187**, **191**, 216, **220**, 307, 311, **314**, 384, 413, 421
   float, 311, 421
   modules, 309, 310
   lighting, 311
   ratio, 44, 56, **314**
   structure, **236**, **473**, **474**
Partitions, 392
Payment request, 467, **472**
Permanent loan, 146, 445
   Sources of, 147
Permits, building, 170, **176**, **178**, **197**, **431**, 445, **471**
   grading, **85**, **176**, **177**, **220**
Permitting, 79, **88**
Photovoltaic, 256
Piling, *see* structure, foundation
Planned Unit Development (PUD), 56, 499, 500
Plant, Ed, 75
Plat, platting, 59
Plazas, 218, 219
Plumbing fixtures, 295, 297, 298, **302**, **304**
   systems, 338, **348**
Products of Combustion (POC), 365
Political issues, 29, 31, 65, 499
Post-tensioned concrete, *see* concrete
Potable water, *see* domestic water.
Power distribution, *see* electrical system
Precast concrete, *see* concrete
Preinstalled items, 426
Prelease, 382, 126
Premises, 411, 418
Prentiss Properties entities, **15**, **16**, **80**, **86–88**, **116**, **150**, **265**, **379**, **400**, **430**, **441**, **442**, **448**, **474**, **471–474**, 503
Prentiss, Michael V., 5, 6, 8
Preparation, 26
Prestressed concrete, *see* concrete
Pro forma, 73, **81**, 125, **139**, **174**, **175**, 382
   cash flow analysis, 127
   executive summary, 127
   input sheet, 126, 130
   project cost report, 127, 129
   spreadsheet calculations, 126
Progress billing, 468
Project, cost report, 126, 127, 129
   Design Criteria, 33, 47, 55, 112, 165, 171, **173**, 181, 182, 184, **189**, 197
   meetings, 121, 467, 468
   web site, *see* web based management
Property Management, 29, 120, 158, 216, 252, 255, 267, 270, 276, 277, **284**, 297, 298, 300, 306, 307, 331, 337–339, 359, 360, 365, 368, 370, **374**, 390, 397, 398, **399**, 411, 421, 428, 463, 467, 469, 472, 479, 480
Proximity device, *see* security
Public art, 218
Public relations, 208
Punch list, 469

R

Rain screen, *see* façade
Raised floor, 332, 361
Rate of return, 11, 23, 30, 40, 47, 65, 73, 74, 108, 111, 125, 127, 128, **139**, **140**, 143, 167, 172, 382, 383, 387, 410, 417, 419, 420, 425, **430**
Recourse loan, 143
Recycling, *see* sustainable design
Redevelopment agency, 60, 61
Reflectance, 256
Reflective, reflectivity, 241, 243, 253, 256
Refrigeration system, *see* HVAC
Reinforcing bars, 226–228, **235**, **236**, **238**, **264**
Relative humidity, 333, 335
Renderings, 209, **213**, **264**, 445
Renewal (extension) term, 412, 427
Rental income, 108
   rate, 36, **48**, 108, 381, 411
Rent, 419
Rentable area, 36, 107, 418, 427
Rentable/useable (R/U) ratio, 108, 200, 293
Request for Proposal (RFP), 410, **414**, 435, 467.
Retail, 47
Retaining walls, **220**, 226
Retention ponds, 216, 501
Return, *see* rate of return
Right of first refusal, 428
opportunity, 428
Risk, 11, 25, 30, 33, 73, 74, 76, 108, 111–115, 125, 143–145, 147, 410, 417, 424, 426, **430**, 438, 439, 463, 464, **471**, 481, 499
   management, 111–115
Rock anchors, 225
Roadways, 216, 501
Roof, 252
   built-up, 254
   design, 255
   single ply, 254
   structure, 230, 233, **265**
   thermoplastic, 254
   thermoset, 254
   types, 254, **267**
   warranties, 255
Room Criterion, 290
R/U ratio, *see* rentable/useable (R/U) ratio
R-value, 242, 256

S

San Diego Corporate Center, **15**, **48**
San Diego Gas & Electric (SDG&E), **62**, **141**, **175**, **176**, **177**, **224**, 347
Sanitary waste, 338, **348**
Schedule (project), 26, 55, 114, 163, 165, 170, 181, 208, 375, **401**, 443–459, 464, **473**
Schematic design, 168, 197, 181, **448**
Schlessinger, Martin, 8
Scripps Bank, **84**, **178**, **213**, **386**, **401**, **415**, **431**, **432**
Sealants, *see* façade
Security, 368, **373**
   CCTV, 369, 374
   proximity devices, 368, 369, **373**
   surveillance, 369
Seismic issues, *see* structure
Sensitivity analysis, 30, 125, 131
Service areas, 317, 359
Shading coefficient, *see* glazing
Sheet piling, 225
Shell and core construction, 36, **53**, 171, 388, **399**, 461
Shop drawings, 444, 463, 467, 469
Single ply roofing, *see* roof
Site, acquisition, 73, **80**, 112
   aggregate base, 217
   coverage, 56
   conditions, 59
   density, *see* floor area ratio

The numbers indicated in bold refer to the Case Study.

design, 215–218, **220**
environmental testing, 58, 448
evaluation, 73
planning, 181, 184, 185, **186**
selection, 45, 71
Study, 29, 31, 55
testing, *see* testing, site
work, 60
Slurry walls, 225
Smoke control, 367, 372
Social issues (concerns), 13, 31, 44, 153, 161, 165, 168, 493, 494
see also sustainable design
Société Générale, 85, **150–152**, 265
Soil borings, 59
Soil-nail(ing), **178**, **179**, 225, **237**, **238**, **471**, **472**, **483**
Solar orientation, *see* sustainable design
Solid state starters, 330, 354
Soldier beams, 225
Sound pressure level, **291**
transmission class (STC), 285, 288, **291**
Space plan(ning), **188** 377
see also floor layout
see also test floor plans
Span, *see* structure
Spandrel, 240
glass, 247
Specifications, 144, 156, 157, 158, 169, 171, 397, 398, **399**, 413, 422, **441**, 465, 469
Speech privacy, 286
Spray and fluid applied roofing, 254
Sprinkler system, 232, 366, 389, 392, **400**, 413, **414**, 426
Stabilized occupancy, 108, 111, 480
Stairways, 294, **302**
Standards, various, 156
Storm drainage, 339, **347**
water management, 215, **348**, 501
Structure(al), 225
base, 217
brace frame, 228, 229, **234**, **235**
efficiency, 230
frame, 189, 225, 230
foundation, 226, 227
K-bracing, 228, **234**
live load, 231, **235**, **236**
moment frame, 228, **234**
seismic issues, 182, 228
span, 229, 231, **234**
steel, 228–232, **234**, **236**, 239, 434, 437, **441**, **448**, 466, **472**
substructure, 22
testing, *see* testing and wind tunnel
Stucco, 249
Subcontractor, 111, 113, 114, 120, 156, **401**, 437, **441**, **448**, 463, **471**
Subdivision, 59, 79
map, 59, 79, 88, 220, 445,
Subletting, 412, 422
Submittal logs, 467
Subordination, 149, 423
Substantial completion, 108, 469, **483**
Substantial Conformance Review (Determination), **62**, **69**, **88**, **89**, **93**, **96**, **97**, **116**, **192**, **193**, 386, **448**, **471**, **485**
Substructure, *see* structure
Supplementary Conditions, 157, 389, 436, 462
Supply, *see* office space supply
Suppression, fire, 366
SureTrak, 443
Surveillance, *see* security
Survey, 55, 58, 74, 76 119, 144–146, 148, 165
topographical survey, 59, 119
Sustainable design, 154, 165, 184, 321, 322, 493
energy conservation, 321, 322, 324, 329, 330, 333, 493, 495, 496
solar orientation, 181, 184
recycling, 154, 161, 163, 165, 493, 495, 498
water, 217, 297, 338, 493, 494, 495
see also lighting and lighting controls
see also social issues
Swinerton & Walberg, **122**, **174**, **400**, **441**, **471**, **474**
Switchgear, *see* electrical
Syska & Hennessy, **122**, **173**, **191**

T

Telephone system, 360, 361, **363**
Temporary Certificate of Occupancy (TCO), **401**, **432**, **448**, **449**, 468, **472**, **473**, **484**
Temporary storm retention, 225
Tenant construction coordinator, 469
delay, **399**, **401**, 413, 418, 425, 426, **430**, 461, 469, 470, **473**
Improvements. (TIs), 31, 44, **48**, **53**, **54**, 171, **345**, 382, 383, 387, 388, 397
retention, 387, 428, 480, 494
Tentative map, **97**
Term, 411, 418
Test floor plans, 202, 377, 389
see also floor layout
see also space plan
Testing, air testing and balancing, 334, 466, 468
façade, 250, 252, **258**, 466
field, 58, 226, 228, 266, 466
laboratories, 466, 467
site, 58, **63**
smoke control, 367, **373**, **473**
structural steel, 466
Thermal break, *see* glazing
Thermal energy storage (TES), *see* HVAC
Thermocycle, *see* HVAC
TIAA, 146
Tie backs, 225
sheeting, 225
Tile panels, 248
Title insurance, 74, **117**, 145, 148, **150**
Toilet, fixtures, *see* plumbing fixtures
partitions, 296, **302**
rooms, 295, **302**
Tombstone, *see* advertising
Topographical survey, *see* survey
Total project cost, 108, 125, 126, **140**, **141**, **484**
Traffic study, 31, 58, 65, **88**, 182, **188**, 216, 307, 308
Transformers, *see* electrical
Trash handling, 306, **314**
Trust Deed, *see* Deed of Trust
Two First National Plaza, 232

U

Uniform Building Code (UBC), 156, **177**, **234**
Uniform Commercial Code (UCC), 148
Unit project cost, 108
Useable area, 107
U.S. Green Building Council, 497, 498
Utilities, 59, 217, **220**, 499, 502
deregulation, 326
U-value, 241, 253, 256

V

Vacancy, 30, 33, 36, 39–41, 71, 126
cost, 38, 108, 125, 129

The numbers indicated in bold refer to the Case Study.

Index

rate, 39, 108, 114, 145, 147
Value engineering, 170, 171, 218, **224**
Variable air volume system (VAV), *see* HVAC
Variable frequency drive (VFD), 330, 354
Vision glass, *see* glazing
Visual comfort probability (VCP), 355, 356
Visual light transmission (VLT), 241
Volatile organic compounds (VOCs), 393, 395, 398, 496

W

Waiver of liens, 146, 467, 469
Wall covering, 393
Walters & Wolfe, **262**, **471**
Warranties, 255, 438, 467
Water, treatment, 298
  conservation, *see* sustainable design
Waterford Development Company, **16**, **54**, **80**, **81**, **83–88**, **93**, **150**, **186**, **441**, **448**
Web-based project management, 157, 461
Web site (home page), *see* marketing
Wet bulb temperature, **346**
Wetlands, 57–59, 499
White noise, 288
"Will Serve" letters, 146, 502
Wind tunnel tests, 58, 168, 169, 229, 243
Window washing equipment, 251–253
Window wall, *see* facade
Wong, Joseph, **122**
Work letter, 210, 389, 392, 413, 426, 427, **429**, **430**.
Working drawings, 113, 120, 157, 162–164, 169,

X

"X" (bracing), 228, **234**

Z

"Z" corridor, *see* corridors
Zones, air, *see* air distribution
Zoning, 29, 31, 40, 47, 55, 56, 60, 67, 71, 73, 74, 76, 79, 119, 144, 146, 148, 164, 166, 197

The numbers indicated in bold refer to the Case Study.

EL CAMINO REAL

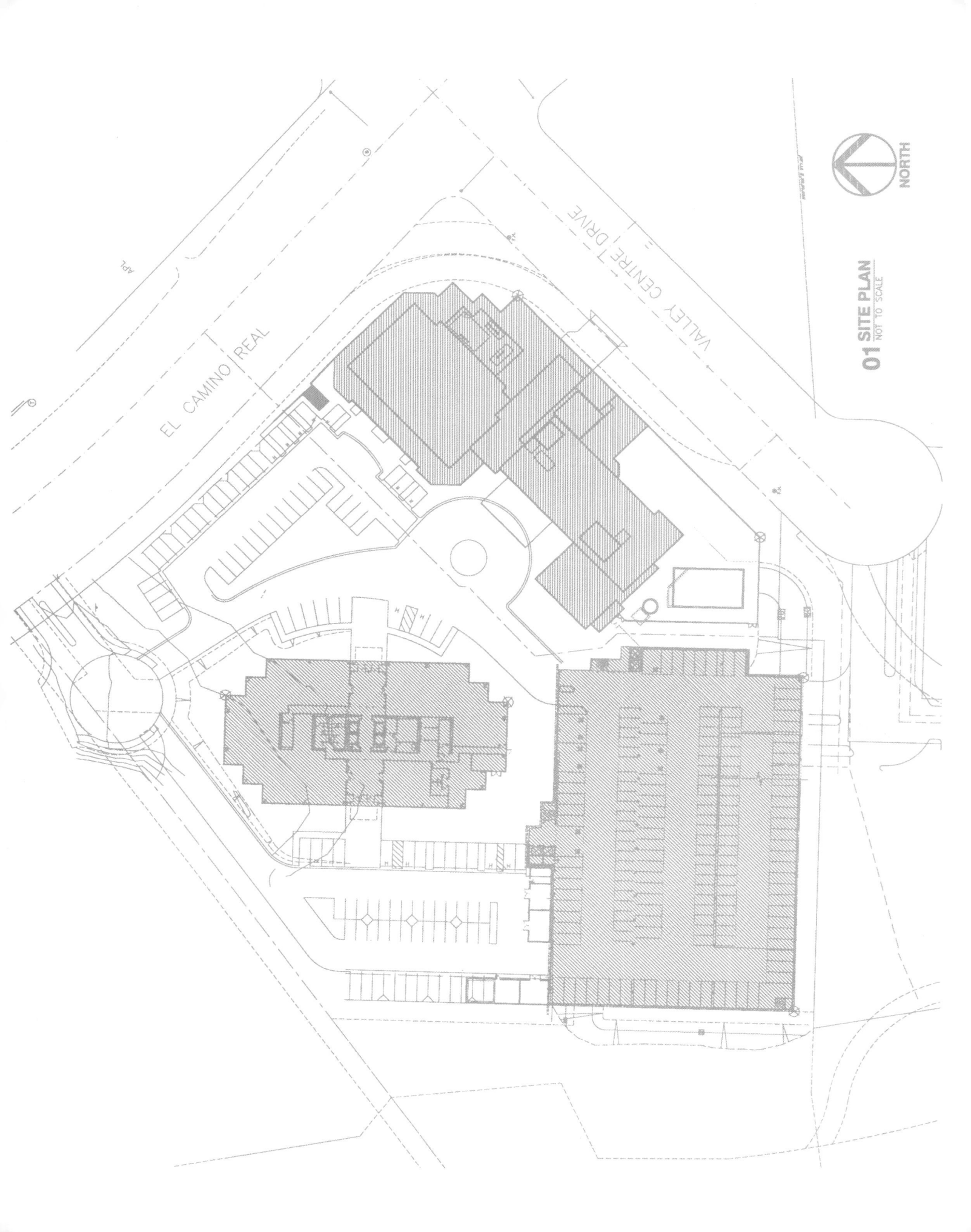

VALLEY CENTRE DRIVE

NORTH

01 SITE PLAN
NOT TO SCALE

PHOTOGRAPHY and GRAPHICS CREDITS

Bank One

BOMA/ULI

Building Operating Management

Business Real Estate Brokerage Co.

Cushman & Wakefield

Destiny Books

Hanna Gabriel Wells

HCB Contractors

HKS Architects

International Parking Design

Joseph Wong Design Associates (JWDA)

Nabih Youssef & Associates

Parking Consultants Council of the National Parking Association

Pardee Homes

Prentiss Properties Trust

Rick Engineering

Robinson, Bill

Swinerton & Walberg

Trane

Wallace, Roberts & Todd

Walters & Wolfe

WDG-Habib Architecture